THE TERRORIST LIST

THE TERRORIST LIST

THE MIDDLE EAST

Volume 2: L–Z

Edward F. Mickolus

PRAEGER SECURITY INTERNATIONAL
Westport, Connecticut • London

Library of Congress Cataloging-in-Publication Data

Mickolus, Edward F.
  The terrorist list : the Middle East / Edward F. Mickolus.
     p.   cm.
  Includes bibliographical references and index.
  ISBN 978–0–313–35766–4 ((set) : alk. paper)—ISBN 978–0–313–35768–8 ((vol. 1) : alk. paper)—
  ISBN 978–0–313–35770–1 ((vol. 2) : alk. paper)
  1. Terrorists—Middle East—Biography—Dictionaries.   2. Terrorism—Middle East.   I. Title.
  HV6433.M5M53   2009
  363.325092′256–dc22   2009003340

British Library Cataloguing in Publication Data is available.

Library of Congress Catalog Card Number: 2009003340
ISBN: 978–0–313–35766–4 (set)
978–0–313–35768–8 (vol. 1)
978–0–313–35770–1 (vol. 2)

First published in 2009

Praeger Security International, 88 Post Road West, Westport, CT 06881
An imprint of Greenwood Publishing Group, Inc.
www.praeger.com

Printed in the United States of America

The paper used in this book complies with the
Permanent Paper Standard issued by the National
Information Standards Organization (Z39.48–1984).

10 9 8 7 6 5 4 3 2 1

For those who protect us in silent service to our country. It is an honor to know you.

CONTENTS

L

Amir Laaraj: an Algerian who, in the mid-2000s, visited the leaders of the Algerian Salafist Group for Preaching and Combat with Muhammad Benhedi Msahel and Anour Majrar, both of whom were arrested while Laaraj remained free.

Essoussi Laaroussi: a Tunisian who had done time in a Belgian jail, he met with Essid Sami Ben Khemais and Tarek Maaroufi in Brussels on February 10, 2000.

Bashir Abu Laban: age 41, one of four Palestinians charged on February 7, 2004, by a Palestinian military tribunal at the Saraya Prison and security compound in central Gaza City in connection with the October 15, 2003 van bomb in the Gaza Strip under a U.S. diplomatic convoy that killed three Americans and injured one. Charges included possessing explosives and weapons and planting mines in the area where the attack occurred. They were not directly charged with the murders. Chief Judge Khalid Hamad adjourned the trial until February 29 to permit the defendants to obtain counsel. Abu Laban was arrested on the day of the blast and was a member of the Popular Resistance Committees, a group of militants from other Palestinian groups, including the al-Aqsa Martyrs Brigades. When the Gaza City military tribunal began in February, the group was charged with possessing explosives and weapons and with planting mines in the vicinity of where the Americans died. The prosecutor said the group was planting mines to take out Israeli tanks. On March 14, 2004, a Palestinian court ruled that there was insufficient evidence against three of them and ordered them released. Their release was delayed pending an official directive to do so by Yasser Arafat. Arafat advisor Bassam Abu Sharif said the trio "were found innocent because they arrested three other guys who are under investigation and interrogation."

Abdullah Abd al-Hamid Labib: variant of Mohammed Abdel Ali Labib.

Mohammed Abdel Ali Labib: variant Abdullah Abd al-Hamid Labib, alias Colonel Hawari, leader of a terrorist group of which Mohammed Rashid, an accused Palestinian serial bomber, was a member. On October 20, 1988, a French court convicted Labib in absentia for his role in several terrorist attacks throughout Western Europe in the mid-1980s aimed at Syrian, Libyan, and U.S. targets, and gave him the maximum 10-year sentence for complicity in transporting arms, ammunition, and explosives and for "criminal association." The United States said he was behind a TWA attack. He had headed the Fatah Special Operations Group's intelligence and security apparat that sometimes served as Yassir Arafat's bodyguard.

Osama bin Laden: variant Usama bin Ladin, alias Usama bin Muhammad bin Awad bin Ladin, Shaykh Usama bin Ladin, the Prince, the Emir, Abu Abdallah, Mujahid Shaykh, Hajj, the Director, the Teacher: founder of al Qaeda. Member of a Saudi family that made its millions in construction, he studied at King 'Abd-al-Aziz University, where he was influenced by two members of the Muslim Brotherhood: 'Abdallah 'Azzam, a Jordanian Palestinian, and Muhammad Qutb, brother of the Egyptian Muslim Brotherhood's most extremist militant, Sayyid Qutb, who was executed by Egypt in 1966.

bin Laden was born on July 30, 1957 in Saudi Arabia. He is left-handed and walks with a cane. He is about six feet five inches and about 160 pounds. He said on November 27, 1996 that his followers were responsible for the June 25, 1996 truck bombing of the U.S. military's compound at Khobar Towers near Dhahran that killed 19 U.S. airmen and wounded 547 others. On February 24, 1998, he issued a fatwa that allows attacks on Americans worldwide. He was placed on the FBI's 10 Most Wanted List in June 1999. The State Department's Rewards for Justice Program offered up to $25 million for his apprehension; the U.S. Senate voted 87 to 1 on July 13, 2007 to double it to $50 million. An additional $2 million is available via the Air Transport Association and Airline Pilots Association.

As of October 2001, his cells were believed to be operating in the United States, Canada, Ecuador, Uruguay, Mauritania, Algeria, Libya, Egypt, Saudi Arabia, Yemen, Sudan, Ethiopia, Eritrea, Somalia, Kenya, Uganda, Tanzania, Qatar, Afghanistan, Pakistan, Tajikistan, Uzbekistan, Jordan, Lebanon, Azerbaijan, Chechnya, Albania, Bosnia, Germany, the United Kingdom, Spain, France, Italy, Bangladesh, Malaysia, and the Philippines.

Saad bin Laden: son of Osama bin Laden. A Saudi who escaped from Afghanistan after 9/11 and into Iran, where he was believed to have been placed under house arrest.

Abu-Ladin: alias of 'Abdallah Salih 'Abd-al-Karim Ibrahim.

Shaykh Usama bin Ladin: variant of Osama bin Laden.

Usama bin Muhammad bin Ladin: variant of Osama bin Laden.

Moustapha Hamid Lafta: a former Iraqi Army officer allegedly behind the November 12, 2003

truck bombing in Nasiriyah, Iraq that killed 19 Italians and 12 Iraqis.

Abu al-Lahd: alias of Walid, a member of the Popular Front for the Liberation of Palestine whom *Ha'aretz* claimed, on November 13, 1986, to be one of the masked suicide terrorists who fired on and threw grenades at worshippers in the Neve Shalom, Istanbul, Turkey synagogue on September 6, 1986; doused the 21 corpses with gasoline; and set them alight. Two terrorists who had barred the door died in the attack when their grenades exploded in their hands. A third escaped. The attack was claimed by the Islamic Jihad, Abu Nidal, the Northern Arab League, the Islamic Resistance, the Palestinian Resistance Organization, the Fighting International Front—'Amrush Martyr Group, and the Organization of the Unity of the Arab North.

Sabir Lahmar: an Algerian suspected of membership in the Armed Islamic Group who was arrested in Bosnia/Herzegovina shortly after the 9/11 attacks. He had earlier made threats against the NATO-led Stabilization Force (SFOR) and U.S. interests.

Loay al-Lahwani: one of two Palestinian suicide bombers who, on February 4, 2008, killed an Israeli woman and injured more than 20 others, including his accomplice, in Dimona, 40 miles from the Gaza Strip. An Israeli officer shot the wounded terrorist five times before he could set off the belt. Abu Walid, spokesman for the al-Aqsa Martyrs Brigades, claimed credit, saying the terrorists lived outside Gaza City and the central Gaza city of Khan Younis. Abu Obeida, spokesman for the Izz al-Din al-Qassam Brigades, a Hamas group, also claimed credit.

Ahmed Laidouni: arrested on January 18, 1999 by French police for ties to Osama bin Laden and charged with criminal association with a terrorist enterprise. He was born in France to Algerian parents. He fought with Bosnian Muslims in 1992–1995 and trained in Afghan camps. On March 17,

2004, he went on trial for "criminal association in relation to a terrorist enterprise," which carries a ten-year sentence.

Boumediene Lakhdar: on January 18, 2002, U.S. troops brought him and five other terrorism suspects out of Bosnia to Guantánamo after a Bosnian court ruled on January 17 that it had too little evidence to press charges. He was accused of plotting to blow up the U.S. Embassy in Sarajevo and conduct other attacks on Americans in Bosnia. Five of the men were naturalized Bosnians; Bosnia stripped them of their citizenship in November 2001. The group had been arrested by Bosnian authorities in October 2001.

Harizi Lakhdar: alleged member of the Islamic Salvation Front who was arrested for involvement in the August 26, 1992 bombing of the Air France ticket counter at Houari Boumedienne Airport in Algeria that killed 12 people and wounded 128. Public sessions of his trial began on May 4, 1993. On May 26, 1993, a special Algiers judicial council sentenced him to five years.

Lakhlaf: alias Abu-Shayma', an Algerian member of al Qaeda in Iraq assigned as a fighter in Mosul in 2007. His phone number was 0021373655279.

Ismail Hafez al-Lami: alias Abu Dura, a leader of Shi'ite extremists based in Iran. In January 2008, he led a pro-Iranian group that has targeted Iraqi officials, Sunni leaders, and others. His group was responsible for the kidnap/torture/murder of Sunnis in Iraq's Ministry of Higher Education in 2006. His assets were subjected to financial sanctions by the U.S. Treasury on January 9, 2008 under Executive Order 13438.

Mr. Lamin: alias of Lamen Khalifa Fhimah.

A. Lapez: alias used by one of two members of the Popular Front for the Liberation of Palestine (PFLP) who hijacked TWA flight 741, a B707 flying from Frankfurt to New York on September 6, 1970. The plane was diverted to Dawson's Field,

Zerka, Jordan, a former Royal Air Force landing strip in the desert. This was the first of several hijackings carried out by the PFLP on this day. The group demanded the release of three PFLP members held in West Germany for an attack on an airline bus in Munich, three held in Switzerland for an attack on an El Al plane in Zurich, several fedayeen held in Israeli prisons, and Leila Khaled, who was held in a UK jail after a foiled hijacking attempt. The planes were blown up after the hostages were deplaned. Jordanian King Hussein ultimately had enough of their antics, and ordered Jordanian troops to battle the fedayeen, during which 7,000 people died.

Mohamed Larbi: one of three Algerians arrested in Naples, Italy on November 17, 2005 who were suspected of being Islamist extremists with ties to international terrorists and who could become "potentially operative" and ready to carry out an attack.

'Abd al-Latif: a Palestinian associate of a Palestinian with a Jordanian passport who was arrested by Larnaca Airport security personnel on December 17, 1985 for trying to smuggle arms aboard a Swiss airplane scheduled to depart for Amman. Police believed he was one of four Arabs who intended to hijack the plane.

Faraj Yasin 'Abd al-Latif: arrested on August 12, 1985 by the Egyptian prosecutor's office on charges of communicating with Libya to the detriment of Egypt's political status and receiving a bribe from Libya to commit murder in the foiled plot to assassinate Ghayth Said al-Mabruk, a political refugee living in Alexandria, Egypt, on August 6, 1985. When arrested, he and two others had a machine gun and pistol. They were later found guilty and sentenced to death.

Shakub 'Abd-al-Latif: variant of Shaqueb Abd Al Latif.

Shaqueb Abd Al Latif: alias Abu Usama, variant Abu Usamah, a Moroccan student born in

1984 who joined al Qaeda in Iraq as a fighter in 2007, bringing his passport, ID, and watch. His recruitment coordinator was Nabil, whom he knew through Saied. He took a bus from Turkey to Syria, where he met Abu Omar. He brought 100 Euros with him. His home phone number was 0021214543342.

Allova Layachi: one of three Algerian hijackers of an Air Algerie Convair 640 flying from Annaba to Algiers on August 31, 1970. The trio wanted to fly to Albania to obtain political asylum, but the Albanian government refused to let the plane land. The group flew to Dubrovnik, Yugoslavia, where they surrendered to police.

Abdelhaq Layda: a member of the Algerian Armed Islamic Group (GIA) whose release was demanded by the GIA in a letter to French President Jacques Chirac on December 24, 1996 in which it suggested that it was responsible for the bombing on December 3 of the Paris Metro. Layda was on Algeria's death row.

Abu Layith: alias of Milad Attia.

Abu-al-Layth: Libya-based recruitment coordinator for foreign fighters for al Qaeda in Iraq in 2006.

Abu-al-Layth: alias of an unnamed Libyan fighter for al Qaeda in Iraq in 2007. His phone number was 00218926226720.

Abu-al-Layth or Abu-Layth: alias of Ahmad Hilmi al-Hasadi.

Abu Hajir Al Zubear Lazardi: alias of Abd Al Aziz Awad Abd Allah Al Shahrani.

Abdullah Hussein Lehebi: age 47, alias Abu Khalid al-Dulaimi, a leader of al Qaeda in Iraq from the Amiriyah section of Anbar south of Fallujah who was interviewed for a February 8, 2008 *Washington Post* article.

Matthew Leibowitz: one of four American Jews who opened fire with M-16 rifles at a bus near Ramallah that was carrying Palestinians to work on March 4, 1984. The four fled in a Subaru but were captured later that day by Israeli security forces. Terror Against Terror claimed credit. He confessed and was sentenced to three years and three months.

Craig Leitner: one of four American Jews who opened fire with M-16 rifles at a bus near Ramallah that was carrying Palestinians to work on March 4, 1984. The four fled in a Subaru but were captured later that day by Israeli security forces. Terror Against Terror claimed credit. He was released when he agreed to turn state's evidence. He fled to the United States, where he was apprehended at Pace University's White Plains campus by a U.S. Marshal.

Said Lekhal: a member of the Algerian Islamic Salvation Front (FIS) committee of elected members who provided safe haven to FIS executive council member Abderrahmane Dhina in Switzerland after he escaped a November 9, 1994 French raid on an FIS safe house.

Abu Faraj Libbi: alias of Abu Faraj Farj.

Abd Muhsin Libi: manager of the bin Laden front Afghan Support Committee's office in Peshawar, Pakistan, and office director for the Revival of Islamic Heritage Society, his assets were blocked by the U.S. Department of the Treasury on January 9, 2002.

Abu Bu Sharia Al Libi: alias of Abd Al Hakim Mustafa Al Oukaley.

Abu Faraj Farj al-Libi: variant al-Liby, alias Dr. Taufeeq, third in command of al Qaeda.

On April 30, 2005 (some reports say May 2), Pakistani authorities, with the assistance of U.S. intelligence, arrested the Libyan citizen, age 42, who was wanted for the two assassination attempts against President Pervez Musharraf and was also believed to have been a key planner of the 9/11 attacks. Pakistan said it would try him for the assassination attempts rather than hand him over to the United States. Pakistan had offered a $350,000 reward for his capture.

He was arrested in the town of Mardan in the North West Frontier Province with three other men following a shootout. He ran from his hideout, jumped over a cemetery wall, and into a guest house, where he was found hiding. Police fired tear gas into the building, and al-Liby emerged. In follow-up raids, Pakistani authorities grabbed more than 20 other suspects, including at least eight in Lahore on May 4. Among them were three Uzbeks, an Afghan, and seven Pakistanis.

al-Liby was also linked to terrorist plans to conduct attacks before the 2004 US elections. In 2003, he had succeeded the arrested Khalid Sheikh Muhammad as al Qaeda's operational planner. On May 11, 2005, Pakistani's interior minister said that al-Liby was also involved in a plot to kill Prime Minister Shaukat Aziz, subject of a suicide bombing in July 30, 2004 near Islamabad. The suicide bomber killed eight other people, including Aziz's driver. On June 6, 2005, Pakistan said it had handed al-Liby to the Americans a few days earlier.

On September 6, 2006, President Bush announced that the last 14 detainees would be transferred from secret foreign prisons to the military detention facility at Guantánamo Bay. The group was identified as Abu Zubaydah, Khalid Sheikh Mohammed, Ramzi Binalshibh, Mustafa Ahmad al-Hawsawi, Hambali, Majid Khan, Lillie, Ali Abd al-Aziz Ali, Ahmed Khalfan Ghailani, Abd al-Rahim al-Nashiri, Abu Faraj al-Libi, Zubair, Walid bin Attash, and Gouled Hassan Dourad.

Abu-Hammad al-Libi: variant Abu Hamam al-Libi, alias of Hafiz Salih al-Masmari, variant Hafez Saleh Al Mismarie.

Abu Laith al-Libi: variant Sheikh Abu Laith al-Qassimi al-Libi. As of September 2007, he was a field commander and spokesman for al Qaeda. He was a leader of the Libyan Islamic Fighting Group. He had fought Russian troops in Afghanistan, was imprisoned in Saudi Arabia for two years, and failed to overthrow Muammar Qadhafi in Libya in the mid-1990s. He was arrested in Saudi Arabia after a November 1995 bombing outside the U.S. office for training the Saudi national guard. He either escaped or was released. He began working with Osama bin Laden in 1999. He led the retreat from Kabul in 2001. He ran training camps in Afghanistan. The U.S. military placed him on its most wanted list in 2006. He organized the suicide attack that killed 23 people in Bagram's U.S. Air Base during the February 2007 visit by Vice President Dick Cheney. He was the target of a rocket attack in June 2007 in Paktia Province, Afghanistan. In October 2007, the U.S. announced rewards ranging from $20,000 to $200,000 for him and 11 other Taliban and al Qaeda leaders. On January 28, 2008, a missile fired by what was reported by the press to be a U.S. Predator drone killed him in Mir Ali, north Waziristan, Pakistan. He was 41 years old at the time of his death.

Abu Yahya al-Libi: variant Abu Yehia al-Libi, alias of Mohamed Hassan, variant Abdulbakar Mohammed Hassan, alias Hasan Qaiid, alias Yunis al-Sahrawi, an al-Qaeda-affiliated religious scholar who, with three other al Qaeda members, escaped from a U.S. military prison in Bagram in July 2005. As of September 2007, he had appeared in more than a dozen Al Sahab propaganda videos. He was suspected of involvement in the February 27, 2007 suicide car bombing at the gates of Bagram Air Base that killed 23 people and injured 24 others during the visit of U.S. Vice President Dick Cheney. His older brother, imprisoned in Libya, was a key figure in the Libyan Islamic Fighting Group. Libi had gone to Afghanistan in the early 1990s, then went back to study Islam for two years in Mauritania. He returned to Afghanistan, and preached about the shariah. He was detained in Pakistan in 2002.

Abu Yehia al-Libi: variant of Abu Yahya al Libi.

Al-Khitab al-Libi: alias of 'Abd-al-Rahman 'Abd-al-'Aziz Darbi.

Anas al-Libi: variant of Anas al-Liby.

Ibn al-Shaykh al-Libi: a suspected al Qaeda commander captured in Pakistan on November 11, 2002. President Bush ordered his U.S. assets frozen on September 24, 2001. He was a senior trainer for al Qaeda and had close contacts with Abu Zubaydah. He headed paramilitary training at Afghanistan's Khaldan camp.

Sheikh Abu Laith al-Qassimi al-Libi: variant of Abu Laith al-Libi.

Abu Abd Al Rahman Al Libie: alias of Abd Al Hakim Mansour Abd Al Qader Al Oulafie.

Abu Anas al-Liby: variant Anas al-Libi, alias Anas al-Sabai, Nazih al-Raghie, Nazih Abdul Hamed al-Ragie, a Libyan indicted in 2000 in New York connection with the August 7, 1988 bombings of the U.S. embassies in Tanzania and Kenya and for conspiracy to kill U.S. nationals, to murder, to destroy buildings and property of the United States, and to destroy the national defense infrastructure of the United States. He faced life in prison without parole on various conspiracy charges. The Rewards for Justice Program offers $5 million for his apprehension. He has claimed to have been born on March 30, 1964 and May 14, 1964 in Tripoli, Libya. He is about six feet tall. He joined al Qaeda in the 1980s or early 1990s. The computer specialist was a member of the group's ruling council, the shura. He left Sudan before Osama bin Laden left in 1996 for Afghanistan and showed up in Qatar and then Manchester, United Kingdom, where he was given political asylum. In 2000, UK arresting authorities found that he had fled, leaving a 180-page terrorist manual on a computer disk. He apparently led the early al Qaeda resistance to U.S. operations in Afghanistan following the 9/11 attacks, then fled to Sudan. The Libyan computer expert is a member of an extremist Islamic group opposed to Muammar Qadhafi. He is between five feet ten inches and six feet two inches.

On March 18 2002, the United States announced his capture in Sudan the previous month. However, on March 19, 2002, the Administration said that the individual in custody was not this Liby, but a person with a sound-alike name who was a "moderately high up" al Qaeda member wanted by a country other than the United States.

Sabbeh Al Liel: alias of Muhammad Ahmad Omar.

Abdul Basit Abu Lifa: a Palestinian Dane in contact with a group of al Qaeda sympathizers in Europe in 2006. On February 15, 2007, a Copenhagen judge sentenced him to seven years in jail for involvement in a failed plot to blow up a European target.

Orjan Lihe: one of five Iranian diplomats arrested in Turkey on October 25, 1988 who were planning to kidnap Said Abu Hassan Mochhadezade, an anti-Khomeini engineer working in Erzincan who reportedly was a member of the Peoples Mujahideen. They were to be tried by a state security court in Istanbul State. The press reported that two of them were members of the Savama or Iranian secret police; the other three were members of the embassy's bodyguard team.

Lilie: variant Lillie, alias of Bashir bin Lap. On September 6, 2006, President Bush announced that the last 14 detainees would be transferred from secret foreign prisons to the military detention facility at Guantánamo Bay. The group was identified as Abu Zubaydah, Khalid Sheikh Mohammed, Ramzi Binalshibh, Mustafa Ahmad al-Hawsawi, Hambali, Majid Khan, Lillie, Ali Abd al-Aziz Ali, Ahmed Khalfan Ghailani, Abd al-Rahim al-Nashiri, Abu Faraj al-Libi, Zubair, Walid bin Attash, and Gouled Hassan Dourad.

Lillie: variant of Lilie.

Menachem Livni: one of three masked Jewish Underground gunmen who fired Kalashnikov submachine guns at students milling about a courtyard at the Hebron Islamic College in Israel on July 27, 1983. They also threw a grenade in the attack that killed three and wounded 30. Livni was arrested for the attack and sentenced to life in prison. On March 27, 1987, President Chaim Herzog commuted the sentences to 24 years each. On December 26, 1990, Israel freed him; a life sentence in Israel usually requires that the convict serve at least 20 years.

Mostafa Lmounatassime: political leader of a group of 32 people arrested on February 20, 2008 by Moroccan authorities who said they were a terrorist network linked to al Qaeda that planned to assassinate Cabinet members, army officers, and members of the local Jewish community. Some of the group belonged to al Badil al Hadari, an Islamist party, the banning of which was announced the same day. The group had conducted holdups and sold stolen goods. One member worked with European criminals to steal $25.65 million from an armored truck in Luxembourg in 2000. The group also stole gold jewelry in Belgium, melting it down and selling it via a goldsmith who belonged to the group.

Faheem Khalid Lodhi: age 36, a Pakistani-born Australian architect charged with four counts of planning to bomb either the nation's electricity grid or defense installations in Sydney. His trial began on April 24, 2006, in Sydney. He had worked at three defense installations in Sydney. He had emigrated to Australia in 1996. Intelligence agents searching his home in October 2003 found "a terrorism manual," according to prosecutors. On June 19, 2006, after five days of deliberations, a New South Wales Supreme Court jury found him guilty of three charges (collecting maps of Sydney's electricity grid, acting in preparation for a terrorist act by gathering information about bomb making, and possessing documents with information about how to manufacture poisons), making him the first man convicted of plotting attacks under new antiterrorism legislation. The first and third charges carry 15-year sentences; the second carries a life sentence. Judge Anthony Whealy announced that Lodhi had been acquitted on the fourth charge of downloading aerial photographs of defense facilities from the Internet. The sentencing hearing would begin on June 29.

Etienne Lona: leader of the militia believed responsible for the February 24, 2005 shooting to death of nine Bangladeshi soldiers serving as part of the UN peacekeeping force near Kafe in the northeast. On March 1, 2005, he turned himself in to UN peacekeepers.

Osama bin London: alias of Mohammed Hamid.

Hamada Mohammed Lotfi: hanged on December 31, 1994 in a Cairo prison after being found guilty of planting explosives at a military base near the Libyan border in hopes of assassinating Egyptian President Hosni Mubarak.

Jamal al-Lounici: a Moroccan sentenced to death in his home country and serving time in a French jail in 1995. He was named as the leader of 12 members of the Algerian Islamic Salvation Front arrested on June 6, 1995 in Milan, Rome, Naples, and Pavia, who had links with terrorists in Algeria, France, Germany, and Belgium. The group was suspected of involvement in the July 7, 1994 attack in Djendjen, Algeria, in which seven Italian sailors were found with their throats cut.

Djamel Lounici: of Algiers, possibly the same person as noted above, was listed by the U.S. Treasury Department on October 24, 2003 as a financier of the Algerian terrorist organization Salafist Group for Call and Combat.

Lua'ai: a Syrian-based facilitator for foreign recruits joining al Qaeda in Iraq in 2007.

Muhammad Lu'Ay: one of the five Guards of Islam gunmen who failed in an assassination attempt against Shahpour Bakhtiar, the Shah's last Prime Minister, in Neuilly-sur-Seine, France on July 17, 1980.

Abu Mohammed Lubnani: alias of Mustapha Darwich Ramadan.

Mostafa Lunani: on February 16, 2006, a Belgian court sentenced him to six years for belonging to the Moroccan Islamic Combatant Group, which was involved in the March 11, 2004 Madrid train bombings and the 2003 bombing in Casablanca that killed 32 people.

Abu Luqman: alias of Fazul Abdallah Mohammed.

Hamadah Muhammad Lutfi: a fugitive Egyptian soldier and member of Gama'at who was sentenced to death by the Sidi Barrani military court on February 16, 1994 for having planned an assassination attempt against Egyptian President Hosni Mubarak, who was to visit the Sidi Barrani military base near the Libyan border.

Hamadah Lutfi: one of three individuals sentenced to death on February 17, 1994 by a Cairo military court for plotting the assassination of President Mubarak by bombing Sidi Barrani Airport and the Presidential guest house in Marsa Matruh. Two of the defendants were executed by firing squad on February 28, 1994.

Jadu Mamim Ahmad Lu'ubaydi: alias Abu 'Abd al-Rahman al-Shanqiti, a Mauritanian student from al-Hawd al-Sharqi (the eastern basin) who was born in 1970 and joined al Qaeda in Iraq as a fighter in 2007, bringing his passport. His recruitment coordinator was Abu-'Abdallah, whom he knew via a sheik who was teaching him. While in Syria, he met Abu-'Umar al-Tunisi and Hamdan, who gave him $100 after taking 3,500 Syrian Lira from him. He knew a scientist whose phone number was 002226250577 who wanted to join al Qaeda in Iraq. Lu-ubaydi could be contacted via his brother at 002226505501.

M

M.: Libyan terrorism suspect, who had been held without charge for two years in London's high-security Belmarsh prison, whose release was ordered by the Appeal Court on March 18, 2004.

Karim M.: a Moroccan detained by German police on April 11, 2002, who had the phone number of Ramzi Binalshibh, who was believed to have initially been scheduled to be the 20th hijacker for the September 11 attacks. He was believed to have been involved in the April 11, 2002 truck bombing of a synagogue in Djerba, Tunisia that killed 17 people, including 11 German tourists, five Tunisians, and a French citizen.

Hammed Saleh Al Ma'abouni: alias Abu Al Barra'a, a Saudi from Mecca's al Khadra'a district who was born in 1402 Hijra and joined al Qaeda in Iraq on 20th Sha'aban 1427 Hijra (2007), bringing cash in dollars and rials, and a bag. His recruitment coordinator was Ra'aed al Shamerie. His phone number was 0507758584.

Samir Basheer Ma'alawi: alias Abu Ikram, a Tunisian mechanic from Benzet who joined al Qaeda in Iraq as a martyr in 2007. Ashraf was his recruitment coordinator. His phone number was 0021696885222.

Habib Maamar: variant Habib Ma'mar, a Tunisian member of the May 15 Organization arrested in Paris in May 1986, who confessed to the bombing in Orchard Street in London on December 25, 1983 near Marks and Spencer and Selfridges. He claimed he was paid $3,000/month by a pro-Iraqi faction of the Palestine Liberation Organization led by Abu Ibrahim to bomb Israeli targets. He also confessed to the February 23, 1985 bombing of Marks and Spencer in Paris that killed one and injured 14, and to the August 21, 1985 bombing of the Israeli Bank Leumi office in Paris. Large quantities of a plastic explosive, penthrite, were found in his Paris home. His trial opened on December 13, 1989. He told police he was asked to photograph Jewish establishments in Paris, London, Athens and Istanbul. He made regular visits to Baghdad to collect money and explosives. He traveled via Madrid under various names and using forged Moroccan passports.

Tarek Maaroufi: a Tunisian with Belgian citizenship, who was wanted on an Italian warrant in October 2001; his Belgian citizenship prevented his extradition. He was one of three Europe-based organizers for the Egyptian Anathema and Exile and the Algerian Salafist Group for Preaching and Combat. He was in contact with Essid Sami Ben Khemais, who was a leader of a European network of al Qaeda cells. He was arrested by Belgian police in December 2001 on charges of forgery, criminal association, and recruiting for a foreign army or armed force. On September 20, 2003, a Belgian court sentenced him to six years for the September 9, 2001 al Qaeda assassination in Afghanistan of Northern Alliance leader Ahmed Shah Massoud. He was accused of involvement in the fake passport ring linked to the Massoud killing. Italy wanted him for ties to known al Qaeda cells.

Amer el-Maati: alias Amro Badr Eldin Abou el-Maati, Amro Badr Abouelmaati, a Canadian wanted for questioning by the FBI in connection with possible terrorist threats in the United States. He claims to have been born in Kuwait on May 25, 1963. He is six feet tall and weighs 209 pounds. The Rewards for Justice program offers $5 million for his apprehension and/or conviction.

Amro Badr Eldin Abou el-Maati: alias of Amer el-Maati.

Mahmud Abu-al-Ma'ati: a Zifta resident who was a member of an Iraqi Ba'ath Party cell in Egypt arrested on April 13, 1991 on charges of plotting to carry out acts of sabotage and terrorism.

Fethi Maatoug: one of five members of the Islamic Tendency Movement arrested for the August 2, 1987 bombing of four tourist hostels in Sousse and Montastir, Tunisia by the Habib al-Dawi Group of the Islamic Jihad Organization in Tunisia. He was given the four bombs by bomb maker Mehrez Bourigga.

Abu Ma'awieah: alias of Mouttaz Hassan Murageh.

Bakour Mabrouk: alleged member of the Islamic Salvation Front who was arrested for involvement in the August 26, 1992 bombing of the Air France ticket counter at Houari Boumedienne Airport in Algeria that killed 12 people and wounded 128. Public sessions of his trial began on May 4, 1993. On May 26, 1993, a special Algiers judicial council passed death sentenced on 38 defendants, including him. The council found him guilty of actual direct participation in the crime as well as taking part in an aggression with the aim of inciting citizens to carry arms against state security, belonging to an armed group, spreading killing and destruction, hiding criminals, possession of forbidden weapons, and heading armed gangs.

Ahmad Salamah Mabruk: variant Ahmed Salama Mabruk, identified by Egyptian authorities on March 20, 1993 as a senior Egyptian fundamentalist abroad who had trained 25 Muslim members of the outlawed Jama'ah al-Islamiyah

group who were arrested at the al-Sallum border post after trying to enter Egypt from Libya with false passports. Police said they were planning to carry out attacks. The senior Egyptian Islamic Jihad member was deported from Baku, Azerbaijan, to Egypt in September 1998. When captured, the group's number three leader was carrying a computer disk listing 100 possible U.S. and Israeli targets. On April 18, 1999, the jailed head of the Egyptian Islamic Jihad's military operations told *Al-Hayat* that the group had chemical and biological weapons that it intended to use in "100 attacks against U.S. and Israeli targets and public figures in different parts of the world." He was sentenced to hard labor for life in a mass trial of Jihad members. He claimed that the plan was on a computer disk that was seized from him during his arrest in Azerbaijan.

Ahmed Salama Mabruk: variant of Ahmad Salamah Mabruk.

'Umar Mabruk: alias 'Abd al-Jalid Khalid Ahmad al-Subbar, was arrested in connection with the attempted assassination on November 29, 1984 in Athens of 'Asim Qutayshat, Jordan's Charge d'Affaires. The gun jammed. Border police arrested him at the Idomeni checkpoint on the Greece–Yugoslavia border. He was traveling under a forged Moroccan passport. Eyewitnesses identified him as the assailant. He had entered Greece on October 28. He was convicted of attempted murder and sentenced to 10 and a half years in prison.

Hamid Salih al-Ma'buni: alias Abu-al-Bara', a Saudi from Hay al-Khadra', Mecca, who was born in 1982 and entered Iraq on September 13, 2006, when he joined al Qaeda in Iraq. His recruitment facilitator was Ra'id al-Shammari. He contributed $1,000, a cell phone, and 2,603 riyals. His phone number was 0507758584.

Abderamane Madami: arrested on August 11, 1994 by French police for "activities in connection with a movement which advocates and practices violence and terrorism."

Abassi Madani: leader of the Algerian Islamic Salvation Front who, in 1993, was serving a 12-year jail sentence in Algeria. Algeria requested the extradition from Germany of his son, Oussama, on June 3, 1993. His release was demanded by the four Algerian Islamic extremists who, on December 24, 1994, hijacked an Air France A300 on the ground at Algiers's Houari Boumedienne Airport and killed a Vietnamese trade councilor and an Algerian policeman.

Abu Abd Allah al Madani: variant of Abu-'Abdallah al-Madani.

Abu 'Abdallah al-Madani: alias of 'Umar.

Abu-'Abdallah al-Madani: alias of 'Umar.

Abu-'Abd-al-Rahman al-Madani: alias of Hasan al-Surayhi.

Abu-'Abdallah al-Madani: variant Abu Abd Allah al Madani, alias of Muhammad 'Ali Munsir, variant Muhammad Ali Munser.

Abu Awef al Madani: variant of Abu-'Uf al-Madani.

Abu-'Uf al-Madani: variant Abu Awef al Madani, alias of 'Abd-al-Rahman Wa'il 'Ammash al-Harbi.

Ibrahim al-Madani: alias of Saif al-Adel.

Khaled Madani: an Algerian arrested in Spain on February 23, 2004 on suspicion of supplying forged documents to the Hamburg, Germany, al Qaeda cell. On April 12, 2004, the FBI and a U.S. prosecutor questioned him about whether he had forged passports for the 9/11 attackers.

Mahmud Madani: Hamas official who was shot in the West Bank on February 19, 2001.

Mahmud Muhammad Madani: arrested by Egyptian police in connection with the February 26, 1993 bombing of the Wadi el-Nil coffee shop in Tahrir Square in Cairo in which four people were killed and 16 wounded. He was tried with 48 other fundamentalist suspects on March 9, 1993 at the military court complex in the Hakstep area east of Cairo. They were charged with damaging national unity and social peace by calling for a change of the system of government and damaging the national economy by attacking tourism. Some were also charged with attempted murder in eight attacks on tour buses and Nile cruise ships. They faced possible death sentences. They were also accused of belonging to an underground organization, attempting to overthrow the government, and illegal possession of arms and explosives.

Oussama Madani: son of the Islamic Salvation Front of Algeria leader Abassi Madani. On June 3, 1993, Algeria asked Germany for the extradition of Oussama.

Sharif 'Abd-al-Rahman Tawfiq al-Madani: alias Umar al-Masri, identified by the Ethiopian government as one of the nine gunmen who, on June 25, 1995, fired on the armored limousine of Egyptian President Hosni Mubarak in Addis Ababa. On August 7, 1995, the Ethiopian Supreme State Security prosecutors charged the nine of forming a terrorist organization to destabilize the country, possessing arms and explosives, communicating with a foreign state to undermine the country's security, attempting to assassinate state figures, and attempting to blow up vital establishments.

'Ali Bin-Muhammad al-Madayyan: alias Abu-Rihanah, a Saudi from Buraydah who was born circa 1987 and joined al Qaeda in Iraq as a martyr circa 2006–2007, contributing $500, a watch, and his passport. His recruitment coordinator was Abu-'Adil, whom he knew via Abu-Usamah. He flew to Syria, where he met Abu-'Uthman and Abu-'Da'a'. He brought 4,500 riyals with him. His home phone number was 0096663235978.

Mohammed Maddy: age 44, an Egyptian charged in New York with sneaking his wife and children past airport security. As of November 2001, he was in federal custody in connection with Immigration and Naturalization Service and FBI investigations of the 9/11 attacks.

Khalid al-Madi: identified by Doha's *al-Sharq* on March 19, 1993 as a former member of the Abu Nidal Group. He was entrusted with financial administration, but left his post for the Far East.

Saed Madjid: Iranian hijacker of a British Airways BAC111 flying from Manchester to London on January 7, 1975. He demanded L100,000 ($235,000), a parachute, and a flight to Paris. The pilot pretended to go to Paris, but instead landed at Stansted Airport, Essex, 40 miles from London. The hijacker got off the plane and tried to escape, holding a steward as a hostage. He was subsequently captured. He was tried in London.

Tahri Madjid: alleged member of the Islamic Salvation Front who was arrested for involvement in the August 26, 1992 bombing of the Air France ticket counter at Houari Boumedienne Airport in Algeria that killed 12 people and wounded 128. Public sessions of his trial began on May 4, 1993. On May 26, 1993, a special Algiers judicial council sentenced him to six years.

Ahmad Madkhil: alias Abu-'Azam, an Algerian born in 1977 who joined al Qaeda in Iraq in 2007. His home phone number was 0021332221101; he could also be found at 0021371479638 and 0021362402666.

Iman al-Madnhom: one of seven male Palestine Liberation Organization (PLO) terrorists being searched for on April 30,1988 by Philippines Angeles Metropolitan District Command and Clark Air Base, after they had arrived from Manila earlier in the week to conduct sabotage and bombing missions and attack nightclubs frequented by U.S. servicemen. The terrorists reportedly arrived on a bus and carried black bags containing explosives to be set off at the Sweet Apple Club and the Capcom information booth. The PLO denied involvement.

Mohammad Abdullah Madni: a 22-year-old Saudi arrested by Pakistani authorities on August 17, 1998 as he was attempting to enter Afghanistan at the Towr Kham border post in the North West Frontier Province. He claimed that he was a bin Laden associate, but authorities said he was not involved with the bombings of the two U.S. embassies in Tanzania and Kenya on August 7, 1998. He was to be handed over to Saudi security agents.

Muhammad Saad Iqbal Madni: age 24, an al Qaeda operative who had worked with shoe bomber Richard Reid. He was arrested on January 9, 2002 by Indonesian authorities. Egypt requested extradition; Iqbal held Egyptian and Pakistani passports. The stocky, bearded Iqbal was wanted on terrorism charges in Egypt. Indonesia sent him quietly to Egypt on January 11 without a court hearing or lawyer. His name appeared on al Qaeda documents found in Afghanistan. Indonesian officials told the media that he had been sent to Egypt because of visa violations—failing to identify a sponsor for his visit. He had arrived in Jakarta on November 17, 2001. He had visited Solo, in central Java, which is believed to be a base for the al Qaeda-affiliated Jemaah Islamiah, a military Muslim group with bases in Indonesia, Singapore, and Malaysia.

'Abd ar-Rida Dawud Madwah: a Kuwaiti acquitted by the Kuwaiti State Security Court in 1984 in connection with the December 12, 1983 truck bombing of the administrative building of the U.S. embassy in Kuwait, killing four people and injuring 59.

Haitham Maghawri: Executive Director of the Holy Land Foundation for Relief and Development (HLF) who once told the Immigration and Naturalization Service that he had been arrested for planting a car bomb in a foreign country. President Bush ordered HLF's assets seized on December 4, 2001. HLF raised $13 million from U.S. residents the previous year; President Bush said some of the money was used to fund Hamas' efforts to "recruit suicide bombers and to support their families." The Texas-based organization had 35 full-time employees and was the largest Islamic charity in the United States. The Treasury Department froze $1.9 million in HLF funds in five U.S. banks. Raids were conducted at HLF offices in California, Illinois, and New Jersey. The FBI noted that the HLF had aided the family of a Hamas terrorist jailed for killing a Canadian Jewish tourist on a Tel Aviv beach.

Maghawri was among those indicted on July 27, 2004, when the Justice Department in Dallas unsealed a 42-count indictment against the HLF, charging it and 7 senior officials of the nation's largest Muslim charity with funneling $12.4 million over six years to individuals and groups associated with Hamas. The charges included providing material support for terrorism, money laundering, and income tax offenses. He had already left the country.

Zayd al-Maghrabi: a Moroccan in Damascus who served as a recruiter and travel facilitator for foreign fighters who wanted to join al Qaeda in Iraq in 2007.

Mua'awia Al Maghribi: recruitment coordinator for foreign fighters for al Qaeda in Iraq in 2007.

Abu Maghrieb: alias of Ahmed Bin Saleh bin Yunes Al Mughrieq.

Said Magri: placed under house arrest in Folembray, France on August 11, 1994 by French police for "activities in connection with a movement which advocates and practices violence and terrorism." He went on a hunger strike on August 16, 1994. He was taken to the hospital in Chauny, Aisne on August 23. Magri, manager of a Lille pizzeria, was suspected of membership in the Algerian Islamic Salvation Front (FIS). He said an uncle and a cousin had been killed by the FIS in Algeria. On August 26, he said he was ready to commit suicide if not released.

Mohamed Maha, age 32 and Omar Maha, age 23: Casablanca-based suicide bombers who, on April 14, 2007, attacked the U.S. consulate and the American Language Center, a privately run school and cultural center on the same Casablanca street within minutes of each other, slightly injuring a bystander.

Muhammad Mahalawi: a 22-year-old student sentenced to death on January 10, 1995 by the Higher Military Court in Cairo in connection with the October 14, 1994 stabbing of Naguib Mahfouz, the only Arab to receive the Nobel Prize for Literature, in a Cairo suburb.

Shadi Mahanna: Islamic Jihad's commander in northern Gaza who was killed in an Israeli air strike on October 27, 2005.

Jasem Mahboule: one of nine members of the Mujahedeen Movement, which has ties to al Qaeda, arrested on November 13, 2001 by Madrid and Granada police on charges of recruiting members to carry out terrorist attacks. Interior Minister Mariano Rajoy said the arrests followed two years of investigations. The leader was initially identified as Emaz Edim Baraktyarkas (variant Imad Eddin Barakat Yarbas), a Syrian with Spanish nationality. The other eight were from Tunisia and Algeria. Spain did not offer details on the terrorists' targets. The next day, police identified three more Islamic suspects. Police seized videos of Islamic guerrilla activities, hunting rifles, swords, fake IDs, and a large amount of cash. Spain—and other European nations—expressed concern about extraditing suspects to the United States for trial by military tribunals announced by President Bush.

On November 17, CNN reported that 11 suspected members of an Al Qaeda cell were arraigned. The *Washington Post* quoted Spanish officials on November 19 as indicating that eight al Qaeda cell members arrested in Madrid and

Granada had a role in preparing the September 11 attacks. Judge Baltasar Garzon ordered eight of them held without bail, because they "were directly related with the preparation and development of the attacks perpetrated by the suicide pilots on September 11." Judge Garzon charged them with membership in an armed group and possession of forged documents. They were also accused of recruiting young Muslim men for training at terrorist camps in Indonesia. They also reportedly sheltered Chechnya rebels and obtained medical treatment for al Qaeda members. They conducted robberies and credit card fraud and provided false documents to al Qaeda visitors. They also forwarded money to Hamburg. The group had connections to Mohamed Bensakhria, head of the Frankfurt-based cell that planned a terrorist attack in Strasbourg, France. He was arrested the previous summer and extradited to France. The group also had connections to six Algerians detained in Spain on September 26 who were charged with belonging to the Salafist Group for Preaching and Combat, a bin Laden-funded Algerian group.

The charges were based on documents and intercepted phone conversations of detainee Imad Eddin Barakat Yarbas, al Qaeda's leader in Spain. His name and phone number were in a document found in a search of a Hamburg apartment of a bin Laden associate. Police believe hijacker leader Atta could have met with some of them when he visited Spain in January and July. The group had links to Mamoun Darkazanli. Judge Garzon released three others who were arrested on November 13, but ordered them to report regularly to the authorities.

al-Mutawakkil 'Ala-Allah Mahdi: alias Abu-al-Fada', variant Abu-al-Fida', a Yemeni from San'a' who offered to be a suicide bomber for al Qaeda in Iraq in 2007. His home phone was 009671544144. He donated his passport and $240. His recruitment coordinators were al-Haram al-Jarbani and Salim al-Dulaymi.

Brahim Mahdi: age 34, an Algerian man believed to be connected to the Algerian Islamic League who coregistered a car with Lucia Garofalo, a Canadian arrested on December 19, 1999 in Vermont and charged with smuggling an alien into the United States.

Abderrazak Mahdjoub: an Algerian and suspected al Qaeda organizer in Germany who asked Mohammed Daki to find shelter for arriving immigrants in early 2003. He was one of two individuals arrested in Rome on November 28, 2003 on suspicion of recruiting suicide bombers against Coalition forces. He was charged with association with the aim of international terrorism. On March 19, 2004, Germany extradited him to Italy. As of March 18, 2005, he was on trial in Italy for links to international terrorists.

Abderrazak Mahdjoub: a resident of Germany and brother of Samir Mahdjoub who was linked to three Algerians and a Spaniard who, on May 14, 2004, were arrested in Spain and jailed pending investigation of their suspected involvement in terrorism. On May 19, High Court Judge Baltasar Garzon said the three Algerians belonged to al Qaeda and were recruiting Muslims across Europe to go to Iraq to fight the United States. The group was directed by Abu Musab Zarqawi. Garzon said the network was linked to one broken up in November in Italy. He said the group was also connected to the 9/11 Hamburg cell. He said Samir Mahdjoub helped others "distribute money to finance the sending of mujaheddin to Iraq" using the infrastructure of Ansar al-Islam in Italy and Syria. He said Mahdjoub and Redouane Zenimi and Mohamed Ayat had formed a Spanish al Qaeda cell lending "economic financing to the rest of the European network." He said the trio took orders from Abderrazak Madhjoub. Zarqawi ordered Abderrazak Mahdjoub and Abdelahi Djaouat to travel "to Damascus in March 2003 with the intention of going to Iraq, where other mujaheddin would be arriving." The duo were arrested in Syria.

Samir Mahdjoub: one of four individuals arrested in Spain on May 14, 2004 and jailed pending investigation of their suspected involvement in terrorism. On May 19, High Court Judge Baltasar Garzon said the three Algerians belonged to al Qaeda and were recruiting Muslims across Europe to go to Iraq to fight the United States. The group was directed by Abu Musab Zarqawi. Garzon said the network was linked to one broken up in November in Italy. He said the group was also connected to the 9/11 Hamburg cell. He said Samir Mahdjoub helped others "distribute money to finance the sending of mujaheddin to Iraq" using the infrastructure of Ansar al-Islam in Italy and Syria. He said Mahdjoub and Redouane Zenimi and Mohamed Ayat had formed a Spanish al Qaeda cell lending "economic financing to the rest of the European network." He said the trio took orders from Abderrazak Mahjdoub, a resident of Germany and a brother of one of the trio.

Abou Khalil Mahfoud: alias of Mahfoud Tadjine.

Abdul Rehman Misri Mahgribi: a Moroccan son-in-law of al Qaeda deputy chief Ayman al-Zawahiri and senior al Qaeda member who was killed when a Predator fired a missile in Damadola, a village near the Afghan border, 120 miles northwest of Islamabad, on January 13, 2006.

Muhammad al-Mahi: a member of Takfir wa Hijrah who was detained by Sudanese authorities after terrorists attacked worshippers in the Ansar al-Sunnah mosque in Khartoum on February 4, 1994, killing 19 worshippers and injuring several others.

Abd Al Mallek Hisham Mahio: alias Abu Hisham, a Syrian student in business administration from Ham'mas who was born in 1981 and joined al Qaeda in Iraq as a martyr in 2007, providing his ID and authorization document. He had experience in English, computers, and explosives. His recruitment coordinator was Abu Suleiman, whom he knew from Abu Abd Allah Al Ansari. His phone number was 0096631474957.

Abu-Mahjan: alias of Karim.

Abu-Mahjin: alias of Hudayban Bin-Muhammad Bin-Hudayban.

Abu Mahjjen: alias of Hamied Al Outtabie.

Mohammed Zeki Mahjoub: age 40, a store clerk arrested in Canada in 2000 and accused of membership in a radical splinter group of the Egyptian Islamic Jihad organization, working on a Sudanese farm run by bin Laden, staying briefly with a senior al Qaeda member, and lying about the visit when he entered Canada in 1995. He was held without formal charge on a security certificate, a procedure that was deemed constitutional by the Ottawa Federal Appeals Court on December 10, 2004. On February 23, 2007, Canada's Supreme Court unanimously struck down the use of secret testimony to imprison and deport foreigners as possible terrorist suspects, saying it violated the Charter of Rights and Freedoms. The court suspended the ruling for a year, leaving six detainees – five Arabs and one Sri Lankan – in limbo. Two were in a special prison, three were free on bond, and the last was ordered released on bond. In mid-February, a federal court ordered Mahjoub moved to house arrest.

Adel Mahjub: alias of Mahjub Husayn Muhammad.

Muhammed Mahjub: a senior leader of the Vanguards of Conquest faction of the Egyptian Islamic Jihad (EIJ). He was arrested on July 7, 2000 by Canadian police because of his links to the EIJ and Osama bin Laden. Egypt requested extradition.

Ali Mahmad: a 48-year-old Lebanese citizen detained in Paraguay on the tri-border area of Argentina, Brazil, and Paraguay on April 27, 1996. Israel announced that he was part of an Iranian-controlled Hizballah terrorist cell on his way to attack a Jewish institution. On April 29, 1996, the Buenos Aires press reported the release of two Lebanese citizens who were held for not presenting identity papers. The duo claimed to be bakers from Fox do Iguacu, Brazil and that their attorney, who was applying for their residency papers, was in possession of their identity papers.

Thabit 'Abd-al-Karim Mahmad: alias Zaydan, identified by Doha's *al-Sharq* on March 19, 1993 as a member of the Abu Nidal Group's Central Committee and deputy director of administration.

Pajiri Mahmed: alias of Hossein Dasgiri.

Abdul Basit Mahmood: alias Arbali Forlani, alias Abdul Karim, who was identified on January 29, 1995 by the Philippine National Police as the leader of an international terrorist group mostly composed of 30 Muslim extremists. The police said he was on the December 11, 1994 Philippine Airline Lines Flight 434 that was bombed by Abu Sayyaf on its way to Tokyo. His group also aimed to kill the Pope when he visited the Philippines in January 1995. He was later identified as Ramzi Ahmad Yusuf.

Sultan Bashir-ud-Din Mahmood: on December 20, 2001, the Bush Administration placed him on the list of banned terrorists and froze his international funds.

Mahmoud: alias given by Uganda to one of two European Popular Front for the Liberation of Palestine hijackers of Air France flight 139, an A300 flying from Tel Aviv to Paris on June 27, 1976 and ultimately diverted to Entebbe.

Mahmoud: a name given by a Shi'ite who, on April 10, 1984, told the *Washington Post* that he had loaded the dynamite into the car that crashed into the Israeli Army's south Lebanese headquarters in Tyre, killing 76 Israeli soldiers, border guards, and security men as well as 14 Palestinian and Lebanese prisoners. The Armed Struggle Organization (Munazmat al Nidal al-Musallah) claimed credit.

Mahmoud: alias of Dr. Ramadan Abdullah Mohammad Shallah.

Abdullah Aboud Mahmoud: an Iraqi fedayeen from a village near Baghdad who was allegedly behind the November 12, 2003 truck bombing in Nasiriyah, Iraq that killed 19 Italians and 12 Iraqis.

Husseini Rad Mahmoud: one of two Black March terrorists who, on April 16, 1979 tried to take over El Al flight 334, a B707 flying from Vienna to Tel Aviv, at Zaventem Airport in Brussels. They conducted a gun battle with police in which a dozen people were injured, then shot seven more Belgians. El Al security men and Belgian police shot one of the terrorists and arrested both. On August 16, 1979, the duo were sentenced to eight years for attempted murder and for carrying illegal weapons and false identity papers.

Mohammed Mahmoud: age 22, a leader of the Global Islamic Media Front, an Internet propaganda arm of al Qaeda, who was held by Austrian police who, on September 12, 2007 detained three al Qaeda sympathizers for posting an Internet video in the spring that threatened to attack Austria and Germany if they did not withdraw their military forces from Afghanistan.

El-Sayed Abdelkader Mahmoud: an Egyptian believed to be the leader of an al Qaeda cell that was broken up by police in Milan, Italy in November 2001.

Taha Mahmoud: South Yemeni terrorist bayoneted by Pakistani police after he had opened fire on Iraqi officials entering their Karachi Consulate General on August 2, 1978.

Youssef Hassan Mahmoud: driver of the car of Egyptian Interior Minister Zaki Badr on December 16, 1989 when gunpowder from a pickup truck exploded 30 yards away, burning Mahmoud. He was arrested. He was a student in Faiyum, a town heavily influenced by antigovernment fundamentalists.

Mohammed Mahmoudi: one of three Iranian youths who hijacked an Iran National Airlines B727 flying between Tehran, Abadan, and Kuwait on October 9, 1970 and diverted to Baghdad, Iraq. The trio threatened to blow up the plane with all passengers if Iran did not release 21 political prisoners. They injured a flight attendant. They were held by Iraqi authorities for questioning.

Mahmud: alias of Bassem Muhammad Khalil Shahin.

Eng 'Abd-al-'Aziz Mahmud: one of 12 Popular Front for the Liberation of Palestine members arrested by Jordanian security forces on October 4, 1989 for questioning about the smuggling of explosives and personnel into Jordan to fire rockets across the cease-fire line.

'Ali Mahmud: alias Ahmad Husan Kamil, 17-year-old nephew of Najib Muhammad Mahmud, who, on March 27, 1996, hijacked to Libya an Egyptair A310. The Egyptian embassy in Libya said that Libya would extradite the hijackers. Qadhafi ordered them handed over to the Egyptians on March 31. They arrived in Cairo that day.

Imad Salim Mahmud: a Lebanese who was resident in West Berlin and believed to be involved in the April 6, 1986 bombing of the La Belle Disco. Libyan terrorists stored weapons in his apartment.

Khalid Mahmud: 17-year-old son of Najib Muhammad Mahmud, who, on March 27, 1996, hijacked to Libya an Egypt Air A310. The Egyptian embassy in Libya said that Libya would extradite the hijackers. Qadhafi ordered them handed over to the Egyptians on March 31. They arrived in Cairo that day.

Mahmud Mahmud: name given by an individual who claimed credit for the Secret Lebanese Army in the June 1, 1987 assassination of Lebanese Prime Minister Rashid Karami when a bomb exploded on his helicopter.

Muhammad Mahmud: one of three Lebanese arrested on July 28, 1994 by Costa Rican police in David when they tried to cross the Panamanian–Costa Rican border with false passports. They were suspected of involvement in the suicide bombing of ALAS Airlines flight HP-1202, a twin-engine Brazilian-made Embraer on July 19, 1994, that killed two crew and 19 passengers, including a dozen Israeli businessmen, shortly after the plane had left Colon Airport in Panama. The Partisans of God, believed to be an Hizballah cover name, claimed credit.

Muhammad 'Isam Mahmud: a Syrian citizen arrested in Iraq who claimed to have been hired by the Syrian Consul in Bahgdad, Nasuh Juwayjati, to engage in acts of terrorism. Mahmud confessed to planting a bomb in a car in Ar-Rashid Street in Baghdad.

Mustafa Mahmud: on January 7, 1987, he was sentenced to death for setting off two time bombs at popular cafes in Kuwait on July 11, 1985 that killed 10 and injured 87.

Najib Muhammad Mahmud: also identified in the press as Muhammad Mahmud Humayd, Muhammad Mahmud Hamid Salim, alias Najib, Egyptian owner of a Luxor restaurant who was joined by his son, age 16, and nephew, age 14, on March 27, 1996 in hijacking an Eygpt Air Airbus A-310 flying from Luxor to Cairo and diverting it toward Tobruk, Libya. The hijackers were initially misidentified as Saudis. The pilot said the lead hijacker had taken "a whole strip of sedative pills and was acting strangely." The trio demanded to meet with Egyptian President Hosni Mubarak, U.S. President Bill Clinton, and Libyan leader Muammar Qadhafi, but surrendered after five hours at Libya's Martubah Airport, 90 kilometers from Tobruk. The trio later told the press that they intended to request political asylum and enhance the status of the Bani Hilal clan.

Egyptian authorities said Mahmud was mentally ill, an alcoholic, and a drug addict. He had lost his restaurant a year earlier for administrative irregularities. The trio had purchased explosives from a merchant on the Idfu mountains. He was flying to Cairo to see his psychiatrist. His son was seeking treatment for a drug habit. The Egyptian embassy in Libya said that Libya would extradite the hijackers. Qadhafi ordered them handed over to the Egyptians on March 31. They arrived in Cairo that day.

Nasser Mahmud: a 37-year-old Lebanese citizen detained in Paraguay on the tri-border area of Argentina, Brazil, and Paraguay on April 27, 1996. Israel announced that he was part of an Iranian-controlled Hizballah terrorist cell on his way to attack a Jewish institution. On April 29, 1996, the Buenos Aires press reported the release of two Lebanese citizens who were held for not presenting identity papers. The duo claimed to be bakers from Foz do Iguacu, Brazil, and that their attorney, who was applying for their residency papers, was in possession of their identity papers.

Shaykh Mahran: an Abu Nidal member who, on August 13, 1992, was hospitalized after being shot five times on al-Sitt Nafisah Street in Sidon, Lebanon.

Hidir Ahmet Mahresh: a Syrian who hijacked Saudi Airlines flight 287, a Lockheed Tristar en route from Damascus to Jeddah on April 5, 1984. He demanded to fly to Stockholm. He agreed to land in Istanbul for refueling. The plane instead landed in Yesilkog, where security forces stormed the plane and arrested him. He suffered a slight head injury.

Ibrahim Maiden: age 51, a condominium manager who trained in Afghanistan in 1993 and was the head of a Malaysian cell of Jemaah Islamiyah, whose members were arrested in December 2001 and January 2002 by Singaporean and Malaysian authorities.

Gazhi Ibrahim Abu Maizar: variant of Gazi Ibrahim Abu Mezer.

Hazam Majali: a Yemeni sentenced to death on August 28, 2004 by a Yemeni court at the end of the trial of 15 individuals convicted for the October 6, 2002 al Qaeda bombing of the *Limburg*, a French supertanker, in the Arabian Sea 5 miles off the coast of Yemen. Majali was sentenced to death for killing a Yemeni policeman at a checkpoint in 2002.

Abdul Karim Majati: an al Qaeda in Saudi Arabia terrorist leader who was killed in April 2005. He was linked to Younis Mohammed Ibrahim Hayari, the Moroccan head of al Qaeda in Saudi Arabia.

Bastawi 'Abd-al-Majid Abu-al-Majd: one of seven terrorists hanged on July 8, 1993 in the appeals prison in Cairo for attacks on tourist buses and installations in the al-Wajh al-Qiblio, Luxor, and Aswan areas, in accordance with the sentence handed down by the Supreme Military Court on April 22, 1993 in Case Number 6.

Majdi: Saudi-based recruitment coordinator for al Qaeda in Iraq foreign fighters in 2007.

Majed: Saudi-based recruitment coordinator for al Qaeda in Iraq foreign fighters in 2007.

Abd Al Aziz Hammed Abd Al Aziz Al Majed: an al Qaeda in Iraq volunteer.

Abd al Aziz Bin Ibrahim Bin Abd Al Aziz Al Majed: alias Abu Al Zubear, a Saudi from Riyadh who was born in 1988 and joined al Qaeda in Iraq as a fighter on 6th Rajab 1428 Hijra (2007), contributing a small amount of cash and bringing his passport, ID, and driver's license. His recruitment coordinator was Abu Abd Allah. His phone number was 5463596; his brother's was 0556001708; his family's was 0541948820.

Aymen Salem Majed: alias Abu Rayan, a Saudi student at an accounting college in Jeddah who joined al Qaeda in Iraq as a martyr in 2007, bringing $300, 30 Egyptian cents, and three watches.

His recruitment coordinator was Abu Musa'ab. His phone numbers were 78312 and 9665046.

Bader Bin Ibrahim Bin Nasser Al Majed: alias Abu Ibrahim, a Saudi mechanic from Riyadh who was born in 1400 Hijra and arrived in Iraq on 8th Sha'aban 1428 to join al Qaeda in Iraq as a martyr, bringing his passport. His recruitment coordinator was Abu Abd Allah. He arrived in Syria via public transportation. There he met Abu Umar, to whom he gave all of his 5,200 Saudi riyals. His phone number was 012680777; his wife's was 0558366658, which was that of Um Muhammad and Um Ahamed.

Abdul Majeed: on December 20, 2001, the Bush Administration placed him on the list of banned terrorists and froze his international funds.

Majid: Saudi-based recruitment coordinator for al Qaeda in Iraq foreign fighters in 2007.

Abd-al-Majid: alias Abu-Khalid, a Saudi from Mecca who was a fighter for al Qaeda in Iraq in 2007. His travel coordinator was Majdi. His home phone number was 5443086; his brother's was 0555570098.

'Abd-al-'Aziz Hamad – 'Abd-al-'Aziz al-Majid: variant Abd Al Aziz Hammed Abd Al Aziz Al Majed, alias Abu-'Amir al-Tamimi al-Najdi, variant Abu Ammer al Tammimi al Najdy, a Saudi from Riyadh who was born in 1982 and joined al Qaeda in Iraq on November 12, 2006 to conduct a martyrdom operation. He contributed his passport, $920, and 200 lira. His father's phone number was 0504198424; Umm -Amir's was 0564301510. His recruitment coordinator was Abu-'Abdallah Makbal.

Abu-'Ali Majid: alias of Mahmud Khalid 'Aynatur.

Hashim Bin-Muhammad Bin-'Abd-al'Aziz al-Majid: alias Abu-Hamzah, a Saudi born in 1988 who joined al Qaeda in Iraq as a martyr on July 20, 2007, contributing a video camera and presenting his passport, driver's license, and ID. His recruitment coordinator was Abu-'Abdallah. His brother's phone number was 0541404209; his father's was 0504198424.

Mohammed Majid: alias Mullah Fouad, an Iraqi Kurd and key Ansar organizer in Parma, Italy who fled to Syria a year earlier and who was allegedly behind the November 12, 2003 truck bombing in Nasiriyah, Iraq that killed 19 Italians and 12 Iraqis.

Rizaq Sayyid 'Abd-al-Majid: alias Walid Khalid, identified by Doha's *al-Sharq* on March 19, 1993 as a member of the Abu Nidal Group's Central Committee and official spokesman for the group in Beirut. He was prominent during the *Silco* ship incident. He was believed to have been assassinated in southern Lebanon in 1992.

Saili Majid: an Iranian man who was sought under an international arrest warrant in connection with the August 6, 1991 assassination of former Iranian Premier Shapur Bakhtiar in his Paris home. On February 7, 1994, French Judge Louis Bruguiere dropped the charges.

Al-Majidi: alias of 'Ali Khidayir Badday 'Abd.

Samir Bin Muhammad Al Majnoni: alias Abu Jawed, a Saudi born in 1401 Hijra who joined al Qaeda in Iraq in 2007. His phone numbers were 0504541147 and 025222597.

Majrah: variant of Majri.

Anour Majrar: arrested in Morocco in late 2005. He said he had visited the Algerian Salafist Group for Preaching and Combat leaders in Algeria with Muhammad Benhedi Msahel and Amir Laaraj, an Algerian. Morocco charged Msahel and Majrar with being part of a terrorist network that was planning to attack the Paris Metro, Orly Airport, the headquarters of France's domestic intelligence agency, Milan's police headquarters, and the Basilica of San Petronio in Bologna, whose fifteenth-century fresco shows the Prophet Muhammad in hell. In February 2007, Majrar was sentenced to seven years in prison.

Majri: variant Majrah, Saudi-based recruitment coordinator for al Qaeda in Iraq foreign fighters in 2007.

Makram Bin Salem al-Majri: alias Abu Mua'az, a Swedish clerk who was born in 1974 and joined al Qaeda in Iraq (AQI) as a fighter circa 2007, contributing his watch. He also brought his passport and driver's license. He turned over all of his $2,700 to his handlers in Syria, who told him it was a donation. He had arrived from Sweden via Egypt and Syria. His recruitment coordinator was Ashraf, whom he met during the Hajj. His home phone number was 0046850022939; his wife's was 00201162833329, although he asked the AQI personnel officer not to contact her.

Abu-'Abdallah Makbal: variant Abu Abd Allah Mukbel, Saudi-based recruitment coordinator for foreign fighters for al Qaeda in Iraq in 2006.

Abu-'Usamah al-Maki: alias of Faris.

Abu-'Abadah al-Makkawi: alias of Turki Muhammad al-Jaza'iri the Algerian.

Muhamad Ibrahim Makkawi: alias of Saif al-Adel.

Muhammad al-Makkawi: alias of Saif al-Adel Almasari, senior al Qaida aide listed by the *Washington Post* in late February 2002 as being at large.

Abu Asim al-Makki: alias of Muhammad Hamdi al-Ahdal.

Abu Asim al-Makki: alias of Sheikh Abd al-Rahim al-Nashiri.

Abu-Dhar al-Makki: alias of Sultan Radi al-Utaybi.

Abu-Hamzah al-Makki: alias of 'Adil Mastur Yahya al-Ka'bi al-Hadhli.

Abu-Khubab al-Makki: alias of Salih Bin Muhammad Nasir al-Ahmadi.

Abu-Mu'ayyad al-Makki: alias of 'Abdullah Sami Ahmad Muhammad.

Abu Suleiman Makki: alias of Khaled Harbi.

Abu-Tariq al-Makki: alias of Muhammad 'Abd-al-Fattah Muhammad Rashad.

Abu-'Umar al-Makki: alias of Sabir 'Isa al-Isma'il.

Omar Abdullah Makki: leader of the terrorist group Lashkar-i-Tayyiba, who was killed on June 20, 2001 near Srinagar, Kashmir.

Ya'arib Faiq Mahdi: an Iraqi sentenced to 15 years in prison by the Kuwaiti State Security Court in 1984 in connection with the December 12, 1983 truck bombing of the administrative building of the U.S. Embassy in Kuwait, killing four people and injuring 59. As of April 1987, none of the death sentences had been carried out. The release of 17 of the 25 prisoners in the case was demanded on numerous occasions by the Islamic Jihad in return for Americans held captive in Lebanon beginning in 1986.

Sa'id Amin Abu-Al-Majd: arrested on November 16, 1992 for being the driver of the taxi used in the getaway from the attack on November 11, 1992 by four Islamic Group gunmen against a busload of 18 German tourists that injuring seven people in Qina, Egypt. He was found in a sugar cane farm near Hujayrat.

Al-Majid: one of two Palestinian students who threw a hand grenade at two other Palestinian students at a Thessaloniki, Greece student hotel on November 8, 1985. They were arrested while attempting to leave the country on a flight from Mikra Airport. Police found an automatic weapon, two grenades, and 420 grams of dynamite in the al Fatah members' apartment.

Issam Ahmad Dibwan Al-Makhlafi: a Yemeni born in Saudi Arabia on 1977, believed by the FBI on February 11, 2002, to be planning a terrorist attack in the United States or on U.S. interests in Yemen.

Nabil Hassan Ahmed Makhlofi: variant of Nabil Hasan Ahmad Makhlufi.

Said Makhloufi: alleged member of the Islamic Salvation Front who was arrested for involvement in the August 26, 1992 bombing of the Air France ticket counter at Houari Boumedienne Airport in Algeria that killed 12 people and wounded 128. Public sessions of his trial began on May 4, 1993. On May 26, 1993, a special Algiers judicial council passed death sentenced on 38 defendants, including him. The council found him guilty of inciting citizens to carry arms against state security, belonging to an armed group, spreading killing and destruction, hiding criminals, possession of forbidden weapons, and heading armed gangs. He remained at large.

Nabil Hasan Ahmad Makhlufi: variant Nabil Hassan Ahmed Makhlofi, alias Abu-Muhammad, a Moroccan from Casablanca who was born on October 21, 1984 and joined al Qaeda in Iraq as a "fearless fighter"/martyr on October 25, 2006, contributing $100, a razor, a watch, a passport, and an ID card. His recruitment coordinators were Sa'd and Sa'id. His phone number was 212 64529351.

Amar Makhulif: alias Abu Doha, alias the Doctor, 36 in September 2001, believed to be a senior Algerian terrorist in London with links to European al Qaeda terrorist cells. He was arrested at Heathrow Airport on charges of orchestrating a foiled plot to bomb Los Angeles International Airport on December 31, 1999. He was in contact with Redouane Dahmani.

Mahmud Makkawi: leader of the Egyptian Vanguards of Conquest Organization, who was believed to be hiding in Pakistan in late November 1993. He had gone to Afghanistan with Ayman al-Zawahiri. Egyptian police wanted him in connection with the November 25, 1993 bombing of the convoy of Egyptian Prime Minister Dr. 'Atif Sidqi that killed a 15-year-old girl and wounded 21 other people. *Middle East News Agency* said that they had also participated in the car bomb explosion in the al-Qulali area a few months earlier and the abortive attempt to assassinate UN Secretary General Dr. Boutros Boutros-Ghali during the Organization of African Unity (OAU) summit in Cairo.

Samir Abduh Sa'id al-Maktawi: born in Saudi Arabia in 1968, the Yemeni was believed by the FBI, on February 11, 2002, to be planning a terrorist attack in the United States or on U.S. interests in Yemen.

Abu-Malak: alias of Anas Isma'il Mula.

Abu-'Abd-al-Malak: a Syrian-based travel facilitator for al Qaeda in Iraq foreign fighters in 2007.

Tayseer Abd Al Mousleh Al Maleeh: variant of Taysir 'Abd-al-Muslih al-Malih.

Abu Abd Al Malek: a Syrian-based facilitator for foreign recruits joining al Qaeda in Iraq in 2007.

Mansouri Maliani: alleged member of the Islamic Salvation Front who was arrested for involvement in the August 26, 1992 bombing of the Air France ticket counter at Houari Boumedienne Airport in Algeria that killed 12 people and wounded 128. Public sessions of his trial began on May 4, 1993. On May 26, 1993, a special Algiers judicial council sentenced him to death, finding him guilty of incitement to carry arms against state security, forming an armed group, heading an armed gang, and carrying forbidden weapons. On August 31, 1993, after exhausting all constitutional and legal appeals, he was executed.

Taysir 'Abd-al-Muslih al-Malih: variant Tayseer Abd Al Mousleh Al Maleeh, alias Abu-Mus'ab, variant Abu Musa-ab, a Saudi from Al-Jawf who was born on December 6, 1980 and joined al Qaeda in Iraq on October 14, 2006, contributing $100, 100 lira, and three electric razors. His home phone numbers were 0096646255589 and 0096656390056.

Abdul Malik: On March 26, 2007, the Pentagon announced that Abdul Malik, who was arrested in East Africa earlier in 2007 and admitted involvement in the November 2002 Kenyan hotel bombing and attempted downing of an airplane, had been transferred to the Guantánamo Bay military prison camp. *Reuters* reported that he was captured in Kenya. He was believed to be connected to al Qaeda suspect Saleh Ali Saleh Nabhan, a Kenyan wanted in the hotel attack.

Malika: alias of Malika El-Aroud.

Sayed Abdul Malike: age 43, a New York cab driver arrested by the FBI on May 22, 2003. He allegedly attempted to buy enough explosives "to blow up a mountain." He allegedly surveilled bridges and cruise ships in Miami and lied to the FBI about his activities. U.S. Magistrate Judge Rosanne L. Mann ordered him held without bail after Assistant U.S. Attorney Catherine Friesen said he could be a terrorist and that she would prove that he tried to buy explosives in Queens. She warned that he might not have acted alone, and was expecting Pakistani-based financing. Malike is a U.S. resident from Afghanistan. He was held on charges of unlawful possession of Valium and lying to law enforcement officers.

Sher Mohammad Malikkheil: alias Sheroo, a Pashtun tribesman with known links to Islamists. On February 28, 2008, a missile strike leveled his home near Kaloosha village in South Waziristan, Pakistan, killing ten suspected al Qaeda and Taliban members and wounding another seven. He was a member of the Yargulkhel subtribe of the Wazir tribe.

Nasser Khamis el-Mallahi: a member of Monotheism and Jihad, the name once used by the group that became Al Qaeda in Iraq. On May 8, 2006, Bedouin trackers led police to the hideout, in an olive grove south of Arish on the Sinai Peninsula. El-Mallahi was married to a Palestinian. After a half-hour gun battle, he was killed. He was believed to have organized the triple bombing on April 24, 2006 of a seaside promenade at the resort of Dahab, Egypt, killing 18 civilians, including six foreigners (among them a 10-year-old German boy who died in a taxi on the way to a hospital, a Swiss, a Russian, and a Lebanese woman, and two unidentified foreign women), and injuring 85, including three Italians and four Americans.

Abdul Rahim Mallouh: deputy secretary general of the Popular Front for the Liberation of Palestine who was arrested by Israel on June 11, 2002.

Habib Ma'mar: variant of Habib Maamar.

Mamaru: alias of Isidro Garalde Bedialauneta.

Captain Mamoud: variant Mahmoud, alias of Zuhair Akache, who fired into a car near Hyde Park in London on April 10, 1977 and killed Qadi Abdullah Ali Hajri, deputy chief of the North Yemen Supreme Court, who had served as his nation's Prime Minister from 1972–1974; his wife, Fatimah; and Abdullah Ali Hammami, a minister in the North Yemeni embassy. Akache escaped into a subway station. He reportedly took an Iraqi Airways jet to Baghdad within five hours. He possibly next surfaced as Captain Mamoud, the leader of the October 13, 1977 Lufthansa flight 181 hijacking, when he died in a shootout with the German rescue squad. Believed by some observers to have been Johannes Gerdus, a Dutch terrorist.

Harda Mamoud: variant Mahmoud, alias used by one of the Organization of Struggle Against World Imperialism hijackers of Lufthansa flight 181, a B737 scheduled to fly from the Spanish resort island of Mallorca to Frankfurt on October 13, 1977. The terrorists demanded the release of the same 11 terrorists in West German jails as had been mentioned in the Schleyer kidnapping of September 5, 1977 and the release of two Palestinian terrorists held in Turkish jails for the August 11, 1976 Popular Front for the Liberation of Palestine machine gun attack on passengers awaiting an El Al flight in Istanbul. They demanded $15 million and that 100,000 DM be given to each prisoner, who were to be flown to Vietnam, Somalia, or South Yemen, all of which indicated an unwillingness to receive them. After the plane had hopscotched to various countries, the terrorists shot the pilot in Aden. A West German GSG9 team ran a successful rescue operation in Somalia on October 18, initially killing two of the hijackers. A third in the first-class compartment opened fire and threw a grenade after being hit. A female hijacker opened fire and was quickly subdued. Harda Mamoud was believed by some observers to have been Johannes Gerdus, a Dutch terrorist, who died in the GSG9 rescue.

Omar Ben Mamoud: Sudanese terrorist and alleged chairman of the International Mollah Force whom Philippines National Police, on November 14, 1995, said had infiltrated into the country to train Abu Sayyaf Muslim extremists in Mindanao. He was linked to Ramzi Ahmad Yusuf and Hadji Murad.

Ahmed Mamour: a Lebanese arrested on April 3, 1985 by Rome police after he fired an antitank rocket at the fourth-floor window of a building housing the Jordanian embassy. He admitted to being a member of Black September, the cover name for Abu Nidal's group.

Daimal Mamud: local chairman of the Popular Front for the Liberation of Palestine in the Philippines in December 1988.

Nu Man: alias of Mustafa Mohamed Fadhil.

Robert S. Manning: a Jewish Defense League member and fugitive in Israel who, in July 1988, was indicted by a federal grand jury on charges of aiding and abetting in the sending of a letter bomb to the Manhattan Beach offices of Prowest Computers owner Brenda Couthamel on July 17, 1980. The bomb killed her secretary, Patricia Wilkerson. Manning had been solicited to send the bomb by William Ross. He faced a life sentence.

Rochelle Ida Manning: wife of Robert S. Manning, she was indicted on charges of aiding and abetting in the sending of a letter bomb to the Manhattan Beach offices of Prowest Computers owner Brenda Couthamel on July 17, 1980. The bomb killed her secretary, Patricia Wilkerson. Manning's husband had been solicited to send the bomb by William Ross. She faced a life sentence. She was in custody awaiting a November 1, 1988 trial.

Mansour: Saudi-based recruitment coordinator for al Qaeda in Iraq foreign fighters in 2007.

Abd Allah Mansour: alias of Adel Lahiq al Qurani.

Abdallahal-Mansour: Egyptian Jihad Secretary General who remained at large as of April 18, 1999, when a military court sentenced nine of his group to death.

Abu Ammer Am Mansour: alias of Zakaria Hussnie al Refa'aie.

Ahmed Ahkir Mansour: a Syrian who was one of two Islamic Dawa gunmen who overpowered a guard and threw a bag of explosives into the fountain in front of the Iraqi consulate in Istanbul, Turkey on December 21, 1983. Prior to the explosion, the two were arrested near the car, which they had intended to move to the Iraqi embassy.

Ali M. Mansour: a Hattiesburg, Mississippi resident and one of a dozen masked, club-wielding Libyan students who took over the Libyan student aid office in McLean, Virginia and took hostages for a few minutes on December 22, 1982. Police raided the site after nine hours and the students surrendered. They were held on three counts of abduction. Bond for four of the students, who had, in 1981, occupied the Libyan UN Mission was set at $30,000; bond for the others was set at $15,000. Fairfax County released the names of the students on December 30, 1982. The Libyan student aid group sued the defendants for $12 million in Fairfax Circuit Court. On February 7, 1983, the students countersued for $15 million. Each of the students pleaded guilty in January 1983 to unlawful assembly, assaulting two office employees, and destroying private property. County prosecutors dropped felony charges of abduction. On March 4, 1983, Judge Barnard F. Jennings sentenced the 12 to one year in jail. On September 9, 1983, a Fairfax County judge released 10 of the 12 protestors after they presented proof to the court that they were enrolled for the fall term at accredited U.S. colleges.

Ali Omar Mansour: a Libyan intelligence officer arrested by French authorities on December 1, 1994 in connection with the UTA 772 bombing of September 19, 1989 that killed 171. He was released on December 5, 1994.

Ben Khalifa Mansour: a Tunisian who was one of six men arrested on March 1, 2002 by Rome police on suspicion of al Qaeda ties. They were held on suspicion of association with a "criminal organization with terrorist intentions" and intent to obtain and transfer arms and weapons. Wiretaps of their conversations included discussions of killing President Bush, a cyanide compound, and weapons needed for terrorist training camps in Afghanistan. Police seized videos, address books, and a plane ticket to Phoenix. They also found a letter with the address of Lotfi Raissi, an Algerian accused in the United Kingdom of giving pilot training to the 9/11 hijackers.

Issam Mansour: one of three gunmen who, on March 16, 1993, shot to death Professor Djilali Liabes, the former Algerian Minister for Higher Education, in Douba, Algeria. Mansour was

found dead 500 meters from the site. He was fatally wounded in the leg.

He was born on February 8, 1962 in Bab el Oued and lived in the Bourouba quarter near Badjarah.

Mohamed Mansour: a resident of Kusnacht, Switzerland; Zurich, Switzerland; the United Arab Emirates; and Egypt who was listed in November 2001 by the United States as a terrorism financier.

Muhammad Sakout Mansour: variant of Muhammad Sakut Mansur.

Shadi Muhammad Saleh Al Mansour: alias Abu Muhammad, a Syrian pathologist from Dyr Al Zur who joined al Qaeda in Iraq as a martyr in 2007, bringing 43,500 lira. His recruitment coordinator was Abu Ahmed. His phone number was 051351243.

Sidi Mohammed ben Mansour: Algerian student at the Vincennes Faculty of the University of Paris who was arrested on April 18, 1971 as a member of the Easter Commando of the Popular Front for the Liberation of Palestine (PFLP). He was accused of furnishing detonators to the group, which had arrived in Israel intending to bomb Israeli buildings for the PFLP. He was sentenced to prison.

Zeinab Mansour-Fattouh: a resident of Zurich, Switzerland who was listed in November 2001 by the United States as a terrorism financier.

Abdallah al Mansouri: variant of Muhammad 'Abdallah al-Mansuri.

Alla'a Abd Allah Al Mansouri: alias Abu Abd Allah, a Libyan from Darnah who was born on March 3, 1977 and joined al Qaeda in Iraq on October 25, 2006, bringing an ID, watch, knife, and flashlight. His recruitment coordinator was Suhil. His home phone number was 0021881631150.

Mansur: on July 6, 1988, Pakistani district court judge Zafar Ahmed Babar ended an eight-month trial in a special court in Rawalpindi's Adiyala maximum security prison and sentenced the Lebanese to death by hanging for the September 5, 1986 hijacking of a Pan Am B747 and for killing 11 passengers at Karachi airport. There was insufficient evidence to convict five terrorists of the deaths of 11 other passengers. The hijacker mastermind, Sulayman al-Turki, said that the group would appeal the sentences and, if they were freed, "we would hijack a U.S. airliner once again." The court also passed a total jail sentence of 257 years on each of the accused on several other charges of murder, conspiracy to hijack, possession of illegal arms, and confinement of the passengers. The terrorists had 30 days to appeal the verdict and the sentence in Lahore's High Court. On July 28, 1988, the press reported that the terrorists reversed their decision, and would now appeal.

'Abdallah Mansur: alias of 'Adil Lahiq al-Qarni.

Abu-'Amir al-Mansur: alias of Zakariyyah Husni al-Rifa'i.

Ahmad Jabir al-Mansur: one of the April 5, 1988 hijackers of Kuwait Airlines flight 422, a B747 flying from Bangkok to Kuwait that was diverted to Mashhad, Iran. He had arrived in Bangkok on March 30, 1988 with a forged Bahraini passport.

Ali Mansur: a Lebanese with German citizenship who was arrested on July 25, 1990 on suspicion of murder. He was believed to have been involved in the April 5, 1986 bombing of La Belle Disco in West Berlin. On August 22, 1990, the examining magistrate at the Tiergarten Court rescinded the arrest warrant at the request of the public prosecutors. He was freed two days later.

Kamal Mansur: alias of Faysal al-Kafri.

May Elias Mansur: a Lebanese woman initially suspected of setting off a bomb on TWA flight 840

en route from Rome to Athens on April 2, 1986. Four people were sucked out of the hole in the side of the B727. Mansur had sat on seat 10F and disembarked before the plane left. She allegedly had past connections with a terrorist act involving an Alitalia flight, but it was determined that authorities had confused her with a man believed responsible for placing a bomb on an Alitalia flight in 1983. She was questioned by Lebanon's military prosecutor and an investigating judge on April 10, 1986, but no arrest warrant was ever issued.

Muhammad Sakut Mansur: variant Muhammad Sakout Mansour, alias Abu-Mus'ab, a Moroccan from al-Dar al-Bayda' in Casablanca, who was born on August 14, 1978 and joined al Qaeda in Iraq on October 10, 2006, contributing $100 and a wristwatch. His brother's phone number was 0021279329855; that of another relative was 0021222321666. His recruitment coordinator was Muhammad al-Jardan.

Umran Mansur: manager of the Libyan Arab Airlines office in Istanbul who met with the two Libyans who were stopped by police on April 18, 1986 in front of the U.S. officer's club in Ankara, Turkey, and threw away a bag containing six grenades and ran. Mansur allegedly selected the target. His trial began in absentia on May 13, 1986 in the State Security Court. On June 7, 1986, the charges were dropped because of diplomatic immunity.

Yasir Muhammad Mansur: arrested by Egyptian police in connection with the February 26, 1993 bombing of the Wadi el-Nil coffee shop in Tahrir Square in Cairo in which four people were killed and 16 wounded. He was tried with 48 other fundamentalist suspects on March 9, 1993 at the military court complex in the Hakstep area east of Cairo. They were charged with damaging national unity and social peace by calling for a change of the system of government and damaging the national economy by attacking tourism. Some were also charged with attempted murder in eight attacks on tour buses and Nile cruise ships. They faced possible death sentences. They were also accused of belonging to an underground organization, attempting to overthrow the government, and illegal possession of arms and explosives.

'Ala' 'Abdallah al-Mansuri: alias Abu-'Abdallah, a Libyan from Darnah who was born on March 5, 1977 and joined al Qaeda in Iraq on October 25, 2006 to become a martyr. His recruitment coordinator was Suhayl. He contributed his ID card, a watch, a knife, and a flashlight. His home phone number was 0021881631150.

Muhammad 'Abdallah al-Mansuri: variant Abdallah al Mansouri, member of the Lebanese Armed Revolutionary Faction (LARF) arrested on August 6, 1984 in Trieste as he entered Italy carrying 6.6 kilograms of explosives. His release was demanded by the gunmen who kidnapped Giles Sidney Peyrolles, the director of the French Cultural Center and a consular official, near his Tripoli office on March 24, 1985. On May 8, 1985, he was charged by an Italian judge with the February 15, 1984 assassination in Rome of Leamon R. Hunt, the American Director General of the multinational force in Egypt's Sinai Peninsula. On June 18, 1985, a Trieste court found him guilty and sentenced him to 16 years and a $510 fine. On October 11, 1985, a Rome appeals court threw out the charges against the LARF member for insufficient evidence. On November 27, 1985, LARF threatened Italy unless he was released. On March 20, 1986 a bomb exploded in the crowded Point-Show shopping mall just off the Champs Elysees in Paris, killing two Lebanese and wounding 30; the Committee of Solidarity with Arab and Middle East Political Prisoners demanded the release of Mansuri.

Salamah Sagar Rahaq Al Manzi: alias Abu Azzam, a Saudi born in 1402 Hijra who joined al Qaeda in Iraq in 2007 and was assigned to Al Anbar. His phone number was 0154560891.

Ishaq Manzoor: a Jaish-e-Muslimeen (a breakaway Taliban faction) commander who claimed

credit for the October 28, 2004 kidnapping of three UN election workers in Kabul.

Abu-al-Maqam: variant of Abu-al-Maqdam.

Abu-al-Maqdam: alias of 'Abd-al-Rahman Bin-'Ali al-Rajihi.

Abu Khatab al-Maqdisi: spokesman for the Palestinian gunmen who on March 12, 2007 kidnapped *BBC* reporter Alan Johnston in Gaza City. He was arrested by Hamas on July 2, 2007.

Sheik Abu-Mohammed Maqdisi: alias of Isam Mohammad Taher Barqawi. He was released from a Jordanian prison on March 12, 2008, having been held without charge since July 2005 despite his acquittal at a trial of al Qaeda sympathizers.

Ahmad 'Abd-al-Maqsud: one of three al-Jama'ah al-Islamiyah extremists who, on February 4, 1993, threw petrol bombs at three South Korean tourists outside their hotel near the Egyptian Pyramids. He was arrested at the scene and told police that he agreed to attack the Korean tourists' bus with Hasan al-Sakran.

Sayyid 'Abd-al-Maqsud: one of seven fundamentalists with terrorist connections who were arrested on September 27, 1998 in London under the immigration law.

Ali Maqtari: Yemeni detained by the United States in October 2001 in connection with the 9/11 investigation.

Nabil al-Marabh: on September 17, 2001, Detroit police raided a two-story brick duplex on Norman Street, searching for the 34-year-old Kuwaiti bin Laden associate who once lived there. They found a day planner that contained a sketch of a U.S. military base in Incirlik, Turkey and an Arabic reference to a planned attack on former Secretary of Defense William Cohen. Chicago police arrested al-Marabh two days later at a liquor store. Nine days later, the Secret Service arrested

Youssef Hmimssa, age 30, a Moroccan Chicago cab driver whose fake ID appeared in the same bedroom as the day planner. al-Marabh had financial dealings with Boston hijackers Ahmed Alghamdi and Satam Al Suqami. al-Marabh was a close friend of Raed Hijazi, a former Boston cabbie on trial in Jordan for his role in an aborted plot to bomb Jordanian hotels and tourist sites filled with Americans and Israelis celebrating the millennium. Hjjazi told American and Jordanian authorities that al-Marabh was a bin Laden agent. Boston cab driver al-Marabh moved among Canada, Boston, and Detroit before his arrest. Canadian Mounties raided three houses and a business in Toronto on September 26, searching for information in connection with al-Marabh.

In June 2001, al-Marabh was then wanted for failing to visit his parole officer after receiving a six-month suspended sentence in Boston for stabbing a roommate during an argument. In June, the Immigration and Naturalization Service caught him in the back of a tractor-trailer, carrying fake Canadian documents and trying to sneak into the United States at Niagara Falls. He was turned over to Canadian authorities, who released him on bond into the custody of his uncle. His uncle worked for a religious school in Canada run by a terrorist, according to news accounts. al-Marabh went back to a new address in Dearborn, Michigan, obtaining a duplicate license in Detroit in August. When federal agents raided al-Marabh's old Norman Street residence on September 17, they arrested three men inside, including Karim Koubriti and Ahmed Hannan, Youssef Hmimssa's old roommates, who denied knowing al-Marabh. Koubriti told agents there were false documents in the bedroom. Agents found a false passport and Social Security card for Michael Saisa, with Hmimssa's photo. They also found the day planner. Moroccans Koubriti, Hannan, and Hmimssa remained in detention as of November 1 on charges of possession of false documents. A Detroit federal grand jury subpoenaed handwriting samples.

In July 2002, al-Marabh agreed to a plea bargain, admitting to conspiring to enter the United States illegally. He was freed for eight months' time served and ordered to be deported to Syria.

'Umar Ibrahim al-Marba'i: variant Omar Ibrahim al Marbaie, alias Abu-Usayd al-Hadrami, variant Abu Aseed al Hadramie, a Saudi from Umm-al-Quraa Street in Mecca who joined al Qaeda in Iraq on September 13, 2006. He was born on January 21, 1982. His phone numbers were 0096394814681, 0096393440867, and 00966556110420. He brought $7,300 and 3,000 lira. His recruitment coordinator was Abu Tamam.

Omar Ibrahim al Marbaie: variant of 'Umar Ibrahim al-Marba'I.

Jamal Alawi Mari: a Yemeni captured a few weeks after 9/11 at his Karachi home by Pakistani and U.S. authorities on suspicion of working for charities that funded al Qaeda. He claimed he was imprisoned in Jordan, then taken to Guantánamo.

Abu Mariam: alias of 'Abdallah Ahmad 'Abdallah.

Mushar Muhammad al-Marishid: alias Abu-Hazim, a Saudi who worked in communications and lived in Riyadh who was born circa 1987 and joined al Qaeda in Iraq to become a martyr on August 11, 2007, contributing 16,400 Saudi riyals and a passport. His recruitment coordinator was Abu-'Umar, whom he knew via a friend in Saudi Arabia. He arrived in a group via Saudi Arabia and Syria, where he met recruitment facilitator Abu-Mur.

Mohammed Markieh: one of 15 Iranian dissidents from Sydney who attacked the Iranian Embassy in Australia on April 6, 1992, beating diplomatic staff and injuring three of them, damaging cars, ransacking files, and setting fires. He was remanded until June 1. Prosecutors opposed bail. A large number of Iranian passports and $65,000 U.S. cash were stolen. The defendants each faced up to ten charges related to attacks on embassy officials and property damage.

Lamine Maroni: age 31, one of five Algerian al Qaeda members whose trial began on April 16, 2002 in Frankfurt on charges of plotting to bomb the Strasbourg marketplace on December 23, 2000. They were charged with forming a terrorist organization, planning to cause an explosion, plotting to commit murder, falsifying documents, dealing drugs, and various weapons charges. His fingerprints matched those of a man living in Sheffield, United Kingdom, who was convicted of bank robbery. On March 10, 2003, the Frankfurt court found him guilty of preparing a bomb in the attack on the Strasbourg Christmas market and of conspiracy to murder. He was sentenced to 10–12 years. He said that the prosecution failed to prove al Qaeda links.

Salem Abu Marouf: arrested in March 1996 by Palestinian security forces at the request of Israel on suspicion of involvement in a recent series of Hamas bombings.

Isam Marqah: alias Salim Ahmad, named by Doha's Al Sharq on March 19, 1993 as the assistant secretary general of the Abu Nidal group as of 1987. He had lost the position in 1991, but kept his membership in the Political Bureau.

Ali Saleh Khalah al-Marri: alias Abdullakareem A. Almuslam, believed to be al Qaeda's senior operative in the U.S. following the 9/11 attacks. The Qatari was believed to be linked to Khalid Sheikh Mohammed, Mustafa Ahmed al-Hawsawi, Abu Khabab al-Masri, and Dhiren Barot.

He arrived in the United States at age 17 in 1982, bouncing around at several colleges. He obtained a business degree from Bradley University in Peoria, Illinois in 1991. In 1996, he left Qatar and moved to Afghanistan, where he trained for 15–19 months in al Qaeda camps, learning about poisons and toxins from Abu Khabab al-Masri. In the summer of 2001, Khalid Sheik Mohammed (KSM) introduced him to Osama bin Laden in Afghanistan, where he was told to go to the United States before 9/11. In August, he went to the United Arab Emirates, where Mustafa Ahmed al-Hawsawi, the 9/11 paymaster, gave him $13,000 in cash. He enrolled at Bradley University on September 11, 2001 to earn his Master's in computer science. On December 12, 2001, the FBI arrested him at his home. Searches of his computer records included research on purchasing large quantities of chemicals used to manufacture hydrogen cyanide. He was later charged with credit card fraud; he held more than 1,000 stolen credit card numbers. On December 23, 2002, he was charged with lying to federal agents about his phone calls to al-Hawsawi and travel. On March 1, 2003, KSM and Hawsawi were captured in Pakistan. KSM went on to give information about al-Marri. Al-Marri's case moved from New York to Illinois on May 12, 2003. On June 23, 2003, President Bush named him an enemy combatant, the only foreigner arrested in the United States to be so named. The President said that he was planning attacks against water reservoirs, the New York Stock Exchange, and U.S. military academies. Al-Marri was held in a Navy brig in Charleston, South Carolina. In August 2005, his lawyers sued the government, saying he was kept in "complete isolation from the world" and denied care for physical and mental ailments. On April 5, 2006, the Pentagon told a court that he "currently possesses information of high intelligence value, including information about personnel and activities of al Qaeda." His case became a cause celebre for human rights activists.

His younger brother, Jarallah, had been in an al Qaeda camp, had met with KSM in the late summer of 2001, and was held as an enemy combatant at Guantánamo Bay.

On August 23, 2007, the Richmond-based U.S. Court of Appeals for the Fourth Circuit granted a federal request that the full 10-member Court review the 2-1 ruling of June 11, 2007 that said the government could not hold him indefinitely without being charged. On April 8, 2008, defense attorney Jonathan Hafetz told the U.S. Court of Appeals for the Fourth Circuit in

Richmond that a 2003 Justice Department memo on military interrogations proved that his detention was illegal.

Hamdi 'Abd-al-Karim al-Marsawi: alias Abu-'Abd-al-Rahman, a Tunisian leather merchant from Ariyanah who was born in 1986 and joined al Qaeda in Iraq as a martyr on May 5, 2007, contributing 1,000 Syria lira, 60 Saudi riyals, and his passport. His recruitment coordinator was Abu-'Ubaydah Saudi, whom he met via his brothers in Tunisia. He arrived via Saudi Arabia and Syria, where he met Abu-'Abbas. He brought $200 and 300 Syrian lira with him. His phone numbers were 002162333686 and 0021671763762.

Marwan: one of three al-'Asifah Forces General Command Palestinian gunman who infiltrated Israel from Egypt on March 7, 1988, hijacked a Renault-4 and then a bus filled with hostages, and were killed in a shootout with Israeli troops.

Marwan: alias of Zulkifli bin Hir.

Marwan: alias Abu-'Abd-al-'Aziz al-Harbi, a Saudi from Jeddah who joined al Qaeda in Iraq as a fighter in 2007, contributing his passport. His recruitment coordinator was Hammam. His home phone number was 6547752; his cell was 0555615572.

Abu Marwan: alias of Muhammad Ahmad Abu-'Assal.

Abu Marwan: alias of Marwan Hadid al-Suri.

Bilal bin Marwan: a Saudi and a senior bin Laden lieutenant for whom the Coalition and Afghans were searching after 9/11 and the overthrow of the Taliban. His U.S. assets were ordered frozen on October 12, 2001.

Hasan Marwan: alias Ali Yusuf, arrested on August 29, 1981 by Austrian police after he attacked a synagogue, killing two and injuring 20. He was believed connected to the May 1, 1981,

murder in Austria of Heinz Nittel, president of the Austrian-Israeli Friendship League, a leading Socialist Party official, and head of the Vienna Traffic Department. Abu Nidal's 'Al-Asifah organization claimed credit for the assassination.

Mustafa Marwi: Hizballah member identified by *Ha'aretz* on January 8, 1990 as one of the three kidnappers of U.S. Marine Lt. Col. William Richard Higgins on February 17, 1988. The paper claimed Syrian forces had detained and interrogated the kidnappers in September 1989. Marwi was allegedly released after two weeks.

Abu Maryam: alias of 'Abdallah Ahmad 'Abdallah.

Abu Maryam: alias of Mohammed Abdullah Warsame.

Baruch Marzel: identified on March 13, 1994 by Israeli authorities as a leader of the extremist group Kach, which the Cabinet unanimously banned for being a terrorist group. He went into hiding since the government issued an arrest warrant, but continued to call radio station from his cell phone. He was captured unarmed at the home of another West Bank settler on April 3, 1994. He was ordered jailed for three months without trial.

Dr. Mousa Muhammad Abu Marzook: variant Musa Abu-Marzuq, head of the Hamas Political Bureau and its representative in Damascus, Syria in December 1994. On July 25, 1995, he was arrested by Immigration and Naturalization Service officers at JFK International Airport when the name of the former resident of Falls Church, Virginia appeared on a terrorist lookout database. Israel believed he oversaw Hamas's terrorist campaign and requested that he be sent to Israel. He had lived in the United States for 14 years and was given Permanent Resident Alien status in 1990. He was returning from the United Arab Emirates via the United Kingdom at the time of his arrest.

He was born in Gaza in 1951. He began graduate studies in engineering at Louisiana State University in 1973, and earned an engineering doctorate in the 1980s. He left the United States for Jordan, where he was expelled in June 1995 after taking public credit for attacks on Israeli soldiers and citizens. Israel linked him to 13 terrorist attacks since March 1988, leading to the deaths of at least 79 Israeli and foreign civilians and 40 military or security personnel. Israel said that, in 1989, he transferred $100,000 to Hamas in Gaza and gave it another $100,000 in 1992 to finance "military operations." His release was demanded on November 13, 1995 by the group that set off a car bomb in a parking lot of a building belonging to the Saudi National Guard in Riyadh, killing five American military trainers and wounding 60 others. On May 8, 1996, New York U.S. District Court Judge Kevin Duffy said he could be extradited to Israel. The United States released him on May 5, 1997, sending him to Jordan, where he pledged to continue working for the political wing of Hamas. He agreed to surrender his U.S. residency and not to contest terrorism accusations that prompted his initial detention. On August 30, 1999, Jordanian police issued an arrest warrant for him. He was deported to Iran on September 22, 1999. On August 22, 2003, President Bush froze his assets and called on allies to join him by cutting off European sources of donations to Hamas.

On August 20, 2004, the Justice Department unsealed the indictment of Marzook; former Howard University professor Abelhaleem Hasan Abdelraziq Ashqar of Fairfax County, Virginia; and Muhammad Hamid Khalil Salah, age 51, of suburban Chicago, who was arrested on August 19. They were charged in a 15-year racketeering conspiracy to funnel money to Hamas, which was deemed a "criminal enterprise." The indictment said that, beginning in 1988, the trio conspired with 20 others to use bank accounts in Mississippi, Ohio, Virginia, Wisconsin, and other states to launder millions to Hamas. The money was used to pay for false passports, kidnappings, murders, and other crimes in Israel. U.S. officials planned to seize $2.7 million.

Marzouk: alias of Abderraouf Ben Habib Jdey.

Hamel Marzouk: Algerian member of the Casablanca Group who was interrogated on September 22, 1994 in Morocco in connection with the August 24, 1994 attack in which terrorists shot to death two Spanish tourists at the Atlas-Asni Hotel in Marrakech. A local newspaper said he confessed to the attack, a planned attack on a Casablanca synagogue, the McDonald's restaurant in Casablanca on September 11, 1993, and the Moroccan Savings and Loan Bank on September 25, 1993 in Oujda.

Yaseen Ali Al Marzouki: variant of Yasin 'Ali-al-Marzuqi.

Amor Marzuki: name on a false Tunisian passport used by one of the three Egyptian Revolution hijackers of Egyptair flight 648 that had left Athens bound for Cairo on November 23, 1985.

Mansur al-Alfi Marzuq: arrested by Egyptian police in connection with the February 26, 1993 bombing of the Wadi el-Nil coffee shop in Tahrir Square in Cairo in which four people were killed and 16 wounded. He was tried with 48 other fundamentalist suspects on March 9, 1993 at the military court complex in the Hakstep area east of Cairo. They were charged with damaging national unity and social peace by calling for a change of the system of government and damaging the national economy by attacking tourism. Some were also charged with attempted murder in eight attacks on tour buses and Nile cruise ships. They faced possible death sentences. They were also accused of belonging to an underground organization, attempting to overthrow the government, and illegal possession of arms and explosives.

Dr. Musa Abu-Marzuq: variant of Mousa Muhammad Abu Marzook.

Yasin 'Ali-al-Marzuqi: variant Yaseen Ali Al Marzouki, alias Abu-al-Khattab, a Tunisian from Kabis, variant Kabess, who was born on April 9, 1976 and joined al Qaeda in Iraq as a combatant on November 12, 2006, contributing a passport, watch, and $170. His recruitment coordinator was Muhsin, variant Mohsen. His home phone number was 0021675392768.

Mohammed Masalhah: alias Esa, leader of the eight members of Black September who broke into the Israeli quarters of the Olympic Games in Munich on September 5, 1972, killing two Israeli athletes and taking nine others hostage. After a shootout with police, the hostages were killed, as were five of the terrorists and a West German policeman. The three surviving terrorists were released in response to demands by hijackers of a Lufthansa jet on October 29, 1972.

Abu Ali Al Masery: alias of Hassan Muhamad Muhamad Hassan.

Fadhil Ibrahim Mahmud Mashadani: alias Abu Huda, a main facilitator of insurgent attacks in Iraq. He was suspected of being a link between senior Ba'athist leaders hiding in Syria and the insurgents. He was named on February 14, 2005 as one of Iraq's 29 most-wanted insurgents; a $200,000 bounty was offered.

Khalid al-Mashhadani: age 41, a senior member of al Qaeda in Iraq arrested on July 4, 2007 by U.S. forces. Iraq experts described Mashhadani as a Salafist extremist who had been imprisoned by Saddam Hussein. He was one inch shorter than six feet tall, and thin. Among his four brothers was a senior enlisted soldier in Saddam Hussein's army. al-Mushhadani had run a car registration business in Baghdad until he joined the Sunni insurgency. al-Mashhadani was the seniormost Iraqi in the branch, which is run by foreigners, including Egyptian Abu Hamza al-Muhajer, alias Abu Ayyub al-Masri.

Abu-Mash'al: alias of 'Abd-al-'Aziz Sanhat 'Abdallah al-Harbi.

Khalid Mash'al: a senior Hamas leader who, in mid-1995, was being considered as a replacement for Abu Marzook, a prominent financier.

Mahmoud Masharka: age 24, a Palestinian from a village near Hebron, on March 30, 2006, was disguised as an Israeli hitchhiker and set off a bomb inside a car that had picked him up near Qedumim, a northern West Bank settlement, killing four Israelis and himself, about 10 P.M. A splinter group of the al-Aqsa Martyrs Brigades from the Balata refugee camp near Nablus claimed credit.

Ismail Mashour: age 25, a Palestinian who, on November 6, 2002, fired into a greenhouse in the Rafih Yam Jewish settlement in the southern Gaza Strip, killing two Israelis and injuring a third. The Hamas terrorist killed Assaf Tsfira, age 18, a member of the family that employed him as a farm laborer, then ran into a textile shop and shot to death Amos Saada, age 51, the owner. He fought his way into a settlement guard's car, injuring him slightly before a second guard shot him after he threatened the guard with a hand grenade. He then was shot to death by a guard.

Muhammad Adam Muhammad al-Masmarani: alias Abu-Turab, a Libyan religious student from Benghazi who was born in 1989 and joined al Qaeda in Iraq to become a suicide bomber on July 28, 2007, contributing $100, 3,000 liras, his passport, and an ID card. His recruitment coordinator was al-Hajj. He came from Libya via Cairo to Syria, staying in Damascus for six days, where he met Abu-'Abbas. He brought 7,000 liras. His father's phone number was 018926938308.

Hafiz Salih al-Masmari: variant Hafez Saleh Al Mismarie, alias Abu-Hammad al-Libi, variant Abu Hamam Ali Libi, a Libyan from Darnah who was born on February 9, 1986 and joined al Qaeda in Iraq on October 10, 2006, contributing $100.

His phone number was 00218925782391. His recruitment coordinator was Hassan.

Mohammed Masmoudi: former Tunisian foreign minister whose release was demanded by three hijackers of a Tunis to Djerba flight of an Air Tunisia B727 on January 12, 1979 that was diverted to Tripoli, Libya.

Majed Azzam Yahiya Al Masouri: alias Abu Omar, a Yemeni high school student who brought his ID, driver's license, $200, and 50 Syrian lira with him in joining al Qaeda in Iraq in 2007 as a martyr. While in Syria, his contacts took his passport. His recruitment coordinators were Faiez and Adel. His phone number was 470037.

Abdel al-Aziz al-Masri: alias of Ali Sayyid Muhamed Mustafa al-Bakri, al Qaeda's nuclear chief, according to Khalid Sheik Mohammed, as reported in George Tenet's memoirs. He was detained in Iran. He reportedly conducted experiments with explosives to test nuclear yields.

Abd Al Wakil Al Masri: alias of Mustafa Mohamed Fadhil.

Abu-'Ali-al-Masri: alias of Hasan Muhammad Muhammad Hasan.

Abu Ayyub al-Masri: variant Abu Ayub al-Masri, alias Abu Hamza al-Muhajir, alias Yusif al-Dardiri, last remaining original member of the Mujahidin Shura Council in Iraq and a central figure as of late 2007 in al Qaeda in Iraq. The Egyptian served as Abu Mus'ab al-Zarqawi's senior operational coordinator and attended the first meetings between Ansar al-Islam commander Umar Baziyani and al-Zarqawi. Authorities believed he was involved in the construction of the car bombs used in the attacks on the UN headquarters and Jordanian Embassy in Baghdad, the Ashura and Arba'in commemoration bombings, and the Assassins Gate attack on the Coalition Provisional Authority. The U.S. State Department offered a $5 million

reward for his capture on June 30, 2006. He was dropped from the Rewards for Justice program in February 2008, and the Department of Defense Rewards Program offered $100,000 for his arrest.

Abu Hafs al-Masri: alias of Mohammed Atef.

Abu Hamza al-Masri: born Mustafa Kamel Mustafa, a London resident and member of the Islamic Army of Aden, which claimed credit for the USS *Cole* bombing. On April 19, 2002, the United States froze his assets.

On May 27, 2004, at U.S. request, a UK antiterrorist squad arrested Masri, age 47, a Muslim cleric whose Finsbury, London mosque was a focal point for radical Islamists. Police had earlier closed his mosque. U.S. officials unsealed a federal indictment charging him with planning terrorist acts in Oregon, Afghanistan, and Yemen. He was accused of planning a military training camp for jihadists in rural Bly, Oregon in 1999 with James Ujaama (who had turned state's evidence) and leading a plot by the Islamic Army of Aden to take 16 Western tourists hostage in Yemen in December 1998 (the group kidnapped 12 Britons and two Americans in Yemen). The indictment said he provided a satellite phone to the group and received three calls in London from them the day before the kidnapping. He offered to serve as an intermediary, speaking to the kidnapping leader. The indictment was handed up on April 19 by a federal grand jury in New York.

The Egyptian had become a UK citizen in 1981. He had earlier worked as a nightclub bouncer. He lost both hands and an eye while fighting the Soviets in Afghanistan. He often praised bin Laden and blamed the Jews for 9/11. UK authorities believed he had recruited Richard Reid, the would-be shoe bomber of December 2001, and Zacarias Moussaoui, the would-be 20th 9/11 hijacker. In 2003, the United Kingdom declared Masri a threat to national security and moved to strip him of his UK citizenship. He was represented by attorney Maddrassar Arani. He was eligible for the death penalty for the kidnapping plot; however, the United Kingdom has no death penalty. The United States requested extradition. He was also wanted in Yemen, which does not have an extradition treaty with the United Kingdom.

Yemen said police had arrested a carload of ten radicals, including Masri's son, around the time of the kidnapping. The group was carrying explosives and planning to attack a British consulate and two churches.

On August 26, 2004, British police arrested al-Masri on suspicion of involvement in "the commission, preparation or instigation or acts of terrorism," holding him at London's high-security Belmarsh prison. On August 27, antiterror police were given until September 2 to question him. He had been held at Belmarsh since May 2004, pending extradition to the United States. In April 2004, a federal grand jury in New York indicted him on charges of seeking to establish a military training camp for Muslim terrorists in Oregon and aiding the kidnapping of 16 Western tourists in Yemen.

On October 19, 2004, British prosecutors charged him with ten counts of soliciting others to murder nonbelievers, including Jews, five counts of "using threatening, abusive or insulting words or behavior with the intention of stirring up racial hatred," and one count of possessing a terrorist document. The charges could lead to a life sentence. Observers believed that this would add years to the U.S. extradition request. He remained in London's Belmarsh Prison. In February 2006, he was sentenced in the United Kingdom to seven years in prison for incitement to kill non-Muslims.

On February 7, 2008, the British Home Office approved his extradition to the United States to face charges in connection with the Oregon terror camp case. He had 14 days to appeal the extradition decision, which he did on February 20, 2008.

Abu Jihad al-Masri: alias of Mohammed Hasan Khalil al Hakim.

Abu Khabab al-Masri: alias Midhat Mursi al-Sayid 'Umar, Egyptian chemical, biological, radiological and nuclear expert who worked with Mustafa Setmariam Nasar at al Qaeda's Derunta terrorist camp in Afghanistan, training hundreds of extremists in poisons and chemicals. He was educated in Egypt in chemical engineering. He apparently trained Ali Saleh Kahlah al-Marri. In the 1980s, he was a member of the Egyptian Islamic Jihad group run by Ayman al-Zawahiri. Since 1999, he has distributed training manuals that contain instructions for making chemical and biological weapons. Some of these training manuals were recovered by U.S. forces in Afghanistan. He was believed to have fled to Chechnya or the Pankisi Gorge of Georgia by 2002, training militants in chemical weapons, then went on to Pakistan. Al-Masri was initially believed killed in an air strike in Pakistan on January 13, 2006, although the *Washington Post* listed him, on September 9, 2007, as being one of the group's key leaders and he appears in the National Counterterrorism Center 2008 calendar. The Rewards for Justice Program offers $5 million for his arrest and/or conviction. He was born on April 29, 1953 in Egypt.

Abu Khalid al-Masri: senior al Qaeda aide listed by the *Washington Post* in late February 2002 as being at large.

Abu Mohamed al-Masri: alias of 'Abdallah Ahmad 'Abdallah.

Abu Mohammad al-Masri: al Qaeda's chief of training, listed by the *Washington Post* in late February 2002 as being at large. He might be hiding in Iran with Saif Adel.

Abu Muhammad al-Masri: alias of 'Abdallah Ahmad 'Abdallah.

Abu Muhayyam al-Masri: the Egyptian leader of an al Qaeda cell in Anbar province who was captured by the Iraqi army on November 10, 2006 in a raid in Rawah.

Abu Obaidah al-Masri: variant Abu Ubaida al-Masri. As of September 2007, an Egyptian explosives expert who was external operations chief for al Qaeda. He allegedly was the mastermind behind the July 7, 2005 bombings of the London Underground, the August 2006 plan to bomb ten U.S.-bound planes from the United Kingdom, and a failed plot in Copenhagen in the fall of 2007. He was believed to be hiding in Pakistan, the government of which believed he was behind the November 1995 suicide bombing of the Egyptian Embassy in Islamabad that killed 17 people. Reports of his demise in airstrikes in January 2006 and October 2006 proved unreliable. He had lost two fingers. He was in his mid-forties. He had fought in Bosnia in the early 1990s, then was wounded in Chechnya. He also spent time in the United Kindom. He requested asylum—a request denied in 1999—under an alias in Munich, where he dealt with a Moroccan computer scientist who was the son-in-law of Ayman al-Zawahiri, and with Jordanians who plotted in 2002 to shoot Jews. He had been jailed in Germany pending deportation, but was later released. He surfaced in 2000 at a training camp near Kabul, teaching explosives, artillery, and topography. He was five feet seven inches tall, with gray-black hair. He was part of the 055 Brigade, a paramilitary unit that fought against the U.S. incursion in 2001. He was believed to have trained recruits from Denmark and Germany in the spring of 2007 at a compound in North Waziristan, Pakistan. On April 9, 2008, the United States announced that he had died of hepatitis C in Pakistan a few months earlier, probably December 2007. He had succeeded Abu Hamza Rabia, an Egyptian killed in a missile strike in 2005 in Pakistan. He was replaced as al Qaeda's number three by Shaykh Sayed al Masri (which means "the Egyptian") who had been head of the group's finances. Others believed he was replaced by Khalid Habib, Hamza al Jawfi, or Midhat Mursi.

Abu Omaram Al Masri: alias of Muhammad Sami Ahmed Ali Attia.

Abu Ubaida al-Masri: variant of Abu Obaidah al-Masri.

Ahmad al-Masri: alias of Ahmad Muhammad Hamid Ali.

Ahmad al-Masri: one of 12 Popular Front for the Liberation of Palestine members arrested by Jordanian security forces on October 4, 1989 for questioning about the smuggling of explosives and personnel into Jordan to fire rockets across the cease-fire line.

Izzedin Masri: age 23, a Hamas suicide bomber who, on August 9, 2001, set off a 10-pound bomb packed with nails at the kosher Sbarro's Pizzeria in Jerusalem, killing 14 other people and injuring more than 100. (Reports varied between 13 and 19 on the number killed.) Six of the dead and many of the wounded were Israeli children or teens.

The terrorist had lived in a village near the West Bank town of Jenin. Some observers said he had been dropped off at the restaurant at Jaffa and King George Streets by a motorcyclist who sped off.

Khaled el-Masri: age 43, a German citizen of Lebanese descent, arrested on May 17, 2007 in Germany on suspicion of arson and sent to a psychiatric ward following a 4:45 A.M. fire in a wholesale market in Neu-Ulm that caused $680,000 in damage. He was represented by attorney Manfred Gnjidic, who claimed his client had experienced a "complete nervous breakdown" because he claimed the Central Intelligence Agency had kidnapped him in Macedonia on New Year's Eve 2003 and tortured him an in Afghan prison. In March 2007, the U.S. Federal Appeals Court in Richmond, Virginia had refused to reinstate his lawsuit, saying it could jeopardize national security by exposing state secrets.

Layla al-Masri: one of seven people, including three Lebanese, arrested on March 5, 1987 by

French police in a raid on her apartment in the Rue de l'Assomption in the 16th District in Paris, in which police found 15.8 kilograms of explosives, two automatic pistols, and another pistol.

Maher Masri: age 20, an armed Palestinian from the village of Beit Hanun in the northern Gaza Strip who was crossing into Israel through a fence on the Gaza Strip border near the Niram kibbutz, who was shot to death by Israeli soldiers on August 10, 2002. The Hamas member was carrying hand grenades and died when one went off. Soldiers found an AK-47 near his body.

Sheikh Sayed al-Masri: former head of al Qaeda finances who became al Qaeda's number three at the 2008 death of Abu Obaidah al-Masri.

Umar al-Masri: alias of Sharif 'Abd-al-Rahman Tawfiq al-Madani.

Usamah al-Masri: alias used by an Egyptian who had lived in Aden for several years before 1998 and was a member of the Islamic Army of Aden. On December 28, 1998, he was 1 of the Islamic militants who kidnapped 16 tourists, including 12 Britons, 2 Americans, and 2 Australians, in the early afternoon on the main road from Habban to Aden in the southern province of Abyan, Yemen. A Yemeni guide and a British man escaped in one of the tourists' five vehicles and told embassies of the kidnappings. The others were believed to have been driven to al-Wadeaa, an area 250 miles south of Sanaa. The next day, authorities tried to free the hostages, but four of the British travelers were killed and an American woman and an Australian were wounded in the battle with the Islamic Jihad. (British Foreign Secretary Robin Cook said three Britons and an Australian were killed.) The Aden-Abyan Islamic Army also claimed credit. The others were rescued from the 15 kidnappers, 3 of whom, including al-Masri, were killed.

Said al Islam el Masry: variant of Saif al Islam el Masry.

Saif al Islam el Masry: variant Said al Islam el Masry, an Egyptian member of the al Qaeda military committee and al Qaeda military instructor. On October 21, 2002, Georgian special forces said they had captured 15 Arab militants linked to al Qaeda in the Pankisi Gorge and turned them over to the United States. Among those caught was Saif al Islam el Masry, who had been trained by Hizballah in southern Lebanon, and was among a group of al Qaeda members chosen to go to Somalia to fight the United States in the early 1990s. He had served as an officer of the Chechnya branch of the Benevolence International Foundation, which was cited in U.S. court as an al Qaeda financial conduit. The detainees had passports from Morocco, Egypt, and European countries. Georgian investigators reported that one team was attempting to obtain explosives to use against a U.S. or other Western installation in Russia. Another six men were developing poisons to use against Western targets in Central Asia.

Izettin Rida Masrojeh: Palestinian guerrilla arrested at Istanbul's Yesilkoy (now Ataturk International) Airport in July 1981. On February 24, 1983, the Martial Law Court of Istanbul acquitted him of "conspiracy to commit a felony" and released him from custody. He had been accused of perpetrating attacks against the Israeli consulate and its personnel and had faced a ten-year prison term.

Ibrahim Massad: one of three Palestinian gunmen who, on December 11, 1996, ambushed and killed a 12-year-old Israeli and his mother and injured four other passengers (three girls, aged four to ten and their father) in their Volkswagen Golf station wagon while they were driving on a new bypass road near Surda on the West Bank. Two gunmen, armed with automatic weapons, and a driver sped off to Ramallah, 12 miles north of Jerusalem. The victims of the evening killing were among the founding families of the Jewish settlement of Bet El. Survivor Yoel Tsur is director of the settlers' pirate radio station Channel 7. The Popular Front for the Liberation of Palestine (PFLP) took credit.

On December 18, the Palestine Liberation Organization's (PLO) State Security Court convicted three 20-year-old Palestinian PFLP members for the murders. Massad, the driver, was jailed for 15 years. The PLO said the trio would not be extradited to Israel.

Mohammad Massari: a Saudi dissident reportedly involved in a Libyan-financed plot in 2003 to assassinate Saudi government leader Crown Prince Abdullah.

Nabil Massoud: one of two suicide bombers who on killed 11 people and wounded more than 20 at the port of Ashdod. The 18-year-old Palestinians were schoolmates and had lived in a Gaza Strip refugee camp. Nabil Massoud and Mohammed Salem recorded a video in which they said that the joint operation between Hamas and the al-Aqsa Martyrs Brigade was in retaliation for recent Israeli attacks against Palestinians. The duo wore Israeli military uniforms and brandished Kalashnikovs. They set off the explosives two minutes apart within 50 yards of each other. The first terrorist set off his bomb inside an open-air warehouse filled with forklifts and heavy machinery. The second terrorist was across the street from the port, near a fish import–export company. The second bombing was much less powerful than the first. They had infiltrated from Gaza.

Maher al-Masti: one of seven male Palestine Liberation Organization (PLO) terrorists for whom Philippines Angeles Metropolitan District Command and Clark Air Base were searching on April 30, 1988 after they had arrived from Manila earlier in the week to conduct sabotage and bombing missions and attack nightclubs frequented by U.S. servicemen. The terrorists reportedly arrived on a bus and carried black bags containing explosives to be set off at the Sweet Apple Club and the Capcom information booth. The PLO denied involvement.

'Abd-al-'Aziz Bin-'Abdallah al-Mas'ud: alias Abu-Rayan, a Saudi from al-Zilfi who was born in 1979 who joined al Qaeda in Iraq in 2007, bringing $2,600. He was deployed to Mosul. His phone numbers were 064220146 and 0554570708.

'Ali Radi Muhammad Mas'ud: arrested by Egyptian police in connection with the February 26, 1993 bombing of the Wadi el-Nil coffee shop in Tahrir Square in Cairo in which four people were killed and 16 wounded. He was tried with 48 other fundamentalist suspects on March 9, 1993 at the military court complex in the Hakstep area east of Cairo. They were charged with damaging national unity and social peace by calling for a change of the system of government and damaging the national economy by attacking tourism. Some were also charged with attempted murder in eight attacks on tour buses and Nile cruise ships. They faced possible death sentences. They were also accused of belonging to an underground organization, attempting to overthrow the government, and illegal possession of arms and explosives.

Husayn Mas'ud: Palestinian who trained Saiqa in explosives at Ad-Damur camp in Beirut in the late 1970s.

Miftah 'Ali Mas'ud: variant Mufti 'Ali Mas'ud, one of two Libyans reported on November 21, 1995 by London's *al-Sharq al-Awsat* to being pursued by Jordanian authorities for having illegally crossed the Syrian border at al-Ramtha and believed to be planning the assassination of Jordanian officials or Libyan dissidents. Amman's *al-Hadath* suggested they were involved in the bombing of the U.S. military mission in Riyadh and were sent by members of Libyan intelligence. They were given passports by a Palestinian organization.

Mufti 'Ali Mas'ud: variant of Miftah 'Ali Mas'ud.

Majid 'Azzam Yahya al-Masura: alias Abu-'Umar, a Yemeni who joined al Qaeda in Iraq to become a suicide bomber in 2007. He had attended high school. His passport was taken in Syria. He presented his ID, driver's license, $200, and 50 Syrian pounds. He met recruitment coordinators Fabiz and 'Adil in a mosque. His phone number was 470037.

Dr. Ahmad Abu-Matar: identified by Doha's *al-Sharq* on March 19, 1993 as a former member of the Abu Nidal Group. He was director of the Sabra publishing, printing, distribution, and press house, who separated from the Abu Nidal group after the house's financing was cut off. He then moved it to Syria.

Hamdi Matar: one of 12 Popular Front for the Liberation of Palestine members arrested by Jordanian security forces on October 4, 1989 for questioning about the smuggling of explosives and personnel into Jordan to fire rockets across the cease-fire line.

Muhammad 'Afifi Matar: an Egyptian poet and member of the Egyptian Ba'ath Party who was among six people arrested on April 3, 1991 in Egypt on suspicion of involvement in an Iraqi-sponsored terrorist plot.

Ahmad Mutahhar Jamil al-Matari: alias Ahmad Mutahhar, a Yemeni who, on April 19, 1992, took the Saudi Ambassador to Yemen, Ali Muhammad al-Qufaydi, hostage in his office, demanding a $1 million ransom. He threatened to blow up the embassy and was armed with two guns and a hand grenade. He was overpowered by Yemeni security forces the next day and was arrested. On April 21, 1992, the Yemeni Interior Ministry said that he had been accused of belonging to extremist political groups and was involved in several bombings in Sana'a in 1984. He was sentenced to three years in jail.

A. Mateen: alias of 'Abdol Matin.

Mullah Mateen: a Taliban leader killed by Afghan security forces on September 4, 2007. He was believed to be behind the July 19, 2007 Taliban kidnapping of 23 South Korean Christian evangelicals from a bus on a highway in Ghazni province.

'Abdol Matin: variant A. Mateen, a Persian-speaking Afghan refugee who was residing in Abbottabad, Pakistan and was arrested on December 25, 1995 in connection with the December 21, 1995 car bombing in Peshawar's shopping center that killed 42 people and injured more than 125. He came to Peshawar the day of the bombing, and was also wanted for other bombs. Police said he and his accomplices purchased the brown Toyota Corolla used for the bomb from a bargain center in Peshawar. The group then fled in a grey double-cabin 1989 Toyota pickup.

Muhammad Salih 'Awad Matrudah: alias Abu-Bakar, a Libyan traffic policeman from Darnah who was born on July 4, 1979 and arrived on May 9, 2007 in Iraq to become a martyr for al Qaeda in Iraq, contributing $450 and 1,750 Syrian lira. He arrived via Libya, Egypt, and Syria, where he met Abu-'Abbas. His recruitment coordinator was Saraj, whom he knew from a new acquaintance. He had completed military training. His home phone number was 00218928009041; his brother's was 00218926228152.

Qasim Mu'in Anwar Matti: arrested on December 5, 1988 in Cyprus on charges of counterfeiting dollars. Three days later, the Palestinian Liberation Movement demanded his release.

Youssef Muhammad Al Saddeq Al Matrawi: alias Al Qa'a Qa'a, a Libyan born in 1985 who joined al Qaeda in Iraq in 2007. His phone number was 00218925104494.

Zahran Nassor Maulid: alias of Khalfan Khamis Mohamed.

Abu Hafs al-Mauritania: alias of Mafouz Ould Walid, an al Qaeda counselor listed as dead by the *Washington Post* as of March 28, 2002.

Jamal Mawas: Lebanese General and a senior officer in the presidential guards who was detained for the February 14, 2005 car bombing that killed former Lebanese Prime Minister Rafiq Hariri, 60, as the billionaire was driving through central Beirut's waterfront just before lunchtime. Another 22 people died and more than 100 people were injured, including the Minister of Economy.

Abu-M'awiah: alias of Yasin.

Mawlana: alias of 'Abd al-Aziz Awda.

Mawlud: alias Abu-Jalal, an Algerian member of al Qaeda in Iraq in 2007. His phone number was 0021332336385.

Mawsuni: alias of Aydir.

Aydir Mawsuni: alias Abu-'Abdallah, an Algerian university student who was born on December 4, 1988 and joined al Qaeda in Iraq as a fighter on January 22, 2007, bringing his passport. His recruitment coordinator was Abu-'Assam, whom he knew through Abu-'Abdallah. He flew from Libya, stopping in Algeria, Tunisia, and Syria, where he met Abu-'Abd-al-Malak, Abu-'Ali, Abu-'Assam, and Abu-Basil. He gave them his 150 euros; he was told he was not permitted to enter Iraq with anything but his passport. His brother's phone number was 0021370952758.

Al Mayeet: variant Al Mayet, a Libya-based recruitment coordinator for al Qaeda in Iraq foreign fighters in 2007.

Al Mayet: variant of Al Mayeet.

Maylud: alias Abu-Sulayman Abu-'Abd-al-Hadi, a Moroccan sent on a suicide mission for al Qaeda in Iraq in 2007. His wife's phone numbers were

011412296 and 063856656. He owned a passport.

Husayn Mazbou: On April 27, 1989, French investigating magistrate Gilles Boulouque issued a warrant for his arrest for conspiracy and illegal possession of explosives.

Mr. Mazeh: alias Gharib, name used to register at London's Beverly Hotel by an Arab terrorist who blew himself up with his own bomb on August 1, 1989. The Organization of the Strugglers of Islam said he had intended to kill Salman Rushdie.

Abu Mazem: alias of Anis Naqqash, Palestinian leader of the five Guards of Islam gunmen who failed in an assassination attempt against Shahpour Bakhtiar, the Shah's last Prime Minister, in Neuilly-sur-Seine, France on July 17, 1980. He was wounded in the attack.

Abu Mazin: alias of Bilal Hasan, commander of Saiqa's militia in the late 1970s.

Abu-Mazin: alias of Musa al-Husayni.

Abu Mazin: name given by an anonymous caller of one of the October 23, 1983 suicide bombers in Lebanon. A truck bomb at the Battalion Landing Team building at Beirut International Airport killed 241 U.S. Marines and injured more than 80 other soldiers, while a car bomb in Beirut's Ramel el-Baida district killed 58 French paratroopers and injured another 15.

Wassim I. Mazloum: age 24, a legal permanent resident alien who came to the United States from Lebanon in 2000 and one of three people living in Toledo, Ohio who were charged by the FBI on February 21, 2006 with planning to attack U.S. troops in Iraq by setting up a Middle Eastern terrorism training camp. Between November 2004 and August 2005, the trio learned to build bombs and shoot handguns while setting up a fraudulent nonprofit organization. Formal charges included conspiracy to kill Americans abroad, providing material support to terrorists, taking weapons training, and trying to acquire or build explosives. They faced life in prison. They had been indicted the previous week. They pleaded not guilty in federal courts in Cleveland and Toledo to charges of conspiracy to kill or maim people outside the United States. During their trial on April 23, 2008, undercover informant Darren Griffin said the trio had met only once during the two years he had investigated them. Mazloum co-owns a Toledo auto dealership with his brother.

Mikdad Mbaied: one of four gunmen who, on March 6, 2004, disguised jeeps to look like Israeli army vehicles and tried to attack an Israeli military checkpoint at the Erez border crossing in the Gaza Strip. Palestinian Authority guards stopped them and shot to death at least four Palestinians before a large explosion took place, killing two Palestinian officers and wounding another 15 people. A car bomb had exploded nearby, apparently a diversion. Islamic Jihad, Hamas, and the al-Aqsa Martyrs Brigades jointly claimed credit, and said the dead were Omar Abu Said and Hatim Tafish of al-Aqsa, Mikdad Mbaied of Islamic Jihad, and Mohammed Abu Daiah of Hamas.

Abu Omar al Meccaie: alias of Sabber Essa Al Ismaieli.

Abu Zer al Meccee: alias of Sultan Raddy al Outabey.

Abu Khibab al Meccey: alias of Saleh Bin Nasser Muhammad Nasser Al Ahmady.

Abu Moua'aied al Meccie: alias of Abd Allah Sammy Ahmed Muhammad.

Abu Tarek al Meccie: alias of Muhammad Abd al Fattah Muhammad Rashad.

Beorg Mechal: alias used by one of two suspected Palestine Liberation Organization members who were arrested on April 26, 1979 at the Passau–Achleiten crossing point on the Austrian–Bavarian border when West German police searching their rental car found 50 kilograms of explosives, time fuses, and 11 passports with photographs not of them. Bonn authorities believed that the duo intended to pass the documents to Palestinians either already in Germany or intending to arrive soon.

Yahia Meddah: a 27-year-old Algerian asylum-seeker arrested in August 1996 by Immigration and Naturalization Service agents on suspicion of involvement in terrorism. Meddah had settled in West Virginia after entering the United States on a false French passport ten months earlier. He requested political asylum, claiming he faced persecution from Algerian opposition forces, whom he claimed had kidnapped his father and sister and killed many of his relatives.

Human Rights Watch used his case to criticize U.S. treatment of immigration detainees, citing two suicide attempts on his part.

In 1997, an immigration judge denied his asylum request and attempt to stop a deportation order. The judge based his decision in part on secret evidence that he said showed Meddah's "connection with international terrorism."

On October 2, 1998, Meddah climbed over an eight-foot fence in a recreation area of Miami's Windmoor psychiatric hospital and fled to Canada.

La Medica: alias of Ivon Consuelo Izquierdo, 1 of the 16 members of the April 19 Movement of Colombia who took over the Embassy of the Dominican Republic on February 27, 1980. The gunmen ultimately flew to Cuba.

Mehri Medieddin: variant of Mahri Muhyi-al-Din.

Tehar Medjadi: alias of Ahmed Ressam.

Youssef Samir Megahed: age 21, one of two Egyptian students from the University of South Florida in Tampa who, on August 4, 2007, were stopped for speeding in their 2000 Toyota Camry near a Navy base in Goose Creek, South Carolina. They were jailed after authorities discovered explosives in the car's trunk. The materiel included a mixture of fertilizer, kitty litter, and sugar; 20 feet of fuse cord; and a box of .22-caliber bullets. On August 31, they were indicted by a federal grand jury on charges of carrying explosive materials across state lines. One of them faced terrorist-related charges of demonstrating how to use pipe bomb explosives, including the use of remote-controlled toys, to the other. The duo claimed they were going to the beach with fireworks purchased from Wal-Mart. With federal charges in place, state charges were expected to be dismissed as of September 4.

Authorities later determined that Ahmed Abdellatif Sherif Mohamed had posted on YouTube.com a 12-minute video on how to use a remote-controlled toy car to set off a bomb. His computer had bomb-making files in a folder called "Bomb Shock."

On December 1, 2007, Mohamed said in a defense filing that the explosives were cheap "sugar rocket" fireworks he had made that would travel only a few feet. On January 31, 2008, the FBI announced that the items were low-grade fireworks. But prosecutors countered on February 5, 2008 that the FBI report had been mischaracterized and that the items met the U.S. legal definition of explosives.

'Abd al-Baset al-Megrahi: variant Abdel Basset Ali al-Megrahi, variant Abd al Basset al Megrahi, alias Abdelbaset Ali Mohmed, alias Mr. Baset, alias Ahmed Khalifa Abdusamad, a Libyan intelligence officer charged on November 14, 1991 by a federal grand jury in Washington with 193 felony counts in the Pam Am flight 103 bombing. He was accused of planting and detonating the bomb, and was believed to be in Libya. The U.S. indictment included 189 counts for killing the 189 U.S. citizens, one count of conspiracy, one count of putting a destructive device on a U.S. civil aircraft resulting in death, one count of destroying a U.S. civil aircraft with an explosive device, and one count of destroying a vehicle in foreign

commerce. The last three charges carry the death penalty. The United Kingdom issued similar arrest warrants for 'Abd-al-Basit 'Ali Muhammad al-Miqrahi. On November 27, 1991, the United States and United Kingdom demanded that Libya hand him over for trial. Muammar Qadhafi refused on November 28, 1991. On December 4, 1991, Libya's new intelligence chief, Colonel Yusuf al-Sabri, announced the detention of the indicted duo. The United States and United Kingdom again demanded extradition, which Qadhafi again declined. On December 8, 1991, Libya announced it would try the two men and it would deliver the death penalty if they were found guilty. But the Libyan Foreign Minister said the government did not think they were guilty.

al-Megrahi was born in Tripoli, Libya on April 1, 1952. He was circa five feet eight inches tall and weighed circa 190 pounds. He was married. He had black hair and dark brown eyes. He was the former security chief of Libyan Arab Airlines.

On December 7, 1988, he bought clothing and an umbrella at Mary's House, a shop near his Malta hotel, and put them in a suitcase. He and partner Lamen Khalifa Fhimah allegedly illegally obtained Air Malta luggage tags and used them to route the bomb-rigged suitcase as unaccompanied luggage on an Air Malta flight to Frankfurt. The suitcase was transferred to Pan Am flight 103A and on arrival in London, put on Pan Am flight 103, which blew up 38 minutes after departing for New York.

A State Department spokesman said al-Megrahi worked with his first cousin Said Rashid Kisha, "the leading architect and implementer of Libya's terrorist policies and a powerful member of Libya's inner circle."

On April 5, 1999, Libya turned him to UN officials for trial. He and his fellow defendant appeared in court the next day, when the names of the 270 victims were read aloud. They were charged in English and Arabic with murder, conspiracy to commit murder, and violations of international aviation security laws. On May 3, 2000, the trial opened, and the defendants pleaded not guilty. On January 10, 2001, the prosecution closed its arguments and dropped the lesser charges of conspiracy and a violation of British aviation law, leaving only the murder counts.

He was found guilty of murder on January 31, 2001 by a Scottish court seated in the Netherlands regarding the December 21, 1989 Pan Am flight 103 bombing. He was sentenced to life in prison with the possibility of parole after 20 years. He lost an appeal on March 14, 2002. On June 28, 2007, the Scottish Criminal Cases Review Commission announced that he may have "suffered a miscarriage of justice" in being convicted for the bombing and granted his request for an appeal before a panel of five appellate judges in Edinburgh.

Abd al Basset al Megrahi: variant of 'Abd al-Baset al-Megrahi.

Abdel Basset Ali al-Megrahi: variant of Abd al-Baset al-Megrahi.

Adel Abd-al-Meguid: at-large Egyptian Jihad terrorist who was one of 62 defendants tried in absentia in a military tribunal in Haekstep, Egypt beginning on February 1, 1999. Charges against 107 defendants included forgery, criminal conspiracy, subversion, membership in an outlawed group, plotting to carry out attacks on officials and police, attempting to prevent security forces from carrying out their jobs, and conspiracy to overthrow the government. He was a leader of the Islamic Observation Center in London.

Farid Abdel Meguid: leader of a group of six Palestine Popular Struggle Front (some reports say it was the Popular Front for the Liberation of Palestine) hijackers of an Olympics Airways B727 flying from Beirut to Athens on July 22, 1970. In Athens, the hijackers negotiated for the release of seven Arab terrorists who were being held for the December 21, 1969 attack on an El Al airliner, the December 21, 1969 attempted hijacking of a TWA plane, and the November 27, 1968 attack on the El Al office in Athens. The Greek government agreed to continue the trial of the November terrorists on July 24, sentencing two terrorists to

11 and 18 years, respectively, then let them go free. The seven freed terrorists flew to Cairo.

Mona Abdel Meguid: Sister of the leader of a group of six Palestine Popular Struggle Front (some reports say it was the Popular Front for the Liberation of Palestine) hijackers (of which she was one) of an Olympics Airways B727 flying from Beirut to Athens on July 22, 1970. In Athens, the hijackers negotiated for the release of seven Arab terrorists who were being held for the December 21, 1969 attack on an El Al airliner, the December 21, 1969 attempted hijacking of a TWA plane, and the November 27, 1968 attack on the El Al office in Athens. The Greek government agreed to continue the trial of the November terrorists on July 24, sentencing 2 terrorists to 11 and 18 years, respectively, then let them go free. The seven freed terrorists flew to Cairo.

Mehdi: alias of Mohamed Zineddine.

Ali Khalik Mehri: a naturalized Paraguayan citizen and Lebanese businessman living in Ciudad del Este who was arrested by Paraguayan authorities in February 2000. He had financial links to Hizballah, and was charged with violating intellectual property rights laws and aiding a criminal enterprise involved in distributing CDs espousing Hizballah's extremist ideals. He also was charged with selling millions of dollars of counterfeit software and sending the proceeds to Hizballah. In a search of his home, police found videos and CDs of suicide bombers calling for others to follow them. He fled the country in June 2000 after faulty judicial procedures allowed his release. He was believed to be an al Qaeda financier, and was a large campaign contributor to members of the ruling Colorado Party.

Abdullah Mehsud: variant Abdullah Mahsud, age 28 as of October 2004, a one-legged former Taliban fighter who had been freed from the U.S. Navy detention facility at Guantánamo Bay, Cuba, in March 2004. He had been held for two years after being captured by Afghan forces in

Kunduz in northern Afghanistan in December 2001 while fighting for the Taliban. Authorities believed he had established ties with al Qaeda after his release. He also had led foreign militants, principally from Uzbekistan. He was the leader of the group that, on October 9, 2004, kidnapped Chinese engineers working with Pakistanis in South Waziristan. He was killed on July 24, 2007 in Pakistan in a raid by security forces on his hideout in Zhob in Baluchistan province, 30 miles from the Afghan border. He blew himself up with a grenade rather than surrender. He was one of seven former Guantánamo detainees named by the Pentagon as having returned to the insurgency upon release.

His brother, Baitullah Mehsud, commands 30,000 fighters supporting al Qaeda in Pakistan.

Baitullah Mehsud: a Taliban commander in South Waziristan, Pakistan, whom Pakistani authorities said was behind the December 27, 2007 assassination of Benazir Bhutto. He was formally charged on March 1, 2008. He remained at large, denying involvement.

Abdel Karim El Mejjati: on September 5, 2003, the FBI put out a worldwide alert for Adan El Shukrijumah, Abderraouf Jdey, Zubayr Al-Rimi, and Karim El Mejjati, who were believed to be engaged in planning for terrorist attacks, according to information provided by Khalid Sheik Mohammed, al Qaeda's operations chief. El Mejjati, 35, was born in Morocco and held a Moroccan ID card. He entered the United States in 1997 and 1999. He had been a medical student. Several passports were issued for him in France. He was suspected in the May 2003 bombings in Casablanca that killed 30 people plus 12 terrorists.

On March 31, 2004, the Spanish investigating judge put out an international arrest warrant for the wealthy Moroccan, who was thought to be the organizer of the March 11, 2004 al Qaeda bombings of commuter trains in Madrid that killed 200 and wounded 2,000. He was also wanted for bombings in Riyadh.

He was sentenced in absentia in Morocco to 20 years. He died in a three-day gun battle with security forces in his hideout in Ar Rass, a small town in Saudi Arabia in April 2005, during which 15 militants, including his teenage son, Adam, died.

Mejjati's name also appeared in threatening e-mails sent to Antwerp newspapers on April 1, 2004, warning of attacks against Jewish targets.

Ali Mohammad al-Mekdad: a Lebanese Shi'ite and one of three Hizballah terrorists reported by the Argentine Foreign Ministry on November 4, 1994 as planning terrorist attacks and as being on their way to Argentina. He was traveling on a Lebanese passport.

Mekki Hamed Mekki: age 30, a Sudanese pilot who, on September 20, 2002, was held in North Carolina for making false statements while applying for a U.S. visa. Investigators were attempting to determine whether he was an al Qaeda terrorist planning to fly a plane into a U.S. target. Several other Sudanese were held elsewhere while federal authorities tried to determine whether they had ties to Mekki. A court date was set for September 23.

Meliani: alias of Mohamed Bensakhiria.

Farid Mellouk: a French national of Algerian extraction identified as one of seven Algerians arrested on March 5, 1998 by Belgian police after a shootout and a 12-hour standoff. The detainees belonged to the European-based support network for Algeria's Armed Islamic Group.

Gamal al-Menshawi: Egyptian arrested at Amman Airport in February 2003 on suspicion of involvement in terrorism. The *Washington Post* claimed he was held in Jordanian custody and, as of December 2007, was in Egypt.

Mohammed Nabil Merhi: one of seven people arrested on November 27, 1984 by Italian police at an apartment in the seaside resort of Ladispoli. Police found a map of the U.S. embassy in Rome that had strong and weak security points marked.

The men were charged with forming an armed gang. Italian authorities speculated that the men belonged to the Islamic Jihad Organization and planned a suicide bombing at the embassy. Some were carrying false passports. All had entered Italy at different times during the year and had registered with several universities in central Italy. On February 8, 1985, an Italian examining magistrate released him; he had claimed to be only a casual acquaintance of five of the defendants.

Abu Meriam: Beirut-based spokesman for Ahmed Jabril's Popular Front for the Liberation of Palestine–General Command, who took credit for the February 21, 1970 bombing of Swissair 330 that killed all 38 passengers and nine crew.

Abdellatif Merroun: age 42, a businessman and one of two British citizens detained in Morocco on August 1, 2003 on suspicion of having ties to the Salafia Jihadia, a group of underground Islamic extremists involved in the May 16, 2003 suicide bombings in Casablanca. The group has ties to al Qaeda. The duo were not suspected of involvement in the attacks.

Abdel Aziz Merzuoghi: one of three Black June terrorists who fired machine guns and threw grenades at Vienna's Schwechat Airport on December 27, 1985. After a car chase and gun battle with police, he was severely injured. Two people were killed and 37 injured. He carried a faked Tunisian passport, having come to Vienna from Beirut. The terrorists had intended to take hostages to obtain an El Al plane, which they would crash into Tel Aviv. He was charged with murder and attempted murder. The Vienna public prosecutor indicted him on March 13, 1987. On May 21, 1987, he was found guilty of two counts of murder and sentenced to life in prison.

Hassan Mesbah: alleged member of the Islamic Salvation Front who was arrested for involvement in the August 26, 1992 bombing of the Air France ticket counter at Houari Boumedienne Airport in Algeria that killed 12 people and wounded 128. Public sessions of his trial began on May 4, 1993. On May 26, 1993, a special Algiers judicial council sentenced him to ten years.

Mohammed El Mesdawi: one of two Libyans who fired pistols and submachine guns at passengers in the international arrival area of Rome's Fiumicino Airport on February 24, 1981, wounding five passengers. Police returned fire, wounding one terrorist and capturing both. On November 22, 1983, Italy's Assizes Court gave El Mesdawi a 15-year sentence. On October 7, 1986, Italy quietly freed the duo. A Red Cross plane flew the Libyans to Tripoli and returned with four Italians who had been held in Libya for the past six years.

Akram Meshal: variant Akram Mishal, former project and grants director of the Holy Land Foundation and cousin of Hamas political bureau leader Khalid Meshal. He was among those indicted on July 27, 2004, when the Justice Department in Dallas unsealed a 42-count indictment against the Holy Land Foundation, charging it and seven senior officials of the nation's largest Muslim charity with funneling $12.4 million over six years to individuals and groups associated with Hamas. The charges included providing material support for terrorism, money laundering, and income tax offenses.

Khaled Meshal: age 41, Jordanian political chief of Hamas in Amman who was the target of an Israeli assassination attempt on September 25, 1997. Two Mossad agents were captured after trying to jab poison into Meshal's left ear as he entered his office on an Amman street. Meshal was treated with a medicine obtained after King Hussein asked American assistance in dealing with the nerve toxin, which generated uncontrollable vomiting and respiratory arrest. Meshal's bodyguards ran down the duo, one of whom was dark and muscular, the other bearded and blond, who had fled in a Hyundai and on foot.

On August 30, 1999, Jordanian police issued an arrest warrant for Meshal. They arrested him on September 22, 1999 as he arrived at Amman's airport on a flight from Iran. He was charged with affiliation with an illegal organization, which carried a one-year prison term.

Meshal, a physicist, became "world leader" of Hamas on March 22, 2004 after Israel assassinated Sheikh Ahmed Yassin.

Abdel Ghani Meskini: alias Eduardo Rocha, age 31 as of March 18, 2000, when prosecutors charged him with aiding Ahmed Ressam's foiled December 15, 1999 attempt to smuggle explosives into the United States from Canada. He was arrested in Brooklyn on December 30, 1999, when police found Ressam's phone number in his pocket. The New York resident pleaded not guilty in January 2000 to charges of providing and concealing support for Ressam. He was indicted in 2000 for conspiring with Mokhtar Haouari since October 1997 to support members and associates of a terrorist group. The six-count indictment charged that they provided and concealed material support to terrorists, transferred fraudulent ID documents, and trafficked in and used fraudulent bank and charge cards. A federal judge set an April 17, 2001 trial date. On March 7, 2001, Meskini pleaded guilty in a Manhattan court to charges that he aided the effort to smuggle explosives into the United States and he agreed to testify against other suspects. He faced 105 years in prison.

Mohammad El-Mezain: the Holy Land Foundation's (HLF) first chairman and later its endowments director, and a cousin of Hamas political bureau chief Mousa Abu Marzook. He was among those indicted on July 27, 2004, when the Justice Department in Dallas unsealed a 42-count indictment against the HLF, charging it and seven senior officials of the nation's largest Muslim charity with funneling $12.4 million over six years to individuals and groups associated with Hamas-controlled committees in the West Bank and Gaza. The charges included providing material support for terrorism, money laundering, and income tax offenses. On October 22, 2007, jurors in Dallas acquitted him of most charges of funneling millions of dollars to Hamas terrorists and deadlocked on the rest. The judge declared a mistrial.

Baghdad Mezaine: age 38, one of two Algerians arrested on September 26, 2001 in Leicester, United Kingdom, where police found propaganda material encouraging the recruitment of young Muslims for jihad training. They also seized money, faked credit cards, and other counterfeit documents. Police found videotapes, including 19 copies of a film of bin Laden's speeches and films of operations in Chechnya and Afghanistan. On April 1, 2003, the Leicester Crown Court found them guilty of raising money for terrorism and sentenced them to 11 years in prison.

Juma Mohammed Ali Mezdawi: a Libyan who was sentenced to 15 years for wounding two Lebanese at Fiumicino Airport in 1981, when the terrorists mistook the victims for opponents of Muammar Qadhafi whom they had been ordered to kill. On October 6, 1986, the Italian government announced that for "humanitarian motives" it had freed three convicted Libyan gunmen, including Mezdawi, in exchange for four Italians being held in Libya for the past six years. A Red Cross plane flew the Libyans to Tripoli and returned with the Italians.

Gazi Ibrahim Abu Mezer: variant Gazhi Ibrahim Abu Maizar, then age 23, arrested with two other people on July 31, 1997 by New York police and federal agents who seized five powerful bombs after a dawn shootout in a Brooklyn apartment at 248 Fourth Avenue. The detainees had planned to blow up transportation facilities, including the subway system in New York City. As police entered the apartment, one man ran toward a bomb. Although police fired, he threw one of several detonating switches. A second man was shot while moving toward the bomb. Abu Mezer told police how to render the bombs harmless and how they were to be used against the subway system's Atlantic Avenue station and a commuter bus. Both terrorists were hospitalized.

Investigators discovered papers in which Abu Mezer identified himself in an application for political asylum, claiming that he was arrested in Israel for "being a member of a known terrorist organization." His relatives in Hebron, West Bank, said he had been arrested once during the 1987–1993 intifada after a clash between teen stone throwers and Israeli soldiers. He was released without charges after a few days. His brother claimed that he had served on the Palestinian negotiating team that reached the last major accord with Israel in September 1995. He claimed that his brother supported the peace process and admired the United States.

On August 12, 1997, FBI investigators suggested that the duo was setting up a hoax designed to extort money from the U.S. State Department's Heroes antiterrorism rewards program. A New York judge issued a permanent order of detention and scheduled a court hearing for August 14. Defense lawyers did not request bail. On August 29, the two were indicted by a federal grand jury in New York for plotting to set off a pipe bomb in the subway. They faced life in prison if convicted of conspiracy to use a weapon of mass destruction. Arraignment was expected within the fortnight. The trial began on July 6, 1998. On July 23, 1998, the jury found him guilty of plotting to blow up the subway station.

Medani Mezerag: commander of the Islamic Salvation Army of Algeria, who said, in Paris on September 24, 1997, that his followers would suspend military operations on October 1. The group is the military wing of the Islamic Salvation Front. Mezerag denounced recent terrorist actions by the Armed Islamic Group.

Baghdad Meziane: age 37, one of two Algerians charged by British police on January 17, 2002 with planning and financing terrorists acts for al Qaeda in Leicester. Local police also detained 11 other men on charges of terrorism and immigration fraud. Prosecutors said Meziane had raised money to finance terrorist acts and had planned an attack overseas. French media said the Leicester cell planned and financed an aborted al Qaeda effort in 2001 to bomb the U.S. Embassy in Paris. The duo were to appear in court next week for a bail hearing.

Julio Cesar Mezich: variant of Julio Cesar Mezzich.

El Smansouri Abdulla' Mhao': arrested near Trieste in December 1984 with 8 kilograms of explosives. His arrest led to the detention of Josephine 'Abduh Sarkis, an alleged member of the Lebanese Armed Revolutionary Faction, on December 18, 1984.

Mohamed Mheni: age 25, one of the five individuals without police records who, on May 16, 2003, conducted suicide bombings in Casablanca that killed 45 and wounded more than 100.

Khalid al-Midhar: variant of Khalid Almihdhar.

Zein al-Abidine al-Midhar: former head of the Islamic Army of Aden in Yemen, who was executed for kidnapping. Authorities were attempting to determine whether he was related to 9/11 hijacker Khalid al-Midhar.

Muhammad Khadir Abu-al-Faraq al-Mihallawi: arrested on October 15, 1994 by Egyptian police in connection with the October 14, 1994 stabbing of Naguib Mahfouz, the only Arab to receive the Nobel Prize for Literature, in a Cairo suburb.

Mansour Hasan 'Abdullah al-Mihaymid: an elementary school teacher and a leader of a radical Shi'ite cell in Kuwait who, during a videotaped confession aired by Saudi television, said that he and his accomplices were responsible for two bombs that exploded on July 10, 1989 in two streets leading to the Great Mosque in Mecca, killing one Pakistani and injuring 16 of the 1.5 million pilgrims from 100 countries attending the hajj. He admitted that his group "collected the explosives from the back door of the Iranian

Embassy in Kuwait. . . . My role in the operation was one of general supervisor."

Abu-al-Hasan al-Mihdar: On December 28, 1998, he led a group of Islamic militants who kidnapped 16 tourists, including 12 Britons, 2 Americans, and 2 Australians, in the early afternoon on the main road from Habban to Aden in the southern province of Abyan, Yemen. A Yemeni guide and a British man escaped in one of the tourists' five vehicles and told embassies of the kidnappings. The others were believed to have been driven to al-Wadeaa, an area 250 miles south of Sanaa. The next day, authorities tried to free the hostages, but four of the British travelers were killed and an American woman and an Australian were wounded in the battle with the Islamic Jihad. (British Foreign Secretary Robin Cook said three Britons and an Australian were killed.) The Aden-Abyan Islamic Army also claimed credit. The others were rescued from the 15 kidnappers, 3 of whom, including al-Mihdar, were detained.

Zein Abidine Mihdar: on December 28, 1998, he joined a group of Islamic militants who kidnapped 16 tourists, including 12 Britons, 2 Americans, and 2 Australians in the early afternoon on the main road from Habban to Aden in the southern province of Abyan, Yemen. A Yemeni guide and a British man escaped in one of the tourists' five vehicles and told embassies of the kidnappings. The others were believed to have been driven to al-Wadeaa, an area 250 miles south of Sanaa. The next day, authorities tried to free the hostages, but four of the British travelers were killed and an American woman and an Australian were wounded in the battle with the Islamic Jihad. (British Foreign Secretary Robin Cook said three Britons and an Australian were killed.) The Aden-Abyan Islamic Army also claimed credit. The others were rescued from the 15 kidnappers.

On May 5, 1999, Judge Najib Mohammed Qaderi announced that his court in Abyan had sentenced three Islamic militants to death for the kidnap/murder. A fourth defendant was sentenced to 20 years in jail; a fifth was acquitted,

as were nine other men tried in absentia. Other charges included highway robbery, sabotage, and forming an armed group aimed at destabilizing the government. On October 17, 1999, a Yemeni firing squad in Sanaa executed Zein Abidine Mihdar, an Islamic fundamentalist leader who was convicted of abducting the Western tourists. He was the first person executed on kidnapping charges under a law passed in August 1998.

Yusuf Miflih: one of two heavily armed Palestinian brothers with Jordanian passports who hijacked a Kuwait Airlines B737 flying from Beirut to Kuwait on July 24, 1980. The duo demanded between $750,000 and $2.7 million they claimed was owed them by a Kuwaiti businessman. They released 37 passengers in Kuwait, then flew on to Bahrain, back to Kuwait, on to Abadan, and back to Kuwait. The hijackers eventually surrendered to a Palestine Liberation Organization representative and were imprisoned.

Abu Mihjen: alias of Hudayban Bin Muhammad Bin Hudayban.

Salim Qasim Mihyu: one of three people arrested on February 4, 1994 in connection with the January 29, 1994 murder by the Al-Awja Palestinian organization in Beirut of Jordanian First Secretary Naeb Umran Maaitah. On February 17, 1994, Beirut's first investigating judge formally issued arrested warrants for the trio under Articles 549 and 72 of the Penal Code on charges of premeditated murder.

Ahmed Salim Mikati: al Qaeda operative in Lebanon who was arrested in a September 17, 2004 raid. Lebanon's top prosecutor said Ismail Mohammed Khatib and Mikati were planning to bomb the Italian and Ukrainian embassies in Beirut. Mikati had been in contact with beheading specialist Abu Musab al-Zarqawi in Iraq.

Hussein Muhammad Hussein Mikdad: a 33-year-old Lebanese terrorist who, on April 12, 1996, was handling an explosive device in his east Jerusalem Lawrence Hotel room when it exploded prematurely. One of his legs was blown off, and he sustained injuries to his face. The resident of Faroun, Lebanon, also lost the use of his other leg and an arm and was blinded. The explosion severely damaged several rooms in the hotel on Salah al-Din Street. Police found two pounds of RDX plastic explosive and a delay mechanism in his room. He had photographed several local mosques, perhaps planning a provocation against the Israelis. Police later determined that the Hizballah terrorist had smuggled enough plastic explosives through Tel Aviv's airport on April 4 to blow up a plane. He had arrived on a Swissair flight from Zurich, carrying a UK passport in the name of Andrew Jonathan Charles Newman, which had been stolen three years earlier. He had planned to set off the bomb on an El Al plane.

Wahid Sa'd Fikri al-Mikkawi: fugitive sentenced to three years and fined 500 Egyptian pounds on March 17, 1994 by the Higher Military Court in Cairo in connection with the November 25, 1993 bombing of the convoy of Egyptian Prime Minister Dr. 'Atif Sidqi that killed a 15-year-old girl and wounded 21 other people.

Nasir 'Abd-al-Rida Husayn al-Mil: variant Nasir 'Abd-al-Rida Husayn al-Sayl, 1 of 11 Iraqis and three Kuwaitis arrested on April 13, 1993 by Kuwaiti authorities in a plot to assassinate former U.S. President George H. W. Bush with a bomb during his visit to Kuwait. The Kuwaiti was an official at the security office at the Juvenile Prison in the Ministry of Social Affairs and Labor. He sheltered suspects in his apartment in the al-Salimiyah area and frequented al-Jakhur with another suspect. On May 10, 1993, Kuwait ruled out extradition, saying it would try the group. He was acquitted on June 4, 1994.

Hasan Qasim Mimr: one of five Palestinians sentenced to death on October 27, 1988 by Sudanese Court President Judge Ahmad Bashir under Article 252 on charges of premeditated murder

for firing submachine guns and throwing tear gas shells in the Acropole Hotel and the Sudan Club in Khartoum on May 15, 1988, killing eight people. The defendants were found guilty on all charges in a four-page list of indictments, with the exception of criminal plotting under Article 95, because the plotting was conducted outside Sudan. On January 7, 1991, the court trying the Palestinians ordered their immediate release because the decree "was based on the fact that the relatives of five British (victims) had ceded their right in qisas (blood vengeance), similar punishment and diya (blood money) but demanded imprisonment of the murderers." The court decreed two years in prison for murder, two years for committing damage, six months for possessing unlicensed weapons, one month for attempted murder at the hotel, and one month for attempted murder at the club. However, the punishments had to be applied concurrently and lapsed on November 15, 1990.

'Ali Minayan: one of 57 people of Middle Eastern and North African origin arrested by French police on June 3, 1987 in connection with the discovery of an arms, explosives, and drugs cache in Fontainebleau forest, south of Paris, the previous week. Threats had been made by the Committee for Solidarity with Arab and Middle East Political Prisoners. He was ordered out of the country.

Sulayman Sayyid Mustafa al-Minyawi: alias found on a forged ID card in a raid on a terrorist safe house in Egypt on November 10, 1995.

Abu-Miqdad: alias of Musbah Sa'id al-Warghami.

Abu-Miqdam: alias of 'Abd-al-Salih.

'Abd-al-Basit 'Ali Muhammad al-Miqrahi: variant of 'Abd al-Baset al-Megrahi.

Abdi Abdullei Mireh: one of four gunmen posing as patients who, on October 22, 1995, shot to death Dr. Graziella Fumagalli, an Italian doctor working at a tuberculosis hospital in Marka, in her surgery, and wounding biologist Dr. Cristofo Andreoli. The triggerman was arrested.

Mohammed Mirmehdi: one of four Iranian brothers of the Mirmehdi family—Mohammed, age 34; Mohsen, age 37; Mojtaba, age 41; and Mostafa, age 45—arrested on October 2, 2001 who had worked in real estate in Los Angeles. On August 24, 2004, the U.S. Board of Immigration Appeals ruled that their ties to the Mujaheddin-e Khalq Iranian terrorist group were inconclusive. Two immigration judges had said that the brothers would be persecuted if forced to return to Iran. But they did not qualify for political asylum because they lied on their applications in 1999. On March 17, 2005, the United States released the four Iranian Mirmehdi brothers, who had been detained since October 2, 2001 as national security risks. The government agreed to ease restrictions on their movements in Los Angeles. The four had been held at the Terminal Island jail near Long Beach. They were represented by attorney Marc Van Der Hout.

They had been arrested initially in 1999 for lying on their applications for asylum. They had been linked to the anti-Iranian Mojaheddin-e Khalq. They were released in 2000, but rearrested in 2001. Immigration appeal judges ruled that they could not be sent to Iran, but the government sought to deport them to a third country for other violations. In February 2005, Immigration and Customs Enforcement offered to free them if they agreed not to travel more than 35 miles from home or talk to anyone with a criminal or terrorist background. They balked, citing the First Amendment.

Mohsen Mirmehdi: one of four Iranian brothers of the Mirmehdi family—Mohammed, age 34; Mohsen, age 37; Mojtaba, age 41; and Mostafa, age 45—arrested on October 2, 2001 who had worked in real estate in Los Angeles. On August 24, 2004, the U.S. Board of Immigration Appeals ruled that their ties to the Mujaheddin-e Khalq Iranian terrorist group were inconclusive. Two

immigration judges had said that the brothers would be persecuted if forced to return to Iran. But they did not qualify for political asylum because they lied on their applications in 1999. On March 17, 2005, the United States released the four Iranian Mirmehdi brothers, who had been detained since October 2, 2001 as national security risks. The government agreed to ease restrictions on their movements in Los Angeles. The four had been held at the Terminal Island jail near Long Beach. They were represented by attorney Marc Van Der Hout.

They had been arrested initially in 1999 for lying on their applications for asylum. They had been linked to the anti-Iranian Mojaheddin-e Khalq. They were released in 2000, but rearrested in 2001. Immigration appeal judges ruled that they could not be sent to Iran, but the government sought to deport them to a third country for other violations. In February 2005, Immigration and Customs Enforcement offered to free them if they agreed not to travel more than 35 miles from home or talk to anyone with a criminal or terrorist background. They balked, citing the First Amendment.

Mojtaba Mirmehdi: one of four Iranian brothers of the Mirmehdi family—Mohammed, age 34; Mohsen, age 37; Mojtaba, age 41; and Mostafa, age 45—arrested on October 2, 2001 who had worked in real estate in Los Angeles. On August 24, 2004, the U.S. Board of Immigration Appeals ruled that their ties to the Mujaheddin-e Khalq Iranian terrorist group were inconclusive. Two immigration judges had said that the brothers would be persecuted if forced to return to Iran. But they did not qualify for political asylum because they lied on their applications in 1999. On March 17, 2005, the United States released the four Iranian Mirmehdi brothers, who had been detained since October 2, 2001 as national security risks. The government agreed to ease restrictions on their movements in Los Angeles. The four had been held at the Terminal Island jail near Long Beach. They were represented by attorney Marc Van Der Hout.

They had been arrested initially in 1999 for lying on their applications for asylum. They had been linked to the anti-Iranian Mojaheddin-e Khalq. They were released in 2000, but rearrested in 2001. Immigration appeal judges ruled that they could not be sent to Iran, but the government sought to deport them to a third country for other violations. In February 2005, Immigration and Customs Enforcement offered to free them if they agreed not to travel more than 35 miles from home or talk to anyone with a criminal or terrorist background. They balked, citing the First Amendment.

Mostafa Mirmehdi: age 42, accused of membership in an Iranian terrorist organization, he was in federal custody as of November 2001 in connection with the FBI's investigation of the 9/11 attacks. One of four Iranian brothers of the Mirmehdi family—Mohammed, age 34; Mohsen, age 37; Mojtaba, age 41; and Mostafa, age 45—arrested on October 2, 2001 who had worked in real estate in Los Angeles. On August 24, 2004, the U.S. Board of Immigration Appeals ruled that their ties to the Mujaheddin-e Khalq Iranian terrorist group were inconclusive. Two immigration judges had said that the brothers would be persecuted if forced to return to Iran. But they did not qualify for political asylum because they lied on their applications in 1999. On March 17, 2005, the United States released the four Iranian Mirmehdi brothers, who had been detained since October 2, 2001 as national security risks. The government agreed to ease restrictions on their movements in Los Angeles. The four had been held at the Terminal Island jail near Long Beach. They were represented by attorney Marc Van Der Hout.

They had been arrested initially in 1999 for lying on their applications for asylum. They had been linked to the anti-Iranian Mojaheddin-e Khalq. They were released in 2000, but rearrested in 2001. Immigration appeal judges ruled that they could not be sent to Iran, but the government sought to deport them to a third country for other violations. In February 2005, Immigration

and Customs Enforcement offered to free them if they agreed not to travel more than 35 miles from home or talk to anyone with a criminal or terrorist background. They balked, citing the First Amendment.

Ahmed Abd Al Salam Saleh Misbah: alias Abu Rakabah, a Libyan born in 1986 who joined al Qaeda in Iraq in 2007, contributing $5. His phone number was 00218925104494, suggesting he may be related to Anas 'Abd-al-Salam Salih Misbah.

Akram Abd Al Salam Saleh Misbah: alias Abu Hamzza, a Libyan born in 1988 who joined al Qaeda in Iraq in 2007. His phone number was 00218925104494, suggesting he may be related to Anas 'Abd-al-Salam Salih Misbah.

Anas 'Abd-al-Salam Salih Misbah: variant Annes Abd Al Salam Saleh Misbah, alias Abu-al-Bara', variant Abu al Barra'a, a Libyan from Benghazi who was born on September 5, 1983 and joined al Qaeda in Iraq as a martyr on October 28, 2006, contributing $100, 20 Libyan dinars, and 3,250 lira. His recruitment coordinator was Suhayl. His phone numbers were 218925104494 and 218926273025.

Annes Abd Al Salam Saleh Misbah: variant of Anas 'Abd-al-Salam Salih Misbah.

Abu Misha'al: alias of Abd Al Aziz Sanhat Abd Allah Al Harbie.

Akram Mishal: variant of Akram Meshal.

Khaled Mish'al: variant of Khaled Meshal, Hamas leader arrested in Jordan on September 22, 1999. The Israelis had attempted to assassinate him by injecting a lethal poison in his ear in Amman. He had been the head of the Hamas office in Damascus. By August 2003, he had become the head of the Hamas Political Bureau and Executive Committee in Damascus. On August 22, 2003, President Bush froze his assets and called on allies to join him by cutting off European sources of donations to Hamas.

Raed Abdul Hamid Misk: age 29, a cleric at the Mosque of the Arches who lived in Hebron and who on August 19, 2003 set off a suicide bomb loaded with ball bearings and other metal objects in a double-cabin Egged No. 2 bus in an ultra-Orthodox Jewish neighborhood in Jerusalem, killing 21 people, including five Americans and six children, and injuring more than 140, including 40 children. Hamas and the Islamic Jihad claimed credit. Israeli authorities blew up the bomber's family home.

Hafez Saleh Al Mismarie: variant of Hafiz Salih al-Masmari.

Abdul Sattar Sharif ul Misri: one of two al Qaeda operatives in Baluchistan arrested on August 30, 2004 by Pakistani authorities at a rented mud house in Quetta. The Egyptian had a bounty on his head.

Abu-Hafs al-Misri: alias of Muhammad 'Atif Mustafa

Abu Obaidah Misri: al Qaeda's chief of operations in Afghanistan's eastern Konar province who was killed on January 13, 2006 when a Predator drone fired a missile in Damadola, a village near the Afghan border, 120 miles northwest of Islamabad

Hani Habib Tahir al-Misri: member of a cell in Kuwait that set two bombs that exploded on July 10, 1989 in two streets leading to the Great Mosque in Mecca, killing a Pakistani and injuring 16 of the 1.5 million pilgrims from 100 countries attending the hajj.

Imad al-Misri: Egyptian al-Gama'at al-Islamiyya member arrested in July 2001 in Bosnia/Herzegovina and extradited to Egypt in October 2001.

Khalid Al-Mitari: a Kuwaiti held by U.S. authorities as of November 2001 in connection with their 9/11 investigations.

Al-Said Hassan Mkhles: variant Mokhles, a suspected Egyptian Islamic Group terrorist whose extradition was requested of Uruguay by Egypt in connection with the 1997 al-Gama'at al-Islamiyya attack on tourists in Luxor, Egypt. He was detained in Uruguay in early 1999 on charges of document fraud after trying to enter the country with a false passport. In July 2003, Uruguay extradited him to Egypt, which had said that he was a member of EIG and a possible al Qaeda associate. Egypt agreed that he would not be subjected to the death penalty, permanent imprisonment, or charged for document fraud, for which he already had served four years.

Mourad el Mnaouar: age 24, one of three individuals arrested with sabers on May 1, 2004. They were injured during an overnight gun battle in Casablanca's southern suburbs.

Sheik Mohammed Ali Hassan Moayad: variant Mouyad, one of two Yemenis arrested in Germany on January 10, 2003 and extradited to the United States, where they were prosecuted in 2005 for conspiracy to send money from Brooklyn to Hamas and al Qaeda. He claimed to have sent millions to the groups. Evidence included documents obtained in Afghanistan, Yemen, and Croatia, sources in the United Kingdom and Israel, and electronic surveillance of their hotel room in Germany where they stayed in 2003. On March 10, 2005, Moayad was convicted of conspiring to funnel money to al Qaeda and Hamas. Moayad was convicted of conspiracy, providing material support to Hamas, and attempting to support al Qaeda, but acquitted of providing support to al Qaeda. Defense attorneys said they would appeal. Moayad was represented by attorney William H. Goodman. Moayad faced 60 years. On July 28, 2005, Moayad was sentenced to 75 years, the maximum allowed. As of 2007, he was held in the Florence supermax prison in Colorado.

Hadi Modarresi: accused by Kuwait's *al-Qabas* news service of supervising the April 5, 1988 hijacking of Kuwait Airlines flight 422, a B747 flying from Bangkok to Kuwait that was diverted to Mashhad, Iran. He was the brother of Mohammad Taqiyodin Modaresi, leader of the Islamic Action Organization, which carried out the hijacking on the orders of Iranian Interior Minister Hojjat ol'Eslam 'Ali Akbar Mohtashemi, according to the newspaper.

Mohammad Taqiyodin Modarresi, leader of the Islamic Action Organization, which carried out the April 5, 1988 hijacking of Kuwait Airlines flight 422, a B747 flying from Bangkok to Kuwait that was diverted to Mashhad, Iran on the orders of Iranian Interior Minister Hojjat ol'Eslam 'Ali Akbar Mohtashemi, according to Kuwait's *al-Qabas* news service. He was the brother of Hadi Modarresi, who allegedly supervised the hijackers.

Khlouloud Moghrabi: a Lebanese arrested on August 2, 1978 and held for a week without bail at the United Kingdom's Marylebone Magistrate's Court on charges of conspiracy to murder Iraqi Ambassador Taha Ahmad ad-Dawud. On July 28, 1978, a grenade was thrown under ad-Dawud's car, killing him.

Mahmoud Said al-Moghrabi: sentenced to six years for complicity to commit murder for helping to make the bombs used in the 1985 bombings of a Copenhagen synagogue and a Northwest Airlines office that killed an Algerian tourist and injured 44 people. On May 10, 1991, the U.S. District Court for the Eastern District of New York said it wanted to question him in connection with the December 21, 1988 bombing of Pan Am flight 103 over Lockerbie, Scotland that killed 270. He was scheduled to be questioned on June 12, 1991 by attorneys representing the Pan Am victims' relatives, who were suing Pan Am for $14 billion in damages. He was believed to have visited Hajj Hafiz Qasim al-Dalqamuni in early October 1988, and might have been with him when a bomb similar to the Pan Am bomb was built.

Mohammed Mohajir: alleged leader in the 1980s of a terrorist support ring in Paris.

Kasim Ben S. Mohamad: one of five Palestinian skyjackers in a February 22, 1972 incident in which Lufthansa flight 594, a B747 flying from New Delhi to Athens, was hijacked by guerrillas armed with hand grenades, dynamite, and pistols. They initially told the pilot to go to the desert along the Red Sea, but they landed at Aden, South Yemen. They demanded the release of the killers of Wasfi Tell in Cairo and the Black September murderers of five Jordanian workers in Cologne, West Germany on February 6, 1972. The group called themselves the Organization for Victims of Zionist Occupation, the Organization for Resistance to Zionist Conquest of Palestine, and the Organization for Resistance to Zionist Occupation. In a letter, terrorists threatened to blow up the plane and the passengers if $5 million was not sent to a secret location outside Beirut. The West Germans announced the ransom payment on February 25. The group freed the passengers and surrendered to South Yemeni authorities, who released them on February 27.

Otoman A. Mohamad: a Milwaukee resident and one of a dozen masked, club-wielding Libyan students who took over the Libyan student aid office in McLean, Virginia and took hostages for a few minutes on December 22, 1982. Police raided the site after nine hours and the students surrendered. They were held on three counts of abduction. Bond for four of the students who, in 1981, had occupied the Libyan UN Mission, was set at $30,000; bond for the others was set at $15,000. Fairfax County released the names of the students on December 30, 1982. The Libyan student aid group sued the defendants for $12 million in Fairfax Circuit Court. On February 7, 1983, the students countersued for $15 million. Each of the students pleaded guilty in January 1983 to unlawful assembly, assaulting two office employees, and destroying private property. County prosecutors dropped felony charges of abduction. On March 4, 1983, Judge Barnard F. Jennings sentenced the 12 to one year in jail. On September 9, 1983, a Fairfax County judge released 10 of the 12 protestors after they presented proof to the court that they were enrolled for the fall term at accredited U.S. colleges.

Shafi Mohamadian: one of 57 people of Middle Eastern and North African origin arrested by French police on June 3, 1987 in connection with the discovery of an arms, explosives, and drugs cache in Fontainebleau forest, south of Paris, the previous week. Threats had been made by the Committee for Solidarity with Arab and Middle East Political Prisoners. He was ordered out of the country.

Abu Qasim son of Mohammad: one of five Libyans arrested on March 27, 1993 by police in Peshawar, Pakistan at a checkpoint near the Gulbahar crossing. Police found in their vehicle two .30 pistols and 30 cartridges, fake passport stamps, U.S. dollars, and Pakistani currency.

Khalid son of Mohammad: one of five Libyans arrested on March 27, 1993 by police in Peshawar, Pakistan at a checkpoint near the Gulbahar crossing. Police found in their vehicle two .30 pistols and 30 cartridges, fake passport stamps, U.S. dollars, and Pakistani currency.

Mahoud M. Mohammad: one of two members of the Popular Front for the Liberation of Palestine (PFLP) who threw grenades and fired a machine gun in Athens Airport at an El Al plane waiting to take off for New York on its way from Tel Aviv on December 26, 1968. Israeli passenger Leon Shirdan was killed and a stewardess suffered a fractured leg and spinal injuries when she jumped out of the plane. The PFLP duo were immediately arrested by Greek police; they were convicted and sentenced on March 26, 1970. Mohammad received 17 years and 5 months for interference with air traffic, arson, and illegal use and possession of explosives. A charge of premeditated murder against him for using the machine gun was lessened to a count of manslaughter by

negligence. Mohammed, age 25, was a Palestinian refugee. The duo was freed on July 22, 1970 when six Palestinians hijacked an Olympic Airways plane to Beirut.

Mohamed the Egyptian: alias of Rabei Osman el-Sayed Ahmed.

Ahmad Yusuf Mohamed: a Sudanese UN diplomat whose expulsion was demanded by the United States on April 10, 1996 for his involvement with the World Trade Center bombing on February 26, 1993 as well as the group that was arrested on June 24, 1993 for plotting to bomb several New York City landmarks, including the UN building, and for planning to assassinate Egyptian President Husni Mubarak during a visit to the United States.

Ahmed Abdellatif Sherif Mohamed: variant Mohamed Ahmed, age 24, one of two Egyptian students from the University of South Florida in Tampa who, on August 4, 2007, were stopped for speeding in their 2000 Toyota Camry near a Navy base in Goose Creek, South Carolina. They were jailed after authorities discovered explosives in the car's trunk. The materiel included a mixture of fertilizer, kitty litter, and sugar; 20 feet of fuse cord; and a box of .22 caliber bullets. On August 31, they were indicted by a federal grand jury on charges of carrying explosive materials across state lines. One of them faced terrorist-related charges of demonstrating how to use pipe-bomb explosives, including the use of remote-controlled toys, to the other. The duo claimed they were going to the beach with fireworks purchased from Wal-Mart. With federal charges in place, state charges were expected to be dismissed as of September 4.

Authorities later determined that Mohamed had posted on YouTube.com a 12-minute video on how to use a remote-controlled toy car to set off a bomb. His computer had bomb-making files in a folder called "Bomb Shock."

On December 1, 2007, Mohamed said in a defense filing that the explosives were cheap "sugar rocket" fireworks he had made that would travel only a few feet. On January 31, 2008, the FBI announced that the items were low-grade fireworks. But prosecutors countered on February 5, 2008 that the FBI report had been mischaracterized and that the items met the U.S. legal definition of explosives.

Ait Bellouk Mohamed: alias Islam, a Moroccan who was arrested on November 21, 1993 by police in the Kouba district of Algiers. He was born on April 29, 1966. He was believed to have prepared and carried out the October 24, 1993 kidnapping in Algiers of three French citizens working with the French consulate. He admitted involvement in several other crimes planned and conducted by the armed group led by Sid Ahmed Mourad, alias Djaafar the Afghan. On January 23, 1995, prosecutors at an Algiers special court demanded the death sentence. On January 24, 1995, the court sentenced him to death.

Ait Mouloud Mohamed: identified as the main defendant in the October 24, 1993 kidnapping in Algiers of three French citizens working with the French consulate. On January 23, 1995, prosecutors at an Algiers special court demanded the death sentence.

Ali A. Mohamed: alias Abu Omar. On October 30, the *New York Times* reported that on September 11, 1998, federal prosecutors had filed sealed charges against the 46-year-old former Army sergeant, a native of Egypt, who was in custody at the Metropolitan Correctional Center in New York.

Mohamed was a former Major in the Egyptian Army. He was granted a visa to the United States in 1985 and eventually became a U.S. citizen. He joined the U.S. Army in 1986, and traveled frequently to New York, where he trained Islamic militants in basic military techniques.

Mohamed had served for three years at the U.S. Army's Special Forces base in Fort Bragg, North Carolina. He was honorably discharged in 1989, and lived for much of the 1990s in California. A witness at the 1995 New York subway trial

testified that he traveled to New York while on active duty to provide military training to Muslims preparing to fight Soviets in Afghanistan. Students included El Sayyid A. Nosair, who killed Meir Kahane.

On May 19, 1999, federal officials indicted Mohamed on charges of training bin Laden's terrorists and Islamic militants, some of whom were later convicted of the New York subway bombing conspiracy and the World Trade Center bombing. He also made at least two trips to Afghanistan to train rebel commanders in military tactics.

He established ties with bin Laden's organization in 1991, and obtained false documents for the group. He assisted with logistical tasks, including bin Laden's 1991 move to Sudan.

On October 20, 2000, he pleaded guilty in a New York federal court to conspiring with bin Laden in the bombings of the U.S. embassies in Kenya and Tanzania on August 7, 1998. He pleaded guilty to five criminal felony counts, including conspiracy to murder, kidnap, and maim Americans in connection with terrorist acts, and to conspiracy to destroy U.S. defense facilities. He had been scheduled to go on trial in January 2001.

He told U.S. District Judge Leonard B. Sand that in 1993 he had briefed bin Laden after scouting possible U.S., UK, French, and Israeli terrorist targets in Kenya. He put together a study replete with sketches and photos. The U.S. Embassy in Nairobi was included. He also arranged a meeting in Sudan between bin Laden and the leader of Hizballah. He said he was involved with the Egyptian Islamic Jihad before he joined the army. He taught Muslim culture at Fort Bragg, North Carolina. He faced a life sentence, but could get substantial time off for his cooperation. He was represented by attorney James Roth.

Imad Mohamed: alleged member of the Islamic Salvation Front who was arrested for involvement in the August 26, 1992 bombing of the Air France ticket counter at Houari Boumedienne Airport in Algeria that killed 12 people and wounded 128. Public sessions of his trial began on May 4, 1993. On May 26, 1993, a special Algiers judicial council passed death sentenced on 38 defendants, including him. The council found him guilty of indirect participation in the crime by helping the perpetrators as well as taking part in an aggression with the aim of destroying the governing regime. On August 31, 1993, after exhausting all constitutional and legal appeals, he was executed.

Manhal Ben Mohamed: one of four accomplices of two Libyan intelligence officers arrested by the FBI on July 20, 1988 on charges of plotting to assassinate former National Security Council aide Marine Colonel Oliver L. North. The Falls Church, Virginia resident was a Manara travel agent. U.S. Magistrate Leonie Brinkema set bond between $25,000 and $50,000 for the Moroccan citizen. The group apparently was planning revenge against U.S. officials believed to have planned the April 1986 air raid against Libya in retaliation for Libyan involvement in several terrorist attacks. On July 28, 1988, a federal grand jury handed down a 40-count indictment, charging the group with conspiracy, money laundering, and violations of U.S. trade sanctions against Libya.

Matlou Mohamed: alleged member of the Islamic Salvation Front who was arrested for involvement in the August 26, 1992 bombing of the Air France ticket counter at Houari Boumedienne Airport in Algeria that killed 12 people and wounded 128. Public sessions of his trial began on May 4, 1993. On May 26, 1993, a special Algiers judicial council acquitted him.

Najib Chaib Mohamed: a Moroccan arrested in January 2002 in Spain for his alleged involvement in a suspected al Qaeda recruiting and logistics cell led by Imad Eddin Barakat Yarkas.

Rouabhi Mohamed: alleged member of the Islamic Salvation Front who, by October 1, 1992, had confessed to involvement in the August 26, 1992 bombing of the Air France ticket counter at Houari Boumedienne Airport in Algeria that killed 12 people and wounded 128. He was born

on July 1, 1942 in Tebessa, and lived in Bazali Avenue, Hocine Dey, Algiers. He was a headmaster of a secondary school and a lecturer. He had a Bachelor of Arts degree in economics, a Bachelor of Arts in literature, a general culture degree, a professional degree, and one in administrative management. He was an active member of the Islamic Call Movement.

Samir Ait Mohamed: age 32, an Algerian accused of helping Ahmed Ressam, who had been arrested on December 15, 1999 while transporting explosives across the Canada–United States border.

Mohamed used a fake French passport in 1991 to move from Algeria to Germany, where he requested political asylum.

On November 15, 2001, U.S. authorities served an extradition warrant for Mohamed, who had been held in Canadian custody in Vancouver since July 28, 2001 for immigration violations. Charges against him had been sealed in October. A criminal complaint was made public on November 15, accusing him of trying to get two hand grenades and a machine gun with a suppressor so Ressam could raise money for a Los Angeles attack via bank robberies. He was also accused of working with Mokhtar Haouari to obtain a "credit card with an alias for Ressam's use in connection with his planned terrorist operation and jihad work," according to the indictment. Court papers said Mohamed provided Ressam with a 9 mm semiautomatic pistol with a suppressor, knowing Ressam planned to conduct a terrorist attack in the United States. He was charged with two counts of conspiracy to commit international terrorism, and faced a life sentence. On November 29, 2001, the FBI released a document in Canada that said that he aimed to get "genuine" Canadian passports to permit a "team of terrorists" to enter the United States. He was to have obtained passports from "an individual working inside" the passport agency. In 1999, he sent four passports to Germany. The recipients had all trained with Ressam at a camp in Afghanistan. He was indicted on December 12, 2001 in New York on charges of obtaining weapons for Ressam.

Abu Mohammed: alias of Ayman al-Zawahiri.

Abu Mohammed: alias of Sa'd al-Sharif, bin Laden's Saudi brother-in-law and financial chief.

Abu Mohammed: alias of Emad Abdelwahid Ahmed Alwan.

Ali Mohammed: in 2000, the Egyptian Islamic Jihad member told a U.S. court he had surveilled and photographed the U.S. Embassy in Nairobi at the direction of Osama bin Laden, who used one of the photos to determine where the truck bomb should go on August 7, 1998.

Azam Mohammed: alias of Ramzi Ahmad Yusuf.

Faqir Mohammed: deputy leader of Pakistan's Taliban movement in May 2008.

Fazul Abdullah Mohammed: alias Fouad Mohammed, in his late twenties as of October 2001, circa five feet four inches tall, circa 130 pounds, Comoran, trained with bin Laden in Afghanistan and led an al Qaeda branch in Kenya. He was charged with planning the August 7, 1998 bombing of the U.S. Embassy in Nairobi, Kenya. He was listed in October 2001 as one of the FBI's 22 most-wanted terrorists. He was linked to four people who were charged on June 23, 2003 by the Kenyan government in the November 28, 2002 suicide bombing of the Paradise Hotel in Kenya, in which 16 died and 80 were injured. He speaks French, Arabic, and English. He carries a Kenyan passport. He taught at an Islamic school in Lamu, Kenya under the alias Abdul Karim. He is married to Mohamed Kubwa's half-sister, Amina. Kubwa was charged in the November 28, 2002 attacks. Kubwa was believed to have been killed on January 8, 2007, when the U.S. conducted an airstrike in Badmadow island off southern Somalia.

Fouad Mohammed: alias of Fazul Abdallah Muhammad.

Sergeant Hussein Abbas Mohammed: a member of the Egyptian Home Guard who was named on November 12, 1981 as one of the assassins of Egyptian President Anwar Sadat on October 6, 1981. He was sentenced to death on March 6, 1982 and shot by firing squad on April 15, 1982.

Hilal Mohammed: Jordanian living in Brooklyn detained as an accomplice of Rashad Baz, a Brooklyn resident who, on March 1, 1994, fired on a convoy of Hasidic Jewish students on Franklin D. Roosevelt Drive near the Brooklyn Bridge in New York, injuring 14 rabbinical students in a van. Officials said he had helped Baz dispose of the guns and the car. He worked at a Brooklyn taxi service that also employed Baz. Bail was set at $20,000. He pleaded not guilty on March 29.

Hussain Youssef Ibrahim Mohammed: a Bahrain University student and 1 of 44 Bahrainis arrested on June 4, 1996 and charged with plotting to overthrow the government. The group's leader had asked the group to gather information on U.S. forces in Bahrain, where the U.S. Fifth Fleet is based. One suspect said that the group had been trained by Hizballah in Lebanon. Mohammed said the training included work with "light, medium, and heavy weapons . . . using explosives, and techniques of making bombs." The group claimed to be the military wing of Hizballah Bahrain.

Jaad Mohammed: a 20-year-old Syrian who was one of three Black June members who took five hostages at the Syrian Embassy in Rome on October 11, 1976. They surrendered after two hours after discovering they had not taken the Ambassador hostage. The attackers were jailed and charged with attempted murder. On November 6, 1976, a Rome court sentenced them to 15 years in jail, to be followed by three years of supervised freedom. The Syrians requested extradition.

Jamal Jafar Mohammed: sentenced to death for the 1983 car bombings of the U.S. and French embassies in which five people died and more than

80 were injured. On February 6, 2007, CNN reported that he was a member of the Iraqi parliament and had parliamentary immunity. He had led an Iraqi arm of the Iranian Armed Forces. He was a member of Iraqi Prime Minister Nouri al-Maliki's Dawa Party.

Jamil Qasim Saeed Mohammed: a 27-year-old Yemeni microbiology student and al Qaeda member who was believed to be involved in the October 12, 2000 al Qaeda bombing of the USS *Cole* in Yemen, in which 17 U.S. sailors were killed and 44 injured. He was captured in Karachi a few weeks after 9/11. On October 26, 2001, Pakistani authorities handed him over to U.S. authorities, who apparently flew him to Jordan.

Khalid Mohammed: a senior al Qaeda in Iraq leader serving as chief of security in the north.

Mustafa Mohammed: alias of Mustafa Mohamed Fadhil.

Rauf Mohammed: age 26, an Iraqi taxi driver acquitted by a London court on August 29, 2006 of making two videos of London landmarks that terrorists could use. He said the 2003 video was a harmless tourist souvenir. He was represented by attorney Lawrence McNulty, who said that the videoed remarks about killing President Bush, Prime Minister Blair, Italian Prime Minister Silvio Berlusconi, and Defense Secretary Donald Rumsfeld had been made in a joking manner. The video included Parliament, the London Eye Ferris wheel, and a police station.

Rawad Jassem Mohammed: age 23, one of three suicide bombers who, on November 9, 2005, attacked Western hotels in Amman, killing 59 and wounding more than 300. Abu Musab al-Zarqawi's group al Qaeda in Iraq claimed credit.

Said Hazan Mohammed: arrested in February 1999 by Uruguayan authorities while he was trying to enter the country from Brazil with a fake Malaysian passport. On February 24, it appeared that Uruguay would extradite him to Egypt to stand trial for the attack in Luxor on November 17, 1997 in which terrorists killed 58 foreigners and four Egyptians.

Salah Abu Mohammed: spokesman for the Al Qaeda in Islamic North Africa group that claimed credit for the February 22, 2008 kidnapping of two Austrian tourists in Tunisia.

Sami Saleem Mohammed: age 21, from the northern West Bank village of Qabatiyah, identified by the Palestinian Islamic Jihad as the suicide bomber who, on April 17, 2006, set off explosives outside the Mayor Falafel and Shawarma fast food restaurant in Tel Aviv during Passover, killing nine other people and wounding more than 60 Israelis. A security guard outside the restaurant, which had been targeted by a suicide bomber in January (when two dozen Israelis were killed by a 22-year-old), stopped the terrorist from entering the building.

Sheik Omar Bakri Mohammed: on August 8, 2005, the Syrian-born radical flew to Lebanon, saying the UK had declared war against Muslims. He was detained by Lebanese authorities, but later released. Bakri had publicly said that he would not tell police if he knew of an Islamist bomb plot. A *Sunday Times* reporter heard him refer to the 7-7-5 bombers of the London subway system as the Fantastic Four. On August 12, 2005, the British government barred his return to the country for medical treatment.

Walter Mohammed: alias used by one of two Organization of Struggle Against World Imperialism hijackers of Lufthansa flight 181, a B737 scheduled to fly from the Spanish resort island of Mallorca to Frankfurt on October 13, 1977. The duo demanded the release of the same 11 terrorists in West German jails as had been mentioned in the Schleyer kidnapping of September 5, 1977 and the release of two Palestinian terrorists held in Turkish jails for the August 11, 1976 Popular Front for the Liberation of Palestine machine-gun attack on passengers awaiting an El Al flight in Istanbul. They demanded $15 million and that 100,000 DM be given to each prisoner, who were to be flown to Vietnam, Somalia, or the People's Democratic Republic of Yemen (commonly known as South Yemen), all of which indicated an unwillingness to receive them. After the plane had hopscotched to various countries, the terrorists shot the pilot in Aden. A West German GSG9 team ran a successful rescue operation in Somalia on October 18, initially killing two of the hijackers. A third in the first-class compartment opened fire and threw a grenade after being hit. A female hijacker opened fire and was quickly subdued.

Ghanim Mohammed Mohammedi: age 37, a welder and former Iraqi Ba'ath Party member who was believed to be an aide to Abu Musab al-Zarqawi. On October 23, 2004, U.S. Marines captured him in a midnight raid in Fallujah.

Yousri Mohareb: a Gaza-trained Egyptian detained by Egyptian police in May 2006 who was in contact with Palestinian Tamer al-Nuseirat, who said he was willing to conduct attacks in Egypt.

Abdelbaset Ali Mohmed: alias of 'Abd al-Baset al-Megrahi.

Abou-Naama Mohmoud: an Algerian arrested on August 2, 1978 and held for a week without bail at Marylebone Magistrate's Court on charges of conspiracy to murder Iraqi Ambassador Taha Ahmad ad-Dawud. On July 28, 1978, a grenade was thrown under ad-Dawud's car, killing him.

Zouheir Mohsen: chief of the Palestine Liberation Organization's military division who, on March 12, 1975, threatened to launch terrorist attacks on Israeli targets in the United States.

Abdul Mohsin: an Egyptian arrested in April 2000 in a police raid on a Peshawar, Pakistan apartment. Mohsin had spent three months in jail in Canada on suspicion of involvement with Osama bin Laden's al-Qaeda group. Police found several forged passports in the apartment. The police had raided the place on a tip that bin Laden's son was living in the apartment with Mohsen and an Algerian, who was also detained.

Ayatollah Mohtashani: Iran's Ambassador to Syria who was reported by Jack Anderson and Dale Van Atta on November 7, 1986 of planning the hijacking of a Kuwaiti A310 en route from Kuwait to Bangkok with intermediate stops in Dubai and Karachi on December 4, 1984.

Ayatollah Mohtashemi: possibly the same individual as above, founder of Hizballah who, in September 1995, threatened to conduct a suicide attack against an Israeli plane in retaliation for the September 19, 1995 hijacking to Israel of an Iranian plane.

Kareem Altohami Mojati: a Moroccan supporter of bin Laden who fought in Afghanistan who helped plan the May 2003 suicide bombings in Casablanca that killed 33 people, and who was number four on the Saudis' 26 most-wanted terrorists list. He died in a gun battle with Saudi authorities on April 3-6, 2005 in a walled compound in Ar Rass.

Al-Said Hassan Mokhles: variant of Al-Said Hassan Mkhles.

Bouchoucha Mokhtar: a Tunisian member of an al Qaeda cell in Italy, who was serving prison terms in Italy for trafficking in arms and explosives when, on April 19, 2002, the US froze his assets.

Mazen Mokhtar: an Egyptian-born imam and political activist, in 2004, operated the Web sites www.azzam.com and www.qoqaz.net, based in Nevada and Connecticut, which the U.S. Justice Department said were "more operational" than scholarly. He works as the imam at the Masjid al-Huda mosque in New Brunswick, New Jersey. Mokhtar's lawyer denied that his client was a terrorist.

Nahrim Mokhtari: an Iranian woman arrested by Argentine police on December 5, 1998. She was linked to Middle Eastern terrorist groups, and had told a former lover of plans to bomb the Israeli Embassy in Argentina before it occurred on March 17, 1992.

Bouchoucha Moktar: one of four Tunisians convicted by a Milan court on February 22, 2002 on terrorist charges, including criminal association with intent to transport arms, explosives, and chemicals, and falsifying 235 work permits, 130 driver's licenses, several foreign passports, and various blank documents. They were acquitted of charges of possession of arms and chemicals. The guilty verdicts regarding the documents were the first in Europe against al Qaeda operatives since the September 11, 2001 attacks. The four belonged to the Salafist Group for Preaching and Combat, an Algerian wing of al Qaeda. Moktar received five years.

Ali Mollahzadeh: one of three Iranian youths who hijacked an Iranian Airlines B727 flying from Tehran to Abadan on June 21, 1970 and diverted it to Baghdad, Iraq, where they were given asylum. His brother was another hijacker.

Hassan Mollahzadeh: one of three Iranian youths who hijacked an Iranian Airlines B727 flying from Tehran to Abadan on June 21, 1970 and diverted it to Baghdad, Iraq, where they were given asylum. His brother was another hijacker.

Christian Moller: suspected of taking part in West German bank raids after he joined the Baader-Meinhof Gang in July 1977. He was arrested with Gabriele Korecher-Tiedemann on December 20, 1977 by Swiss authorities after the duo drove their French-registered auto from France into Switzerland. He was wounded in a gun battle with police. Some of the money paid in the ransom of Walter Palmers, who was kidnapped on November 9, 1977 in Austria, was found in their car.

Yousef Magied Molqi: a Palestinian convicted of killing Leon Klinghoffer, age 69, a wheelchair-bounded Jewish American who was murdered and thrown overboard in the takeover of the *Achille Lauro* cruise ship on October 7, 1985 in Greece. On February 25, 1996, Molqi, age 34, disappeared during a prison furlough at a church-run shelter in Prato, near Florence, Italy. He was scheduled to return to Rebibbia Prison in Rome at the end of his 12-day pass. He was serving a 30-year term, but had been permitted short release periods four times earlier. On March 13, 1996, Italy offered a "substantial" reward for his arrest. The U.S. Department of State offered a $2 million reward and resettlement in the U.S. for informants and their families.

On March 22, 1996, Spanish Civil Guard detectives, aided by Italian police, arrested him in Estepona. On December 4, 1996, Spain extradited him to Italy, which put him back in a Rome prison cell.

Abdullamajed Apaase-al-Habeb al-Momany: one of 16 Middle Eastern terrorists the Saudi Embassy, on March 20, 1990, told Thai officials were planning to attack Saudi diplomats and officials overseas. He carried a Lebanese passport.

Azita Monachipur: arrested in September 1986 by French counterintelligence agents following a wave of bombings that left 13 dead. On April 24, 1988, Paris police jailed the Iranian anti-Khomeini leftist for possession of explosives he said would be used for attacks in Iran. He was sentenced to 30 months.

Abdul-Majeed Mohammed Abdullah Moneea: former number 18 on the Saudi's 26 most-wanted terrorist list, was killed in a gun battle in a house in eastern Riyadh by Saudi forces on October 12, 2004.

Mohamed Hashem el Moneiry: one of two hijackers of an Egyptian Misrair Antonov-24 flying from Cairo to Aswan on August 18, 1969 and diverted to a small airstrip north of Jeddah, Saudi Arabia. He and his brother were arrested by Saudi Arabia and returned on the same plane under guard to Luxor, Egypt. El Moneiry was an army physician who was accompanied by his wife and three children.

Soliman Hashem el Moneiry: one of two hijackers of an Egyptian Misrair Antonov-24 flying from Cairo to Aswan on August 18, 1969 and diverted to a small airstrip north of Jeddah, Saudi Arabia. He and his brother were arrested by Saudi Arabia and returned on the same plane under guard to Luxor, Egypt. Soliman was sentenced to life in prison.

'Abd-al-Hakim Monib: a member of the Taliban council who, on September 15, 1995 in a *BBC Radio* interview, warned foreign embassies and organizations to leave Kabul.

Said Monsour: a Moroccan identified by the FBI in 1995 as one of seven men with ties to Hamas and the Islamic Group who helped plan the February 26, 1993 World Trade Center bombing. He had lived in Denmark since 1984, and had hosted blind radical Sheik Omar Abd-al-Rahman when he visited Denmark in 1990. He was believed to be a European organizer for the Islamic Group, the spiritual leader of which is Sheik Rahman.

Montazer: driver of the getaway motorcycle used by one of the three Iranian government agents believed to have assassinated Abdolrahman Qassemlou, secretary general of the Kurdish Democratic Party, in Vienna, Austria on July 13, 1989.

Bagher Moomeney: one of eight Iranian students arrested in the United States on November 15, 1979 for attempting to smuggle three disassembled Winchester 30.06 rifles, matching scopes, 15 boxes of ammunition, and a street map of Washington, DC with certain embassies marked, as one of the men was about to board TWA 900 from Baltimore-Washington International Airport to New York's JFK International Airport. The Iranians spoke of taking the rifles to Iran. They claimed to be attending Baltimore-area colleges, and were jailed on bonds ranging from $25,000 to $250,000. The group was charged with dealing in firearms without a license, placing firearms on an interstate commercial airliner without notifying the carrier, and conspiracy. Moomeney was to travel to Iran with the weapons. On February 25, 1980, Moomeney pleaded guilty to placing guns on a common carrier. On April 10, 1980, a federal judge gave him a suspended sentence and told him to leave the country "with reasonable haste."

Munir Moqda: a prominent Palestinian guerrilla leader based in Lebanon, who was tried in absentia in Jordan in connection with the foiled December 13, 1999 28-person al Qaeda plot to attack Israelis, Americans, and other Christian tourists. On September 18, 2000, the military court sentenced him to death for the plot, but acquitted him on charges of links to bin Laden.

Majed Moqed: age 22, one of the al Qaeda hijackers who, on September 11, 2001, took over American Airlines flight 77, a B757 headed from Washington's Dulles International Airport to Los Angeles with 64 people, including four flight attendants and two pilots on board. The hijackers, armed with box cutters and knives, forced the passengers and crew to the back of the plane. The plane made a hairpin turn over Ohio and Kentucky and flew back to Washington, with its transponder turned off. It aimed full throttle at the White House, but made a 270-degree turn at the last minute and crashed into the Pentagon in northern Virginia at 9:40 A.M. The plane hit the helicopter landing pad adjacent to the Pentagon, sliding into the west face of the Pentagon near Washington Boulevard. The plane cut a 35-foot wedge through the building's E, D, C, and B rings between corridors 4 and 5. More than 100 people were killed.

Mrayan Morak: one of six Iranian Hizballah members detained on May 2, 1992 by Ecuadoran police in Quito on suspicion of involvement in the March 17, 1992 car bombing at the Israeli Embassy in Buenos Aires that killed 29 and injured 252. They had intended to go to Canada via the United States. On May 9, the Crime Investigation Division in Quito said that the group was not involved in the bombing, but would be deported to Iran through Bogota and Caracas. They were released on May 12, 1992 and given 72 hours to leave the country.

Seyed Abrahim Mosavi: one of eight Iranian students arrested in the United States on November 15, 1979 for attempting to smuggle three disassembled Winchester 30.06 rifles, matching scopes, 15 boxes of ammunition, and a street map of Washington, DC with certain embassies marked, as one of the men was about to board TWA 900 from Baltimore–Washington International Airport to New York's JFK International Airport. The Iranians spoke of taking the rifles to Iran. They claimed to be attending Baltimore-area colleges, and were jailed on bonds ranging from $25,000 to $250,000. Mosavi purchased the rifles for more than $1,000 cash, and had spoken to a gun dealer about purchasing machine guns, pistols, a 12-gauge riot control shotgun, and a Heckler and Koch assault rifle. The group was charged with dealing in firearms without a license, placing firearms on an interstate commercial airliner without notifying the carrier, and conspiracy. On March 5, 1980, jurors acquitted Mosavi of attempting to smuggle rifles and ammunition aboard the plane.

Safal Mosed: age 24, residing in Lackawanna, a suburb of Buffalo, New York, was identified as a member of an al Qaeda-trained terrorist cell on American soil. He and four others had attended an al Qaeda training camp in Afghanistan, learning how to use assault rifles, handguns, and other weapons, in June 2001, and left the camp before the 9/11 attacks. They were charged with providing, attempting to provide, and conspiring to provide material support and resources to a foreign terrorist group (al Qaeda), which entail a

maximum 15-year prison sentence. The recruits at the al-Farooq camp, which is located near Kandahar, were addressed by bin Laden. The camp was also attended by American Taliban John Walker Lindh.

The defendants were identified as Faysal Galab, age 26; Sahim Alwan, age 29; Yahya Goba, age 25; Safal Mosed, age 24; and Hasein Taher (variant (Ther), age 24; who lived within a few blocks of one another. Two associates were believed to be in Yemen; another was out of the country. The associates, identified only as A, B, and C, included two U.S. citizens from Lackawanna. Prosecutors later identified the ringleader as unindicted coconspirator Kamal Derwish, 29, believed to be living in Yemen. The defendants were later joined by Mukhtar al-Bakri, age 22, who, with Alwan, admitted attending the camp.

At the September 19 bail hearing, attorney Patrick J. Brown, representing Mosed, said "If Mr. Alwan is the head of a sleeper cell, he is not to be trusted. There was no proof that Mosed was there."

The defendants were well-known in the local community. One was voted the high school's friendliest senior. Four are married; three have children.

Prosecutors noted that Mosed had spent $89,000 at the Casino Niagara in Canada within the year.

The FBI had begun an investigation when the men came to Lackawanna in June 2001. The Bureau said there was no evidence that they were planning a specific attack in the United States.

Federal prosecutors noted on September 27 that some of the accused had tapes and documents in their homes that called for suicide operations against Islam's "enemies." Shafal Mosed had 2 different Social Security cards in his possession and 11 credit cards for 6 different names.

On October 8, Judge Schroeder released on $600,000 bond Sahim Alwan, but ordered the other five held without bail.

On October 21, a federal grand jury indicted the six on charges of providing and attempting to provide support to al Qaeda, and with conspiring to provide material support to the terrorists. They pleaded not guilty the next day to charges that they trained at an al Qaeda camp. They faced 15 years in prison.

On March 24, 2003, Shafal Mosed, the college student and marketer, pleaded guilty in federal court in Buffalo to providing "material support" to al Qaeda by attending the al Farooq camp, a stronger charge than Galab's charge of "funds and services." His attorney, Patrick Brown, said "he is ashamed that he went. He absolutely does not buy into that, the al Qaeda party line." This was the first time an individual had been convicted of providing material support to al Qaeda. The conviction carries a ten-year sentence, but his cooperation was expected to shorten it to eight years. Sentencing was scheduled for July 16. Brown said Mosed agreed to the plea because he feared the government would tack on more serious charges, including treason and serving as an enemy combatant.

On December 9, Shafal Mosed, then age 25, received eight years.

Imran Motala: on May 9, 2007, British police arrested the 22-year-old on suspicion of commissioning, preparing, or instigating acts of terrorism, i.e., assisting the suicide bombers who attacked the London subway system on July 7, 2005.

Mounir El Motassadeq: age 27 as of September 2001, was a Moroccan studying at Hamburg's Technical University. He had transferred money to 9/11 hijack leader Muhammad Atta and Ramzi Binalshibh. He also had power of attorney for 9/11 UA 175 hijacker Marwan Al-Shehhi. He was one of two Muslim witnesses to Atta's will, although he denied having seen the will. He said he transferred $1,000 to Atta in 2000 to pay for a computer. He did not explain his transferring $2,350 to Binalshibh. On November 28, 2001, Hamburg police arrested El Motassadeq on "urgent suspicion of supporting a terrorist group." He might have visited an al Qaeda terrorist camp in Afghanistan in the summer of 2000; Pakistan said that he was in Pakistan in July 2000. While

in Pakistan, he stayed at the same Karachi hotel as fugitive Said Bahaji and probably fugitives Binalshibh and Essabar using aliases. Police said he managed one of Marwan Al-Shehhi's accounts, into which large sums of money were deposited from May to November 2000 to finance flight lessons and pay for the upkeep in the United States of Al-Shehhi, Atta, and Ziad Jarrahi. El Motassadeq is married to a Belarussian and has a son. He came to Hamburg in 1995 to study for a degree in electrical technology. Atta helped him to find a Goeschen Street apartment, around the corner from Atta's Marien Street apartment. El Motassadeq flew to Istanbul in May 2001, where he met with a man who transported Islamic fighters to and from Afghanistan and Chechnya. He apparently had contact with people affiliated with Mamdouh Mahmud Salim, a suspected al Qaeda financier extradited by Germany to the United States in 1998. He had signed up to tour a Stade nuclear power plant near Hamburg in 2001. He, Atta, Al-Shehhi, Jarrahi, and Essabar attended Bahaji's 1999 wedding at the al-Quds mosque in Hamburg.

On August 28, 2002, German federal prosecutors filed charges in Hamburg Superior Court against the 28-year-old Moroccan electrical engineering student. He was charged with more than 3,000 counts of accessory to murder and membership in a terrorist organization. On September 30, 2002, the U.S. and German governments blocked his financial assets. On October 23, 2002, he told the court that he transferred $2,500 from al-Shehhi's account to pay for his military training in Afghanistan at the request of Binalshibh. On February 19, 2003, the German court convicted him of the 3,000 counts. He was sentenced to 15 years in prison. On March 4, 2004, a German appeals court ordered a new trial, saying the proceeding had been compromised by U.S. refusal to give Motassadeq access to Binalshibh. He was freed by the Hamburg court on April 7, 2004, pending a retrial in June. His retrial began on August 10, 2004.

On May 13, 2005, the United States sent six pages of summaries from interrogations of Ramzi

Binalshibh and Mohamedou Ould Slahi to a Hamburg court retrying Mounir el Motassadeq. On August 19, 2005, a German court convicted Motassadeq and sentenced him to seven years as a member of the Hamburg cell, but found him not guilty of more than 3,000 counts of accessory to murder in the 9/11 attack, ruling that he did not play a direct role in the plot. On February 7, 2006, Motassadeq was unexpectedly freed from a Hamburg prison, pending appeals. On October 12, 2006, a German court began a hearing on whether it should reinstate the accessory-to-murder charges.

On November 16, 2006, Germany's Federal Court of Justice overturned the Hamburg court's acquittal of Motassadeq, who now faced 15 years when he was to be resentenced in Hamburg. On January 12, 2007, Germany's Federal Constitutional Court refused to take up his appeal of helping three of the 9/11 hijackers. The appeal was separate from his appeal of the 15-year sentence he received on January 8, 2007 for being an accessory to the deaths of the 246 people who died on the planes.

Ahamed Bin Saleh Bi Yunes Al Moughriq: variant of Ahmed Bin Saleh bin Yunes Al Mughrieq.

Mohamed Mouhajef: variant of Muhammad Muhajir.

Youssef Bin Muhamad Mouhirayer: alias Abo Khaoulah, a Moroccan from Hie al Hanna'a who was born on April 1, 1979 and joined al Qaeda in Iraq as a martyr on October 25, 2006, bringing a passport, ID, watch, and $100. His home phone number was 067987672.

Michel (variant Michael) Waheb Moukharbel: assistant of Carlos, the Venezuelan Popular Front for the Liberation of Palestine (PFLP) terrorist. He ran the PFLP's European operations. He was involved in the planning of the RPG-7 attack on an El Al 707 in Orly Airport on January 13, 1975. Carlos killed him when French police raided his Paris apartment in July 1975.

Ammar Moula: alias of Zakariya Essabar.

Noureddinne Mouleff: an Algerian charged on December 3, 2003 with terrorism and fraud offenses. He was among 14 people arrested the previous day.

Maroona Mouna: name used on the Iranian passport of the female hijacker who joined the Organization of Struggle Against World Imperialism hijackers of Lufthansa 181, a B737 scheduled to fly from the Spanish resort island of Mallorca to Frankfurt on October 13, 1977. The duo demanded the release of the same 11 terrorists in West German jails as had been mentioned in the Schleyer kidnapping of September 5, 1977 and the release of two Palestinian terrorists held in Turkish jails for the August 11, 1976 Popular Front for the Liberation of Palestine machine-gun attack on passengers awaiting an El Al flight in Istanbul. They demanded $15 million and that 100,000 DM be given to each prisoner, who were to be flown to Vietnam, Somalia, or the People's Democratic Republic of Yemen (commonly referred to as South Yemen), all of which indicated an unwillingness to receive them. After the plane had hopscotched to various countries, the terrorists shot the pilot in Aden. A West German GSG9 team ran a successful rescue operation in Somalia on October 18, initially killing two of the hijackers. A third, in the first-class compartment, opened fire and threw a grenade after being hit. A female hijacker opened fire and was quickly subdued. She was wearing a Che Guevara t-shirt and shouting "Palestine will live" in Arabic when she was captured.

Mansour Mourad (variant Mansur Seifeddin Mourad): terrorist held by the Greek government for a November 27, 1968 (or 1969) attack on the El Al office in Athens. The 21-year-old Jordanian member of the Palestine Popular Struggle Front joined Elie Karabetian in throwing two hand grenades into the Athens office of El Al, killing a $2\frac{1}{2}$-year-old Greek child and wounding 15 others, including three Americans, a Briton, 10

Greeks, and a 3-year-old Greek child. His release was demanded by the hijackers of an Olympic Airways B727 flying from Beirut to Athens on July 22, 1970. The hijackers agreed to let his trial go ahead as scheduled on July 24, 1970. After the trial, the hostages would go free. He was sentenced to 11 years. He was released into the custody of the International Committee of the Red Cross and flown to Cairo. The prosecutor who had tried him on charges of murder and had succeeded in convicting him of premeditated manslaughter told him that he hoped to see him again in his country as a tourist.

Mourad: alias of Mohamed Zineddine.

Sid Ahmed Mourad: alias Djaafar the Afghan, alleged to be the leader of an armed group that, on October 24, 1993, kidnapped three French citizens working with the French consulate in Algiers. The chief of the Armed Islamic Group was killed by Algerian authorities in a gun battle on February 26, 1994. He was also linked to the kidnapping of Cheikh Mohamed Bouslimani, the chairman of the Guidance and Reform charity society, from his home in Blida in November 1993.

Walid Majib Mourad: one of three individuals arrested in Richford, Vermont on October 23, 1987 after they illegally crossed into the United States from Canada with a terrorist bomb made from two metal canisters filled with smokeless gunpowder. A black hood found with the bomb and bomb-making equipment resembled hoods used in terrorist attacks in the Middle East. On October 28, 1987, U.S. Magistrate Jerome J. Niedermeier ordered them held without bail. They said they were Canadian citizens living in Montreal, but were believed to be Lebanese. On January 26, 1988, Mourad pleaded guilty to conspiring to transport explosives and to an immigration violation, for which he faced ten years in prison. On May 17, 1988, the U.S. government reported that the trio were members of the Syrian Social National Party, a Syrian

terrorist organization that assassinated Lebanese President-Elect Bashir Gemayel in 1982.

Javad Mousavi: one of four Iranians who were detained on December 15, 1989 in Manchester's Stretford Police Station under the Prevention of Terrorism Act on suspicion of planning to kill Salman Rushdie. Mousavi was released on December 19, 1989. His UK-born wife, Dawn, said he was a father of four and disabled from multiple sclerosis.

Shiraz Mousazadeh: one of three Iranians arrested by Turkish police at Esenboga Airport on September 13, 1986 while trying to sneak an attaché case wired to hold explosives onto a Turkish Airlines flight bound for Cyprus. Although there were no explosives in the case, the wires would set if off when the case's handle was touched. The trio had entered Turkey at a border point on the eastern frontier with Iran on September 4, 1986. They claimed they were flying to the Turkish Republic of Northern Cyprus, recognized only by Turkey, to take exams, and claimed no knowledge of the mechanism. On September 17, 1986, the Ankara Security Court charged them with founding a criminal organization and being members of an armed band.

Mahmoud Ibrahim Moussa: Imam of Rome's main mosque, who was suspended on June 13, 2003 from the national Muslim league after he praised Palestinian suicide bombers at Friday prayers, calling on Allah to "annihilate the enemies of Islam."

Samir Moussaab: alias of Samir Saioud.

Mehdi Hachem Moussaoui: on March 11, 2002, he pleaded guilty to racketeering conspiracy in a Charlotte court. He faced 20 years in prison for funneling profits from cigarette smuggling to Hizballah.

Zacarias Moussaoui: age 34, a French Moroccan arrested on August 11, 2001 on immigration charges in Eagen, Minnesota, and later suspected of being the missing 20th 9/11 hijacker. He offered $8,000 in cash to a flight training school to teach him how to steer a jetliner, but not how to land or take off. On September 1, according to the *Washington Post*, French intelligence reported that Moussaoui was linked to "radical Islamic extremists" and that he had spent two months in Pakistan and possibly in Afghan training camps. Police found information in his computers on jetliners, crop dusters, wind patterns, and the way chemicals can be dispersed from airplanes, similar to research conducted by 9/11 hijack operation leader Muhammad Atta. The FBI temporarily grounded all crop dusters in the United States. The German magazine *Stern* reported that two large sums of money were sent to Moussaoui from Duesseldorf and Hamburg on August 1 and 3. Police later suspected that Moussaoui was sent as a replacement 20th hijacker when Ramzi Binalshibh, age 29, a Yemeni fugitive in Hamburg, could not get a visa to enter the United States. Moussaoui became the first person indicted in the attacks when, on December 11, a federal grand jury in Alexandria charged him on six counts of criminal conspiracy, including involvement in the murder of federal employees and committing terrorist acts; four charges carry the death penalty, the others, life. On December 19, Moussaoui was ordered by U.S. Magistrate Judge Thomas R. Jones, Jr. in U.S. District Court in Alexandria, Virginia to be held without bond until his arraignment on conspiracy charges, set for January 2, 2002 before U.S. District Judge Leonie M. Brinkema. He was charged with conspiracy to commit international terrorism, conspiracy to use airplanes as weapons of mass destruction, and other charges. Ahmed Ressam linked Moussaoui to al Qaeda, claiming he recognized him from photographs because they both attended the Khalden al Qaeda training camp in Afghanistan in 1998. Moussaoui was represented by Donald DuBoulay; Gerald Zerkin, age 52, a senior litigator with the Federal Public Defender's office; Federal Public Defender Frank W. Dunham, Jr.; and Edward MacMahon, age 41. Moussaoui's family was represented by

Isabelle Coutant Peyre, fiancee and attorney of Illich Ramirez Sanchez, the Venezuelan Popular Front for the Liberation of Palestine terrorist also known as Carlos the Jackal, who was serving a life term with parole in a French prison.

On January 10, 2005, attorneys for Zacarias Moussaoui asked the U.S. Supreme Court to prevent the government from seeking the death penalty and from presenting evidence related to the 9/11 attacks. On March 21, 2005, the U.S. Supreme Court declined to hear Moussaoui's request to review a lower court ruling that denied him access to al Qaeda detainees Khalid Sheik Mohammed and Ramzi Binalshibh. On April 22, 2005, Moussaoui pleaded guilty to taking part in an al Qaeda conspiracy that led to 9/11; he said that he was to conduct a follow-up plane attack on the White House. U.S. District Judge Leonie Brinkema said he was competent to enter the plea and began deliberations on setting up a jury trial regarding a death penalty. The penalty phase of the trial began on February 6, 2006 with the selection of jurors. He was thrown out of court four times after yelling "I am al Qaeda," fired his lawyers, and said he would testify. Opening statements were scheduled for March 6. He was in and out of court throughout February for his antics.

Judge Brinkema halted the trial on March 13 and said she was considering removing the death penalty after Carla J. Martin, a Transportation Security Administration lawyer, improperly shared testimony and coached seven witnesses, all of them current and former federal aviation employees, via e-mails. The judge had earlier ruled that witnesses could not attend or follow the trial or read transcripts. The judge ordered the prosecution to not use those witnesses. On March 17, she relented slightly, letting the prosecution use other, untainted, aviation witnesses, and said she would also let the government pursue the death sentence.

Moussaoui testified on March 27 that he was to lead a five-man team that included convicted shoe bomber Richard Reid that was to have hijacked a fifth 9/11 plane and crash it into the White House. He did not indicate what happened to the other three would-be hijackers. He also claimed that he knew only about the World Trade Center planes, and claimed that he had lied earlier to investigators.

On March 28, the testimony of two al Qaeda operatives was read to the jury. Sayf al-Adl, a senior member of the group's military committee, said that the defendant was "a confirmed jihadist but was absolutely not going to take part in the September 11, 2001 mission." Waleed bin Attah, alias Khallad, mastermind of the Cole bombing and an early 9/11 planner, said he knew of no part that Moussaoui was to play in the 9/11 attack. Khallad had been captured in April 2003. Testimony by Khalid Shaikh Mohammed indicated that Moussaoui was to be used for a post–9/11 wave of attacks.

The prosecution team argued that Moussaoui was telling the truth, and thus deserved the death penalty. Moussaoui had offered to testify for the prosecution so that he could be heard, but was told that he had a constitutional right to testify. The defense team argued that he was lying. On April 3, 2006, the jury found Moussaoui eligible for the death penalty. Later that week, the final phase of the penalty hearing began, with the prosecution putting on the stand former New York City Mayor Rudolph W. Giuliani and nearly 40 family members of victims and survivors, running videos of people jumping from the doomed buildings, and releasing some of the 911 tapes from the World Trade Center and 32 minutes of cockpit recordings from Flight 93.

On April 13, 2006, Moussaoui took the stand, mocked the victims and their families, and said that he regretted that more Americans didn't die and that Oklahoma City bomber Timothy McVeigh was "the greatest American." The next day, Judge Brinkema vacated her earlier order that the federal government produce Richard Reid to testify. The jury deliberated for 41 hours over seven days, then rejected the death sentence on May 3. The next day, the judge sentenced him to life. As Prisoner 51427-054, he would be in solitary for 23 hours/day in a maximum security prison. He tried, but failed, to withdraw his guilty plea and spark a new trial.

On February 15, 2008, the court papers were unsealed and revealed that his attorneys asked the U.S. Court of Appeals for the Fourth Circuit to overturn the guilty plea and life prison sentence because he could not choose his own counsel or learn much of the evidence against him.

Ibrahim and Mohamed Moussaten: two Moroccan brothers detained by Spanish police on February 1, 2005. They had regular contacts with their maternal uncle, Youssef Belhadj, age 28, who was believed to have made the al Qaeda confessor video in the 3-11-04 Madrid bombing attacks. The duo were jailed on February 5 on provisional charges of collaborating with a terrorist group. Their parents were ordered freed. On October 31 2007, Mohamed Moussaten was acquitted in the trial related to the March 11, 2004 train bombings in Spain.

Sayyed Abbas Moussawi: Hizballah's senior commander who was killed in an Israel air strike in 1992.

Al Mouttasem: alias of Abd Al Salam Khalil Haboub.

Sheik Mohammed Ali Hassan al Mouyad: variant Moayad, age 54, an aide of Abd al Rahim al-Nashiri, chief of al Qaeda operations in the Persian Gulf (al-Nashiri was arrested in the United Arab Emirates in October 2002), who was arrested on January 10, 2003 with his assistant, Mohammed Moshen Yaya Zayed, age 29, both Yemenis, at an airport hotel in Frankfurt. Moayad had been an imam at a large mosque in Sana'a, Yemen, and was an al Qaeda financier. The Germans believed the duo could have been transiting through Frankfurt to an undisclosed location. The Germans considered an extradition request from the United States to send him to New York to face federal charges of providing material support to a terrorist organization. Moayad was represented by attorney Achim Schlott-Kotschote.

The *Washington Post* later reported details of the sting operation. A man claiming to be a Muslim from New York named Mohammed Aansi (variant Alanssi) approached Moayad in Yemen and attempted to get him to come to the United States to meet with a financier. When Moayad balked, he suggested Germany as a safe place to meet. Moayad flew from Yemen and was met at the airport and driven in a Mercedes to the airport's Sheraton to meet a wealthy American Muslim from New York who wanted to donate to Moayad's Middle Eastern charities. The man claimed to be a U.S.-born Muslim convert, Said Sharif bin Turi. For three days, the duo met to discuss monthly $50,000 tranches, not all for charity, some for bin Laden. Moayad claimed he was one of bin Laden's spiritual advisors and had been involved in fundraising and recruiting for al Qaeda. German police arrested him the morning of January 10. He was believed to be a major funder of al Qaeda and the Palestinian Islamic Resistance Movement (Hamas). Yemeni diplomats said that in 1998, Moayad cofounded Sana'a's Al Ehsan Mosque and Community Center, which feeds 9,000 poor families each day and provides free education and medical care. He is a senior member of Islah, an Islamic opposition political party. The FBI said he had collected money for several years from individuals and a Brooklyn mosque and sent the money to al Qaeda. On January 5, 2003, a federal judge in the Eastern District of New York had issued a sealed warrant for his arrest.

On March 4, 2003, the U.S. Attorney General indicted al-Moayab and Zayed for fundraising for al Qaeda in Brooklyn's al Farouq mosque and hosting a service for suicide bombers. The FBI had taped meetings with five Brooklyn residents regarding money for al Qaeda. Moayad had bragged of delivering $20 million to bin Laden before the 9/11 attacks. The United States requested extradition, and was given 30 days to provide enough evidence. The duo faced possible life sentences. The al Farouq mosque had previously been used by Egyptian cleric Sheik Omar Abd-al-Rahman, who was later convicted for the 1993 World Trade Center bombing. An FBI informant said he attended a wedding hosted by

Moayad in September 2002 in Yemen in which a senior Hamas official said that they would read about an operation the next day. That day, a suicide bomber blew up a Tel Aviv bus, killing five and injuring 50.

On July 21, a Frankfurt court approved extradition of the duo to the United States, which had guaranteed that they would not be tried by a military or other special court. The German government administration had the final say on whether to extradite. On November 16, 2003, the duo were extradited to the United States, arriving at John F. Kennedy International Airport. Moayad was arraigned in U.S. District Court in Brooklyn on November 18 on charges of supplying arms, recruits, and more than $20 million to al Qaeda and Hamas. Moayad faced 60 years in prison; Zayed faced 30 years. Court papers filed on December 6, 2004 indicated that when he arrived in New York, Moayad told FBI agents that "Allah will bring storms" to the United States because of his arrest, undercutting defense claims that Moayad did not speak English. "Allah is with me. I am Mohammed al Moayad. Allah will bring storms to Germany and America."

On May 11, 2004, Judge Charles Sifton in New York ruled that Yemeni-born ice cream shop owner Abad Elfgeeh did not understand the consequences of pleading guilty in October 2003 to charges of transferring tens of thousands of dollars to bank accounts in Yemen, Switzerland, Thailand, and China. Elfgeeh had acknowledged sending money to Moayad, who had pleaded not guilty to funding terrorist groups.

On November 15, 2004, at 2:05 P.M., Yemeni-born informant Mohamed Alanssi, alias Mohamed Alhadrami, age 52, of Falls Church, Virginia, asked the security detail outside the White House to deliver a message to President Bush and then set himself on fire, critically injuring himself. He had also sent a note to the *Washington Post* and to FBI agent Robert Fuller indicating that he intended to torch himself. Alanssi had acted as a translator between the FBI operative and Moayad. Alanssi was apparently distraught over his role as a witness and claiming that the FBI had mishandled his case. He claimed that he was not permitted to travel to Yemen to visit his seriously ill wife and their six children because the FBI held his passport. He also claimed he had yet to receive U.S. residency papers and a million dollars (he said the FBI had paid him $100,000). Two days later, he remained in serious condition at Washington Hospital Center, with burns over 30 percent of his body. The defense had claimed that Alanssi had ineptly translated comments by Moayad, making embellishments. In May 2004, Alanssi had been charged in federal court in Brooklyn, New York with felony bank fraud for writing bad checks.

Mouzzah: Libya-based recruitment coordinator for al Qaeda in Iraq foreign fighters in 2007.

Abed Mreish: a Lebanese man in his thirties who, on December 10, 2003, was arrested while he was attempting to enter the U.S. Embassy. He was stopped at an army checkpoint 500 yards from the complex. He was carrying a bag containing TNT, nitroglycerin, and a detonator.

Abu Mrouwah: Iraqi Mukhabarat intelligence agent named by 1 of 11 Iraqis and three Kuwaitis arrested on April 13, 1993 by Kuwaiti authorities as involved in a plot to assassinate former U.S. President George Bush with a bomb during his visit to Kuwait. He told the defendant who named him to kill Bush.

Muhammad Benhedi Msahel: a Tunisian who was the leader of a dozen Islamic militants convicted of terrorism charges in Morocco on March 2, 2007. He led an Islamic cell in Milan with ties to the Algerian Salafist Group for Preaching and Combat, which had changed its name in January 2007 to Al Qaeda of the Islamic Maghreb. Msahel and the other defendants were arrested in March 2006 after the late-2005 arrest in Morocco of Anour Majrar, who said he had visited the Group's leaders in Algeria with Msahel and Amir Laaraj, an Algerian who remained at large. Morocco charged him with being part of a terrorist network that was planning to attack the Paris Metro, Orly Airport, the headquarters of France's domestic intelligence agency, Milan's police headquarters, and the Basilica of San Petronio in Bologna, whose 15th century fresco shows the Prophet Muhammad in hell.

Fahid Mohammed Ali Msalam: variant Fahid Mohammed Ally Msalam, alias Fahid Muhammad 'Alim Salam, Fahid Mohammed Ally, Fahid Mohammed Ali Musalaam, Usama al-Kini; a fugitive Kenyan who, on December 16, 1998, was indicted by the U.S. District Court in Manhattan on 238 counts in the bombing of the U.S. Embassy in Nairobi, Kenya on August 7, 1998. The charges carried the death penalty. The State Department announced a $5 million reward for his capture, similar to the $5 million reward for bin Laden's arrest. State circulated posters printed in English, Arabic, French, Dhari, and Baluchi at all of its diplomatic facilities. State also announced that it would advertise the reward on the Internet. He met with three other conspirators in a Dar es Salaam house in late July and the first week of August 1998 to plan the bombing. He was charged with helping to buy the truck used in the Tanzania bombing, along with Fadhil and others. He packed it with explosives and transported it to the embassy. Charges include murder of U.S. nationals outside the United States; conspiracy to murder U.S. nationals outside the United States; and attack on a federal facility resulting in death. He is circa five feet seven inches tall, and weighs circa 185 pounds. He was born in Mombasa, Kenya on February 19, 1976. He speaks Swahili, Arabic, and English. He has worked as a clothing vendor.

Fahid Mohammed Ally Msalam: variant of Fahid Mohammed Ali Msalam, Fahid Muhammad 'Alim Salam.

Maamoun Msouh: sentenced to eight years on September 29, 2004 by a Yemeni court for helping USS *Cole* bomber Jamal al-Badawi in handling funds and forging identity papers. By May 2008, he was free.

Abu Mua'az: alias of Makram Bin Salem al-Majri.

Abu-Mu'adh: alias of Samir Ahmad 'Ali al-'Amiri.

Abu-Mu'adh: alias of Ibrahim.

Abu-Mu'adh: alias of Ahmad.

Abu-Mu'adh: alias of Salim Sa'd al-Khunayshi.

Abu-Mu'adh: alias of Samir.

Abu Mua'az: alias of Samir Ahmed Ali Al A'ameri.

Seif Muadi: a lieutenant in the Israeli Army, admitted on January 25, 1981 that, on January 12, 1981, he had fired six shots that killed Sheik Mohammed Abu Rabia, the only Bedouin member of Israel's Knesset. He and his two brothers had been arrested in the case. The brothers were the sons of Sheik Jaber Muadi, a Druze rival of Abu Rabia. Seif said that his brothers and father did not know of his murderous intentions.

Muhammed Muassir: an Iranian who was one of two Islamic Dawa gunmen who overpowered a guard and threw a bag of explosives into the fountain in front of the Iraqi consulate in Istanbul, Turkey on December 21, 1983. Prior to the explosion, the two were arrested near the car, which they had intended to move to the Iraqi embassy.

Abu-Mu'awiyah: variant Abu Ma'awieah, alias of Mu'tazz Hasan Muraji'.

Muaz: alias of Atilla Selek.

Abdel Muaz: alias of Ayman al-Zawahiri.

Abu Muaz: an aide of Abu Musab al-Zarqawi, arrested in early May 2003 in Baghdad by U.S. military units.

Mubarak: alias of Abogado Gado.

Zaiad Muchasi: Black September contact of the KGB in Cyprus who was killed on April 9, 1973 when he switched on a light in his Nicosia hotel room after returning from a meeting with the KGB. The switch triggered a detonating device. He had arrived in Cyprus two days earlier as the replacement for the Black September KGB contact who had been killed three months earlier.

'Imad Mudayhili: an individual from Tyre, Lebanon, and one of six individuals reported by Beirut's *al-Nahar* on August 6, 1990 as appearing at an Amal news conference on charges of kidnapping, assassination, setting of explosions, and bringing booby-trapped cars into Tyre. They admitted involvement in the kidnapping of U.S. Marine Lt. Col. William Richard Higgins on February 17, 1988. The group also admitted planting explosive devices at centers of the UN forces in the south; blowing up Mustafa Mahdi's clothing store in Tyre, as well as the Lebanese-African Nasr Bank in Tyre; and bringing three booby-trapped cars into Tyre and al-Bisariyah to kill Amal officials. They said they coordinated their actions with Hizballah and the Iranian Revolutionary Guards.

Qusine E. Muftah: a Milwaukee resident and one of a dozen masked, club-wielding Libyan students who took over the Libyan student aid office in McLean, Virginia and took hostages for a few minutes on December 22, 1982. Police raided the site after nine hours and the students surrendered. They were held on three counts of abduction. Bond for four of the students who, in 1981, had occupied the Libyan UN Mission was set at $30,000; bond for the others was set at $15,000. Fairfax County released the names of the students on December 30, 1982. The Libyan student aid group sued the defendants for $12 million in Fairfax Circuit Court. On February 7, 1983, the students countersued for $15 million. Each of the students pleaded guilty in January 1983 to unlawful assembly, assaulting two office employees, and destroying private property. County prosecutors dropped felony charges of abduction. On March 4, 1983, Judge Barnard F. Jennings sentenced the 12 to one year in jail. On September 9, 1983, a Fairfax County judge released 10 of the 12 protestors after they presented proof to the court that they were enrolled for the fall term at accredited U.S. colleges.

Mohammad Yusuf Mughal: one of four Pakistani members of the Pakistan People's Party who, on March 26, 1991, hijacked a Singapore Airlines B-747 on the Kuala Lumpur–Singapore route. After nine hours of negotiations, the Singapore Army stormed the plane and killed the hijackers, who had threatened violence against the passengers if their demands were not met in five minutes. Mughal was a member of the al-Zulfiqar Organization.

Wassem Mughal: age 22, arrested on October 21, 2005 in the United Kingdom, he may have been planning to bomb the White House and U.S. Capitol. Mughal was charged with having in his bedroom in Chatham, Kent, a DVD titled "Martyrdom Operations Vest," an Arabic document entitled "Welcome to Jihad," a piece of paper with the words "Hospital=attack," a recipe for rocket propellant and "guidance-containing explosion." Younis Tsouli and Mughal were charged with conspiracy to murder and to cause an explosion. Prosecutors said they ran Web sites that linked terrorists in Denmark, Bosnia, Iraq, the United States, and the United Kingdom. The sites included beheading videos. One of their laptops included a PowerPoint presentation entitled *The Illustrated Booby Trapping Course* that included how to create a suicide vest loaded with ball bearings. Tsouli had been asked by al Qaeda to translate into English its e-book, *The Tip of the Camel's Hump.* The two also stole data for hundreds of credit cards which they used to purchase supplies for operatives, and laundered money through 350 transactions at 43 Internet gambling sites, including absolutepoker.com, betfair.com, betonbet.com, canbet.com, eurobet.com, noblepoker.com, and paradisepoker.com, using 130

credit card accounts. They had made more than $3.5 million in fraudulent charges for global positioning system devices, night-vision goggles, sleeping bags, telephones, survival knives, hundreds of prepaid cell phones, tents, and more than 250 airline tickets using 110 different credit cards at 46 airline and travel agencies. They used 72 credit card accounts to register more than 180 domains at 95 Web hosting firms in the United States and Europe. On July 5, 2007, the biochemistry graduate student was sentenced to 7 and a half years after pleading guilty.

Ahmad Ibrahim al-Mughassil: alias Abu Omran, a Saudi leader of Saudi Hizballah's military wing, indicted in the Eastern District of Virginia for the June 25, 1996 bombing of the Khobar Towers military housing complex in Dhahran, Saudi Arabia. He drove the tanker truck bomb and was overall coordinator of the Khobar bombing. He is wanted on multiple conspiracy charges against U.S. nationals and property, including murder, conspiracy to kill U.S. nationals; conspiracy to murder U.S. employees; conspiracy and use of weapons of mass destruction against U.S. nationals; conspiracy to destroy U.S. property; conspiracy to attack national defense utilities; bombing resulting in death; murder while using a destructive device during a crime of violence; and murder and attempted murder of federal employees. The Rewards for Justice Program offers $5 million for his apprehension. He claimed to have been born on June 26, 1967 in Qatif-Bab al Shamal, Saudi Arabia. He is five feet four inches tall and weighs 145 pounds. On April 4, 1997, the Saudis claimed that the Syrians refused to help them capture him—he was with Hizballah in Lebanon—because they did not want to risk a clash with Hizballah. The *New York Times* reported on May 1, 1997 that Iran was harboring him.

Adel Mughrabi: one of three men arrested on January 11, 2002 by the Palestinian Authority in connection with the *Karine*, a cargo ship that was boarded by Israeli navy commanders on January 3, 2002 in the Red Sea. They found 50 tons of weapons, including Katyusha rockets, antitank missiles, mortars, mines, and sniper rifles, believed to have originated in Iran and headed for the Palestinian Authority. The weapons were in quantities banned by the 1993 Oslo peace agreement. Israel said interrogation of the 13 crewmen determined that the arms smuggling was coordinated by Lebanese Hizballah.

Dalal Mughrabi: a Palestinian woman member of the Operation Martyr Kamal Adwan Fatah terrorists who entered Israel on March 11, 1978, seizing a tour bus and leaving 46 dead and 85 wounded before being stopped. She died in a gun battle.

Ahmed Bin Saleh bin Yunes Al Mughrieq: variant Ahamed Bin Saleh Bi Yunes Al Moughriq, alias Abu Maghrieb, an unemployed Saudi from Jawaf who was born on 14-08-1409 Hijra and joined al Qaeda in Iraq as a martyr on 22nd Rabi'al thani (2007), contributing 100 Saudi riyals and 2,800 Syrian Lira. His recruitment coordinator was Abu Abd Allah, whom he knew through friends. He arrived in Syria via Jordan. He met Abu Abbas, who took 19,800 of his 20,000 Saudi riyals. His brother's phone number was 00966557444544. He said he had experience with computers and a modest amount of forensic (sic).

Fu'ad Mughniyah: a Hizballah security officer killed on December 21, 1994 when a booby-trapped Volkswagen van exploded in the Sfayr area near the al-Umara' bakery and al-Inma' Consumers Cooperative in the Bir Abed district of Beirut's Shi'ite Muslim suburb, killing three and injuring 16 others. He headed a hijacking team that killed two U.S. Agency for International Development officers in Kuwait in the 1980s. His brother is 'Imad Fayiz Mughniyah.

Imad Fayez Mughniyah: variant of 'Imad Fayiz Mughniyah.

Imad Fa'iz Mughniyah: variant of 'Imad Fayiz Mughniyah.

'Imad Fayiz Mughniyah: variant Imad Fayez Mugniyah, variant Imad Fa'iz Mugniyah, Imad Mughniyeh, alias Imad Fayiz, Imad Fa'iz, Jahh, Haj, al-Haj, Haji Rudwan, The Fox, Muqniyah, head of the security apparatus for Lebanese Hizballah. He was indicted for his role in planning and participating in the June 14, 1985 hijacking of a TWA commercial airliner that resulted in assaults on various passengers and crew members and the murder of one U.S. citizen. He is wanted for conspiracy to commit aircraft piracy, to commit hostage-taking, to commit air piracy resulting in murder, to interfere with a flight crew, to place a destructive device aboard an aircraft, to have explosive devices about the person on an aircraft, and to assault passengers and crew.

He claimed to have been born in Tir Dibba in southern Lebanon in 1962. He was circa five feet seven inches tall and weighed 150 pounds. He studied engineering briefly at the American University of Beirut. He joined Fatah in his teens, serving in Yasser Arafat's Force 17 security unit. He joined several Shi'ite radical groups in Lebanon, helping to form the Islamic Jihad Organization, a terrorist wing of Hizballah. He may have had contacts with Osama bin Laden, meeting him once in the 1990s.

He was involved in the kidnapping of U.S. hostages in Lebanon in the 1980s; the 1983 bombing of the U.S. Embassy in Beirut, in which 63 people died; and the 1984 kidnap/murder of Chief of Station/Beirut William Buckley. An Iranian intelligence defector told the Germans that Mugniyah joined Iranian diplomats in organizing the July 1994 bombing of a Jewish community center in Buenos Aires that killed 85 people. The Argentines wanted him for the March 17, 1992 bombing of the Israeli Embassy in Buenos Aires in which 23 died. He was believed behind the 1983 bombing of the U.S. Marine barracks in Beirut that killed 241 U.S. soldiers, and the kidnappings of six Americans and five French citizens. He was believed to be behind the June 17, 1987 kidnapping in Beirut of Charles Glass, a former *ABC Television News* and *Newsweek* reporter; 'Ali 'Usayran, son of Defense Minister Adel 'Usayran; and their driver, police officer Ali Sulayman. U.S. officials believed he was one of the April 5, 1988 hijackers of Kuwait Airlines flight 422, a B747 flying from Bangkok to Kuwait that was diverted to Mashhad, Iran.

The Shi'ite joined Force 17, Arafat's personal security force.

He was taken into custody on November 16, 1992.

On April 19, 1993, his trial began at the 29th Grand Criminal bench of the Berlin Regional Court regarding the bombing of the West Berlin La Belle Disco on April 5, 1986. The stateless Palestinian pleaded not guilty to charges of planning attacks on members of the U.S. military.

On April 7, 1995, the FBI went to Saudi Arabia to arrest him for the 1983 truck bombing of the U.S. Marine barracks in Lebanon that killed 241 servicemen; the 1985 TWA hijacking; and numerous kidnappings and bombings against Westerners in the 1980s. However, the Saudis did not permit his Middle East Airlines B707 to land for a scheduled stopover in Jeddah on its way from Khartoum—where he was attending an Islamic conference—to Beirut.

His brother-in-law, Mustafa Badreddin, was one of 17 prisoners held for years in Kuwaiti prisons for a series of 1983 bombings, and was believed to have been the explosives expert involved in the 1983 Marine barracks bombing. U.S. hostages were abducted in Lebanon to obtain the prisoners' release after Badreddin was sentenced to death. Badreddin was freed during the 1990 Iraqi invasion of Kuwait.

Mughniyah was one of ten Shi'ite Muslims identified in November 17, 1992 by the Lebanese newspaper *Nida' al-Watan* as suspected of instigating the kidnappings of U.S. hostages William Buckley, William Higgins, and Peter Kilburn.

On September 2, 1999, Argentina's Supreme Court issued an arrest warrant for planning the March 17, 1992 bombing of the Israeli Embassy. Evidence backing the warrant included handwriting from Hizballah representatives on documents associated with the purchase of the truck used in the bombing.

In mid-February, Israel claimed that he had purchased the arms carried by the *Karine,* a cargo ship that was boarded by Israeli navy commanders on January 3, 2002 in the Red Sea. They found 50 tons of weapons, including Katyusha rockets, antitank missiles, mortars, mines, and sniper rifles, believed to have originated in Iran and headed for the Palestinian Authority. The weapons were in quantities banned by the 1993 Oslo peace agreement. Israel said interrogation of the 13 crewmen determined that the arms smuggling was coordinated by Lebanese Hizballah.

The Rewards for Justice Program offered $5 million for his arrest and/or conviction.

In January 2006, he had allegedly traveled with Iranian President Mahmoud Ahmadinejad to Damascus to meet with Hassan Nasrallah, Hizballah's Secretary General; Palestinian Islamic Jihad leader Ramadan Abdullah Shallah; Hamas leader Kahled Meshaal; and Popular Front for the Liberation of Palestine-General Command leader Ahmed Jibril. He might have organized the kidnapping of an Israeli soldier that led to the Israel-Hizballah war in the summer of 2006.

He was killed in an explosion in a Mitsubishi Pajero in Tantheem Kafer Souseh, an upscale residential section of Damascus, Syria on February 12, 2008. Israel denied responsibility.

Imad Mughniyeh: variant of Imad Fayiz Mughniyah.

Ahmed Mugrabi: detained by Israeli soldiers on May 30, 2002 on suspicion of being behind the May 22, 2002 suicide bombing in Tel Aviv that killed two Israelis and injured more than 25, and preparing explosives for other missions.

Abu al A'ainaa al Muhajer: variant of Abu-'Ayna' al-Muhajir.

Abu Muhamed Al Muhajer: alias of Muhammad Bin Mishal Bin Ghodayb Al Sub'baie.

Abu Obieda Al Muhajer: alias of Jamal Shaka.

Muhammad Muhajer: variant of Muhammad Muhajir.

Abdul Rahman al-Muhajir: alias of Muhsin Musa Matwalli Atwah.

Abdullah al Muhajir: alias of Jose Padilla.

Abu 'Abd al-Rahman al-Muhajir: alias of Muhsin Musa Matwalli Atwah.

Abu Al Muhajir: alias of Muhammad Rashed Ghaleb Al Hourie.

Abu-'Ayna' al-Muhajir: variant Abu al A'ainaa al Muhajer, alias of Muhammad al-Tubayhi.

Abu-Bakr al-Muhajir: alias of Bara'.

Abu-Hakim al-Muhajir: alias of Ahmad Yahya Muhammad Saghiri.

Abu Hamza al-Muhajir: alias of Abu Ayyub al-Masri.

Abu Saggar Al Muhajir: alias of Naif Abd Allah Al Muhajir.

Muhammad Muhajir: variant Muhammad Muhajer, Mohamed Mouhajef, a Lebanese who was one of eight individuals suspected of being Islamic terrorists arrested on March 21, 1987 in Paris by the Department of Territorial Security (DST). The other seven people were of Tunisian origin. Authorities seized 12 liters of a liquid explosive, two Sten guns, and ammunition from the Rue de la Voute safe house in Paris's 12th District. Some of the detainees were members of Islamic Jihad. On March 26, 1987, the group was charged with "belonging to a terrorist network preparing to commit particularly dangerous attacks in France." He was charged with infringement of the legislations of weapons, explosives, and ammunition and of criminal association aimed at disturbing public order by intimidation of terror. He claimed he was born in Ba'labakk, Lebanon and

was a Sorbonne postgraduate theology student. *Paris Domestic Service* said he was a founder of Hizballah. The Lebanese was released on March 25, 1988 after a year in custody because of insufficient evidence to bring him to trial for a series of bombing attacks in France on September 1986 by the Committee for Solidarity with the Arab and Middle Eastern Prisoners. He was married to a French woman.

Naif Abd Allah Al Muhajir: alias of Abu Saggar Al Muhajir. He joined al Qaeda in Iraq in 2007 as a martyr, contributing $100 and his passport. His recruitment coordinator was Abu Kafi, whom he knew through Abu Saleh. He traveled from Dubai to Syria, where he met Abu Khudaier, Abu Yaser, Abu Abd Al Rahman, and Abu Omar Al Tunisi, to whom he gave his 5,500 riyals. They gave him $100 back. His home phone number was 009663690615; his father's was 009665005600800. He lived in Bariedah.

Essa Ismail Muhamad: charged by a Spanish judge with financing the al Qaeda truck bombing on April 11, 2002 that killed 19 people in a synagogue in Djerba, Tunisia. He remained at large.

Ahmad Isa Muhamed: an Iraqi who was one of six men arrested on March 1, 2002 by Rome police on suspicion of al Qaeda ties. They were held on suspicion of association with a "criminal organization with terrorist intentions" and intent to obtain and transfer arms and weapons. Wiretaps of their conversations included discussions of killing President Bush, a cyanide compound, and weapons needed for terrorist training camps in Afghanistan. Police seized videos, address books, and a plane ticket to Phoenix. They also found a letter with the address of Lotfi Raissi, an Algerian accused in the United Kingdom of giving pilot training to the 9/11 hijackers.

Fathi Ali Muhamed: alias Abu Al Balaa'a, a Libyan born in 1981 who joined al Qaeda in Iraq in 2007, bringing $4,100 and 2,750 Syrian lira.

His home phone number was 0925317564; his father Ali's was 0925114389; his brother Muhammad's was 0625103865.

Faysal Salah Muhamed: an Iraqi who was one of six men arrested on March 1, 2002 by Rome police on suspicion of al Qaeda ties. They were held on suspicion of association with a "criminal organization with terrorist intentions" and intent to obtain and transfer arms and weapons. Wiretaps of their conversations included discussions of killing President Bush, a cyanide compound, and weapons needed for terrorist training camps in Afghanistan. Police seized videos, address books, and a plane ticket to Phoenix. They also found a letter with the address of Lotfi Raissi, an Algerian accused in the United Kingdom of giving pilot training to the 9/11 hijackers.

Muhammad: alias of 'Abd-al-Quddus al-Qadi.

Muhammad: alias Abu Fahd, a Saudi who joined al Qaeda in Iraq as a fighter in 2007, contributing his watch and bringing his passport. His recruitment coordinator was Majri, variant Majrah. His home phone numbers were 015551162 and 050000209.

Muhammad: alias Abu-'Abdallah, a Tunisian member of al Qaeda in Iraq assigned in 2007 as a fighter in Mosul. His phone number was 0021697116643.

Muhammad: alias Abu-'Abdallah, a Syrian fighter for al Qaeda in Iraq in 2007 whose phone number was 0096214652280.

Muhammad: alias Abu-Ayat, a Libyan from Sarat who was born in 1977 and was a member of al Qaeda in Iraq in 2007, owning a passport and $500. His travel coordinators were Abu-'Umar and Abu-Samir. His phone number was 2201892749195.

Muhammad: alias Abu-al-Hasan, a Saudi from al-Baha, variant al-Bahah, who joined al Qaeda in Iraq in 2007. His recruitment coordinator was Bassam. His home phone was 077281830; his cell was 0508282415.

Muhammad: alias Abu-al-Khattab, a Yemeni fighter for al Qaeda in Iraq in 2007 who owned a passport. His home phone number was 009671245723; his cell was 00967967733720352.

Muhammad: alias Abu-Abd-al-Rahman, a Tunisian member of al Qaeda in Iraq in 2007. He owned a passport. His phone number was 0021623015130.

Muhammad: alias Abu-al-Walid, a Tunisian from Ibn-'Arus, variant Bin 'Arus, who joined al Qaeda in Iraq as a fighter in 2007, bringing his passport. His recruitment coordinator was al-Hajj. His home phone number was 0021696813566.

Muhammad: alias Abu-al-Fadl, variant Abu al-Fadil, an Algerian who joined al Qaeda in Iraq as a fighter in 2007, bringing his passport. His recruitment coordinator was Abu-al-Bara'. His home phone number was 0021377006638.

Muhammad: alias Abu-Hamzah, a Syrian from Al-Hasakah who joined al Qaeda in Iraq in 2007, donating his watch. His recruitment coordinator was Abu-'Ammar. His home phone number was 0096352362194.

Muhammad: alias Abu-'Asim, a Saudi student at the College of Communications who lived in Ta'if and was born on February 10, 1982. He joined al Qaeda in Iraq as a martyr on February 15, 2007, contributing $4,100 and 1,000 liras, plus his passport. His recruitment coordinator was Abu-al-Zubayr, a colleague at school. He flew to Syria, meeting 'Abd-al-Hadi, to whom he gave 4,700 of his 5,200 riyals. He had weapons training. His phone numbers were 00966553300455 and 00966555717745.

Muhammad: alias Abu-Mundhir: a Libyan member of al Qaeda in Iraq who was to conduct a suicide mission in Mosul in 2007. He owned a watch. His phone number was 00218927478512.

Muhammad: alias Abu-al-Qa'qa', an Algerian who was born in January 1985 and was sent on a suicide mission by al Qaeda in Iraq in 2007. His travel coordinator was Abu-'Asim. He owned a passport and held 800 liras that belonged to Abu-'Usamah. His brother's phone number was 072030319.

Muhammad: alias Abu-Qutaybah, a Tunisian member of al Qaeda in Iraq in 2007 who brought his passport, driver's license, and ID. His home phone number was 0021679408123; his brother's was 0021696930018.

Muhammad: alias Abu-al-Sadiq, a Syrian fighter specializing in media for al Qaeda in Iraq in 2007 whose home phone number was 0096648380851. He could also be contacted on 0096315315587 and 0096315315578. He owned a watch.

Muhammad: alias Abu-Saraqah, a Libyan member of al Qaeda in Iraq who was to conduct a suicide mission in Mosul in 2007. He owned $100 and a watch. Salim, his colleague, could be found at 00218927875755.

Muhammad: alias Abu-Yusuf, variant Abu Yusif, a Tunisian from Tunis who joined al Qaeda in Iraq as a martyr in 2007, contributing $200, his passport, and ID. His recruitment coordinator was Abu-Ibrahim. His home phone number was 0021671781842.

Muhammad: alias Abu-al-Harith, a Jordanian member of al Qaeda in Iraq in 2007 who owned a passport and whose phone number was 0777480805.

Muhammad: alias Abu-Yasir al-Maki Z., a Saudi from Mecca who was born in 1985 and was a fighter for al Qaeda in Iraq in 2007. He owned a passport and ID. His travel coordinator was Basim. His home number was 25274176; his brother Muhana's was 506036469.

'Abd al-'Aziz 'Arfan Muhammad: arrested on August 12, 1985 by the Egyptian prosecutor's office on charges of communicating with Libya to the detriment of Egypt's political status and receiving a bribe from Libya to commit murder in the foiled plot to assassinate Ghayth Said al-Mabruk, a political refugee living in Alexandria, Egypt, on August 6, 1985. When arrested, he and two others had a machine gun and pistol. They were later found guilty and sentenced to death.

Abd Allah Sammy Ahmed Muhammad: alias Abu Moua'aied al Meccie, a Saudi from Mecca who was born on September 29, 1978 and joined al Qaeda in Iraq as a martyr on November 10, 2006, bringing a watch and $8,000. His recruitment coordinator was Hussam. His family's phone number was 00966559686100.

Abd-al-Bad'i Maylud Muhammad: alias Harithah. According to al Qaeda in Iraq's captured Sinjar personnel records, he lived in Darnah, Libya. His coordinator was Bashar, whom he knew via a friend. His phone was 00218925797714. His family's phone number was 00218926969303. He came to Syria via Egypt. He met a Syrian, Fadil, who facilitated his travel from Syria. He was given 15,000 lira. He wanted to be a fighter.

'Abd-al-Hadi Muhammad: alias Hamzah, an Egyptian Islamic Group terrorist who was injured during the failed June 26, 1995 assassination attempt against Egyptian President Hosni Mubarak in Addis Ababa, Ethiopia. He later died of his wounds.

Abd-al-Karim Muhammad: alias 'Awni Jabar, identified by Doha's *al-Sharq* on March 19, 1993 as a member of the Abu Nidal Group's Central

Committee. He was transferred as the group's representative for Sudan, Aden, and Libya.

Abd an-Nasir Jamal Muhammad: alias of Salah Mohammed Khaled.

'Abdallah Idris Muhammad: chairman of the Eritrean Liberation Front in 1989.

'Abdullah Sami Ahmad Muhammad: alias Abu-Mu'ayyad al-Makki, a Saudi from Mecca who was born on September 29, 1978 and joined al Qaeda in Iraq as a martyr on November 10, 2006, contributing a watch and $8,000. His recruitment coordinator was Hussam. His family's phone number was 00966559686100.

'Abd-Rabbuh 'Ali Muhammad: alias of Ilich Ramirez Sanchez.

Abu Muhammad: alias of Abu Mus'ab al-Zarqawi.

Abu Muhammad: alias of Ayman al-Zawahiri.

Abu Muhammad: alias of Moua'aied Khalef Shehaza.

Abu Muhammad: alias of Shadi Muhammad Saleh Al Mansour.

Abu Muhammad: a Palestinian whom *Ha'aretz* claimed on November 13, 1986 of being the leader of the masked suicide terrorists who fired on and threw grenades at worshippers in the Neve Shalom, Istanbul, Turkey synagogue on September 6, 1986, doused the 21 corpses with gasoline, and set them alight. Two terrorists who had barred the door died in the attack when their grenades exploded in their hands. A third escaped. The attack was claimed by the Islamic Jihad, Abu Nidal, the Northern Arab League, the Islamic Resistance, the Palestinian Resistance Organization, the Fighting International Front–'Amrush Martyr Group, and the Organization of the Unity of the Arab North. Muhammad served as the terrorist team's squad

leader as he had been in Turkey several times. He left Istanbul and returned to Tehran three days before the attack, leaving the operation to the two remaining terrorists.

Abu Muhammad: alias of Mamdouh Muhammad Bikhet al Saaedi.

Abu-Muhammad: alias of an unnamed Yemeni sent on a suicide mission by Al Qaeda in Iraq in 2007. His phone numbers were 009677770510104 and 00967777660889.

Abu-Muhammad: alias of Al-Bassari 'Abdallah.

Abu-Muhammad: alias of Mahir Muhammad 'Abd-al-Baqi.

Abu-Muhammad: a Syrian-based travel facilitator for al Qaeda in Iraq in 2007.

Abu-Muhammad: alias of Mamduh Muhammad Bakhit al-Sa'idi.

Abu-Muhammad: alias of Nabil Hasan Ahmad Makhluf.

Abu-Muhammad: alias of 'Abdallah al-Qadhafi.

Abu-Muhammad: alias of Mubsit Rashid.

Abu-Muhammad: alias of Ibrahim Yahya Ahmad Rakid.

Abu-Muhammad: alias of 'Abd-al-'Aziz Muhammad al-Jahni.

Abu-Muhammad: alias of Abd-al-Hakim.

Abu-Muhammad: alias of Muhammad Bin-'Abd-al-'Aziz Bin-Sulayman al-Dubaykhi.

Abu-Muhammad: alias of Abdallah Awlad al-Tumi.

Abu-Muhammad: alias of Yazid.

Abu-Muhammad: alias of Sami.

Abu-Muhammad: alias of Sulayman Muhammad al-'Utaybi.

Abu-Rawan Muhammad: a Saudi-based recruitment coordinator for foreign fighters for al Qaeda in Iraq in 2007.

Ahmad 'Ali al-Muhammad: alias Abu-al-Fadl, a Syrian third-year college chemical engineering student from Dayr az Zawr who was born in 1983 and joined al Qaeda in Iraq as a combatant on August 9, 2007, contributing $400 and bringing a watch and ID. His recruitment coordinator was Abu-'Umar, whom he knew via a friend and a relative. He met Abu-'Umar Abu-Sa'd in Syria. He had experience in computers and chemical engineering. He brought $500. His home phone was 051727489; his father's mobile phone was 0999863573.

Ahmad 'Asad Muhammad: alias Salim 'Abd al-'Aziz, alias Salim, a Lebanese among three Abu Nidal members arrested by Peruvian police on July 16, 1988 for the Egyptair hijacking of November 24, 1986 as well as the December 1986 Rome and Vienna airport attacks. The trio were trying to form links with the Shining Path. The group planned to attack the Jewish Synagogue of Peru, the Israeli Embassy in Lima, the U.S. consulate, the Shalom Travel Agency, and national and international maritime transportation companies. Peruvian police planned to expel the trio in early August 1988 for breaking the immigration law.

Ahmed Abd Allah Muhammad: alias Abu Obieda, a Yemeni taxi driver from Aden who was born in 1986 and joined al Qaeda in Iraq on 14/7/1428 Hijra as a martyr, contributing his passport, ID, $180, and a ticket. His recruitment coordinator was Abu Abd Allah, a friend of his brother. In Syria, he met Abu Al Abbas. He brought $200. His home phone number was 009672270267; his cousin's

was 00967733164927; his father-in-law's was 0096777803381.

'Ali 'Id Muhammad: an Egyptian terrorist arrested by Pakistani authorities on May 14, 1994 and deported to Egypt. He was detained by Cairo airport authorities upon arrival on May 14. He had left Cairo in 1990 and settled in Peshawar until he was arrested in Karachi. The arrest fell within Interpol's jurisdiction to arrest Arab Afghans after the expiration of the Afghan government's deadline for them to leave the country. He was wanted in the Vanguard of Conquest case.

'Ali Nasir Muhammad: leader of a group that fled on February 17, 1987 after People's Democratic Republic of Yemen police opened fire on the occupants of an armored Toyota laden with 16 kilograms of dynamite sticks in Shabwah Governorate.

Al-Arab Sadiq Hafiz Muhammad: alias Khalifah, identified by the Ethiopian government as one of the nine Egyptian Islamic Group gunmen who, on June 25, 1995, fired on the armored limousine of Egyptian President Hosni Mubarak in Addis Ababa. On August 7, 1995, the Ethiopian Supreme State Security Prosecution charged the nine of forming a terrorist organization to destabilize the country, possessing arms and explosives, communicating with a foreign state to undermine the country's security, attempting to assassinate state figures, and attempting to blow up vital establishments.

Awad Ahmed Salem Muhammad: name on a passport used by Hamam Ali Ahmed Salem.

Awad Faraj Muhammad: alias Abu Hajjir, a Libyan from Benghazi who was born in 1983 and joined al Qaeda in Iraq as a martyr on 8th Jumada al-Awal 1428 Hijra (2007), donating $100. His recruitment coordinator was Abu Hamzza, whom he knew via a friend. Upon arrival in Syria from Libya and Egypt, he met Abu Omar, bringing

1,400 Libyan dinars. His phone number was 0021892549623.

Bastawi 'Abd-al-Hamid Abu-al-Majd Muhammad: a student at Qina Trade School who was arrested on November 11, 1992 holding the weapon he used in the attack as one of four Islamic Group gunmen against a bus load of 18 German tourists that injured seven people in Qina, Egypt. He was carrying an automatic rifle and two magazines, one empty and the other containing 29 rounds.

Emad Muhammad: alias Carlos the Iranian, identified by "Witness A," an Iranian citizen who testified on December 28, 1994 in the investigation of the AIMA (Asociacion Mutual Israelita de Argentina) bombing, as the mastermind of the attack.

Faraj 'Umran Muhammad: alias Abu-Sulayman, a Libyan from Benghazi who was born in 1985 and joined al Qaeda in Iraq as a combatant on June 19, 2007. His recruitment coordinator was Zurwaq. He traveled from Libya to Egypt and Syria, where he met Abu-'Umar, who took his 3,000 Syrian lira. He brought $100. His phone number was 00218925318121.

Fazul Abdallah Muhammad: variant Fazul Abdallah Mohammed, alias Abdallah Fazul, Abdalla Fazul, Abdallah Mohammed Fazul, Fazul Abdilahi Mohammed, Fazul Abdallah, Fazul Abdalla, Fazul Mohammed, Haroon, Harun, Haroon Fazul, Harun Fazul, Fadil Abdallah Muhamad, Fadhil Haroun, Abu Seif al Sudani, Abu Aisha, Abu Luqman, Fadel Abdallah Mohammed Ali, Fouad Mohammed, Abu al Fazul al-Qamari, 'Abdallah Fazul, Abu Sayf al-Sudani, indicted on September 17, 1998 in the Southern District of New York for involvement in the bombings of the U.S. embassies in Tanzania and Kenya on August 7, 1998 and the attacks on Mombasa, Kenya, on November 28, 2002. He was wanted for murder of U.S. nationals outside the United States, conspiracy to murder U.S. nationals outside the United States, and attack on a federal facility resulting in death.

The Rewards for Justice Program offers $5 million for his apprehension. He has used August 25, 1972 and December 25, 1974 as his date of birth, and claims to have been born in Moroni on the Comoros Islands. He is about five feet, four inches tall and weighs between 120 and 140 pounds. He claims Comoran and Kenyan citizenship.

On May 14, 2003, he was reported to be in Kenya. Mohammed was seen in Mogadishu after the bombing of the Paradise Hotel in Mombasa. On May 15, the United Kingdom suspended flights to and from Kenya. The UK government warned of a "clear terrorist threat" in Uganda, Ethiopia, Tanzania, Somalia, Eritrea, and Djibouti." On May 16, U.S. and UK Marines searched the borders with Somalia and Sudan during heightened fears of an al Qaeda attack.

Hatim Yazid Muhammad: variant Hattem Yazeed Muhammad, alias Abu-Rawaha, variant Abu Rawha, a Moroccan from Casablanca who was born on August 22, 1978 and joined al Qaeda in Iraq on October 25, 2006 to become a martyr. He contributed $100, a watch, and a passport. His recruitment coordinator was Sa'd. His brother's phone number was 071983611; his friend's was 079410739.

Hattem Yazeed Muhammad: variant of Hatim Yazid Muhammad.

Jamal Ja'afar Muhammad: an Iraqi sentenced in absentia to death by the Kuwaiti State Security Court in 1984 in connection with the December 12, 1983 truck bombing of the administrative building of the U.S. Embassy in Kuwait, killing four people and injuring 59. As of April 1987, none of the death sentences in the case had been carried out. The release of 17 of the 25 prisoners in the case was demanded on numerous occasions by the Islamic Jihad in return for Americans held captive in Lebanon beginning in 1986.

Joseph Muhammad: one of three terrorists who, on July 11, 1988, fired machine guns and threw hand grenades at the *City of Poros*, a Greek island ferryboat that was carrying tourists in the Aegean Sea, killing 11 and injuring 98.

Khadir Samir Muhammad: alias of Hijab Jaballah.

Khalid Sheikh Muhammad (KSM): alias Muktar Balucci, alias The Brain, planner of the 1990s Bojinka plan to bomb a dozen American planes, and of the 9/11 attacks. Born in 1965 in Pakistan, son of two Baluchistan immigrants. An ethnic Pakistani, his parents moved to Kuwait, where he grew up. One of his brothers joined the Muslim Brotherhood in the 1980s, and invited KSM to join. In 1983, he obtained a visa to study at Chowan College in Murfreesboro, North Carolina. He graduated from North Carolina State Agricultural and Technical State University in 1986. He later turned up in Afghanistan, and moved on to Peshawar, where he met Osama bin Laden. He was arrested on March 1, 2003 in Rawalpindi, Pakistan.

In March 2003, Tunis issued a warrant for the arrest of Khalid Sheikh Mohammed for his role in the truck bombing on April 11, 2002 that killed 19 people in a synagogue in Djerba, Tunisia.

At the beginning of his trial with 13 other detainees in Guantánamo Bay, Cuba, on March 10, 2007, he said that he was responsible for 30 planned and actual terrorist attacks, including 9/11. "I was responsible for the 9/11 operation from A to Z." He also claimed credit for:

- the 1993 bombing of the World Trade Center, carried out by his nephew, Ramzi Yousef;
- the November 2003 attacks in Istanbul against UK and Israeli targets that killed 57 and wounded 700;
- the would-be downing of a trans-Atlantic aircraft by shoe bomber Richard Reid;
- the 2002 bombing of a Kenya beach resort frequented by Israelis;
- the failed 2002 missile attack on an Israeli passenger jet at Mombasa, Kenya;
- the 2002 bombing of two nightclubs in Bali, Indonesia that killed 202;

- the 2002 shooting to death of a U.S. Marine in Kuwait's Fikla Island;
- planned attacks against U.S. nuclear power plants; suspension bridges in New York; U.S. embassies in Indonesia, Australia, and Japan; Israeli embassies in India, Azerbaijan, the Philippines, and Australia; U.S. naval vessels and oil tankers around the world; an oil company he claimed was owned by former Secretary of State Henry Kissinger on Sumatra, Indonesia; the Sears Tower in Chicago; the Empire State Building; the New York Stock Exchange; the Library Tower (now known as the U.S. Bank Tower) in Los Angeles; the Plaza Bank in Washington State; the Panama Canal; Big Ben; and London's Heathrow Airport;
- planned assassination attempts against former U.S. Presidents Carter and Clinton;
- assassination attempts against Pope John Paul II and Pakistani President Pervez Musharraf;
- supervising the "cell for the production of biological weapons, such as anthrax and others, and following up on dirty-bomb operations on American soil";
- personally beheading *Wall Street Journal* reporter Daniel Pearl in February 2002. "I decapitated with my blessed right hand the head of the American Jew Daniel Pearl in the city of Karachi, Pakistan. For those who would like to confirm, there are pictures of me on the Internet holding his head."
- a plot to blow up a dozen airliners heading from the Philippines and other locations in Asia to the United States;
- a plot to blow up a flight from London to the United States;
- planned attacks on U.S. military vessels in the Straits of Hormuz, Gibraltar, and the Port of Singapore;
- planned hijackings of planes leaving Saudi Arabia that would be crashed into buildings in Eilat, Israel;
- sending fighters into Israel to conduct surveillance;
- surveilling U.S. nuclear power plants;

- a planned attack against NATO headquarters in Brussels, Belgium;
- planned attacks against Israeli passenger jets at Bangkok Airport;
- planned attacks against U.S. military bases and nightclubs in South Korea.

He did not claim credit for the August 1998 bombings of two U.S. embassies in Tanzania and Kenya, the USS *Cole* bombing in October 2000 in Yemen, or the attack on a U.S. consulate in Pakistan in June 2002. Many observers doubted that he was this active, suggesting that it would deflect attention away from the true planners.

On September 6, 2006, President Bush announced that the last 14 detainees would be transferred from secret foreign prisons to the military detention facility at Guantánamo Bay. The group was identified as Abu Zubaydah, Khalid Sheikh Mohammed, Ramzi Binalshibh, Mustafa Ahmad al-Hawsawi, Hambali, Majid Khan, Lillie, Ali Abd al-Aziz Ali, Ahmed Khalfan Ghailani, Abd al-Rahim al-Nashiri, Abu Faraj al-Libi, Zubair, Walid bin Attash, and Gouled Hassan Dourad.

On August 9, 2007, the Pentagon declared Muhammad an enemy combatant, a legal status that permitted the military authorities to hold him indefinitely at the detention center and put him on trial for war crimes.

On February 11, 2008, the Pentagon announced it would seek the death penalty in the war crimes charges of six individuals detained at Guantánamo who were believed to have planned the 9/11 attacks: Khalid Sheikh Muhammad, Ramzi bin al-Shibh, Ali Abd al-Aziz Ali alias Ammar al-Baluchi, Mohammed al-Qahtani, Mustafa Ahmed al-Hawsawi, and Walid bin Attash alias Khallad. The six were charged with conspiracy, murder in violation of the laws of war, attacking civilians, attacking civilian objects, intentionally causing bodily injury, destruction of property, terrorism, and material support for terrorism. KSM, bin Attash, Binalshibh, and Ali were also charged with hijacking or hazarding an aircraft. His arraignment was scheduled for June 5. His defense team included Navy Reserve Judge Advocate General Prescott L. Prince, Army Lt. Col. Michael Acuff, and civilian attorneys Scott McKay and David Nevin.

Mahjub Husayn Muhammad: alias Adel Mahjub, hijacker on April 6, 1994 of a Sudanese B737 flying between Khartoum and al-Danaqilah that he diverted to Luxor, Egypt, where he surrendered and requested political asylum. He told Egyptian authorities his real name was 'Adil Mahjub Muhammad Ahmad. On October 18, he appeared before the high state security court in Cairo on charges of armed hijacking. He was accused of threatening the pilots and forcing them to take the plane to Luxor. On October 27, Sudan requested extradition. Egypt denied the asylum and extradition requests. On January 1, 1995, Egypt sentenced him to 15 years of hard labor.

Mahmud Muhammad: one of two Iraqi terrorists arrested on January 21, 1991 in Bangkok, Thailand who were part of an international terrorist network financed and armed via Iraqi diplomatic pouches. He was deported on January 28, 1991, but ultimately flew to Nepal on January 31. He was not charged in Thailand, but he was arrested by Nepalese police upon arrival. Nepal deported him back to Bangkok on February 3, 1991. On February 7, both terrorists were deported to Athens.

Mazen Yahiya Muhammad: variant of Mazin Yahya Muhammad.

Mazin Yahya Muhammad: variant Mazen Yahiya Muhammad, alias Abu-Dajanah, a Saudi from Mecca who was born on October 25, 1983 and joined al Qaeda in Iraq on September 23, 2006. His recruitment coordinator was Abu-Sa'id. He contributed $700 and a cell phone. His brother Abu-Khayriyyah's, variant Kharireah, phone number was 00966564522908; Abu-Hamam's was 0096655454990.

Muhammad Al Alhajj Muhammad: alias Abu Hassan, a Syrian veterinary student from al Dyr who had also served as a coordinator in Syria and who joined al Qaeda in Iraq as a martyr in 2007, bring 2,400 lira. His recruitment coordinator was al Hajji. His phone numbers were 039523618 and 093762025.

Muhammad Jubarah Muhammad: a Sudanese Army corporal born in 1968 who was accompanied by his wife Vam when, on January 4, 1995, he hijacked a Sudan Air Fokker taking off from Khartoum on a flight to Marawi and asked to fly to Cairo. The plane landed in Port Sudan airport, where the couple was arrested. Muhammad said he wanted to take his wife to Cairo for a honeymoon, but was unable to afford the fare. He came from Omdurman.

Muhammad Kazim 'Abd al-Qawi Muhammad: a heavy machinery driver for a sewage company born on May 27, 1961. He used a fake identity card for Lufti Ahmad al-Sayyid Abu al-'Aynayn, born in February 1965. He was identified by Egyptian police as being a suspected in the attempted assassination, on August 13, 1987, by four gunmen who fired on Major General Muhammad al-Nabawi Isma'il, former deputy prime minister and interior minister, in front of his house in Cairo.

Muhammad Saqr Muhammad: alias Abu-Hudhayfah, a Libyan born in 1981 who joined al Qaeda in Iraq in 2007.

Al-Mukanna Muhammad: arrested on October 15, 1994 by Egyptian police in connection with the October 14, 1994 stabbing of Naguib Mahfouz, the only Arab to receive the Nobel Prize for Literature, in a Cairo suburb. He carried a false ID card in the name of Muhammad Naji Muhammad Mustafa. The electrician was sentenced to death on January 10, 1995 by the Higher Military Court in Cairo.

Mustafa 'Abd-al-Aziz Muhammad: alias al-Turki, identified by the Ethiopian government as one of the nine Egyptian Islamic Group

gunmen who, on June 25, 1995, fired on the armored limousine of Egyptian President Hosni Mubarak in Addis Ababa. On August 7, 1995, the Ethiopian Supreme State Security Prosecution charged the nine of forming a terrorist organization to destabilize the country, possessing arms and explosives, communicating with a foreign state to undermine the country's security, attempting to assassinate state figures, and attempting to blow up vital establishments.

Mu'tasim Bin-Sadiq Bin Muhammad: variant Mutassem Bin Sadiq Bin Muhammad, alias Abu-Khattab, an Omani who was born in 1980 and joined al Qaeda in Iraq on September 19, 2006, depositing 1,522 riyals and 20 Dirham. His brother Baker's phone number was 00973506806001; his father's 00973505121646.

Mutassem Bin Sadiq Bin Muhammad: variant of Mu'tasim Bin-Sadiq Bin Muhammad.

Rafi' Muhammad Juma'h Muhammad: one of two Jordanians arrested for setting off two time bombs at popular cafes in Kuwait on July 11, 1985 that killed 10 and injured 87. He was acquitted on January 7, 1987.

Sa'd Amin Abu-al-Majd Muhammad: one of seven terrorists hanged on July 8, 1993 in the appeals prison in Cairo for attacks on tourist buses and installations in the al-Wajh al-Qiblio, Luxor, and Aswan areas, in accordance with the sentence handed down by the Supreme Military Court on April 22, 1993 in Case Number 6.

Salah 'Abd-al-Hamid Shaker Muhammad: variant of Shalah 'Abd-al-Hamid Shakir Muhammad.

Salah 'Abd-al-Hamid Shakir Muhammad: variant Shaker, 27-year-old Palestinian Islamic Jihad suicide bomber from Rafiah who, on January 22, 1995, set off his bomb outside a bus stop snack bar at the Beit Lid Junction of Israel, killing 18 soldiers and one civilian and wounding another 65 people. The psychotherapist had been wounded six times by Israeli soldiers and detained for 18 days during the intifadah.

Tagun Mehemet Muhammad: a Libyan arrested in Limassol, Cyprus on September 17, 1990 at an offshore company office that publishes Arabic newspapers and magazines. He was held on suspicion of planning terrorist activities and was expected to be deported. He had arrived in Cyprus a month and a half earlier and had vanished. His short-stay visa expired. No incriminating evidence was found in his Limassol apartment, but he was charged with living in Cyprus illegally.

Tariq Muhammad: alias of Ibrahim al-Tamimi.

Tariq 'Abd-al-Samad Muhammad: sentenced to death on July 16, 1994 by a Cairo military court for involvement with the Vanguard of the Conquest gunmen who, on August 18, 1993, fired on the motorcade of Egyptian Interior Minister Hassan Alfi. Five people died and 17 were wounded when a remotely detonated bomb exploded as Alfi's convoy passed by. He was also accused of murdering a dissident member of their group and the main prosecution witness in the trial of militants convicted of trying to kill Prime Minister 'Atif Sidqi in November 1993. Sidqi escaped unharmed, but a 15-year-old girl was killed. The prosecution failed to make the case that he was responsible for plotting to assassinate UN Secretary General Boutros Boutros-Ghali during an African summit in Cairo in June 1993. He had pleaded not guilty to the charges. On August 22, 1994, he was hanged in Cairo's Appeals Prison.

Usama Hattab Muhammad: alias Abu Sa'ayed, a Tunisian university student from Bin A'arous who was born on November 9, 1982 and joined al Qaeda in Iraq as a fighter on 7th Muharram (circa 2007). He gave $200 of his $400 to his handlers in Syria. His recruitment coordinator was Abu Ahmed, whom he knew via a Tunisian friend he met in Syria. He flew from Tunisia to Turkey, then drove to Syria. His phone number was 0021611443302.

Ya'lushin al-Muhammad: alias Abu-Safwan, a Moroccan from Tangier who was born on April 17, 1973 and joined al Qaeda in Iraq on October 14, 2006, contributing a watch and two MP3 players. His recruitment coordinator was Sa'd. His mother's phone number was 0021270828273; colleague Yasin's was 0021278783318.

Zuzant Muhammad: one of three terrorists who, on July 11, 1988, fired machine guns and threw hand grenades at the *City of Poros*, a Greek island ferryboat that was carrying tourists in the Aegean Sea, killing 11 and injuring 98.

Abu Muhammed: alias of Fawaz Mukhlef Aweda al Qeddie.

Ali Muhammed: an al Qaeda weapons trainer who was arrested in the United States on September 10, 1998. He had served in the Egyptian army and was also a former noncommissioned officer in the U.S. Special Forces.

Haj Muhammed: Hizballah member alleged to have handled the cargo transfer of the *Karine*, a cargo ship that was boarded by Israeli navy commanders on January 3, 2002 in the Red Sea. They found 50 tons of weapons, including Katyusha rockets, antitank missiles, mortars, mines, and sniper rifles, believed originating in Iran and headed for the Palestinian Authority. The weapons were in quantities banned by the 1993 Oslo peace agreement. Israel said interrogation of the 13 crewmen determined that the arms smuggling was coordinated by Lebanese Hizballah.

Jamel Hahmud Talid Muhammed: one of three Lebanese Palestinians identified in a March 16, 1989 FAA warning of a possible plan to hijack a U.S. airliner in Europe. The FAA said the trio might be carrying false passports issued in Bahrain, Pakistan, or North Yemen.

Mahdi Muhammed: variant Mahde, one of two Popular Front for the Liberation of Palestine terrorists who threw grenades and fired submachine guns at a crowd waiting to board El Al flight 582, a B707 bound for Tel Aviv from Istanbul on August 11, 1976. They killed four and wounded 26 before surrendering. They claimed Libya had financed the operation. On November 16, 1976, a Turkish court sentenced them to death but commuted the sentences to life in prison. Muhammed's release was demanded by the Organization of Struggle Against World Imperialism hijackers of Lufthansa flight 181, a B737 scheduled to fly from the Spanish resort island of Mallorca to Frankfurt on October 13, 1977.

Noor Uthman Muhammed: a Sudanese captured at an al Qaeda safe house with Abu Zubaydah on March 28, 2002. He had trained at the Khaldan terrorist training camp in Afghanistan, later become a weapons instructor there for hundreds of terrorists. From 1996–2000, he was the facility's deputy commander. On May 23, 2008, U.S. military prosecutors at Guantánamo charged him with war crimes, including conspiracy and providing support to terrorism. The five foot, two inch defendant faced life in prison.

Abu Mahdi al Muhandis: alias of Ja'afar al-Ibrahimi, a senior Badr Brigade operative in Iraq with ties to Hizballah and the Iranian Revolutionary Guards. He was believed to have been involved in the 1980s-era bombing of the U.S. Embassy in Kuwait.

Amjad al-Muhanna: a Syrian whom the Jordanian prosecutor said had joined the Islamic Jihad—Al-Aqsa Battalions by August 1992.

Sana Muhaydali: a 16-year-old who killed herself and two Israeli Defense Forces soldiers and slightly injured two others when she set off a bomb in her car at a roadblock in Lebanon on April 9, 1985. The Lebanese National Resistance Front claimed credit. On a televised tape, she said she was "going to join several other saints."

Abu Abed Al Muhaymen: alias of Hammoud al Hawarie.

Yusuf Ibn-Muhammad Muhayrir: alias Abu-Khawlah, a Moroccan from al-Hana' who was born on April 1, 1979 and joined al Qaeda in Iraq as a martyr on October 25, 2006, contributing a passport, $100, and a watch. His recruitment coordinator was Sa'd. His home phone number was 067987672.

Zayn-al-Abidin al-Muhdar: leader of the Islamic Aden-Abyan Army that was linked to Osama bin Laden. The group kidnapped 16 Westerners in Yemen in December 1998 and executed three British citizens and an Australian. In October 1999, Yemen executed him.

Abu Muhjeen: alias of Kariem.

Abu Muhjin: leader of the Lebanese 'Asbat al-Ansar group in October 2001. He had been sentenced to death in absentia by Lebanese courts.

Abu-Muhjin: alias of Hamid al-'Utaybi.

Muhammad Baqir al-Muhri: leader of a cell in Kuwait that was responsible for two bombs that exploded on July 10, 1989 in two streets leading to the Great Mosque in Mecca, killing a Pakistani and injuring 16 of the 1.5 million pilgrims from 100 countries attending the hajj.

Abu-Muhammad al-Muhrib: Syria-based travel facilitator for foreign fighters for al Qaeda in Iraq in 2007.

Abu-Muhammad al-Muharib: a Syria-based travel facilitator for al Qaeda in Iraq foreign recruits in 2007.

Abu-'Abd-al-Muhaymin: alias of Humud al-Hawari.

Muhriz: alias Darrar, a Tunisian fighter for al Qaeda in Iraq in 2007 who owned a passport and 1030 euros. His brother, who lives in Denmark, could be called on 004527191449 or 004521408616.

Zuhair Muhsen: chief of Saiqa (Thunderbolt), a Syrian-sponsored Palestinian organization, and head of the Palestine Liberation Organization's (PLO's) military department. He was assassinated on July 25, 1979 as he was returning to his apartment in Cannes' Gray d'Albion Hotel after an evening at the Palm Beach Casino. He was born on the West Bank in 1936. He joined the Syrian Baath party in 1953 and Saiqa in 1968. He had been a math teacher and had graduated from Lebanese University with a political science degree. He was a member of the PLO's 15-member Executive Committee.

Muhsin: Tunisia-based recruitment coordinator for foreign fighters for al Qaeda in Iraq in 2006.

Abd-al-Muhsin: alias al-Battar, a Saudi fighter for al Qaeda in Iraq in 2007. He owned a passport, cell phone, and watch. His home phone number was 0096663698696; his cell was 0966503982923.

Abu al-Mu'iz: alias of Ayman al-Zawahiri.

Abu Mujahed: a Lebanese who fled to Denmark in 2000, where he contacted bin Laden cells. He was an associate of Danial Ahmed al-Samarji.

Abu Mujahed: alias of Ali Al Awdi.

Abu-Majahed: alias of Muhammad bin Querqa.

Abu Al Muhajer: alias of Muttaz Saleh Ba'amer.

Abu Hamza al-Mujaher: alias of Abu Ayub al-Masri.

Abu-Mujahid: alias of 'Ali al-'Udah.

Jamil Daud Mujahid: alias of James Stubbs.

Zabiullah Mujahid: a Taliban spokesman who took credit for the January 14, 2008 attack on the Serena Hotel that killed six.

Abu Abdullah al-Mujamie: variant al-Majemaai, a deputy of the leader of al Qaeda in Iraq who was killed on February 15, 2007 in a shootout with police near Balad.

Abu Abdullah al-Majemaai: variant of Abu Abdullah al-Mujamie.

Ayerbe Mujica: one of 11 Euskadi Ta Askatasuna (ETA) members expelled by Algiers to Caracas, Venezuela on May 27, 1989.

Salam Muhammad Mukahhal: an Abu Nidal member who, on August 10, 1992, was ambushed and shot to death as he was traveling by car to Ba'labaak in Lebanon's al-Biqa' Valley.

Abu Abd Allah Mukbel: variant of Abu 'Abdallah Makbal.

Kamal Muhamad Mukbel: alias Abu Salaman, a Yemeni from Aden with experience in business science who joined al Qaeda in Iraq in 2007, bringing his watch. His recruitment coordinator was Abu Musa'ab. His phone number was 711346295.

El Sa'id Hassan Ali Mohamed Mukhlis: an Egyptian living in Ciudad del Este who was arrested on January 29, 1999 by Montevideo police. He was tied to Egypt's Islamic Group and was en route to Europe to meet an al Qaeda cell. He was believed to be a member of an Egyptian militant group that wants to establish a Muslim state in Egypt. Muhklis was picked up attempting to enter the country from Brazil on a false Malaysian passport. The *London Sunday Times* claimed that, based upon intercepted phone calls, authorities believed that he was about to fly to London to form a terrorist cell that would conduct attacks against the British embassies in Paris and Brussels. He was suspected of involvement in the 1997 Gama'at massacre of 58 tourists in Luxor. He faced extradition to Cairo on murder charges. Muhklis had lived in Brazil for five years. He took his wife and their three children, all under age five, to the border. They were all carrying false Malaysian passports. They arrived in Chui, a border town on the Atlantic coast, and checked into a hotel. He told neighbors he had lived in Brazil for ten years, yet he knew no Portuguese.

'Abd-al-Rahman 'Abd-al-Mu'az al-Mukhtar: alias Abu-Hazim, a Yemeni born in 1983 who joined al Qaeda in Iraq as a fighter in 2007. His Yemeni phone number was 009671249846; his Riyadh phone number was 0096614354996.

Majid Yusuf al-Mukly: variant of Majid Yusuf al-Mulki.

Muktarmar: alias of Dulmatin.

'Abbas 'Abbuz Mul: an Iraqi intelligence captain posing as an Egyptian citizen who was arrested on March 20, 1991 on his arrival at Cairo airport. He had been ordered to join a terrorist group that was to assassinate Egyptian officials, including Interior Minister Major General Muhammad 'Abd-al-Halim Musa, and blow up vital installations.

Anas Isma'il Mula: alias Abu-Malak, Saudi from Mecca born in 1982 who joined al Qaeda in Iraq in 2007, bringing 40 lira and 1,367 Saudi riyals. He was deployed to Anbar. His phone numbers were 0504531973 and 0553551559.

Majid Yusuf al-Mulki: variant Majid Yusuf al-Mukly, one of the four Palestine Liberation Front hijackers on October 7, 1985 of the Italian cruise ship *Achille Lauro*, which set sail from Genoa, Italy, on a 12-day Mediterranean excursion with planned stops at Naples, Syracuse, Alexandria, Port Said, and Ashdod, Israel with 116 passengers and 331 crew members as hostages. He killed Leon Klinghoffer, age 69, an American confined to a wheelchair, and dumped the body overboard. The hijacking ended in Egypt. The United States requested extradition from the Egyptians, but President Hosni Mubarak told reporters that the

hijackers had left for an unknown destination. However, U.S. fighters forced the getaway plane to land and took the four hijackers into custody. The four hijackers were formally arrested by Italian authorities; the United States planned to request extradition. On October 17, 1985, after the Craxi government resigned, murder warrants were issued in Genoa against the four hijackers. A fellow hijacker identified al-Mulki as Klinghoffer's killer. His trial began on November 18, 1985 on charges of arms smuggling. He was found guilty and sentenced to eight years. On June 18, 1986, his trial began in Genoa for murder and kidnapping. On July 10, 1986, he was sentenced to 30 years. On May 24, 1987, a Genoa appeals court upheld the conviction. On May 11, 1988, Italy's Supreme Court of Cassation confirmed an appeals court's 30-year sentence.

Abu-Mu'min: alias of Yasir al-Saddi.

Mohammad Munaf: a panel of the Washington, DC Circuit ruled that the Iraqi-American had no right to U.S. courts. He had traveled to Iraq in 2005 to serve as a guide to a group of Romanian journalists, who soon were kidnapped. Authorities believed he was involved in the kidnapping. U.S. authorities said he confessed but recanted when tried in Iraq. He was convicted by the Iraqi Central Criminal Court and sentenced to death. In December 2007, the U.S. Supreme Court agreed to hear the case of *Munaf v. Geren*. Arguments were scheduled for March 2008, the same month that an Iraqi appeals court overturned the conviction.

Mohammed Ahmed Munawar: On July 6, 1988, Pakistani district court judge Zafar Ahmed Babar ended an eight-month trial in a special court in Rawalpindi's Adiyala maximum security prison and sentenced the Lebanese to death by hanging for the September 5, 1986 hijacking of a Pan Am B747 and for killing 11 passengers at Karachi airport. There was insufficient evidence to convict five terrorists of the deaths of 11 other passengers. The hijacker mastermind, Sulayman al-Turki, said that the group would appeal the sentences and if they were freed, "we would hijack a U.S. airliner once again." The court also passed a total jail sentence of 257 years on each of the accused on several other charges of murder, conspiracy to hijack, possession of illegal arms, and confinement of the passengers. The terrorists had 30 days to appeal the verdict and the sentence in Lahore's High Court. On July 28, 1988, the press reported that the terrorists reversed their decision not to appeal.

Abu-Mundhir: alias of Muhammad.

Abu-al-Muni'm: alias of 'Abdallah.

'Id'Abd-al-Mun'im: an Egyptian fundamentalist extradited by the South Africans to Egypt in November 1998.

Muhammad Ali Munser: variant of Muhammad 'Ali Munsir.

Muhammad 'Ali Munsir: variant variant Muhammad Ali Munser, alias Abu-'Abdallah al-Madani, variant Abu Abd Allah al Madani, a Saudi from Medina who was born on July 7, 1973 and joined al Qaeda in Iraq on October 14, 2006, contributing 502 riyals, 300 lira, a wristwatch, an MP3 player, and a recorder. His recruitment coordinator was Abu-Ahmad. His home phone number was 8380731; his wife's was 0505327482; his brother Zaki's was 0505301360 and his father's was 050307967.

Abu Abu Al Munzer: alias of Hanni Muhammad Al Sagheer.

Ibrahim Muqadmeh: a senior Hamas military leader who was released in early March 1997 from a Gaza City jail. He was rearrested on March 22, 1997 in connection with the previous day's Hamas suicide bombing that killed three Israeli soldiers (other reports said three women) and injuring 47 other people in Apropo, a Tel Aviv café.

Abu-Muqbil: alias of Ahmad.

Ahmad 'Alawi al-Muqbuli: a North Yemeni who, on March 17, 1985, hijacked Saudi Arabian Airlines flight 208, a B737 en route from Jeddah to Kuwait with a stop in Riyadh, as it was preparing to land at Dharhan Airport. He demanded to be flown to an undisclosed destination. Security guards shot and killed the hijacker when he attempted to set off his grenade.

Abu Muqdad: alias of Ammash Mishan al Bedyre.

Abu al Muqdad: alias of Abd Allah Bin Turkey Bin Abd Allah Al Qahtani.

'Ali al-Muqdad: Hizballah member and one of three terrorists reported by Paraguay's *Noticias* on August 31, 1994 to have entered the country on August 27, 1994 to conduct a bombing against the Jewish community in Buenos Aires. They were to travel from Barcelona, Spain via Hungary and Germany then to Rio de Janeiro or Sao Paulo, then to Foz do Iguacu or Asuncion, to Ciudad del Este, then onward with their explosives to Buenos Aires for a September 3 attack.

Abdel Aziz Muqrin: variant of Abdulaziz Muqrin.

Abdulaziz Muqrin: variant Abdel Aziz Muqrin, al Qaeda leader in Saudi Arabia in mid-2004. Saudi authorities killed him in a raid on June 18, 2004, hours after Muqrin's group had beheaded American hostage Paul Johnson, who was kidnapped on June 12, 2004. Authorities said they killed Muqrin and three other Most Wanted terrorists in a two-hour shootout at a roadblock in Riyadh; 12 other terrorists were detained. Police said the cell was involved in the November 9, 2003 bombing of a foreigners' residential compound in Riyadh and the May 2004 Khobar bombing that killed 22. Police found a car used by a gunman who shot to death a BBC cameraman and wounded a BBC reporter in Riyadh on June 6. They also detained a planner of the October 2000 USS *Cole* bombing.

Abu Muqtad: alias Misbah Saied Al Warghami.

Abu Qattada Al Murabett: alias of Fahed Bin Manawer Bin Za'ar Al Etteri.

Murad: alias Abu-Wahid, a Tunisian from Ibn-'Arus, variant Bin 'Arus, who joined al Qaeda in Iraq in 2007. His recruitment coordinator was 'Abdallah. His home phone number was 71300406.

Abdul Hakim Murad: alias Saeed Ahmed, arrested on January 6, 1995 in the Philippines on suspicion of plotting with Ramzi Ahmad Yusuf with plotting to assassinate Pope John Paul II during his visit to the islands. He was turned over to the United States by Philippine authorities on March 8, 1995. On April 13, 1995, federal officials in New York charged him with conspiring with others to plant bombs on numerous commercial U.S. aircraft. He faced 45 years. On October 5, 1995, U.S. officials charged Yusuf with possessing a letter threatening to conduct additional terrorist attacks and demanding Murad's release. On February 23, 1996, he was indicted for the December 1, 1994 bombing of the Greenbelt Theater in Manila, Philippines, that injured several moviegoers. On September 5, 1996, he was found guilty on all seven counts in the conspiracy to set off the airplane bombs. Defense attorneys said they would appeal. On April 4, 2003, the U.S. Court of Appeals for the Second Circuit upheld his convictions in the 1993 World Trade Center and the Bojinka plot.

Mustafa Murad: alias Abu-Nizar, one of two dissident former members of the Central Committee and Political Bureau of Fatah–The Revolutionary Council said, on October 31, 1989, to have been killed, along with 156 of Abu Nidal's followers, by Abu Nidal in Libya on October 17, 1988. Other dissidents said he was killed in Abu Nidal's office on October 17, 1989.

Ahmad al-Muragah: one of 12 Popular Front for the Liberation of Palestine members arrested by Jordanian security forces on October 4, 1989 for questioning about the smuggling of explosives and personnel into Jordan to fire rockets across the ceasefire line.

Mouttaz Hassan Murageh: variant of Mu'tazz Hasan Muraji'.

Ahmad Bin-'Abd-al-Ghafur Mura'i: alias 'Abd-al-Baqi, a Syrian agricultural engineer from Adlab who was born in 1982 and joined al Qaeda in Iraq as a martyr on July 9, 2007. His recruitment coordinator was Abu-Ishaq, whom he met on the Internet. He also dealt with Abu-'Umar in Syria. His home phone number was 0236351.

Mu'tazz Hasan Muraji': variant Mouttaz Hassan Murageh, alias Abu-Mu'awiyah, variant Abu Ma'awieah, a Libyan from Darnah who was born on July 1, 1979 and joined al Qaeda in Iraq on October 25, 2006 to become a martyr. He contributed his passport and $100. His recruitment coordinator was Abu-'Umar. His phone numbers were 00218926754197 and 00218632696. His brother Ihab's phone was 002189262220556.

Abu-Muram: alias of 'Abd-al-Mun'im Maqshar al-'Amrani, variant Abd Al Mounaem Mekshar al Oumrani.

Khalid Muhammad Rakan Al Murshed: alias Abu Al Walied, a Saudi bank clerk at Bank Al Raghie from Riyadh/al Rawddah who was born on 1401 Hijra and joined al Qaeda in Iraq as a fighter on 26th Rajab 1428 (2007), contributing 16,000 of his 17,000 Saudi riyals, his passport, and his ID. His recruitment coordinator was Mansour, whom he knew through his cousin, Abu Usama. He arrived in Syria by bus via Riyadh and Jordan. In Syria, he met Abu Yaser, Abu Haziefah, and Abu Omar. His brother Abd Al Aziz's phone number was 0504145554.

Musa Ibrahim Muhammad al-Murshid: alias Abu-Yusuf, variant Abu Youssef, a Saudi student from Riyadh who was born on May 22, 1985 and joined al Qaeda in Iraq as a fighter on November 12, 2006, contributing his passport, $520, 165 riyals, and sunglasses. His recruitment coordinator was Abu-Suhayb, variant Abu Suhib. His home phone number was 0096614280952; his brother's was 00966505181804.

Mohammad Abu Murshud: head of the Islamic Jihad's armed wing in central Gaza who was killed on December 27, 2007 by an Israeli air strike in Gaza.

Midhat Mursi: an Egyptian chemist in charge of al Qaeda's unconventional weapons program who may have become al Qaeda's external operations chief, succeeding Abu Ubaida al Masri, who died of hepatitis C in December 2007. He attended a meeting with recruits from northern Europe who trained in Pakistan in the spring of 2007.

Tariq 'Ali Mursi: on November 8, 1998, the Egyptian fundamentalist and bin Laden associate, who was extradited the previous month by South Africa, refused to make any statements before the Egyptian State Security High Court.

Fadlallah Fadlallah Murtadi: a Lebanese who was 1 of 13 members of the Iranian Lebanese Hizballah reported by Madrid *Diario 16* on October 20, 1987 as having entered Spain on October 13, 1987 to attack diplomats from Saudi Arabia, Kuwait, and Iraq.

'Abd-al-Qadir Salih Musa: alias Abu-Khalid, a Libyan from Darnah who was born in 1985 and joined al Qaeda in Iraq in 2007, bringing $1,000. His recruitment coordinator was Abu-Sa'd. He flew from Libya via Egypt to Syria, where he met Abu-Nasir. His phone numbers were 0913265422 and 0927482119.

Abu Musa: on May 22, 1985, the Jordanian state prosecutor's office issued a summons for him in connection with a foiled plot by the Libyans and the Abu Nidal organization to set off a bomb at the U.S. Embassy in Egypt.

Ahmad 'Ali Musa: alias Abu-Mus'ab, a Jordanian merchant from Zarqa who was born on April 25, 1981 and joined al Qaeda in Iraq as a martyr on November 18, 2006, contributing his passport. His recruitment coordinator was 'Abd-al-Hamid. His brother's phone number was 0745478503.

Haji Abu Musa: official in charge of Fatah-Revolutionary Council troops in Lebanon. He was one of two dissident former members of the Central Committee and Political Bureau of Fatah-The Revolutionary Council who, on October 31, 1989, were said to have been killed, along with 156 of Abu Nidal's followers, by Abu Nidal in Libya in 1987 or 1988.

Hasan Hodge Hajji Musa: a Lebanese student arrested at Larnaca Airport on May 10, 1988 after police found that he was carrying a radio cassette player with a silencer-equipped pistol and two full magazines of ammunition inside his bag. He admitted that he had intended to murder someone in Cyprus.

Tawfiq Musa: a 45-year-old from Milwaukee and one of four members of the Abu Nidal group jailed on April 1, 1993 by St. Louis police for planning to blow up the Israeli Embassy and murder Jews. He was listed in the indictment as having discussed blowing up the Israeli Embassy. He ordered that all records of the meeting be destroyed. In July 1994, he pleaded guilty to federal racketeering charges of smuggling money and information, buying weapons, recruiting members, illegally obtaining passports, and obstructing investigations and helping plot terrorist attacks. On November 22, 1994, U.S. District Judge Donald Stohr sentenced him to 21 months in prison. With credit for time served, he was due to be released in January 1995. Jewish groups protested, noting that he was eligible for 20 years and a $250,000 fine.

Abu Musa'ab: variant of Abu Mus'ab.

Abu Musa'ab: alias of Ahamed Hussein Al Hamadi.

Abu Musa'ab: alias of Rabie Bin Muhammad al Hamadi.

Abu Musa'ab: alias of Ahmad Ali Mussa.

Abu Musa'ab: alias of Khalid Jummah Masoud al Shalieah.

Abu Musa'ab: alias of Abd Al Rahman Al Vaitouri Hammed Al Zaytoni.

Abu Musab: alias of Ghasoub Abrash Ghalyoun.

Abu Musab: alias of Isnilon Totoni Hapilon.

Abu-Mus'ab: alias of an unnamed Moroccan member of al Qaeda in Iraq sent on a suicide mission in 2007. His home phone number was 0021237908446; his sister's was 0021266277543.

Abu-Mus'ab: alias of Fahd.

Abu-Mus'ab: alias of 'Abd-al-Rahman Muhammad Ibrahim al-Dubaykhi.

Abu-Mus'ab: alias of Hasan.

Abu-Mus'ab: Saudi-based recruitment coordinator for foreign fighters for al Qaeda in Iraq in 2006.

Abu-Mus'ab: variant Abu Musa'ab, alias of Taysir 'Abd-al-Muslih al-Malih, variant Tayseer Abd Al Mousleh Al Maleeh.

Abu-Mus'ab: alias of Muhammad Sakut Mansur, variant Muhammad Sakout Mansour.

Abu-Mus'ab: alias of Ahmad 'Ali Musa.

Abu-Mus'ab: alias of Muhammad 'Ayn-al-Nas.

Abu-Mus'ab: alias of 'Abd-al-Razzaq.

Abu-Mus'ab: alias of 'Abd-al-Rahman Bin Muhammad Bin Farhan al-Shammari.

Abu-Mus'ab: alias of 'Abid 'Abd-'Abid al-Shari.

Abu-Mus'ab: alias of Khalid Jum'ah Mas'ud al-Shu'liyyah.

Abu-'Mus'ab: alias of Khalfallah 'Abd-al-Mu'min Walid.

Abu-Mus'ab: alias of 'Abd-al-Rahman al-Fayturi Hamad al-Zaytuni.

Khaled Musaid: on September 29, 2005, Egyptian police in the Sinai Peninsula shot to death Musaid and Tulub Murdi Suleiman in a gun battle in the Mount Halal area, near where fellow Sharm el-Sheik bombing suspect Moussa Badran had been shot earlier that day. The duo were suspected of having organized the multiple bombings on July 23, 2005 in the Sharm el-Sheik resort that killed 88 and wounded 119.

Fahid Mohammed Ali Musalaam: variant of Fahid Mohammed Ally Msalam, Fahid Muhammad 'Alim Salam.

Khamis Muhammad Musallam: one of three members of the Egyptian Jihad Organization serving life sentences for the October 6, 1981 assassination of Egyptian President Anwar Sadat who, on July 17, 1988, escaped from Turrah prison at dawn after attacking two prison guards. He was 165 centimeters, dark, of medium build, and slightly bald.

Seyyed Rexa Asyhar Musavi: one of two Iranians who hijacked an Iran Air B727 flying from Tehran to Bushehr Port on June 26, 1984 and demanded to go to Baghdad. The plane landed in Qatar and Cairo. The hijackers were denied asylum in Egypt, but received it in Iraq.

Abdullah Ahmed Khaled al-Musawah: name on a lease for an apartment in Yemen that was used as a lookout site for the October 12, 2000 al Qaeda bombing of the USS *Cole* in Yemen in which 17 U.S. sailors were killed and 44 injured.

'Abd-al-Kamil Bin-Ahmad Musawi: alias Abu-'Abdallah, an Algerian from Al-Wadi who was born on October 26, 1973 and joined al Qaeda in Iraq as a fighter on November 18, 2006, contributing a passport, 1,150 lira, and two Libyan dinars. His recruitment coordinator was Abu-Jalal. His home phone number was 0021378194557; his friend's was 0021361326321.

Husayn Musawi: leader of the Islamic Amal in 1983. The group was believed to be responsible for the October 23, 1983 bombings in Beirut that killed 241 U.S. Marines and 58 French paratroopers. On August 2, 1985, he denied U.S. State Department charges that his family was behind the kidnapping of seven Americans to obtain the freedom of a relative held in Kuwait for the December 1983 bombings of the U.S. and French embassies.

Husayn al-Sayyid Yusif al-Musawi: a Lebanese sentenced to life in prison by the Kuwaiti State Security Court in 1984 in connection with the December 12, 1983 truck bombing of the administrative building of the U.S. Embassy in Kuwait, killing four people and injuring 59. As of April 1987, none of the death sentences had been carried out. The release of 17 of the 25 prisoners in the case was demanded on numerous occasions by the Islamic Jihad in return for Americans held captive in Lebanon beginning in 1986.

Muhamad Musawi: variant Mohamed al Mussawi, a Lebanese detained by French counterintelligence on July 22, 1987 in connection with a wave of bombings in Paris between December 1985 and September 1986 that killed 13 and wounded 250. He was indicted three days later for "associating with criminals linked with an individual or collective undertaking aiming to disturb public order by intimidation or terrorism." On October 31, 1990, the Paris Appeals Court overruled an earlier decision to free him and announced a five-year prison sentence against him. An arrest warrant was issued.

Muhammad Musawi: one of ten Shi'ite Muslims identified in November 17, 1992 by the

Lebanese newspaper *Nida' al-Watan* as suspected of instigating the kidnappings of U.S. hostages William Buckley, William Higgins, and Peter Kilburn.

Rashim Musawi: an individual tried with two Arabs who were arrested in April 1979 trying to smuggle 50 kilograms of explosives through Austria into West Germany. He denied membership in any Palestinian organization. The geography student said he had met Iranian Mohammad Zahedi in Rome by accident. On July 20, 1979, the Passau regional court sentenced him to four months for forging documents and unlawful entry into West Germany.

Shaykh 'Abbas Musawi: Hizballah General Secretary who was killed in an Israeli helicopter ambush in Lebanon on February 16, 1992.

Amin Isma'il Musaylihi: sentenced to death on March 17, 1994 by the Higher Military Court in Cairo in connection with the November 25, 1993 bombing of the convoy of Egyptian Prime Minister Dr. 'Atif Sidqi that killed a 15-year-old girl and wounded 21 other people.

Ahmad Salih Muslih: one of 12 Popular Front for the Liberation of Palestine members arrested by Jordanian security forces on October 4, 1989 for questioning about the smuggling of explosives and personnel into Jordan to fire rockets across the cease-fire line

Abu-Muslim: alias of Wisam 'Abdallah Jum'ah Al-Sharif.

Ahmad Ali Mussa: alias Abu Musa'ab, a Jordanian merchant from Zarqah who was born on April 25, 1981 and joined al Qaeda in Iraq as a martyr on November 17, 2006, bringing his passport. His recruitment coordinator was Abd Al Hamied. His brother's phone number was 0745478503.

Abu Mussab: alias of Abd Al Razik.

Abu Mussab: alias of Al Abd Aalah Al Karshami.

Abu Mussab: alias of Watsef Allal Nelly Mussab.

Abu Mussab: alias of Khalid Badah Raziuq Muttaire.

Abu Mussab: alias of Wassem Belqas Haroun.

Abu Mussab: alias of Abd Al Rahman Muhammad Ibrahim Al Dubikhi.

Abu Mussab: a Yemeni-based recruiter for al Qaeda in Iraq foreign fighters in 2007.

Watsef Allal Nelly Mussab: alias Abu Mussab, an Algerian college student in chemistry and computers who lived in Kalitous and was born on March 29, 1978. He joined al Qaeda in Iraq on 7/1/1428 Hijra (2007) as a fighter, contributing his watch, ring, MP3 player, and passport. His recruitment coordinator was Ashraf, whom he met during Hajj through brother Tawansah. In Syria, he met Safwan, giving him 100 of his 400 euros. He had experience in computer software. His home phone number was 00213500247; his brother's was 0021372449620.

Abu Mussam: alias of Jihad Bu Alla'aq.

Abd Al Kamel Bin Ahamed Mussawi: alias Abu Abd Allah, an Algerian clerk from al Wad who was born on October 26, 1973 and joined al Qaeda in Iraq on November 17, 2006 as a fighter, bringing a passport, 1,150 lira, and two Libyan dinars. His recruitment coordinator was Abu Jalal. His home phone number was 0021378194557; a friend's was 0021361326321.

Mohamed al Mussawi: variant of Muhamad Musawi.

Abu Musayyib: a member of the Hamas 'Izz-al-Din al-Qassam battalion who, on July 18, 1995, shot to death two Israeli youths, one of them a soldier, who were hiking in a nature reserve in Wadi al-Qilt on the West Bank.

Walid 'Abd al-Nabi Muhammad Moussa al-Musshewen: one of two occupants of a car bomb who were killed when it exploded in Hilaly Street in Kuwait City on May 18, 1988.

Mustafa: variant Mustafah: alias Abu al-'Abbas, an Algerian who joined al Qaeda in Iraq as a media expert in 2007, bringing his passport. His recruitment coordinator was Abu-al-Bara'. His home phone number was 021532561.

Mustafa: alias of Mohbar Hussain, leader of the four hijackers of the Libyan Revolutionary Cells and the Organization of the Soldiers of God—Martyr Zulfikar Ali Bhutto Group who took over Pan Am flight 73 at Karachi airport on September 5, 1986. After the hijackers threw grenades and fired machine guns at the passengers, killing 22 and injuring 100 others, he ordered a fellow hijacker to shoot him in the stomach, where he was wearing explosives. The compatriot winged him, then fled, and Mustafa was arrested. On September 8, he was charged with hijacking an aircraft, murder, attempted murder, and several other crimes. He carried a Bahraini passport. On July 6, 1988, Pakistani district court judge Zafar Ahmed Babar ended an eight-month trial in a special court in Rawalpindi's Adiyala maximum security prison and sentenced the Lebanese to death by hanging for the hijacking and for killing 11 passengers at Karachi airport. There was insufficient evidence to convict five terrorists of the deaths of 11 other passengers. The hijacker mastermind, Sulayman al-Turki, said that the group would appeal the sentences and if they were freed, "we would hijack a U.S. airliner once again." The court also passed a total jail sentence of 257 years on each of the accused on several other charges of murder, conspiracy to hijack, possession of illegal arms, and confinement of the passengers. The terrorists had 30 days to appeal the verdict and the sentence in Lahore's High Court. On July 28, 1988, the press reported that the terrorists reversed their decision not to appeal.

Abu Mustafa: alias of Ziyad Bu Souhilah.

Abu-Mustafa: alias of Wajih Mustafa.

Abu Ali Mustafa: alias of Mustafa Zibri, Popular Front for the Liberation of Palestine leader killed on August 27, 2001 when Israeli helicopters fired two U.S.-made missiles at an apartment building housing several Palestinian American families in El Bireh on the West Bank. He was sitting at his desk in his third-floor corner office. Colleagues said a missile hit him directly, decapitating him.

'Awad Mustafa: a Sudanese who attempted to hijack a Sudanese plane en route from Baghdad to Khartoum on July 5, 1986 and divert it to Israel. The pilot instead landed in Khartoum, where security personnel arrested Mustafa. The hijacker's father said that his son had been having mental problems after the drowning death of his brother in Baghdad.

Djamal Mustafa: one of several men who were convicted in Dusseldorf on October 26, 2005 of plotting to attack Jewish sites and supporting a terrorist group. He was sentenced to five years in prison.

Hasan Ahmad Mustafa: one of two farmers in Imbabah who were arrested on January 5, 1993 by Egyptian investigators in Al-Minya for importing arms for terrorists in Asyut, in an ambush on the desert road in Al-Minya. The duo were carrying 4 machine guns, 2 pistols, and 35 spare parts for weapons. They had previously been accused in seven cases of arms trading.

Hassam Mustafa: alias of 'Ad-al-Karim al-Banna.

Isham Mustafa: Algerian and one of two assassins of Izz Ad-Din al-Qalaq, Paris Palestine Liberation Organization chief, and his aide, Hammad

Adnan, on August 3, 1978. The Rejection Front of Stateless Palestinian Arabs, and Black September and June claimed credit.

Khaled ben Mustafa: one of five former inmates of Guantánamo Bay sentenced by a French court on December 19, 2007 for "criminal association with a terrorist enterprise." The prosecution said they had used false IDs and visas to "integrate into terrorist structures" in Afghanistan. They admitted to being in the military camps, but said they had not used their combat training. They were not sent back to prison, although they were formally sentenced. Mustafa was sentenced four years in prison, three suspended and one year as time served. His attorney said he would appeal. The group were among seven French citizens captured in or near Afghanistan by the U.S. in 2001 following 9/11. They were held for two years at Guantánamo, then handed over to Paris in 2004 and 2005. One was freed immediately upon arrival. The others spent up to 17 months in French prisons.

Maget Mustafa: age 36, one of two Egyptians arrested by Albanian police on June 29, 1998 and accused of attempting to organize an Islamic fundamentalist network throughout the country. They led the Renaissance of the Islamic Heritage, which has been active in charitable work for a year. Such groups were also suspected of being covers for terrorist groups. The duo rented an apartment in the Tirana suburbs, which contained forged documents, two automatic pistols, two rifles, and ammunition. On July 4, the Albanian newspaper *Tirana Koha Jone* claimed that the duo were arrested in Elbasan, escorted to Rians Airport, and put onto a military plane. The paper claimed that the duo were wanted for two murders committed in France and Algiers and were thought to belong to a Saudi terrorist group. A judge had allegedly freed them, but the police helped to spirit them out of the country after they were declared persona non grata.

The *Tirana Gazeta Shqiptare* on July 14 claimed that the duo would set up a training camp in

Elbasan for young Muslims who, upon graduation, would infiltrate the Kosova Liberation Army. They were alleged to be members of the Selephist sect.

Majed Mustafa: an Egyptian Islamic Jihad/al Qaeda member who was arrested in Albania in 1998 and sent to Egypt. He had material indicating a planned bombing of the U.S. Embassy in Tirana. He had worked in the Tirana branch of the Kuwaiti Society for the revival of the Islamic Heritage.

Muhammad Mustafa: wanted by Egyptian police in connection with the November 25, 1993 bombing of the convoy of Egyptian Prime Minister Dr. 'Atif Sidqi that killed a 15-year-old girl and wounded 21 other people. *Middle East News Association* said that they had also participated in the car bomb explosion in the al-Qulali area a few months earlier and the abortive attempt to assassinate UN Secretary General Dr. Boutros Boutros-Ghali during the Organization of African Unity (OAU) summit in Cairo.

Muhammad Amad Mustafa: one of three Lebanese arrested on July 28, 1994 by Costa Rican police in David when they tried to cross the Panamanian border with Costa Rica with false passports. They were suspected of involvement in the suicide bombing of ALAS flight HP-1202, a twin-engine Brazilian-made Embraer, on July 19, 1994 that killed two crew and 19 passengers, including a dozen Israeli businessmen, shortly after the plane had left Colon Airport in Panama. The Partisans of God, believed to be an Hizballah cover name, claimed credit.

Muhammad 'Atif Mustafa: alias Abu-Hafs al-Misri, a bin Laden aide in November 1998 about whom the Egyptian authorities were making inquiries.

Muhammad Naji Muhammad Mustafa: alias of al-Mukanna Muhammad.

Mustafa 'Abd-al-Hamid Mustafa: said by the Ethiopian Supreme State Security Prosecution on August 7, 1995 to be one of five terrorists who had confessed to training in the al-Kamp and Kangu camps in Khartoum with two of the nine Egyptian Islamic Group gunmen who, on June 25, 1995, fired on the armored limousine of Egyptian President Hosni Mubarak in Addis Ababa.

Mustafa Kamel Mustafa: birth name of Abu Hamza al-Masri.

Otman Saleh Mustafa: a 22-year-old resident of the Jabiliya refugee camp in the Gaza Strip and Hamas member on an Israeli list of wanted terrorists who, on July 1, 1993, was wounded in the head when two Palestinian gunmen fired on a commuter bus in northern Jerusalem, then carjacked a rental car. He was believed to be a partner of the gunmen. He was hospitalized in serious condition. Police found bullets in his pocket but no weapon.

Shehada Ahmed Mustafa: one of three Fatah members who were captured by Israeli troops two miles south of the Lebanese border on April 21, 1973. The group had planned to attack civilians at a bus station in Safad, 14 miles southeast. Mustafa confessed at an April 22 news conference that they were on a "suicide mission to sabotage the bus station, a restaurant, and other public places" and had been ordered to "kill as many as we could and not permit ourselves to be captured."

Shibli Mustafa: an alleged associate of Osama bin Laden arrested on March 17, 1999 by Karachi Airport police who also detained four of his associates from Turbat, Balochistan. They were picked up following an Interpol report when they arrived at the Jinnah Terminal after being deported from Dubai. Mustafa was returning from London after having served five years in prison for involvement in arms smuggling.

Shukri Ahmed Mustafa: leader of At-Takfir wa al-Hijrah (variously translated as Repent and Migrate, Society for Atonement and Flight from Evil, and Atonement and Migration Society), which kidnapped and killed Shaykh Muhammad Husayn adh-Dahahabi, the former Egyptian minister of religious affairs. The victim had been kidnapped on July 3, and apparently been killed on July 4. Upon his arrest the following week, Mustafa admitted to planning the kidnapping.

Wajih Mustafa: alias Abu-Mustafa, identified by Doha's *al-Sharq* on March 19, 1993 as a former member of the Abu Nidal Group.

Mustafah: variant of Mustafa.

Hadi Mustafavi: one of three Iranian government agents believed to have assassinated Abdolrahman Qassemlou, secretary general of the Kurdish Democratic Party, in Vienna, Austria on July 13, 1989. Austria issued an arrest warrant for him on charges of leaving injured persons whose lives were in danger.

Salah Mahdi Mustafi: alias Jamil Abdel Hassan Ayoub, would-be hijacker of an Alia Caravelle flying from Cairo to Amman on February 19, 1972. He waved a hand grenade, hoping to divert the plane to Tripoli, Libya as it left Cairo. He was overpowered by Jordanian security guards. The Jordanian National Liberation Movement claimed responsibility.

Mustapha: alias of Abderraouf Ben Habib Jdey.

Abdul Rahim Mustapha: a Major in Fatah's Force 17 believed to have been the mastermind of the killing of Ali Naji Awad al-Adhami, a Palestinian political cartoonist, on July 22, 1987 in the United Kingdom. He was expelled from the United Kingdom in April 1987, but reentered the United Kingdom using false ID papers. Investigators linked him to the murdered man.

Abdel-Rahman Saleh Abdel-Rahman al-Mutab: age 26, number 4 on the Saudi government's Most Wanted Terrorists list, was killed on December 27, 2005 following a shootout in the desert. He and a fellow terrorist shot to death two policemen outside Buraydah, northwest of Riyadh. They drove 12 miles southwest and fired on a security checkpoint near Al-Midhnab, killing another three officers. Meanwhile, Mutab escaped, hijacked a woman's car and forced her and her driver out. Police chased him to the Nefoud Umm Khashaba desert, and shot him to death in a gun battle. Mutab had been wanted for killing two policemen in Qusaym in April, along with other shootings and fundraising for militant groups.

Ahmad Mutahhar: alias of Ahmad Mutahhar Jamil al-Matari.

Abdullah Mutlaq Nasser Mutairi: age 32, along with his brother Ahmad Mutlaq Mutairi, two of three Kuwaiti Islamic radicals and supporters of bin Laden arrested by Kuwaiti authorities on February 24, 2003 for planning attacks against U.S. forces. Police seized arms and ammunition during the arrests of the individuals, who were planning to ambush a U.S. military convoy. The men had been under surveillance for some time.

Ahmad Mutlaq Mutairi: age 29, along with his brother Abdullah Mutlaq Nasser Mutairi, two of three Kuwaiti Islamic radicals and supporters of bin Laden arrested by Kuwaiti authorities on February 24, 2003 for planning attacks against U.S. forces. Police seized arms and ammunition during the arrests of the individuals, who were planning to ambush a U.S. military convoy. The men had been under surveillance for some time. Ahmad had traveled to Afghanistan in 2001.

Ali Ahmed al-Mutaqawi: one of 44 Bahrainis arrested on June 4, 1996 and charged with plotting to overthrow the government. The group's leader had asked the group to gather information on U.S. forces in Bahrain, where the U.S. Fifth

Fleet is based. One suspect said that the group had been trained by Hizballah in Lebanon. The group claimed to be the military wing of Hizballah Bahrain. He said the Iranian Revolutionary Guard trained them in Qom, Iran, in May 1994.

Ali Ahmad Kadhem Mutaqawwi: one of two ringleaders of a group of 44 Iranian-trained Shi'ite members of Hizballah Bahrain who were arrested in June 1996 on charges of plotting to overthrow the ruling Khalifa family. He was sentenced to 14 years.

Abu Mu'tarzz: alias of Husayn Nasvi al-Kebir, a Palestinian refugee from Syria, one of six Arabs arrested in Lebanon on March 15, 1974, after they attempted to smuggle arms and explosives in food containers and luggage aboard a KLM Royal Dutch Airlines B747 en route from Amsterdam to Tokyo via Beirut. Reports claimed they were from the Popular Front for the Liberation of Palestine and the Arab National Youth Organization for the Liberation of Palestine.

Mu'tasim: alias of Muhammad 'Abd al-Rahman 'Abid.

Al-Mu'tasim: alias of 'Abd-al-Salam Khalil Hubbub.

Ahmad Bin Mukhallad Bin Hamad al-Mutayri: alias Abu-Sulayman, a Saudi from al-Qasim who joined al Qaeda in Iraq as a martyr in 2007. His recruitment coordinator was Abu-Kafa. He flew from Dubai to Syria, where he met Abu-'Abd-al-'Aziz, Abu al-'Abbas, and Abu 'Umar al-Tunusi. He gave them $100 of his $300. He also brought his passport. His brothers' phone numbers were 00966555171383 and 00966505961144.

Hamad 'Abdallah al-Mutayri: alias Abu Hajir, variant Abu Hajar, a Saudi suicide bomber who offered his services to al Qaeda in Iraq in 2007. His phone number was 009664545217. He brought with him a passport and donated a watch and $400.

Sami al-Mutayri: age 25, a Kuwaiti man who supports al Qaeda and, on January 23, 2002, confessed to the January 21, 2003 drive-by killing of U.S. software engineer Michael Rene Pouliot and injury of fellow San Diegan David Caraway. He was arrested by Saudi border guards as he tried to get into Saudi Arabia; he was handed over to Kuwaiti authorities. He had visited Pakistan to meet with militant groups soon after 9/11. He majored in social studies at Kuwait University and once worked at the Social Services Ministry. Authorities found the rifle and ammunition at his workplace. He acted alone but had assistance in planning the attack. No group claimed credit. On June 4, 2003, a Kuwaiti court sentenced the killer to death.

Mahmud Al Mutazzim: alias of Mahmud Faruq Brent.

Turki bin Fheid al-Muteiri: alias Fawaz al-Nashmi, one of the trio wanted for the May 29, 2004 attack in which 22 were killed at the Oasis Residential Resorts compounds in Khobar, Saudi Arabia. He and three other terrorists died on June 18, 2004 in a two-hour shootout at a roadblock in Riyadh; 12 other terrorists were detained. Police said the cell was involved in the November 9, 2003 bombing of a foreigners' residential compound in Riyadh and the May 2004 Khobar bombing. Police found a car used by a gunman who shot to death a BBC cameraman and wounded a BBC reporter in Riyadh on June 6, 2004. They also detained a planner of the October 2000 USS *Cole* bombing.

On June 13, 2006, an al Qaeda media outlet said that "Turki bin Fheid al-Muteiri–Fawaz al-Nashmi–may God accept him as a martyr (was) the one chosen by Sheikh Osama bin Laden to be the martyrdom-seeker number 20 in the raid on September 11, 2001.... The operation was brought forward for some circumstances that brother Mohamed Atta explained to the general leadership." He was to have been the fifth UA93 attacker. IntelCenter, a U.S. government contractor, obtained a

54-minute video produced by *al-Sahab* featuring al-Nashmi.

Abu al-Muthana: a spokesman for the Army of Islam in Israel in June 2006.

Abu Al Muthanah: alias of Salah Majied Hessen Bu Jaydar.

Abu Muthanna: a Syrian-based facilitator for foreign recruits joining al Qaeda in Iraq in 2007.

Abu-Muthanna: alias of Salim 'Umar Sa'id Ba-Wazir.

Abdulaziz Bin Fahd Bin Nasser al-Mu'thim: age 24, one of four Saudi terrorists who, on April 22, 1996, confessed to the November 13, 1995 bombing of a building used by U.S. military personnel in Saudi Arabia and said that they had planned other attacks but feared arrest. He claimed to have fought in the Afghan War.

He said he was born in al-Kharq, had a secondary education diploma, was self-employed, and lived in the al-Shifa' district in Riyadh.

Abdel Karim Muti': leader in 1985 of Morocco's Secret Islamic Youth Organization.

Fahd Hamid Mutlaq: alias of Ra'd 'Abd-al-Amir Abbud al-Asadi.

Khalid Badah Raziuq Muttaire: alias Abu Mussab, a Saudi with prior military service from Riyadh who was born in 1400 Hijra and joined al Qaeda in Iraq as a fighter in 2007, bringing his passport and $1,500. The money was taken from him by his Syrian contact, Abu Yasser. His recruitment coordinator was Abu Abd Allah. His phone number was 0096656947601.

Darawi Muhammad Ibrahim 'Abd-al-Muttalib: one of seven terrorists hanged on July 8, 1993 in the appeals prison in Cairo for attacks on tourist buses and installations in the al-Wajh al-Qiblio, Luxor, and Aswan areas, in accordance with the sentence handed down by the Supreme Military Court on April 22, 1993 in Case Number 6.

Muhammad Souleh Faleh Al Muttary: alias Abu Bilal, a Saudi born in 1405 Hijra who joined al Qaeda in Iraq in 2007, bringing 1,400 Saudi riyals. He was deployed to Al Anbar. His phone numbers were 0500510928 and 0503000746.

Muyugi: variant of Mullagy.

'Abdallah Mustafa 'Abdallah al-Muzayni: variant Abd Allah Mustafa Abd Allah Al Muzanie, alias Abu-al-Harith, a Libyan from the eastern shore of Darnah who joined al Qaeda in Iraq on October 4, 2006, contributing $100. His phone number was 00218925782391.

Abdelghani Mzoudi: as of late November 2001, he remained in Hamburg, where German authorities were investigating his involvement in the 9/11 attacks. On July 3, 2002, in an early morning raid, Hamburg police arrested seven Islamic radicals, including Mzoudi, age 29, a United Arab Emirates citizen, who had roomed with 9/11 hijacking leader Mohamed Atta in a Marien Street apartment in August 1999 and had witnessed Atta's last will and testament. One of the suspects, who had worked as an archivist for the state police in Hamburg, fell under suspicion for credit card fraud. Surveillance of him led to the others. The seven were questioned, photographed, and fingerprinted. By the end of the evening, five were back on the streets for lack of evidence. The suspects included Moroccans, Egyptians, Afghans, and a German citizen. The men were aged 28 to 51. They met regularly at the Attawhid bookshop near the al Quds mosque in Hamburg that had been frequented by Atta. They had been overheard saying that they wanted to "give their lives for Islam." They also used "secret knocks" to enter meetings at the bookstore. Mzoudi replaced fugitive Said Bahaji, who left Hamburg shortly before 9/11, as Atta's roommate.

On October 10, 2002, Hamburg police arrested Mzoudi, an electrical engineering student from Marrakech, Morocco, on suspicion of providing logistical support to 9/11 hijack leader Mohammed Atta's al Qaeda cell in Hamburg. He had been questioned frequently in the investigation. Authorities seized a laptop, books, and other materials from his apartment; he had been arrested at the home of friends in Hamburg where he was staying overnight. Police had a witness statement that indicated the Mzoudi and the other members of the Hamburg cell had visited Afghan terrorist training camps in 2000. Mzoudi and Mounir Motassadeq, also from Marrakech, had signed Atta's will. Mzoudi had been briefly held in July with Abderrasak Labied, his roommate, along with five other men who had met in the back room of the Attawhid Islamic bookstore in Hamburg to plan suicide attacks. They were released for lack of evidence. A court ruled that the bookstore could reopen. Mzoudi had shared a Hamburg apartment with Ramzi Binalshibh and Zakariya Essabar, a Moroccan who remained at large. Mzoudi provided money to Essabar to attend a flight school in the United States; Essabar failed to obtain a U.S. visa. Mzoudi was in the wedding video of Said Bahaji, a German Moroccan fugitive who left Hamburg shortly before 9/11. Atta also appears in the video.

On May 9, 2003, German prosecutors charged Mzoudi with membership in a terrorist organization and 3,066 counts of accessory to murder in the 9/11 attacks. On June 6, 2003, the U.S. Treasury Department blocked his assets.

On December 11, 2003, Hamburg Presiding Judge Klaus Ruehle announced that the five-judge court had decided to release Mzoudi after determining that the German federal police had provided information, apparently taken from Ramzi Binalshibh, that Mzoudi had no advance knowledge of the 9/11 plot. The trial would continue. On February 5, 2004, the Hamburg State Court acquitted Mzoudi and freed him for lack of evidence. The prosecution appealed the acquittal two days later.

On May 12, 2005, German prosecutors petitioned a Berlin federal court to retry Mzoudi, age 32. On June 9, 2005, a German appeals court upheld his acquittal. Hamburg's top security official, Udo Nagel, said he was a threat and he would expel him within two weeks. Mzoudi arrived in Agadir, Morocco on June 21, 2005.

N

Abed Nabhan: age 25, a Hamas field commander believed to be responsible for the September 29, 2004 attack in which Palestinian Hamas terrorists fired rockets from the Gaza Strip into Sderot, an Israeli city, killing two Ethiopian immigrant children and wounding ten other people. On October 9, Israeli soldiers shot to death Nabhan and four other terrorists preparing to fire an antitank missile from the Jabalya refugee camp. Israeli authorities believed he also was behind a September 30 attack on an army post in northern Gaza that killed an Israeli soldier and injured two others.

Abdul Nabi: one of two Taliban gunmen on a motorcycle who, on November 15, 2003, shot to death Bettina Goislard, age 29, a French woman working for the UN High Commissioner for Refugees in Ghazni. Two men fired on her vehicle with a pistol. Her Afghan driver sustained gunshot wounds. Goislard had been in Ghazni since June 2002. She had also worked for the UN in Rwanda and Guinea. She was the first foreign UN worker to be killed in Afghanistan since the fall of the Taliban in November 2001. On February 10, 2004, a Kabul court convicted Abdul Nabi and Zia Ahmad of murdering her and sentenced them to death. The duo appealed.

Khalid Abd-al-Nabi: leader of the Aden-Abyan Islamic Army (AAIA) who surrendered to Yemeni authorities in October 2003. He was released from custody and, as of April 2004, was not facing charges for any of his activities.

Nabil: one of the three Egyptian Revolution hijackers of Egyptair flight 648 that had left Athens bound for Cairo on November 23, 1985. He executed two female Israeli passengers and injured two Americans.

Nabil: alias of Rifaat Alwan.

Nabil: a Syrian-based al Qaeda in Iraq travel facilitator in 2007; a person of the same name had those duties in Morocco.

Nabil: alias Abu-'Ubaydah, a Yemeni sent on a suicide mission by al Qaeda in Iraq in 2007. He owned $200 and a passport. His phone number was 00967258909.

Abu Nibil: alias of 'Abdallah Hasan.

Albert Nacache: arrested by French police on May 13, 1981 in connection with the May 9, 1981 firing of shots on Pessah (Passover) at the Syrian Airlines office in central Paris.

Anis Naccache: variant Naqqash, variant Nakkash, one of the five Guards of Islam gunmen who failed in an assassination attempt against Shahpour Bakhtiar, the Shah's last Prime Minister, in Neuilly-sur-Seine, France on July 17, 1980. On March 10, 1982, a Nanterre jury sentenced four of them, including Naccache, to life in prison. His release was demanded on July 31, 1984 by the three Guardsmen of Islam hijackers of an Air France B737 flying from Frankfurt to Paris. He was moved to La Sante maximum security prison on September 22, 1986. On February 2, 1989, he claimed that the French had reneged on an agreement for his release after kidnapers had freed French hostages Marcel Carton, Marcel Fontaine, and Jean-Paul Kauffman on May 5, 1988. The next day, Iran also claimed that France had broken the "gentlemen's agreement" to give amnesty to Naccache. On February 12, 1989, French President Francois Mitterrand publicly stated that France had made no commitment to Iran or anyone else to release Naccache. On April 5, 1989, Naccache, claiming to be the European spokesman of Hizballah, said all Muslims in Europe should use "all legal means" to obtain the banning of Salman Rushdie's *The Satanic Verses*. He began a hunger strike on September 8, 1989. In January 1990, Naccache ended a 19-week hunger strike in which his weight dropped from 164 to 105 pounds. He resumed eating after being assured that he would be released later that year. On July 27, 1990, France pardoned Naccache and four accomplices (Mehdi Nejad-Tabrizi, Mohammed Javad Janab, Fawzi Mohammed al-Sattari, and Selaheddin Mohammed Alkara). They were deported to Tehran that day. Sattari, the group's lone Palestinian, flew on to Baghdad.

Said Nacir: member of the Fatah-Revolutionary Council sentenced in Belgium for the 1980 attack against Jewish children in Antwerp. He was expected to be released circa July 27, 1990, after having served a third of his prison sentence.

Youssef Nada: Egypt-born Italian-Tunisian citizen who lived in Campione d'Italia, Switzerland for decades. He also had residences in Capione d'Italia, Italy; and Alexandria, Egypt. In 2001, the UN Security Council blacklisted the then-69-year-old on suspicion of funding the 9/11 attacks. He and Ahmed Idris Nasreddin had founded the Bank al Taqwa, which was also blacklisted. Acting on a Swiss request, Italian police raided his home, seizing papers and computer disks. He was questioned by Swiss police for six hours. Nada denied meeting bin Laden or dealing with his organization, although he admitted membership in the Egyptian Muslim Brotherhood. As of November 2007, Nada remained on the blacklists of the United States and United Nations.

Luis Alberto Nader: one of six Lebanese suspected of involvement in the March 17, 1992 car bombing at the Israeli Embassy in Buenos Aires that killed 29 and injured 252 and the July 18, 1994 bombing of the Argentine-Israeli facility in Buenos Aires. Three of the detainees expressed pro-Hizballah sentiments, but denied involvement. He was arrested on January 30, 1995 in Paraguay. He had lived with fellow detainee Johnny Moraes Baalbaki in Italy but had temporary residence in Fox do Iguacu. They were charged with drug trafficking, violating immigration law, and illegal possession of weapons. He was believed to be a Brazilian of Lebanese origin who was a contact of the Cali cocaine cartel in Italy and Russia. Argentina requested extradition on February 24, 1995 for stockpiling explosives and combat weapons on an island in the Tigre River delta. They were extradited from Paraguay on July 23, 1995 in connection with the discovery of an arsenal near Buenos Aires. They were released on July 27, 1995 in Argentina.

'Abd-al-Karim al-Nadi: named by Cairo's *Middle East News Agency* on May 16, 1996 as having confessed to the Ethiopians for involvement in the attempted assassination on June 26, 1995 in Ethiopia of Egyptian President Hosni Mubarak. Al-Nadi and two others said they had visited Pakistan, Afghanistan, Saudi Arabia, Yemen, and Sudan.

Ismail Abu Nadi: one of three 15-year-old Palestinian boys who, on April 23, 2002, were shot to death near the Netzarim settlement by Israeli soldiers firing a .50 caliber machine gun. The trio had planned to set off a crude pipe bomb, and were also armed with knives. The trio had competed for top honors at Salahuddin School in Gaza City. They left confessor letters to their families, saying they were seeking to be heroes. Hamas condemned the boys' gesture and forbade adolescent attacks.

Mahmud Nadi: Palestinian driver for the bomber of a disco in Tel Aviv. He was charged with murder in Israel on July 10, 2001.

Hammid Nadim: was found by Israeli authorities on a getaway ship that was to be used by eight Fatah terrorists who attacked the Hotel Savoy in Tel Aviv on March 5, 1975. He said he was born in Nablus, on the occupied West Bank. He claimed that he had been ordered to join the attack squad but refused, staying on board the craft to supervise the operation.

Ibrahim Naeli: variant Nayili, a member of the Libyan intelligence service for whom an arrest warrant was issued on October 30, 1991, in connection with the September 19, 1989 Union des Transports Aeriens (UTA) bombing that killed 171. He had left Brazzaville, Congo, the day of the bombing. He was charged with violations of French law by conspiring to commit murder, destroying property with explosives, and taking part in a terrorist enterprise. Observers expected French Investigating Judge Jean-Louis Bruguiere to issue an arrest warrant following his July 5–18, 1996 visit to Libya. On June 12, 1998, France announced that it would try him, along with five other Libyans, in absentia. On March 10, 1999, a French antiterrorism court imposed life in prison on the six in absentia. If any of the six were to fall into French hands, they would automatically be given a retrial under French law. The prosecutor said the evidence showed that the Libyan officials had organized the attack. France had never formally requested extradition of the six. Muammar Qadhafi had earlier said he would turn the six over to France, but also had said he would consider making the six serve any sentence imposed by a French court in Libyan prison.

Mohammed Naeli: alias Mohammed Naydi.

Abdel Karim Abu Nafa: one of two Palestinian terrorists who, on November 27, 2001, fired assault rifles on shoppers and pedestrians at the main bus station in Afula's main shopping district, killing a young man and woman and badly injuring nine other Israelis. One woman attacked a gunman, but they shot her at point-blank range. Two dozen others suffered minor injuries or

shock. Police trapped the duo in a parking lot and shot them to death. They were from two Palestinian militant groups, the Islamic Jihad and the al-Aqsa Brigade. The duo had made a videotape in advance, saying that the attack was to avenge the deaths of Palestinian militants killed by Israel. Mustafa Abu Srieh of Islamic Jihad said "we hope our people will continue in the path of holy war." The other terrorist was Abdel Karim Abu Nafa, age 20, a Palestinian policeman and Fatah activist. The terrorists had stolen a white Subaru sedan with yellow Israeli license plates and drove directly to the bus station.

Radwin al Nafati: alias Abu-'Abdallah, a Tunisian born in 1982 who joined al Qaeda in Iraq in 2007. His home phone number was 0021671724327. He contributed 4700 Euros, $560 and 826 lira, and left a computer with Abu-Muhammad al-Muharib and $5,275 security for Abu-Shayma' in Lebanon. He also brought a passport, ID, driver's license, and student ID. He knew coordinator Abu-Shayma' in Lebanon through a friend in Turkey. He arrived in Syria via Germany and Turkey. The student offered to be a martyr. He said he had studied Russian and mechanics.

Ahmad Mahmud Muhammad Nafi': a member of an Egyptian extremist group who was arrested at Jeddah Airport in Saudi Arabia on January 5, 1993 and handed over to Mahmud Hajjaj, an EgyptAir security officer. Although handcuffed, he bit the officer on the shoulder, causing a deep gash, in an escape attempt. He was deported to Egypt for interrogation in connection with previous charges against him. He had arrived in Saudi Arabia on the pretext of performing a minor pilgrimage. He was born in Damanhur in 1959 and worked as a freelance accountant. Entry and exit visa stamps to Pakistan and Sudan were found in his passport.

Basheer Nafi: a Palestinian, age 43, arrested on June 27, 1996 in Herndon, Virginia and deported to London on July 1 on charges of violating his immigration status. He was believed to be a leader of Islamic Jihad. He worked as a researcher and editor at the International Institute of Islamic Thought (IIIT) in Herndon. His Irish wife, Imelda Ryan, said that he was going to leave the United States permanently anyway, having resigned from the IIIT and booked a flight to London. Nafi had last entered the United States in August 1994. Nafi admitted knowing Fathi Shiqaqi, the assassinated leader of Islamic Jihad. The two attended a university in Cairo in the 1970s. Nafi had earlier worked for the Tampa-based World and Islam Studies Enterprise, whose former administrator, Ramadan Abdullah Shallah, 37, succeeded Shiqaqi as the Islamic Jihad leader.

Nourredine Nafia: a captured Moroccan extremist who told Italian investigators that in 1998 in Turkey, Libyans provided expertise about communications to al Qaeda cells.

Abdullmer Nagh: alias of one of three terrorists allegedly working for Iraqi intelligence whom the Saudi Embassy in Thailand said in September 1991 had made threats against senior diplomats.

Mohammed Naguid: a 21-year-old Palestinian working in Kuwait who was one of three Abdel Nasser Movement (the Palestine Revolution Movement also took credit) hijackers of an Egyptian B737 flying from Cairo to Luxor on August 23, 1976. They demanded the release of five would-be assassins from Egyptian jails. Commandos boarded the plane and overpowered and wounded all three hijackers. The trio said they received their directions in Libya, which promised $250,000 to divert the plane to Libya. On September 18, 1976, they were fined and sentenced to hard labor for life but were acquitted of charges of collusion with Libya.

Mohammed Faez Nahaal: an unemployed Palestinian who, on March 21, 1993, tried to stab a female Israeli soldier with a kitchen knife in Afula. He was seized by other soldiers. He said he was "sick of life" and hoped to be killed.

Ahmad 'Umar Bin-Sha'b al-Nahdi: alias Abu-Suhayb, a Yemeni from Al-Mukalla who was born in 1981 and joined al Qaeda in Iraq as a combatant on July 21, 2007, contributing $500 and bringing his passport and ID. His recruitment coordinator was 'Abd-al-Qadidr. His home phone number was 00967053851211; colleague 'Abdallah Sa'id's was 0097777385615.

Bassam Abdullah Bin Bushar Al-Nahdi: born in Saudi Arabia in 1976, the Yemeni was believed, by the FBI, on February 11, 2002, to be planning a terrorist attack in the United States or on U.S. interests in Yemen.

Jamal al-Nahdi: Yemeni officials said, on December 23, 1992, that he had planned the bombings on December 29, 1992 of the Gold Mohur Hotel in Aden and the Aden Movenpick Hotel, both of which house U.S. Marines. London's *al-Sharq al-Awsat* said he confessed that he intended to blow up a U.S. Navy Galaxy aircraft parked at Aden airport.

Awen Muhammad Raff Allah Nahidd: alias Abu Assem, a Libyan high school student from Dernah who was born in 1988 and joined al Qaeda in Iraq as a martyr on 25th Rabia al Thani (circa 2007), bringing his passport. His recruitment coordinator was Basset Alsha'ari. He came from Libya to Egypt and on to Syria, bringing 350 lira and his passport. His home phone number was 0021881928813; his brother's was 00218926008701.

Mohammed Ali Nail: one of four Libyans arrested on March 22, 1976 in Tunisia on charges of trying to kidnap or assassinate President Habib Bourguiba or Premier Hedi Nouira, Bourguiba's designated successor, in Tunis. He was sentenced to death on April 23, 1976 by the Tunisian state security court.

Taha Naimi: one of three Kurdish sympathizers who hijacked an Iraqi Airways B737 flying from Mosul to Baghdad on March 1, 1975. They demanded $5 million and the release of 85 political prisoners. During the flight, an Iraqi security officer engaged in a shootout with the hijackers, leaving two passengers dead and ten others, including a hijacker, wounded. The plane landed in Tehran, Iran, where the hijackers surrendered. Naimi was executed by an Iranian firing squad on April 7, 1975.

Jihad Abu-al-Naja: a Palestinian Islamic Jihad member whose trial for setting off a bomb that killed seven people in Patras, Greece on April 19, 1991 began on May 8, 1992 in a courtroom within the Kordhallos prison in Piraeus. He was acquitted by an Athens appeals court on July 6, 1992.

Yusuf Sulayman Najah: release from an Israeli jail was demanded on June 27, 1976 by the Popular Front for the Liberation of Palestine hijackers of Air France 139, an A300 Aerospatiale Airbus flying from Tel Aviv to Paris and ultimately diverted to Entebbe.

Talal Muhammad al-Najashi: alias Abu-al-Zubayr, a Saudi student at a teachers' school in Riyadh who was born in 1987 and joined al Qaeda in Iraq as a suicide bomber on May 12, 2007, bringing his passport. His recruitment coordinator was Abu-Salmah. He flew directly to Damascus, spending four days there. A smuggler took his $500 and 22,000 liras. His phone number was 0096612440691; his brother's was 009665555486115; 'Abd-al-'Aziz al-Shahrani's was 00966567054471. He had experience as an urban warfare trainer and in boxing.

'Abadi al-Najdi: alias of 'Abd-al-Rahman Bin-'Ali Bin-Muhammad al-'Ashiri.

Abdur Rahman Najdi: variant Abu Abdel-Rahman Najdi, a Saudi-born al Qaeda terrorist sought by the United States who, in an audiotape aired on August 18, 2003 on Pakistan's *al-Arabiya* television, called on Muslims to join the fight in Iraq against the U.S.-led occupation and

to overthrow the Saudi royal family, whom he termed U.S. puppets. He released another audio on September 7, 2003.

Abu Abdel-Rahman Najdi: variant of Abdur Rahman Najdi.

Abu-'Amir al-Tamimi al-Najdi: alias of 'Abd-al-'Aziz Hamad–'Abd-al-'Aziz al-Majid.

Abu-'Ammar al-Najdi: alias of 'Abd-al-Rahman Muhammad al-Jaryi.

Abu Baher al Najdi: variant of Abu-Bahr al-Najdi.

Abu-Bahr al-Najdi: alias of 'Abdallah Ibrahim al-'Arifi.

Miqdam al-Najdi: variant Mqdam al Njdi, alias of Fahd 'Abd-al-'Aziz 'Abdallah al-'Ajlan.

Qutaybah al-Najdi: the 9/11 Commission said that he was initially scheduled to be a 9/11 hijacker, but backed out after being stopped and briefly questioned by Bahrain Airport security officers.

Abu Ammer al Tammimi al Najdy: variant of Abu-'Amir al-Tamimi al-Najdi.

Abu Naji: alias of Muhamad Shariff.

Yusif Naji: alias Abu-Hamzah, variant Abu Hammza, a Yemeni mechanical automotive engineer who joined al Qaeda in Iraq in 2007 to become a suicide bomber. He left his passport, $200, and 1,000 lira in Syria. His recruitment coordinator was Abu-'\'Azzam, variant Abi Azzam. His phone number was 777877630.

Ahmad Ibrahim al-Najjar: an Egyptian Islamic Jihad/al Qaeda member who was arrested in Albania on June 28, 1998 and sent to Egypt. He had material indicating a planned bombing of the U.S. Embassy in Tirana. He had worked in the

Tirana branch of the Kuwaiti Society for the Revival of Islamic Heritage. He was under a death sentence in Egypt for his role in the attack on Cairo's Khan el Khalil bazaar.

Husayn Ja'far Sadiq al-Najjar: on June 26, 1996, the Bahrain State Security Court sentenced him to 10 years for the February 11, 1996 bombing of the Diplomat Hotel in Manama, the January 17, 1996 bombing of the Le Royal Meridien Hotel, and the bombing of two branches of the Bahrain Corporation for International Shipping and Trade located in the Diplomatic Quarter.

Mazen A. al-Najjar: In 1997, the U.S. Justice Department and the Immigration and Naturalization Service (INS) said that the 43-year-old former professor of Arabic at the University of South Florida in Tampa had ties to the Syria-based Palestinian Islamic Jihad (PIJ). The Palestinian, born in Gaza and raised in Saudi Arabia, was linked to two groups that laundered PIJ money. One was the now-defunct World and Islam Studies Enterprise, based in Tampa, which employed Ramadan Abdullah Shallah, who became the PIJ leader in 1995. He was ordered deported when his visa expired in 1997. He was jailed after the INS presented secret evidence under the 1996 Anti-Terrorism and Effective Death Penalty Act.

U.S. District Judge Joan Lenard ruled in Miami in May 2000 that al-Najjar must be told enough about the evidence to have a fair chance of responding. If freed, he and his wife, Fedaa, faced deportation hearings. Their three daughters were U.S. citizens. On December 12, 2000, Attorney General Janet Reno blocked the release of al-Najjar, who had been jailed for more than three years without criminal charges on secret evidence. Reno said she would review the evidence. The previous week, Immigration Judge R. Kevin McHugh ordered al-Najjar freed on $8,000 bond. Reno released al-Najjar on December 15, 2000. Deportation hearings were set for January 9, 2001. He sought political asylum as a stateless Palestinian. The INS wanted to send him to the United Arab Emirates, where he resided for two years before entering the United States in 1981.

Mohammed Youssef el Najjar: alias Abu Youssef. In 1973, Black September detainee Abu Daoud said that he had been a key planner of the November 28, 1971 assassination of Jordanian Prime Minister Wasfi Tell in Cairo. At the time, Najjar was a member of the Palestine Liberation Organization's political department and chairman of the Higher Committee for Palestinian Affairs in Lebanon. He apparently died on April 10, 1973 in an Israeli raid on Black September facilities in Beirut.

'Abd-al-Karim al Naji: alias of Yasin, an Egyptian Islamic Group terrorist who was arrested one day after the failed June 26, 1995 assassination attempt against Egyptian President Hosni Mubarak in Addis Ababa, Ethiopia.

Ahmed Naji: an Egyptian Islamic Jihad member who fled Albania but was arrested by Italian police in early October 1998. He reportedly had planned the failed attack on the U.S. Embassy in Tirana.

Eyad Ismail Najim: variant of Eyad Mahmoud Ismoil Najim.

Eyad Mahmoud Ismoil Najim: variant Eyad Ismail Najim, variant Iyad Mahmud Isma'il Najm, a Kuwaiti-born Palestinian who carried a Jordanian passport who was arrested in Jordan on August 1, 1995. He was flown to the United States the next day. He had gone to school in Kuwait with Ramzi Ahmad Yusuf. On August 3, 1995, he was charged in a New York federal court with planning and executing the World Trade Center bombing. He was held without bail for a hearing on August 16. He faced a life sentence without parole. Investigators said he was with Yusuf when he gassed up the bomb vehicle and drove the Ryder van into a garage beneath the towers. He entered the United States on a student visa in 1989. He last reported to the Immigration and Naturalization Service in

1990, when he was granted a student work permit. His mother claimed he had studied languages and computer science at a Kansas university, then moved to Dallas. He had been charged in a sealed indictment in September 1994.

'Ali Samih Najm: alias of Joseph Salim Abdallah, deputy head of the Saiqa security office in al-Hamra' in Beirut. The Lebanese was arrested on April 15, 1979 upon his arrival at Cairo airport from Beirut when police discovered that his suitcase contained explosives. The Egyptians said Syrian intelligence had sent him to blow up the Sheraton Hotel, in offices in At-Tahrir Square, and anywhere he chose. The Egyptians said he provided information on Cuban supervision of Saiqa training and planning. Police said he was trained by Abu Salim and his explosives were prepared by Ahmad al-Hallaq. His release was demanded by terrorists who took over the Egyptian Embassy in Ankara on July 13, 1979.

Iyad Mahmud Isma'il Najm: variant of Eyad Mahmoud Ismoil Najim.

Nabil Najm: one of 12 Popular Front for the Liberation of Palestine members arrested by Jordanian security forces on October 4, 1989 for questioning about the smuggling of explosives and personnel into Jordan to fire rockets across the cease-fire line.

Samir Hassan Najmeddin: head of the SAS import–export company that was ordered shut down in August 1987 by Poland after the United States said it was financing Palestinian terrorism. He left the country on January 14, 1988. No expulsion had been ordered, but Poland did not renew his visa.

Abu Najr: alias of Faysal.

Abu-Najr: alias of Fysal.

Abdel Hadi Nakaa: one of two Black September members who were seriously injured when their explosives-laden car blew up on a Rome street on June 17, 1973. He was a Syrian. It was believed they were driving their booby-trapped car toward their next mission, which may have been against the transit camp for Soviet Jewish émigrés in Austria. Some reports claim that Mossad arranged for the bombs' premature detonation.

Anis Nakkash: leader of a pro-Khomeini assassination squad that killed two in a failed assassination attempt against former Iranian Prime Minister Shapur Bakhtiar in July 1980. On February 3, 1986, the Committee of Solidarity with Arab and Middle East Political Prisoners who bombed the Claridge shopping arcade off the Champs-Elysees in Paris demanded his release.

Omar Nakhcha: age 24, a Moroccan who was one of 18 suspected radical Islamists charged on October 23, 2007 by Spanish National Court Judge Baltasar Garzon with belonging to a terrorist organization and 22 radicals with collaboration with it in sending Islamist fighters to Iraq "so they might join in terrorist activity sponsored and directed by al-Qaeda." Nakhcha was also charged with helping some of the March 11, 2004 Madrid train bombers to escape from justice.

Jum'ah Zayd al-Nakhlah: one of the April 5, 1988 hijackers of Kuwait Airlines flight 422, a B747 flying from Bangkok to Kuwait that was diverted to Mashhad, Iran. He had arrived in Bangkok on March 23, 1988 with a forged Bahraini passport.

Mohamed Suleiman Nalfi: a Sudanese who was arrested on March 22, 2001 by the FBI when he was lured from his home with a false job offer in Amsterdam. He was detained by the Bureau when he changed planes. He was indicted in New York for having links to bin Laden and charged in federal court with forming and leading a Sudanese jihad group, following bin Laden's al Qaeda organization, and helping bin Laden start an investment business in Sudan. He was added to the list of 22 defendants in the bin Laden conspiracy, which included the August 7, 1998 bombings of the U.S. embassies in Kenya and Tanzania.

On January 31, 2003, Nalfi, age 40, admitted he worked for bin Laden in Sudan in the early 1990s and pleaded guilty to conspiring to destroy national defense materials, which carries a maximum 10-year sentence. He said he created a jihad group in Sudan in 1989 and helped to build businesses there that aided al Qaeda, which used the firms as fronts to procure explosives, chemicals, and weapons. In 1990, Nalfi and others traveled to Egypt in a camel caravan to establish an al Qaeda weapons smuggling route. Nalfi told U.S. District Judge Kevin Thomas Duffy in New York that, in 1992, he attended a meeting in which al Qaeda leaders discussed how to oust U.S. and UN forces from Somalia and Saudi Arabia. Nalfi had been arrested in 2000 in a conspiracy case involving the 1998 bombings of the U.S. embassies in Tanzania and Kenya. The government agreed to a lesser charge.

Nalini: a Sri Lankan Tamil woman suspected of involvement in the murder of Rajiv Gandhi, India's former prime minister, on May 22, 1991. She was arrested on June 14, 1991 on a State Transport Corporation bus going between Villupuram and Madras during the night. She was held under the Terrorists and Disruptive Activities Act. She was remanded to police custody for 28 days.

Mohammed K. A. al-Namer: alias of Muhsin Musa Matwalli Atwah.

Said Namouh: age 34, arrested by Canadian authorities in Quebec on September 12, 2007. They charged him with conspiracy. The member of the Global Islamic Media Front, an Internet propaganda arm of al Qaeda, was planning to detonate a car bomb.

Nizar Naouar: variant of Nizar bin Mohammed Nawar.

Walid Naouar: brother of Nizar bin Mohammed Nawar, he was arrested by French police on November 5, 2002 in connection with Nizar's involvement as one of the truck bombers who on April 11, 2002 killed 19 people in an explosion at a synagogue in Djerba, Tunisia.

Naoufel: a Moroccan in Spain believed to be involved in the 2003 suicide bombings in Casablanca, Morocco, that killed 45 people. He was in contact with several individuals arrested in October 2003 on suspected terrorism planning.

'Abd al-Rahim 'Ali Isma'il 'Ali Naqi: sentenced to death by Kuwait on June 6, 1987 for the January 19, 1987 sabotage of Kuwaiti oilfields. He remained at large. On June 7, 1987, the Prophet Muhammad's Forces in Kuwait told a Western news agency that they would kill Kuwaiti leaders if the emirate carried out death sentences on six members of its group.

Khalid 'Abd al-Majid 'Abd al-Nabi 'Ali Naqi: sentenced to two years and fined 300 dinars by Kuwait, on June 6, 1987, for the January 19, 1987 sabotage of Kuwaiti oilfields.

Naqibullah: an Afghan judge who hid the two organizers of the bombing that killed a dozen people, including four Americans working for DynCorp, on August 29, 2004. He was arrested in late December 2004. He was head of a preliminary court in the Panjshir Valley.

Anis Naqqash: alias Abu Mazem, Palestinian leader of the five Guards of Islam gunmen who failed in an assassination attempt against Shahpour Bakhtiar, the Shah's last Prime Minister, in Neuilly-sur-Seine, France on July 17, 1980. He was wounded in the attack.

Muhammad Ayn-al-Nas: age 26, alias Abu-Mus'ab, a Moroccan listed in the captured al Qaeda in Iraq personnel documents in the fall of 2007. He flew from Casablanca to Turkey and to Damascus, then showed up at an Iraqi border town on January 31, 2007. The university economics student said he wanted to be a martyr and had experience as a driver. He was born on April 7, 1984. His phone number in Casablanca was 0021260262674. He contributed 100 euros, 1,100 lira, and 15 Turkish lira. He brought a passport and ID. His coordinator in Afghanistan was 'Abd-al-Salam; in Damascus, Zayd al-Maghrabi. His travel facilitator in Syria was Abu-'Uthman. He brought with him 200 euros and $50.

Mustafa Setmariam Nasar: variant Mustafa Sitmaryan Nassar, alias Abu Musab al-Suri, Umar Abd al-Hakim, a Spanish citizen via marriage who might also have Syrian citizenship and who was a leading al-Qaeda ideologue. While a member of the Syrian Muslim Brotherhood, he fled Syria in the 1980s, roaming through the Middle East and North Africa, where he became associated with the Algeria Islamic Group.

He claims to have been born on October 26, 1958 in Aleppo, Syria.

He settled in Madrid in 1987 and married a Spaniard, obtaining Spanish citizenship. In Spain, he wrote inflammatory essays under the pen name Umar Abd al-Hakim. In 1995, he moved to the UK, serving as a European contact for al Qaeda. He roamed throughout Europe and Afghanistan through the late 1990s. He moved his family to Afghanistan in 1998. He was a trainer at the Derunta and al-Bhuraba terrorist camps in Afghanistan, working closely with Midhat Mursi al-Sayid 'Umar, alias Abu Khabab al-Masri, training extremists in poisons and chemicals. Following the 9/11 attacks, he swore loyalty to Osama bin Laden as an al Qaeda member. The United States announced a $5 million reward for his arrest. He was indicted in Spain in September 2003 for terrorist activities of al-Qaeda, and was linked to Imad Yarkas, a Syrian-born Spaniard who ran the group's Spanish cell. He was indicted in Spain for al Qaeda membership and was suspected of having a role in the March 11, 2004 Madrid train bombings. British authorities wanted to question him in connection with the multiple bombings of the London subway system on July 7, 2005.

He was captured by Pakistani forces in a Quetta shop that serves as an office of an Islamic charity tied to a radical group, near the Afghan border, on November 4, 2005. He was transferred to Syrian custody. Nasar had written a 1,600 page tome on how to attack Islam's enemies. He had traveled to Sudan, Afghanistan, Iran, Iraq, Syria, and two European capitals. *UPI* reported on October 19, 2006 that he was in U.S. custody. There had been a $5 million bounty for him.

Balik Nasban: a Lebanese named by Cypriot authorities on August 6, 1986 as having been involved in the August 3, 1986 attack by rockets, machine guns, and mortars at the British air base at Akrotiri by the Unified Nasirite Organization. A car in which spent shells were found had been rented by him.

Abdul Raouf Naseeb: a leading al Qaeda member who was arrested with more than a dozen other militants on March 3, 2004 in Yemen in a nighttime raid in the mountains of Abyan province, 292 miles south of Sanaa. He was wanted for planning the April 2003 prison break of ten terrorists detained in connection with the bombing of the USS *Cole* in October 2000.

Naseer: He was shot to death on September 12, 2003 in a gunfight in central Bombay. He and another man were fleeing in a car in which were hidden detonators, explosives, and guns. He was believed to be the mastermind of two taxi bombs that went off on August 25, 2003 in Bombay, killing 53 people and injuring another 160.

Sajjad Naseer: variant of Sajjad Nasser.

Nagi Nashal: age 53, a Yemeni-born naturalized U.S. citizen who runs a Manhattan newsstand, who, on May 21, 2005 was arrested on charges of threatening to blow up the *New York Post*'s offices for publishing photographs of Saddam Hussein in his underwear. He was denied bail.

Magdy Mahmoud Nashar: a biochemist who had studied at North Carolina State University for a semester in 2000. He was arrested on July

15, 2005 by police in Cairo, Egypt. He allegedly helped rent the July 7, 2005 London subway terrorists' Leeds townhouse. He was freed on August 9 after being in custody for questioning for three weeks. He said he knew bombers Germaine Lindsay and Hasib Hussain casually.

Abdullah Nasheri: age 22, a suspected Islamic extremist from Sanaa, Yemen, on July 27, 1998 shot to death three Roman Catholic medical nuns in Hodeidah, 140 miles west of Sanaa. They were on their way from their home to work as nurses at a charity organization affiliated with an international order founded by the late Mother Teresa when the killer fired on them with a Kalashnikov assault rifle. The killer confessed and said he would go to heaven. He said he killed the nurses because they were "preaching Christianity." The gunman said he had fought in Bosnia as a volunteer in 1992. He had lived there since 1992, and had acquired Bosnian nationality. He married a Bosnian woman.

Sheikh Abd al-Rahim al-Nashiri: alias Abu Asim al Makki, alias Sheik Mohammed Omar al Harazi, who worked with Walid bin Attash in planning the October 12, 2000 bombing in Yemen of the USS *Cole*. He was believed to have given the order to three Saudi members of al Qaeda who were planning to attack U.S. and British warships in the Strait of Gibraltar in May 2002. He was mentioned by some of the defendants as having obtained funds for the October 6, 2002 al Qaeda bombing of the *Limburg*, a French supertanker, in the Arabian Sea five miles off the coast of Yemen. The news media reported that the Mecca-born Nashiri was arrested in November 2002. He had fought against the Russians in Afghanistan. He spent time in Yemen, where he owned Al Mur Honey, a terrorist money laundry. He was detained in Saudi Arabia in 1998 and deported the next year. He may have trained terrorists for the August 7, 1998 bombings of the U.S. embassies in Tanzania and Kenya. On July 7, 2004, a Yemeni court charged him and five other Yemenis in the USS *Cole* bombing. On September 29,

2004, Yemeni Judge Najib al-Qaderi sentenced him to death.

On September 6, 2006, President George W. Bush announced that the last 14 detainees would be transferred from secret foreign prisons to the military detention facility at Guantánamo Bay. The group was identified as Abu Zubaydah, Khalid Sheikh Mohammed, Ramzi Binalshibh, Mustafa Ahmad al-Hawsawi, Hambali, Majid Khan, Lillie, Ali Abd al-Aziz Ali, Ahmed Khalfan Ghailani, Abd al-Rahim al-Nashiri, Abu Faraj al-Libi, Zubair, Walid bin Attash, and Gouled Hassan Dourad.

On March 14, 2007, al-Nashiri told the military Combatant Status Review Tribunal in Guantánamo that he had been coerced into making false confessions about the *Cole* bombing and the August 7, 1998 attacks on the U.S. embassies in Kenya and Tanzania. He had been sentenced in absentia to death in Yemen for his role in the *Cole* case. He said that he was merely involved in a fishing business with the *Cole* bombers. He claimed to have become a millionaire at age 19 and to have met with bin Laden several times in Afghanistan.

Fawaz al-Nashmi: alias of Turki bin Fheid al-Muteiri.

Abdu Nashri: an operational coordinator listed by U.S. Central Command on January 8, 2002 as being at large.

Antoinette Nasif: a Palestinian housewife carrying a Lebanese passport who was arrested on September 17, 1986 by Greek police while she was carrying 248 rounds of automatic weapon ammunition in a secret compartment as she was boarding Cyprus Airways flight 337 for Larnaca and Damascus, which included as a passenger Cypriot President Spiros Kiprianou. She had arrived at Ellinikon Airport on a Scandinavian Airlines flight from New York via Copenhagen. She claimed she was to board a ship for Lebanon from Larnaca. She said she did not know that it was illegal to import ammunition into Greece.

Ilyas Nasif: signature used by one of the Palestinian gunmen who, on September 26, 1986, signed a statement asking their comrades not to seize hostages to obtain their release. He had been sentenced to life in prison in Cyprus in February 1986 in connection with the takeover of an Israeli-owned yacht, the *First*, taking two Israeli hostages after killing a woman in the initial assault in Cyprus on September 25, 1985. After nine hours of negotiations, the terrorists killed the hostages and surrendered. Fatah Force 17 claimed credit.

'Abd al-Husayn Karam Dawish Nasir: member of a cell in Kuwait that set two bombs that exploded on July 10, 1989 in two streets leading to the Great Mosque in Mecca, killing a Pakistani and injuring 16 of the 1.5 million pilgrims from 100 countries attending the hajj.

'Abd al-Karim Husayn Muhammad al-Nasir: variant Abdelkarim Hussein Mohamed al-Nasser, Saudi, leader of Saudi Hizballah indicted in the Eastern District of Virginia for the June 25, 1996 bombing of the Khobar Towers military housing complex in Dhahran, Saudi Arabia. The U.S. Department of State's Rewards for Justice Program offers $5 million for his apprehension. He is wanted for conspiracy to kill U.S. nationals; conspiracy to murder U.S. employees; conspiracy to use weapons of mass destruction against U.S. nationals; conspiracy to destroy U.S. property; conspiracy to attack national defense utilities; bombing resulting in death; use of weapons of mass destruction against U.S. nationals; murder of federal employees; and attempted murder of federal employees. He was born in Al Ihsa, Saudi Arabia. He is five feet eight inches tall and weighs 170 pounds. He was born circa 1942–1952. The Rewards for Justice Program offers $5 million for his apprehension.

Abu-Nasir: alias of Ibrahim.

Faysayl Falih al'Sahim al-Nasir: sentenced to seven years of hard labor by Kuwait on June 6, 1987 for the January 19, 1987 sabotage of Kuwaiti oilfields.

Mahmud Abd an'Nasir: his release from an Israeli jail was demanded on June 27, 1976 by the Popular Front for the Liberation of Palestine hijackers of Air France flight 139, an A300 flying from Tel Aviv to Paris and ultimately diverted to Entebbe.

Sa'id Nasir: a Palestinian arrested circa 1981 by Belgium for an attack on Jewish school children in Antwerp in which a French youth was killed. Nasir had been serving a life sentence. His release was demanded during the shipjacking of the *Silko* that began on November 8, 1987 in the Mediterranean. He was released in January 1991.

Sami Nasir: a Palestinian with a Jordanian passport who was arrested by Larnaca Airport security personnel on December 17, 1985 trying to smuggle arms aboard a Swissair plane scheduled to depart for Amman. His hand luggage contained three hand grenades, two pistols, two magazines, a silencer, and 90 rounds of ammunition. Police believe he intended to hijack the plane with three others who did not board. His sister's apartment contained five grenades and two silencers. On January 15, 1986, he was sentenced to six years for arms possession at the airport. He was also sentenced to five years for the arms found at his sister's apartment. On July 31, 1986, he was quietly deported. Some sources indicated that he had been exchanged for two Cypriot students—Panayiotis Tirkas and Tavros Yiannaki—held by a Muslim group in Beirut. Cypriot authorities said Nasir had a heart ailment.

Sharif Mutlaq Nasir: acquitted by the Kuwaiti State Security Court in 1984 in connection with the December 12, 1983 truck bombing of the administrative building of the U.S. Embassy in Kuwait, killing four people and injuring 59.

Tawfiq Nasir: on December 30, 1994, Judge Nasri Lahhud, the Lebanese government's representative in the military court, issued charges against the Lebanese citizen on charges of committing terrorist acts in accordance with Articles 5 and 6 of law No. 11 in connection with the December 21, 1994 incident when a booby-trapped Volkswagen van exploded in the Sfayr area near the al-Umara' bakery and al-Inma' Consumers Cooperative in the Bir Abed district of Beirut's Shi'ite Muslim suburb, killing three and injuring 16 others.

William Nasir: release from an Israeli jail was demanded on June 27, 1976 by the Popular Front for the Liberation of Palestine hijackers of Air France flight 139, an A300 flying from Tel Aviv to Paris and ultimately diverted to Entebbe.

Yusuf abu-Nasir: alias of Mohammed Ahmad Hasan Abu Nasser.

Yusuf Hisham al-Nasir: variant Nisir. On November 13, 1985, Italian authorities issued an arrest warrant for the Palestine Liberation Front member in connection with the hijacking of the Italian cruise ship *Achille Lauro* on October 7, 1985. The hijackers killed Leon Klinghoffer, age 69, an American confined to a wheelchair, and dumped the body overboard. The hijacking ended in Egypt. On August 1, 1986, al-Nasir was arrested in Viechtach, West Germany. He had been sentenced in absentia to six years and six months for providing weapons to the hijackers. On May 24, 1987, a Genoa appeals court upheld the conviction.

Hassan Mustafa Osama Nasr: The Italian media claimed that he was whisked off the streets of Milan and flown to Cairo on February 17, 2003. As of mid-December 2006, he was in prison in Egypt.

Mehidi Ben Nasr: leader of a Milan-based network that was wrapped up on November 6, 2007 in coordinated raids in Italy, France, Portugal, and the United Kingdom that netted 17 Algerians and Tunisians suspected of terrorist ties in Salafist jihadi militant cells that were recruiting would-be suicide bombers for Iraq and Afghanistan. Milan prosecutors ordered the raids in Milan, Bergamo, Verese, and Reggio Emilia. Police found poisons, remote detonators, and manuals. The leaders were identified as Dridi Sabri, Mehidi Ben Nasr and Imed Ben Zarkaoui, all operating in Italy. Three suspects remained at large. Police said the investigation began in 2003. The detainees were charged with illegal immigration, falsifying ID documents, and helping to hide people sought for terrorist activity.

Mohammed Mahmoud Nasr: a 28-year-old Palestinian suicide bomber who, on August 12, 2001, ran into a coffee shop on Wall Street in Kiryat Motzkin, a suburb of Haifa, Israel and set off a belt of explosives wrapped around his torso, killing himself and injuring 15 others, one critically. He ran up to a waitress and pulled up his yellow shirt, saying "Do you know what I have here?" The Islamic Jihad terrorist then yelled "Allahu Akhbar!" and detonated the bomb. Restaurant owner Aaron Roseman said he had enough time to throw a chair at the terrorist before ducking.

Sayed Seif el-Nasr: would-be hijacker of an Egyptian Airlines Antonov 24 flying between Cairo and Luxor on September 16, 1970. He wanted to go to Saudi Arabia. He was disarmed by a security officer. El-Nasr was sentenced to ten years in prison.

Hadi Nasrallah: 18-year-old son of Hizballah secretary general Said Hassan Nasrallah was killed in a gun battle on September 12, 1997 with Israeli troops in the Jabal al-Rafei area of southern Lebanon. The Hizballah leader declared his son's death a victory over Israel.

Said Hasan Nasrallah: in September 1997, he was the Secretary General of Hizballah.

Abdul-Hafiz Mohammed Nassar: a Jordanian active in Palestinian affairs who was sentenced to five years in prison after pleading guilty to one count of conspiring to illegally possess and transport explosives across state lines. He had placed explosives and electronic gear in a storage locker in Alexandria, Virginia. Reporters suggested that the material had been intended for the assassination of President Ronald Reagan and Israeli Prime Minister Menachem Begin during the latter's visit to the White House in September 1981. The explosives were placed in the locker the day before Begin arrived. He was indicted by a grand jury on firearms and conspiracy charges on October 19, 1982. He was held in a Washington, DC jail in lieu of $750,000 bond. He had made four trips to Beirut in the previous 19 months and may have been planning to smuggle the explosives into Lebanon.

Ibrahim Nassar: a member of the Hamas military wing who, on September 13, 1995, was killed and a woman, wounded, when a bomb they were preparing exploded in the al-Shaja'iyah neighborhood of Gaza.

Mustafa Sitmaryan Nassar: variant of Mustafa Setmariam Nasar.

William Nassar: early member of Fatah whose release from an Israeli prison was demanded during the Black September hijacking on May 8, 1972 of Sabena Airlines flight 517, a B707 flying the Vienna-Athens-Tel Aviv route over Zagreb by two male and two female Black September Organization members.

Yassin Nassari: age 27, husband of Bouchra el-Hor, a young Dutch Moroccan mother from Zutphen. They were detained in May 2006 at Luton Airport outside London. Police found suspicious files in his laptop computer, such as instructions for making explosives and a rocket launcher. When police searched their home, they found *A Training Schedule for Committing Jihad.* They found a letter by el-Hor in which she offered herself and their six-month-old son as martyrs. She was charged with failing to disclose

information to prevent a terrorist attack. Nassari was charged with possessing documents for terrorism. Their trial was set for May 23, 2007 in London. The duo had lived in the United Kingdom and traveled often to the Netherlands.

Abdelkarim Hussein Mohamed al-Nasser: variant of 'Abd al-Karim Husayn Muhammad al-Nasir.

El Sayyid A. Nasser: variant of El Sayyid A. Nosair.

Gamal Shawki Abdel Nasser: variant of Khaled Abdel Nasser.

Khaled Abdel Nasser: variant Gamal Shawki Abdel Nasser, eldest son of the late Egyptian President Gamal Abdel Nasser. On February 18, 1988, Egyptian prosecutor Mohammed Guindi asked for the death sentence in absentia for him on charges of murder and conspiracy by the Egypt's Revolution group, which had attacked Israeli and U.S. diplomats. In 1984, the group shot and wounded an Israeli security guard in Cairo. In 1985, it assassinated an Israeli administrative attaché. In 1986, it killed a young woman working at the Israeli Embassy. In May 1987, gunmen fired on the car of three U.S. diplomats. On February 20, 1988, Egypt requested extradition from Yugoslavia. On February 21, 1988, Nasser said he would voluntarily return from self-exile to face the charges. On January 3, 1989, he was granted bail after returning to Egypt to stand trial. Defense lawyers claimed that the shootings were justified.

Mohammed Ahmad Hasan Abu Nasser: alias Yusuf abu-Nasir, a former security prisoner and member of the Popular Front for the Liberation of Palestine (PFLP). He was identified by the victim as one of the three Palestinians who kidnapped U.S. citizen Chris George, director of the Save the Children Fund in Gaza, on June 22, 1989. On June 28, 1989, Israeli soldiers shot Nasserdead after he fired a pistol at soldiers arresting him. During the evening he had hijacked a taxi at gunpoint.

He was wanted for two other terrorist attacks and was described as mentally unstable. In the early 1970s, he was jailed for killing a woman whom he suspected of collaborating with Israel, and for carrying out attacks in Jerusalem. He had been released in a mass prisoner exchange in 1985 between Israel and the PFLP-General Command. He had belonged to the PFLP, but was expelled because of erratic behavior. He then joined the Democratic Front for the Liberation of Palestine. On June 14, 1989, he wounded a guard at a military tank truck outside Beit Lahia, Gaza. On June 18, 1989, he wounded an Israeli army officer and killed a Palestinian outside the main military government office in Gaza City.

Nabila al-Riyami Nasser: an Omani and one of six Arabs arrested on April 1, 1995 by Philippine authorities in Kaloocan for being members of the little-known Islamic Saturday Meeting. The group had ties to Ramzi Yusuf. Documents taken from the six detainees indicated that they planned to attack U.S. and Saudi citizens in the Philippines. They were charged with illegal possession of firearms and explosives. Police had seized several M-16 Armalite rifles, dynamite, and detonators. Police said they were preparing for a series of bombings to disrupt the May 8 elections. In December 1995, they were tried before the Kaloocan City Regional Trial Court for illegal possession of firearms and explosives.

Najim Nasser: one of six Iraqis who were among nine suspected terrorists, including the brother of Ramzi Yusuf, who were arrested on December 29, 1995 by Philippines police, who also seized explosives, 50 Philippine passports, and maps of Metro Manila.

Saud bin Ali bin Nasser: age 30, a naturalized Saudi of Yemeni origin who worked at a car dealership, who, on February 20, 2003, shot to death Robert Dent, a British Aerospace Engineering (BAE) Systems employee, in his car while waiting at a Riyadh traffic light. Nasser had recently traveled to Pakistan and named his youngest son Osama. No group claimed credit.

Wael Nasser: arrested on August 18, 1995 by the Palestinian Authority (PA) following a five-hour shootout/standoff in Gaza City. The Hamas terrorist had been planning a suicide attack. Israel had sealed its border with Gaza for 10 days while the PA agents searched for him.

Nassim: member of a cell of the Salafist Group for Preaching and Combat based in Milan that was wrapped up by Italian police on October 10–11, 2002. Intercepted conversations showed the suspects talking about obtaining explosives in southern France. In September, they referred to an upcoming "soccer game," believed to be code for an attack. They also said they would take revenge against Italy for supporting U.S. antiterrorist efforts. Nassim said "You'll see what happens now in Italy. Now they are causing problems. Maybe you'll find 300 or 400 dead in the subway."

Khaled Salah Nassr: an Egyptian arrested in Evansville, Indiana and later released. He was initially held as a possible grand jury witness in the 9/11 case.

Tahir Nasur: age 44, who works for the Sanabel Relief Agency in the United Kingdom, which the U.S. claimed in February 2006 finances Libyan Islamic Fight Group terrorists, was one of eight people, including five foreigners, arrested on May 24, 2006 for "facilitating terrorism abroad" in 18 raids in London and Manchester. The United States said it is an al Qaeda affiliate that attempted to overthrow Libyan leader Muammar al-Qadhafi. The threats were not against UK facilities. Michael Todd, Chief Constable of the Greater Manchester Police, said "we are not talking today about a direct threat to the UK. We are talking about the facilitation of terrorism overseas. That could include funding, providing support and encouragement to terrorists." The five foreigners were held under the government's power to "deport individuals whose presence in the UK is not conducive to the public good for reasons of national security." The other trio was held under antiterrorist legislation.

Hasan Taysir al-Natshah: a resident of the Ra's al-Amud neighborhood of East Jerusalem and one of the Hamas terrorists who, on October 9, 1994, kidnapped Israeli Corporal Nachshon Mordekhay Wachsman from Jerusalem's 'Atarot junction.

Samir al-Natur: one of three Hizballah terrorists reported by the Argentine Foreign Ministry on November 4, 1994 as planning terrorist attacks and on their way to Argentina. He was traveling on a Lebanese passport.

Navir: alias of Hocine Abderrahim.

Nawaf: variant Nawwaf, alias Abu Al Harith, a Saudi from Mecca who joined al Qaeda in Iraq in 2007, bringing his passport. His phone number was 5458753.

Belgacem Nawar: an uncle of suicide bomber Nizar Nawar. In April 2004, he remained in Tunisian custody, charged with complicity in the truck bombing on April 11, 2002 that killed 19 people in a synagogue in Djerba, Tunisia.

Nizar bin Mohammed Nawar: age 25, variant Naouar, alias Sword of the Faith, the Tunisian, who had lived in Lyon. In a will dated July 5, 2000 and sent to *Al-Quds Al-Arabi* newspaper, Nawar called on his family to contribute to a holy war "with their souls and money." He was one of the men who on April 11, 2002, drove a truck transporting natural gas that exploded outside the outer wall of North Africa's oldest synagogue on the island of Djerba, Tunisia, killing 17 people, including 11 German tourists, five Tunisians, and a French citizen. On April 16, the Islamic Army for the Liberation of the Holy Sites, which has links to bin Laden, claimed credit.

Tunisia, on April 22, 2002, blamed the attack on Nawar and a relative living in the country. Police had discovered a phone call to Germany by

Nawar shortly before the blast. Nawar phoned Christian Ganczarski, age 35, a Polish-born German convert to Islam. He was asked if he needed anything, and replied, "I only need the command."

Zayd 'Ali Muthanna al-Nawar: variant Nawwar, alias Abu-Jihad, a Yemeni from Sana'a who joined al Qaeda in Iraq in 2007 as a suicide bomber, contributing his watch, $200, and 40 Yemeni riyals. He met his recruitment coordinator, Abu-'Azzam, through his teacher at the mosque, 'Adil al-Watari, variant al-Watri, variant Adel al Watery. He came from Jaddah al-Sham, Yemen. His Syrian contacts took a passport and $100 from him. His phone number was 204356. He had military experience.

Ahmad Mustafa Nawawah: a fugitive in Sudan said by the Ethiopian Supreme State Security Prosecution on August 7, 1995 to have helped five terrorists who had confessed to training in the al-Kamp and Kangu camps in Khartoum with two of the nine Egyptian Islamic Group gunmen who, on June 25, 1995, fired on the armored limousine of Egyptian President Hosni Mubarak in Addis Ababa.

Nawwaf: variant of Nawaf.

Zayd 'Ali Muthanna al-Nawwar: variant of Zayd 'Ali Muthanna al-Nawar.

Sheik Haq Nawaz: chief suspect in the December 19, 1990 murder of Sadiq Ganji, an Iranian diplomat who headed the Iranian Cultural Center in Lahore. On December 27, 1990, Pakistani police said they would prosecute the killers in Rawalpindi. Some of the eight suspects belonged to the Soldiers of the Companions of the Prophet Mohammad (Anjuman Sipahe Sahaba), a Pakistani religious group. The detainees said they wanted to avenge the murder of the group's leader, Maulana Haq Nawaz Jhangvi, in February 1990 at Jhang, their base in Punjab. Haq Nawaz was seriously wounded when he tried to commit suicide by shooting himself when he was surrounded by police soon after the murder. On March 13,

1991, a special court in Lahore sentenced him to death for killing Ganji.

Yusri 'Abd al-Mun'im Nawfal: identified by Egyptian police as being a suspect in the attempted assassination of Major General Muhammad al-Nabawi Isma'il, former deputy prime minister and interior minister, on August 13, 1987, by four gunmen who fired on him in front of his house in Cairo. Nawfal was arrested on August 30, 1987 while carrying a pistol in Cairo. On August 31, 1987, he confessed that he was driving the Datsun pickup truck from which the suspects opened fire on former interior minister Hasan Abu Basha in May. He was injured in the neck when Abu Basha's guard fired back.

'Ammar Nayazi: arrested on October 27, 1992 by Egyptian police in connection with the Muslim Group's October 21, 1992 attack on a tour bus near Dayrut that killed a British tourist and injured two others. He served as the lookout who whistled when the coast was clear.

Muhammad Nayazi: at-large brother of 'Ammar Nayazi, who was arrested on October 27, 1992 by Egyptian police in connection with the Muslim Group's October 21, 1992 attack on a tour bus near Dayrut that killed a British tourist and injured two others.

Mohammed Naydi: a senior Libyan intelligence official. U.S. authorities said in 1991 that they were preparing a case against him in connection with the December 21, 1988 bombing of Pan Am flight 103 over Lockerbie, Scotland that killed 270. The flight 103 detonator matched photos of timers seized from Naydi when he was arrested in February 1988 in Dakar, Senegal. He was also in N'Djamena, Chad on March 10, 1984 when an earlier Union des Transports Aeriens (UTA) flight 772 exploded on the runway, injuring 24 people.

Ibrahim Nayili: variant of Ibrahim Naeli.

Faysal Ahmad Karam Nayruz: a Kuwaiti who was believed to have set off an explosion on May 22, 1987 that caused a fire at one of the natural gas storage tanks in the port of Al-Ahmadi, Kuwait. A body found at the scene was believed to be his. He was believed killed while planting the bomb.

Mohammed Nazal: Hamas representative to Jordan. On August 30, 1999, Jordanian police issued an arrest warrant for him.

Attef Nazch: one of 16 Middle Eastern terrorists the Saudi Embassy told Thai officials on March 20, 1990 were planning to attack Saudi diplomats and officials overseas. He carried a Lebanese passport.

Nazeeh: alias of Fawaz Younis.

Nazih: alias given by Fawaz Younis, the spokesman of the six Brigades of the Marches of Lebanese Resistance hijackers who took over Royal Jordanian Airlines flight 402, a B727 boarding passengers at Beirut International Airport on June 11, 1985. The plane hopscotched through Europe and the Middle East. The hijackers escaped after setting off a bomb on the plane in Beirut.

Osama Nazir: deputy chief of Jaish-e-Muhammad, who was arrested on November 17, 2004 by Pakistani authorities for the March 17, 2002 attack on the Protestant International Church in Islamabad's diplomatic quarter. The terrorists threw hand grenades, killing five people, including an Afghan; a Pakistani; Barbara Green, an American who worked for the U.S. Embassy; and Kristen Wormsley, age 17, her daughter who was a senior at the American School in Islamabad; and an unidentified person (possibly an assailant); and wounding 46 others. Nazir was found at a madrasa in Faisalabad, the city where al Qaeda leader Abu Zubayda was captured in 2002. Nazir was also believed involved in the failed assassination attempts on President Pervez Musharraf in December 2003 and on Prime Minister Shaukat Aziz. Authorities confiscated cell phones, computer disks, documents, and other materials related to the organization. The Pakistani daily *Dawn* said Nazir had direct links with bin Laden. He met with July 7, 2005 London bomber Shahzad Tanweer in Pakistan in 2004.

Mahmud Nazmi: during a trial on February 24, 1989 against Egypt's Revolution Organization, a witness told the court that the accused had participated in the August 20, 1985 murder of Israeli diplomat Albert Artkash.

Khalid al-Karim Nazzal: an Algerian senior official of the Popular Front for the Liberation of Palestine who was killed by two gunmen on motorcycles on June 9, 1986 outside his hotel at 87 Alexandra Avenue in Athens, Greece.

Muhammad Nazzal: Hamas representative in Jordan in mid-1994 who, in mid-1995, was being considered as a replacement for Abu Marzook, a prominent financier.

Salah Nazzal: alias of Saleh Abdel Rahim Souwi.

Yusaf Nazzal: Abu Daoud claimed that he had traveled on an Algerian passport and was involved in the Black September Olympics attack of September 5, 1972.

Mohamed Nechle: on January 18, 2002, U.S. troops brought him and five other terrorism suspects out of the country to Guantánamo after a local court ruled on January 17 that it had too little evidence to press charges. He was accused of plotting to blow up the U.S. Embassy in Sarajevo and conduct other attacks on Americans in Bosnia. Five of the men were naturalized Bosnians; Bosnia stripped them of their citizenship in November 2001. The group had been arrested by Bosnian authorities in October 2001.

Mohammed Nedjar: one of three Algerian men claiming membership in the Union of Peaceful Citizens of Algeria who, on November 12, 1994, hijacked an Air Algerie F27 flying between Algiers and Ouargla to Palma de Majorca's Son Sant Joan Airport. They asked not to be repatriated to Algeria because they feared they would be killed. They demanded liberation of Algeria's political prisoners, resumption of elections in Algeria, refueling the plane, and passage to Marseilles. They surrendered to authorities.

Fowzi Badavi Nejad: an Iranian dockworker who was the only surviving terrorist of the six Iranian Khuzestanis who took over the Iranian Embassy in London on April 30, 1980. He was charged with the murder of two hostages, assault, unlawful imprisonment, and several other offenses. During his January 1981 trial, he claimed the attack was planned and organized by the Iraqis. He was sentenced to life in prison.

'Abdl al-Rahim Ismail 'Ali Neqqi: at-large Kuwaiti teacher and 1 of 16 people accused on March 9, 1987 of a 1987 bombing in a parking lot near Salehiyeh complex in downtown Kuwait, bomb explosions in two oil wells and an artificial island in Al-Ahmadi, setting fire to Mina 'Abdallah refinery in June 1986, and a mob riot before the Bayan police station in 1987.

Khalid 'Abdl al-Masid 'Ali al-Neqqi: at-large Kuwaiti and 1 of 16 people accused on March 9, 1987 of a 1987 bombing in a parking lot near Salehiyeh complex in downtown Kuwait, bomb explosions in two oil wells and an artificial island in Al-Ahmadi, setting fire to Mina 'Abdallah refinery in June 1986, and a mob riot before the Bayan police station in 1987. He was under detention pending trial. He was a student of Kuwait University's faculty of commerce.

Andrew Jonathan Charles Newman: his passport, stolen in 1993, was used by Hizballah would-be bomber Hussein Muhammad Hussein Mikdad, who was severely injured when his bomb went off prematurely on April 12, 1996.

Prof. Hameedullah Khan Niazi: Faisalabad leader of the banned Lashkar-i-Taiba (Holy

Army) who was arrested on March 27, 2002 in Pakistan.

Hasan Kamal Nicholas: release from an Israeli jail was demanded on June 27, 1976 by the Popular Front for the Liberation of Palestine hijackers of Air France flight 139, an A300 flying from Tel Aviv to Paris and ultimately diverted to Entebbe.

Abu Nidal: alias Sabri al-Banna, Iraq-based leader of a Fatah splinter faction in the 1970s. On May 22, 1985, the Jordanian state prosecutor's office issued a summons for him in connection with a foiled plot to set off a bomb at the U.S. Embassy in Egypt. On January 23, 1986, an international arrest warrant was issued in Italy for him for masterminding the December 27, 1985 attack on Rome's Fiumicino Airport in which 16 died and 73 were wounded. On February 12, 1988, a Rome court sentenced him in absentia to life in prison for the Rome attack. He and three others were tried in absentia in Jordan on June 12, 2001 for the 1994 murder of a Jordanian diplomat in Lebanon.

Ahmad 'Abd ak-Karim Niimah: alias Karim, an Iraqi acquitted by the Kuwaiti State Security Court in 1984 in connection with the December 12, 1983 truck bombing of the administrative building of the U.S. Embassy in Kuwait, killing four people and injuring 59.

Luie Nijmeh: one of four members of the Abu Nidal group jailed on April 1, 1993 by St. Louis, Missouri police for planning to blow up the Israeli Embassy and murder Jews. He was listed in the indictment as having discussed blowing up the Israeli Embassy. He had received his instructions in Mexico in 1987. His brother, Saif, was held on similar charges. In July 1994, he pleaded guilty to federal racketeering charges of smuggling money and information, buying weapons, recruiting members, illegally obtaining passports, and obstructing investigations and helping plot terrorist attacks. On November 22, 1994, U.S.

District Judge Donald Stohr sentenced him to 21 months in prison. With credit for time served, he was due to be released in January 1995. Jewish groups protested, noting that he was eligible for 20 years and a $250,000 fine.

Saif Nijmeh: one of four members of the Abu Nidal group jailed on April 1, 1993 by St. Louis police for planning to blow up the Israeli Embassy and murder Jews. He was listed in the indictment discussing a rocket-propelled grenade launcher he had obtained. He had received his instructions in Mexico in 1987. His brother, Luie, was held on similar charges. In July 1994, he pleaded guilty to federal racketeering charges of smuggling money and information, buying weapons, recruiting members, illegally obtaining passports, and obstructing investigations and helping plot terrorist attacks. On November 22, 1994, U.S. District Judge Donald Stohr sentenced him to 21 months in prison. With credit for time served, he was due to be released in January 1995. Jewish groups protested, noting that he was eligible for 20 years and a $250,000 fine.

Mohammad Jafar Nikham: Iranian Embassy's press attaché to Madrid who was withdrawn on July 27, 1984 by his government when Spanish police accused him of ties to four Iranian members of the Martyrs of the Iranian Revolution who were arrested on July 23, 1984 while carrying two antitank grenade launchers, six 40 mm grenade launchers and two .45 caliber machine guns in Barcelona and Madrid. They were charged with plotting to hijack a Saudi airliner. Authorities believed their Barcelona safe house was used in the coordination and perpetration of terrorist acts in Spain and elsewhere in Europe, including attacks against a Saudi plane and the U.S. Embassy in 1983. The terrorists planned to shoot down another Saudi plane and to assassinate Masud Rajavi, leader of the Mojahedine-e Khalq in Paris. When police searched Nikham's apartment, they found diplomatic bags loaded with guns and explosives, and found details of the plans of the terrorists to hijack a Saudi plane on a flight from Madrid to

Jeddah and Riyadh. Police said he was using his diplomatic status to pass weapons to three of the terrorists while in the transit lounge at Madrid airport.

Abu-Muhammad al-Ni'man: alias of Fahd Hilal al-Muqadi al-'Atibi.

Rauhi Ibrahim Abdul-Latif Nimr: a Jordanian who worked as a guard at the Kuwaiti Fatah offices who was sentenced to death by a Kuwaiti court on November 15, 1980 for the July 12, 1980 bombing of the newspaper *al Rai al Aam* that killed two people. He had been charged with murder and possession of explosives.

Shaul Nir: one of three masked gunmen who fired Kalashnikov submachine guns at students milling about a courtyard at the Hebron Islamic College in Israel on July 27, 1983. They also threw a grenade in the attack that killed three and wounded 30. He was arrested for the attack and sentenced to life in prison. On March 27, 1987, President Chaim Herzog commuted the sentences to 24 years each. On December 26, 1990, Israel freed him; a life sentence in Israel usually requires that the convict serve at least 20 years.

Ilyas Abu Nizar: alias of Mustafa Murad, one of two dissident former members of the Central Committee and Political Bureau of Fatah-The Revolutionary Council who, on October 31, 1989, was said to have been killed, along with 156 of Abu Nidal's followers, by Abu Nidal in Libya in 1988. The dissidents said he was killed in Abu Nidal's office on October 17, 1989. Doha's *al-Sharq* on March 19, 1993 said he was killed in Libya on October 17, 1988.

Muhammad Batal Muhammad Nizar: variant Muhamad Battel Muhammad Nizar, alias Abu-al-Walid al-Shami, a Syrian from Aleppo who was born on March 24, 1976 and joined al Qaeda in Iraq on October 1, 2006, contributing $100, 5,000 lira, two watches, and an MP3 player. His

home phone number was 2261713; his brother's was 3639508.

Muhamad Battel Muhammad Nizar: variant of Muhammad Batal Muhammad Nizar.

Mustafa Murad Abu-Nizar: assistant secretary general of the Abu Nidal group until 1987.

Mqdam al Njdi: variant of Miqdam al-Najdi.

Abu Ahmad Yones Njeim: Name used by "Gueye," a hijacker, for his colleague who joined him in the September 6, 1970 hijacking of Pan Am flight 93.

Ramez Noaman: age 27, a Yemeni detained on September 19, 2001 in Rowland Heights, California. The California Polytechnic University student was held in New York as a material witness in the 9/11 attacks until his October 2 release. He lived in the same house as the hijackers after they moved out.

Benham Nodjaumi: Iranian businessman charged in the United Kingdom in March 1983 with kidnapping six Iranians in London and Belgium.

Ebadollah Nooripur: on June 9, 1988, the Iranian terrorist who was serving 12 years for blowing up London's Queen's Gardens Hotel in May 1981 was released early by the United Kingdom and deported. The press speculated that she was freed to help release kidnapped Anglican envoy Terry Waite.

Benni Antoine Norris: alias of Ahmed Ressam.

El Sayyid A. Nosair: variant Noseir, Nosir, Nasser, El Sayyd Abdulaziz El Sayyd, shot in the neck and killed Rabbi Meir Kahane, founder of the Jewish Defense League and head of the Israeli Kach movement, on November 5, 1990 at the Marriott Marquis East Hotel in New York City. While attempting to commandeer a taxi at gunpoint, he traded gunfire with a local police officer; both were wounded. Nosair was critically wounded in the chin.

Nosair was born in Egypt and left Cairo for the United States in 1981. He obtained U.S. citizenship in 1989. The maintenance worker was not a member of any terrorist organization. He had lived in Cliffside Park, New Jersey, but also used a Brooklyn address. He was married to American-born Caren Ann Mills, a convert to Islam who met her husband in a Pittsburgh mosque. They had three children.

He was a deeply religious man who prayed several times during the work day. He had been displaced as a teen from his Sinai Peninsula home after the Israeli occupation. He was fired as a diamond setter in Pittsburgh because his efforts to convert coworkers to Islam interfered with his work. He lied on his employment application about his residence because the city hires only residents. When arrested, he was carrying three driver's licenses with three different addresses. He was on sick leave from his job at the time of the attack.

He was charged with second-degree murder, attempted murder in the second-degree, aggravated assault of a police officer, second-degree assault, reckless endangerment, coercion, three counts of weapons possession, and unlawful imprisonment (for commandeering the taxi). The murder charge carried a maximum sentence of 25 years to life.

On November 13, 1990, he appeared in Manhattan Criminal Court for a hearing on murder charges. On November 20, 1990, a New York grand jury indicted him for murder, to which he pleaded not guilty the next day.

On November 30, 1990, in a search of his home, the FBI found a list of six prominent New Yorkers, including a member of Congress and two federal judges, and warned that they could be terrorist targets. On December 11, 1990, police searching his home found ammunition and literature on bomb-making.

On December 18, 1990, New York State Supreme Court Justice Alvin Schlesinger revoked Nosair's $300,000 bail. He said that a passport in a different name indicated that Nosair might flee.

The trial began on November 19, 1991. The jury began deliberations on December 18, 1991. On December 20, 1991, he was acquitted of the murder charge regarding Kahane and the attempted murder charge of shooting a postal worker during his escape. He was convicted of assaulting the postal worker and another man, of gun possession, and coercing the cab driver by pointing his gun at his head. Nosair faced jail terms of two to seven years for each assault charge and the coercion charge, and five to 15 years for the weapons charge, and was held without bail. On January 29, 1992, Manhattan Judge Alvin Schlesinger said that the jury's not guilty verdict defied the evidence, and imposed the maximum allowable sentence of 7 and a half to 22 years.

He was the cousin of Egyptian-born Ibrahim Elgabrowny, who was arrested on March 4, 1993 in connection with the February 26, 1993 bombing of the World Trade Center in which seven people were killed and more than 1,000 wounded.

In March 1993, FBI agents seized documents from Nosair's prison cell in Attica state prison. He was believed to be corresponding with Mohammed A. Salameh, who had been arrested for renting the truck used in the 1993 bombing of the World Trade Center.

On January 13, 1995, federal prosecutors said that he had carried out the bombing of a popular Manhattan gay bar on April 28, 1990 in which three people were injured, and that he had plotted to murder Soviet President Mikhail Gorbachev.

On October 1, 1995, a jury found him guilty of seditious conspiracy, which carries a life term. He was also convicted of assault on Irving Franklin, who was at the Kahane shooting, attempted murder and assault of postal police officer Carlos Acosta, and numerous other charges involving possession and use of firearms. He was acquitted of any direct role in the plot to bomb city landmarks.

On January 17, 1996, U.S. District Judge Michael B. Mukasey sentenced him to life plus 75 years.

El Sayyid A. Noseir: variant of El Sayyid A. Nosair

El Sayyid A. Nosir: variant of El Sayyid A. Nosair.

Mohammed Nouami: alias of Abdul Rahim Khalid.

Akbar Nouchedehi: one of the 25 members of the People's Majority, an anti-Khomeini group, who seized the Iranian Interests Section in Washington, DC and held six Iranian employees hostage for an hour on August 7, 1981. The group was arrested by police. On October 23, they were put on probation after being convicted of forcible entry and ordered to complete 25 hours of community service. Nouchedehi was charged with carrying a pistol without a license in the wounding of Iranian employee Mohammed Shamirza.

Abu Muhammad al Nouman: alias of Fahid Hilal al Muqady al Outaby.

Abu Nourah: alias of Ahmed Mussfer Mufleh Al Ka'abie Al Hazlie.

Abu Nourah: alias of Fahid Hammed Muhammad al Rashied.

Mahmoud Nourami: Iranian charge d'affaires in Lebanon reported by Jack Anderson and Dale Van Atta of planning the hijacking of a Kuwaiti A310 en route from Kuwait to Bangkok with intermediate stops in Dubai and Karachi on December 4, 1984.

Drissi Noureddine: on January 26, 2005, Italy's Justice Ministry sent inspectors to Milan after Judge Clementina Forleo dropped terrorism charges against three Tunisians and two Moroccans on January 24, saying they were "guerrillas," not "terrorists." She said their actions in recruiting for and financing training camps in northern Iraq during the U.S.-led invasion did not "exceed the activity of a guerilla group." She claimed the 1999 UN Global Convention on Terrorism said

that paramilitary activities in war zones could not be prosecuted according to international law unless they were designed to create terror among civilians and broke international humanitarian laws. Prosecutors said they would appeal. Noureddine was to be tried again in another court in Brescia.

Saver al-Nouri: one of two al Qaeda Martyrs Brigades members from Nablus who, on January 5, 2003, set off suicide bombs on parallel streets that killed 23 and injured 107.

Abu Nsser: alias of Nawaf Nasser Jali Al Harabi.

'Abd-al-Latif al-Nu'aymi: charge d'affaires at the Iraqi Embassy in Beirut identified on October 9, 1990 by the London-based Kuwaiti newspaper *al-Qabas al-Duwali* as being a leader of a worldwide Iraqi terrorist network.

As'ad al-Nubani: variant of Asir al-Nubani.

Asir al-Nubani: variant As'ad al-Nubani, arrested on April 23, 1991 in connection with the explosion of a parcel bomb on April 19, 1991 that killed seven and injured ten others at the Patras, Greece offices of Air Courier Service. The Palestine Liberation Organization had arranged for his surrender to the Ministry of Public Order. His trial began on May 8, 1992 in a courtroom within the Kordhallos prison in Piraeus. He was sentenced by an Athens appeals court on July 6, 1992 to life in prison plus 25 years for forming a terrorist group and supplying, making, and transporting a bomb causing loss of human life.

Abu Jihad al-Nubi: alias of Mustafa Mohamed Fadhil.

Kamal Numayr: release from an Israeli jail was demanded on June 27, 1976 by the Popular Front for the Liberation of Palestine hijackers of Air France flight 139, an A300 flying from Tel Aviv to Paris and ultimately diverted to Entebbe.

Nur: alias of Ayman al-Zawahiri.

Abu-al-Nur: alias of Ibrahim.

Samir Nur'Ali: an Iranian member of Ayatollah Sadegh Khalkhali's Fedaye Islam group who threw a hand grenade into a student gathering in Baghdad's al-Mustansiriyah University on April 1, 1980 in an attempt to assassinate Iraqi Prime Minister Tariq Aziz.

Mahmoud Nureddin: arrested in Egypt on September 19, 1987 in connection with the killing of an Israeli diplomat at the Cairo trade fair in early 1986 and the attack on a U.S. Embassy station wagon on May 26, 1987 in Cairo by the Revolution Group.

Nuri: alias of Yusif Salam.

Adnan Ahmad Nuri: one of two hijackers of a British Airways flight from Bombay to London on March 3, 1974. The duo diverted the plane after its Beirut stopover and demanded to fly to Athens, where they intended to demand the release of Black September terrorists in the Athens airport attack on August 5, 1974. Greece denied landing permission, so the plane flew to Amsterdam's Schipol Airport. The terrorists allowed everyone to leave before torching the plane. The two were captured by police. The had claimed membership in the Palestine Liberation Army, but later the Organization of Arab Nationalist Youth for the Liberation of Palestine claimed credit. On June 6, 1974, a Dutch court convicted them on charges of air piracy and arms violations and sentenced them to five years.

The Palestinian next surfaced on October 26, 1974, when he and another imprisoned Arab terrorist, joined by two Dutch criminals, took 22 hostages at the prison chapel at Scheveningen, Netherlands. Guns had been smuggled into the prison. After a 105-hour siege, police raided the chapel. The Dutch attorney general said the four would be charged with unlawful deprivation of liberty.

Nuri and Sami Houssin Tamimah, his fellow March 3 hijacker, were released on November 24, 1974, and flown to Tunis as part of an agreement reached with four hijackers of a British Airways plane in Dubai on November 22, 1974. On December 7, 1974, the two terrorists went to Libya with the four hijackers who had demanded their release and five other terrorists released from Egypt. The two hijackers of the VC-10 apparently were given their freedom in Libya.

Tamer al-Nuseirat: a Palestinian who said he was willing to conduct attacks in Egypt. He may have been involved in the triple bombing on April 24, 2006 of a seaside promenade at the resort of Dahab, Egypt, killing 18 civilians, including 6 foreigners (among them a 10-year-old German boy who died in a taxi on the way to a hospital, a Swiss, a Russian, and a Lebanese woman, and two unidentified foreign women), and injuring 85, including three Italians and four Americans.

Mohammad Nuzzal: head of the Jordanian branch of Hamas, who said he had no information regarding Hamas kidnapping Israeli Senior Master Sergeant Nissim Toledano on December 13, 1992.

O

Abu Anwar al-Obaidi: an al Qaeda in Iraq spokesman in Garma, east of Fallujah, Anbar Province, who said that videos discovered in December 2007 of al Qaeda teaching children how to kidnap and kill were authentic.

Ahmed Obeid: aide of Sheik Abdel Karim Obeid, both of whose release was demanded on July 30, 1989 by the Organization of the Oppressed on Earth, who threatened to hang U.S. Marine Lt. Col. William Richard Higgins, whom the group kidnapped on February 17, 1988.

Mahmoud Abu Obeid: age 24, a West Bank leader of Islamic Jihad who was shot to death on February 21, 2007 in the West Bank by undercover Israeli soldiers as he traveled by car. He fired an M-16 in the air, then aimed it at the troops. He had been wanted for recruiting a Palestinian from Jenin who was caught on February 20 while trying to carry out a suicide bombing. Abu Obeid had supplier the bomber with the explosives.

Sheikh Abdel Karim Obeid: variant Ubayd, Hizballah cleric who was arrested on July 28, 1989 by Israeli commandos in Lebanon. His release was demanded on July 30, 1989 by the Organization of the Oppressed on Earth, who threatened to hang U.S. Marine Lt. Col. William Richard Higgins, whom the group kidnapped on February 17, 1988. Israel announced the next day that Obeid had acknowledged involvement in Higgins' abduction, saying that the chief kidnapper left the getaway car at his house for a month after the kidnapping. He also admitted involvement in two car bombings, two other abductions, and the capture of three Israeli soldiers held in Lebanon. After Higgins was murdered on July 31, 1989, the Revolutionary Justice Organization threatened to kill hostage Joseph Cicippio if Obeid was not freed. The Oppressed on Earth also threatened to kill UK hostage Terry Waite.

Abu Obeida: spokesman for the Izz al-Din al-Qassam Brigades, a Hamas group, in February 2008.

Abu Obeida: alias of Yasser Sheik Youssef.

Abu Obeied: alias of Muhammad Abd Al Ghafour Abd Al Baqie.

Oum Obeyda: alias of Malika El-Aroud.

Abu Obieda: alias of Ahmed Abd Allah Muhammad.

Abu Obieda: alias of Tawfieq Muhammad Al Akhder Al Rahimi.

Hamed Obysi: age 21, one of two people arrested on August 6, 2005 by Turkish police for links to al Qaeda. Police grabbed Obysi at a Turkish border post when he tried to bribe police.

Abd al Aziz Odeh: alias of 'Abd al-Aziz Awda.

Abdel Aziz Odeh: alias of 'Abd al-Aziz Awda.

Abed Al Aziz Odeh: alias of 'Abd al-Aziz Awda.

Abdel Basset Odeh: age 24, a Palestinian who lived in Tulkarm, who, on March 27, 2002, conducted a Hamas suicide bombing that killed 28, including an American, Hannah Rogen, and injured 172, 48 of them seriously, at the seaside Park Hotel in Netanya during a Seder dinner at the start of Passover. Odeh had worked in hotels in Netanya and elsewhere in Israel, and had been on Israel's wanted list. The hotel's guards did not spot him. When a reception clerk asked what he was doing, he ran into the dining room and set off the 20-pound bomb strapped to his waist and hidden by an overcoat.

He had disappeared several months before the bombing after being told to report for questioning to the Palestinian Authority. He was one of eight children. He was to be married to a Palestinian woman he had met in Baghdad, but was refused entry to the Allenby Bridge to Jordan at the beginning of his return visit. Iraqi President Saddam Hussein had pledged to send $25,000 to each suicide bomber's family. Posters of Odeh named him "The Lion of the Holy Revenge." The attack led Prime Minister Ariel Sharon to invade the West Bank in an effort to shut down the bombers.

Mohammed Odeh: age 29, of East Jerusalem, one of 15 men arrested on August 17, 2002 by Israeli police who broke up the terrorist cell responsible for eight bombings in the previous six months (including the March 9, 2002 suicide bombing of the Moment Café in Jerusalem that killed 11, the May 7, 2002 attack at the Rishon Letzion pool hall that killed 16, and the July 31, 2002 bombing at Hebrew University that killed nine and wounded 87). The Israelis said they had learned that the Hamas cell was about to set off another bomb in central Israel. Odeh worked at Hebrew University as a contract painter, and used his university ID card to carry out the bombing. He hid the bomb in some shrubs the night before the attack, then placed it on a table in the cafeteria the next day. He set it off with a cell phone. Officials said the site was chosen because "they were looking for a place with no Arabs." On September 12, 2002, an Israeli court charged four Arab residents of East Jerusalem with murder, attempted murder, and conspiracy to murder in the case. They faced life in prison. They were also accused of having chosen the targets and transporting the suicide bombers to attacks on Café Moment and at the Rishon Letzion pool hall.

Mohammed Sadiq Odeh: variant Mohammed Saddiq Odeh, variant Howeida, age 33, a Pakistani engineer (other reports said a Jordanian-born Palestinian) arrested on August 7, 1998 at Karachi Airport in connection with the al Qaeda bombing of the U.S. Embassy in Kenya on August 7, 1998. He was returned to Kenya on August 14 for traveling on a false Yemeni passport with a fake visa, using the name Abdull Bast Awadah. An immigration official noted that the photograph in his passport was not of him. He had flown to Pakistan on August 6 on a Pakistan International Airways flight 943, departing Nairobi at 10 P.M. and arriving in Karachi at 8:25 A.M., the day of the blast. He said his spiritual guide was bin Laden and that he was attempting to seek refuge with him in Afghanistan. He claimed that the bomb contained 1,760 pounds of TNT, and was assembled over several days at the hotel under his direction. Kenyan television claimed that he was married to a Kenyan. Police held three other people in connection with the attack. Two were identified as Mohammed Saleh and Abdullah. Odeh also claimed that his group had taken part in the October 3–4, 1993 attack on U.S. forces in Mogadishu, Somalia which killed 18 Americans. Former Ambassador Robert Oakley and several journalists who had covered the attack said they were unaware of any foreign involvement in the Somalia killings. Islamabad's *The News* claimed Odeh had confessed to conducting other missions for bin Laden in the Philippines, Cairo, and Jordan.

Odeh's Yemeni passport, No. 0011061, was stamped for entry into Mombasa, Kenya on August 3. He apparently took a ten-hour bus ride to the capital.

On August 27, 1998, Odeh was brought out of Nairobi and arrived in New York City the next day to be arraigned. In the affidavit, federal prosecutors accused bin Laden's al Qaida group of bombing the embassy in Kenya. Odeh was charged with 12 counts of murder, one count of murder conspiracy, and one count of conspiracy to use weapons of mass destruction. His court-appointed attorney, Jack Sachs, said that Odeh lives in Jordan with his wife and one girl and was last employed making and selling furniture. The affidavit said that Odeh joined al-Qaida in 1992, and received explosives training at bin Laden's camps. Odeh later trained other Islamic radicals opposed to the UN humanitarian mission in Somalia. In 1994, he moved to Mombasa, Kenya, where he used al Qaida money to establish a fishing business, the profits from which supported al Qaida members in Kenya. He met with senior al Qaida commanders and was shown TNT and detonators obtained in Tanzania. On August 2, he met with al Qaida members, including an explosives expert who ran the Kenyan cell. On August 4, the group, minus Odeh, surveilled the U.S. Embassy in Nairobi. On August 6, all but one member of the group left Nairobi. Odeh was told that al Qaida members in Afghanistan were also moving "to avoid retaliation from the U.S."

He was indicted on 238 counts on October 7, 1998 by a federal grand jury in New York. He was charged with 224 counts of murder and with training the Somalis. On October 8, he pleaded not guilty.

He was convicted on May 29, 2001 for conspiracy in the bombing of the U.S. Embassies in Kenya and Tanzania and sentenced to life in prison.

Sheik Odeh: alias of 'Abd al-Aziz Awda.

Riyadh al-Ogaidi: age 39, a leader of al Qaeda in Iraq in the Garma region of Iraq's eastern Anbar Province who was interviewed for a February 8, 2008 *Washington Post* article.

Azim Musa Ogiedo: release from an Israeli jail was demanded on June 27, 1976 by the Popular Front for the Liberation of Palestine hijackers of Air France flight 139, an A300

flying from Tel Aviv to Paris and ultimately diverted to Entebbe.

Muhammad Oglah: a Jordanian whose expulsion from France was ordered on December 24, 1986 in connection with the discovery of an arms cache in Aulnay-sous-Bois near Paris on December 18, 1986.

Nabil Okal: leader of 23 Islamists linked to Osama bin Laden who were arrested by Israeli and Palestinian security services in June–August 2000. He had trained in al Qaeda camps in Afghanistan and was allegedly funded by Hamas, which the group denied.

Abdelhakim Okaly: a 28-year-old from Darnah, Libya who joined al Qaeda in Iraq in early 2007. His father tried to prevent him from leaving Libya, asking the local emigration office to withhold his travel permit, but the young cab driver got out of town.

Yunus Okut: one of three people arrested after Turkish border police at the Cilvegozu gate from Jordan arrested the driver of a Mercedes carrying 30 kilograms of highly explosive materials. The driver said he had received $400 to drive the car to Turkey. Two Iraqis with Jordanian passports were arrested; police also were searching for a holder of a Jordanian passport. The car's documents were forged.

Hossein Shyrh Olya: an Iranian armed with a submachine gun who hijacked a U.S. commuter plane in Killeen, Texas and demanded to be flown to Cuba on February 15, 1983. He forced the pilot to land in Nuevo Laredo, Mexico, where he turned himself in to the Federal Security Directorate after being promised safe passage. He was flown to Mexico City, where he was indicted on March 4, 1983 for hijacking and hostage taking. The U.S. requested extradition.

Omar: alias of Commander Senen Dario Rangel Osorio.

Omar: alias of Soussan Said.

Abu Omar: alias of Ahmed Ali Ahmed.

Abu Omar: alias of Ali A. Mohamed.

Abu Omar: alias of Isnilon Totoni Hapilon.

Abu Omar: alias of Majed Azzam Yahiya Al Masouri.

Abu Omar: alias of Hatim Ahmed Hamdan Al Shamrani.

Abu Omar: alias of Abd Al Rahman Suleiman Al Wakeel.

Abu Omar: alias of Abd Al Aziz Abd Al Rab Saleh Al Yafea'a.

Abu Omar: alias of Basem Muhammad Shebli.

Abu Salsabil Hassan Omar: alias of Ali Sayyid Muhamed Mustafa al-Bakri.

Amah Hi Omar: alias of Isnilon Totoni Hapilon.

Badadi Omar: leader of the Popular Front for the Liberation of Saquia El Hamra and Rio de Oro (POLISARIO) in Morocco. On July 20, 1996, he applied for political asylum in Spain.

Fazal Omar: Sudanese student at Peshawar's Engineering and Technology University and one of six accomplices of Ramzi Ahmad Yusuf who were arrested on March 11, 1995 by Pakistani police. He was held under the (Section)14 (Amendment) Foreigners Act.

Jaseem Kahtan Omar: an Iraqi fedayeen from Balad who was allegedly behind the November 12, 2003 truck bombing in Nasiriyah, Iraq that killed 19 Italians and 12 Iraqis.

Kisoume Omar: one of six Islamic extremists who, on March 28, 1994, assassinated Konstantin Kukushkin, a driver at the Russian Embassy, and senior Algerian diplomat Belkacem Touati in front of his wife and children in Bordj el Kiffan.

Muhammad Ahmad Omar: alias Sabbeh Al Liel, a Saudi student from Jeddah who was born in 1402 Hijra and joined al Qaeda in Iraq as a fighter in 2007, bringing his passport. His recruitment coordinator was Hussam, a coworker. He arrived by bus to Syria, where his contacts took his 1,000 rials. His home phone number was 6252680; his brother's was 0501490705; friend Abu Al Bara'a, a mujahedeen supporter, was at 0555277141.

Mullah Omar: led the Taliban regime in Afghanistan that sheltered al Qaeda. He sustained a shrapnel wound to his right eye. He was born circa 1966 in Uruzgan Province, Afghanistan. The Rewards for Justice program offers $10 million for his arrest and/or conviction.

Omar Uthman Abu Omar: more commonly known as Abu Qatada.

Ramzi Omar: alias of Ramzi Binalshibh.

Shawqi Ahmad Omar: a Jordanian-American arrested in Baghdad in October 2004 for sheltering an Iraqi insurgent and four Jordanian jihadis in his residence, which contained explosives, and for aiding Abu Musab al-Zarqawi's terrorist network. The Iraqi government said he was planned to kidnap foreigners. Coalition forces wanted to turn him over to the Central Criminal Court of Iraq for prosecution. The Washington, DC district court blocked his transfer. A panel of the U.S. Court of Appeals for the District of Columbia Circuit upheld the decision, saying the court had jurisdiction to hear his claim to the writ of habeas corpus. In December 2007, the U.S. Supreme Court agreed to hear the case of *Geren v. Omar*. Arguments were scheduled for March 2008.

Tarek Eid Omar: an Egyptian arrested in Evansville, Indiana and later released. He was initially held as a possible grand jury witness in the 9/11 case.

Mohamed Omari: age 24, a Moroccan parking lot attendant believed to have prepared the five May 16, 2003 suicide bombings in Casablanca that killed 45 and wounded more than 100. He gave five teams Casio watches to ensure simultaneous explosions at 9:30 A.M. One of Omari's compatriots set off the explosions early, killing himself and another terrorist and injuring Omari, who attempted to flee.

Abu Mohammed Omari: alias of Fakhri al-Umari.

Mohammed Fakr Omari: alias of Fakhri al-Umari.

Mashor Adnam Om-rah: one of 16 Middle Eastern terrorists who, on March 20, 1990, the Saudi Embassy told Thai officials were planning to attack Saudi diplomats and officials overseas. He carried a Lebanese passport.

Abu Omran: alias of Ahmad Ibrahim al-Mughassil, indicted in the Eastern District of Virginia for the June 25, 1996 bombing of the Khobar Towers military housing complex in Dhahran, Saudi Arabia. He is wanted on multiple conspiracy charges against U.S. nationals and property, including murder and the use of weapons of mass destruction. The Rewards for Justice Program offers $5 million for his apprehension. He claimed to have been born on June 26, 1967 in Oatif-Bab, Saudi Arabia. He is five feet four inches tall and weighs 145 pounds.

Marrwam al-Hady Omran: one of 16 Middle Eastern terrorists who, on March 20, 1990, the Saudi Embassy told Thai officials were planning to attack Saudi diplomats and officials overseas. He carried a Libyan passport.

Charles Orfaly: name given by one of two Iraqi terrorists arrested on January 21, 1991 in Bangkok, Thailand who were part of an international terrorist network financed and armed via Iraqi diplomatic pouches. He was deported on January 28, 1991, but ultimately flew to Nepal on January 31. He was not charged in Thailand, but he was arrested by Nepalese police upon arrival. Nepal deported him back to Bangkok on February 3, 1991. On February 7, he and the others were deported to Athens.

Nazmi Ortac: arrested on March 1, 1992 after two individuals threw two hand grenades near the Neve Shalom synagogue in Istanbul, slightly injuring a Jewish passerby. Turkish Hizballah was blamed. On April 2, two Hizballah members were sentenced to 39 years by the Istanbul State Security Court.

Samih Osailly: arrested on April 12, 2002 by Antwerp, Belgium police on charges of diamond smuggling and illegal weapons sales. He is an associate of ASA Diam, which served as a key facilitator for al Qaeda diamond-purchase operations in Liberia and Sierra Leone. His cousin, Aziz Nassour, is a Lebanese diamond merchant associated with ASA Diam. Nassour pressed Sierra Leonean Revolutionary United Front (RUF) rebels to step up diamond production. Osailly pleaded not guilty. Belgian investigators said bank records showed ASA turned over almost $1 billion in the year before 9/11. They also found phone records of calls to Afghanistan, Pakistan, Iraq, and Iran.

Abu Osama: alias of Adel Nasser al Sowda.

Ustad Osama: alias of Mohammed Yasin.

Amar Sherin Osman: on April 8, 1986, the Egyptian said he had a bomb in his briefcase on Eastern Airlines flight 119 en route from New York's La Guardia Airport to Atlanta, Georgia. After an emergency landing in Philadelphia, it was determined to be a hoax. He was charged with providing false information and interfering with a flight crew.

Hussein Osman: variant of Osman Hussein, Osman Hussein, alias Isaac Hamdi.

Semi Osman: a Lebanese imam who was arrested in May 2002 by the Puget Sound Joint Terrorist Task Force at Seattle's Dar-us-Salaam (Taqwa) mosque and charged with immigration fraud and illegal possession of a semiautomatic .40 caliber handgun with its serial numbers removed. Police seized from his residence additional firearms, military field manuals, instructions on poisoning water supplies, a visa application to Yemen, various items associated with Islamic radicalism, and papers by London-based Muslim radical Sheik Abu Hamzi al-Masri, who had publicly supported the 9/11 attacks. British citizen Osman is an active-duty U.S. Navy reservist and a former Army enlistee who lives in Tacoma. Osman lived for a time on a ranch in Blye, Oregon, which was raided in June 2002 by FBI agents investigating reports of a 1999 "jihad training camp," conducted by al-Masri. Others who visited Osman's mosque included "9/11 20th hijacker" Zacarias Moussaoui and would-be shoe bomber Richard Reid.

Police were also investigating mosque members James and Mustafa Ujaama, brothers who grew up in Seattle and converted to Islam. Police believed James posted radical Islamic teachings on a web site for al-Masri's London mosque and escorted two representatives from the mosque to the Oregon ranch.

On August 2, 2002, Semi Osman, of Tacoma, pleaded guilty to a weapons violation in exchange for immigration charges being dropped. Prosecutors had stated that Osman "was committed to facilitate an act of international terrorism," which defense attorney Robert Leen denied. On April 25, 2003, a Seattle judge sentenced Osman to 11 months in prison.

Akhtar Mohammad Osmani: a senior Taliban commander and a close associate of Osama bin Laden who was killed on December 19, 2006 in a U.S. airstrike in Afghanistan's Helmand Province near the Pakistani border. He was the most senior Taliban leader killed since 2001.

Adel Ismail Eisa Otaibi: variant of 'Adil Isma'il 'Isa al-'Utaybi.

Saud Homood Obaid Otaibi: a Saudi who was number 7 on the Saudis' 26 most-wanted terrorists list. He died in a gun battle with Saudi authorities on April 3–6, 2005 in a walled compound in Ar Rass.

Abdulaziz Muhammad Saleh Bin Otash: born in Saudi Arabia in 1975, on February 11, 2002, the Yemeni was believed by the FBI to be planning a terrorist attack in the United States or on U.S. interests in Yemen.

Abu Othman: a Saudi-based recruitment coordinator for al Qaeda in Iraq foreign fighters in 2006.

Ali Kathry Othman: on October 30, 1984, he was deported to Tripoli, Libya in connection with several bombs that went off in London during mid-March 1984. Evidence was insufficient to press charges.

Omar Mahmoud Mohammed Othman: more commonly known by the alias Abu Qatada.

Mohammed Oudeh: a house painter from East Jerusalem who, on November 5, 2002, admitted planting the bomb in Hebrew University's cafeteria that killed nine people in the summer of 2001.

Muhammad Abu Abd Allah Al Oujaylly: alias Abu Yacoub, a Saudi who was born in 1986 and joined al Qaeda in Iraq as a fighter in 2007, bringing his passport. His recruitment coordinator was Abu Usama, whom he met via his friend Abu Shaker. He arrived from Jordan by bus in Syria, where he met Abu Omar, Abu Omar al Tunisi, Abu Al Abbas, and Abu Muhammad Al Shayep, who relieved him of all but $200 of his $1,400, 4,000 lira, and 70 rials. His home phone number was 0096626721489; Rahime's was 0096656938184.

Abd Al Hakim Mustafa Al Oukaley: alias Abu Bu Sharia Al Libi, a Libyan from Dernah who was born in 1980 and joined al Qaeda in Iraq as a martyr in 2007, contributing $100 and his passport. His recruitment coordinator was Al Mayeet, whom he knew from the area. He brought $100 with him. His brother's phone number was 00218926219150; his father's was 00218925894602.

Abd Al Hakim Mansour Abd Al Qader Al Oulafie: alias Abu Abd Al Rahman Al Libie, a Libyan carpenter from Dernah who was born in 1977 and joined al Qaeda in Iraq as a fighter in 2007, providing his passport, military service certificate, and watch. His recruitment coordinator was Jalal al Kilani. He had experience with the AK-47. His home phone number was 00218735.

Abu Oumier: alias of Ali Othman Hammed al Ourfi.

Muhammad Mussa Oumran: alias Abu Al Walied, a Libyan born in 1985 who joined al Qaeda in Iraq on October 4, 2006, bringing $100 and a watch. His recruitment coordinator was Abu Omar. His phone number was 0926188074.

Mansour Oumrane: one of two Libyans arrested on February 19, 1988 by Senegalese security officials as they were attempting to illegally enter the country with explosives and weapons at Dakar-Yoff Airport during the night. They had come from Cotonou via Abidjan. They were turned over to the State Security Court on April 8, 1988, and faced three to five years in prison for "acts and maneuvers likely to threaten public security." On June 15, 1988, they were to be released without charges being brought and were to leave the country the next day.

Abd Al Mounaem Mekshar al Oumrani: variant of 'Abd-al-Mun'im Maqshar al-'Amrani.

Abd Al Rahman Muhammad Ouqael: alias Abu Hazifah Al Yamani, a Saudi from Jeddah who was born in 1983 and joined al Qaeda in Iraq as a fighter in 2007, bringing his passport. His recruitment coordinator was Abu Usama. His took a bus from Jordan to Syria, where he met Abu Omar, Abu Al Abbas, Abu Omar Al Tunisi, and Abu Muhammad Al Shayeb, who took $2,100 of his $2,400. His brother Ahamed's phone number was 00966569710233.

Abd Al Munaem Essa Muhammad Ouqaiel: alias Abu Yacoub, a Libyan student from Benghazi who was born in 1983 and joined al Qaeda in Iraq as a fighter in 2007, contributing his ID and passport. His recruitment coordinator was Abu Qassem, whom he knew through Abd Al Hamied inside Iraq. He took a bus from Egypt and Jordan to get to Syria, where he met Abu Omar and Loua'aie.

Samar Ourfali: a Palestinian who had lived in the Neuss, West Germany apartment that was raided on October 26, 1988, resulting in the arrests of 14 Arabs suspected of Popular Front for the Liberation of Palestine-General Command terrorist ties. On July 29, 1990, *Washington Post* reporter Jack Anderson said that in July 1990, Sweden had released from jail and expelled 11 Palestinians, including Ourfali, who might have been connected to the December 21, 1988 bombing of Pan Am 103 over Lockerbie, Scotland that killed 270.

Ali Othman Hammed al Ourfi: alias Abu Oumier, a Libyan from Dernah who was born on February 16, 1985 and joined al Qaeda in Iraq in 2006, 18th Ramadan, bringing 500 lira. His recruitment coordinator was Abu Hazifa. His father's phone number was 00218927598830; his uncle's was 0021881626604.

Muhammad Ousath: Yemen-based recruitment coordinator for al Qaeda in Iraq foreign fighters in 2007.

Issa Saad Oushan: one of Saudi Arabia's 26 most-wanted terrorists, he was killed on July 21, 2004 in a police raid on a terrorist safe house in Riyadh's

King Fahd district. Police found the severed head of U.S. hostage Paul Johnson, who had been kidnapped on June 12, 2004, in a refrigerator freezer. Police killed two terrorists on the 26 Most Wanted list, including Oushan, and captured three others, including the wife and three children of Saleh Awfi, the self-proclaimed leader of the group.

Sultan Raddy al Outabey: alias Abu Zer Al Meccee, a Saudi from Mecca who was born on 27/4/1405 Hijra and joined al Qaeda in Iraq on 22 Ramadan 1427 Hijra (2006), bringing a watch and 845 riyals. His brother's phone number was 0553272394; Munief's was 0566416525.

Fahed Naief Hajraf Al Outabi: alias Abu Azzm Al Hassawi: a Saudi who joined al Qaeda in Iraq in 2007, bringing $100. His personnel coordinators were Abu Omar Al Libi and Abu Hider. His home phone number was 0096635880796; Muhammad's was 00966559666691; and his brother Muhammad's were 09665046229138 and 00966504229138.

Fahid Hilal al Muqady al Outaby: alias Abu Muhammd al Nouman, a Saudi from al Sharqiea who was born in 1980 and joined al Qaeda in Iraq on 9th Ramadan 1427 Hijra (2006), bringing $100. His recruitment coordinator was Abu Musa'ab. His phone number was 0096655616680; Abu Mishbeb's was 0966504805048.

Nasser Bin Fisel Bin Nasser Al Outaby: alias Abu Azzam, a Saudi from Riyadh who joined al Qaeda in Iraq as a fighter on 6th Rajab 1428 Hijra (2007), contributing 4,500 Saudi riyals and his passport. His recruitment coordinator was Majed. His uncle's phone number was 0096605770433; his father's was 0966505496867.

Abu Obieda al Outaibe: alias of Muhammad Saud Muhammad al Jadiee.

Hamied Al Outtabie: alias Abu Mahjjen, a Saudi from Mecca who was born on 18/10/1401 Hijra

and joined al Qaeda in Iraq on 20th Sha'aban 1427 (circa 2007), bringing $900. His recruitment coordinator was Abu Tamam. His phone number was 0556555712.

Owaiss: alias al-Kini Abdallah, arrested in Qatar and extradited to Yemen in May 2004. He had trained in explosives in al Qaeda's al-Farouq camp in Afghanistan. In turn, he was a close associate of Saif al-Adel, al Qaeda's military chief who was a key planner of the 1998 U.S. embassy bombings in Africa, and Khallad, the one-legged Afghan fighter and architect of the USS *Cole* bombing. Owaiss was also connected to Abu Musab al-Zarqawi.

Mustafa Khan Owasi: age 33, one of five men for whom, on December 29, 2002, the FBI asked the public to be on the lookout. They were believed to have entered the U.S. illegally circa December 24, possibly from Canada. The Bureau's Seeking Information: War on Terrorism Web site said there was no specific information tying them to terrorist activities, but that the Bureau wanted to locate and question them. The FBI said the names and ages could be faked. The Bureau later said that they were "terror suspects" connected with a passport smuggling operation with possible ties to terrorists. The men may have lived in Pakistan and could be part of a larger group planning New Year's attacks. The *Washington Post* reported they were part of a group of 19 who had sought fake documents to use to enter the United States. The *Toronto Sun* said that the five arrived at Toronto's Pearson International Airport two weeks earlier, lived in the Toronto area for a few days, then were smuggled into the United States. A British Columbia woman saw two of them on a Vancouver Island ferry on December 10.

Pakistani Jeweler Muhammad Asghar, age 30, said that his photo was that used to identify Mustafa Khan Owasi. Asghar said he had never traveled abroad, having been stopped two months ago from traveling to the United Kingdom when United Arab Emirates police found he had a forged passport. He suggested that those who faked his passport had gone on to use his photo with this latest crop.

By January 2, 2003, the investigation into the manufacture of fake IDs had extended into Canada, Pakistan, and the United Kingdom, and the United States was considering publishing the names of six, and possibly 14, others. There was no record at the U.S. Immigration and Naturalization Service of anyone by any of the involved names coming into the United States.

On January 6, 2003, the FBI called off the hunt for the would-be terrorists, saying it was a hoax.

Mohamed Rashed Daoud al-Owhali: alias Khalid Salim Saleh bin Rashed, a Yemeni who rode on the truck in the August 7, 1998 bombing of the U.S. Embassy in Nairobi, was flown to the United States on August 26, 1998. He was arraigned the next day in a Manhattan courthouse on 12 counts of murder, one for each American killed, one count of conspiracy, and one count of using weapons of mass destruction. FBI Director Louis Freeh told a news conference that al-Owhali had admitted that he was trained in Afghan camps affiliated with Osama bin Laden, that he had attended meetings with bin Laden, and that he had expected to die in the bombing. Al-Owhali traveled to Nairobi on July 31 from Lahore, Pakistan. A week later, he threw the grenade at the guard at the embassy. He was hospitalized in Nairobi with lacerations on his hands and face and a large wound on his back. He was questioned by Kenyan police two days later, then arrested. At the hospital, he discarded two keys that fit a padlock on the rear of the truck, and three bullets from a gun he had in the truck. Hospital employees later found the evidence. On August 12, he initially told the FBI that he had been standing in a bank near the embassy when the bomb went off, and claimed that he was wearing the same clothing as on August 7. The affidavit doubted this claim, because "his clothes bore no traces of blood." He later admitted lying. On August 20, al-Owhali confessed to the FBI, saying he'd been trained in explosives, hijacking, and kidnapping in Afghan camps. Some were affiliated with al Qaida, which, according to the affidavit, was "an international terrorist group led by Osama bin Laden, dedicated to opposing non-Islamic governments with force and violence." He was aware that bin Laden had issued a fatwa calling for the killing of Americans. He was ordered held without bail pending a September 28 court appearance. Al-Owhali applied for free legal services, saying he was single, unemployed, and had received $12,000 from his father in the past year. His only asset was a 1992 Chevrolet Caprice.

Ekrem Ozel: alias of Louai al-Sakka.

P

Ghousror Abdallah Pahhoul: one of five Iranian diplomats arrested in Turkey on October 25, 1988 who were planning to kidnap Said Abu Hassan Mochhadezade, an anti-Khomeini engineer working in Erzincan who reportedly was a member of the Peoples Mujahideen. They were to be tried by a state security court in Istanbul State. The press reported that two of them were members of the Savama Iranian secret police; the other three were members of the embassy's bodyguard team.

Papa: alias of Abderraouf Ben Habib Jdey.

Abderrazak Para: alias of Amari Saifi.

Ali Akbar Parvaresh: on August 9, 1994, Argentine Judge Galeano ordered the Iranian Embassy Third Secretary's arrest in connection with the July 18, 1994 bombing of the Argentine-Israeli Mutual Aid Association (AIMA) in Buenos Aires that killed 96 and wounded 231. He had already left for Iran prior to the blast. On March 8, 2003, Argentine Judge Juan Jose Galeano issued a 400-page indictment against four Iranian diplomats, including Parvaresh, accusing them of the 1994 bombing of the Argentine Israeli Mutual Aid Association community center that killed 85 people. Parvaresh was a former Minister of Education and former Speaker of the Iranian Majlis (parliament).

Yahia Payumi: Palestinian arrested on June 7, 2004 in Milan, Italy with his houseguest, Rabei Osman el-Sayed Ahmed, who was linked to an al Qaeda network in Europe.

Adam Pearlman: alias of Adam Yahiye Gadahn.

Gideud Peli: on June 14, 1984, he was convicted of plotting to blow up the Al Aqsa Mosque. In a plea bargain, he was sentenced to five years for planning terrorist operations and another five for stealing and illegally transporting army weapons.

Adil Pervez: age 19, one of five men for whom, on December 29, 2002, the FBI asked the public to be on the lookout. They were believed to have entered the United States illegally circa December 24, possibly from Canada. The Bureau's Seeking Information: War on Terrorism Web site said there was no specific information tying them to terrorist activities, but that the Bureau wanted to locate and question them. The FBI said the names and ages could be faked. The Bureau later said they were "terror suspects" connected with a passport smuggling operation with possible ties to terrorists. The men may have lived in Pakistan and could be part of a larger group planning New Year's attacks. The *Washington Post* reported that they were part of a group of 19 who had sought fake documents to use to enter the United States. The *Toronto Sun* said that the five arrived at Toronto's Pearson International Airport two weeks earlier, lived in the Toronto area for a few days, then were smuggled into the United States. A British Columbia woman saw two of them on a Vancouver Island ferry on December 10.

By January 2, 2003, the investigation into the manufacture of fake IDs had extended into Canada, Pakistan, and the United Kingdom, and the United States was considering publishing the names of six, and possibly 14, others. There was no record at the U.S. Immigration and Naturalization Service of anyone by any of the names involved coming into the United States.

On January 6, 2003, the FBI called off the hunt for the would-be terrorists, saying it was a hoax.

Tiran Polack: identified on March 13, 1994 by Israeli authorities as a leader of the extremist group Kach, which the Cabinet unanimously banned for being a terrorist group.

Hadi Soleiman Pour: age 47, former Iranian Ambassador to Argentina who was arrested by UK officials on August 21, 2003. He was wanted for the 1994 bombing of the Argentine Israeli Mutual Aid Association community center that killed 85 people. Police detained him at his Durham home on an extradition warrant. He was freed on November 12, 2003, when the UK government said there was not enough evidence to continue the case.

Hassan Ellaj-Pour: variant of Hassan Alad-Push, a terrorist member of the People's Strugglers of Iran.

The Prince: alias of Osama bin Laden.

The Professor: alias Michael Raphael, alias Hedschab Dschaballah, alias Samir al Ahad. On March 20, 1989, *Radio Free Lebanon* claimed that Lebanese student Khalid Ja'far was given a cassette recorder rigged with explosives by a Libyan explosives expert called "The Professor" in Bonn one week before the December 21, 1988 Lockerbie bombing of Pan Am 103 that killed 270 people. Hamburg's *Bild*, on March 22, 1989, claimed that he used passports from Jordan, Lebanon, Syria, Morocco and Libya, and that his real name might have been Samir Qadar.

Hassan Alad-Push (variant Hassan Ellaj-Pour): People's Strugglers of Iran (Mujahiddin e Khalq) driver of a Volkswagen used to cut off the car of three U.S. employees of Rockwell International who were assassinated on August 28, 1976 as they were being driven to work at an Iranian air force installation, Doshen Tappeh, in southeastern Tehran. He was killed on September 5, 1976 by security agents who traced him through the car's dealer. A pistol used in the assassination was found with him. It was believed he had used it to administer the coup de grace.

Q

Abu al Qa'a Qa'a: alias of Hamzza Abu al Qa'a Qa'a.

Al Qa'a Qa'a: alias of Youssef Muhammad Al Saddeq Al Matrawi.

Hamzza Abu al Qa'a Qa'a: alias of Abu al Qa'a Qa'a, a Libyan from Dernah who was born on March 27 1982 and joined al Qaeda in Iraq on October 28, 2006, bringing 300 lira and a watch. His recruitment coordinator was Abu Abd Allah. His phone number was 081623949.

Samir Qadar: on March 2, 1989, Hamburg's *Bild* claimed that the Libyan was the mastermind of the December 21, 1988 Lockerbie bombing of Pan Am 103 that killed 270 people. The paper claimed that he had killed Egyptian journalist Yusuf Sebai in Cyprus on February 12, 1978, and was released from prison in 1982 after Abu Nidal threats. It claimed he organized the attacks on the U.S. Embassy and a synagogue in Rome in 1983 that killed 37, the attack on Leonardo da Vinci Airport in Rome on Christmas 1985, the September 5, 1986 hijacking of a Pan Am plane in Karachi, and the June 11, 1988 *City of Poros* shipjacking. In 1986, he married a Finnish woman and moved to Stockholm.

Muhammad Havi Qaddur: alias of Qaddura Muhammad Abd al-Hamid.

Abdel-Qadar Abdel Qader: a Syrian scrap dealer arrested on December 27, 2005 on suspicion of involvement in the December 12, 2005 car bombing in Beirut, Lebanon that killed 4 people, including anti-Syrian journalist and member of Parliament Gebran Tueni, age 48, and injured 39. He was one of three Syrians detained earlier for questioning in the case. He was questioned about phone calls made around the time of the bombing. He rented a plot of land near the scene of the crime.

Muhammad Abdel Qader: a medical student arrested in the Islamic Liberation Organization attack on the Military Technical Academy in Cairo on April 18, 1974, which killed 11 and injured 27 in a gun battle with police. The group's leader had visited Libya in June 1973 to discuss the attack with Muammar Qadhafi. The raid apparently was to lead to a coup attempt against President Sadat.

'Abdallah al-Qadhafi: alias Abu-Muhammad, a Libyan Islamic studies student from Massratah who joined al Qaeda in Iraq on July 4, 2007, contributing his passport. His recruitment coordinator was Abu-'Asim. He flew from Libya to Syria. His friend's phone number was 0928514123; his brother's was 0927989902.

Abd al-Latif Qadi: release from an Israeli jail was demanded on June 27, 1976 by the Popular Front for the Liberation of Palestine hijackers of Air France flight 139, an A300 flying from Tel Aviv to Paris and ultimately diverted to Entebbe.

'Abd-al-Quddus al-Qadi: alias Muhammad, an Egyptian Islamic Group terrorist who died during the failed June 26, 1995 assassination attempt against Egyptian President Hosni Mubarak in Addis Ababa, Ethiopia.

Yasin Al-Qadi: alias Shaykh Yassin Kadi, from Jiddah, Saudi Arabia, head of the Muwafaq Foundation, an al Qaeda front funded by wealthy Saudi businessmen. His U.S. assets were ordered frozen on October 12, 2001. His defunct Muwafaq (Blessed Relief) Foundation was listed as "an al Qaeda front that receives funding from wealthy Saudi businessmen" and was used for "transferring millions of dollars to bin Laden." He was named in August 19, 2003 as a major investor in BMI, Inc., an Islamic investment company in New Jersey that passed the money to terrorist groups, according to a federal affidavit.

Abd-al-Qadir: Yemen-based recruitment coordinator for al Qaeda in Iraq foreign fighters in 2007.

Ahmad Sayyid Qadir: *al-Musawwar* reported on March 29, 1996 that the Canadian government had asked the Pakistanis to release the Canadian of Egyptian descent who was believed involved in the November 19, 1995 truck bombing at the Egyptian Embassy in Pakistan that killed 19 and wounded more than 80.

Bid-al-Qadir: alias of 'Abd-al-Rahim.

Hasan Hamdan Hasan 'Abd-al-Qadir: one of a group of Jordanian Afghans sentenced on December 21, 1994 by the Jordanian State Security Court for belonging to an illegal society, participating in a conspiracy to carry out terrorist acts, and possessing explosives for illegal purposes. The Muslim fundamentalists bombed cinemas, wounding nine people, including an attack on January 26, 1994 at an Amman cinema showing what they perceived to be pornographic films, and another bombing on February 1, 1994. The group had been seized in a crackdown on Muslim radicals in January 1994. Their trial began on August 27, 1994, when they were accused of

planning to assassinate leading Jordanians, including 'Abd-al-Salam al-Majali, Jordan's former chief peace negotiator with Israel. One of those sentenced to death was Muhammad Jamal Khalifah, a Saudi fugitive son-in-law of Osama bin Laden. 'Abd-al-Qadir, a juvenile, was sentenced to 12 years.

Samir Muhammad Ahmad al-Qadir: variant Samir Muhammad Ahmad Khudayr, alias 'Ajjab Jabalah, alias Michel Nabih Raphael, alias Zahir al-Rabi'. On February 21, 1994, a Swedish court issued a warrant for his arrest; he was suspected of being the mastermind in the shipjacking of the *Achille Lauro* in the Mediterranean on October 7, 1985 in which U.S. citizen Leon Klinghoffer was murdered. Al-Qadir settled in Sweden in 1986 under another name. He was an operations officer of the Abu Nidal group. On February 27, 1992, French Judge Jean-Louis Bruguiere issued an international arrest warrant for him in connection with the July 11, 1988 Abu Nidal attack on the Greek ship *City of Poros* that killed nine people and injured 80. The warrants charged him with murder and attempted murder. The Palestinian carried a Libyan passport. He was identified by Doha's *al-Sharq* on March 19, 1993 as a former member of the Abu Nidal Group and a prominent member of its intelligence group. He was purged after he was suspected of contacting an Arab country's intelligence agency. Some reports indicate that he was killed in Athens by a car bomb in 1988.

Ahmed Abdul Qadus: captured with Khalid Sheikh Mohammed, a senior al Qaeda operative, on March 1, 2003 in Pakistan.

Islam Yousef Qafisha: a Nablus suicide bomber who, on August 12, 2003, killed Erez Hershkovitz, age 21, a recent high school graduate and resident of Elon Moreh settlement, and injured three other hitchhikers at a small bus kiosk at the highway intersection near the Ariel settlement. The bombing injured six people. Hamas claimed credit. The terrorist wore a green shirt and an explosive belt.

Nidal al-Qahiri: alias Abu-Sa'd, a Tunisian doctor from Tunis who was born in 1979 and joined al Qaeda in Iraq to become a suicide bomber in 2007. He was proficient in four languages. He brought a passport. He traveled from Germany to Turkey and Syria. His home phone number was 002675292329; colleague Farras's was 004916092766161.

Fu'ad Mansur 'Ali Sa'id Qahtan: alias Abu-'Abadah, a Yemeni who joined al Qaeda in Iraq in 2007, bringing $200. His personnel coordinators were Abu-Zubayr and Abu-Hadi. His phone number was 0096625426937.

Abd Allah Bin Turkey Bin Abd Allah Al Qahtani: alias Abu Al Muqdad, a Saudi from Riyadh who was born in 1978 and joined al Qaeda in Iraq as a martyr in 2007. His recruitment coordinator was Binder.

Abdullah Hamid al Muslih al Qahtani: a Saudi held at Guantánamo as of January 2004.

Hasan 'A'id al-Qahtani: variant Hassan A'aedd al Qahtani, alias Abu-Julaybib, variant Abu Julaibib, a Saudi from Riyadh who was born on July 27, 1982 and joined al Qaeda in Iraq as a fighter on October 28, 2006, contributing a flash memory/thumb drive and a watch. His recruitment coordinator was Abu-Sarab. His phone numbers were 0505474943 and 0555264746.

Hassan A'aedd al Qahtani: variant of Hasan 'A'id al-Qahtani.

Jabir Hasan al Qahtani: a Saudi held at Guantánamo as of January 2004. In the first week on August 2001, a Saudi named al Qahtani was refused entry to the United States by U.S. Customs officials in Orlando. He may have been intending to meet Mohamed Atta, the 9/11 leader, who was in Orlando at the time. He said he planned to visit friends in the United States but could not name them. Al Qahtani was later taken prisoner in Pakistan or Afghanistan and was held in the U.S. Navy's prison in Guantánamo Bay, Cuba.

Jabran Said bin al-Qahtani: a Saudi held at Guantánamo Bay who was charged on May 30, 2008 by the Pentagon with having attended al Qaeda training camps and studying bomb-making. He faced a life sentence.

Mohammed al-Qahtani: on February 11, 2008, the Pentagon announced that it would seek the death penalty in the war crimes charges of six individuals detained at Guantánamo who were believed to have planned the 9/11 attacks: Khalid Sheikh Muhammad, Ramzi bin al-Shibh, Ali Abd al-Aziz Ali alias Ammar al-Baluchi, Mohammed al-Qahtani, Mustafa Ahmed al-Hawsawi, and Walid bin Attash alias Khallad. The six were charged with conspiracy, murder in violation of the laws of war, attacking civilians, attacking civilian objects, intentionally causing bodily injury, destruction of property, terrorism, and material support for terrorism. Al Qaida members Khalid Sheik Mohammed (KSM), bin Attash, Binalshibh, and Ali were also charged with hijacking or hazarding an aircraft. Al-Qahtani was often described as the 20th hijacker who was to have been on UA flight 93 that crashed into the Pennsylvania countryside. He was denied entry into the United States by immigration agents at Orlando Airport on August 4, 2001. He allegedly provided cash to the 9/11 hijackers. His civilian attorney was Gitanjali Gutierrez of the New York Center for Constitutional Rights. On May 13, 2008, Susan Crawford, the legal officer supervising the trials, dismissed the capital charges against him.

Mohammed ibn-Abdullah Qahtani: presented as the Mahdi by the hundreds of heavily armed rebels who took over the Grand Mosque at Mecca on November 20, 1979.

Mohammed Jaafar al-Qahtani: an al Qaeda figure who escaped from an Afghan prison, was recaptured, and handed over to Saudi authorities by the United States on May 7, 2007.

Muhammad Abd Al Aziz Al Qahtani: alias Abu Haffas, a Saudi prayer caller from Tathlith who joined al Qaeda in Iraq as a martyr in 2007, bringing 1,100 lira. His recruitment coordinator was Abu Omar. His phone number was 00966500535954.

Muhammad 'Abd-al-'Aziz al-Qahtani: variant Muhammad Abd Al Aziz al Qahttani, alias Abu-Basir, variant Abu Baseer, a Saudi from Riyadh who was born on June 8, 1982 and joined al Qaeda in Iraq as a fighter on October 6, 2006, contributing 1,000 euros, a flash memory card, and a mobile phone. His recruitment coordinator was Abu-Sarab, variant Abu Serrab. His phone number was 0555215646.

Muhammad Abd Al Aziz al Qahttani: variant of Muhammad 'Abd-al-'Aziz al-Qahtani.

Abu Bakr Qaidah: an Egyptian Afghan Arab who was killed in the raid by Ibn Khattab's Chechen/Afghan Arabs on December 22, 1997 against the cantonment of the Russian Army's 136th Mechanized Brigade General Command.

Hasan Qaiid: alias of Abu Yahya al-Libi.

Abdel Nasser Qaisi: one of three Palestinian gunmen who, on December 11, 1996, ambushed and killed a 12-year-old Israeli and his mother and injured four other passengers (three girls, aged 4 to 10 and their father) in their Volkswagen Golf station wagon while they were driving on a new bypass road near Surda on the West Bank. Two gunmen, armed with automatic weapons, and a driver sped off to Ramallah, 12 miles north of Jerusalem. The victims of the evening killing were among the founding families of the Jewish settlement of Bet El. Survivor Yoel Tsur is director of the settlers' pirate radio station Channel 7. The Popular Front for the Liberation of Palestine (PFLP) took credit.

On December 18, the Palestine Liberation Organization's (PLO) State Security Court convicted three 20-year-old Palestinian PFLP members for the murders. Qaisi was sentenced to life in prison at hard labor for killing Etta Tsur and Ephraim Tsur. The PLO said the trio would not be extradited to Israel.

Kamal Ali Hammed Qaisse: alias Abu Basser, a Saudi from Jeddah who was born in 1403 Hijra and joined al Qaeda in Iraq in 2007, bringing 1,000 Saudi riyals. He was deployed to Al Anbar. His phone numbers were 0501063682, 0502684315, and 0509685187.

Ibrahim Qam: one of three Palestinian gunmen who, on December 11, 1996, ambushed and killed a 12-year-old Israeli and his mother and injured four other passengers (3 girls, aged 4 to 10 and their father) in their Volkswagen Golf station wagon while they were driving on a new bypass road near Surda on the West Bank. Two gunmen, armed with automatic weapons, and a driver sped off to Ramallah, 12 miles north of Jerusalem. The victims of the evening killing were among the founding families of the Jewish settlement of Bet El. Survivor Yoel Tsur is director of the settlers' pirate radio station Channel 7. The Popular Front for the Liberation of Palestine (PFLP) took credit.

On December 18, the Palestine Liberation Organization's (PLO) State Security Court convicted three 20-year-old Palestinian PFLP members for the murders. Qam was sentenced to life in prison at hard labor for killing Etta Tsur and Ephraim Tsur. The PLO said the trio would not be extradited to Israel.

Abu al Fazul al-Qamari: alias of Fazul Abdallah Muhammad.

'Isam al-Din Muhammad Kamal al-Qamari: one of three members of the Egyptian Jihad Organization serving life sentences for the October 6,

1981 assassination of Egyptian President Anwar Sadat who, on July 17, 1988, escaped from Turrah prison at dawn after attacking two prison guards. He was 160 centimeters tall with grey hair and a reddish complexion. On July 25, 1988, he was fatally shot by Egyptian police in a gun battle in the Shobra district of Cairo. Two policemen were wounded when Qamari fired a submachine gun and threw two grenades at the police.

'Ali Mustafa Bal'idal-Qamati: alias Abu-Turab, a Libyan from Benghazi who was born in 1986 and joined al Qaeda in Iraq in 2007. He said colleague Al-Bayana's phone number was 0926434691.

Qambar Khamis 'Ali Qambar: variant of Qumbar Khamis 'Ali Qumbar.

'Umar al-Mabruk Qammadi: one of two Libyans claiming membership in the Libyan Revolutionary Committees who, on June 26, 1987, gunned down an exiled opponent of Libyan leader Muammar Qadhafi on a Rome street near President Francesco Cossiga's residence.

Hisham Mustafa Qanbar: Syrian from Idlib Province who worked as the Third Secretary in the Syrian Embassy in Amman, and who was believed to have provided the explosive charge the went off inside the Cinderella grocery in Jabal Amman on January 11, 1982, wounding five people.

Mohammed Qandeel: Islamic Jihad's deputy commander in northern Gaza who was killed in an Israeli air strike on October 27, 2005.

Imad Qandil: one of 40 Shi'ite terrorists arrested in Egypt on August 19, 1989 for planning to carry out attacks against U.S., Israeli, Saudi, Iraqi, and Kuwaiti interests, including embassies and airlines. He was one of four dissident members of the Repudiation and Renunciation Group in al-Gharibiyah Governorate who formed the terrorist cell in 1985.

Abu-al-Qa'qa: alias of 'Abd-al-Sattar.

Abu-al-Qa'qa': alias of Hamzah 'Ali 'Awwad.

Abu-al-Qa'qa': alias of Muhammad.

Salad-Din al-Q'arah: one of the five Guards of Islam gunmen who failed in an assassination attempt against Shahpour Bakhtiar, the Shah's last Prime Minister, in Neuilly-sur-Seine, France on July 17, 1980.

'Adil Lahiq al-Qarni: alias 'Abdallah Mansur, a Saudi from Al-Madinah Al-Munawarah, Al-Jazirah who was born on December 24, 1972 and joined al Qaeda in Iraq on September 23, 2006. His recruitment coordinator was Abu-'Ibada. He contributed $400, a cell phone, and an "alphabetical device." He said colleague Abu-Lahiq's phone number was 0508193458 and his brother's was 0501851873.

Bader Bin Eied Bin Ali Al Qarni: variant of Badr Bin-'Id Bin-'Ali al-Qurni.

Musa al-Qarni: an Islamic cleric detained in Saudi Arabia on February 2, 2007 who had past associations with bin Laden during the Afghan war against the Soviets.

Salah Nasser Salim Ali Qaru: Yemeni arrested in Indonesia in August 2003 on suspicion of involvement in terrorist activities. The *Washington Post* claimed he was held in Jordan for ten days. As of December 2007, he was believed to be free in Yemen.

Jihad al-Qashah: alias of Ibrahim Mohammed Zein al-Abedeen.

'Ali Qashshur: an individual from Dayr Qanun al-Nahr and one of six reported by Beirut's *al-Nahar* on August 6, 1990 as appearing at an Amal news conference on charges of kidnapping, assassination, setting of explosions, and bringing booby-trapped cars into Tyre, Lebanon. They admitted involvement in the kidnapping of U.S. Marine Lt. Col. William Richard Higgins on February

17, 1988. The group also admitted planting explosive devices at centers of the UN forces in the south; blowing up Mustafa Mahdi's clothing store in Tyre as well as the Lebanese-African Nasr Bank in Tyre; and bringing three booby-trapped cars into Tyre and al-Bisariyah to kill Amal officials. They said they coordinated their actions with Hizballah and the Iranian Revolutionary Guards.

Qasim: an individual from Al 'Abbasiyah and one of six reported by Beirut's *al-Nahar* on August 6, 1990 as appearing at an Amal news conference on charges of kidnapping, assassination, setting of explosions, and bringing booby-trapped cars into Tyre, Lebanon. They admitted involvement in the kidnapping of U.S. Marine Lt. Col. William Richard Higgins on February 17, 1988. The group also admitted planting explosive devices at centers of the UN forces in the south; blowing up Mustafa Mahdi's clothing store in Tyre as well as the Lebanese-African Nasr Bank in Tyre; and bringing three booby-trapped cars into Tyre and al-Bisariyah to kill Amal officials. They said they coordinated their actions with Hizballah and the Iranian Revolutionary Guards.

Abd ar'Rahman Qasim: release from an Israeli jail was demanded on June 27, 1976 by the Popular Front for the Liberation of Palestine hijackers of Air France flight 139, an A300 flying from Tel Aviv to Paris and ultimately diverted to Entebbe.

Adam Ali Qasim: alias of Ramzi Ahmed Yusuf.

Ahmad Khalid al-Qasim: arrested on February 24, 1995 as one of two attackers of Gilles Haine, Second Secretary at the French Embassy in Amman, Jordan. Some speculated that Haine and his wife were shot at for eating in the open during Ramadan. A judicial source said that the gunmen sought to undermine tourism. The furniture shop assistant was from al-Karak. On September 5, 1995, the Jordanian State Security Court held a public session during which the defendants were charged with possessing and manufacturing

unlicensed explosives with the aim of using them illegally and of participating in a plot to carry out terrorist attacks.

Hafidh Qasim: release from an Israeli jail was demanded on June 27, 1976 by the PFLP hijackers of Air France flight 139, an A300 flying from Tel Aviv to Paris and ultimately diverted to Entebbe.

Ibrahim Qasim: his release from a Kenyan jail was demanded on June 27, 1976 by the Popular Front for the Liberation of Palestine hijackers of Air France flight 139, an A300 flying from Tel Aviv to Paris and ultimately diverted to Entebbe.

Muhammad 'Abd-al-Qadir Bil-Qasim: alias Abu-Hurayrah, a Libyan Arabic language teacher who claimed to be a weapons expert and was born in 1981. He joined al Qaeda in Iraq as a suicide bomber on June 7, 2007, bringing with him $200. His recruitment coordinator was Akram. He arrived via Egypt in Syria, where he stayed 13 days, meeting Abu-'Umar and giving him 2,000 Syrian lira. His phone numbers were 0021892690636 and 00218630236.

Muhammad Salam Bin Qasim: a Libyan diplomat accused by the Tunisian government of having brought letter bombs into Tunisia in a diplomatic pouch on board a Libyan Arab airliner. Authorities believed he took the bag to the Libyan General Commission in Tunis before he left Tunisia. One letter bomb injured a mail handler at the central post office on September 25, 1985. Tunisia severed diplomatic relations with Libya the next day.

Mustafa Qasim: alias Mustafa 'Arif al-Rifa'i, one of five Palestinians sentenced to death on October 27, 1988 by Sudanese Court President Judge Ahmad Bashir under Article 252 on charges of premeditated murder for firing submachine guns and throwing tear gas shells in the Acropole Hotel and the Sudan Club in Khartoum on May 15, 1988, killing eight people. The defendants were found guilty on all charges listed in a four-page list of indictments, with the exception of criminal plotting under Article 95, because the plotting was conducted outside Sudan. On January 7, 1991, the court trying the Palestinians ordered their immediate release because the decree "was based on the fact that the relatives of five British (victims) had ceded their right in qisas (blood vengeance) similar punishment and diya (blood money) but demanded imprisonment of the murderers." The court decreed two years in prison for murder, two years for committing damage, six months for possessing unlicensed weapons, one month for attempted murder at the hotel, and one month for attempted murder at the club. However, the punishments had to be applied concurrently and lapsed on November 15, 1990.

Mu'tasim Qasim: alias of Muhammad 'Abd al-Rahman 'Abid.

Tal'at Fu'ad Qasim: alias Abu-Talal al-Qasimi, media spokesman for the Egyptian Islamic Group, who was arrested on September 12, 1995 by Croatian authorities after he had escaped from Denmark to a military zone in Bosnia-Hercegovina. Cairo requested his extradition on September 14. Egypt's Higher Military Court passed a death sentence against him in December 1992 in the "returnees from Afghanistan" case. He had been charged in the al-Jihad case of 1981 and spent three years in jail. He then left for an unnamed Arab country, then moved to Peshawar, Pakistan, where he published the magazine *Al-Murabitun*. He obtained political asylum in Pakistan in 1992. He traveled to several European and African countries, including Sudan, during the next three years. He later changed his name to Ibrahim Ya'qub 'Izzat. On September 25, 1995 the Vanguards of Islamic Conquest threatened "severe" reprisals against Croatia and Egypt if he was extradited to Egypt. Croatia announced that he had left the country for an unknown destination on September 18. On October 20, 1995, his release was demanded by the Egyptian Gama'at members

who set off a car bomb in the parking lot of the police department of Primorje-Gorani county in Rijeka, Croatia, killing one person and injuring 29. On October 25, London's *al-Hayah* reported that the Danish government had been informed that Tal'at was abducted from Croatia, possibly by the Israelis, who took him to France.

Zakariya Muhammad Dawud Qasim: one of a group of Jordanian Afghans sentenced to death on December 21, 1994 by the Jordanian State Security Court for belonging to an illegal society, participating in a conspiracy to carry out terrorist acts, and possessing explosives for illegal purposes. The Muslim fundamentalists bombed cinemas, wounding nine people, including an attack on January 26, 1994 at an Amman cinema showing what they perceived to be pornographic films, and another bombing on February 1, 1994. The group had been seized in a crackdown on Muslim radicals in January 1994. Their trial began on August 27, 1994, when they were accused of planning to assassinate leading Jordanians, including 'Abd-al-Salam al-Majali, Jordan's former chief peace negotiator with Israel. One of those sentenced to death was Muhammad Jamal Khalifah, a Saudi fugitive son-in-law of Osama bin Laden.

Abu-Talal al-Qasimi: alias of Tal'at Fu'ad Qasim.

Muhammad Ahmad Qasir: a Lebanese Shi'ite associate of the hijacker of Air Afrique RK-056 on July 24, 1987. He was arrested on August 24, 1987 by Bangui, Central African Republic police. He lived in Sibut, 200 kilometers from Bangui, and was said to have given refuge to the terrorist for two weeks in July 1987.

Musa Ja'far Qasir: a Lebanese Shi'ite associate of the hijacker of Air Afrique RK-056 on July 24, 1987. He was arrested on August 24, 1987 by Bangui, Central African Republic police.

Yabu Qasiz: release from an Israeli jail was demanded on June 27, 1976 by the Popular Front for the Liberation of Palestine hijackers of Air France flight 139, an A300 flying from Tel Aviv to Paris and ultimately diverted to Entebbe.

Nihad Qasmar: one of the April 5, 1988 hijackers of Kuwait Airlines flight 422, a B747 flying from Bangkok to Kuwait that was diverted to Mashhad, Iran. On May 21, 1988, the Kuwaiti paper *al-Qabas* said that he was killed during clashes between Hizballah and Amal in Burj al-Barajinah, Beirut, at the beginning of the week.

Abu Qassem: Libyan-based recruitment coordinator for al Qaeda in Iraq foreign fighters in 2007.

Abu Qatada: alias of Omar Uthman Abu Omar, variant Omar Mahmoud Mohammed Othman, 44 in early 2005, a Jordan-born (some reports say he was born in Bethlehem in 1960) Palestinian Islamic cleric involved in the European operations of al Qaeda accused of inspiring the March 11, 2004 Madrid train bombers. British officials arrested him in October 2002, in a raid on his hideout in a south London house. He had been underground since December 2001. He was wanted for questioning in France, Spain, Italy, and Germany for recruiting for al Qaeda in Europe. He had been convicted and sentenced to life in prison in absentia by Jordan for a plot to bomb tourist sites and an American school. He also conducted prayer meetings attended by shoe bomber Richard Reid and Zacarias Moussaoui. French Judge Jean-Louis Bruguiere said Abu Qatada laundered money and planned and financed attacks throughout Europe. Spanish Judge Baltasar Garzon said he was a contact between al Qaeda and Abu Dahdah, a Spanish-based terrorist suspect, and terrorists in Germany, France, Italy, and Belgium. Hamburg authorities had found tapes by Abu Qatada in 9/11 hijack leader Mohammad Atta's last known apartment. Abu Qatada had been given asylum in the United Kingdom in 1994 after fleeing Jordan. But his travel documents were seized, assets frozen, and $600 weekly welfare payments suspended in October 2001 after it was determined that he had an unexplained $270,000 in his bank

account. He had expressed admiration for Osama bin Laden in interviews.

On March 11, 2005, after the British Parliament passed the government's antiterrorism law, a special immigration appeals judge freed eight terrorism suspects, including Abu Qatada. The eight foreign citizens had been held without charge or trial for up to 3 and a half years. Their freedom, however, included nighttime curfews, electronic tagging, regular searches of their homes, and a ban on the use of cell phones and computers. British authorities detained him on August 11, 2005. He was expected to be deported to Jordan.

On February 26, 2007, a special immigration court ruled that he faced no abuse if deported to Jordan. Jordan had twice convicted him in absentia and sentenced him to life in prison for plotting to bomb U.S. and Jewish sites. After 2 and a half years in Belmarsh Prison, he was released under "control orders," a form of house arrest. He was represented by attorney Gareth Peirce, who planned to appeal.

His release was demanded by the Palestinian gunmen who, on March 12, 2007, kidnapped BBC reporter Alan Johnston in Gaza City.

On April 9, 2008, a three-judge panel of the Court of Appeals for England and Wales denied deportation, saying there were reasonable grounds to believe that Jordan would jail him for life. An immigration appeals commission ordered the release of the "godfather of Londonistan" on May 8, 2008.

Hamza al-Qatari: senior al Qaeda financial aide listed by the *Washington Post* in late February 2002 as having died.

Abu-Qatibah: alias of Wa'il Muhammad Bishtawi.

Muhammad Kazim 'Abd al-Qawi: identified by Egyptian police as being a suspected in the attempted assassination on August 13, 1987 by four gunmen who fired on Major General Muhammad al-Nabawi Isma'il, former deputy prime minister and interior minister, in front of his house in Cairo. On August 28, 1987, police found his hideout in the fields of Santaris village, Ashmun District, al-Minufiyah Governorate. He fired a handgun at the police, who returned fire, killing him. He had been hiding in the house of pharmacist 'Abd al-Hamid Isma'il, who was later arrested.

Mahmud Ja'Far Qawwash: release from an Israeli jail was demanded on June 27, 1976 by the Popular Front for the Liberation of Palestine hijackers of Air France flight 139, an A300 flying from Tel Aviv to Paris and ultimately diverted to Entebbe.

Munsir al-Qaysar: variant of Monzer al-Kassar.

Isma'il al-Qaysiyah: a Palestinian Islamic Jihad member whose trial for setting off a bomb that killed seven people in Patras, Greece on April 19, 1991 began on May 8, 1992 in a courtroom within the Kordhallos prison in Piraeus. He was sentenced by an Athens appeals court on July 6, 1992 to 4 and a half years.

Fawaz Mukhlef Aweda al Qeddie: alias Abu Muhammed, a foreign fighter for al Qaeda in Iraq who was born in 1979 and lived in al Jaziera/al Gawef. His home phone number was 009666244146. He knew coordinator Abu Abdallah via al Akhal. He drove to Syria, stopped in al Keryatl al Sham and Dayr az Zawr and arrived in Iraq on the 22nd of Muahrem. He met with the al Qaeda in Iraq personnel specialist on 23 Muharem 1428 Hijiri. He presented 3,500 riyals from Abdallah to Abu al Muthanna, along with a passport, ID, and driver's license. While in Syria, he also met Lua'ai and Abu Abd al Malek. The facilitators took 3,200 riyals from him in Syria. He offered to be a martyr. He had been a prayer caller.

Faud al-Qeitan: one of three Kurdish sympathizers who hijacked an Iraqi Airways B737 flying from Mosul to Baghdad on March 1, 1975. They demanded $5 million and release of 85 political prisoners. During the flight, an Iraqi security officer engaged in a shootout with the hijackers, leaving two passengers dead and ten others, including a hijacker, wounded. The plane landed in Tehran, Iran, where the hijackers surrendered. Al-Qeitan was executed by an Iranian firing squad on April 7, 1975.

Ali Qhorbanifar: an Iranian expelled by the British Home Office to France on May 17, 1984 for "preparing acts of terrorism."

Ya'qub Qirrish: in a raid on a residence on October 3, 1992, Jordanian police uncovered weapons, documents, and photographs indicating that the Shabab al-Nafir al-Islami group planned to attack the United States, United Kingdom, and French embassies. On October 5, the prosecutor told the State Security Court that the Lower House member had pleaded not guilty to charges of affiliation with a group plotting to overthrow the regime and possession of illegal weapons. The group had financial support from the Popular Front for the Liberation of Palestine-General Command.

Ibrahim Qita'i: alias of Ibrahim 'Ali.

Amir 'Abd-al-Qadir Sadiq 'Umar Qishu: alias Abu-'Abd-al-Rahman, an Algerian student from Qasantinah who was born in 1984 and joined al Qaeda in Iraq as a fighter in 2007, bringing a passport. His recruitment coordinator was Jamal, who knew him through a friend who was a fellow student at the institute. He flew to Damascus, where he met Abu-'Uthman, who took from him $5 and two mobile phones. He also brought 50 euros and 450 lira. His home phone number was 0021391201607; his brother's was 00213233498619; a friend's was 0033620932612.

Ibrahim Ahmed Mahmoud al Qosi: a Khartoum-born Sudanese who was one of two bin Laden bodyguards detained at the Guantánamo Bay military prison who were charged by the United States on February 24, 2004 with conspiracy to commit war crimes, terrorism, attacking civilians, murder, and destruction of property. They became the first detainees to stand trial before the special military tribunals established after 9/11. Military prosecutors would not seek the death penalty.

Qosi was a key al-Qaeda accountant. He wore an explosive belt to thwart assassination attempts against bin Laden. He joined al-Qaeda at its 1989 founding. In the early 1990s, he was an al-Qaeda courier in Sudan. He completed military training at an al-Qaeda terrorist camp in Afghanistan and served as an al-Qaeda accountant in Pakistan, eventually becoming a top financial officer. He managed and distributed money via Muslim charities, and helped run Taba Investment Company. He signed checks for bin Laden and exchanged money on the black market. He moved explosives and ammunition around Sudan for the terrorist group. In 1994, after a failed assassination attempt, he was chosen to be a bodyguard. He often was bin Laden's driver. He served in an al Qaeda mortar crew from 1998 to 2001. He also ran the kitchen at bin Laden's Star of Jihad compound in Jalalabad. He was one of 40 al Qaeda members captured by Pakistani forces in December 2001 near Tora Bora. He was represented by attorney Air Force Lt. Col. Sharon Shaffer. On August 27, 2004, he appeared before a military commission and was formally charged with conspiring to commit terrorism, which carries a life sentence. He did not enter a plea.

On February 9, 2008, a new Congressionally approved military commission charged the 47-year-old Qosi with being an al Qaeda conspirator. He was accused of helping bin Laden's family flee Kandahar to Kabul, then Jalalabad, then to Tora Bora around the 9/11 attacks. The Pentagon said it would seek life in prison. On March 6, 2008, the Pentagon added charges of war crimes, material support for terrorism, and conspiring with bin Laden. His arraignment was scheduled for April 10, 2008.

Mohammad Rateb Qteishat: one of five Islamic militants who, on March 12, 2006, were convicted in Jordan of plotting terrorist attacks against Jordanian intelligence agents, foreign tourists, and upscale hotels. They were sentenced to ten years of hard labor to life. Qteishat, the plot's organizer who remained at large, received a life sentence. He was believed to be holed up in Iraq.

Muhammad Yasin Qu'adduh: a Lebanese who was 1 of 13 members of the Iranian Lebanese Hizballah reported by Madrid *Diario 16* on October 20, 1987 as having entered Spain on October 13, 1987 to attack diplomats from Saudi Arabia, Kuwait, and Iraq.

Ahmed Hassan Quaily: age 33, an Iraqi arrested in October 2004 by the FBI in a sting operation in which he trying to buy machine guns and hand grenades from undercover agents. He threatened to "go jihad" against the United States. On May 31, 2005, he pleaded guilty to federal weapons charges in Nashville, Tennessee.

'Ali Ghassan Mahmud Qubaysi: a Lebanese who was 1 of 13 members of the Iranian Lebanese Hizballah reported by Madrid *Diario 16* on October 20, 1987 as having entered Spain on October 13, 1987 to attack diplomats from Saudi Arabia, Kuwait, and Iraq.

Taysir al-Qubba'ah: Popular Front for the Liberation of Palestine Executive Committee member who, in a July 1977 interview with Madrid's *Cambio* in Algiers, vowed to kill several Arab personalities, including Yasir Arafat.

Abu-Qudamah: alias of Faysal 'Abdallah Ahmad al-Faraj.

'Adil al-Sayyid 'Abd-al-Quddous: variant of 'Adil al-Sayyid 'Abd-al-Quddus.

'Adil al-Sayyid 'Abd-al-Quddus: variant Quddous, fugitive sentenced to death on March 17, 1994 by the Higher Military Court in Cairo in connection with the November 25, 1993 bombing of the convoy of Egyptian Prime Minister Dr. 'Atif Sidqi that killed a 15-year-old girl and wounded 21 other people. The at-large Egyptian Jihad terrorist was one of 62 defendants tried in absentia in a military tribunal in Haekstep, Egypt beginning on February 1, 1999. Charges against 107 defendants included forgery, criminal conspiracy, subversion, membership in an outlawed group, plotting to carry out attacks on officials and police, attempting to prevent security forces from carrying out their jobs, and conspiracy to overthrow the government. He remained in London.

Walied Abd Allah Muhammad Quehaiel: alias Asad Allah, a Libyan teacher from Dernah who was born on September 13, 1980 and joined al Qaeda in Iraq as a martyr on 22nd Rabi al-thani 1428 Hijra (2007), contributing 1,550 Syrian Lira. He had experience in weight lifting. His recruitment coordinator was Bashar. He arrived in Syria via Egypt. While in Syria, he met Abu Abbas. He brought with him $400. His phone number was 32189928036889.

Muhammad bin Querqa: alias Abu-Mujahed, a Tunisian recruit to al Qaeda in Iraq who wanted to serve as a fighter, claiming to be a shooting expert. His phone number was 21227529. He was born on January 9, 1980, and arrived in Iraq on 8 Muharem 1428. He contributed 2205 Lira and other cash and also brought his passport and ID. His coordinator was Safwan al Tunisian, whom he knew from Al Sham, Syria. He flew from Turkey to Damascus, then moved on to Iraq. He met Abu-Muhammad while in Syria. He brought $1,200 with him; none was taken from him in Syria.

Abu-Quhafah: Saudi-based recruitment coordinator for al Qaeda in Iraq foreign fighters in 2007.

Aldemar Quintari: an Afghan explosives expert identified in December 1995 by the *World*, a Philippines newspaper, as having been chosen to replace terrorist Shah in carrying out planned terrorist activities in Manila.

Muhammad 'Abdallah al-Qulaysi: alias Abu-al-Hur, a Yemeni mechanical engineer from Sana'a who was born in 1987 and joined al Qaeda in Iraq as a fighter on June 19, 2007. His recruitment coordinator was Muhammad. He flew from Yemen to Damascus, where he met Abu-'Umar, who took $100 of his $300. His phone number was 711782833.

Muhammad Qumayl: on January 30, 1995, the Janin military court sentenced him to life plus 10 years in prison for aiding Raid Zakarna, a 19-year-old Palestinian who, on April 6, 1994, drove an Opel car bomb next to an Egged bus number 340 at a bus stop in 'Afula, Israel, killing eight, including himself, and wounding more than 50 people. He was also sentenced for planning several other aborted attacks, including a suicide attack near an Israel Defense Forces bus in his native Janin.

Qumbur Khalis 'Ali Qumbur: variant Qambar Khamis 'Ali Qambar, a 23-year-old laborer who was one of four suspects from Sutrah, Bahrain who confessed in front of an investigating judge to pouring gasoline and throwing Molotov cocktails at the al-Zaytun Restaurant in Sitrat Wadiyan on March 14, 1996, killing seven Bangladeshi workers. On July 1, 1996, the State Security Court sentenced him to life for premeditated arson.

Fhad al-Quoso: Yemeni accused of involvement in the October 12, 2000 al Qaeda bombing of the USS *Cole* in Yemen in which 17 U.S. sailors were killed and 44 injured. He reportedly told investigators that an associate of bin Laden gave him more than $5,000 to finance the *Cole* attack's planning and videotaping of the suicide bombing.

Hanni Abd Allah Al Quraishy: alias Abu Suleiman, a Saudi student from al Ta'aef who joined al Qaeda in Iraq as a martyr in 2007, contributing 25 lira and a passport. His recruitment coordinator was Abu Rowan. He flew to Syria, where he met Abu Umar, Abu Fisel, and Abu Muhammad. He gave them 25,000 Syrian lira. He had some media experience. His home phone was 0095527387673; his brother's was 0096650355605; a friend's was 00966552447916.

Adel Lahiq al Qurani: alias Abd Allah Mansour, a Saudi from Al Madina born on 13/11/1392 Hijra who joined al Qaeda on 1st Ramadan 1427 Hijra (circa 2006), bringing $400 and label makers. His recruitment coordinator was Abu Ebbadah. He said Abu Lahiq's phone number was 0508193458; his brother's was 0501851873.

Hassan Bin Alalmah Muhammad Al Qurani: alias Abu Abfd Al Rahman, a Saudi born in 1391 Hijra who joined al Qaeda in Iraq in 2007, bringing $41,732. He said colleague Ahmed's mobile phone was 0504547853; Ahmed could also be contacted at 072813158 and 0556891683.

Tariq Quraysh: variant of Tariq al-Qurayshi.

Tariq al-Qurayshi: variant Tariq Quraysh, wanted in connection with the Muslim Group's October 21, 1992 attack on a tour bus near Dayrut, Egypt that killed a British tourist and injured two others. His brother died on October 6, 1992 when a bomb he was carrying exploded in Dayrut station, killing four other people. Tariq was one of seven Islamic militants shot dead by police in a raid in Cairo on February 3, 1994.

Badr Bin-'Id Bin-'Ali al-Qurni: variant Bader Bin Eied Bin Ali Al Qarni, alias Abu-Usamah, a Saudi from al-Sharai', variant Al Shara'ah, Mecca, who joined al Qaeda in Iraq on September 13, 2006. He was born on November 2, 1981. His phone number was 0504502049; he listed a home number of 5241302. His recruiter was

Abu-Tamam. He contributed $1,000 and was assigned to the al-Fallujah area.

Fahad al-Quso: variant of Fahd Mohammed Ahmed al-Quso.

Fahd Mohammed Ahmed al-Quso: variant Fahad al-Quso, alias Fahd Mohammed Ahmed al-Awlaqi, Abu Huthaifah, Abu Huthaifah al-Yemeni, Abu Huthaifah Al-Adani, Abu al-Bara, indicted with Jamal al-Badawi by the United States in 2003 following Badawi's confession to the FBI in January 2001 that he had been recruited by al Qaeda to lead a terrorist attack. Al-Quso was born in Aden, Yemen on November 12, 1974 and has Saudi citizenship. He is five feet six inches tall and weighs 150 pounds. He is wanted in connection with the October 12, 2000 bombing of the USS *Cole*. He was being held by Yemeni authorities for the *Cole* attack when he escaped from prison in April 2003. He was indicted on May 15, 2003 by a federal grand jury on 50 counts, including murder and conspiracy to murder U.S. nationals and U.S. military personnel; conspiracy to use and using a weapon of mass destruction; damaging and destroying government property and defense facilities; and providing material support to a terrorist organization. The Rewards for Justice Program offers $5 million for his arrest and/or conviction. He was convicted in a Yemeni court for involvement in the USS *Cole* attack. He was released from prison in May 2007.

Abu Quitaibay: variant of Abu-Qutaybah.

Abu-Qutadah: alias of Sa'id Awlad al-Sheikh.

Abu-Qutaybah: alias of Al-Tahir Ayat Billa.

Abu-Qutaybah: variant Abu Quitaibah, alias of Fathallah Khayrallah ;Abd-al-Karim, variant Fattah Alah Khaier Allah Abd Al Karim.

Abu-Qutaybah: alias of Muhamad.

Sayyid Qutb: an extremist militant of the Egyptian Muslim Brotherhood who was executed by Egypt in 1966. His ideas influenced Osama bin Laden.

Abu Quttaibah: alias of al Taher Ayett Bala.

Saleh Quuwaye: one of two Saudis who were among the nine suspected terrorists arrested on December 29, 1995 by Philippines police, who also seized explosives, 50 Philippine passports, and maps of Metro Manila.

R

Ezzat Ahmad Rabah: one of four members of Black September who assassinated Jordanian Prime Minister Wasfi Tell in Cairo's Sheraton Hotel on November 28, 1971. Jordanian Foreign Minister Abdullah Sallah was slightly injured, and an Egyptian policeman was seriously wounded. The foursome was immediately captured. Rabah, the shooter, said "We wanted to have him for breakfast, but we had him for lunch instead." The group said it was avenging the killing of Palestinian guerrillas in the Jordanian civil war of September 1970, which Palestinians referred to as Black September. Their release was demanded by the hijackers of Lufthansa 649 on February 22, 1972. After great pressure by Arab nations, Egypt released them on bail of 1,000 Egyptian pounds ($2,300) each. Some reports said that the Palestine Liberation Organization provided their bail on February 29, 1972. Other reports said that the Popular Front for the Liberation of Palestine claimed credit. They were never brought to trial. Some reports said they lived in Cairo for a year with Libyan financing. They were then told to leave Cairo and were given transit documents for Beirut. But the judiciary balked and prevented their travel.

Mohammed Ahmed Rabbah: name given by a caller to Ophir Zadok, an Israeli security officer at the Israeli embassy in Brussels on September 11, 1972 who was lured to Prince's Café in De Brouckere Square. The caller claimed to have information about a terrorist plot against the embassy. Two fedayeen terrorists fired at him, critically wounding him. Some accounts credited Fatah or Black September; others said he was an undercover Mossad officer, and the caller was one of his Palestinian contacts.

Mohammad Nasir Rabbini: one of four Iranian members of the Martyrs of the Iranian Revolution who were arrested on July 23, 1984 while carrying two antitank grenade launchers, six 40 mm grenade launchers and two .45-caliber machine guns in Barcelona and Madrid. They were charged with plotting to hijack a Saudi airliner. Authorities believed their Barcelona safe house was used in the coordination and perpetuation of terrorist acts in Spain and elsewhere in Europe, including attacks against a Saudi plane and the U.S. Embassy in 1983. The terrorists planned to shoot down another Saudi plane and to assassinate Masud Rajavi, leader of the Mojahedine-e Khalq in Paris.

Mohsen Rabbani: former cultural attaché at the Iranian Embassy in Buenos Aires until December 1997. He was believed to have been involved in the planning of the March 17, 1992 bombing of the Israeli Embassy in Argentina and the July 1994 bombing of the Jewish Community Center in Buenos Aires. He was aided by four local police officers who were arrested and four Iranian intelligence officers who entered the country through Ciudad del Este, Paraguay. On March 8, 2003, Argentine Judge Juan Jose Galeano issued a 400-page indictment against four Iranian diplomats, including Rabbani, accusing them of the 1994 bombing of the Argentine Israeli Mutual Aid Association community center that killed 85 people.

Ashraf Sa'id 'Abd-Rabbuh: one of seven terrorists hanged on July 8, 1993 in the appeals prison in Cairo for attacks on tourist buses and installations in the al-Wajh al-Qiblio, Luxor, and Aswan areas, in accordance with the sentence handed down by the Supreme Military Court on April 22, 1993 in Case Number 6.

Salah Sa'ib 'Abd-Rabbuh: arrested by Egyptian police in connection with the February 26, 1993 bombing of the Wadi el-Nil coffee shop in Tahrir Square in Cairo in which four people were killed and 16 wounded. He was tried with 48 other fundamentalist suspects on March 9, 1993 at the military court complex in the Hakstep area east of Cairo. They were charged with damaging national unity and social peace by calling for a change of the system of government and damaging the national economy by attacking tourism. Some were also charged with attempted murder in eight attacks on tour buses and Nile cruise ships. They faced possible death sentences. They were also accused of belonging to an underground organization, attempting to overthrow the government, and illegal possession of arms and explosives.

Fawaz Yahya al-Rabeei: variant Fawaz al-Rabi'l, alias Furqan the Chechen, a Yemeni believed born in Saudi Arabia in 1979. On February 11, 2002, he and perhaps 16 others from Saudi Arabia, Yemen, and Tunisia were believed by the FBI to be planning a terrorist attack in the United States or on U.S. interests in Yemen. He was behind the 2002 attack on the French tanker *Limburg* off the Yemeni coast, in which a Bulgarian crew member died and 90,000 barrels of oil spilled into the Gulf of Aden. al-Rabeei had also been convicted for the attack on a Hunt Oil Company helicopter in 2002 and setting off a bomb at a Civil Aviation Authority building.

In early April 2003, Yemeni authorities arrested him. He apparently escaped an explosion on August 9, 2002 that killed two accomplices in a Sana'a warehouse, where terrorists had hidden 650 pounds of Semtex in pomegranate crates. Yemeni officials also seized weapons, including rocket-propelled grenades.

At 4:30 A.M. on February 3, 2006, 23 convicted al Qaeda members, including al-Rabeei, broke out of a Sana prison by crawling through a 140-yard-long tunnel they had dug in cooperation with outsiders. They used a broomstick with a sharpened spoon and three pots tied together as a U-shaped scoop to dig beneath the Political Security Office basement compound. They had been sentenced in 2005 on terrorism charges. The escape occurred before the scheduled February 4, 2006 trial of Mohammed Hamdi Ahdal, a senior al Qaeda suspect, and 14 others charged with involvement in several terrorist attacks in the country, including the USS *Cole* bombing and the *Limburg* ship bombing. Observers suggested the escape was an inside job.

On October 1, 2006, Yemeni antiterrorist authorities killed al-Rabeei.

Fawaz Yayha al Rabeiei: variant of Fawaz Yahya al-Rabeei.

Zahir al-Rabi': alias of Samih Muhammad Khudayr.

Abdelghani Rabia: an Algerian acquitted on December 18, 2002, by a Rotterdam court on charges of planning attacks on the U.S. Embassy in Paris. He was turned over to immigration authorities for being in the country illegally.

Hamza Rabia: served as external operations chief for Osama bin Laden before he and four other al Qaeda terrorists were killed by a missile from a Predator drone on December 1, 2005 in Pakistan in a tribal area along the Afghan border. The Egyptian citizen was a top operational planner against U.S. and European targets. He had replaced Abu Faraj Libbi, who had been the third-ranking leader of al Qaeda. Local authorities said the men, including two Arabs, died while making bombs at 1:45 A.M.

Ashrai Rabii: wife of Massoud Rajavi, Paris-exiled leader of the Iranian Mujaheddin-e- Khalq Iran. She was killed in a security raid on a northern Tehran house on February 8, 1982.

Fawaz al-Rabi'l: variant of Fawaz Yahya al-Rabeei.

Muhammad Bin Abd Al Rahm'man Bin Abd Rabuh: alias Abu Klash, a Saudi student from Mecca who was born on September 19, 1404 Hijra and joined al Qaeda in Iraq as a fighter on 5th Jumada al-awal (2007), bringing 2,500 Saudi Riyals. His recruitment coordinator was Abu Abd Allah, whom he knew via Abu Abbas. He arrived in Syria where he met Abu Khalaf Abu Hussien, a tall man with a red face. His phone number was 0551708038; his father's was 0508826704.

Rachid: alias of Abdelylah Ziyad.

Hchaichi Rachid: alleged member of the Islamic Salvation Front who, by October 1, 1992, had confessed to involvement in the August 26, 1992 bombing of the Air France ticket counter at Houari Boumedienne Airport in Algeria that killed 12 people and wounded 128. He was born in May 1946 at el Biar, Algiers and lived in its Rabia district. He was a captain with Air Algerie airlines. Had had a Bachelor of Arts degree in mathematics and a professional pilot's degree from Yugoslavia. Public sessions of his trial began on May 4, 1993. On May 26, 1993, a special Algiers judicial council passed a death sentence on 38 defendants, including him. The council found him guilty of actual, direct participation in the crime as well as taking part in an aggression with the aim of destroying the governing regime. On August 31, 1993, after exhausting all constitutional and legal appeals, he was executed.

Ayman Kamel Radi: variant Iman Ghadi, a 21-year-old resident of Khan Yunis in the Gaza Strip who died on December 25, 1994 when a bomb he was carrying exploded prematurely and wounded 13 people as he was putting the satchel of explosives near a bus full of Israeli airmen near the Jerusalem Convention Center on Zalman Shazar Avenue. He was a member of the Gaza Strip's Palestinian Authority police force. Hamas claimed credit.

Muhammad 'Abd-al-Radi: an Egyptian Islamic Group terrorist who was injured during the failed June 26, 1995 assassination attempt against Egyptian President Hosni Mubarak in Addis Ababa, Ethiopia. He later died of his wounds.

Radwan: alias of Dr. Ramadan Abdullah Mohammad Shallah.

Ahmad 'Abd-al-Rahim Radwan: alias Ahmad 'Abd-al-Ghani, one of seven terrorists hanged on July 8, 1993 in the appeals prison in Cairo for attacks on tourist buses and installations in the al-Wajh al-Qiblio, Luxor, and Aswan areas, in accordance with the sentence handed down by the Supreme Military Court on April 22, 1993 in Case Number 6.

Captain Rafat: an alias of Ali Shafik Ahmed Taha, alias Ahmed Mousa Awad, one of three Popular Front for the Liberation of Palestine (PFLP) hijackers of an El Al B707 going from Rome to Tel Aviv's Lod Airport on July 22, 1968. The plane was diverted to Algiers, where the hijackers demanded the release of 1,200 Palestinian prisoners from Israeli jails. The Algerians held the trio at a military camp for the balance of the negotiations.

Rafat led a Black September hijacking on May 8, 1972 of Sabena Airlines flight 517, a B707 flying the Vienna–Athens–Tel Aviv route over Zagreb by two male and two female Black September members. The group landed at Lod Airport in Israel and demanded the release of 317 fedayeen prisoners, most of them held at Ramleh prison. They threatened to blow up the plane and all aboard. He was killed when Israeli forces stormed the plane.

In 1969, he had supervised the two Young Tigers of the PFLP's Ho Chi Minh section, who bombed the Brussels office of El Al. He was also a member of the Revolution Airstrip commando squad in 1970, during the PFLP's multiple hijackings. In 1971, he joined Black September.

His release was demanded by the four Black September terrorists who took over the Israeli Embassy in Bangkok on December 28, 1972.

Salama Abdel Hakeem Radwan: an Islamic Group member who was killed in an April 23, 1996 gun battle with hundreds of police. The terrorists were holed up near Ashmouneen in Minya Province, Egypt, and were suspected of involvement in the April 18, 1996 firing on the Europa Hotel on al-Haram Street in Cairo that killed 18 Greek tourists and wounded 21 other people.

Salih Ra'fat: official spokesman in 1993 for the Democratic Front for the Liberation of Palestine's Yasir 'Abd-Rabbuh wing.

Mohamed Rafik: a Moroccan imam who preached at a mosque in Cremona, outside Milan. On July 13, 2005, a judge in Brescia, Italy, sentenced him to four years and eight months for membership in a cell that planned attacks, including one against Milan's subway system.

Abd al Rahman Bin Ali Al Ragahi: variant of 'Abd-al-Rahman Bin-'Ali al-Rajihi.

Yahya Ragheh: age 23, whom al Qaeda member Rabei Osman el-Sayed Ahmed was training to become a suicide bomber, received five years on November 6, 2006, from a court in Milan.

Abu Raghib: alias of Abd Al Ghani Hibab Al Sa'awi.

Ibrahim Abdul Azis Raghif: alias Abu Safwat, a member of Fatah's office in Beirut, who was assassinated in Cyprus on December 15, 1979 by a gunman who ran off. Israel said he was in Cyprus to organize raids against Egyptian and Israeli targets.

Nazih al-Raghie: alias of Anas al-Liby.

Raghu: variant of Rasu.

Nazih Abdul Hamed al-Ragie: alias of Anas al-Liby.

Mohammed Jahir Abbas Rahal: alias Muhammad Ghali, a Lebanese arrested with a pistol that was used in the shooting of Libyan Embassy official Mohammed Idris, who was driving to the embassy in Madrid on September 12, 1984. Rahal had grown up in west Beirut and was a member of the Imam Musa as-Sadr Brigade. Rahal confessed that he had shot Idris on orders of the group's leader. On October 10, 1984, the kidnappers of Spanish Ambassador Pedro Manuel de Aristegui demanded his release. On June 18, 1985, the hijackers of TWA flight 847 demanded his release. He and an accomplice were scheduled to stand trial on June 19, 1985 in Madrid. The Spanish government refused to release them. On June 25, 1985, the duo were sentenced to 23 years in prison for attempted murder. There were rumors that they would be sent to Lebanon to serve out their sentences. On January 17, 1986, Rahal's relatives abducted a Spanish diplomat and two Lebanese Spanish Embassy consular staffers and demanded Rahal's release. The Black Flag also demanded his release. He was pardoned by the Spanish government on July 14, 1986 and returned to Beirut.

Abd Al Raheem Fathie Abd Al Raheem: alias Abu Hamzza, a Libyan from Dernah who was born in 1986 and joined al Qaeda in Iraq as a fighter in 2007, bringing his passport. His recruitment coordinator was Basha'ar. He arrived via Egypt and Syria, where he was given 1,500 Syria lira. The phone number of colleague Abu Abd Al Rahman was 00218924925123.

Mohsem Rahgohzar: one of two People's Mujahedin-e Khalq hijackers of an Iranian Airbus en route from Tehran to Jeddah on August 7, 1984 that was diverted to Cairo and Rome, where they surrendered. On August 13, 1984, a Rome court acquitted him. He had requested political asylum in Italy. The Iranian government pressured him to return home to face trial and "a light sentence."

Zaydan Abd Al Alsalam Abd Al Rahiem: alias Abd Al Rahman, a self-employed Libyan from Benghazi who was born in 1985 and joined al Qaeda in Iraq on the 8th Jumada al-Awal 1428, hoping to become a martyr. His recruitment coordinator was Usama, whom he knew through a friend. He arrived via Libya, Egypt, and Syria, where he met Abu-'Umar. He brought with him 650 Libyan dinars.

Abd al-Rahim: one of four individuals who were seen on al Qaeda videotapes seized in the home of the late al Qaeda commander Muhammad Atef. On January 17, 2002, they were believed to be at large and planning suicide attacks against Western targets. Possibly the same individual as Abdul Rahim-Riyadh.

'Abd-al-Rahim: alias Bid al-Qadir, a Moroccan sent on a suicide mission by al Qaeda in Iraq in 2007. He owned a passport, 245 liras, and 100 euros. Khalid, his brother, could be phoned on 0021278642442.

'Abd al-Rahim Isma'il Muhammad Taqi 'Abd al-Rahim: one of five people for whom the Kuwaiti Interior Ministry on February 3, 1987 issued arrest warrants on suspicion of involvement in recent bombings.

Abdel Rahim: alias of Richard Reid, the shoe bomber.

'Alayni 'Abd al-Rahim: a Palestinian who, on March 13, 1984, was chased down in front of the Israeli Embassy in Palaion Psikhikon, an Athens suburb, and found to be carrying a loaded pistol. He confessed that he and four other members of the Lebanese National Resistance Front had intended to assassinate Yehezkel Barnea, the Israeli charge d'affaires in Greece. He had made an earlier

trip to Athens on February 2 and had stayed until March 2 to plan the assassination. His Moroccan passport said he was born in Tripoli, Lebanon. On March 15, 1984, he was charged with the attempted assassination and jailed to await trial. On April 19, 1984, the trial was postponed indefinitely while the judicial decision on his indictment was translated into Arabic.

Atta Tayem Hamida Rahim: an Egyptian engineer and former reserve officer in the Egyptian Air Defense Command who was named on November 12, 1981 as one of the assassins of Egyptian President Anwar Sadat on October 6, 1981. He was sentenced to death on March 6, 1982 and hanged on April 15, 1982.

Iyad Wasif 'Abd al-Rahim: one of three men arrested for the November 24, 1985 Abu Nidal Group assassination of Husayn 'Ali Ibrahim al-Bitar and his son, Mohammad, in the Al-Rashid suburb of Amman, Jordan. The trio entered Jordan on November 14 from Kuwait carrying Jordanian passports.

Muhammed Rahim: an Afghan al Qaeda associate of Osama bin Laden who was turned over to the U.S. military at Guantánamo Bay on March 14, 2008. The "high value detainee" was captured in Pakistan in the summer of 2007. He had helped bin Laden escape from Tora Bora, Afghanistan in 2001. He had served bin Laden as a courier, personal facilitator, and translator. He sought chemicals for an attack against U.S. forces in Afghanistan and tried to recruit people who could get onto U.S. bases.

Rabah Abdul-Rahim: an aide to Abu Nidal who was assassinated on August 23, 1989 as he was driving with his bodyguards to Sidon from Beirut, Lebanon. He was a senior member of the Fatah-Revolutionary Council.

Saeed Abdul Rahim: on July 6, 1988, Pakistani district court judge Zafar Ahmed Babar ended an eight-month trial in a special court in Rawalpindi's

Adiyala maximum security prison and sentenced the Lebanese to death by hanging for the September 5, 1986 hijacking of a Pan Am B747 and for killing 11 passengers at Karachi airport. There was insufficient evidence to convict five terrorists of the deaths of 11 other passengers. The hijacker mastermind, Sulayman al-Turki, said that the group would appeal the sentences and if they were freed, "we would hijack a U.S. airliner once again." The court also passed a total jail sentence of 257 years on each of the accused on several other charges of murder, conspiracy to hijack, possession of illegal arms, and confinement of the passengers. The terrorists had 30 days to appeal the verdict and the sentence in Lahore's High Court. On July 28, 1988, the press reported that the terrorists reversed their decision not to appeal.

Saleem Abdel Rahim: Syrian-born director of the Islamic Releif Agency, a Kuwaiti-financed organization in Peshawar, and one of six accomplices of Ramzi Ahmad Yusuf who were arrested on March 11, 1995 by Pakistani police. He was charged under the Maintenance of Public Order Act.

Rahimi: alias of Mohammed Jaafari Sahraroodi.

Tawfieq Muhammad Al Akhder Al Rahimi: alias Abu Obieda, a Tunisian college student from Bin Arouss who was born on May 6, 1983 and joined al Qaeda in Iraq as a fighter on 7/1/1428 Hijra (2007), contributing 500 euros and an MP3 player, along with his passport and ID. His recruitment coordinator was Abu Ahmed, whom he met in Syria. He flew from Tunisia to Turkey, then arrived in Syria, where his contact took $200 of his $2,000. His home phone number was 0021671444149; his brother's was 0021622520160.

Abd al Rahman: alias of Zaydan Abd Al Alsalam Abd Al Rahiem.

'Abd-al-Rahman: Moroccan-based recruitment coordinator for al Qaeda in Iraq in 2006.

'Abd-al-Rahman: alias of Na'im Bil-Qasim Faraj Ibrahim al-Kadiki.

'Abd-al-Rahman: alias of Muhammad.

Abdul Rahman (variant Abdel Rahman): alias of Muhsin Musa Matwalli Atwah.

Abu Abd Al Rahman: alias of Saied Harbala.

Abu Abd Al Rahman: alias of Hamdi Muhammad Abd al Samed.

Abu Abd Al Rahman: alias of Hassan Bin Alalmah Muhammad Al Qurani.

Abu-'Abd-al-Rahman: alias of Kamal Bin-'Azzuz.

Abu-'Abd-al-Rahman: alias of Amir 'Abd-al-Qadir Sadiq 'Umar Qishu.

Abu 'Abd-al-Rahman: alias of Adam Salah-al-Din.

Abu-'Abd-al-Rahman: alias of Usamah Bin-'Abd-al-Rahman al-Wahibi.

Abu-'Abd-al-Rahman: alias of Bilal 'Abd-al-Rahman al-Sharqawi.

Abu-'Abd-al-Rahman: alias of Hamid Muhammad Shu'ayb.

Abu-'Abd-al-Rahman: alias of Hamdi 'Abd-al-Karim al-Marsawi.

Abu-'Abd-al-Rahman: alias of al Qaeda in Iraq suicide bomber Walid.

Abu-'Abd-al-Rahman: alias of Sultan Salih al-Harbi.

Aseraf Abdul Alzouri Rahman: a United Arab Emirates citizen and one of six Arabs arrested on April 1, 1995 by Philippine authorities in

Kaloocan for being members of the little-known Islamic Saturday Meeting. The group had ties to Ramzi Yusuf. Documents taken from the six detainees indicated they planned to attack U.S. and Saudi citizens in the Philippines. They were charged with illegal possession of firearms and explosives. Police had seized several M-16 Armalite rifles, dynamite, and detonators. Police said they were preparing for a series of bombings to disrupt the May 8 elections. In December 1995, they were tried before the Kaloocan City Regional Trial Court for illegal possession of firearms and explosives.

Ataur Rahman: alias Sunny, military commander of the banned Jamatul Mujaheddin Bangladesh, which wants to establish sharia law and claims to have 10,000 members. He is also the younger brother of Abdur Rahman, the group's leader. Ataur was arrested in a December 13, 2005 raid on Tejgaon Polytechnic College in Dhaka, Bangladesh.

Ata-ur-Rahman: alias of Naeem Bukhari.

Atiyah Abd al-Rahman: variant of Atiyeh Abd al-Rahman.

Atiyeh Abd al-Rahman: variant Atiyah Abd al-Rahman, a Libyan who fought against the Algerian government in the mid-1990s before becoming Osama bin Laden's liaison to the Salafist Group for Preaching and Combat, renamed in January 2007 to al Qaeda in the Islamic Republic, and its leader, Abdelmalek Droukdel. The United States offers $1 million for his capture The *Washington Post* identified him on September 9, 2007 as the group's liaison to Islamists in Iraq and Algeria; the National Counterterrorism Center (NCTC) says he is the al Qaeda emissary to Iran. He recruits and facilitates talks with other Islamic groups to operate under the banner of al-Qaida. He is also a member of the Libyan Islamic Fighting Group and Ansar al-Sunna. He is an explosives expert and viewed as an Islamic scholar. He is five feet five inches tall and was born in the late 1960s in Libya.

'Isam Muhammad 'Abd-al-Rahman: sentenced to death on March 17, 1994 by the Higher Military Court in Cairo in connection with the November 25, 1993 bombing of the convoy of Egyptian Prime Minister Dr. 'Atif Sidqi that killed a 15-year-old girl and wounded 21 other people.

Khidr Abu 'Abd-al-Rahman: alias of Ahmad Saeed.

Midhat Abd-al-Rahman: left Egypt in 1993 for Pakistan and Sudan, where he received military training and was involved with Islamic Group leaders. On November 17, 1997, he was one of six Muslim militants dressed in black sweaters similar to the winter uniforms of the Egyptian police. The militants got out of a car and fired on tourists at Luxor, killing 58 foreigners and four Egyptians (including two policemen). The terrorists were armed with six machine guns, two handguns, and police-issue ammunition. They also had two bags of homemade explosives.

After an hour-long gun battle in which one terrorist died, the five surviving terrorists hijacked the tour bus of Hagag Nahas, age 36, who had dropped off 30 Swiss an hour earlier. The terrorists forced him to drive "to another place so they could shoot more people." He drove for an hour before stopping near the access road to the Valley of the Queens, half a mile away from the temple. A terrorist clubbed Nahas in the chest with the butt of his rifle. Police fired on the gunmen, killing a terrorist. The rest fled. Police said they had caught up to the bus and killed all five gunmen, who had fired into the crowds along the plaza facing the 3,400-year-old Hatshepsut temple.

One of the dead terrorists was identified as Midhat Abd-al-Rahman.

Mohammad Omar Abd-al-Rahman: alias Assadullah, son of Sheik Omar Abd-al-Rahman, the blind sheik. Mohammad was listed as dead by the *Washington Post* as of March 28, 2002.

Sharif 'Abd-al-Rahman: a member of the Islamic Group in Egypt who was killed on July 1, 1995 in Addis Ababa, Ethiopia. He had fled Egypt for Afghanistan a few years earlier. He moved to Peshawar, Pakistan before moving on. He was a prominent member of the Islamic Group's military wing in Qina. He was identified by the Ethiopian government as the leader of the nine Egyptian Islamic Group gunmen who, on June 25, 1995, fired on the armored limousine of Egyptian President Hosni Mubarak in Addis Ababa.

Sheikh Omar Ahmed Abdel Rahman: "blind sheikh" leader of an al Qaeda-linked Islamist faction in the United States that bombed the World Trade Center in New York City on February 26, 1993.

On July 1, 1993, Attorney General Janet Reno authorized federal agents to detain him in connection with the arrests of eight foreign Islamists on June 24, 1993 by the FBI who charged them with planning to bomb the UN headquarters building in Manhattan; 26 Federal Plaza, which includes the local FBI headquarters and other agencies; the 47th Street diamond district, which is run principally by Orthodox Jews; and the Lincoln and Holland tunnels connecting Manhattan and New Jersey; and planning to assassinate Senator Alfonse M. D'Amato (R-NY), Assemblyman Dov Hiking, an Orthodox Jewish legislator from Brooklyn, UN Secretary General Boutros Boutros-Ghali, and Egyptian President Hosni Mubarak. Authorities revoked his immigration parole status that permitted him to remain at large while appealing his deportation. He surrendered to police on July 2 after a 20-hour standoff between police and his followers.

His release was demanded in numerous terrorist threats, and by the hijacker on August 15, 1993 of a Dutch KLM B747-400 in Tunisia.

On April 28, 1994, Egypt sentenced him in absentia to seven years' hard labor for inciting a riot and attempting to kill two policemen in 1989. He was acquitted on the charges in 1989, but President Mubarak cancelled the verdict in January 1994 and ordered the retrial.

On August 25, 1994, a federal grand jury in Manhattan issued a 20-count indictment against

Rahman and 14 others on terrorist conspiracy charges, linking him and his followers to the 1990 murder of Rabbi Meir Kahane, and to "murder in aid of racketeering."

On January 23, 1995, U.S. President Bill Clinton ordered an immediate freeze on his U.S. assets, as his actions constituted a terrorist threat to the Middle East peace process.

He was convicted on October 1, 1995 for a plot to blow up landmarks in New York City, including the UN building. He called on his followers to conduct terrorist activities upon his death. On January 17, 1996, U.S. District Judge Michael B. Mukasey sentenced him to life without parole plus 65 years.

He was held at the Medical Center for Federal Prisoners in Springfield, Missouri since September 2003 because of diabetes and other problems. In early December 2006, he was rushed to a Missouri hospital for a blood transfusion. On November 12, 1981, he had been indicted for saying "it is God's will" when told about the assassination plot that led to the murder of Egyptian President Anwar Sadat on October 6, 1981. Rahman was a theology professor from Cairo's Al Zahar University and had taught at Asyut. He was acquitted of the Sadat charges on March 6, 1982. The Egyptian Gama'at intended to obtain his release in the November 17, 1997 attack in Luxor at the Hatshepsut Temple that killed 58 foreign tourists and four Egyptians and wounded 26 other tourists. His release was demanded on November 13, 1995 by the group that set off a car bomb in a parking lot of a building belonging to the Saudi National Guard in Riyadh, killing five American military trainers and wounding 60 others.

He was named as an unindicted coconspirator on October 7, 1998 by a federal grand jury in New York for his role in the August 7, 1998 bombings of the U.S. Embassies in Dar es Salaam, Tanzania and Nairobi, Kenya.

On August 16, 1999, a three-judge panel of the U.S. Court of Appeals for the Second Circuit upheld his seditious conspiracy conviction.

His release was demanded on March 20, 2000 by the Abu Sayyaf rebels who took more than

70 hostages, many of them children from two Philippine schools.

Saleh Abder Rahman: a Jordanian and one of three Action Group for the Liberation of Palestine terrorists who attempted to hijack an El Al B707 in Munich on February 10, 1970. They were thwarted in their attempt and threw hand grenades at a shuttle bus and the transit lounge. He was injured when he crashed through a skylight attempting to escape. The trio was charged with murder, but they were freed during the September 6, 1970 multiple hijacking by the Popular Front for the Liberation of Palestine, which had claimed credit for the attack, as did the Action Organization for the Liberation of Palestine.

Salim 'Abd-al-Rahman: alias of Muhammad Habib.

Soufiane Raifa: on April 15, 2005, National Court Judge Juan del Olmo filed provisional terrorism charges against the Moroccan suspected of helping to obtain the explosives used in the March 11, 2004 Madrid train bombings.

Lotfi Raissi: on September 21, 2001, London police arrested the 27-year-old Algerian pilot who was believed to be the flight instructor for the four 9/11 pilot/hijackers. He was held without bond. On October 10, 2001, he was indicted in Arizona for providing false information on a Federal Aviation Administration form to obtain a commercial pilot's license. The United States was seeking extradition. Raissi was believed to have links to a suspected Algerian wing of al Qaeda. On November 27, a federal grand jury in Phoenix added conspiracy charges against him. The indictment said he conspired with his Phoenix apartment mate, Redouane Dahmani, an Algerian, to falsify an asylum claim that would permit Dahmani to stay in the United States. Dahmani was in custody in Phoenix on charges of forgery and perjury, held in lieu of a $1 million bond, and was suspected of having contacts with a senior Algerian terrorist in London. He had listed his address as a Phoenix

apartment on N. 23rd Avenue, the address Raissi gave in June when he was stopped for speeding in Yarnell, Arizona. Dahmani's phone number was found on a paper in the London home of Abu Doha, age 36, alias The Doctor, alias Amar Makhulif, believed to be a senior Algerian terrorist in London with links to European al Qaeda terrorist cells. Raissi was arrested at Heathrow Airport on charges of orchestrating a foiled plot to bomb Los Angeles International Airport on December 31, 1999. London prosecutors said they seized a video of Raissi in an aircraft with 9/11 hijack pilot Hani Hanjour. Raissi trained on 30 aircraft at four flight schools. He was represented by Hugo Keith and Richard Egan. Magistrate Timothy Workman denied a bail hearing for the second time on December 14. The next court date was set for January 11, 2002. Investigators backed off from initial claims that he was in contact with three of the hijackers.

Raissi bought a fake ID in the name of Fabrice Vincent Algiers to get a job as a short-order cook. In 1993, he was arrested for stealing a briefcase at Heathrow Airport; he pleaded guilty, was not jailed, then returned to Algeria. In 1996, Italian police arrested him in Rome when he was carrying faked French ID papers; he was expelled with his French girlfriend. In 1998, he trained on the same flight simulator with Hani Hanjour five times. In January 1999, he received a U.S. commercial pilot's license for flying B737s. On November 18, 2000, he married Sonia Dermolis, a French Catholic and aspiring dancer. He was ticketed for speeding from Las Vegas to Phoenix on June 18, 2001. On June 23, 2001, he and Hanjour enrolled at Sawyer Aviation on the same day. Raissi trained at the simulator for seven days; Hanjour continued his training through July 29. On September 21, Raissi, his wife, and his brother Mohammed were arrested.

On February 12, 2002, ignoring U.S. protests, Judge Timothy Workman at Belmarsh Magistrate's Court in southeastern London released him on $15,000 bail. Police kept his passport. On April 24, 2002, Judge Workman dismissed the extradition case and freed him. On September 16,

2003, Raissi sued the FBI and U.S. Department of Justice for $10 million.

On March 1, 2002, Italian police who arrested six al Qaeda sympathizers found a letter with his address.

On February 14, 2008, a British appeals court said that he had been "completely exonerated" and could seek compensation from the UK government for wrongful arrest and detention.

'Arif Ahmad Raja: one of two Lebanese hijackers of a Romanian B707 chartered by the Libyan Arab Airways to fly from Athens to Tripoli on June 23, 1983. The hijackers demanded to be flown to Beirut. The plane landed in Rome to refuel, and were denied landing permission in Beirut. After hopscotching, the plane landed at Larnaca Airport in Cyprus. The hijackers demanded to go to Tehran. The hijackers surrendered. The hijackers were members of a Shi'ite Moslem militia group who wanted an independent investigation to look into the 1978 disappearance in Libya of Musa as-Sadr, the group's spiritual leader. On August 2, 1983, the hijackers were sentenced to seven years in jail after pleading guilty in a Nicosia court.

Tariq Raja: possibly the true name of Richard Reid, the would-be shoe bomber.

Arif Rajan: on July 8, 2002, the FBI and Immigration and Naturalization Service announced that, in June, they had raided 75 jewelry stores and kiosks, most of them called Intrigue Jewelers, in shopping malls in eight states as part of an investigation into al Qaeda money laundering. A dozen men, mostly Pakistanis, were taken into custody on immigration charges. Authorities also seized documents, computer records, and other evidence against the Orlando, Florida-based company Gold Concept, Inc., owned by naturalized U.S. citizen Arif Rajan of Ocoee, Florida. The press had reported that, in the weeks after 9/11, authorities had raided an Intrigue Jewelers in Allentown, Pennsylvania. The operators had come under suspicion after developing World Trade Center photographs; one fled the United

States, another was charged with immigration violations.

Maryam Rajavi: wife of Iraq-based leader Massoud Rajavi, she was arrested on June 17, 2003 on suspicion of plotting Mujaheddin-e Khalq terrorist attacks in France and building a support base for operations abroad. Police seized $1.3 million in U.S. currency, mostly in $100 bills, plus computers and satellite telecommunications equipment from the walled compound in Auvers-Sur-Oise, north of Paris. The head of French intelligence said the group was planning to attack Iranian diplomatic missions in Europe and elsewhere. An individual in London set himself on fire outside the French Embassy in protest. German police arrested 50 demonstrators after they broke into the Iranian consulate in Hamburg. On June 18, three Iranians set themselves on fire to protest the arrests. As of June 20, nine people had self-immolated; one died. On July 2, a Paris court ordered the release of Maryam Rajavi.

Massoud Rajavi: Paris-exiled leader of the Iranian Mujaheddin-e-Khalq Iran in the 1980s who left for Iraq on June 7, 1986.

Saleh Rajavi: brother of Massoud Rajavi, he was among 159 people arrested on June 17, 2003 on suspicion of plotting Mujaheddin-e Khalq terrorist attacks in France and building a support base for operations abroad. Police seized $1.3 million in U.S. currency, mostly in $100 bills, plus computers and satellite telecommunications equipment from the walled compound in Auvers-Sur-Ooise, north of Paris. The head of French intelligence said the group was planning to attack Iranian diplomatic missions in Europe and elsewhere.

Saleh al-Rajhi: a former member of the McLean, Virginia-based Peoples Committee for Libyan Students, was one of two Libyan intelligence officers arrested by the FBI on July 20, 1988 on charges of plotting to assassinate former National Security Council aide U.S. Marine Colonel Oliver

L. North. Al-Rajhi reportedly gathered information in June 1987 "concerning the identities, home addresses, and phone numbers of government officials" working in U.S. intelligence agencies and sent the data to Mohamed Madjoub, a top intelligence officer in Libya. U.S. Magistrate Leonie Brinkema ordered him held without bond, as he was an illegal alien and would probably flee. He entered the United States in 1976, and was a graduate student at George Washington University. The group apparently was planning revenge against U.S. officials believed to have planned the April 1986 air raid against Libya in retaliation for Libyan involvement in several terrorist attacks. On July 28, 1988, a federal grand jury handed down a 40-count indictment, charging the group with conspiracy, money laundering, and violations of U.S. trade sanctions against Libya. He allegedly prepared a document including the names and addresses of "over 1,000 federal employees" in military and intelligence agencies.

Husham Mohammed Rajih: arrested on August 29, 1981 by Austrian police after he attacked a synagogue, killing 2 and injuring 20. The Iraqi confessed to the May 1, 1981, murder in Austria of Heinz Nittel, president of the Austrian–Israeli Friendship League, a leading Socialist Party official, and head of the Vienna Traffic Department. Abu Nidal's Al Asifah organization claimed credit for the assassination. Rajih had lived in Austria since December 1978 and was a student at Vienna's technical university. He was sentenced by a Vienna court to life in prison on January 21, 1982 for the Nittel murder.

'Abd-al-Rahman Bin-'Ali al-Rajihi: variant Abd al Rahman Bin Ali Al Ragahi, alias Abu-al-Maqdam, variant Abu-al-Maqam, a Saudi attorney from Riyadh who was born in 1984 and joined al Qaeda in Iraq as a fighter in 2007, bringing his passport. He met his unnamed recruitment coordinator via Abu Abd Allah. He flew from Jeddah to Syria, bringing 10,000 Saudi riyals; his Syrian contacts told him to give them half. His phone number was 009664584911.

Abu Rakabah: alias of Ahmed Abd Al Salam Saleh Misbah.

Rakan: alias Abu-al-Battar, a Saudi member of al Qaeda in Iraq in 2007 who owned a passport. His travel coordinator was Abu-Sa'd. His phone numbers were 05021320008 and 043822147.

Ibrahim Yahya Ahmad Rakid: alias Abu-Muhammad, an Algerian painter from Algiers who was born in 1980 and joined al Qaeda from Iraq as a fighter circa 2006–2007. He knew his recruitment coordinator, Samir, through a friend. He flew to Damascus. He gave his Syrian contacts 50 of the 170 euros he had with him. His phone number was 0021321263423.

'Abd-al-Shafi Ahmad Ramadan: on June 8, 1992, the motorcycle-riding masked gunman shot to death Dr. Faraj Fudah, variant Farag Fouda, a Muslim writer, near the Heliopolis, Nasr area of Cairo. Ramadan resided in the al-Zawiyah al-Hamra' and was a member of Islamic Jihad.

'Ali al-Ajafli Ramadan: variant of Ali Ecefli Ramadan.

Ali Ecefli Ramadan: variant 'Ali al-Ajafli Ramadan, one of two Libyans who, when stopped by police on April 18, 1986 in front of the U.S. officer's club in Ankara, Turkey, threw away a bag containing six grenades and ran. They were apprehended. The attack was to occur during a wedding party attended by 100 people. The terrorists were aided by a Libyan diplomat at the local embassy. On April 28, 1986, the duo were charged with conspiracy to kill a group of people and with smuggling arms. The duo had entered Turkey on April 16, 1986 and had contacted Umran Mansur, manager of the Libyan Arab Airlines office in Istanbul. Ramadan allegedly selected the target. The grenades were supplied by Mohammad Shaban Hassan, a Libyan Embassy employee in charge of administrative affairs who met with the duo on April 17 and 18. The trial began on May 13, 1986 in the State Security Court. On

June 7, 1986, he was convicted of possession of explosives and was sentenced to five years in prison. The duo were acquitted of the more serious conspiracy charges. The Court of Appeals revoked the decision on the grounds that they were not punished for establishing an organization for the aim of committing a crime. During a retrial, the court insisted on its previous decision, causing a second revocation by the Court of Appeals Criminal Assembly. On April 14, 1988, he was sentenced to eight years and four months in prison for establishing an armed organization with the purpose of killing more than one person. He was also fined 62,500 Turkish lira.

Ghalib Ramadan: a resident of Ayios Pavlos, Nicosia who, on February 1, 1990, was arrested along with a member of the Palestine Liberation Organization diplomatic mission to Cyprus following a police chase after the duo were involved in a nighttime shooting involving machine guns in the Ayios Dhometios, Nicosia area while trying to sell heroin and hashish.

Mustapha Darwich Ramadan: age 40, alias Abu Mohammed Lubnani, one of several thieves who stole more than $300,000 from an armored car in Copenhagen in 1997. He had been under surveillance as an Islamic extremist. He was arrested shortly before he planned to take a flight to Amman, Jordan. He was convicted of robbery and served 3 and a half years in prison. After his June 2001 release, he robbed a money-transfer store of $15,000, then escaped to either Jordan or Lebanon. He became a leader of the Ansar al-Islam in Iraq. He was believed to be operating a network that recruits young Muslims in Europe to join the Iraqi insurgency.

Said Ramadan: a Palestinian gunman who, on January 22, 2002, fired at people on busy Jaffa Street near Zion Square in West Jerusalem during the afternoon, shooting an M-16 assault rifle into a crowded bus stop, fatally wounding two women and injuring 14 other Israelis before being shot to death by policeman Sgt. Hanan

Ben Naim. The Al-Aqsa Martyrs Brigades claimed credit.

Sa'id 'Ali Tharauni Ramadan: one of two Libyans claiming membership in the Libyan Revolutionary Committees who, on June 26, 1987, gunned down an exiled opponent of Libyan leader Muammar Qadhafi on a Rome street near President Francesco Cossiga's residence.

Rambo: alias Zeba Hamid, alias used by one of the four hijackers of the Libyan Revolutionary Cells and the Organization of the Soldiers of God—Martyr Zulfikar Ali Bhutto Group who took over Pan Am flight 73 at Karachi airport on September 5, 1986.

Rachid Ramda: alias Abou Fares, an Algerian Islamic Group member arrested in London on November 4, 1995 and charged in connection with the series of bombings in Paris in the fall of 1995 that killed 10 and injured 180, including the bombing at the St. Michel Metro Station in Paris on July 25, 1995 in which eight were killed and 30 were injured. He was held pending a French extradition request, which was issued on November 8. He was to appear in court again on November 16. On June 27, 2002, the UK High Court ruled against extradition, overturning the government's 2001 extradition decision. On March 29, 2006, a French court sentenced him to 10 years in jail for assisting terrorists who bombed Paris Metro rail stations in 1995.

Rami: a Syrian from Al-Dir who was born in 1982 and joined al Qaeda in Iraq as a martyr in 2007, donating 2,230 lira. His home phone number was 051356414. His recruitment coordinator was Abu-Ibrahim.

Abu Rami: a Syrian from Aleppo and member of the Popular Front for the Liberation of Palestine-General Command who, on November 25, 1987, flew a motorized hang glider for 80 kilometers across the border and over an Israeli Defense Forces encampment near Qiryat

Shemona, firing machine guns and throwing grenades. He killed six Israeli Defense Forces soldiers and wounded seven others before being killed.

Ilich Ramirez Sanchez: alias Carlos, a Venezuela-born Popular Front for the Liberation of Palestine (PFLP) terrorist. He also used the aliases Naqi Abu-Bakr Ahmad, the Jackal, Carlos Andres Martinez-Torres, Hector Lugo Dupont, Glenn Gebhard, Cenon Marie Clark, Adolf Jose Muller Bernal, and Ahmad Adil Fawaz, Dr. Murad Shakir 'Aziz, Martinez Torres, 'Abdallah Barakat, Dr. 'Abdallah Burhan, and 'Abd-Rabbuh 'Ali Muhammad.

He was believed to have been involved in the planning of the September 28, 1973 takeover of a train of Soviet Jewish émigrés in Austria by Saiqa.

He was believed to have fired a shot at Joseph E. Sieff, president of the Marks and Spencer store chain, honorary vice-president of the Zionist Federation of Britain, and President of the Joint Palestinian Appeal in London on December 31, 1973. The shot lodged in Sieff's head. The PFLP gunman escaped.

An individual vaguely matching his description threw a bomb into the Bank of Hapoalim, Israel's third largest bank, in London on January 24, 1974, injuring a typist. The PFLP claimed credit.

He was rumored to have been involved in the August 3, 1974 bombings of two small cars and a minibus parked outside the offices of two anti-Arab newspapers, L'Aurore and Minute, and a the United Jewish Social Fund, in Paris. On August 5, the PFLP claimed credit in the name of Commando Muhammad Boudia. Detailed diagrams of all three offices, carefully annotated, were found among his papers when his apartment was raided in 1975.

He was believed to have thrown a grenade into the Drugstore Saint-Germaine, a popular Paris shopping complex, on September 15, 1974, killing two Frenchmen and wounding 34 others. The Mohammad Boudia Commando claimed credit, as did the Group for the Defense of Europe.

He might have been the shooter of Alan Quartermaine, a London insurance broker, who was hit twice in the neck and killed when his chauffeur-driven Rolls Royce stopped at a King's Road traffic light in London on November 18, 1974. Observers believed Carlos mistook him for a Jewish member of Parliament who drove a Rolls and lived nearby. Others suspected Irish Republican Army involvement.

He was involved in the planning of the RPG-7 attack on an El Al B707 in Orly Airport on January 13, 1975.

Three French DST police visited his apartment at 9 Rue Toullier in Paris at 9:40 P.M. on July 27, 1975. After questioning him for 30 minutes, they asked him to come to the Paris police headquarters. He excused himself to go to the restroom, then emerged with a Czech automatic pistol, killing Michael Waheb Moukharbal, a PFLP Muhammad Boudia Commando member who had fingered him, plus officers Raymoud Dous and Jean Donatini, and wounding Commissaire Principal Jean Herranz in the throat. He escaped. A few days later, the French expelled three members of Cuba's embassy whom they claimed were members of the Direccion General de Inteligencia who had extensive contacts with Carlos. A bag of weapons and explosives left by Carlos was found in an apartment of friends with whom he had stayed.

He next surfaced on December 21, 1975, when he led six members of the Arm of the Arab Revolution, a PFLP cover name, who took over a ministerial meeting of the Organization of Petroleum Exporting Countries (OPEC) in Vienna, Austria and took 70 hostages, including 11 oil ministers. An arrest warrant was handed down in the OPEC case by the Vienna criminal court on December 23, 1975.

In August or September 1979, he opened fire on the occupants of a passenger car in Budapest, Hungary.

On July 13 1990, Budapest MTI news agency blamed him for the February 21, 1981 bombing of the Radio Free Europe building in Munich.

In a letter sent to the West German embassy in Saudi Arabia, he claimed credit for the August 25, 1983 bombing of the French consulate in West Berlin's Kurfurstendamm shopping mall that killed one and injured 23. His fingerprint was on the letter.

In October 1983, he sent a letter to the same embassy, threatening to kill Bonn interior minister Friedrich Zimmermann if authorities prosecuted Gabriele Kroecher-Tidemann for her role in the 1975 Carlos-led attack on the OPEC headquarters in Vienna.

He sent a letter to the *Agence France-Presse* office in Berlin claiming credit for the December 31, 1983 bombing of a French TGV high-speed train en route from Marseilles to Paris that killed three and injured 10. Experts said that the handwriting was his. He was believed to be hiding in East Berlin.

On June 21, 1990, a Vienna, Austria newspaper reported that he had operated from East Berlin during the Erich Honecker regime with the consent of Honecker and former minister of state security Erich Mielke.

On November 28, 1991, the French press agency, AFP, reported that Syria had expelled him on September 21, 1991 and that he was probably now in Yemen after Libya refused to have him. He and his family—Magdalena Kopp of the West German Red Army Faction and their two children—reportedly had Yemeni diplomatic passports. His passport said he was Aden-born diplomat Naqi Abu-Bakr Ahmad, age 43.

He had been found guilty and sentenced to life in prison in absentia in 1992.

He was arrested in Sudan on August 14, 1994 and extradited to France.

Sante Prisoner 872686/X went on trial on December 12, 1997 for killing French security officers Raymond Dous and Jean Donatini and Lebanese informant Michel Moukarbal on June 27, 1975.

On December 24, 1997, France found him guilty and sentenced him to life in prison for three murders in 1975. On December 26, 1997, he asked France's highest court to overturn the conviction, claiming he was not permitted to confront his accusers.

On November 9, 1998, he was in the first week of a hunger strike in a French jail.

In April 1999, Venezuela's newly elected President Hugo Chavez wrote him a letter of solidarity, addressing him as a "distinguished compatriot."

By May 1999, he began writing a newspaper column for *La Razon*, a Venezuelan weekly.

On June 23, 1999, France's highest court rejected a final appeal.

On March 12, 2003, he went on trial in Berlin on charges of murder, attempted murder, and causing explosions in five attacks in Western Europe that killed six people. On March 17, 2003 his wife, Magdalena Kopp, age 54, refused to testify against him.

Munzir Rammal: sentenced on April 13, 1994 to life at hard labor for being an accomplice to Husan Muhammad Tulays, who confessed to firing six bullets on September 18, 1986 at Colonel Christian Goutierre, the French military attaché in Beirut, killing him. The Anti-Imperialist International Brigades, the Revolutionary Brigades, and the Front for Justice and Revenge separately claimed credit.

Abu Rana: alias of Jumaa Farid al-Saeedi.

Rashid Randa: an Arab Afghan who led the nine bombings during July-October 1995 by the Algerian GIA (French acronym for the Armed Islamic Group) in France that killed nine and wounded 160. He had known Osama bin Laden since the 1980s.

Dr. 'Abd al-Aziz al-Rantisi: Hamas Gaza Strip leader killed by an Israeli helicopter raid on April 17, 2004. The pediatrician was the group's spokesman in July 30, 1997, having been released that spring from an Israeli jail. On August 22, 2003, President Bush froze his assets and called on allies to join him by cutting off European sources of donations to Hamas. He had become head of Hamas in the Gaza Strip on March 22, 2004 after Israel killed Sheikh Ahmed Yassin. Thousands attended Rantisi's funeral.

Michel Nabih Raphael: alias of Samir Muhammad Ahmad al-Qadir.

Marwan Hazzam Raqeh: variant of Marwan Hazzam Raqih.

Marwan Hazzam Raqih: variant Marwan Hazzam Raqeh, alias Abu-Dajanah, a Yemeni who joined al Qaeda in Iraq as a fighter in 2007. He provided his passport and $170 to his Syrian contacts. His phone number was 03209372. His recruitment coordinator was Khalil, variant Khaliel.

Yislam Abu-Ra'sayn: self-declared tribal chieftain of Yemen's Shabwah Governorate. Yemeni officials said he had planned the bombings on December 29, 1992 of the Gold Mohur Hotel in Aden and the Aden Movenpick Hotel, both of which house U.S. Marines. London's *al-Sharq al-Awsat* said he confessed that he intended to blow up a U.S. Navy Galaxy aircraft parked at Aden airport.

Rashad: alias of Dr. Ramadan Abdullah Mohammad Shallah.

Khalid Rashad: one of three individuals sentenced to ten years in prison on February 17, 1994 by a Cairo military court for plotting the assassination of President Mubarak by bombing Sidi Barrani Airport and the Presidential guest house in Marsa Matruh.

Muhammad 'Abd-al-Fattah Muhammad Rashad: alias Abu-Tariq al-Makki, variant Abu Tarek al Meccie, a Saudi from Mecca who was born on May 14, 1952 and joined al Qaeda in Iraq as a martyr on November 10, 2006, contributing a watch and $12,400. His recruitment coordinator was Abu-Hussam. His home phone number was 00966559686100.

Usamah Muhammad Rashad: sentenced to death on July 16, 1994 by a Cairo military court

for involvement with the Vanguard of the Conquest gunmen who, on August 18, 1993, fired on the motorcade of Egyptian Interior Minister Hassan Alfi. Five people died and 17 were wounded when a remotely-detonated bomb exploded as Alfi's convoy passed by. He was also accused of murdering a dissident member of their group and the main prosecution witness in the trial of militants convicted of trying to kill Prime Minister 'Atif Sidqi in November 1993. Sidqi escaped unharmed, but a 15-year-old girl was killed. The prosecution failed to make the case that he was responsible for plotting to assassinate UN Secretary General Boutros Boutros-Ghali during an African summit in Cairo in June 1993. He had pleaded not guilty to the charges. On August 22, 1994, he was hanged in Cairo's Appeals Prison.

Khalaf al-Rashdan: alias Abu-Ahmad, variant Abu Ahmed, a Syrian from Dar'a, variant Derah who joined al Qaeda in Iraq on September 13, 2006. He was born on January 2, 1985. His phone number was 015880295. His recruitment coordinator was Abu-al-Basr, variant Abu Al Beser.

Khalid Salim Saleh bin Rashed: alias of Mohamed Rashed Daoud al-Owhali.

Abdul Rasheed: age 27, a Syrian held in U.S. federal custody as of November 2001 in connection with the FBI's investigation of the 9/11 attacks.

Saud Abdulaziz Saud Al-Rasheed: variant al-Rashid. On August 20, 2002, the FBI issued a worldwide alert for the arrest the 21-year-old, who was believed to have ties with the 9/11 hijackers, and was considered "armed and dangerous." The information on him came from material recovered overseas, including an image of a Saudi passport issued to him in May 2000 in Riyadh, which was found in a CD-ROM that included information on some of the hijackers. He surrendered to Saudi Interior Ministry officials in Riyadh on August 22 and was being questioned. His family doubted that he had connections to the attackers, claiming that he spent a year working in Afghanistan on humanitarian projects, returning to Saudi Arabia four months before the attacks. Al-Rasheed was on vacation in Egypt when he saw his photo on *CNN*. He had trained in Afghanistan.

Rashid: alias Abu al-'Abbas, a Tunisian fighter for al Qaeda in Iraq in 2007, who owned a passport, $200, and 300 lira. His phone number was 002167130190.

Abu Rashid: an Iranian linked to 40 Shi'ite terrorists arrested in Egypt on August 19, 1989 for planning to carry out attacks against U.S., Israeli, Saudi, Iraqi, and Kuwaiti interests, including embassies and airlines.

Ahmad Rashid: alias of Ramzi Ahmad Yusuf.

Ata Abdoulaziz Rashid: age 31, arrested on December 3, 2004 at a safe house of three radical Islamic members of the Iraqi group Ansar al-Islam, hours before they planned to attack Iraqi Prime Minister Ayad Allawi during a state visit. On November 16, 2005, Germany charged Rashid; Mazen Ali Hussein, age 23; and Rafik Mohamad Yousef, age 31, with plotting to assassinate Allawi. Their trial began on June 19, 2006.

Faisal Rashid: Lebanese Brigadier General detained for the February 14, 2005 car bombing that killed former Lebanese Prime Minister Rafiq Hariri, 60, as the billionaire was driving through central Beirut's waterfront just before lunchtime. Another 22 people died and more than 100 people were injured, including the Minister of Economy.

Hasan Rashid: a Lebanese associate of a Palestinian with a Jordanian passport who was arrested by Larnaca Airport security personnel on December 17, 1985 for trying to smuggle arms aboard a Swissair plane scheduled to depart for Amman. Police believed he was one of four Arabs who intended to hijack the plane.

Hussein Muhammed al Rashid: one of two Popular Front for the Liberation of Palestine terrorists

who threw grenades and fired submachine guns at a crowd waiting to board El Al 582, a B707 bound for Tel Aviv from Istanbul on August 11, 1976. They killed four and wounded 26 before surrendering. They claimed Libya had financed the operation. On November 16, 1976, a Turkish court sentenced them to death but commuted the sentences to life in prison. Rashid's release was demanded by the Organization of Struggle Against World Imperialism hijackers of Lufthansa 181, a B737 scheduled to fly from the Spanish resort island of Mallorca to Frankfurt on October 13, 1977.

Izzat Bin Rashid: release from an Israeli jail was demanded on June 27, 1976 by the Popular Front for the Liberation of Palestine hijackers of Air France flight 139, an A300 flying from Tel Aviv to Paris and ultimately diverted to Entebbe.

Mas'ud Mahmud Rashid: alias Abu-'Azzam, a Libyan secondary school student from Darnah who was born in 1985 and joined al Qaeda in Iraq as a martyr, probably in 2007, bringing his passport. His recruitment coordinator was Bashar. He traveled to Egypt and on to Syria, where he met Abu al-'Abbas. He brought $100. His phone number was 00218925470864.

Mohammed Rashid: arrested in 1973 for smuggling hashish in Greece and served three years of a six-year term. He was arrested by Greece on May 30, 1988 while entering the country on a forged Syrian passport in the name of Mohammed Hamdan. On June 13, 1988, the United States requested extradition in connection with charges stemming from the August 11, 1982 explosion on board Pan Am 830 from Honolulu to Tokyo that killed a Japanese teen and wounded 15 other passengers. He was also suspected of planting a bomb on a TWA flight from Rome to Athens in April 1986 that killed four Americans. Greece denied the extradition request for that incident on June 6, 1988. On July 14, 1988, the Palestinian was sentenced by the First Magistrates Court in Athens to seven months in Koridhallos Prison on the passport charge. He was believed to be a member of the Abu Nidal group, or a group run by Mohammed Abdel Ali Labib, alias Colonel Hawari. On August 3, 1988, the Supreme Court Council in Athens rejected his appeal of his seven-month sentence. On October 10, 1988, the Appeals Court announced that the council had ruled in favor of extradition to the United States. On October 28, 1988, during the extradition hearing, the Direct Revolutionary Action for the Liberation of Palestine told Reuters, "We warn the Greek government against continuing to hold our struggling brother Mohammed Rashid and extraditing him to the American authorities. All Greek governmental, civilian, and diplomatic institutions in Greece as well as outside will be the target of attacks." On November 16, 1988, the Supreme Court requested more evidence from the United States regarding his identity. On March 28, 1989, the Court of Appeals in Piraeus sentenced him to eight months for possession of arms inside the prison where he was being detained. On September 13, 1990, Deputy Prime Minister Athanasios Kanellopoulos announced that he would not be extradited but would be tried in Greece. On September 18, 1990, the Athens prosecutor brought criminal charges of premeditated manslaughter, provocation, and illegal capture of an aircraft against Rashid. The trial began on October 7, 1991, with him charged with premeditated manslaughter, seizing an airplane, and planting a bomb on an airplane.

On January 7, 1992, a three-member Greek criminal court sentenced him to 18 years in prison for premeditated manslaughter and damaging an airplane. The court ordered that he be deprived of his civil rights for five years and be deported after completion of his sentence. The 43 months he had already served were to be subtracted from his sentence. Two of the three judges found him guilty of voluntary homicide but the third declared him innocent because of lack of proof of identity. He was found innocent of charges of an act of violence against an aircraft and of actually placing the bomb. On November 21, 1992,

his trial in Greece was adjourned. On March 3, 1993, a five-member court began hearings in Koridhallos, western Athens's top security prison, on his bid to overturn his 18-year sentence. His appeal had been postponed several times because of a lawyers' strike. On June 18, 1993, a Greek appeals court cut his sentence to 15 years. On December 9, 1994, the Supreme Court rejected his application to overturn the verdict by the Athens appeals court that sentenced him in June 1994 to 15 years for premeditated manslaughter and causing damage to an airplane.

On December 4, 1996, a Greek court released him from Athens's Korydallos Prison. He was then deported to Tunisia. Greece had rejected a U.S. extradition request. The United States pointed out that Rashid was the ringleader of a prison riot and that his cell had been found full of contraband and weapons. Rashid was arrested, apparently in Egypt, on June 2, 1997 and flown to the United States. On June 3, 1997, he was arraigned in a U.S. court in Washington, DC on a nine-count indictment for conspiracy to murder, assault, and aircraft sabotage. He pleaded not guilty and claimed he was being subjected to double jeopardy because he Greek court had convicted him in 1992. U.S. District Judge Aubrey Robinson ordered him held for a hearing. The indictment also named as an accomplice Rashid's wife, Christine Pinter, alias Fatima, who remained at large. U.S. officials had earlier accused him of planting a bomb, which did not explode, on a Pan Am plane in Brazil in 1982 and of setting off a bomb on a TWA airliner approaching Athens in 1986 that killed four Americans. He said it was a case of mistaken identity, claiming to be Rashid Salah Mohammed Alzaghary of Palestine. He was believed to be a member of the Iraq-based Arab Organization of May 15 terrorist group. The prosecution said it would seek life in prison. In December 2002, he secretly pleaded guilty to conspiracy and murder charges.

On March 24, 2006, he was sentenced by U.S. District Judge Royce C. Lamberth to seven years for setting off a bomb on Pan Am flight 830. He also was detained for two years in

Egypt. He is due to be released and deported in 2013.

Mohammed Rashid: identified by confessed bomber Asif Zaheer as receiving from him the car bomb that, on May 8, 2002, exploded next to a pink and white 46-seat Pakistani Navy Mercedes Marco Polo bus outside the upscale Karachi Sheraton Hotel and Towers on Club Road, killing 16 people, including 11 French citizens working for a technical company on a submarine project; two Pakistani beggars; and the driver, of unidentified nationality; and wounding 22 others, including 12 French citizens and eight Pakistanis. Police arrested but did not immediately charge, two other people on January 7, 2003 as a result of Zaheer's information. On June 30, 2003, the Pakistani antiterrorism court sentenced three Islamic militants to death for the bombing.

Mohammed Rashid: an Iraqi member of Ansar al-Islam who was allegedly behind the November 12, 2003 truck bombing in Nasiriyah, Iraq that killed 19 Italians and 12 Iraqis.

Mohammed Hussein Rashid: alias Youssef Awad, arrested after confessing to the April 10, 1983 assassination of 'Isam as-Sartawi, Palestine Liberation Organization representative at the Socialist International Conference held in Albufeira, Portugal. Abu Nidal claimed credit, as did the Antiterrorist Iberian Command. The Abu Nidal group threatened Portuguese interests and citizens worldwide if he was not released. On January 11, 1984, he was acquitted of the murder charge and sentenced to three years for using a forged passport. During the trial, he had claimed that his confession was meant to draw attention away from the true killers. In June 1984, the Supreme Court overturned the lower court's acquittal. On May 10, 1985, a second trial acquitted him of murder and sentenced him to three years for using a false passport.

Moubsett Rashid: variant of Mubsit Rashid.

Mubsit Rashid: variant Moubsett Rashid, alias Abu-Muhammad, a Moroccan from Casablanca who was born on October 15, 1974 and joined al Qaeda in Iraq as a martyr on November 10, 2006, contributing a watch, cell phone, and passport. His recruitment coordinator was Sa'id. His brothers' phone numbers were 00212061437585 and 00212061791751.

Muhammad Rashid: manager of the al-Rafidayn Bank who was arrested on April 15, 1994 in connection with the April 12, 1994 assassination by an Iraqi gunman of Talib al-Suhayl al-Tamimi, a leading member of the London-based Free Iraqi Council opposition group in Beirut during the night. He apparently had helped the gunmen reach the house of the victim. The order from Baghdad for the assassination came in a coded telex message to the bank's center in al-Sadat Street in Ra's Beirut.

Muhammad Bin-'Abdallah Bin-Ahmad al-Rashid: alias Abu-al-Bara', a Saudi teacher from Riyadh who was born in 1982 and joined al Qaeda in Iraq on August 21, 2007 as a suicide bomber, bringing his passport. His recruitment coordinator, Abu-'Abdallah, was an old friend. He flew directly from Saudi Arabia to Syria, where he met Abu-Yasir, Abu-Ayat, and Abu-'Umar. He gave some of his 22,300 euros to Abu-Yasir. His phone numbers were 0555686764 and 0555400679.

Musa Ahmad Rashid: Fatah-Revolutionary Council representative in Kuwait who two dissident former members of the Central Committee and Political Bureau of Fatah-The Revolutionary Council said on October 31, 1989, was killed, along with 156 of Abu Nidal's followers, by Abu Nidal in Libya in 1988.

Nazih Nushi Rashid: named by Egyptian police and a Muslim militant defendant as being one of the Vanguard of the Conquest gunmen who, on August 18, 1993, fired on the motorcade of Egyptian Interior Minister Hassan Alfi.

Five people died and 17 were wounded when a remotely-detonated bomb exploded as Alfi's convoy passed by. Rashid was believed to be the head of the group's military wing.

Saud Abdulaziz Saud al-Rashid: variant of Saud Abdulaziz Saud al-Rasheed. The 9/11 Commission said that he was initially scheduled to be a 9/11 hijacker, but backed out after being pressured by his Saudi family. He had trained in Afghanistan.

Ali-Amin al-Rashidi: alias Abu Ubaydah al-Banshiri, an Egyptian senior member of the Egyptian Islamic Jihad who supervised al Qaeda Afghanistan camps and led bin Laden's forces against the United States in Somalia. He had served as an Egyptian security officer before leaving for Afghanistan in 1983.

He was identified by Egyptian authorities on March 20, 1993 as a senior Egyptian fundamentalist abroad who had trained 25 Muslim members of the outlawed Jama'ah al-Islamiyah group who were arrested at the al-Sallum border post after trying to enter Egypt from Libya with false passports. Police said they were planning to carry out attacks.

Rashidi had worked to unite the Egyptian Islamic Jihad and the Gama'at al-Islamiyah. He drowned in a Tanzania ferry accident in Uganda's Lake Victoria in May 1996.

Abu Rashied: alias of Sa'ad Eeybouh.

Fahid Hammed Muhammad al Rashied: alias Abu Nourah, a Saudi who joined al Qaeda in Iraq in 2007. His recruitment coordinator was Abu Sumahia. His Syrian contact was Hayider. His phone numbers were 0096612301135 and 096612269973.

Ratib Salih Rashwan: charged by Egypt with crossing the border at illegal places to serve as a driver in the foiled plot to assassinate Ghayth Said al-Mabruk, a political refugee living in Alexandria, Egypt, on August 6, 1985.

Ibrahim Rasool: variant of Ibrahim Rasul.

Ibrahim Rasul: variant Rasool, alias Abdul Shakoor, an Iranian displaced person holding a UN High Commission for Refugees card and one of six accomplices of Ramzi Ahmad Yusuf who were arrested on March 11, 1995 by Pakistani police. He was arrested at the Cantt Railway Station while carrying explosives. He was charged at the time of his arrest, under the Maintenance of Public Order Act, with plotting to kill Prime Minister Bhutto. He implicated Yusuf in the June 20, 1994 bombing of the Imam Reza mausoleum in Mashad, Iran that left 25 dead and 70 injured. He settled in Peshawar in the 1980s to join the Afghan war against the Russians. On April 3, 1995, he was brought from Peshawar to Karachi for investigation into the alleged attempt against Prime Minister Bhutto. He alleged that three million rupees remained in the vaults of a foreign bank in Karachi, to be paid to them for the attempt. He was remanded for five days to the physical custody of the Crimes Investigation Department on August 20, 1995. He was a resident of Askari Lane, Mohalla Juman Shah near the Smani Mosque. He was a member of a terrorist group based in Karachi. He was suspected of involvement in the murder of several leaders of the Sipah-e Sahaba Pakistan, including Haq Nawaz Jangvi.

Sayid Ahmad Sayid 'Ali Sayid Abbas 'Abd-al-Rasul: member of a cell in Kuwait that set two bombs that exploded on July 10, 1989 in two streets leading to the Great Mosque in Mecca, killing a Pakistani and injuring 16 of the 1.5 million pilgrims from 100 countries attending the hajj.

Khalil Said Ratib: arrested on September 27, 1981 by Larnaca airport police in connection with the Black June attack in which a grenade was thrown into the Shoham, Limassol, Cyprus offices of an Israeli shipping firm on September 23, 1981, injuring three female and two male Greek Cypriot employees.

Ahmad Rauf: Palestinians alleged that he was involved in an attempt to kill Popular Front for the Liberation of Palestine (PFLP) hijacker Leila Khaled, then a schoolteacher, and PFLP deputy Wadi Haddad when six Katyusha rockets were fired at his Beirut home on July 11, 1970. Rauf had come from and returned to West Germany.

Hani 'Abdallah 'Abd-al-Ra'uf: sentenced to 15 years with hard labor on March 17, 1994 by the Higher Military Court in Cairo in connection with the November 25, 1993 bombing of the convoy of Egyptian Prime Minister Dr. 'Atif Sidqi that killed a 15-year-old girl and wounded 21 other people.

Mohammad Rauf: alias of Iman Faris.

Munir 'Abd-al-Ra'uf: a Lebanese Hizballah member mentioned on August 18, 1994 by *Buenos Aires LS84 Television* as having been identified by a woman to Paraguayan police investigating the July 18, 1994 bombing of the Argentine-Israeli Mutual Aid Association (AIMA) in Buenos Aires that killed 96 and wounded 231.

Avishai Raviv: leader of the right-wing Eyal group, who was arrested and ordered held for seven days on a conspiracy charge in connection with the November 4, 1995 assassination of Israeli Prime Minister Yitzak Rabin. He was a follower the slain U.S. rabbi Meir Kahane, founder of the Jewish Defense League.

Ibrahim Rawaf: one of two men indicted in the United States on July 26, 1984 on charges of planning to assassinate Mohammad Fassi, a Saudi sheik living in London. Rawaf offered Martindale, the chief of American International Trade Group, Inc., $50,000 to assassinate Fassi. As of August 1984, Rawaf was a fugitive in Lebanon from a U.S. arrest warrant.

Abu-Rawaha: alias of Hatim Yazid Muhammad.

Hani Rawajbeh: age 22, Hamas militant who, on October 11, 2001, blew himself up while planting a bomb along a road used by Israelis in the West Bank. He was the longtime deputy of Mahmoud Abu Hanoud, a senior Hamas military leader.

Abu Rawha: alias of Hattem Yazeed Muhammad.

Sayf Din Rawi: named on February 14, 2005 as one of Iraq's 29 most-wanted insurgents. A bounty of between $50,000 and $200,000 was offered.

Mahir al-Rawsan: alias Walid, identified by Doha's *al-Sharq* on March 19, 1993 as a member of the Abu Nidal Group's Central Committee. His brother, Nawwaf al-Rawsan, alias 'Uthman, was imprisoned in the United Kingdom for attempting to assassinate Israeli Ambassador Argov on June 3, 1982 after the Israeli invasion of Lebanon.

Nawwaf al-Rawsan: alias 'Uthman, alias 'Uthman al-Rawsh, imprisoned in the United Kingdom for attempting to assassinate Israeli Ambassador Argov on June 3, 1982 after the Israeli invasion of Lebanon. After he announced his resignation from the Fatah-Revolutionary Council (Abu Nidal Group), his sentence was suspended. His brother, Mahir al-Rawsan, alias Walid, was identified by Doha's *al-Sharq* on March 19, 1993 as a member of the Abu Nidal Group's Central Committee.

'Uthman al-Rawsh: alias of Nawwaf al-Rawsan.

'Abdallah Bin-Rawwahah: alias of Muhammad 'Ali Farah.

Mustafa Abu-Rawwash: suspected leader of al-Gama'at al-Islamiyah was killed on Cairo on June 9, 1997. Four members of the group were arrested.

Wail at Rayamy: one of 16 Middle Eastern terrorists whom the Saudi Embassy told Thai officials on March 20, 1990 were planning to attack Saudi diplomats and officials overseas. He carried a Libyan passport.

Abu Rayan: alias of Aymen Salem Majed.

Abu-Rayan: alias of 'Abd-al-'Aziz Bin-'Abdallah al-Mas'ud.

Abdelfettah Raydi: a suicide bomber in Morocco who, on March 11, 2007, killed only himself but injured four others in a busy Internet café in a Casablanca slum right after the café owner told him to stop looking at jihadi Web sites.

Ayyoubi Raydi: brother of Abdelfettah Raydi, on April 10, 2007 set off his explosives as Moroccan police searched his Casablanca neighborhood. A police officer died and a 7-year-old boy and a policeman were injured.

Ibrahim Mohammed Abdullah Rayes: on December 8, 2003, Saudi security forces raided a gas station and killed the Saudi, who was on the list of the country's 26 most-wanted men, all of whom were connected to recent suicide bombings in Riyadh. A second terrorist was also killed in the raid in Riyadh's Sweidi neighborhood.

Tawfiq Muhammad al-Akhdar al-Rayhami: alias Abu-'Ubaydah, a Tunisian who joined al Qaeda in Iraq on January 25, 2007. He was born on May 6, 1983, and lived in Bin 'Arus, Tunisia. His home phone number was 0021671444149; his brother's phone number was 002162250160. He contributed 500 Euros and an MP3 player. He brought with him a passport and ID card. He met Abu-Ahmad, his coordinator, in Syria. He flew from Tunisia to Turkey, then to Syria, arriving in Iraq by land. He brought $2,000 with him; $200 was taken from him in Syria. He offered to be a fighter; he had been a university student.

'Arif Rayya: a Lebanese prisoner said to be in ill health whose release was demanded on February 7, 1985 by the hijackers of a Cyprus Airways B707 in Lebanon. He was not released by Cypriot officials.

Abu-Rayyan: Saudi-based recruitment coordinator for al Qaeda in Iraq foreign fighters in 2007.

Abd al'Latif Abd al'Razaq: France believed he was a 43-year-old Iraqi friend of Wadi Haddad and was one of the Popular Front for the Liberation of Palestine hijackers of Air France flight 139, an A300 flying from Tel Aviv to Paris on June 27, 1976 and diverted to Entebbe, Uganda.

Abd Al Razik: alias Abu Mussab, an Algerian from Al Wadd who joined al Qaeda in Iraq (AQI) as a fighter in 2007, claiming computer experience. He claimed to know AQI member Abu Baker Sunaikhara, an expert in explosives who was from Taghazout Village District Qam'mar in Qam'mar city. His phone number was 0021390926639.

Muzir Daire Razoki: assistant trade attaché at the Iraqi Embassy in Thailand who was one of five men detained by the Immigration Police in January 1991 as part of a terrorist plot against U.S., UK, Israeli, and Australian installations and airlines. He claimed to be a member of the Iraqi intelligence agency Mukhabarat.

'Abd-al-Razzaq: alias Abu-Mus'ab, an Algerian from al-Wad who joined al Qaeda in Iraq as a fighter in 2007. He had experience with computers. His phone number was 0021390926639. He knew Ab-Bakr, Saniqriyah, who had expertise in improvised explosive devices, and who could be contacted in Taghurt Village, Qamar administrative district, Qamar municipality.

Seyam Reda: a German of Afghan ancestry who worked for a German television network and who some news sources said had been rejected as a cameraman for *al-Jazeera*. He was arrested on September 17, 2002 by Indonesian authorities and held on suspicion of involvement in terrorism and misusing his tourist visa by working as a journalist. Police thought he could be Abu Daud, wanted in Singapore and Malaysia for links to international terrorism. Police believed he was involved with Omar al-Farouq, an al Qaeda operative from Kuwait who was arrested in June. Al-Farouq claimed he was to be the triggerman for a failed 1999 assassination attempt against President Megawati Sukarnoputri; his wife served as translator for the plot. Al-Farouq said he was part of a second assassination plot in 2002; the bomb exploded prematurely at a mall, blowing off the assassin's leg. The burly Reda speaks Arabic and German but little Indonesian. He was arrested in a $4,000/month South Jakarta home with a swimming pool and internal camera system. In a search of the home, police found videos of al-Farouq giving weapons and military instruction to Islamic militants in eastern Indonesia. German police arrived the next week to assist in the investigation. Some observers believe he was the financier of the October 12, 2002 bombings of two Bali nightclubs that killed 202 people.

Aberrahmani Redouane: alias Riad Le Blond, an Armed Islamic Group leader in Algiers who was among 11 rebels killed by the government on July 7, 1998 in the forested heights of the La Vigie District of Algiers.

Zakaria Hussnie al Refa'aie: alias Abu Ammer Am Mansour, a Syrian from Dera'ah who was born on April 2, 1984 and joined al Qaeda in Iraq as a martyr on November 10, 2006, bringing a passport. His recruitment coordinator was Abu Amer. His phone number was 015235784.

Mohammed Refai: age 40, a Syrian held in federal custody as of November 2001 in connection with the FBI's investigation of the 9/11 attacks.

Hafid Regraji: an Algerian expelled by the British Home Office to Algeria on May 17, 1984 for "preparing acts of terrorism."

Kassem Rehan: a Lebanese Hizballah leader abducted by Israeli soldiers on July 23, 1994 on accusations of plotting attacks against Israel. He was taken while driving from Ruhmoor in the Beka'a Valley to the market town of Nabatiyeh in southern Lebanon.

Abdur Rehman: a soldier from Helmand and would-be assassin who was shot to death on September 5, 2002 by U.S. troops guarding Afghan President Hamid Karzai in Kandahar. Karzai had just stepped into a car outside the provincial governor's office when Rehman, still in uniform, fired on the vehicle. Karzai was unhurt. Governor Gul Agha Shirzai, a passenger in the vehicle, was hit in the neck. A U.S. Special Operations soldier suffered minor injuries and was in stable condition. Rehman had joined Gul Agha Shirzai's security force less than three weeks earlier. No one claimed credit. Local officials blamed al Qaeda and the Taliban. Others suggested the work of Gulbuddin Hekmatyar, former Afghan prime minister and now a fugitive who had called for jihad against the Americans and the government.

Khidr Abu Abdur Rehman: alias of Ahmad Saeed.

Richard Reid: age 28, a drifter who boarded American Airlines flight 63 in Paris on December 22, 2001 and attempted to set off explosives hidden in his shoes with a match. The six foot four inch, 220-pound Middle Eastern-looking man carried a British passport issued on December 7 in Belgium, but some authorities said it was "questionable." Reid had torn several pages out of his old passport. He boarded without any luggage or additional ID, traveled alone, and had a one-way ticket—all tipoffs that should trigger suspicions. He lit a match and, when confronted by a flight attendant, put it in his mouth. After she alerted the pilot by intercom and returned, he tried to set alight the inner tongue of his sneaker, which had been drilled out and had protruding wires. She tried to stop him, but Reid threw her against the bulkhead. Reid bit a second flight attendant on the thumb. The crew and several passengers, including Kwame James, a six foot eight inch pro basketball player, overpowered him; several passengers suffered minor injuries. Two French doctors on board used the plane's medical kit to sedate him three times; other passengers tied him to his window seat in row 29. The pilot diverted the flight to Boston's Logan International Airport, escorted by two U.S. Air Force F15 fighter jets. The crew questioned Reid, who claimed his father is Jamaican and his mother, British and that he was traveling to the Caribbean to visit family members. Some media outlets reported that he was a Muslim convert. The passengers gave the pilot two audiotapes Reid was carrying. The FBI took the man into custody for "interference with a flight crew," a felony. Reid was jailed and placed on suicide watch at the Plymouth County Correctional Facility south of Boston in Plymouth, Massachusetts. He faced charges that could lead to a sentence of 20 years and a $250,000 fine. On December 24, he was formally charged in court in Boston with interference with flight crews by assault or intimidation. He requested a court-appointed attorney for his December 28 court appearance.

Tests on the shoes indicated a substance consistent with C-4. The ignition devices were later "disrupted" and the shoes were detonated in an open field. The FBI said there were two "functional improvised explosive devices" inside the sneakers.

French police said that the suspect was born in Sri Lanka and named Tariq Raja, alias Abdel Rahim. Other reports said may have had dual citizenship. U.S. officials said he might be mentally unstable. French media reported that he had tried to board the same flight on December 21, but was stopped by police unsure of his passport.

On December 11, the U.S. Federal Aviation Administration had warned airlines to be on the alert for individuals smuggling weapons or bombs in their shoes. Following the incident, some airports began random inspections of passenger footwear.

Reid and al Qaeda suspect Zacarias Moussaoui attended the primarily black Brixton Mosque in London, although worshipers could not establish that the two attended together. Some al Qaeda detainees in Afghanistan said they recognized Reid from photos that appeared in the media.

The French *La Provence* newspaper quoted police and intelligence sources as indicating that Reid was part of the Tabliq Islamic movement, but he left because it was not "radical enough." The *Boston Globe* cited FBI speculation that Reid had an accomplice to put together the explosive device. Reid had previous run-ins with London police for mugging and robbery. Interpol said he had 13 theft charges, one case of offenses against people, and two cases of offenses against property. While in jail, he converted to Islam and moved on to radicalism.

Reid spent the night before the incident in a $175 airport hotel room paid for by American Airlines because he missed the previous day's flight due to extensive questioning by French border police.

Investigators determined that Reid had traveled to Israel, Egypt, the Netherlands, and Belgium, and that the shoes contained PETN (pentaerythritol tetranitrate), a C-4 type of explosive and key ingredient in Semtex; TATP (triacetone triperoxide); and nonmetal fuses, which may have made them more difficult to set off.

Despite being a drifter, Reid somehow had enough money for international travel. His estranged father said Reid had traveled to Iran three or four years earlier. Reid was in Israel in June for a week, possibly testing El Al security. He was quizzed when he arrived at Tel Aviv's Ben Gurion Airport. El Al put him on a seat next to a sky marshal. He may have purchased the sneakers in Amsterdam. In Brussels, he picked up the British passport, which he was carrying, along with his old one, when he showed up at the Paris airport.

At an initial hearing on December 28, 2001, FBI witness Margaret Cronin said that the bomb could have blown a hole in the plane's fuselage, leading to explosive decompression of the cabin. Because Reid was in a window seat, the blast could also have ignited the fuel tanks. U.S. Magistrate Judge Judith G. Dein ruled that there was probable cause for the arrest and ordered Reid held without bail. She ruled that he posed a serious flight risk, and would pose a danger to the public if released. He faced charges punishable by up to 20 years in prison and a $250,000 fine. Prosecutors, including Colin Owyang, could file additional charges, and had three weeks to present evidence to a grand jury. Reid was represented by public defender Tamar Birckhead.

On January 16, 2002, he was indicted in Boston for attempting to blow up the plane. Five the nine charges carried life sentences, including attempted use of a weapon of mass destruction and using a destructive device. He pleaded not guilty on January 18, 2002 in U.S. District Court to eight of the charges. Defense attorneys challenged the ninth charge of attempting to wreck a mass transportation vehicle. On June 11, 2002, U.S. District Judge William Young threw out one of the nine charges, saying that a plane is not a vehicle under the Patriot Act. On October 4, 2002, after initially asking that references to al Qaeda training be dropped in the indictment in return for a guilty plea, he pleaded guilty to all eight charges, including attempt into blow up the airliner. On January 30, 2003, he was sentenced to life in prison.

Azri Saleh Reifi: on March 17, 1992, the Palestinian from the occupied territories slashed a sword at passersby in Tel Aviv's Jaffa section, killing two Israelis and wounding 20. A policeman killed him with two shots. He apparently was avenging the death of his father, who died in Israeli detention in 1989 from diabetes complications. He carried a leaflet from Hamas. Islamic Jihad later claimed credit, saying it was retaliating for the killing of Abbas al Musawi by Israeli commandos.

Abdelhalim Hafed Remadna: an Algerian, age 35, arrested on November 15, 2001 by Milan police as he was boarding a train. He had false Italian residency papers and was trying to leave the country. He was held in the investigation into the 9/11 attacks.

Maryan Remesani: one of six Iranian Hizballah members detained on May 2, 1992 by Ecuadoran police in Quito on suspicion of involvement in the March 17, 1992 car bombing at the Israeli Embassy in Buenos Aires that killed 29 and injured 252. They had intended to go to Canada via the United States. On May 9, the Crime Investigation Division in Quito said that the group was not involved in the bombing, but would be deported to Iran through Bogota and Caracas. They were released on May 12, 1992 and given 72 hours to leave the country.

Ahmed Ressam: alias Tehar Medjadi , alias Benni Antoine Norris, an Algerian with a fake Canadian passport, attempting to enter Port Angeles, Washington, as he arrived by ferry from Canada, who was arrested on December 15, 1999 by Washington State Police and customs officials. He was transporting two 22-ounce bottles of nitroglycerin, more than 100 pounds of urea, and homemade timers in his rental car. The detonating device consisted of circuit boards linked to a Casio watch and a 9-volt battery, similar to one used early by bin Laden associates. He was born in Algeria in 1967 and was arrested and jailed for 15 months for arms trafficking with terrorists. He and his associates in Canada were members of Algeria's Armed Islamic Group and were believed to be working for Osama bin Laden. In March 1998, he attended an al Qaeda camp in Afghanistan.

Ressam attempted to flee after being questioned and asked to step out of his Chrysler 300, the last car off the ferry. Customs inspector Diana M. Dean asked him to step out of his car. Inspector Carmon Clem removed the trunk floor board and discovered suspicious packages. Customs agents found 118 pounds of a fine white powder used to manufacture explosives, 14 pounds of a sulfate, two jars of nitroglycerine, and four small, black boxes believed to be detonators. Senior inspector Mark Johnson patted down Ressam for weapons and felt something in a jacket pocket. Ressam slipped out of his jacket and ran. He was chased down six blocks away from the ferry customs port. He was carrying a false Canadian passport and driver's license with two different names. Witnesses said they saw a possible accomplice walk off the Coho Ferry as Ressam was being arrested.

On December 22, 1999, Ressam appeared before U.S. Magistrate David Wilson, and was charged in a Seattle federal court with knowingly transporting explosives across the Canadian border, having false identification papers, and making false statements to U.S. Customs Service officials. He was represented by court-appointed attorney Tom Hillier, who pleaded not guilty for his client.

Ressam speaks French and Arabic, and had planned to stay at the Best Western Loyal Inn in Seattle, close to a variety of holiday events. He had a reservation on an American Airlines flight from Seattle to New York via Chicago, and a ticket for a connecting British Airways flight to London. The Seattle hotel had a reservation made on December 14 for "Benni Norris," the name on the faked passport. A van parked near his apartment was registered to a Benni Antoine Norris. The individual who used a Best Western national 800 number left a credit card number and a contact telephone number in Quebec.

Ressam had been denied refugee status in Canada because of his links to the Algerian Armed Islamic Group (GIA). He was earlier arrested in Canada and served a brief sentence for stealing computers and car phones. He had arrived in Canada on February 20, 1994, requesting refugee status. He claimed the Algerian police had arrested him in 1992 on charges of selling guns to the rebels. He said he was held in prison for 15 months and tortured until he signed a false confession. Upon release, he fled to Morocco, Spain, and France, before arriving in Canada. His French passport was for Tehar Medjadi, but he soon admitted that the document and his Catholic birth certificate were faked. In 1995, he failed to show up for a hearing and was detained, but the court let him go free. An arrest warrant was issued on February 8, 1998, in the theft of a computer from

a parked car, a charge for which he served two weeks in jail. Around that time, a deportation order was issued, on the basis of three outstanding criminal arrest warrants, two involving thefts from cars and one in a breaking and entering. In May 1998, a nationwide immigration arrest warrant was issued, but Canadian officials were unable to find him.

He was held without bail pending his trial, scheduled for February 22. He could be sentenced to 40 years in prison if convicted of the five counts in the indictment, which did not contain conspiracy charges.

The Canadian *Globe and Mail* claimed that U.S. counterintelligence agents had alerted the Mounties about Ressam in Vancouver. The Mounties had him under surveillance for three weeks at the 2400 Motel in Vancouver.

A spokesman for the Montreal police said that Ressam lived for a time with Karim Said Atmani, who was extradited by Canada to France on charges that he participated in the 1995 Paris subway bombing that killed four and injured 86. Montreal police announced that they had arrested 11 men, mostly Algerians, during the past four months for thefts during the previous two years that obtained 5,000 items, such as computers, cell phones, passports, and credit cards. Some were believed to be aiding Islamic radicals.

French officials said Ressam was linked to Fateh Kamel, an Algerian veteran of the Afghan war, who was tied to the 1996 bombers in Paris who left one bystander and several Islamic radicals dead. French officials sent a team to Canada in October 1999 to interview Ressam and Atmani, but neither could be located.

On December 18, 1999, the Customs Service put all 301 ports of entry on high alert. U.S. authorities searched for an accomplice who was with Ressam at British Columbia's 2400 Motel in Vancouver for three weeks. Ressam paid cash for the $325/week suite of two rooms, kitchen, and bath. Mounties raided Ressam's apartment house at 1250 Fort Street, in Montreal's East End. Breaking in a window, the police found a .357 Magnum pistol and instructions for making bombs.

Police were searching for three possible accomplices of Ressam, two of whom were a man he shared a motel room with in Vancouver and another who may have been on the ferry with him.

On December 19, Montreal police found an orange van registered to Benni Norris, the alias on Ressam's passport. A bomb squad searched the 1989 GMC and a house.

Montreal police suggested that Ressam had ties with Mourad Gherabli, age 40, an Algerian believed to be part of a ring of thieves who have stolen cell phones and computers and used them to finance Islamic terrorist groups around the world. Gherabli denied the charges by observing "I like girls. I like cocaine. I have a big, big problem with the poker machines. So I steal. But I'm not a terrorist. I don't have enough money to send to anyone." Police believed that the theft money moved from Canada via France, Belgium, Italy, Kovoso, Pakistan, and on to Algeria.

Ressam reportedly had been seen in training camps used in the 1980s by Islamic militants fighting the Russians in Afghanistan. Ressam had told Canadian immigration officials that he had been wrongly accused in Algeria of being an Islamic radical.

Police were searching for a Ressam associate, Abdelmajed Dahoumane, age 32, as of December 17. On December 25, the FBI interviewed Horizon Air ticket agents; one of them had sold a ticket to a man of his description. He had a French passport and paid in Canadian currency for a ticket from Bellingham, 90 miles north of Seattle, to Seattle, with a connecting flight to Las Vegas. Canadian police had issued an arrest warrant accusing him of illegally possessing explosives with the intent to cause damage or injury. He had stayed with Ressam in the Vancouver hotel room, which reeked of a rotten egg smell, consistent with the theory that they had been making nitroglycerin.

Ressam reportedly had received terrorist training in Afghanistan and Pakistan, and had fought in Muslim military units in Bosnia against Croatian and Serbian militias. French sources said he was suspected of involvement in the 1996

bombing of the Paris subway that killed four and injured 91, as well as holdups near Lille.

Ressam used a 9 mm semiautomatic pistol supplied by Samir Ait Mohamed in an August 1999 holdup attempt at a Montreal currency exchange.

On December 28, 1999, Seattle Mayor Paul Schell announced the cancellation of Seattle's millennium party at the Space Needle because of fears of a terrorist attack.

Authorities announced on December 29 that Ressam was not carrying nitroglycerine, but the more deadly RDX (cyclotrimethylene trinitramine), one of the world's most powerful explosives, often used by military services for demolitions. It can be combined with PETN to form Semtex, a plastic explosive.

Ressam's attorneys asked for a change of venue on January 22, 2000, claiming that media coverage had harmed his chances for a fair trial. They requested a move to San Francisco or Los Angeles. Assistant U.S. Attorney Harold Malkin opposed the change.

Ressam was arraigned on January 27, 2000 in federal court in Seattle on four new counts that superseded the original indictment. U.S. District Judge John Coughenour moved the trial date from February 28 to July 10. On March 3, 2000, the judge moved the trial to Los Angeles. His trial began on March 12, 2001 in Los Angeles. He was convicted on April 7, 2001 in the New Year's Day 2000 bomb plot and sentenced in June to 130 years in prison. The jury found him guilty on nine criminal counts, including terrorism and assorted charges involving transporting explosives, smuggling, and using false passports. The same day, he was convicted in absentia by a Paris court for belonging to a terrorist group of Islamic militants; he was sentenced to five years. On May 25, he offered to testify in the July 2001 trial of Mokhtar Haouari in New York. On July 3, 2001, he told a federal jury in U.S. District Court in Manhattan that his group planned to set off a huge bomb at the Los Angeles International Airport.

On July 27, 2005, U.S. District Judge John C. Coughenour sentenced Ressam, age 38, to 22 years in prison. The Algerian had cooperated with international investigators regarding Afghan terrorist training camps, but stopped talking in 2003. Prosecutors hoped that he would testify against his coconspirators—Samir Ait Mohamed and Abu Doha—who were awaiting extradition from Canada and the United Kingdom. On August 26, 2005, prosecutors said they would appeal the sentence, which was shorter than the 35 years they requested and less than the 65 years to life that was the standard sentencing range. With credit for time served and three years for good behavior, he could be released in 14 years, then be deported or sent to France, where he had been convicted in absentia of other terrorism-related crimes. Judge Coughenour had also taken the opportunity to criticize the Bush administration's handling of terrorist suspects. "We did not need to use a secret military tribunal, detain the defendant indefinitely as an enemy combatant or deny the defendant the right to counsel. The message to the world from today's sentencing is that our courts have not abandoned our commitment to the ideals that set our nation apart." On January 16, 2007, a three-judge panel of the U.S. Court of Appeals for the Ninth Circuit reversed Ressam's conviction on one of nine charges and threw out the sentence. The court sent the case back to the lower court for a new sentence.

On March 25, 2008, Attorney General Michael B. Mukasey made his first argument before the U.S. Supreme Court in asking them to reinstate the 22-year term given to Ressam. The Ninth Circuit had claimed that the statute used for the one count was too open-ended, calling for a 10-year mandatory term for anyone who "carries any explosive during the commission of any felony." On May 19, 2008, the Supreme Court, on an 8–1 decision, upheld his conviction on a federal explosives charge that increased his sentence.

Bassam Reyati: Jordanian living in Brooklyn detained as an accomplice of Rashad Baz, a Brooklyn resident who, on March 1, 1994, fired on a convoy of Hasidic Jewish students on Franklin D. Roosevelt Drive near the Brooklyn Bridge in New York, injuring 14 rabbinical students in a van. He was charged with hindering prosecution and weapons possession. Officials said he had helped Baz dispose of the guns and the car. Reyati owned the Brooklyn taxi service that employed Baz and another accomplice. Bail was set at $20,000. He pleaded not guilty on March 29.

Ali Reza: one of three Iranian youths who hijacked an Iran National Airlines B727 flying between Tehran, Abadan, and Kuwait on October 9, 1970 and diverted to Baghdad, Iraq. The trio threatened to blow up the plane with all passengers if Iran did not release 21 political prisoners. They injured a flight attendant. They were held by Iraqi authorities for questioning.

Ali Reza: an Iranian refugee detained for 24 hours at Karachi airport on September 24, 1989 in connection with a possible attempt to hijack Saudi Airlines SV-353 from Karachi to Jeddah. He was released after close interrogation. He had come to Karachi as a refugee in February 1989, and had been living in a slum behind the airport. He was planning to emigrate to the United States.

Mohammad Reza: one of six Iranian Hizballah members detained on May 2, 1992 by Ecuadoran police in Quito on suspicion of involvement in the March 17, 1992 car bombing at the Israeli Embassy in Buenos Aires that killed 29 and injured 252. They had intended to go to Canada via the United States. On May 9, the Crime Investigation Division in Quito said that the group was not involved in the bombing, but would be deported to Iran through Bogota and Caracas. They were released on May 12, 1992 and given 72 hours to leave the country.

Sadiq 'Ali Reza: identified on Saudi television on September 21, 1989 as one of two Iranians who claimed that they were working at the Iranian Embassy, who were to provide explosives to a cell in Kuwait that set two bombs that exploded on July 10, 1989 in two streets leading to the Great Mosque in Mecca, killing a Pakistani and injuring

16 of the 1.5 million pilgrims from 100 countries attending the hajj.

Reza Rezai: leader of an Iranian leftist group killed by security forces on June 2, 1973 in a raid on his home. A pistol used by Rezai was the weapon taken from the body of Iranian General Taheri by his assassins. He was leader of a group that shot to death U.S. military advisor Lt. Col. Lewis L. Hawkins on June 2, 1973.

Omar Mohammed Ali Rezaq: at the opening of his trial in Valletta, Malta on November 1, 1988, the Palestinian pleaded guilty to the murder of an American woman and an Israeli man in the Egyptair hijacking of November 24, 1985. He was sentenced to 25 years in 1986 but served only seven years before being granted amnesty by the government of Malta. Upon being freed, he flew to Ghana on February 25, 1993. From there, he boarded a flight to Lagos, Nigeria, on July 15, 1993. Nigeria barred him from entering the country and on July 16, 1993, turned him over to the United States. The Abu Nidal member was charged in the United States with air piracy. He appeared on July 16, 1993 in federal court in Washington DC. U.S. District Judge Royce Lamberth entered a plea of not guilty in his behalf after his court-appointed lawyer, Santha Sonenberg, refused to enter a plea. He was held without bond pending an August 2, 1993 court hearing. He was scheduled to be tried for air piracy in the United States on April 9, 1996. Attorneys Robert Tucker and Teresa Alva offered an insanity defense. On July 19, 1996, a federal jury convicted Rezaq of air piracy. He was sentenced to life on October 7, 1996. Judge Lamberth recommended that he never win parole. Rezaq was ordered to pay $264,000 to the victims' relatives, who did not accept Rezaq's apology. On February 6, 1998, the U.S. Court of Appeals for the District of Columbia Circuit upheld his air piracy conviction.

Samir Rhadir: Jordanian sentenced to death in Nicosia for the February 18, 1978 Black June

assassination of Yusef el-Sebai. In April 1978, Cyprus's High Commission in London received a phone call warning that the building would be blown up if the killers were executed.

Abbas Rhayel: a Lebanese asylum seeker in Germany and Hizballah member who, on September 17, 1992, shot to death four Democratic Party of Kurdistan politicians in Berlin's Mykonos restaurant at the behest of the Iranians. On April 10, 1997, a German tribunal sentenced him to life in prison.

Ali Bin Riad: alias Abu Zakker, an Algerian who joined al Qaeda in Iraq in 2007. His recruitment coordinator was Abu Jalal. His phone number was 0021332247318.

Aham Rial: on April 10, 2008, Shin Bet announced that Aham Rial, age 21 and Ana Salum, age 21, two Palestinians from Nablus, had confessed to plotting to poison food they would serve at the Grill Express restaurant near the Diamond Exchange in Ramat Gan. They were members of the al-Aqsa Martyrs Brigade in Nablus, which also asked them to smuggle a suicide bomber into Israel. They were arrested on March 19. They were in the country illegally and lacked work permits.

Craig Richter: one of four American Jews who opened fire with M-16 rifles at a bus near Ramallah that was carrying Palestinians to work on March 4, 1984. The four fled in a Subaru but were captured later that day by Israeli security forces. Terror Against Terror claimed credit. He confessed and was sentenced to five years.

'Abdullah Asad 'Abdullah 'Ali Rida: member of a cell in Kuwait that set two bombs that exploded on July 10, 1989 in two streets leading to the Great Mosque in Mecca, killing a Pakistani and injuring 16 of the 1.5 million pilgrims from 100 countries attending the hajj.

Badir Ibrahim 'Abd ar-Rida: an Iraqi sentenced to death by the Kuwaiti State Security Court in

1984 in connection with the December 12, 1983 truck bombing of the administrative building of the U.S. Embassy in Kuwait, killing four people and injuring 59. As of April 1987, none of the death sentences had been carried out. The release of 17 of the 25 prisoners in the case was demanded on numerous occasions by the Islamic Jihad in return for Americans held captive in Lebanon beginning in 1986.

Youssef Abdulkusser Rida: name on a forged passport carried by Mohammad Ali Hamadei at the time of his arrested in West German on January 13, 1987.

Essam al-Ridi: an Egyptian who had fought against the Soviets in Afghanistan in the 1980s. He purchased a plane in the United States to help ship Stinger missiles from Pakistan to Sudan for al Qaeda. He was a prosecution witness in the trial of the bombers of the U.S. embassies in Kenya and Tanzania on August 7, 1998.

Lamin Rif: alias of Abu-'Abdallah, an Algerian welder born on September 13, 1982 who joined al Qaeda in Iraq on January 22, 2007 as a fighter, bringing his watch. His recruitment coordinator was Abu-Isam, whom he knew via Abu-al-Qa'qa'. He came via Algeria, Tunis, and Libya to Syria, where he met Abu-'Abd-al-Malik, Abu-'Ali, Abu-'Asim and Abu-Basal, who took his 150 euros. They told him nothing was permitted to go into Iraq with him except passports. His home phone number was 80021321532991.

Mustafa 'Arif al-Rifa'i: alias of Mustafa Qasim.

Zakariyyah Husni al-Rifa'i: alias Abu-'Amir al-Mansur, a Syrian from Dar'a born on April 2, 1984 who joined al Qaeda in Iraq on November 10, 2006 as a martyr, contributing a passport. His recruitment coordinator was Abu-'Amir. His phone number was 015235784.

Muhammad Rihal: Hizballah member identified by *Ha'aretz* on January 8, 1990 as one of the three kidnappers of U.S. Marine Lt. Col. William Richard Higgins on February 17, 1988. The paper claimed Syrian forces had detained and interrogated the kidnappers in September 1989. Rihal was arrested in Beirut on August 31, 1989. He was allegedly released after two weeks.

Abu-Rihanah: alias of 'Ali Bin-Muhammad al-Madayyan.

Yahia Rihane: alias Krounfil (Algerian slang for "mole"—he had a large mole on his face), identified on August 28, 1995 by police as the organizer of the four Algerian Islamic extremists who, on December 24, 1994, hijacked an Air France A300 on the ground at Algiers's Houari Boumedienne Airport and killed a Vietnamese trade councilor and an Algerian policeman. The hijackers were killed in a rescue attempt at Marseilles airport. Rihane organized the July 25, 1995 bombing in Paris that killed seven and injured 86 to avenge the killing of the four hijackers.

Mahmed Fahmi Rimawi: positioned a backup car near the hotel during the Popular Front for the Liberation of Palestine assassination on October 17, 2001 of Israel's right-wing Minister of Tourism, Rehavam Zeevi. He was arrested soon after escaping to the home of Tzalah Alawi in an Arab village just beyond the Old City walls.

Zubayr al-Rimi: a suspected al Qaeda militant believed involved in the May 12, 2003 triple truck bombing of a residential complex in Riyadh that killed 34 and injured 190. Al-Rimi was born in Saudi Arabia and married a Moroccan woman who was arrested in June raids. On September 5, 2003, the FBI put out a worldwide alert for Adan El Shukrijumah, Abderraouf Jdey, Zubayr al-Rimi, and Karim El Mejjati, who were believed to be engaged in planning for terrorist attacks, according to information provided by Khalid Sheik Mohammed, al Qaeda's operations chief. On September 23, 2003, Saudi forces killed three terrorists, including al-Rimi. The gun battle occurred at a housing complex in Jizan, near the Yemen border. One security officer died. Two suspects were arrested.

Samir 'Abd al-Latif Muhammad Riqz: a Lebanese who was one of 18 Arab terrorists reported by Madrid *Diario 16* on October 20, 1987 as having entered Spain in August to attack Middle Eastern diplomatic missions and assassinate Saudi Ambassador Muhammad Nuri Ibrahim. They had received weapons and casing reports on the ambassador from a Lebanese student resident in Spain whose initials were HMI.

Sajida Mubarak Atrous al-Rishawi: age 35, wife of Ali Hussein Ali al-Shamari, age 35, one of three suicide bombers who, on November 9, 2005, attacked Western hotels in Amman, killing 59 and wounding more than 300. Abu Musab al-Zarqawi's group Al Qaeda in Iraq claimed credit. On November 13, 2005, she confessed on Jordanian television that she had walked into the hotel with her husband, wearing an explosives belt that contained ball bearings. Her belt failed to detonate; his went off. She was picked up in a raid in Salt (earlier misidentified as Amman). She was wearing the suicide vest during the broadcast. Her brother, Thamer, was an al-Qaeda member who was killed in a U.S. assault in Fallujah in April 2004. She had fled to a hotel that she and the three other bombers had rented in Amman's suburbs. She then ran off to Salt. Some pundits speculated that she was turned in to authorities by her sister's relatives. On March 14, 2006, Jordan indicted al-Zarqawi, al-Rishawi, and six others for the attacks. On July 9, 2006, a military prosecutor demanded the death penalty for al-Rishawi, the only defendant in custody. On January 27, 2007, Jordan's seniormost court rejected her appeal.

Aline Ibrahim Riskalah: a Lebanese Maronite Catholic woman arrested on October 20, 1988 after deplaning from a Middle East Airlines flight from Beirut at Milan's Linate Airport when police found that a false bottom of her suitcase hid large black-and-white photographs of U.S.

hostages Terry Anderson, Thomas Sutherland, and Alann Steen. She also carried a handwritten letter to a northern Italian businessman signed by Steen, $1,000 in counterfeit U.S. bills, and 50 grams of heroin. A spokesman for the Christian Lebanese Forces said she lived in Beirut's Christian southern suburb of 'Ayn al-Rummanah, had been divorced several times, and had unspecified "suspicious relations." Islamic Jihad denied any links with her. On November 3, 1988, someone claiming membership in the Islamic Jihad threatened to kidnap Italians in West Beirut if Italy did not release her.

Abdul Rahim-Riyadh: a senior al Qaeda facilitator listed by U.S. Central Command on January 8, 2002.

Nabil Nasser al-Riyami: an Omani and one of six Arabs arrested on April 1, 1995 by Philippine authorities in Caloocan for being members of the little-known Islamic Saturday Meeting. The group had ties to Ramzi Yusuf. Documents taken from the six detainees indicated that they planned to attack U.S. and Saudi citizens in the Philippines. They were charged with illegal possession of firearms and explosives. Police had seized several M-16 Armalite rifles, dynamite, and detonators. Police said they were preparing for a series of bombings to disrupt the May 8 elections.

Reem Saleh Riyashi: age 22, a first-ever Islamic Resistance Movement (Hamas) female suicide bomber, who, on January 14, 2004, killed two Israeli soldiers, a border patrol officer, and a private security guard and wounded eight Israelis and four Palestinians in a morning attack at the entrance to an Israeli industrial park on the Gaza Strip border. In a videotape, she said "I have two children and love them very much. But my love to see God was stronger than my love for my children, and I'm sure that God will take care of them if I become a martyr. . . . I am proud to be the first female martyr." She had hidden explosives on her body, and feigned a limp, telling security officials that a metal plate in her leg would set off their metal detectors. She was the first suicide mother against Israelis in the ongoing 3-year Palestinian uprising. Hamas and the al-Aqsa Martyrs Brigades jointly took credit. Relatives said she left behind a $3^1/_2$-year-old son, Obedia, and an 18-month-old daughter, Doha.

On January 20, the *Washington Times* and *Yediot Ahronot* reported that she was atoning for an adulterous affair; her husband, a Hamas operative, said she could restore the family's good name by carrying out the suicide attack. Her lover gave her the suicide bomb; her husband drove her to the Erez crossing for the attack.

'Umar Muhammad 'Ali al-Rizaq: sole surviving Egyptian Revolution hijacker of Egyptair flight 648 that had left Athens bound for Cairo on November 23, 1985. The terrorists executed several passengers before a government rescue operation. The final death toll was 61, with another 26 injured. Egypt requested extradition on November 27, 1985; the request was denied on December 4, 1985. On December 12, 1985, he was charged in Malta with two murders, hijacking sequestration, and attempted murder. He had arrived in Athens on the morning on November 23 on a flight from Tripoli, and had met the other two hijackers only 30 minutes before the attack. He pleaded not guilty on January 6, 1986.

'Irfan Rizq: one of five Palestinians arrested on July 9, 1987 when Egyptian authorities discovered an Iranian-backed terrorist group that had chosen a governorate in Lower Egypt for their operations. Police seized explosives from a group collaborating with the al-Jihad Organization.

Pierre Rizq: alias Akram, a Lebanese Forces official accused by the Lebanese Voice of the People as being responsible for setting off a 1-kilogram bomb inside a suitcase at Beirut International Airport that killed five persons and injured 73 on November 11, 1987. The bomb killed the blonde Palestinian woman who was carrying the suitcase. The Lebanese Liberation Organization claimed credit.

Mullah Roazi: claimed to be the senior Taliban official in Zabol province, and claimed credit for the October 30, 2003 kidnapping in Afghanistan of Hasan Onal, a Turkish engineer.

Mulla Rocketi: alias of Mulla Abdol Salam.

Mechthild Rogali: possibly one of six members of the Arm of the Arab Revolution, a Popular Front for the Liberation of Palestine cover name, who took over a ministerial meeting of the Organization of Petroleum Exporting Countries (OPEC) in Vienna, Austria and took 70 hostages, including 11 oil ministers. She was the girlfriend of Hans-Joachim Klein, a Second of June Movement member who participated in the OPEC raid. A warrant was handed down in the OPEC case by the Vienna criminal court on December 23, 1975.

Novoff Nagib Meflehel Rosan: on January 26, 1983, the Iraqi pleaded not guilty to charges of shooting Israeli Ambassador Shlomo Argov in London on June 4, 1982. On March 5, 1983, he was convicted in London's Central Criminal Court. He received a 35-year sentence. He was an Iraqi intelligence service colonel and deputy commander of Abu Nidal's special operations section.

Abdullah Mohammed Rashid al-Roshoud: al Qaeda's chief ideologue in the Saudi region, he was killed on June 30, 2004 during a car chase and shootout with police in the al-Quds neighborhood of eastern Riyadh, during which a police officer also died. The cleric was number 24 on the list of Saudi Arabia's 26 most-wanted terrorists. He had called for holy war against the Saudi royal family and Westerners in the Gulf. There is some dispute on his date of death. On June 23, 2005, Abu Musab al-Zarqawi, the Jordanian head of al Qaeda in Iraq, said in a Web statement that al-Roshoud was killed in a U.S. airstrike in northwest Iraq. He was one of only three terrorists on the list still at large.

Freedom Rostami: one of eight Iranian students arrested in the United States on November 15,

1979 for attempting to smuggle three disassembled Winchester 30.06 rifles, matching scopes, 15 boxes of ammunition, and a street map of Washington, DC with certain embassies marked, as one of the men was about to board TWA 900 from Baltimore-Washington International Airport to New York's JFK International Airport. The Iranians spoke of taking the rifles to Iran. They claimed to be attending Baltimore-area colleges, and were jailed on bonds ranging from $25,000 to $250,000. The group was charged with dealing in firearms without a license, placing firearms on an interstate commercial airliner without notifying the carrier, and conspiracy. On February 22, 1980, he pleaded guilty to lesser crimes in exchange for agreeing to leave the United States at the end of the semester in civil engineering at the Community College of Baltimore.

Najib Rouass: a Tunisian who on July 13, 2005 was sentenced by a judge in Brescia, Italy to 14 months for inciting violence.

Hamsa Abu Roub: age 35, an Islamic Jihad leader killed in an Israeli raid in Qabatiya on December 26, 2002.

Abd Allah Bin Rouha: alias of Muhammad Ali Farah.

Nassim Abu Rous: one of two Hamas members arrested on January 14, 1998 by Palestinian officials. After a three-hour trial, they were sentenced to 15 years in prison at hard labor for building bombs and recruiting the five suicide bombers who killed 26 people in attacks in Israel on July 30 and September 4, 1997.

Abu Rowan: Saudi-based recruitment coordinator for foreign fighters for al Qaeda in Iraq in 2007.

Omar Abu Rub: cousin of Yousef Abu Rub, who joined him on November 28, 2002 as the two al-Aqsa Martyrs Brigades gunmen jumped out of a stolen white Mazda and fired hundreds of AK-47 bullets and threw a grenade at the Likud Party headquarters in Beit Shean, killing five Israelis and wounding 20 before being shot to death in a five-minute gun battle with local guards. An explosive belt one of them was wearing failed to detonate. Voters were casting ballots in a nationwide primary that selected incumbent Ariel Sharon to run as prime minister in January. Among the injured were the three sons of former Israeli Foreign Minister David Levy. On November 29, Israeli troops blew up the Jalboun homes of the two Palestinian gunmen, both in their twenties.

Yousef Abu Rub: cousin of Omar Abu Rub, who joined him on November 28, 2002 as the two al-Aqsa Martyrs Brigades gunmen jumped out of a stolen white Mazda and fired hundreds of AK-47 bullets and threw a grenade at the Likud Party headquarters in Beit Shean, killing five Israelis and wounding 20 before being shot to death in a five-minute gun battle with local guards. An explosive belt one of them was wearing failed to detonate. Voters were casting ballots in a nationwide primary that selected incumbent Ariel Sharon to run as prime minister in January. Among the injured were the three sons of former Israeli Foreign Minister David Levy. On November 29, Israeli troops blew up the Jalboun homes of the two Palestinian gunmen, both in their twenties.

Abu Bakr al-Rubaei: confessed that he and 31 other al Qaeda members planned to attack Western and U.S. interests and the homes of foreign diplomats in Yemen. He was sentenced to eight years on November 7, 2007. The Yemeni court convicted 32 Yemeni al Qaeda members of planning attacks on oil and gas installations in the country. They were sentenced to up to 15 years. Six convicts were tried in absentia. Four others were acquitted. They had been charged with forming an armed gang and planning attacks against oil installations with rocket-propelled grenades (RPGs) in September 2006. The trial began in March 2007.

Fawzi Hamza al-Rubay': a mujahedin opponent of the Iraqi regime expelled by France to Baghdad. He had been pardoned by Iraq on March 12, 1986 following French intervention. On August 27, 1986, the Al-Rafidayn Vanguard of the Hezbollah in Iraq kidnapped an Iraqi, Kamil Abd al-Husayn al-Zubaydi, in Cyprus and said they would exchange him in Beirut for al-Rubay' and another muj, Muhammad Hasan Khayr al-Din.

Haji Rudwan: alias of Imad Mugniyah.

'Awdah Misbah Rujub: arrested in a raid on the house of his uncle, Rizq, after the May 17, 1996 arrest by Israeli police of Hamas leader Hasan Salamah after a gun battle.

Hasan Rujub: arrested in a raid on the house of his brother, Rizq, after the May 17, 1996 arrest by Israeli police of Hamas leader Hasan Salamah after a gun battle.

Rizq 'Abdallah Rujub: arrested in a raid on his house after the May 17, 1996 arrest by Israeli police of Hamas leader Hasan Salamah after a gun battle. Police charged him with transporting the suicide bombing mastermind in his car. Police also arrested Rujub's brother, Hasan, and his nephew, 'Awdah Misbah.

Ahmed Rukhar: a convenience-store owner from La Rioja region who, on January 13, 2004, was charged by a Spanish judge with financing the al Qaeda truck bombing on April 11, 2002 that killed 19 people in a synagogue in Djerba, Tunisia. He was arrested in March 2003 and held on $127,000 bond on suspicion of helping to finance the bombing by sending money to al Qaeda contacts.

Jalal Rumaneh: a 30-year-old Palestinian member of Hamas who was severely injured on July 19, 1998 when he prematurely ignited a car bomb in his Fiat van on Jerusalem's Jaffa Road at 8:30 A.M. The bomb contained 160 gallons of flammable liquid and a large quantity of nails. The mixture caught fire but failed to explode. The terrorist lived in the Amari refugee camp near Ramallah. He was hospitalized with extensive burns and was reported in serious condition.

Badi Farhan al-Rumman: alias Abu-al-Basr, variant Abe al Besser, a Syrian from Dar'a, variant Derrah who was born in 1980 and joined al Qaeda in Iraq on October 14, 2006 to be a combatant. His home phone number was 015880733.

Yunus Yunus Fatihallah Abu-Ruqbah: alias Abu-'Abbas. According to the captured Sinjar personnel records of al Qaeda in Iraq, he arrived in Iraq on May 9, 2007, having traveled from Darnah, Libya to Egypt, then Syria. He hoped to become a martyr. He signed up through coordinator Qamar and contributed 2,200 Syrian Lira and 30 Marks. His Syrian coordinator was Abu 'Abbas. He claimed to have training in light weapons.

Fawwaz Shabbab al-Ruqi: alias Abu-al-Zubayr, a Saudi from Riyadh who was born in 1985 and joined al Qaeda in Iraq in 2007, contributing 1,000 SR and 6,000 Syrian Lira, along with his bank ID and passport. His recruitment coordinator was Abu-Sa'ud, whom he knew through a brother. He took a smuggling route to Iraq via Syria, where he had met Abu-'Uthman, an Iraqi who charged him 3,000 riyals.

Abu Rusdan: temporary leader of Indonesia's Jemaah Islamiyah, who was arrested on April 23, 2003.

Ibrahim al-Russan: a Jordanian whose expulsion from France was ordered on December 24, 1986 in connection with the discovery of an arm cache in Aulnay-sous-Bois on December 18, 1986.

Mohamed Rustin: Syrian member of a hijacking trio who took over KLM 366, a DC-9 flying from Malaga, Spain to Amsterdam on September 4, 1976. The plane landed in Tunis and Cyprus for refueling. While circling off Israel's shore, the trio demanded the release by Israel of eight prisoners, including Kozo Okamoto and Archbishop Hilarion Capucci. The trio surrendered in Cyprus. They claimed they were members of a Libyan-based Popular Front for the Liberation of Palestine unit. They were believed to have obtained asylum in an undisclosed country.

'Abdallah Bin-Ruwahah: alias of 'Abdallah Ahmad Imhayrith.

Abu Ruwan: Saudi-based recruitment coordinator for foreign fighters for Al Qaeda in Iraq in 2007.

'Adil Muhammad 'Abdallah Ruwayhil: alias Abu-Dujanah al-Tabuki, a Saudi power company worker from Tabuk who was born in 1981 and joined al Qaeda in Iraq as a suicide bomber on 22 Rabi' al-Thani (probably 2007), bringing his passport. He flew to Amman and on to Syria, where he spent six days and met Abu al-'Abbas, who took all of his 11,000 Saudi riyals. He had some experience as a sniper. His phone number was 00966551891409.

S

Abu-Saad: Saudi-based recruitment coordinator for foreign fighters for al Qaeda in Iraq in 2006.

Abu Sa'ad: alias of Saied Bin Al Sadeeq Bin Al Khelfah.

Abu Sa'ad: alias of Abd Al Rahman Sa'ad Harries Al Sarwani.

Ibrahim Bin Masoud Sa'ad: alias Abu Zer, an Algerian clerk from Constantinople who was born on September 20, 1983 and joined al Qaeda in Iraq on November 17, 2006 as a fighter, bringing his passport. His recruitment coordinator was Abu Jalal. His father's phone number was 02139942378.

Mohamed Yahya Ould Saad: one of six people arrested by Mauritanian authorities in March 1999 for having ties to Osama bin Laden. Saad was in Afghanistan from 1993 to 1997 and was believed to have had military training at an al Qaeda camp.

Sabah Saddiq Saad: an Iraqi diplomat who arrived in Manila on January 14, 1991. The Philippine government soon denied his accreditation because of his involvement with two terrorists who were trying to plant a 200-pound bomb at the U.S. Information Service's Thomas Jefferson Library that exploded prematurely in Manila on January 19, 1991.

Al-Sharif Hassan Sa'ad: Egyptian al-Gama'at al-Islamiyya member arrested in July 2001 in Bosnia-Herzegovina and extradited to Egypt in October 2001.

Yusuf Ahmed Saad: convicted of having supplied money, passports, and other logistical support to the four shipjackers of the *Achille Lauro* cruise ship on October 7, 1985. On December 24, 1990, a Genoa magistrate freed the Palestinian under an amnesty program that had no public notice and expelled him to Algeria.

Lotfi Abu Saada: age 21, variant Lutfi Amin Abu Saadeh, from Illar (variant Kfar Rai), a village near Tulkarm in the West Bank, and a suicide bomber who, on December 5, 2005, killed five people and injured 40 in an attack on a mall in Netanya, the third such attack on the mall since 2001. The Islamic Jihad and the al-Aqsa Martyrs Brigades claimed credit. Security officers became suspicious of the bomber as he stood in line at a security checkpoint. When they approached him, he set off the bomb.

Slah Saadaoui: age 25, arrested on March 11, 2003, in Lyon, France. He allegedly supplied Nizar Nawar with fake ID papers used in the truck bombing on April 11, 2002 that killed 19 people in a synagogue in Djerba, Tunisia.

Ahmed Saadat: Popular Front for the Liberation of Palestine (PFLP) leader after the death of Mustafa Zibri in a missile attack on August 27, 2001. He instructed the killers of Rehavam Zeevi, 75, Israel's right-wing Minister of Tourism, on October 17, 2001. The Palestinian Authority announced Saadat's arrest on January 15, 2002. On June 19, 2007, Israeli authorities arrested 12 PFLP members who planned to kidnap Americans to demand his release.

Lutfi Amin Abu Saadeh: variant of Lotfi Abu Saada.

Mongi Ben Adollah Saadequi: one of three Black June terrorists who fired machine guns and threw grenades at Vienna's Schwechat Airport on December 27, 1985. After a car chase and gun battle with police, he died of his wounds. Two people were killed and 37 injured. He carried a faked Tunisian passport, having come to Vienna from Beirut. The terrorists had intended to take hostages to obtain an El Al plane, which they would crash into Tel Aviv.

Abdelkader Saadi: alias of Georges Ibrahim 'Abdallah.

Abdul Kader Saadi (variant 'Abd al-Qadir al-Sa'di, Abdelkader Saadi): alias of Georges Ibrahim 'Abdallah, the alleged leader of the Lebanese Armed Revolutionary Faction. His release was demanded by the gunmen who kidnapped Giles Sidney Peyrolles, the director of the French Cultural Center and a consular official, near his Tripoli office on March 24, 1985.

Abu Munder al-Saadi: spiritual leader of a Libyan militant group who was arrested in the Hong Kong airport in the early 2000s, according to Noman Benotman, a former member of the group.

Luay Saadi: an Islamic Jihad West Bank military leader killed by Israeli forces in Tulkarm on October 24, 2005.

Wailed Abd Allah Ali Al Sa'adi: alias Abu Khalid Al Ammani, a Saudi with a 2007 Bachelor of Arts degree in education who joined al Qaeda in Iraq as a fighter on 26th Rajab 1428 Hijra (circa 2007), contributing 2,302 Saudi Riyals, his passport, and ID. His recruitment coordinator was Abu Abd Allah. In Syria, he met Abu Sa'ad and Abu Hajjir, whom he gave 3,700 Saudi Riyals. His phone number was 0966555256661.

Amar Bin Hammed Bin Aqeel Al Sa'adoun: alias Abu Jarah, a Saudi from Riyadh who was born in 1983 and joined Al Qaeda in Iraq as a fighter on 7th Rajab 1428 Hijra (circa 2007), bringing his passport, driver's license, and ID. His recruitment coordinator was Wailed. His phone number was 05555591720.

Abd Baqi Abd Karim Abdallah Saadun: former Ba'ath Party regional chairman in Diyala and regional chairman of southern Iraq. He was wanted for crimes against humanity that took place during a 1999 uprising during his leadership of the Ba'ath Party district of Basra. He was named on February 14, 2005 as one of Iraq's 29 most-wanted insurgents; a $1 million bounty was offered.

Mamdouh Muhammad Bikhet al Saaedi: alias Abu Muhammad, a Saudi from Mecca who was born on 1/5/1399 Hijra who joined al Qaeda in Iraq on 1st Ramadan 1427 Hijra (circa 2006), bringing $600 and a watch. His recruitment coordinator was Shady Abu Hussam. His home phone number was 5729172; Abd Allah's number was 050870058; Mashour's was 0559011511.

Abd Al Ghani Hibab Al Sa'awi: alias Abu Raghib, a Syrian lawyer from Dyr al Zur who joined al Qaeda in Iraq as a martyr in 2007, bringing 1,000 lira and four million Iraqi dinars. Al Hajji was his recruitment coordinator. His phone numbers were·092223933, 368863, and 351131.

Abu Sa'ayed: alias of Usama Hattab Muhammad.

Anas al-Sabai: alias of Anas al-Liby.

Shawan al-Sabaawi: on February 23, 2005, *Iraqiya* state television ran a video of the former Lieutenant Colonel in Saddam Hussein's army, who said Syrian intelligence trained him in beheading hostages.

Rafed Latif Sabah: alias Abi Tagrid, alias Abi Azad, an Al Qaeda in Iraq leader who was killed on September 21, 2007 during counterterrorism operations in Baghdad. He had been involved in kidnapping foreign diplomats in 2006 and in several car bombings. He was ousted from the group after stealing $200,000, but returned to help during the ongoing Coalition sweeps in Baghdad.

Yusuf al-Sabatin: an at-large merchant sentenced to hang on January 16, 1994 in connection with a plot to assassinate Jordanian King Hussein during the graduation ceremony at Muta University, a Jordanian military academy, which was foiled on June 26, 1993. He was also found guilty of belonging to the Islamic Liberation Party, which aimed to topple the regime through violence and establish an Islamic caliphate state. He was found guilty of conspiring to kill Hussein, but found innocent of trying to change the Constitution due to lack of evidence.

Ahmad Umar Nasir al-Sabawi: the al Qaeda in Iraq emir in East Mosul who was captured in April–May 2008.

Salim al-Sabbagh: one of 40 Shi'ite terrorists arrested in Egypt on August 19, 1989 for planning to carry out attacks against U.S., Israeli, Saudi, Iraqi, and Kuwaiti interests, including embassies and airlines. He was one of four dissident members of the Repudiation and Renunciation Group in al-Gharibiyah Governorate who formed the terrorist cell in 1985.

Walid Abd Allah Abd Al Rahman Al Sabbeh: alias Abu Abd Allah, a Saudi born in 1989 who joined al Qaeda in Iraq in 2007, bringing $2,600. His phone numbers were 050675138 and 0555146793.

The Saber: alias of Essid Sami Ben Khemais.

Mansour Omran Saber: a Libyan intelligence agent. The detonator used in the bombing of Pan Am flight 103 on December 21, 1988 that killed 270 over Lockerbie, Scotland matched photos of timers seized from him when he was arrested in February 1988 in Dakar, Senegal.

Fajkumar Naraindas Sabnani: on July 25, 2002, SEPRINTE, the Paraguayan counterterrorism secretariat, raided the Ciudad del Este office and apartment of the alleged Hizballah-connected money launderer. Police found letters detailing the sale of military assault rifles and other military weapons, receipts for large wire transfers, and what appeared to be bomb-making materials. Although police arrested three of his employees, he remained in Hong Kong.

Fouhad Sabour: age 38, one of five Algerian al Qaeda members whose trial began on April 16, 2002 in Frankfurt on charges of plotting to bomb the Strasbourg marketplace on December 23, 2000. They were charged with forming a terrorist organization, planning to cause an explosion, plotting to commit murder, falsifying documents, dealing drugs, and various weapons charges. The French citizen moved to London in July 2000 after having been in Bosnia and Pakistan. He flew to Frankfurt in October 2000. He was convicted in absentia in a French court for bombings in Paris in 1995. On March 10, 2003, the Frankfurt court found him guilty of preparing a bomb in the attack on the Strasbourg Christmas market and with conspiracy to murder. He was sentenced to 10 to 12 years. He said that the prosecution failed to prove al Qaeda links.

Dridi Sabri: age 37, variant Sabri Dridi, leader of a Milan-based network that was wrapped up on November 6, 2007 in coordinated raids in Italy, France, Portugal, and the United Kingdom that netted 17 Algerians and Tunisians suspected of terrorist ties in Salafist jihadi militant cells that were recruiting would-be suicide bombers for Iraq and Afghanistan. Milan prosecutors ordered the raids in Milan, Bergamo, Verese, and Reggio Emilia. Police found poisons, remote detonators, and manuals. The leaders were identified as Dridi Sabri, Mehidi Ben Nasr, and Imed Ben Zarkaoui, all operating in Italy. Three suspects remained at large. Police said the investigation began in 2003. The detainees were charged with illegal immigration, falsifying ID documents, and helping to hide people sought for terrorist activity.

Shuhour Abdullah Mukbil al-Sabri: born in Saudi Arabia in 1976, the Yemeni was believed by the FBI on February 11, 2002, to be planning a terrorist attack in the United States or on U.S. interests in Yemen.

Sad: his release from a Kenyan jail was demanded on June 27, 1976 by the Popular Front for the Liberation of Palestine hijackers of Air France flight 139, an A300 flying from Tel Aviv to Paris and ultimately diverted to Entebbe.

Sa'd: Morocco-based recruitment coordinator for foreign fighters for al Qaeda in Iraq in 2006.

Abu-Sa'd: alias of 'Abd-al-Rahman Sa'd Haris al-Sirwani.

Abu-Sa'd: alias of Faysal Sa'd all-'Utaybi.

Abu-Sa'd: a Saudi-based recruitment coordinator of foreign fighters for al Qaeda in Iraq in 2006.

Abu-Sa'd: alias of Nidal al-Qahiri.

Hamdan Sa'ud Sa'd: alias of Bandar Ajil Jabir al-Shammari.

Ibrahim Ibn-Mas'ud Sa'd: alias Abu-Dhar, an Algerian from Constantine who was born on September 20, 1983 and joined al Qaeda in Iraq as a fighter on November 18, 2006, contributing his passport and ID. His recruitment coordinator was Abu-Jalal. His father's phone number was 002139942378.

Marwan al-Sadafi: variant Safadi, alias Marwan Adib Adam Kadi, alias Ibrahim Mahmood Awethe, a 40-year-old Lebanese arrested on November 7, 1996 by Paraguayan authorities on suspicion of involvement with Hizballah. He was extradited to New York the next day. He was placed in a Chicago jail on November 9 on charges of passport fraud. He was later extradited to Canada, where he had escaped while serving a nine-year prison sentence for drug trafficking.

He was linked to an alleged plan to bomb the U.S. Embassy in Paraguay on the anniversary of the November 1995 bombing of a U.S. military facility in Saudi Arabia. He apparently had conducted surveillance of the area. Argentine officials apparently told the Paraguayans about his Hizballah connections. Sadafi was arrested along with another Arab man–who was later released–at a hotel (or apartment house) in Ciudad del Este, on the Argentine–Brazil–Paraguay border. He was picked up during a raid against smugglers during which police discovered double-barreled shotguns, revolvers, pistols, and Canadian passports.

U.S. officials later said Sadafi's nationality was unclear. He obtained a valid U.S. passport in Chicago by using a fake driver's license and birth certificate for Ibrahim Mahmood Awethe.

Abd al Hamied Omar Ali Al Sadai: alias Abu Ubidah, a Saudi from Shadourah who joined al Qaeda in Iraq as a fighter in 2007, providing his watch. His phone numbers were 0096655474776 and 00966554747746.

Yasir al-Saddi: alias Abu-Mu'min: identified by Doha's *al-Sharq* on March 19, 1993 as a former member of the Abu Nidal Group and a prominent member of the People's Army who was assassinated in 1987.

Muhammed Usman Saddique: age 24, lived on Albert Road in East London. He was arrested in the United Kingdom on August 10, 2006 in connection with a foiled plot by al Qaeda to use liquid explosives and common electronic devices as detonators to destroy at least ten planes flying from the United Kingdom to the United States. Two dozen people were detained in the United Kingdom; the number rose to 41 by the next day.

Abdallah al-Sadeq: a Libyan apprehended in Thailand in spring 2004, according to Noman Benotman, a former member of the Libyan militant network.

Abu al Sadeq: alias of Abd Al Aziz Muhammad Ali Karim.

Al Bara'a Muhammd Sadeq: alias Abu Turab, a Syrian from Durra'a who was born on March 21, 1984 and joined al Qaeda in Iraq on 9th Ramadan 1427 Hijra (2006), bringing a watch, $100, 100 lira, and a knife. His recruitment coordinator was Abu Hamzza. His home phone number was 015226823; his father's was 00962795031899.

Hoseyn Qader Sadeqi: an Iranian arrested by Kuwaiti police on January 12, 1985 for plotting to set fire to the Kuwaiti information complex and for distributing subversive literature.

Mustafa Bin Ibrahim Bin Sader: alias Abu Abbad, a Sudanese who joined al Qaeda in Iraq in 2007 He said Abu Mallek's phone number was 0966506534821; his brother in-law Abu Al Abbas's was 00966683691533.

Abd al-Qadir al-Sa'di: variant of Abdul Kader Saadi.

'Abd al-Rahim Muhammad Hasan Sadiq: sentenced to death by Kuwait on June 6, 1987 for the January 19, 1987 sabotage of Kuwaiti oil fields. The next day, the Prophet Muhammad's Forces in Kuwait told a Western news agency that it would kill Kuwaiti leaders if the emirate carried out death sentences on six members of its group.

Abu-al-Sadiq: alias of Muhammad.

Abu-al-Sadiq: alias of 'Abd-al-'Aziz Muhammad 'Ali Karim.

Al-Arab Sadiq: alias of Khalifah, an Egyptian Islamic Group terrorist who was arrested after the failed June 26, 1995 assassination attempt against Egyptian President Hosni Mubarak in Addis Ababa, Ethiopia.

Al-Bara' Muhammad Sadiq: alias Abu-Tirah, a Syrian from Di'ah who was born on March 21, 1984 and joined al Qaeda in Iraq on October 1, 2006, donating a watch, knife, $100, and 100 lira. His home phone number was 015226823; his father's was 00962795031899.

Yasir Fahd al-Sadiq: alias Abu-Hanin, a Saudi computer institute student from Mecca who was born in 1982 and joined al Qaeda in Iraq as a combatant on January 22, 2007. His recruitment coordinator was Abu-'Ali, who lives with al 'Utaybah. He flew from Jeddah to Damascus, where his contacts took $200 from him. He also brought 1,500 riyals. His father's phone number is 0096657288246; his sister's is 009665424042.

'Abd-al-Salam Sadmah: alleged on November 11, 1989 by Rome's *Avanti* as being close to Muammar Qadhafi and top leaders of Libyan Revolutionary Committees who had planned a series of terrorist attacks in Italy. The paper said he had trained the gunmen who killed dissident Ibn-Yusuf Salam Khalifah in Rome in June 1987. He was also suspected of planning attacks on Italian airlines and killing a UK police officer in London in 1984.

Mohammed ben Sadok: sentenced to life in prison at hard labor on December 11, 1957 for the May 26, 1957 assassination in Paris of Ali Chekkal, former vice president of the Algerian Assembly.

Abdulhadid Hadi Sadun: a security guard at the Libyan Embassy who was linked to two Libyans who were stopped by police on April 18, 1986 in front of the U.S. officers' club in Ankara, Turkey, and threw away a bag containing six grenades and ran. His trial began in absentia on May 13, 1986 in the State Security Court. On June 7, 1986, the charges were dropped because of diplomatic immunity.

Abu Saed: also known as Abdul Karim Abu Hamid, Popular Front for the Liberation of Palestine-General Command leader of six Fatah dissidents who claimed to be members of the Friends of Arabs, who hijacked a B707 leased to Kuwait Airways by British Midland Airways as it was flying out of Beirut on July 8, 1977. Abu Saed had served as the Palestine Liberation Organization's post office communications chief during the 1975–1976 civil war in Lebanon. He had received foreign intelligence assistance in his jailbreak shortly before the hijacking. He was an accused thief, defrauder, and extortionist. The group demanded the release of 300 prisoners in Arab jails. They also demanded the release of Archbishop Hilarion Capucci. The hijackers became frustrated with Saed, and two of the hijackers and three hostages overpowered him. The group surrendered to Syrian authorities on July 10.

Abu Saeed: a lieutenant of Abu Musab al-Zarqawi who was captured in late November 2004.

Ahmad Saeed: variant Sa'id, variant Ahmad Saeed Khadr, alias Khidr Abu Abdur Rehman, variant 'Abd-al-Rahman, director of Human Concern International Peshawar, who was arrested by Pakistani authorities on the frontier with Afghanistan on December 3, 1995 on suspicion of financing the November 19, 1995 truck bombing at the Egyptian Embassy in Pakistan that killed 19 and wounded more than 80. Police raided his Hayatabad residence, but he was in Afghanistan. He surrendered to police upon his return to Pakistan, where he had worked since the early 1980s. By December 20, 1995, he was in the 17th day of a hunger strike. He had been moved from the Federal Investigation Agency headquarters to the Pakistan Institute of Medical Sciences. He was an Egyptian with Canadian citizenship. His son-in-law, Khalid, was also suspected of involvement in the attack and had fled to Afghanistan.

Jumaa Farid al-Saeedi: variant Saeidi, alias Abu Humam, alias Abu Rana, deputy chief of al Qaeda in Iraq, who had served in Saddam Hussein's intelligence service. He was detained by U.S. and Iraqi authorities in August 2006 while hiding among women and children. His lieutenant, Haitham al-Badri, had bombed the golden-domed Shi'ite shrine in Samarra on February 22. He had claimed to be running al Qaeda operations in Baghdad and Diyala and Salahuddin provinces.

Jumaa Farid Saeidi: variant of Jumaa Farid al-Saeedi.

Mahmud el Safadi: alias of Abdel Kadir el Dnawy, one of eight members of Black September who broke into the Israeli quarters of the Olympic Games in Munich on September 5, 1972.

Marwan al-Safadi: variant of Marwan al-Sadafi.

Fadi Safah: one of 57 people of Middle Eastern and North African origin arrested by French police on June 3, 1987 in connection with the discovery of an arms, explosives, and drugs cache in Fontainebleau forest, south of Paris, the previous week. Threats had been made by the Committee for Solidarity with Arab and Middle East Political Prisoners. On June 11, 1987, the Lebanese was put on a plane to Beirut.

Abdul Rehman Al Safani: a Saudi of Yemeni descent with ties to Osama bin Laden. He was identified by a detainee on June 14, 2001 to Indian police as being behind a plot to bomb the U.S. Embassy in India. He fled India by mid-August. U.S. and Yemeni officials said he played a central role in organizing the October 12, 2000 USS *Cole* bombing using the name Mohammed Omar Al Harazi. They also said he was involved in the August 7, 1998 bombings of U.S. embassies in Kenya and Tanzania.

Hussein Abdul Hassan Safaoui: one of seven people arrested on November 27, 1984 by Italian police at an apartment in the seaside resort of Ladispoli. Police found a map of the U.S. embassy in Rome that had strong and weak security points marked. The men were charged with forming an armed gang. Italian authorities speculated that the men belonged to the Islamic Jihad Organization and planned a suicide bombing at the embassy. Some were carrying false passports. All had entered Italy at different times during the year and each had registered at one of several universities in central Italy. On October 17, 1985, an Italian court acquitted five defendants, including Safaoui, of charges that they were planning an attack on the U.S. Embassy. On October 1, 1986, an appeals court in Rome overturned the lower court decision and handed the case to the public ministry for further action. But only one defendant was still in custody.

Fu'ad al-Safarini: alias 'Umar Hamdan, identified by Doha's *al-Sharq* on March 19, 1993 as a former member of the Abu Nidal Group. He reached Jordan after contacting Jordanian intelligence in 1987.

Zayd Hassan Abd al-Latif Masud al-Safarini: a Kuwaiti-born Jordanian arrested on September 28, 2001 after his release from a Pakistani prison where he had served 14 years for membership in the Abu Nidal organization and for the September 5, 1986 hijacking of Pan Am flight 73 on the ground in Karachi in which 22 passengers were killed. He shot U.S. passenger Rajesh N. Kumar in the head. He was rendered to justice in September 2001. On October 1, 2001, the United States charged him with murder. He was arraigned in U.S. District Court on charges contained in a 126-count indictment issued in 1991. On July 31, 2002, he appeared in federal court in Washington, DC for serving as the ringleader of the hijackers. Charges included murder, conspiracy, and air piracy. Prosecutors said he gave the orders to the other gunmen to shoot at the passengers and throw grenades at them. Prosecutors sought the death penalty. On November 12, 2003, the 41-year-old pleaded guilty to the 95 counts of murder, air piracy, and terrorism to avoid a death penalty. On December 16, 2003, U.S. District Judge Emmet G. Sullivan sentenced him to life

in prison. On May 13, 2004, Safarini was given three consecutive life sentences plus 25 years as part of a plea agreement approved by the judge, who said he would recommend that Safarini never be paroled and be sent to a super-maximum security prison in Florence, Colorado.

Shaykh Hasan al-Saffar: a Shi'ite Saudi residing in Damascus and in charge of the youth worldwide in the Shirazi cult. He was linked to 40 Shi'ite terrorists arrested in Egypt on August 19, 1989 for planning to carry out attacks against U.S., Israeli, Saudi, Iraqi, and Kuwaiti interests, including embassies and airlines.

Safi: leader of al Qaeda operations in the northern city of Mosul who was killed by coalition forces in the summer of 2007.

Ahmed Safi: age 23, one of four Palestinians charged on February 7, 2004, by a Palestinian military tribunal at the Saraya Prison and security compound in central Gaza City in connection with the October 15, 2003 van bomb in the Gaza Strip under a U.S. diplomatic convoy that killed three Americans and injured one. Charges included possessing explosives and weapons and planting mines in the area where the attack occurred. They were not directly charged with the murders. Chief Judge Khalid Hamad adjourned the trial until February 29 to permit the defendants to obtain counsel. Safi was arrested in December 2003. The Gaza City military tribunal began in February. The prosecutor said the group was planting mines to take out Israeli tanks. On March 14, 2004, a Palestinian court ruled that there was insufficient evidence against the trio and ordered them released. Their release was delayed pending an official directive to do so by Yasser Arafat. Arafat advisor Bassam Abu Sharif said the trio "were found innocent, and because they arrested three other guys who are under investigation and interrogation."

Ali Safi: age 38, a former Afghanistan university lecturer who had been jailed by the Taliban for playing chess, he led a group that, on February 6, 2000, hijacked an Afghan Ariana Airlines B727 domestic flight carrying 151 people after leaving Kabul. The hijackers diverted it to Tashkent, Uzbekistan; Aktyubinsk, Kazakhstan; Moscow, Russia; and, finally, London. The hijackers surrendered after 75 hours of negotiations on February 10. They never made any political demands. British officials suspected it was a plot for mass asylum. Police arrested 21 people who were on the plane; there were believed to be only 8 to 10 hijackers. About 90 percent of the hostages expressed interest in staying in London; more than half of the passengers, plus the entire cockpit crew, filed formal petitions for asylum within hours. Nineteen men were arrested in connection with the hijacking and were due to appear in court on February 14. Police said they would face charges of hijacking or air piracy—which carries a life prison sentence—and possession of firearms. Another man was charged on February 16. The British government announced that the hijacking and its aftermath had so far cost $5.8 million.

In January 2001, nine defendants were tried but a jury could not agree on a verdict. On December 5, 2001, a London court convicted nine Afghan men of hijacking, false imprisonment of passengers and crew, possessing grenades, and possessing firearms. A 10th man was acquitted. On January 18, 2002, Safi and his brother, Mohammed, 33, were sentenced to five years in prison for the hijacking. The maximum sentence is life in prison, with possibility of parole. The defendants were members of the Young Intellectuals of Afghanistan, and had pleaded not guilty. Of those on the plane, 74, including the accused, had requested asylum. Nineteen applications were granted; the rest were appealing. The judge said they had shown callous disregard for the safety of the passengers and crew.

Mohammed Safi: member of a group that, on February 6, 2000, hijacked an Afghan Ariana Airlines B727 domestic flight carrying 151 people after leaving Kabul. The hijackers diverted it to Tashkent, Uzbekistan; Aktyubinsk, Kazakhstan;

Moscow, Russia; and, finally, London. The hijackers surrendered after 75 hours of negotiations on February 10. They never made any political demands. British officials suspected it was a plot for mass asylum. Police arrested 21 people who were on the plane; there were believed to be only 8 to 10 hijackers. About 90 percent of the hostages expressed interest in staying in London; more than half of the passengers, plus the entire cockpit crew, filed formal petitions for asylum within hours. Nineteen men were arrested in connection with the hijacking and were due to appear in court on February 14. Police said they would face charges of hijacking or air piracy—which carries a life prison sentence—and possession of firearms. Another man was charged on February 16. The British government announced that the hijacking and its aftermath had so far cost $5.8 million.

In January 2001, nine defendants were tried but a jury could not agree on a verdict. On December 5, 2001, a London court convicted nine Afghan men of hijacking, false imprisonment of passengers and crew, possessing grenades, and possessing firearms. A 10th man was acquitted. On January 18, 2002, Safi and his brother, Ali, 38, were sentenced to five years in prison for the hijacking. The maximum sentence is life in prison, with possibility of parole. The defendants were members of the Young Intellectuals of Afghanistan, and had pleaded not guilty. Of those on the plane, 74, including the accused, had requested asylum. Nineteen applications were granted; the rest were appealing. The judge said they had shown callous disregard for the safety of the passengers and crew.

Abu Safian: a Pakistani associate of Ramzi Ahmad Yusuf who was arrested on May 5, 1995 by Pakistani police on charges of selling Yusuf's property in Quetta. He worked at the United Arab Emirates' Red Crescent mission in Quetta.

Safiullah: one of seven individuals sentenced to life in prison on March 13, 1991 by a special antiterrorism court in Lahore, Pakistan for the December 19, 1990 murder of Sadiq Ganji, an

Iranian diplomat who headed the Iranian Cultural Center in Lahore.

'Ala' al-Saftawi: a leader of the Shaqaqi faction of the Islamic Jihad in late 1995.

Majdi al-Safti: a physician and member of Those Salvaged from Hell, a splinter of the Egyptian Islamic Jihad, who was arrested on September 2, 1987 in connection with the attempted assassination, on August 13, 1987, by four gunmen who fired on Major General Muhammad al-Nabawi Isma'il, former deputy prime minister and interior minister, in front of his house in Cairo.

Safwan: a Yemen-based recruitment coordinator for al Qaeda in Iraq foreign fighters in 2007.

Safwan: a Tunisian in Syria who was a recruitment coordinator for al Qaeda in Iraq foreign fighters in 2007. He was a student at a Shariea Institute in Syria.

Abu-Safwan: alias of Ya'lushin al-Muhammad, variant Yaloushen al Muhammad.

Abu Safwat: alias of Ibrahim Abdul Azis Raghif, a member of Fatah's office in Beirut, who was assassinated in Cyprus on December 15, 1979 by a gunman who ran off. Israel said he was in Cyprus to organize raids against Egyptian and Israeli targets.

Hanni al-Sagheer: a Yemeni computer technician whose name appeared in the al Qaeda in Iraq personnel documents that were seized by coalition forces in fall 2007. The suicide volunteer provided his phone number and that of his brother.

Hanni Muhammad Al Sagheer: alias Abu Abu al Munzer, a Yemeni computer technician from Ramah who was born in 1408 Hijra and joined al Qaeda in Iraq as a martyr in 2007, contributing his passport, ID, and watch. His recruitment coordinator was Abu Abd Allah, whom he knew through contacts in Iraq. He flew to Syria, where

he met Abu Fisel and Loua'aie, with whom he was not happy, since he took from him $2,300, two mobile phones, and 1,500 lira. He brought with him another 1,600 rials. His home phone number was 009666234830; his brother's was 0966505616211.

'Abd al-Hadi Ahmad al-Saghir: arrested on November 13, 1992 as one of the gunmen in the November 11, 1992 attack by four Islamic Group gunmen against a busload of 18 German tourists that injured seven people in Qina, Egypt. He was detained in al-Hijayrat in Qina Province while in possession of an automatic rifle used in the crime. He had earlier been arrested on other charges.

'Abd-al-Nasir Haws Bilqasim al-Saghir: alias Abu-Tulhah, a Libyan soldier from Darnah who was born in 1970 and joined al Qaeda in Iraq as a martyr on July 25, 2007, contributing $200 and his passport. He knew his recruitment coordinator, Bashar, through a neighbor. He arrived in Syria via Egypt, then was stuck at the Iraqi border for four days. While in Syria, he met Abu-al-'Abbas. He brought $200 with him.

Ahmad Yahya Muhammad Saghiri: alias Abu-Hakim al-Muhajir, a Yemeni legal-religious student who was born in 1986 and joined al Qaeda in Iraq as a suicide bomber on August 18, 2007, bringing his passport and ID. His recruitment coordinator was Safwan. He traveled from Egypt and Amman, to Syria, where he spent seven days and met Abu-'Umar, a friend of Abu-Hasan. He took from Saghiri 700 of his 1,000 Saudi riyals for a smuggler to bring to Iraq. His home phone number was 009673252626.

Fayez Sahawneh: arrested as an accomplice in the March 29, 1986 bombing of the Arab-German Friendship Society in West Berlin.

Ahamed Bin Bendar Bin Darry Al Sahian: alias Abu Satty, a Saudi from Jawaf who was born in 1390 Hijra and joined al Qaeda in Iraq on 26th

Sha'aban 1427 Hijra (circa 2007, bringing 6,950 lira and 5,507 riyals. His brother Khalid's phone number was 00966508341756; his other brothers' were 0966503398582 and 0096646243876.

Osman Sahin: Chairman of the Union Islamique in eastern France, he was arrested on October 28, 1994 by French authorities and handed over to the border police for expulsion. He had been living with his family in the Montbeliard region for 15 years, and had run the mosque at Sochaux for two years. He was a member of the Anatolian Federal Islamic State, a radical fundamentalist movement.

Zayid Sahmud: alias Basil, identified by Doha's *al-Sharq* on March 19, 1993 as a former member of the Abu Nidal Group. He was a People's Army commander who joined the Emergency Command, an Abu Nidal splinter.

Abu Sahour: alias of Muhammad Bin Saud Bin Sa'ad Al Thabtie.

Mohammed Jaafari Sahraroodi: variant Mohammad Ja'fari Sahrarudi, alias Rahimi, one of three Iranian government agents believed to have assassinated Abdolrahman Qassemlou, secretary general of the Kurdish Democratic Party, in Vienna, Austria on July 13, 1989. He carried an Iranian diplomatic passport. He was taken to a hospital with bullet wounds apparently accidentally sustained. On November 28, 1989, Austria issued an arrest warrant for him on charges of murder.

Nabil Sahraoui: head of the Salafist Group for Call and Combat, an al Qaeda-linked group, who was killed on June 20, 2004, along with three of his aides, by Algerian soldiers in the Kabylie region.

Mohammad Ja'fari Sahrarudi: variant of Mohammed Jaafari Sahraroodi.

Yunis al-Sahrawi: alias of Abu Yahya al-Libi.

Ahmad Bin-Bandar Bin-Dari-al-Sahyan: alias Abu-Sati, a Saudi from al-Jawf who joined al Qaeda in Iraq on September 19, 2006, when he was assigned to Mosul. He contributed 6,950 Liras and 5,507 Riyals. His brother Khalid's phone number was 00966508341756; other brothers' phone numbers were 009556033988582 and 0096646243876.

Thurayya Kamal Sahyoun: possibly a hospital employee and a drowsy and possibly drugged woman who, on November 14, 1987, carried a ribboned Swiss chocolate box past security guards at the American University Hospital. A 1-kilogram TNT bomb attached to an Energa shell and nails inside exploded inside the box, killing her and 6 others and wounding 31. Police put out a warrant for one of her friends and later announced that Karimah Shuqayr had given her the box.

Elias Fu'a Sa'ib: a Lebanese sentenced to death by the Kuwaiti State Security Court in 1984 in connection with the December 12, 1983 truck bombing of the administrative building of the U.S. Embassy in Kuwait, killing four people and injuring 59. As of April 1987, none of the death sentences had been carried out. The release of 17 of the 25 prisoners in the case was demanded on numerous occasions by the Islamic Jihad in return for Americans held captive in Lebanon beginning in 1986.

Sa'id: alias of Mohamed Zineddine.

Sa'id: Moroccan-based recruitment coordinator for foreign fighters for al Qaeda in Iraq in 2006.

Sa'id: Saudi-based recruitment coordinator for foreign fighters for al Qaeda in Iraq in 2006.

Sa'id: alias Abu-al-Yaqin, an Algerian fighter for al Qaeda in Iraq in 2007 who owned a passport. His home phone number was 0021353482221. His brother's number was 0021361553434.

Sa'id: alias Abu-'Ali, a Syrian fighter and doctor for al Qaeda in Iraq in 2007. He owned a passport and ID. His phone number was 052427212.

Sa'id: alias Abu-Rashash al-Zahrani, a Saudi from al-Baha who joined al Qaeda in Iraq in 2007, contributing $275. His recruitment coordinator was Bassam. His home phone number was 177282800; his cell was 0503773299.

Abu Sa'id: alias of Zaki al-Hilu, commander leader for the Popular Front for the Liberation of Palestine. On August 17, 1984, gunmen on a motorcycle fired at him at point-blank range in Madrid, Spain, hitting him in the neck. On August 19, 1984, his condition had improved.

Abu-Sa'id: Saudi-based recruitment coordinator for al Qaeda in Iraq in 2006.

Aha Said: release from an Israeli jail was demanded on June 27, 1976 by the Popular Front for the Liberation of Palestine hijackers of Air France flight 139, an A300 flying from Tel Aviv to Paris and ultimately diverted to Entebbe.

Ahmad Sa'id: variant of Ahmed Saeed.

Ahmad 'Ali Sa'id: alias Abu-Hamzah, a Yemeni from Aden who was born in 1988 and joined al Qaeda in Iraq as a martyr circa 2006–2007. He had trained in Lebanon then entered Iraq via Syria, where he had met Abu-'Uthman. His recruitment coordinator was Abu-Mus'ab. He contributed his passport. His home phone number was 0096722403.

Ahmad Ghassan Said: on January 26, 1983, the Jordanian pleaded not guilty to charges of shooting Israeli Ambassador Shlomo Argov in London on June 4, 1982. On March 5, 1983, he was convicted in London's Central Criminal Court. He received a 30-year sentence for firing the two shots.

Cheikh Mohamed Said: initially named by the Algerian Armed Islamic Group as its new emir in October 1994.

Haithem Said: alias Abu Ahmed, a Lieutenant Colonel in the Syrian Air Force and second in command of the Syrian intelligence service for whom an international arrest warrant was issued on November 26, 1986 by West Germany in connection with the March 29, 1986 bombing of the German-Arab Friendship Society in the Kreuzberg District of West Berlin. One of the bombers said it was conducted at Said's behest.

Hamzah Abu Sa'id: variant of Hamza Abu Zayd.

Jaba Buram Said: one of ten suspected terrorist members of the Sudanese Socialist Popular Front-Revolutionary Committees Movement arrested on July 28, 1984 in the Sudan for plotting terrorist acts in Khartoum. They were charged with plotting the assassinations of President Jafar Muhammad Numayri and the first vice president, the bombing of the U.S. Embassy in Khartoum, and the bombing of military and economic establishments in Sudan. Government sources said the detainees admitted to training at the 2 March camp and the 7 April camp, located on the Tripoli-Sudan Highway inside Libya.

Jabr Rajeh Hassan al-Said: alias Aboud Bakr, alleged by the Swiss on August 21, 2004 as having had "close contact with several members of the hard-core bin Laden movement."

Khaled bin Ahmed bin Ibrahim al-Sa'id: age 24, one of four Saudi terrorists who, on April 22, 1996, confessed to the November 13, 1995 bombing of a building used by U.S. military personnel in Saudi Arabia and said that they had planned other attacks but feared arrest. He claimed to have fought in the Afghan War. He lived in the Urayji quarter of Riyadh and was self-employed.

Mohamed Salem Said: one of four Libyans who arrived in France on August 20, 1987, were arrested by Paris police on September 2–3, 1987, and were deported on September 4, 1987. The U.S. Embassy and French Interior Ministry said that the Libyans were plotting a series of attacks on French soil to mark the 18th anniversary of the September 1 takeover of Libya by Colonel Muammar al-Qadhafi and to "punish France" for its support of the Chadian government.

Muhmad Sa'id: would-be hijacker of a Swiss airliner who ran toward the cockpit brandishing a pocket knife. Security agents overpowered him and handed him over to Israeli police.

Muktar Mohammed Said: alias of Muktar Said Ibrahim.

Naradim Bou-Said: name on a false Moroccan passport used by one of the three Egyptian Revolution hijackers of Egyptair flight 648 that had left Athens bound for Cairo on November 23, 1985.

Omar Abu Said: one of four gunmen who, on March 6, 2004, disguised jeeps to look like Israeli army vehicles and tried to attack an Israeli military checkpoint at the Erez border crossing in the Gaza Strip. Palestinian Authority guards stopped them and shot to death at least four Palestinians before a large explosion took place, killing two Palestinian officers and wounding another 15 people. A car bomb had exploded nearby, apparently a diversion. Islamic Jihad, Hamas, and the al-Aqsa Martyrs Brigades jointly claimed credit, and said the dead were Omar Abu Said and Hatim Tafish of al-Aqsa, Mikdad Mbaied of Islamic Jihad, and Mohammed Abu Daiah of Hamas.

Salah Muhammad Umar Sa'id: an Egyptian Islamic Jihad/bin Laden associate who died in a gunfight with Albanian police on October 25, 1998. He was part of the team that had planned to attack the U.S. Embassy in Tirana.

Seddou Said: one of four Islamic extremists who were hunted down and shot to death by police after the terrorists assassinated Konstatin Kukushkin, a driver at the Russian Embassy, and senior Algerian diplomat Belkacem Touati in front of his wife and children in Bordj el Kiffan on March 28, 1994.

Soussan Said: alias Omar, alleged member of the Islamic Salvation Front who, by October 1, 1992, had confessed to involvement in the August 26, 1992 bombing of the Air France ticket counter at Houari Boumedienne Airport in Algeria that killed 12 people and wounded 128. He was from Taourirt-Ighil, Bejaia, had a secondary education degree, and lived in Bouzaria. He was arrested on November 26, 1986 of involvement in the case of Bouya Ali Mustapha and sentenced to three years in prison. He was pardoned on June 7, 1989. Public sessions of his trial began on May 4, 1993. On May 26, 1993, a special Algiers judicial council passed death sentenced on 38 defendants, including him. On August 31, 1993, after exhausting all constitutional and legal appeals, he was executed.

Tibani Said: alleged member of the Islamic Salvation Front who was arrested for involvement in the August 26, 1992 bombing of the Air France ticket counter at Houari Boumedienne Airport in Algeria that killed 12 people and wounded 128. Public sessions of his trial began on May 4, 1993. On May 26, 1993, a special Algiers judicial council sentenced him to ten years.

'Abd al-Salam Saidi: variant Abdulssalam Seaidi, a Lebanese/Iranian dishwasher who was one of eight men arrested by the French Department of Territorial Security (DST) on March 30, 1987 suspected of planning attacks against Israeli targets. He was charged with illegal arms possession and conspiracy following the discovery of arms caches near Paris that included 9.9 kilograms of explosives, guns, grenades, and documents that mentioned plans for attacks on Arab, Israeli, and U.S. figures, as well as a plan involving El Al and TWA. Three grenades, a gun, a submachine gun, and a Colt .45-caliber revolver were found in Romainville in the Paris Seine-St. Denis suburbs.

He was suspected of belonging to a Syrian guerrilla network linked with an extremist Middle Eastern group. He was in contact with an at-large Syrian linked to the Popular Front for the Liberation of Palestine.

Mamduh Muhammad Bakhit al-Sa'idi: alias Abu-Muhammad, a Saudi from Makkah, al-Jazirah who was born on March 29, 1979 and joined al Qaeda in Iraq on September 23, 2006, contributing a watch and $600. His coordinator was Shadi Abu-Husam. His home phone number was 5729172; 'Abdallah's was 0508700558; and Mashhur's was 0559011511.

Saied: Moroccan-based recruitment coordinator for al Qaeda in Iraq foreign fighters in 2006.

Naif Abd Al Rahman Muhammad Al Saied: alais Abu Thamer, from Jazeerat Al Arab who was born in 1400 Hijra and joined al Qaeda in Iraq in 2007. His home phone number was 0096612351079; his brother Muhammad's was 00966555426838; Binder Al Saied's was 00966509751119.

Mustafa Saif: alias of Mustafa Elnore.

Amari Saifi: alias Abderrazak Para, leader of the Salafist Group for Call and Combat, and the former Algerian paratrooper behind the kidnappings of 28 European tourists in February 2003 in Algeria. On May 24, 2004, the Movement for Democracy and Justice in Chad said that, in March, it had captured 10 Algerian extremists, including Amari Saifi, after a brief firefight. They were being held in a rebel-controlled zone. The rebel spokesman said the group had attempted to contact Algeria, France, Germany, Niger, and the United States about handing over the terrorists. A government would have to pick them up, because the Movement did not have the means to transfer them. On October 27, 2004, Libya extradited Saifi to Algeria.

Shaykh Saiid: variant Sai'id, alias of Mustafa Muhammad Ahmad, which, in turn, might be an alias of Mustafa Ahmed al-Hawsawi. He was reported on Christmas 2001 to be bin Laden's brother-in-law and Saudi al Qaeda financier. President Bush ordered his U.S. assets frozen on September 24, 2001.

Shaykh Sai'id: variant of Shaykh Saiid.

Rakan Saikhan: one of Saudi Arabia's 26 most-wanted terrorists and an alleged conspirator in the October 12, 2000 bombing of the USS *Cole*. He was arrested on June 18, 2004 following a two-hour shootout at a roadblock in Riyadh; 12 other terrorists were detained. Police said the cell was involved in the November 9, 2003 bombing of a foreigners' residential compound in Riyadh and the May 2004 Khobar bombing that killed 22. Police found a car used by a gunman who shot to death a BBC cameraman and wounded a BBC reporter in Riyadh on June 6, 2004.

Samir Saioud: alias Samir Moussaab, coordinator for the Salafist Group for Preaching and Combat. He was killed on April 26, 2007 in a clash with the Algerian Army in the Si Mustapha region, 50 kilometers east of Algiers. He was the deputy leader of al Qaeda of the Islamic Mahgreb.

Abdul Latif Sairfani: on July 6, 1988, Pakistani district court judge Zafar Ahmed Babar ended an eight-month trial in a special court in Rawalpindi's Adiyala maximum security prison and sentenced the Syrian to death by hanging for the September 5, 1986 hijacking of a Pan Am B747 and for killing 11 passengers at Karachi airport. There was insufficient evidence to convict five terrorists of the deaths of 11 other passengers. The hijacker mastermind, Sulayman al-Turki, said that the group would appeal the sentences and if they were freed, "we would hijack a U.S. airliner once again." The court also passed a total jail sentence of 257 years on each of the accused on several other charges of murder, conspiracy to hijack, possession of illegal arms, and confinement of the passengers. The terrorists had 30 days to appeal the verdict and the sentence in Lahore's High Court.

On July 28, 1988, the press reported that the terrorists reversed their decision not to appeal.

al-Raway'i Salim Sa'id al-Sa'iri: alias Abu-al-Zubayr, a Saudi from Shararah who was born in 1980 and joined al Qaeda in Iraq to become a martyr circa 2006 or 2007. His recruitment coordinator was Sa'id.

Michael Saisa: alias of Youssef Hmimssa.

Mohammed Sajid: a Pakistani bin Laden operative arrested in Bangladesh on January 30, 1999. He was charged with attacking the country's leading poet, Shamsur Rahman.

Luay Ben Mohammed Saka: named on February 14, 2005 as one of Iraq's 29 Most Wanted Insurgents. A bounty of between $50,000 and $200,000 was offered.

Sakhkhan: an individual from Al 'Abbasiyah and one of six individuals reported by Beirut's *al-Nahar* on August 6, 1990 as appearing at an Amal news conference on charges of kidnapping, assassination, setting of explosions, and bringing booby-trapped cars into Tyre, Lebanon. They admitted involvement in the kidnapping of U.S. Marine Lt. Col. William Richard Higgins on February 17, 1988. The group also admitted planting explosive devices at centers of the UN forces in the south; blowing up Mustafa Mahdi's clothing store in Tyre as well as the Lebanese-African Nasr Bank in Tyre; and bringing three booby-trapped cars into Tyre and al-Bisariyah to kill Amal officials. They said they coordinated their actions with Hizballah and the Iranian Revolutionary Guards.

Louai al-Sakka: variant Louasi Sakka, alias Louai al-Turki.

Louasi al-Sakka: variant of Louai al-Sakka, one of two people arrested on August 6, 2005 by Turkish police for links to al Qaeda. Al-Sakka was a liaison between al Qaeda and a Turkish cell that carried out bombings in Istanbul in November 2003,

financing the attack. Police put out an alert after a suspicious fire in apartment 1703 in Antalya on August 4 at 3 A.M., where they discovered a large quantity of explosives, two fake passports, and other documents. Al-Sakka had been fabricating a bomb, which exploded prematurely. Al-Sakka was stopped while trying to board a flight to Istanbul from Diyarbakir, using a fake name. Al-Sakka was represented by attorney Ilhami Sayan.

Turkish police arrested al-Sakka in August 2005 when he was planning to steer a bomb-filled yacht into an Israeli cruise ship carrying U.S. soldiers. On August 11, a Turkish court charged al-Sakka in connection with the plot. More than 5,000 Israelis on five ships were diverted from Turkish ports to Cyprus after the threat was received. He yelled to reporters, "I have prepared one ton of explosives. I was going to hit the Israeli ships. No Turks were going to be hurt, only Israelis." The press said he was a senior al Qaeda operative involved in major terrorist plots in Turkey, Jordan, and Iraq, and that he had worked with Abu Musab al-Zarqawi.

Sakka had also been involved in the millennium plot to attack hotels in Amman on December 31, 1999. A Jordanian court had earlier convicted him in absentia for the millennium plot. He also planned the 2003 truck bombing in Istanbul that killed 57 people. That plot was financed with $160,000 in al Qaeda money. He also provided false passports to jihadis. Al-Sakka also was involved in attacks on U.S. bases, commanded forces in Fallujah, Iraq, and was involved in the murder of a Turkish truck driver.

On February 10, 2006, an Ankara court charged the Syrian with planning the 2003 bombings that killed 58 people and wounded 750 in Istanbul. Prosecutors said Osama bin Laden had ordered the man to conduct the attacks. On March 20, 2006, al-Sakka, 32, initially told the court he was someone else—Ekrem Ozel—but had also admitted working beside Abu Musab al-Zarqawi. Prosecutors said he had provided other terrorists $170,000 to carry out the four truck bombings. He was being prosecuted along with 72 Turks. The judge recessed the trial for two months. Al-Sakka's attorney, Osman Karahan, was ordered off the case on the first day of the trial, accused of aiding and abetting a terrorist organization. He represented 14 other defendants in the Istanbul terrorism case. He said the indictment falsely linked him to the July 7, 2005 London rail bombings. Al-Sakka faced prison in Jordan, where he and al-Zarqawi were convicted in absentia for plotting to blow up hotels on December 31, 1999. His attorney said that al-Sakka had moved across Turkish borders 55 times on 18 different passports. On February 16, 2007, a Turkish court sentenced seven men, including al-Sakka, to life in prison.

Nazmi Sakka: a member of a Syrian-backed guerrilla organization who was arrested in Lebanon on April 23, 1983 on suspicion of throwing a hand grenade at a 12-man patrol stationed near the Beirut airport, wounding five U.S. Marines on March 16, 1983. The Islamic Jihad claimed credit.

Abdallah Yosef Abu Sakran: a 21-year-old Hamas member arrested in March 1996 in Gaza.

Hasan al-Sakran: identified by a fellow terrorist as one of three al-Jama'ah al-Islamiyah extremists who, on February 4, 1993, threw petrol bombs at three South Korean tourists outside their hotel near the Egyptian Pyramids.

Jum'ah Hamad al-Muhaiydi Sakran: variant Jummah Hammed Al Muhaidy Sakran, alias Abu-al-Walid, variant Abu al Walied, a Libyan from Darnah who was born on August 9, 1982 and joined al Qaeda in Iraq on October 28, 2006 as a "fearless fighter"/martyr, contributing a watch and a ring. His recruitment coordinator was Faraj. His phone number was 625893.

Jummah Hammed Al Muhaidy Sakran: variant of Jum'ah Hamad al-Muhaiydi Sakran.

Abd Allah Sala'as: alias Abu Al Muta'asem Bellah, a Syrian from Al Tel born in 1983 who joined

al Qaeda in Iraq in 2007, bringing 2,500 Syrian lira. His phone numbers were 05910413 and 0941839.

Abdul Latif Salah: dual Albanian-Jordanian citizen deported by Albania on November 12, 1999. He was believed to be an Egyptian Islamic Jihad associate of Osama bin Laden. He had lived in Tirana from 1992 to 1999 and had connections to several local political parties. He worked with several Islamic nongovernmental organizations and had set up the local Egyptian Islamic Jihad network.

Abu Salah: a Jordanian associate of a Palestinian with a Jordanian passport who was arrested by Larnaca Airport security personnel on December 17, 1985 while trying to smuggle arms aboard a Swissair plane scheduled to depart for Amman. Police believed he was one of four Arabs who intended to hijack the plane.

Ahmad Muhammad Muhsin Salah: variant Ahmed Muhammad Mohsen Saleh, alias Abu-Zir, a Yemeni from Sana'a who was born on November 28, 1983 and joined al Qaeda in Iraq on September 23, 2006, contributing $430, his watch, and a cell phone. His recruitment coordinator was Ismail Abu-Suwayd, variant Ismail Abu Sweede. His home phone number was 009671354854; his brother Abu Ibrahim's number was 00967711333244.

'Ali Fu'ad Salah: leader of a group of eight individuals suspected of being Islamic terrorists who were arrested on March 21, 1987 in Paris by the Department of Territorial Security (DST). Authorities seized 12 liters of a liquid explosive, two Sten guns, and ammunition from the Rue de la Voute safe house in Paris's 12th District. Some of the detainees were members of Islamic Jihad. On March 26, 1987, the group was charged with "belonging to a terrorist network preparing to commit particularly dangerous attacks in France." He was a theology student at the Sorbonne and married to a French woman of Algerian extraction, Faraid Karima.

Ayad Said Salah: the Palestinian leader of the group that conducted three car-bomb attacks in the Taha resort area of Egypt on October 7, 2004. He died accidentally in the blasts. He had lived in el-Arish, in the northern Sinai near the Gaza border.

Muhammed Salah: alias Nasr Fahmi Nasr Hasanayn, a member of the Egyptian Islamic Jihad leadership council who was killed in Khowst, Afghanistan in October 2001. President George W. Bush had ordered his U.S. assets frozen on September 24, 2001.

Khalil Khudayr Salahat: alias Mu'min Adham, identified by Doha's *al-Sharq* on March 19, 1993 as a member of the Abu Nidal Group's Central Committee.

Sirous Salahvarzi: one of eight Iranian students arrested in the United States on November 15, 1979 for attempting to smuggle 3 disassembled Winchester 30.06 rifles, matching scopes, 15 boxes of ammunition, and a street map of Washington, DC with certain embassies marked, as one of the men was about to board TWA 900 from Baltimore-Washington International Airport to New York's JFK International Airport. The Iranians spoke of taking the rifles to Iran. They claimed to be attending Baltimore-area colleges, and were jailed on bonds ranging from $25,000 to $250,000. The group was charged with dealing in firearms without a license, placing firearms on an interstate commercial airliner without notifying the carrier, and conspiracy. On February 22, 1980, Salahvarzi pleaded guilty to lesser crimes in exchange for agreeing to leave the United States at the end of his semester of study in civil engineering at the Community College of Baltimore.

'Abd-al-Salam: Afghanistan-based recruiter for al Qaeda in Iraq in 2007.

'Abd-al-Salam: alias Abu-Ayman, a Tunisian from Ibn-'Arus who joined al Qaeda in Iraq in 2007. His home phone number was 713001337.

Mulla Abdol Salam: alias Mulla Rocketi, former member of the Hezb-e Eslami (Islamic Party) faction of Afghan premier Gulbuddin Hekmatyar, said that six of his followers on June 21, 1993 had kidnapped two Chinese hydrology engineers in Balochistan, Pakistan and had taken them to Afghanistan. He demanded release of his brother, who was held for gun running, from a Pakistani jail, compensation for the death of his nephew, and return of shoulder-carried antiaircraft Stinger missiles. By July 10, 1993, it was reported that he had also been holding hostage seven Pakistani government employees since the previous winter.

Fahid Muhammad 'Alim Salam: variant Fahim Mohammed Ally Msalam, alias Fahid Mohammed Ally, Fahid Mohammed Ali Musalaam, Fahid Mohammed Ali Msalam, Fahid Muhamad Ali Salem, Mohammed Ally Msalam, Usama al-Kini, Fahad Ally Msalam, a Kenyan citizen indicted on December 16, 1998 in the Southern District of New York for his involvement in the August 7, 1998 bombings of the U.S. embassies in Tanzania and Kenya and for conspiring to kill U.S. nationals; the murder of U.S. nationals outside the United States; conspiracy to murder U.S. nationals outside the United States; and attack on a federal facility resulting in death. The Rewards for Justice Program offers $5 million for his apprehension. He claims to have been born in Mombasa, Kenya on February 19, 1976. He is circa five feet seven inches, weighs circa 165 pounds, and has worked as a clothing vendor.

Hasan Salam Salam: one of five members of the Egyptian al-Jihad organization arrested on July 15, 1991 in raids on two arms depots that contined five automatic rifles, 60 Russian-made handguns, 61 locally made shotguns, 111 revolvers, one large Grinev handgun, and boxes filled with explosives.

Wadi' Salim Salam: one of six Arabs for whom the Nicosia District Court issued an eight-day arrest warrant on May 30, 1989 in connection with the discovery by fishermen of two Soviet-made SAM-7 missiles in the McKenzie seashore area near Larnaca International Airport two days earlier. A group of six young Arabs were plotting to shoot down the helicopter of Lebanon's Christian leader, Major General Michel 'Awn, who was scheduled to arrive in Cyprus en route to Casablanca. All six were charged, inter alia, with illegal entry into Cyprus and with possession of weapons and explosives. On June 2, 1989, Lebanon requested extradition. On June 22, 1989, the Larnaca District Court set June 30 as the date for the opening of the preliminary hearing. The trial began on October 9, 1989. All pleaded guilty to illegally possessing and transporting weapons and explosives. Five pleaded guilty to illegal entry. The trial was moved from Larnaca to Nicosia for security reasons. On October 13, 1989, the court sentenced the six on eight charges. Five received jail sentences ranging from one to eight years; the sixth received one to five years. All of the penalties were to be concurrent, effective the date of arrest. The court president said he took the psychological state of the sixth accused into consideration in determining the verdict. On April 15, 1991, Cypriot authorities deported the six Lebanese to Beirut after they had served only 17 months of their sentences.

Yahya Abdus Salam: a Libyan commercial pilot trainee detained on October 1, 1986 by Pakistan's Federal Investigation Agency. He was suspected of being an associate of Salman Tariki, a Libyan who was arrested on September 10, 1986 in Pakistan in connection with the hijacking by the Libyan Revolutionary Cells and the Organization of the Soldiers of God—Martyr Zulfikar Ali Bhutto Group who took over Pan Am flight 73 at Karachi airport on September 5, 1986. The hijackers threw grenades and fired machine guns at the passengers, killing 22 and injuring 100 others. Police believed Tariki was the mastermind of the attack, meeting with the Palestinians, arranging for weapons after casing the airport.

Yusif Salam: alias Yasir Chraydi, alias Nuri, a Palestinian who worked in the Libyan People's Bureau in East Germany in 1986 and was viewed by the Stasi as a killer. He was believed to have orchestrated the bombing of La Belle disco on April 5, 1986 in West Berlin. He instructed Imad Salim Mahmud, a Lebanese who was resident in West Berlin, to select a building suitable for a bomb attack.

Amin Salamah: leader of four al-Saiqa terrorists who were arrested by Amsterdam police detectives on September 5, 1975 while planning to take over the daily 0836 D train from Moscow at Amersfoort station the next day. They intended to kidnap immigrating Russian Jews and demand a plane to fly them and their hostages out of the country. Three days later, they were sentenced to 18 months. Salamah said that the group had been trained in 1972 in a village outside Moscow. Their preliminary six-month course covered the use of arms and explosives, as well as propaganda and interrogation survival techniques.

Hasan Salamah: a Hamas leader arrested on May 17, 1996 by Israeli police after a gun battle. He was believed to have planned three of four then-recent suicide bombings. He was caught during a vehicle search in which guns were found. He was taken to a Hebron hospital after being injured.

Kayid Muhammad Salamah: one of three people who, on February 25, 1994, stabbed two Russians with a penknife in Jordan. The trio fled when police arrived. On March 28, the trio were sent to the head of the preventive security section and later sent to the General Intelligence Directorate.

Sa'id Sayyed Salamah: an Egyptian financial advisor to Osama bin Laden and Egyptian Islamic Jihad member who was deported to Egypt by the Saudis in June 1998. He traveled from Sudan to Pakistan and Europe.

Wadi' Salim Salamah: one of six Muslims detained on May 26, 1989 at Larnaca, Cyprus for conspiring to murder General Michel 'Awn, leader of the Lebanese Phalangists, and for possession of arms, missiles, and munitions. The six were due to be tried by a Larnaca criminal court on October 9, 1989. On August 30, 1989, the Muslim 14 March group threatened to hijack a Cyprus Airlines plane if the government did not release them. The group seeks to avenge the 40 Lebanese Muslims who were killed by 'Awn's troops on March 14, 1989.

Yazeed Bin Abd Al Rahman Al Salamah: variant of Yazid Bin-'Abd-al-Rahman al-Salamah.

Yazid Bin-'Abd-al-Rahman al-Salamah: variant Yazeed Bin Abd Al Rahman Al Salamah, alias Abu-Hudhayfah, variant Abu Hazifah, a Saudi from Buraydah, variant Baridah, who was born on January 23, 1985 and joined al Qaeda in Iraq on October 4, 2006, contributing $100. His recruitment coordinator was Abu-Khalaf. He said the phone number of Abu-Malik was 0504896220; that of Abu-Ahmad was 0506140262; and of Abu Nasir was 0548962220.

Abu Salaman: alias of Ghoriesh Saleh Abd Al Karim Al Ghoriesh

Abu Salaman: alias of Kamal Muhamad Mukbel.

Hara Salame: she had served at the Palestine Liberation Organization office in Sweden for eight years but was ordered expelled by Stockholm on November 21, 1986 on suspicion of aiding terrorism. In 1982, she was suspected of having connections with Fatah and was judged a security risk. In 1986, she was suspected of being an agent of Abu Nidal. She agreed to leave Sweden by November 30, 1986.

Ali Hassan Salameh: alias Abu Hassan, senior member of Razd, the Fatah intelligence organization, believed responsible for several Black September attacks, including the attempted assassination of Jordanian Ambassador Zaid Rifai in London on December 15, 1971, the 1972 Munich Olympics massacre, and the July 20, 1973 Japan Airlines (JAL) hijacking by the Popular Front for the Liberation of Palestine and Japanese Red Army. He was critically wounded on October 8, 1976 when he was shot in the stomach as he walked along a Beirut street. He died on January 22, 1979 when a bomb exploded in a car his entourage was passing in Beirut.

Salameh was a refugee from the Jaffa area of Israel. His father, also a Palestinian militant, was killed when his Ramleh headquarters was blown up by Haganah in 1948. Salameh joined Fatah before the 1967 Middle East war and rose to become chief of security for Yasir Arafat. Georgina Rizk, the 1971 Miss Universe, became his second wife in 1978.

Farouk Salameh: a Palestinian with Jordanian papers who was arrested for the April 5, 1986 bombing of La Belle Discotheque in West Berlin and the March 29, 1986 bombing of the German-Arab Friendship Society in the Kreuzberg District of West Berlin. Hasi said on April 30, 1986 that he and Salameh were responsible for the Friendship Society bombing at the behest of Haithem Said (Abu Ahmed), a lieutenant colonel in the Syrian Air Force and second in command of the Syrian intelligence service. On July 31, 1986, attempted murder charges were brought against Hasi and Salameh for the Friendship Society bombing. The trial began on November 17, 1986, and the duo were convicted on November 26. Salameh was sentenced to 13 years.

Ziad Salameh: a 19-year-old Palestinian resident of the Gaza Strip who, on March 1, 1993, stabbed to death two Israeli men and wounded nine others in Tel Aviv. The Islamic Jihad claimed credit. He said he wanted to hurt Jews because he could not find work in Israel. One of his brothers had been jailed for 15 months for belonging to Islamic Jihad.

'Abdolhasan Ahmad Salami: an Iranian arrested by Kuwaiti police on January 12, 1985 for plotting to set fire to the Kuwaiti information complex and for distributing subversive literature.

Hihad Ibrahim Salami: one of two Palestinians arrested by Spanish police on July 12, 1985 for plotting to blow up the Syrian Embassy in Madrid. They were believed to be members of Force 17, part of Fatah. Police found 12 kilograms of explosives on the men. On November 5, 1986, he was sentenced by the Spanish National High Court to four years and four months for being accessory to the illegal possession of arms and explosives. The offense of preparing to attack the Syrian Ambassador was "not proven."

Irma Salazar: arrested on June 30, 1989 in connection with the May 24, 1989 machine gun murders of two U.S. Mormon missionaries by the Zarate Willka Armed Forces of Liberation of Bolivia.

Najati Saljuq: an Iranian arrested on July 9, 1987 when Egyptian authorities discovered an Iranian-backed terrorist group that had chosen a governorate in Lower Egypt for their operations. Police seized explosives from a group collaborating with the al-Jihad Organization. Saljuq served as liaison between the two groups.

Abu Mohammed al-Salmni: a senior al Qaeda in Iraq leader in 2007 who had served as emir of Habiniyah in western Iraq, and worked with weapons supplies and financiers.

Mohammed Salamollah: alias of Mohammed Alam Gir.

Mohammed Salamouni: one of the 24 defendants in the October 6, 1981 assassination of Egyptian President Anwar Sadat. At the announcement of the sentencing on March 6, 1982, he read a statement in English saying "Sadat made of himself the last pharaoh in our country. He made of himself the last shah. Sadat killed himself by his behavior here in Egypt."

'Ali Saleem: alias of Ali Sayyid Muhamed Mustafa al-Bakri.

Sadeer Saleem: age 26, one of three men arrested on March 22, 2007, by British police "on suspicion of the commission, preparation, or instigation of acts of terrorism" in the July 7, 2005 bombings of the London subway system. He was picked up at his Leeds house. On July 5, 2007, British authorities charged the trio with conspiring with the bombers between November 1, 2004 and June 29, 2005, saying they handled reconnaissance and planning. On August 10, 2007, Mohammed Shakil, Sadeer Saleem, and Waheed Ali, age 24, pleaded not guilty of conspiracy to cause explosions "of a nature likely to endanger life or cause serious injury."

Saleh: alias of 'Abdallah Ahmad 'Abdallah.

Abd Allah Adnan Al Saleh: alias Abu Khalid, a Saudi born in 1980 who joined al Qaeda in Iraq in 2007, bringing 1,200 Syria lira. He was deployed to Al Anbar. His phone number was 01181290632.

Abdel Fattah Saleh: on June 11, 2004, he fired an automatic rifle on worshippers in a mosque in Dhamar province, 40 miles south of Sanaa, during midday prayers, killing four and wounding six. He fled to his home, which police stormed, killing Saleh. Police said a domestic dispute might have motivated him.

Abu Saleh: alias of Abdelkader Mahmoud Es Sayed.

Ahmed Muhammad Mohsen Saleh: variant of Ahmad Muhammad Muhsin Salah.

Ali Al Mabrouk Saleh: a Libyan from Serret's residential district number 2 who was born on May 15, 1985 and joined al Qaeda in Iraq on

20th Sha'aban 1427 Hijra (circa 2007). His recruitment coordinator was Abu Omar. His phone numbers were 0927029697 and 0912183434.

Ali Hussein Saleh: a Hizballah member who worked as a driver for the Iranian Embassy in Beirut, was killed with his passenger on August 2, 2003 by a car bomb.

Ali Muhammad Saleh: a former Yemeni Interior Ministry employee sentenced to five years on September 29, 2004 by a Yemeni court for helping USS *Cole* bomber Jamal al-Badawi in handling funds and forging identity papers.

Fouad Ali Saleh: a Tunisian indicted on May 19, 1987 for the drive-by bombing on September 17, 1986 of the Tati clothing store on the Rue de Rennes in the Montparnasse section of Paris that killed seven and injured 61, including 15 foreigners. He was believed to be the ringleader of the pro-Iranian Arabs. He was accused of being part of a terrorist cell that French police unraveled in March-April 1987. Charges against him were based on evidence provided by Abdel Hamid Badoui and Omar Agnaoui, two Moroccans indicted with him. On October 31, 1990, the Paris Appeals Court upheld his 20-year sentence issued by a Paris court in March 1990, which found him guilty of setting up a terrorist network and drug trafficking. The court said that he must serve two thirds of his prison term and imposed a subsequent permanent ban on his entering France. On April 13, 1992, he was found guilty of organizing a series of bombings that killed 13 and wounded 303 and was jailed for life. The court ruled that he should stay in prison for 18 years before parole could be considered.

Ismaiel Tuhami Saied Bin Saleh: alias Abu Abd Allah, a Moroccan student at a Shariea Instiute in Syria who lived in Tatwan and was born in 1986. He joined al Qaeda in Iraq as a martyr in 2007, presenting his ID. He brought 1,500 lira. His recruitment coordinator was Safwan the Tunisian in Syria, a friend from school, which he had attended for a year. In Syria, he met Abu Al Abbas, who gave him money. His father's phone number was 0021271354702; his phone number was 0021267425391.

John Saleh: name on a Somali passport carried by Johannes Weinrich.

Mahmoud Saleh: one of two hijackers of Lufthansa flight 615, a B727 flying on the Damascus-Beirut–Ankara–Munich run on October 29, 1972. The hijackers threatened to blow up the plane if the surviving three members of the Black September killers in the Munich massacre were not released. The duo was armed with revolvers and two grenades and had used Yemeni and Lebanese passports. The West Germans agreed to free them. The hijackers ultimately landed in Tripoli, Libya, where they were given a heroes' welcome.

An individual of the same name, former temporary Palestine Liberation Organization (PLO) Paris representative after the assassination of Mahmoud el Amchari in 1972, Fatah member, and Rejectionist, was assassinated on January 3, 1977 by two men. Saleh owned the Arabic bookshop in the Rue Saint Victor in Paris's Latin Quarter. The PLO blamed Harley Libermann, former military attaché of the Israeli Embassy in Paris. The PLO said Saleh was born in Sabastiyah in Nablus district. Israel refused to allow Saleh to be buried in his homeland. His Paris funeral was to be attended by a high-level PLO delegation, which sparked a major diplomatic incident on January 7, 1977.

Matarawy Mohammed Said Saleh: alias Wahid, alias Wahid Saleh, identified on July 7, 1993 by U.S. federal prosecutors as a 10th suspect in the plot broken up by the FBI on June 24, 1993 involving individuals who were charged with planning to bomb the UN headquarters building in Manhattan; 26 Federal Plaza, which includes the local FBI headquarters and other agencies; the 47th Street diamond district, which is run principally by Orthodox Jews; and the Lincoln and Holland tunnels connecting Manhattan and New

Jersey; and planning to assassinate Senator Alfonse M. D'Amato (R-NY), Assemblyman Dov Hiking, an Orthodox Jewish legislator from Brooklyn, UN Secretary General Boutros Boutros-Ghali, and Egyptian President Hosni Mubarak. On July 22, 1993, the Egyptian-born detainee was arrested at the Wildwood, New Jersey beach-front Sea Wolf Inn, along with his longtime friend Ashraf Mohammed, who was charged with harboring a fugitive. They were ordered held without bail.

Prosecutors said he brokered a shipment of rocket-propelled grenade launchers from Jordan to Egypt, was involved in counterfeiting and international transportation of stolen cars, and was convicted for heroin trafficking.

In August 1995, he pleaded guilty to a bomb conspiracy count. He had tried to turn state's evidence and the government dropped a charge of attempted bombing. On December 19, 1995, he was sentenced to the 29 months he had already served in jail and was placed on three years probation.

Mazen Ali Saleh: arrested by Paraguayan police on October 3, 2001 on criminal association and tax evasion charges. He was linked to Hizballah.

Mohammad Saleh: one of eight foreign Islamists arrested on June 24, 1993 by the FBI and charged with planning to bomb the UN headquarters building in Manhattan; 26 Federal Plaza, which includes the local FBI headquarters and other agencies; the 47th Street diamond district, which is run principally by Orthodox Jews; and the Lincoln and Holland tunnels connecting Manhattan and New Jersey; and planning to assassinate Senator Alfonse M. D'Amato (R-NY), Assemblyman Dov Hiking, an Orthodox Jewish legislator from Brooklyn, UN Secretary General Boutros Boutros-Ghali, and Egyptian President Hosni Mubarak. They were also tied to the individuals charged with the February 26, 1993 bombing of the World Trade Center. Five of them were arrested in a Queens safe house, assembling explosives by combining fertilizer nitrates and diesel fuel in 55-gallon drums. The FBI seized 400 to 500 pounds of explosives, components of a crude timing device, and other bomb-making equipment. Other arrests occurred in Yonkers, Brooklyn, and Jersey City.

On June 25, the eight defendants appeared before a magistrate in U.S. District Court and were charged with conspiracy and attempting to "destroy by means of fire and explosive" buildings used in interstate commerce. The charges included maximum terms of 15 years in prison, plus fines of $500,000.

The Palestinian provided the fuel needed to build the bomb from his Gulf gas station in Yonkers. He was held without bail. He was accused of providing the 255 gallons of diesel oil found in the safe house and directing his employees to destroy records of the transaction.

On October 1, 1995, he was found guilty of seditious conspiracy, bombing conspiracy, and attempted bombing. On January 17, 1996, U.S. District Judge Michael B. Mukasey sentenced him to 35 years.

Mohammed Saleh: individual arrested by Pakistani authorities on August 7, 1998 in connection with the bombings that day of the U.S. embassies in Kenya and Tanzania.

Suheila Saleh: a Palestinian from Kuwait, identified by the London newspaper *Al Manar* as the female hijacker who joined the Organization of Struggle Against World Imperialism hijackers of Lufthansa flight 181, a B737 scheduled to fly from the Spanish resort island of Mallorca to Frankfurt on October 13, 1977. The terrorists demanded the release of the same 11 terrorists in West German jails as had been mentioned in the Schleyer kidnapping of September 5, 1977 and the release of two Palestinian terrorists held in Turkish jails for the August 11, 1976 Popular Front for the Liberation of Palestine machine gun attack on passengers awaiting an El Al flight in Istanbul. They demanded $15 million and that 100,000 DM be given to each prisoner, who were to be flown to Vietnam, Somalia, or South Yemen, which all indicated an unwillingness to receive them. After the plane had hopscotched to various countries, the terrorists shot the pilot in Aden. A West German GSG9 team ran a successful rescue operation in Somalia on October 18, initially killing two of the hijackers. A third, in the first-class compartment, opened fire and threw a grenade after being hit. A female hijacker opened fire and was quickly subdued. She was wearing a Che Guevara t-shirt and shouting "Palestine will live" in Arabic when she was captured.

Wahid Saleh: alias of Matarawy Mohammed Said Saleh.

Zaharia Abu Saleh: Black September gunman arrested on April 27, 1973 after shooting in the stomach Vittorio Olivares, an Italian employee of El Al in Rome. The Lebanese claimed the victim was an Israeli agent responsible for the death of Black September operative Abdel Zuiater in Rome in October 1972. Abu Saleh was committed to an Italian psychiatric institution and not brought to trial on the grounds that he was mentally unfit. On July 17, 1975, he was released on a 30 million lire bond. It was believed that he left Italy.

Abdul Saleh-U: variant of 'Abd-al-Latif Salih.

Salehah: one of three Afghans who were arrested on April 15, 1981 by Afghan authorities as they were attempting to smuggle two bombs and four revolvers onto a Bakhtar Ariana Afghan Airlines B727 scheduled to fly from Qandahar to Kabul, hoping to divert it to Quetta, Pakistan. The government said the hijackers belonged to the Islamic Society of Afghanistan.

Salem: one of six people mentioned in a warrant of arrest handed down on December 23, 1975 by the Vienna, Austria criminal court for the December 21, 1975 takeover of the Organization of Petroleum Exporting Countries ministerial meeting. Salem was aged about 30, 180-cm tall, with a slender but sturdy figure, round face, and bold-shaped Roman nose.

Abu Salem: Deputy chief of Fatah's Khartoum office, who drove a Land Rover through the unguarded gate of the Saudi Arabian Embassy on March 1, 1973. He and seven other Black September members seized the embassy, took hostages, and murdered U.S. Ambassador Cleo A. Noel, Jr., departing U.S. Charge George C. Moore, and Belgian Charge Guy Eid. They demanded the release of Robert F. Kennedy's assassin, Sirhan Sirhan; imprisoned members of the Baader-Meinhof Gang; Abu Daoud and 16 other Black Septembrists; and two surviving hijackers of a Sabena plane; plus Major Rafreh Hindawi, a Jordanian officer who had been sentenced to life for plotting against the Amman government.

Essa Waqeh Salem: alias Abu Annes, a shepherd from Ba'ag Mujameh Al Badia Mousel who was born in 1985 and joined al Qaeda in Iraq as a martyr in 2007. His recruitment coordinator was Faris. He met Anssari in Syria.

Fahid Muhamad Ali Salem: variant of Fahid Muhammad 'Alim Salam.

Hamam Ali Ahmed Salem: alias Abu Hussein, who used an alias passport in the name of Awad Ahmed Salem Muhammad, a Yemeni from Rabiben who joined al Qaeda in Iraq as a fighter in 2007, bringing his watch. His phone numbers were 00777660889 and 0077560654.

Hesham Salem: an Egyptian arrested in Evansville, Indiana and later released. He was initially held as a possible grand jury witness in the 9/11 case.

Mohammed Salem: one of two suicide bombers who killed 11 people and wounded more than 20 at the port of Ashdod. The 18-year-old Palestinians were schoolmates and had lived in a Gaza Strip refugee camp. Nabil Massoud and Mohammed Salem recorded a video in which they said that the joint operation between Hamas and the al-Aqsa Martyrs Brigade was in retaliation for recent Israeli attacks against Palestinians. The duo wore Israeli military uniforms and brandished Kalashnikovs. They set off the explosives two minutes apart within 50 yards of each other. The first terrorist set off his bomb inside an open-air warehouse filled with forklifts and heavy machinery. The second terrorist was across the street from the port, near a fish import–export company. The second bombing was much less powerful than the first. They had infiltrated from Gaza.

Sergio Rodrigo Salem: one of six Lebanese suspected of involvement in the March 17, 1992 car bombing at the Israeli Embassy in Buenos Aires that killed 29 and injured 252 and the July 18, 1994 bombing of the Argentine-Israeli Mutual Aid Association community center in Buenos Aires. Three of the detainees expressed pro-Hizballah sentiments, but denied involvement. They were charged with drug trafficking, violating immigration law, and illegal possession of weapons. Argentina requested extradition on February 24, 1995 for stockpiling explosives and combat weapons on an island in the Tigre River delta. They were extradited from Paraguay on July 23, 1995 in connection with the discovery of an arsenal near Buenos Aires. They were released on July 27, 1995 in Argentina.

Zainab Abu Salem: age 19, a Palestinian suicide bomber who, on September 22, 2004, walked toward a busy bus stop in northeastern Jerusalem at 3:50 P.M. and set off her explosives when two Israeli policemen asked to search her bag. Border Patrol officers Mamoya Tahio, 20, and Menashe Komemi, 19, along with the terrorist, died and another 16 bystanders were hospitalized. If she had gotten farther, she might have killed 40 people standing at the bus stop/hitchhike point in the French Hill neighborhood. The al-Aqsa Martyrs Brigades said that she was a resident of the Askar refugee camp near Nablus. Later that day, the Israeli Army demolished Salem's family's house.

Mohammed A. Salameh: alias Kamal Ibraham, a Jordanian-born Palestinian living in Jersey City who, on March 4, 1993, was charged by the FBI with aiding the abetting the February 26, 1993 bombing of the World Trade Center in which seven people were killed and more than 1,000 wounded. The handyman was arrested that morning after investigators determined that he had rented the bomb-carrying Ford Econoline E-350 van on February 23. Police searching his apartment found bomb-making equipment and explosives residue. He had given the apartment's address on the van rental slip found at the Ryder truck rental agency. Several hours after the bombing, he returned to the agency with a companion in a red GM sedan and reported that the Econoline had been stolen from a nearby grocery store parking lot. He also went to a Jersey City police station to report the theft. The rental documents had traces of chemical nitrates, which are often found in explosives. When he returned to the agency with the police documents confirming that the van had been stolen, he asked for return of the $400 security deposit. The FBI arrested him as he walked to a nearby bus stop.

He was born in Biddya, in the Nablus subdistrict, on September 1, 1967. His father was a Jordanian of Palestinian origin. He had no criminal record in Jordan. He was the eldest of his mother's 11 children. He had a degree from the Islamic studies faculty of the University of Jordan, and wanted to obtain a Masters of Business Administration in the United States. He had entered the United States on February 17, 1988 on a six-month tourist visa, and had apparently been in the United States illegally since its expiration.

On May 26, he was named in an eight-count indictment for planning and carrying out the World Trade Center attack. He pleaded not guilty on May 28, 1993. The trial began in September 1993. On March 4, 1994, after five days of deliberation, the jury found him guilty on all counts of conspiracy, explosives charges, and assault. On May 24, 1994, U.S. District Judge Kevin Duffy sentenced him to 240 years in prison, a life-term calculated by adding the life expectancy of each of the people killed in the blast, plus 30 years for two other counts.

He went on a hunger strike on August 22, 1993 that lasted for at least five days.

Yasser Ali Salem: tried in absentia, received ten years on August 28, 2004 from a Yemeni court for being a key plotter and buying and delivering the explosives used in the al Qaeda bombing on October 6, 2002 of the *Limburg*, a French super-tanker, in the Arabian Sea five miles off the coast of Yemen.

Abumason Sali: one of six Iranian Hizballah members detained on May 2, 1992 by Ecuadoran police in Quito on suspicion of involvement in the March 17, 1992 car bombing at the Israeli Embassy in Buenos Aires that killed 29 and injured 252. They had intended to go to Canada via the United States. On May 9, the Crime Investigation Division in Quito said that the group was not involved in the bombing, but would be deported to Iran through Bogota and Caracas. They were released on May 12, 1992 and given 72 hours to leave the country.

Barahama Sali: variant of Barhama Sali.

Barhama Sali: variant Barahama Sali, alias Amir, an Abu Sayyaf leader in the Philippines in mid-1994. He was believed to be responsible for the kidnap/murder in June 1994 of 15 civilians. He was killed by the military during a two-month pursuit operation in June 1994.

Krikor (KoKo) Saliba: a Lebanese-Armenian immigrant wanted for questioning in the January 28, 1982 Justice Commandos of the Armenian Genocide assassination in Los Angeles of Turkish Consul General Kemal Arikan.

Elie Louis Salibi: a Labnese Army private arrested on July 31, 1987 by a member of the Board of Immigration's refugee camp outside Motala, Sweden in connection with the June 1, 1987 assassination of Lebanese Prime Minister Rashid Karami when a bomb exploded on his helicopter. He was believed to have planted the bomb, then

left Lebanon. On August 9, 1987, Judge Walid Ghamrah, head of a judicial mission to Sweden, returned home after failing, for five days, to obtain Salibi's extradition for murder and attempted murder on the basis of Articles 549 and 550/201 of the Panel Code. Sweden does not extradite persons threatened with the death penalty. Sweden extended the precautionary detention of Salibi under September 10, 1987. On August 18, 1987, Ghamrah rescinded the arrest warrant, and two days later Sweden released Salibi.

Salih: alias Abu-al-Bara', a Syrian from Al-Dir who was born in 1978 and joined al Qaeda in Iraq as a martyr ("fearless fighter") in 2007, donating 100 lira. His recruitment coordinator was Abu-Ibrahim. His home phone number was 218977; his wife's was 218485.

Salih: alias Abu-Dujanah, a Saudi from al-Qasim who joined al Qaeda in Iraq as a fighter in 2007, contributing his passport. His recruitment coordinator was Abu-'Adil. His home phone number was 063350701; his cell was 00503140701.

Salih: alias Abu-Zakariyah, a Saudi from Mecca who was sent on a suicide mission by al Qaeda in Iraq in 2007. His travel coordinator was Abu al-Zubayr. He owned a passport and $200. Colleague Bandar's phone number was 0555579925; Fahd's was 0553377801, and Abu-Riyad's was 0555712314.

'Abd-al-Salih: alias Abu-al-Miqdam, a Yemeni figher for al Qaeda in Iraq in 2007 who owned a passport. His phone numberwas 00967733246532.

'Abd-al-Husayn Ibrahim Salih: on June 26, 1996, the Bahrain State Security Court sentenced him to 10 years for the February 11, 1996 bombing of the Diplomat Hotel in Manama, the January 17, 1996 bombing of the Le Royal Meridien Hotel, and the bombing of two branches of the Bahrain Corporation for International Shipping and Trade located in the Diplomatic Quarter.

'Abd-al-Latif Salih: variant Abdul Saleh-U, age 42, an associate of Osama bin Laden arrested on November 12, 1999 by Albanian police. The Egyptian, who had obtained Albanian citizenship, was expelled to an undisclosed location. He was also believed to be a member of the Muslim Brotherhood that advocates turning Egypt into a strict Muslim state. He had arrived in Albanian in the early 1990s, and was a key figure in channeling aid from Islamic states to build mosques and hospitals. He also invested heavily in the construction industry. Reuter reported that a source indicated "there is evidence that he was connected to other Egyptian nationals extradited from Albanian last year and to an Albanian involved in planning an attack on the U.S. Embassy."

Abu-Salih: Saudi-based recruitment coordinator for foreign fighters for al Qaeda in Iraq in 2006.

'Ali al-Mabruk Salih: alias Abu-Hasan, a Libyan who lived in Residential Area 2 in Sart and joined al Qaeda in Iraq on September 13, 2006. He was born on May 15, 1985. His phone numbers were 0927029697 and 0912183434. His recruitment coordinator was Abu-'Umar.

'Azmi Husayn Mahmud Salih: a North Yemeni arrested in the October 4, 1984 bombing of a rental car parked at the Israeli Embassy in Nicosia, Cyprus. The Abu Musa Organization claimed credit and threatened Nicosia police if the two suspects, who had gone on a hunger strike, were not released. On October 22, 1984, the duo were deported; the government said that there was insufficient evidence to convict.

Faysal Salih: an official in the Abu Nidal Group who was killed in Sidon, Lebanon on April 14, 1993 when gunmen opened fire with machine-guns as he was carrying his six-month-old son in his house, killing them both.

Fu'ad 'Ali Salih: a Tunisian member of Hizballah charged on December 3, 1987 by Paris judge Gilles Boulouque with four attacks carried out in 1986, including attacks against the post office at the Paris town hall in the Rue de Rennes in Paris, and the bombing by the Committee for Solidarity with Arab and Middle East Political Prisoners on September 12, 1986 of the crowded Casino cafeteria in the La Defense shopping center in Paris, which injured 41 people. By February 1990, he was on trial in Paris with nine others, charged with illegal possession of explosives and setting up a terrorist network linked to the pro-Iranian Hizballah. On March 9, 1990, he was sentenced to 20 years.

Ghannam Salih: identified by Doha's *al-Sharq* on March 19, 1993 as a member of the Abu Nidal Group's Central Committee.

Hamdi Salih: Imbabah resident arrested by Egyptian police in connection with the February 26, 1993 bombing of the Wadi el-Nil coffee shop in Tahrir Square in Cairo in which four people were killed and 16 wounded.

Muhammad Ahmad Sa'id Salih: an Egyptian conscript and member of Gama'at who was sentenced to death by the Sidi Barrani military court on February 16, 1994 for having planned an assassination attempt against Egyptian President Hosni Mubarak, who was to visit the Sidi Barrani military base near the Libyan border. He remained at large.

Muhammad Hasan Salih: one of five alleged Iraqi agents and members of the October 17 Movement for the Liberation of the Syrian People who were arrested by Syria in connection with the multiple bombings of public buses in Syria on April 16, 1986 that killed 27 people and wounded 100. The five were tried and convicted. They were executed on August 24, 1987.

Salim: A Lebanese tied in 1979 to a group of Palestinians in West Germany. Salim, also a French citizen, claimed to not know anything about explosives that were found in a car at a border crossing in April 1979 and said that he was on a business trip. On July 20, 1979, the Passau regional court found him guilty of having prepared a bombing attack and sentenced him to 2 and a half years.

Salim: name used by the leader of the three Egyptian Revolution hijackers of Egyptair flight 648 that had left Athens bound for Cairo on November 23, 1985. He was killed by an Egyptair security guard during the hijacking.

Salim: alias of Ahmad 'Asad Muhammad.

Abdullah Joseph Salim: alias Joseph Salim Abdallah, alias of 'Ali Samih Najm, deputy head of the Saiqa security office in al-Hamra' in Beirut. The Lebanese was arrested on April 15, 1979 upon his arrival at Cairo airport from Beirut when police discovered that his suitcase contained explosives. The Egyptians said Syrian intelligence had sent him to blow up the Sheraton Hotel, offices in At-Tahrir Square, and anywhere he chose. The Egyptians said he provided information on Cuban supervision of Saiqa training and planning. Police said he was trained by Abu Salim and his explosives were prepared by Ahmad al-Hallaq. His release was demanded by terrorists who took over the Egyptian Embassy in Ankara on July 13, 1979.

Abed Qader Abu Salim: a 19-year-old Palestinian from Rantis on the West Bank who, on September 9, 2003, set off explosives at a hitchhiking and bus stop 150 feet from Tzrifin military base, one of the country's largest military bases, 12 miles south of Tel Aviv near Rishon Letzion, killing seven Israeli soldiers, three of them women, and wounding 15 others. His mother, Itaf Mirshed, 46, said "he has taken revenge for the Palestinian people." The Hamas terrorist was a journalism student at Bir Zeit University. He was a friend and distant cousin of bomber Ramez Simi Izzedin Abu Salim. The two bombers had been arrested in December 25, 2002 on suspicion of being Hamas operatives and had spent three months in prison.

Abu Salim: deputy commander of Saiqa security forces in the late 1970s.

Abu-Salim: Jordan-based recruitment coordinator for foreign fighters for al Qaeda in Iraq in 2006.

Ali Salim: name used by one of three terrorists reported by Paraguay's *Noticias* on August 31, 1994 to have entered the country on August 27, 1994 to conduct a bombing against the Jewish community in Buenos Aires. They were to travel from Barcelona, Spain via Hungary and Germany then to Rio de Janeiro or Sao Paulo, then to Foz do Iguacu or Asuncion, to Ciudad del Este, then onward with their explosives to Buenos Aires for a September 3 attack. He was born in 1969, was 1.65 meters tall, slim, and dark skinned.

'Ali 'Abd-al-Hadi Salim: sentenced to five years on July 16, 1994 by a Cairo military court for involvement with the Vanguard of the Conquest gunmen who, on August 18, 1993, fired on the motorcade of Egyptian Interior Minister Hassan Alfi. Five people died and 17 were wounded when a remotely-detonated bomb exploded as Alfi's convoy passed by.

'Ali Qasim Sayf Salim: said by the Ethiopian Supreme State Security Prosecution on August 7, 1995 to be one of five terrorists who had confessed to training in the al-Kamp and Kangu camps in Khartoum with two of the nine Egyptian Islamic Group gunmen who, on June 25, 1995, fired on the armored limousine of Egyptian President Hosni Mubarak in Addis Ababa.

Amin Isma'il Musaylihi Salim: executed by the Egyptian government on May 3, 1994 in connection with the November 25, 1993 bombing of the convoy of Egyptian Prime Minister Dr. 'Atif Sidqi that killed a 15-year-old girl and wounded 21 other people.

Hassan Rostom Salim: alias of Ali Atwa.

Khalid Salim: on September 2, 1998, the Yemeni government newspaper *Al-Wihdah* said that authorities had no record of Salim in the country's population registry. He was reportedly a Yemeni national who threw grenades at the U.S. Embassy in Kenya during the August 7, 1998 bombing attack.

Mamdouh Mahmoud Salim: alias Abu Hajir al-Iraqi, born to Iraqi parents in Sudan, he studied electrical engineering in Baghdad and was an Iraqi army communications officer from 1981 to 1983. After deserting, he moved to Pakistan. In 1986, he met Osama bin Laden in Peshawar, trained in an al Qaeda weapons camp, and became the group's purchaser of communications gear and weapons, including chemical, biological, radiological, and nuclear materials. He was arrested at age 40 on September 16, 1998 by German authorities. The al Qaida member was described as a major financial operative who also procured weapons. A sealed warrant seeking his arrest was filed in Manhattan. He carried a Sudanese passport and claimed to have been born in Khartoum. Some believed he was of Iraqi descent. He was arrested while visiting a friend near Freising in Bavaria. His plane ticket would have taken him to Turkey. He told investigators that he planned to purchase 20 used cars in Germany, but he was not carrying a large amount of money.

Federal prosecutors in New York unsealed the criminal complaint against Salim on September 25. The complaint charged Salim with conspiracy to commit murder and use weapons of mass destruction. It said Salim helped bin Laden to found al Qaeda and that he sat on the group's majlis al-Shura, the advisory council that approves military attacks, and on the fatwa committee, which issued Islamic edicts promoting attacks on Americans. It noted that Salim had worked for al Qaeda in Sudan, Afghanistan, Malaysia, the Philippines, and Pakistan. He obtained communications equipment and "electronic items necessary for the detonation of explosives." It indicated that bin Laden, in conjunction with the governments of Iran and Sudan, sent individuals around the world in the early 1990s to obtain nuclear weapons. The prosecutors charged that Salim met with Iranian officials in Tehran and Khartoum to arrange for al Qaeda members to receive explosives training in Lebanon from Hizballah. The complaint mentioned attempts in 1993 to purchase enriched uranium to fabricate a nuclear bomb. On September 29, federal prosecutors in Manhattan expanded the charges against him, saying that between 1992 and 1998 he had taken part in a conspiracy to attack U.S. military sites abroad and had conspired to transport explosives. They said they would seek his extradition from Germany. On October 6, the Delhi, India *Pioneer* reported that Indian intelligence was investigating Salim. He was indicted on 238 counts on October 7, 1998 by a federal grand jury in New York.

On November 30, a Munich court approved Salim's extradition to the United States to face, in U.S. District Court in New York, charges of murder, conspiracy and use of weapons of mass destruction in an international plot to kill U.S. citizens. Germany's highest court approved the extradition on December 11, 1998. By December 19, Bavarian regional justice authorities and the Foreign Ministry agreed to hand him over to the United States. He was turned over to U.S. officials the next day, flying from Munich Airport to the United States on a U.S. government plane. He was held without bail after appearing in a New York City court and charged with murder, conspiracy, and use of weapons of mass destruction in an international plot to kill U.S. citizens. His court-appointed lawyer, Paul J. McAllister, said that the charges were vague.

On November 2, 2000, Salim and Khalfan Khamis Mohamed stabbed Louis Pepe, a 43-year-old guard, in the eye with a comb filed down to a point at the Metropolitan Correctional Facility in New York. The guard lost his eye and the implement penetrated his brain. On December 20, 2000, Salim was indicted by a federal grand jury in New York on charges including conspiracy to escape, possession of dangerous weapons in a prison, hostage taking, conspiracy to murder, and attempted murder for the attack on the guard.

German authorities said he was connected to Aldy Attar, an Egyptian surgeon in Neu-Ulm.

On April 3, 2002, he pleaded guilty to charges of conspiracy to murder and attempted murder in the stabbing of the guard. On May 3, 2004, he was sentenced to 32 years in prison for the stabbing of Pepe, who was permanently brain-damaged, partially paralyzed, and blinded.

Muhammad 'Abd-al-'Ati Salim: alias Abu-al-Bara', a Libyan student in the college of economics from Darnah who was born in 1984 and joined al Qaeda in Iraq as a suicide bomber in 2007, presenting his passport. His recruitment coordinator was Asadallah. Traveling from Libya to Eygpt to Syria, he met Abu-al-'Abbas, whom he gave $230. His home phone number was 00218924623005; his brother's was 00218925542177.

Muhammad Salim: Islamic Group's military wing leader in Asyut, Egypt in 1993.

Muhammad Mahmud Hamid Salim: alias of Najib Muhammad Mahmud.

Nabil Muhammad 'Abdallah Salim: alias Sari 'Abdallah, identified by Doha's al-Sharq on March 19, 1993 as a member of the Abu Nidal Group's Central Committee.

Ramez Simi Izzedin Abu Salim: age 22, friend and distant cousin of fellow Hamas suicide bomber Abed Qader Abu Salim. The two bombers had been arrested in December 25, 2002 on suspicion of being Hamas operatives and had spent three months in prison. A few hours after Abed's attack, on September 9, 2003, Ramez walked past sidewalk tables and set off his bombs when a guard tried to stop him inside the entrance of Café Hillel on Emek Refaim Street in an affluent Jerusalem neighborhood, killing seven people and injuring 30. The terrorist was studying Islamic law at Al-Quds Open University.

Rashid 'Abdallah Salim: one of three Arabs charged on May 16, 1987 in a Limassol, Cyprus, district court with plotting to murder two British citizens on April 20, 1987, attempted murder, carrying and using automatic weapons, carrying explosives, and possessing forged passports. The attackers were members of the al-Mehdi Ben Barka organization. They were also suspected in the bombing on August 3, 1986 of the Akrotiri military airport. On January 29, 1988, the Kuwaiti citizen was jailed for nine years. On June 28 1989, the Supreme Court ratified the sentenced handed down by the Limassol Assize Court.

Salim Abu Salim: according to *Paris International Service* in March 1987, he was the leader of the Popular Front for the Liberation of Palestine-Special Operations, a PFLP dissident wing, which might have been responsible for a wave of bombings in Paris in September 1986.

Salim Ahmad Salim: sentenced to five years on July 16, 1994 by a Cairo military court for involvement with the Vanguard of the Conquest gunmen who, on August 18, 1993, fired on the motorcade of Egyptian Interior Minister Hassan Alfi. Five people died and 17 were wounded when a remotely detonated bomb exploded as Alfi's convoy passed by.

Jussef Sallata: a Libyan who was arrested after three gunmen killed Abdel Belil Aref, a wealthy Libyan businessman, as he was dining at the Café du Paris on the Via Veneto in Rome on April 18, 1980. On October 6, 1986, the Italian government announced that for "humanitarian motives" it had freed the three convicted Libyan gunmen in exchange for four Italians being held in Libya for the previous six years. A Red Cross plane flew the Libyans to Tripoli and returned with the Italians.

Abu-Salmah: a Saudi-based recruitment coordinator for foreign fighters for al Qaeda in Iraq in 2007.

Abu Salman: alias of Muhammad Rida Dawud.

'Ali Salman: one of three Lebanese terrorists for whom Spanish police issued arrest warrants after the press reported, on October 27, 1991, that a group of seven terrorists was planning assassination attempts at the October 30 opening of the Middle East peace conference in Madrid. Five of the terrorists belonged to the Popular Front for the Liberaton of Palestine, two to Abu Nidal, and all were aided by the Euskadi Ta Askatasuna (Basque Homeland and Liberty, ETA).

Mustafa Salman: an Iraqi sentenced by an Iraqi court on June 5, 2006 to life in prison for aiding and abetting the kidnap/murder of Margaret Hassan, an Iraq–British aid worker killed on October 19, 2004. Pundits believed it was the first trial of a suspect accused in a kidnap or murder of a foreign-born civilian since the overthrow of Saddam Hussein.

Yazeed Al-Salmi: age 23, a Saudi picked up at a San Diego mosque in late September 2001 and held as a material witness in New York for two weeks. The Grossmont Community College student was released on October 9. He briefly lived with Abdussattar Shaikh, who had rented an apartment to two 9/11 hijackers, Nawaf Alhamzi and Khalid Almihdhar. He shared a car insurance policy with Alhamzi to save money.

Mohamed Abdou Saloum: one of two Libyans arrested on February 19, 1988 by Senegalese security officials as they were attempting to illegally enter the country with explosives and weapons at Dakar-Yoff Airport during the night. They had come from Cotonou via Abidjan. They were turned over to the State Security Court on April 8, 1988, and faced three to five years in prison for "acts and maneuvers likely to threaten public security." On June 15, 1988, they were to be released without charges being brought and were to leave the country the next day.

Sals: his release from a Kenyan jail was demanded on June 27, 1976 by the Popular Front for the Liberation of Palestine hijackers of Air France flight 139, an A300 flying from Tel Aviv to Paris and ultimately diverted to Entebbe.

Abu Salsbil: alias of Ali Sayyid Muhamed Mustafa al-Bakri.

Ana Salum: on April 10, 2008, Shin Bet announced that Aham Rial and Ana Salum, both 21, two Palestinians from Nablus, had confessed to plotting to poison food they would serve at the Grill Express restaurant near the Diamond Exchange in Ramat Gan. They were members of the al-Aqsa Martyrs Brigade in Nablus, which also asked them to smuggle a suicide bomber into Israel. They were arrested on March 19. They were in the country illegally and lacked work permits.

Samir Salwan: variant Samir Salwwan, alias of Hasan Izz-al-Din.

Imad Abu Samahadana: a member of the Popular Resistance Committees and one of three Palestinian gunmen who, on September 23, 2004, snuck into an Israeli military post at the Morag settlement and killed three Israeli soldiers by firing into a trailer where they were quartered. Two of the attackers were killed at the site. The third hid among nearby greenhouses and attacked again four hours later, shooting a regional reporter for the Israeli daily *Yedioth Aharonoth* in the leg before dying in a hail of gunfire. He failed to lure the soldiers to an area where he had planted a land mine. In a joint communiqué, three terrorist groups claimed credit and identified the attackers as Mohammed Azazi of Islamic Jihad; Imad Abu Samahadana of the Popular Resistance Committees, and Yousef Amr of the Ahmed Abu Rish Brigades, an offshoot of Fatah.

Maitham Abdulla Jaber Samar: age 39, brother of Qassim Abdulla Jaber Samar, both of whom were swept up on March 20, 2003, when federal agents in the Operation Green Quest terrorist financing task force arrested nine people and executed nine search warrants. The two Iraqi brothers in Denver were arrested for operating an unlicensed money transferring business that sent more than $7 million to Iraq in 2 and a half years. Samar did business as Alrafden Transactions.

Qassim Abdulla Jaber Samar: brother of Maitham Abdulla Jaber Samar, both of whom were swept up on March 20, 2003, when federal agents in the Operation Green Quest terrorist financing task force arrested nine people and executed nine search warrants. The two Iraqi brothers in Denver were arrested for operating an unlicensed money transferring business that sent more than $7 million to Iraq in 2 and a half years.

Jasser Samara: one of two Hamas members arrested on January 14, 1998 by Palestinian officials. After a three-hour trial, they were sentenced to 15 years in prison at hard labor for building and placing bombs and recruiting the five suicide bombers who killed 26 people in attacks in Israel on July 30 and September 4, 1997.

Zaid Saad Zaid al-Samari: number three on the Saudi's most-wanted terrorists list, he was killed on September 6, 2005 in a three-day siege at a seaside villa in Damman's Almubarakia neighborhood.

Danial Ahmed Al Samarji: age 22, one of two members of the Isbat Al Ansar, a Sunni Muslim radical group with bin Laden links, arrested in early October 2001 by Lebanese authorities in Tripoli. The two were handed to the military prosecutor's office for involvement in terrorist activities, arms trafficking, and planning to conduct other acts targeting U.S. interests in the region. Samarji said that after 9/11, he decided to form a new group aimed at attacking U.S. interests, and purchased new weapons for that aim. He named Abu Mujahed, who fled to Denmark in 2000, where he contacted bin Laden cells. Lebanese troops had battled his group in northern Lebanon.

Samarkand: alias of Habis Abdallah al-Sa'ub.

Mohammed Hassan Samarrai: one of two terrorists who, on May 17, 2004, set off a suicide car bomb at the military checkpoint to the entrance to the Green Zone in Baghdad, site of U.S. Headquarters, killing Izz-al-Din Salim, aka Abdul Zahra Othman Muhammad, a Shi'ite Muslim and head of the Iraqi Governing Council, and six other Iraqis, and wounding two U.S. soldiers and six other Iraqis. The Arab Resistance Group al-Rashid Brigades claimed credit.

Khelfa Same: alias of Frazeh Khelfa, an Algerian member of Black September who attempted to assassinate Jordanian Ambassador Zaid Rifai in London on December 15, 1971. Khelfa fired 30 rounds into the ambassador's car in London. He was arrested in Lyons in January 1972. The Lyons court recommended that France grant the United Kingdom's extradition request, but the French Ministry of Foreign Affairs sent him to Algeria.

Abu Ahmad al Samed: alias of Amien Ali Hassan al Ahmadi.

Hamdi Muhammad Abd al Samed: alias Abd Abd al Rahman, an Egyptian from al Buhirah who was born on May 3, 1964 and joined al Qaeda in Iraq on October 14, 2006. His brother's home phone was 0020453802086; his brother's other number was 0020453808083.

Abdennour Sameur: age 34, an Algerian arrested at Luton Airport, north of London, on December 19, 2007. He was one of two British residents who were among the three who had been released from Guantánamo's prison after four years in captivity. He was held under the Terrorism Act on suspicion of the commission, preparation, or instigation of acts of terrorism. He was later released without charge.

Jamal Abu Samhadana: on April 20, 2006, the Hamas-led Palestinian Authority announced the appointment of Samhadana, head of the Popular Resistance Committees, as Director General of the Ministry of Interior with the rank of Colonel. He was suspected of involvement in the attack on a U.S. Embassy convoy in Gaza that killed three U.S. Marine Security Guards in October 2003.

Sami: during a trial on February 24, 1989 against Egypt's Revolution Organization, a witness told the court that the accused had participated in the August 20, 1985 murder of Israeli diplomat Albert Artkash.

Sami: alias Abu-Muhammad, a Saudi from al-Ta'if who was born in 1984 and sent on a suicide mission by al Qaeda in Iraq in 2007. He owned a passport and $200. His home phone number was 7366628. His father's phone number was 0555702102.

Abu-Sami: Saudi-based recruitment coordinator of foreign fighters for al Qaeda in Iraq in 2006.

Abu-Ahmad al-Samid: alias of Amin 'Ali Hasan al-Ahmadi.

Samir: alias of Hocine Buzidi.

Samir: Algeria-based recruitment coordinator for al Qaeda in Iraq of foreign fighters in 2007.

Samir: alias Abu-Mu'adh, an Algerian member of al Qaeda in Iraq in 2007 who owned a passport. His phone number was 0021379549327.

Samir: alias Abu-al-'Abbas al-Tunusi, who came from France to join al Qaeda in Iraq in 2007, donating his MP3 player. He did not have a passport. He apparently went abroad for unspecified medical treatment. His home phone number was 003321153200—ask for Shukri.

Abdullah Samir: variant Samer Mohammed Abdullah, one of eight members of Black September who broke into the Israeli quarters of the Olympic Games in Munich on September 5, 1972, killing two Israeli athletes and taking nine others hostage. After a shootout with police, the hostages were killed, as were five of the terrorists and a West German policeman. The three surviving terrorists, including Samir, were released after the hijacking of a Lufthansa jet on October 29, 1972. They were picked up at Zagreb airport and flew on to Libya, where they disappeared.

Abu Samir: Tunisian-based recruitment coordinator for foreign fighters for al Qaeda in Iraq in 2006.

Salahem Samir: a Palestinian laborer from Amman arrested by Athens police on August 30, 1985, 90 meters from the Jordanian Embassy, while carrying an Austrian-made Steyer automatic weapon, a grenade, a knife, and three magazines of bullets. He admitted that he was on a Black September mission to assassinate the Jordanian Ambassador. His release was demanded by the Revolutionary Organization of Socialist Moslems (an alias of the Abu Nidal group) on September 3, 1985, after one of them members threw two hand grenades at the Hotel Glifadha in an Athens suburb, injuring 18 British tourists.

Jihad 'Awwad al-Samiri: alias Abu-Jandal, a Saudi from Medina who joined al Qaeda in Iraq in 2007, offering to be a fighter. He arrived by caravan from Saudi Arabia to Syria, contributing $1300. His phone number was 00966553322329.

Abdel Razzark Sammarraie: Uganda claimed that he was one of the dead Popular Front for the Liberation of Palestine hijackers of Air France flight139, an A300 flying from Tel Aviv to Paris on June 27, 1976 and ultimately diverted to Entebbe.

Sammer: alias Abu Abd Allah, a Syrian from Al Tal who was born in 1974 and joined al Qaeda in Iraq in 2007. His phone numbers were 0910413 and 0115941849.

Jihad Awad Al Sammery: alias Abu Jandel, a Saudi from Medina who was born in 1404 Hijra and joined al Qaeda in Iraq as a fighter in 2007, contributing $1,300, his passport, and his ID. He arrived in Syria by bus. He brought $1,700 with him, and gave 2,000 rials to his contact in Syria. He said Hatim's phone number was 00966553322329.

Sammy: alias of Mohammed Mansour Jabarah.

Sulayman Samrin: alias Dr. Ghhassan al-'Ali, identified by Doha's *al-Sharq* on March 19, 1993 as first secretary of the Abu Nidal group's Central Committee, member of the Political Bureau, and director of the political office of the General Secretariat.

Hamza Samudi: age 16, a Jenin-based Islamic Jihad terrorist who, on June 5, 2002, set off a car bomb that exploded next to an Egged number 80 bus in Megiddo, killing 17 people, including himself and 13 soldiers, and wounding 45 people. Islamic Jihad said it timed the bombing to coincide with the 35th anniversary of the Arab–Israeli war of 1967. Police said the car was stolen inside Israel in February and driven to the scene from the West Bank. Megiddo (Hebrew for Armageddon) Junction lies near the area the Book of Revelation identifies as the location of the final battle between good and evil before the end of the world.

Hassam Samun: age 27, a Palestinian member of Hamas shot to death on January 12, 2003 by Israeli soldiers who said he had fired on an oil delivery truck in Hebron.

Mustapha Sannoun: arrested in September 1994 near El Jadida, Morocco, in connection with the August 24, 1994 attack in which terrorists shot to death two Spanish tourists at the Atlas-Asni Hotel in Marrakech. He belonged to the Casablanca Group with Algerian Hamel Marzouk, who was interrogated on September 22, 1994.

Nder Ako Santen: one of 16 Middle Eastern terrorists the Saudi Embassy told Thai officials on March 20, 1990 were planning to attack Saudi diplomats and officials overseas. He carried a Swedish passport.

Husayn Ahmad al-Sanuri: one of three Arab Nationalist Youth for the Liberation of Palestine hijackers of a KLM B747 flying from Beirut to New Delhi and Tokyo on November 25, 1973. The hijackers forced the pilot to fly to Damascus, where it was denied refueling privileges. It flew on to Nicosia, Cyprus, where the group demanded the release of seven of their colleagues who were jailed in April 1973 for attacks in Cyprus against Israeli interests. The demands were rejected, but the seven were quietly amnestied by President Makarios and flown to Cairo on December 6. The plane next flew to Tripoli, Libya, where they were rebuffed, and then landed at Valletta, Malta, where the gunmen freed all of the 247 passengers and eight flight attendants. They flew on to Dubai. KLM agreed to halt transporting arms to Israel. The Dutch government pledged on November 25 not to "allow the opening of offices or camps for Soviet Jews going to Israel" and to ban "transportation of weapons or volunteers for Israel." The hijackers went on to Aden, South Yemen, but were denied landing permission. They returned to Dubai, where they surrendered after promises of safe passage to an undisclosed country. On December 8, 1973, the hijackers were taken to Abu Dhabi, where they presumably were turned over to the Palestine Liberation Organization.

Dr. Hasan 'Ali al-Sanusi: a Libyan leaving for Tripoli who was arrested on October 23, 1989 by Cairo International Airport police when they discovered 12 starter guns in his luggage.

'Abdallah Sanussi: Muammar Qadhafi's brother-in-law and deputy chief of the Libyan intelligence service, for whom an arrest warrant was issued on October 30, 1991, in connection with the September 19, 1991 UTA bombing that killed 171. He was charged with violations of French law by conspiring to commit murder, destroying property with explosives, and taking part in a terrorist enterprise.

Habis Abdulla al Saoub: variant of Habis Abdallah al-Sa'ub.

Loa'i Mohammad Haj Bakr al-Saqa: a Syrian who Turkish authorities say masterminded the 2003 bombing of two synagogues, a UK-based bank, and the British consulate in Istanbul that killed 58 people. The authorities said he moved $170,000 between al Qaeda and the Turkish militants.

Ziyad 'Abdallah Salih al-Saq'abi: alias Abu-'Abdallah, a Saudi student from al Jawf who was born in 1986 and joined al Qaeda in Iraq as a combatant in 2007, bringing his passport, ID, and al-'Asr watch. His recruitment coordinator was Abu-'Abdallah. He traveled by land from Jordan to Syria, meeting Abu-'Uthman, who took 2,000 of his 4,000 riyals as a donation. His friend Abu-Rayyan's phone number was 009665002170651.

Ziyad Saqiti: a Palestinian living in Jerusalem, aroused suspicion when he arrived on August 9, 1980 at the Palestine Liberation Organization (PLO) office in Ankara from Athens. He confessed that he had been ordered by Israeli agents to kill the PLO representative.

Ihab Abdullah Saqr: a senior Egyptian Islamic Jihad member who was deported from Baku, Azerbaijan, to Egypt in September 1998. The explosives expert was involved in the November 1995 attack on the Egyptian Embassy in Pakistan.

Abu-Sarab: variant Abu Serrab, a recruitment coordinator in Saudi Arabia of foreign fighters for al Qaeda in Iraq in 2006.

Ibraham Sarachne: a Palestinian Muslim from Bethlehem's Deheisheh refugee camp, who, on May 22, 2002, drove Al Aqsa suicide bomber Issa Bdeir to the scene of the bombing of a suburban Tel Aviv pedestrian mall in which he killed 2 and injured 25. Sarachne and his wife, Medina Pinsky, a Russian immigrant initially thought to be Jewish, had also driven to the town a Palestinian woman, Arin Ahmed, age 20, who intended to set off a suicide bomb against the rescuers. (She apparently had second thoughts. The duo drove her back to Bethlehem after hiding her explosive belt in a car. She was arrested in Beit Sahour.). On June 1, 2002, police said that the wife was Irena Plitzik, age 26, a Ukrainian Christian, not an Israeli Jew. She was carrying a forged ID card for Marina Pinsky, who saw her name in the Israeli papers and alerted authorities to the error.

Saraj: recruiter of foreign fighters for al Qaeda in Iraq in 2007.

Nabil Sarama: a Palestinian who was arrested circa November 2001 near an Orlando pay phone that had been used to make bomb threats. His suitcase contained fake IDs and box cutters. He was charged with making false statements to obtain a residency card.

Saraqah: alias of Mara'ai Hammed Omar al Sheik.

Abu Saraqah: alias of Muhammad.

Saragot Sardi: one of six Iranian Hizballah members detained on May 2, 1992 by Ecuadoran police in Quito on suspicion of involvement in the March 17, 1992 car bombing at the Israeli Embassy in Buenos Aires that killed 29 and injured 252. They had intended to go to Canada via the United States. On May 9, the Crime Investigation Division in Quito said the group was not involved in the bombing, but would be deported to Iran through Bogota and Caracas. They were released on May 12, 1992 and given 72 hours to leave the country.

Zeyal Sarhadi: variant Zia Sarhadi, variant Zeynalabedine Sarhadi, an Iranian arrested by Swiss authorities on December 23, 1991 in connection with the August 6, 1991 assassination of former Iranian Premier Shapur Bakhtiar in his Paris home. Swiss authorities said that while he had been staying at the Iranian Embassy in Bern, he did not work there. The arrest was on the basis of an international warrant by France via Interpol. France had 18 days to make a formal extradition request. French authorities were seeking him on a charge of accessory to murder. He had entered Switzerland on a tourist visa in September 1991. He filed a request for freedom on December 30, 1991, claiming to be an embassy employee with immunity from prosecution. On December 31, 1991, the French requested extradition. On May 26, 1992, French Judge Jean-Louis Bruguiere charged him with "complicity in the murder" of Bakhtiar after he was extradited to France from Switzerland. He was acquitted on December 6, 1994.

Zeynalabedine Sarhadi: variant of Zeyal Sahardi.

Zia Sarhadi: variant of Zeyal Sarhadi.

Mohammad Sarham: alias of Mahmoud Ibrahim Khaled, one of four Martyrs of Palestine terrorists who, on December 27, 1985, fired Kalashnikovs and lobbed grenades in Rome's Fiumicino Airport terminal. He was the only terrorist who survived a gun battle with police. He was born in the Shatila refugee camp. The Abu Nidal group claimed credit for killing 16 people and wounding 73 others. On December 28, 1985, he was indicted for murder in Rome. On February 5, 1987, Italian prosecutor Domenico Sica asked Judge Rosario Priore to indict him.

Ibrahim Muhammad Yahiya Al Sarhie: alias Abu Al Hassan Abu Al Barra'a, a self-employed Yemeni from Sana'a who was born in 1980 and joined al Qaeda in Iraq as a fighter on 4th Jumada al-thani 1428 Hijra (2007), contributing $300 of his $500. He arrived via Saudi Arabia and Syria. He had military experience. His phone number was 711893493.

Abd al-Munim Mutawaali Abu Sari: an Egyptian Islamic Jihad member who was deported by South Africa to Egypt in November 1998. He had been collecting funds from local Muslims and sending them to the Egyptian Islamic Jihad in Egypt.

Saleh Abdalla Sariya: leader of the members of the Islamic Liberation Organization who attacked the Military Technical Academy in Cairo on April 18, 1974, killing 11 and injuring 27 in a gun battle with police. Sariya carried Iraqi and Libyan passport and had worked in Cairo with the Arab League. He had been a political assassin since 1960, when, as a refugee in Iraq, he was sponsored by Haj Amin Hasaini, the grand mufti of Jerusalem. He had also been a member of the Jordanian Communist Party, the Muslim Brotherhood, the Islamic Liberation Party, and numerous Palestinian organizations. He had visited Libya in June 1973 to discuss the attack with Muammar Qadhafi. The raid apparently was to lead to a coup attempt against President Sadat.

Josephine 'Abdu al-Sarkis: variant Josephine Abdo Sarkis, member of the Lebanese Armed Revolutionary Faction (LARF) arrested on December 19, 1984 in Ostia, Italy and charged on May 8, 1985 by an Italian judge with the February 15, 1984 assassination in Rome of Leamon R. Hunt, the American Director General of the multinational force in Egypt's Sinai Peninsula. On June 18, 1985, a Trieste court found her guilty and sentenced her to 15 years and a $510 fine. On October 11, 1985, a Rome appeals court threw out the charges against the LARF member for insufficient evidence. On November 27, 1985, the group threatened Italy unless she was released. On March 20, 1986, a bomb exploded in the crowded Point-Show shopping mall just off the Champs Elysees in Paris, killing two Lebanese and wounding 30 other people; the Committee of Solidarity with Arab and Middle East Political Prisoners demanded the release of Sarkis.

Abu-Sarmad: alias of Jawwad Ahmad 'Arif al-Badawi.

'Abd as-Samad Jawad 'Abdallah as-Sarr: a Kuwaiti acquitted by the Kuwaiti State Security Court in 1984 in connection with the December 12, 1983 truck bombing of the administrative building of the U.S. Embassy in Kuwait, killing four people and injuring 59.

Dr. Issam Sartwi: leader of the Action Organization for the Liberation of Palestine, who had split from Fatah in early 1970 but rejoined.

Abd Al Rahman Sa'ad Harries Al Sarwani: alias Abu Sa'ad, a Saudi from Mecca who was born on 11/12/1404 Hijra and joined al Qaeda in Iraq on 18th Ramadan 1427 Hijra, bringing $100. His recruitment coordinator was Abu Al Zubear. His brother's phone number was 00966502015503.

Adel Bin Mussaed Bin Herees al Sarwani: variant of 'Adi Bin-Musa'id Bin-Hurays al-Sarwani.

'Adi Bin-Musa'id Bin-Hurays al-Sarwani: variant Adel Bin Mussaed Bin Herees al Sarwani, alias Abu-'Adnan, a Saudi from Mecca who was born on March 7, 1985 and joined al Qaeda in Iraq on October 10, 2006, contributing $100. His recruitment coordinator was Al-Zubayr. His brother's phone numbers were 0555568389 and 0556688277.

Bader Ghazi Al Sarwani: variant of Badr Ghazi al-Sarwani.

Badr Ghazi al-Sarwani: variant Bader Ghazi Al Sarwani, alias Abu-'Asim, variant Abu Assem, a Saudi from Mecca who was born on April 24, 1983 and joined al Qaeda in Iraq on October 10, 2006, contributing $300 and a mobile phone. His recruitment coordinator was Abu al-Zubayr. His cousin's phone numbers were 0555568389 and 0556688277. He appears to be related to 'Adi Bin-Musa'id Bin-Hurays al-Sarwani.

Mohammed Shamim Sarwar: an accomplice of indeterminate nationality (initially reported as Indian) who was arrested with Abdel Raouf Hawas on June 14, 2001 in India on suspicion of planning to bomb the U.S. Embassy. They were charged with possession of 13 pounds of explosives, detonators, and timers.

Amari Sasifi: deputy chief of the Salafist Group for Preaching and Combat, who was convicted in absentia on June 25, 2005 in an Algerian court for creating an armed terrorist group and spreading terror among the population. The court sentenced him to life in prison. He was wanted in Germany for kidnapping 32 European tourists in the Sahara desert in various attacks in 2003.

Osama Salah din Abdel Satar: on September 24, 1982, he fired on a tourist bus at the Great Pyramids of Giza, wounding an Egyptian guide and two Soviet tourists. A camel driver struck him on the head, allowing police to arrest the 18-year-old, who was protesting recent Egyptian government arrests of members of the Jihad extremist organization.

Abdel Fatah Satari: arrested in March 1996 by Palestinian security forces at the request of Israel on suspicion of involvement in a recent series of Hamas bombings.

Faouzi Satari: one of the five Guards of Islam gunmen who failed in an assassination attempt against Shahpour Bakhtiar, the Shah's last Prime Minister, in Neuilly-sur-Seine, France on July 17, 1980. On March 10, 1982, a Nanterre jury sentenced four of them, including Satari, to life in prison. His release was demanded on July 31, 1984 by the three Guardsmen of Islam hijackers of an Air France B737 flying from Frankfurt to Paris.

Yasir 'Abd-al-Salam 'Abd-al-Qadir al-Satari: one of three people who, on February 25, 1994, stabbed two Russians with a penknife in Jordan. The trio fled when police arrived. Al-Satari was immediately arrested. He was formerly from al-Ramlah and was currently a resident of an al-Husayn Camp. He confessed that he was accompanied by two other residents of the camp. On March 28, the trio were sent to the head of the preventive security section and later sent to the General Intelligence Directorate.

Abu-Sati: alias of Ahmad Bin-Banfdar Bin-Dari-al-Sahyan.

Jamal Sati: a Sunni Moslem suicide bomber riding a mule with saddlebags full of explosives who died in an attack on a headquarters of the Israel-backed South Lebanon Army on August 6, 1985. A Lebanese civilian was injured.

'Abd-al-Sattar: alias Abu-al-Qa'qa', an Algerian member of al Qaeda in Iraq who was assigned as a fighter in Mosul in 2007. He owned 360 euros. His phone numbers were 0021373911636 and 0021378302489.

Hisham Hikmat Abdul Sattar: an Iraqi political science student in Manila who was arrested by Philippine authorities on January 22, 1991 for his involvement with two terrorists who were trying to plant a 200-pound bomb at a building housing the U.S. Information Service Thomas Jefferson Library. It exploded prematurely in Manila on January 19, 1991. His brother, Husham, was later arrested. Police found bomb-making precursor chemicals in their apartment, along with belongings of the bombers and an address book containing the names of suspected associates of the bombers. Their father was an Iraqi diplomat posted in Somalia who had earlier served in Manila. Sattar was a leader of the National Union of Iraqi Students and Youth—Philippine Branch, and was active in organizing anti-U.S. demonstrations. He had traveled to North Korea. On January 24, Immigration Commissioner Andrea Domingo ordered the brothers' deportation.

Husham Sattar: arrested by Philippine authorities for his involvement with two terrorists who were trying to plant a 200-pound bomb at a building housing the U.S. Information Service Thomas Jefferson Library. It exploded prematurely in Manila on January 19, 1991. His brother, Hisham, was arrested earlier. Police found bomb-making precursor chemicals in their apartment, along with belongings of the bombers

and an address book containing the names of suspected associates of the bombers. Their father was an Iraqi diplomat posted in Somalia who had earlier served in Manila. On January 24, Immigration Commissioner Andrea Domingo ordered the brothers' deportation.

Mohammed Sattar: a member of the Revolutionary Action Organization (RAO) imprisoned in Iraq whose release was demanded by the RAO following the December 25, 1986 hijacking of Iraqi Airways flight 163, a B737 flying from Baghdad to Amman and diverted to Arar, Saudi Arabia, where it crashed, killing 65, according to Iraqi news sources.

Fawzi Mohammed al-Sattari: one of five terrorists jailed for trying to assassinate former Iranian Prime Minister Shahpour Baktiar in France on July 17, 1980 who were pardoned on July 27, 1990 and deported to Tehran. The lone Palestinian in the group, he flew on to Baghdad.

Abu Satty: alias Ahamed Bin Bendar Bin Darry Al Sahian.

Bassam Dalati Satut: one of nine members of the Mujahedeen Movement, which has ties to al Qaeda, arrested on November 13, 2001 by Madrid and Granada police on charges of recruiting members to carry out terrorist attacks. Interior Minister Mariano Rajoy said the arrests followed two years of investigations. The leader was initially identified as Emaz Edim Baraktyarkas (variant Imad Eddin Barakat Yarbas), a Syrian with Spanish nationality. The other eight were from Tunisia and Algeria. Spain did not offer details on the terrorists' targets. The next day, police identified three more Islamic suspects. Police seized videos of Islamic guerrilla activities, hunting rifles, swords, fake IDs, and a large amount of cash. Spain—and other European nations—expressed concern about extraditing the suspects to the United States for trial by military tribunals announced by President George W. Bush.

On November 17, CNN reported that 11 suspected members of an Al Qaeda cell were arraigned. The *Washington Post* quoted Spanish officials on November 19 as indicating that eight al Qaeda cell members arrested in Madrid and Granada had a role in preparing the September 11 attacks. Judge Baltasar Garzon ordered eight of them held without bail, because they "were directly related with the preparation and development of the attacks perpetrated by the suicide pilots on September 11." Judge Garzon charged them with membership in an armed group and possession of forged documents. They were also accused of recruiting young Muslim men for training at terrorist camps in Indonesia. They also reportedly sheltered Chechnya rebels and obtained medical treatment for al Qaeda members. They conducted robberies and credit card fraud and provided false documents to al Qaeda visitors. They also forwarded money to Hamburg. The group had connections to Mohamed Bensakhria, head of the Frankfurt-based cell that planned a terrorist attack in Strasbourg, France. He was arrested and extradited to France. The group also had connections to six Algerians detained in Spain on September 26 who were charged with belonging to the Salafist Group for Preaching and Combat, a bin Laden-funded Algerian group.

The charges were based on documents and intercepted phone conversations of detainee Imad Eddin Barakat Yarbas, al Qaeda's leader in Spain. His name and phone number were in a document found in a search of a Hamburg apartment of a bin Laden associate. Police believe hijacker leader Atta could have met with some of them when he visited Spain in January and July. The group had links to Mamoun Darkazanli. Judge Garzon released three others who were arrested on November 13, but ordered them to report regularly to the authorities.

On April 16, 2008, Judge Ismael Moreno of the National Court indicted Syrian-born Imad Eddin Barakat Yarkas, age 44; Syria-born Muhamed Galeb Kalaje Zouaydi, age 47; and Bassam Dalati Satut, age 48, on suspicion of financing terrorist cells. The indictment said that the trio removed $76,500 in December 2006 from Zouaydi's company and gave the money to Yarkas. Satut had been on provisional liberty. The indictment said that police found, in his home, two bank checks "issued in December 2006, which have as the beneficiary—without any justifying cause—Imad Eddin Barakat Yarkas, for the financing of terrorist cells." Satut was charged with collaboration with a terrorist group. The trio were arraigned on April 24, and denied the charges.

Habis Abdallah al-Sa'ub: variant Habis Abdulla al Saoub, alias Habis Abdulla al-Saub, Abu Tariq, Abu Tarek, Samarkand, Habisabdulla al-Saub, a former anti-Soviet mujahid who fought in Afghanistan then resided in Peshawar, Pakistan until 1993, when he emigrated to the United States. He is a permanent resident alien in the United States and a radical fundamentalist Sunni. He departed the United States on October 17, 2001, intending to enter Afghanistan to fight alongside al Qaeda and the Taliban against Coalition forces. He was accompanied by four U.S. citizens who were apprehended on October 4, 2002. They were all indicted on charges of conspiracy to levy war against the United States, provide material support and resources to foreign terrorist organizations, and contribute services to al-Qaeda and the Taliban. He was last seen on May 23, 2002, when he departed mainland China. The Rewards for Justice Program offers $5 million for his apprehension. He is six feet three inches tall and weights 210 pounds. He was born on November 19, 1965 in Jordan.

Sa'ud: alias Abu-'Umar, a Saudi from Ta'if assigned to a suicide mission by al Qaeda in Iraq in 2007. He owned a passport. His phone number was 0557177707.

Abu-Sa'ud: a Saudi-based recruitment coordinator for al Qaeda in Iraq foreign fighters in 2007.

Abu-Sa'ud: alias of Hamad Bin-Sa'ud al-Harbi.

Abu Ahmed al Saudi: Saudi-based recruitment coordinator for foreign fighters for al Qaeda in Iraq in 2007.

Abu-'Ubaydah Saudi: Tunisia-based recruitment coordinator for al Qaeda in Iraq in 2007.

Mona Saudi: Name given by a female Popular Front for the Liberation of Palestine (PFLP) member who joined the three PFLP hijackers of BOAC 775, a VC-10 flying from Bombay to London and diverted to Beirut on September 9, 1970. It went on to Zerka's Dawson's field near Amman, Jordan. The hijackers joined in the demands of the other hijackers of planes on September 6, 1970 who called for the release of hijacker Leila Khaled and others. The hijackers named their plane Leila. They were joined by three other PFLP members, including Saudi.

Ibrahim Savant: age 25, a British–Iranian soccer fan who converted to Islam and was originally named Oliver. He lived in Stoke Newington, north London. He was arrested in the United Kingdom on August 10, 2006 in connection with a foiled plot by al Qaeda to use liquid explosives and common electronic devices as detonators to destroy at least 10 planes flying from the United Kingdom to the United States. Two dozen people were detained in the United Kingdom; the number rose to 41 by the next day. He was charged in the United Kingdom on August 21, 2006 with conspiracy to commit murder and preparing acts of terrorism. He was ordered held without bail until a September 18 court appearance, when ten other suspects were to appear in court. Prosecutors had said that the trials might not begin until March 2008. His trial, along with that of seven others, began on April 3, 2008. They were charged with conspiracy to murder, contrary to the 1977 Criminal Law Act, between January 1 and August 11, 2006. They were also charged with conspiracy to commit an act of violence likely to endanger

the safety of an aircraft between January 1 and August 11, 2006.

Oliver Savant: birth name of Ibrahim Savant.

Ahmed Muhammad Al Sawahri: alias Abu Ayesha, a Saudi student from Jabal Al Nour, Mecca, who was born in 1407 Hijra and joined al Qaeda in Iraq as a fighter on 26th Rajab 1428 (2007), contributing his passport, 3,500 Saudi Riyals and 100 Syrian Lira. His recruitment coordinator was Abu Abd Allah Al Shamalie. He took a bus from Jordan to Syria, where he met Abu Hajjer, who took 3,000 Syrian Lira from him, leaving him with 3,500 Saudi Riyals and 1,000 Syrian Lira. His phone numbers were 5757432 and 0500260493.

Iyad Sawalha: age 28, head of Islamic Jihad's military wing in the northern West Bank, who was killed on November 9, 2002 when Israeli Army soldiers shot him during a house-to-house hunt in Jenin. He had thrown grenades at the soldiers in an escape attempt. He was behind suicide attacks that killed more than 30 people.

Nabil Sawalhe: an Islamic Jihad suicide bomber who, on November 4, 2002, set off an explosive outside a Shekem home electronics store in a Kfar Saba mall north of Tel Aviv, killing himself and two other people. Some reports indicated that the store's security guard died fighting with the terrorist. Sawalhe was a resident of the Balata refugee camp in Nablus.

Hayha 'Uwaydat Muhammad al-Sawarikah: fugitive member of a group of Jordanian Afghans sentenced to death on December 21, 1994 by the Jordanian State Security Court for belonging to an illegal society, participating in a conspiracy to carry out terrorist acts, and possessing explosives for illegal purposes. The Muslim fundamentalists bombed cinemas, wounding nine people, including a January 26, 1994 attack at an Amman cinema showing what they perceived to be pornographic films, and another bombing on February 1, 1994. The group had been seized in a crackdown on Muslim radicals in January 1994. Their trial began on August 27, 1994, when they were accused of planning to assassinate leading Jordanians, including 'Abd-al-Salam al-Majali, Jordan's former chief peace negotiator with Israel. One of those sentenced to death was Muhammad Jamal Khalifah, a Saudi fugitive son-in-law of Osama bin Laden.

Salem Sa'ad Salem bin Saweed: hanged as the gunman who shot to death U.S. Agency for International Development officer Laurence Foley in Jordan on October 28, 2002 at the behest of Abu Musab al-Zarqawi.

Abu Sayaf: alias of Mubarak 'Ali Ahmad al-Hamami.

Abu Sayaff: alias of Mohammad Ahmad Chalabi.

Abu Sayaff: alias of Muhammad Bin Abd Allah Al Hajari.

Sa'id Bin-'Abd-al-Qadir Salih al-Say'ali: alias Abu-Jubayr, a Saudi from al-Kharj who was born on April 30, 1976 and joined al Qaeda in Iraq as a martyr on November 2, 2006, providing a cell phone, watch, 1,000 riyals and 30,000 Syria Lira. His recruitment coordinator was Abu-Ahmad. His home phone number was 015455532; his brother Salim's was 0555104945.

Yasir Husayn Muhamad Saydat: a Palestinian from Bani Na'im who led four Arab terrorists who fired small arms and threw grenades at Jewish religious students in the West Bank on May 2, 1980, killing five settlers and injuring 17. The Palestine Liberation Organization's Unit of the Martyr Ibrahim Abu Safwat claimed credit. On September 16, 1980, Israeli security forces arrested the four terrorists plus six Fatah accomplices who had helped them hid in caves in the Hebron hills.

Abbas Sayed: a Hamas militant sentenced on January 10, 2006, by the Tel Aviv district court to 35 consecutive life sentences for organizing the 2002 Passover suicide bombing at the Park Hotel in Netanya in which 30 Israelis died. The head of the military wing of Hamas in Tulkarm was also found guilty of a 2001 bombing at a shopping center in Tulkarm in which five people died.

Abdelkader Mahmoud Es Sayed: alias Abu Saleh, an Egyptian organizer of al Qaeda's Milan cell. He was convicted in Egypt for killing 58 foreign tourists at Luxor in 1997. He fled Italy in July 2001 after Italy had given him asylum. On April 19, 2002, the United States froze his assets. He might have been killed in Afghanistan in 2001 during Coalition bombing. He had contacts with several individuals who were arrested on July 11, 2002 in Milan and other Italian cities for making false documents for al Qaeda. A January 2001 wiretap revealed him talking to a Tunisian about false documents easing entry to the United States, saying at one point, "If you have to speak to me about these things, you should come to me and speak in my ear. This subject is secret, secret, secret." He was also linked to Essid Sami Ben Khemais, a major Algerian al Qaeda organizer in Europe who was sentenced to five years in prison in February 2002 for arms trafficking, manufacturing false papers, and arranging illegal immigration.

Farog al-Sayed: one of 16 Middle Eastern terrorists the Saudi Embassy told Thai officials on March 20, 1990, were planning to attack Saudi diplomats and officials overseas. He carried an Egyptian passport.

Mohamed bin Mohamed El-Amir Awad El-Sayed: alias of Mohammad Atta.

Mustafa el Wali Bayyid Sayed: former secretary general of the Polisario Front who was killed in a raid on Nouakchott, Mauritania in June 1976.

On July 7, 1977, the Mustafa el Wali Bayyid Sayed International Brigade claimed credit for firing six pistol shots through the limo window of the Mauritanian Ambassador to France, Ahmed Ould Ghanahalla, injuring him in the jaw, arm, and shoulder.

Sayf: Algeria-based recruitment coordinator for al Qaeda in Iraq foreign fighters in 2007.

Abu-Sayf: alias of 'Abduh 'Abdallah Muhammad al-Asmari.

Anis Sayegh: director of the Palestine Liberation Organization research center in Beirut, Lebanon who was partially blinded when a package bomb exploded on July 19, 1972. His brother, Fayez Sayegh, was director of the Arab League's information service in the United States.

Hani Abdel-Rahim Hussein al-Sayegh: a 28-year-old Saudi detained on March 18, 1997 by Ottawa immigration officials as "a security risk to Canada." The FBI wanted to question him in the June 25, 1996 truck bombing of the U.S. military's compound at Khobar Towers near Dhahran that killed 19 U.S. airmen and wounded 547 others. U.S. officials believed he was a Shi'ite Muslim, possibly the driver of the truck or the getaway car. Shi'ite activists said the Sayegh family comes from Tarut, 25 miles northwest of the Khobar Towers. He claimed he had lived in Syria for the previous two years to avoid government harassment for his dissident views. He had studied Islam in Qom, Iran, in 1987. He claimed his wife wanted to visit her family in Tarut and was to meet him in Kuwait. After the bombing, she was placed under house arrest. He was carrying an international driving permit issued in Syria on August 3, 1994. He was held in the Ottawa Detention Center. On May 5, 1997, Canadian Federal Judge Donna McGillis ruled that there was conclusive evidence that he participated in the bombing, clearing the way for deportation. He declined to take the stand in his own defense. The *Los Angeles Times* quoted Canadian intelligence officials as saying that he

kept surveillance on the target, was at the wheel of the car that signaled the driver of the truck bomb, and assisted in the terrorists' escape. Canada issued a conditional deportation order on May 14, 1997. On May 16, 1997, he expressed interest in cooperating with U.S. authorities. He said that he had studied in Shi'ite Muslim schools in Iran for 10 years and was a member of Hizballah in Saudi Arabia. He claimed to have close contacts with Iranian intelligence. He dismissed his Canadian attorney, Douglas Baum, on May 29, 1997, saying that he did not want to cooperate with the United States. The FBI took custody of him on June 17, 1997. He had agreed to cooperate in the investigation and to enter a guilty plea to surveying U.S. installations for a planned 1995 attack that never took place. He was represented by New York City immigration attorney Michael Wildes when indicted on one count of conspiracy on June 18, 1997. The charge carried a 10-year prison term. The grand jury indictment said that in December 1995, he had traveled to Jizan in the southwest of Saudi Arabia determine the availability of weapons and explosives for use against U.S. targets.

On July 9, 1997, he decided he wanted to explore political asylum in Cuba. He derailed the plea bargain on July 30, 1997, pleading not guilty to the conspiracy charge and saying that he had no information about the Khobar attack. On September 8, 1997, the Justice Department announced it was dropping charges because it lacked sufficient evidence to prosecute. The department said U.S. immigration authorities would seek to deport him to Saudi Arabia. On October 21, 1997, U.S. District Judge Emmet Sullivan formally dropped the bomb-plot charges. On January 22, 1998, the Immigration and Naturalization Service ordered him deported from the United States. He was deported to Saudi Arabia on a U.S. government plane on October 11, 1999.

Suhaila Sayeh: a 43-year-old Palestinian woman convicted by Hamburg's State Supreme Court on November 19, 1996 of murder and other crimes and sentenced to 12 years for her role in the

October 13, 1977 Landshut hijacking. She was one of the four hijackers, but claimed she had no role in killing the plane's pilot during the stop in Aden. The court ruled that she had been complicit. She was the only hijacker to survive the GSG 9 rescue in Somalia. She was arrested in 1994 in Oslo, Norway, and extradited to Germany.

Abdulrab Muhammad Muhammad Ali al-Sayfi: a Yemeni believed by the FBI, on February 11, 2002, to be planning a terrorist attack in the United States or on U.S. interests in Yemen.

Nimer Abu Sayfien: a Palestinian suicide bomber who, on December 9, 2001, injured 29 people (other reports said 11) at a bus stop in Haifa in the late morning. He was carrying the bomb in a bag when approached by Police Officer Hannan Malka. "I could see he was worried in his eyes. He didn't look like he was supposed to be there. He knew I was going to question him, so he blew himself up in front of my eyes." The bomber's body caught fire. Police detonated a second bomb strapped to his body. Abu Sayfien left a suicide note in his Yamoun home, saying he wanted to avenge the November 23, 2001 assassination of Hamas leader Mahmoud Abu Hanoud.

Yezid Gasper Sayiagh: a Palestinian holding a U.S. passport who was arrested on December 18, 1985. He was an associate of a Palestinian with a Jordanian passport who was arrested by Larnaca Airport security personnel on December 17, 1985 when trying to smuggle arms aboard a Swissair plane scheduled to depart for Amman. He was released for lack of evidence that he was part of a plot to hijack the plane.

Nasir 'Abd-al-Rida Husayn al-Sayl: variant of Nasir 'Abd-al-Rida Husayn al-Mil.

Nosrallah Matuk Saywan: an Iraqi sentenced to life in prison by the Kuwaiti State Security Court in 1984 in connection with the December 12, 1983 truck bombing of the administrative building of the U.S. Embassy in Kuwait, killing four people and injuring 59. As of April 1987, none of the death sentences had been carried out. The release of 17 of the 25 prisoners in the case was demanded on numerous occasions by the Islamic Jihad in return for Americans held captive in Lebanon beginning in 1986.

Abu-Sayyaf: alias of Muhammad Bin-'Abdallah al-Hajari.

Abu-Sayyaf: alias of 'Adil Husayn 'Ali Hadi.

El Sayyd Abdulaziz El Sayyd: variant of El Sayyid A. Nosair.

Abdel Wahhab al-Sayyed: a Gaza-born member of the Popular Front for the Liberation of Palestine's (PFLP) political bureau. Twelve rounds were fired at him and his wife, Khaldiyeh, a sister of hijacker Leila Khaled, in their western Beirut home on December 24, 1976. In the 1960s, he was expelled from Egypt and Syria because of his radical activities. He had served as PFLP representative to South Yemen.

Jamil el-Sayyed: Brigadier General and Lebanon's former chief of general security who, on September 1, 2005, was charged by a Lebanese prosecutor with murder, attempted murder, and carrying out a terrorist act in the February 14, 2005 car bombing that killed former Lebanese Prime Minister Rafiq Hariri, age 60, as the billionaire was driving through central Beirut's waterfront just before lunchtime. Another 22 people died and more than 100 people were injured, including the Minister of Economy. El-Sayyed and three other suspects were detained on August 30, 2005. The foursome had been viewed as Syria's chief proxies in Lebanon.

Khaldiyeh al-Sayyed: a sister of hijacker Leila Khaled and wife of Abdel Wahhab al-Sayyed, a member of the Popular Front for the Liberation of Palestine's (PFLP) political bureau. She joined the PFLP in 1969 and held military assignments.

Ahmad 'Isam al-Din al-Sayyid: During a trial on February 24, 1989 against Egypt's Revolution Organization, a witness told the court that the accused had not participated in the August 20, 1985 murder of Israeli diplomat Albert Artkash.

Muhammad al-Sayyid: on March 8, 1990, the Syrian Embassy in Athens denied press charges that the Syrian diplomat was involved in killing Pavlospa Konanis. The Embassy said he started his career with a mission to the Arab League, then worked as a Secretary General of the Arab–Greek Chamber of Commerce before becoming a commercial advisor at the Syrian Embassy.

Sami Bin Rashid Bin Sulayman al-Sayyifi: alias Abu-Yunus, a judge's assistant who hailed from Al-Qasim, 'Unayzah who joined al Qaeda in Iraq as a fighter in 2007, contributing 1,030 Saudi Riyals and bringing his passport, ID, driver's license, and Visa bank cards for al-Rajhi 50631 branch 372, and his watch. His recruitment coordinator was Ibrahim. He took a bus to Damascus, where he met Abu-'Umar and Lu'ay, who took 3,000 of his 4,500 riyals. His home phone number was 0096663640479; his son's was 00966506158667; his brother's was 50789002.

Walid Sbeh: an al-Aqsa Martyrs Brigades activist who, on June 17, 2002, was shot and killed by Israeli soldiers as he was in his car leaving al-Khader, a village near Bethlehem. Military sources said he was responsible for sending suicide bombers into Israel, and had been fingered by three would-be bombers who had been arrested.

Abdul Schalam: Palestinian wanted by Paraguayan authorities on February 20, 1991. He was believed responsible for 47 terrorist attacks in the Middle East and Europe. He reportedly entered Paraguay through Ponta Pora and was to contact foreigners, including Iraqis, who had arrived in Asuncion two weeks earlier. They were believed to be planning terrorist attacks in Paraguay and Argentina.

Luitz Schewesman: name of an alleged member of a Libyan-sponsored Popular Front for the Liberation of Palestine hit team targeting President Reagan and other senior government officials in November 1981. Some reports had the assassins in Mexico or Canada.

Arik Schwartz: a 21-year-old sergeant in an elite Army combat unit who, with his father, was arrested on November 10, 1995 in connection with the November 4, 1995 assassination of Israeli Prime Minister Yitzak Rabin. Police found weapons and explosives during a search at their home in the Tel Aviv suburbs. On December 4, 1995, he was charged with providing bricks of army explosives, detonators, bullets, and fuses to the Amirs—the primary assassination suspects—for use in attacking Palestinians. The seven-count indictment did not mention the Rabin killing.

Naftali Schwartz: Israeli dentist arrested on November 10, 1995 for trying to hide his son, Arik Schwartz.

Todd Michael Schwartz (he Hebraized his named to Tuvia): In January 1975, he set fire to a car belonging to John Artukovich, whose brother, Andrea, was a Croatian Nazi leader sentenced to death in absentia in Yugoslavia for the murder of 800,000 people. The arsonist said he was unable to get to the brother. He jumped a $10,000 bail in Los Angeles and arrived in Israel as a tourist in February 1976. He became an Israeli citizen in April 1976 and joined the Israeli armed forces. On June 16, 1976, members of the Israeli Knesset attempted to prevent his extradition to the United States.

Abdulssalam Seaidi: variant of 'Abd al-Salam Saidi.

Abu Seba: alias of Khamis Farhan Khalaf Abdul Fahdawi.

Merban Seban: one of four Palestinian terrorists who were found guilty on February 17, 1983 in

Turkey and again sentenced to death for their part in the July 13, 1979 raid on the Egyptian Embassy in Ankara, which resulted in the death of two security guards. They had been tried twice before at the Ankara Martial law Command's First Military Court and the Ankara First High Criminal Court, but both times their sentences were annulled.

Malek Mohammed Seif: on October 25, 2001, Phoenix police arrested Seif, age 36, a Djibouti (or French) citizen who trained at two Arizona flight schools in the 1990s but failed instrument tests for his commuter pilot's license. He remained in Arizona trying to change his immigration status. He left the country for a new home in France before 9/11, but was asked to return to the United States voluntarily for questioning. He alleged investigators said they would not arrest him. But an indictment was filed under seal the day before he returned, and he was detained by the FBI when he arrived in Arizona and arrested shortly thereafter. He began a hunger strike in the Maricopa County jail on October 28, and by December 7 had lost 35 pounds. He dropped the hunger strike on December 10. He told the FBI that he met 9/11 hijacker Hani Hanjour at a Tucson dinner party and saw him at a local mosque. Seif faced 41 counts of using a false ID to obtain a Social Security number that he used to apply for jobs, bank accounts, credit cards, and a driver's license. California prosecutors planned to file additional charges for lying on an application for asylum. He was represented by attorney Thomas Hoidal. Seif was to undergo a psychiatric exam to determine whether he was competent to stand trial in January 2002.

Salim Sejann: alias used by one of two suspected Palestine Liberation Organization members who were arrested on April 26, 1979 at the Passau–Achleiten crossing point on the Austrian–Bavarian border when West German police searching their rental car found 50 kilograms of explosives, time fuses, and 11 passports with photographs not of them. Bonn authorities believed that the duo intended to pass the documents to Palestinians either already in Germany or intending to arrive soon.

Abu Selim: Palestine Liberation Organization mediator who was believed to have been involved in the preparation and planning of the Red Eagles of the Palestinian Revolution takeover of the Egyptian Embassy in Ankara on July 13, 1979.

Mohammed Selim: alias Abu Imad, Abu Nidal group commander in Syrian-occupied northern Lebanon who was killed on December 11, 1986 in an Israeli air strike.

Awad Selmi: a senior Hamas leader on a wanted list, who was killed during a terrorist mission in Israel on December 4, 2000.

Gaby Eid Semaan: alias of Mahmoud Slimane Aoun.

Adel Senossi: a Denver man arrested in conjunction with the arrest of two Libyan intelligence officers arrested by the FBI on July 20, 1988 on charges of plotting to assassinate former National Security Council aide U.S. Marine Colonel Oliver L. North. On July 28, 1988, a federal grand jury handed down a 40-count indictment, charging the group with conspiracy, money laundering, and violations of U.S. trade sanctions against Libya. He was charged with using the People's Committee for Libyan Students to acquire information about North.

Abdullah Senoussi: brother-in-law of Mu'ammar Qadhafi and de facto chief of Libyan intelligence. French authorities claimed to have evidence that he was involved in the September 19, 1989 bombing of a Union des Transports Aeriens (UTA) plane and the September 21, 1988 bombing of Pan Am flight 103 over Lockerbie, Scotland. On June 12, 1998, France announced that it would try him, along with five other Libyans, in absentia. On March 10, 1999, a French antiterrorism court imposed life in prison on the six in absentia. If any of the six were to fall into French hands, they would automatically be given a retrial under French law. The prosecutor said the evidence showed that the Libyan officials had organized the attack. France had never formally requested extradition of the six. Qadhafi had earlier said he would turn the six over to France, but also had said he would consider making the six serve any sentence imposed by a French court in Libyan prison.

Khaled Serai: one of three Algerians arrested in Naples, Italy on November 17, 2005 who were suspected of being Islamist extremists with ties to international terrorists and who could become "potentially operative" and ready to carry out an attack.

Ahmed Hossein Abu Sereya: a Palestinian who was arrested and charged after he ran from the scene of two grenade explosions at the Café de Paris on Via Veneto in Rome on September 16, 1985. The explosions killed 39 people. A search of his apartment disclosed a round-trip ticket from Damascus to Vienna to Rome. He was carrying $1,000 and a fake passport. The Revolutionary Organization of Socialist Moslems claimed credit. On August 6, 1986, Assistant Attorney General Domenico Sica recommended that Sereya stand trial for the grenade attack. The prosecutor's office said that Sereya is a member of the Palestinian Martyrs, a group led by Abu Nidal. The trial was scheduled for July 3, 1987.

Abu Serrab: variant of Abu Sarab.

Faouzi Ben Rachid Serraj: implicated in the August 2, 1987 bombing of four tourist hotels in Sousse and Montastir, Tunisia by the Habib al-Dawi Group of the Islamic Jihad Organization in Tunisia.

Alim Seyann: one of two suspected Palestine Liberation Organization members who were arrested on April 26, 1979 at the Passau–Achleiten crossing point on the Austrian–Bavarian border when West German police searching their rental car found 50 kilograms of explosives, time fuses, and

11 passports with photographs not of them. Bonn authorities believed that the duo intended to pass the documents to Palestinians either already in Germany or intending to arrive soon. They had planned to bomb an Israeli ship in Hamburg harbor. They were also suspected of involvement in the April 24, 1979 bombing of a Jewish synagogue in Vienna. They were held in Munich for trial.

Abu Omar As-Seyf: an Arab alleged to represent al Qaeda in Chechnya who was alleged by *Tass* to have financed the Chechen terrorist attack on the elementary school in Beslan, Russia on September 1, 2004.

Jehad Shaaban: a Palestinian who had lived in the Neuss, West Germany apartment that was raided on October 26, 1988, resulting in the arrests of 14 Arabs suspected of Popular Front for the Liberation of Palestine-General Command terrorist ties. On July 29, 1990, *Washington Post* reporter Jack Anderson said that, in July 1990, Sweden had released from jail and expelled 11 Palestinians, including Shaaban, who might have been connected to the December 21, 1988 bombing of Pan Am flight 103 over Lockerbie, Scotland that killed 270.

Abd Al Qader Abd Al Aziz Al Sha'aerie: alias Abu Al Zubear, a Libyan merchant from Dernah who was born in 1984 and joined al Qaeda in Iraq in 2007, presenting his ID and passport. His recruitment coordinator was Bashar Al Darsi, whom he knew through a relative. He came to Syria via Egypt, spending four days in Syria and four days on the border. In Syria, he met Abu Al Abbas. He brought $200 with him.

Abdel Muati Shaban: age 18, a Palestinian suicide bomber disguised as an ultraorthodox Jew, who, on June 11, 2003, set off his bomb in the middle of Bus 14 in downtown Jerusalem during the 5 P.M. rush hour, killing 16 others, including the driver and three passersby, and wounding more than 70. Hamas claimed credit for the Jaffa Road attack, saying it was retaliating for Israel's attempted assassination of senior Hamas leader Abdel Aziz Rantisi in Gaza City on June 10. The attack occurred at the stop at Mahane Yehuda, an open-air market near Klal Center.

Anwar Shaban: leader of the Egyptian Gama'at until his death in 1994.

Yusuf Mahmud Sha'ban: variant Yusuf Muhammad Sha'ban, alias Wa'il Mahmud 'Ali, a Palestinian arrested on February 4, 1994 who confessed to the January 29, 1994 murder in Beirut of Jordanian First Secretary Naeb Umran Maaitah. He admitted membership in the Abu Nidal group. On February 17, 1994, Beirut's first investigating judge formally issued arrest warrants for three terrorists, including Sha'ban, under Articles 549 and 72 of the Penal Code on charges of premeditated murder. On March 24, 1994, he was formally indicted as the triggerman. The prosecution called for the death penalty.

Yusuf Muhammad Sha'ban: variant of Yusuf Mahmud Sha'ban.

Mohamed A. Shabata: a former student at Weber State College who was arrested in Chicago on July 17, 1981, a few hours after the bullet-riddled body of Nibail A. Mansour, a Libyan student, was found stuffed in the trunk of his car, parked in front of the Ogden, Utah, apartment of Shabata. Shabata was carrying a large amount of cash and tickets to Tripoli, Libya via London. He was convicted of second-degree murder on November 25, 1981 and sentenced to five years to life on December 2, 1981.

Ibrahim Bin Muhammad Al Shabi: alias Abu Walid, a Tunisian from Tunisia who was born in 1984 and joined al Qaeda in Iraq as a fighter in 2007, bringing $210, 3,000 lira, his passport, his student ID, and a delayed military service document. His recruitment coordinator was Abu Omar the Tunisian. He flew from Turkey to Syria, where he met Abu Omar al-Ansari and Abu Omar the Tunisian. His home phone number was 0021671709054.

Yusuf Shadid: on May 22, 1985, the Jordanian state prosecutor's office issued a summons for him in connection with a foiled plot by the Libyans and the Abu Nidal organization to set off a bomb at the U.S. Embassy in Egypt.

Fatah Shaddini: one of the five Guards of Islam gunmen who failed in an assassination attempt against Shahpour Bakhtiar, the Shah's last Prime Minister, in Neuilly-sur-Seine, France on July 17, 1980.

Shadi: Yemeni-based recruitment coordinator for foreign fighters for al Qaeda in Iraq in 2006.

Al-Shaer: alias of Dr. Ramadan Abdullah Mohammad Shallah.

Raed Shaghnoubi: on March 3, 1996, he set off a bomb on the No. 18 Egged bus on Jaffa Road and Rashbag Street between the central post office and police headquarters in Jerusalem, killing 19, including 6 Romanians, and wounding 10 others. Israeli soldiers blew up the two-room house of his family.

Mullah Ahmad Shah: alias of Mullah Ismail.

Timoor Shah: head of an Afghan criminal gang that on May 16, 2005 kidnapped Clementina Cantoni, age 32, an Italian employee of CARE International, in Kabul during the night.

Wali Khan Amin Shah: alias Osama Azmiry, a Saudi who accompanied Osama bin Laden to Afghanistan in 1980 and fought with him in the 1989 Jalalabad battles. He was involved in plots to assassinate Pope John Paul II and President Bill Clinton in Manila, and the Boyinka plot to blow up 11 aircraft flying to the United States from the Philippines. He was captured in Malaysia on December 9, 1994 and flown to New York, where he was charged with six counts of conspiracy to bomb airliners, which carries a life sentence without parole. On February 23, 1996, he was indicted for the December 1, 1994 bombing of the Greenbelt

Theater in Manila, Philippines, that injured several moviegoers. On September 5, 1996, he was found guilty on all seven counts in the conspiracy to set off the airplane bombs, and of attempting to escape from prison. Defense attorneys said they would appeal.

Abbas Mohammed 'Ali Shahadi: on March 24, 1988, he threw two hand grenades—which failed to explode—and fired four shots at a van taking a 12-man flight crew to a hotel at Bombay's Sahar International Airport, seriously wounding the Italian pilot in the stomach and throat. Police arrested him and seized his automatic pistol and two magazines of ammunition. He carried no travel documents and was suspected of membership in the Abu Nidal group. He claimed to be a Lebanese, although earlier press reports said he was an Iranian. He said he shot the pilot to avenge the death of his parents who were killed 18 months earlier in an Alitalia crash in Rome. Indian police did not believe the story. The Cells of the Arab Fighters claimed credit.

Ismael Shahbakhsh: leader of a group that, on August 12, 2007, kidnapped a Belgian woman and her Belgian partner. He demanded that his jailed brother be freed.

Muhammad Hasan Abu Shahda: member of a group opposed to Yasir Arafat who was arrested on August 15, 1978 from a Lahore house for suspected involvement in the August 5, 1978 attack on the Palestine Liberation Organization (PLO) offices in Islamabad that killed four people in an attempted assassination of PLO representative Yusuf Abu Hantash. A Rawalpindi magistrate remanded him to police custody for 13 days.

Samir Arif El Shahed: one of two hijackers of Lufthansa flight 615, a B727 flying on the Damascus-Beirut-Ankara-Munich run on October 29, 1972. The hijackers threatened to blow up the plane if the surviving three members of the Black September killers in the Munich massacre were not released. The duo was armed with

revolvers and two grenades and had used Yemeni and Lebanese passports. The West Germans agreed to free them. The hijackers ultimately landed in Tripoli, Libya, where they were given a heroes' welcome.

Ibn Shaheed (Son of the Martyr): alias of Moammar Abdullah Awamah.

Ibn al-Shahid: believed to be associated with the 'Asbat al-Ansar in Lebanon, he was arrested in October 2003 and charged with masterminding the bombing of three fast food restaurants in 2003 and the McDonald's attack on April 5, 2003 that wounded 10.

Bassem Muhammad Khalil Shahin: alias Mahmud, an Egyptian Gama'at leader killed by Egyptian police on October 15, 1994. He was a fugitive who had been sentenced to three years in prison in 1992 in connection with the killing of secular writer Farag Foda. He was believed to be the mastermind of the October 14, 1994 stabbing of Naguib Mahfouz, the only Arab to receive the Nobel Prize for Literature, in a Cairo suburb.

Husayn Shahin: one of three Lebanese terrorists for whom Spanish police issued arrest warrants after the press reported, on October 27, 1991, that a group of seven terrorists were planning assassination attempts at the October 30 opening of the Middle East peace conference in Madrid. Five of the terrorists belonged to the Popular Front for the Liberation of Palestine, two to Abu Nidal, and all were aided by the Basque Nation and Liberty (ETA).

Walid Shahin: an at-large merchant sentenced to be hanged on January 16, 1994 in connection with a plot foiled on June 26, 1993 to assassinate Jordanian King Hussein during the graduation ceremony at Muta University, a Jordanian military academy. He was also found guilty of belonging to the Islamic Liberation Party, which aimed to topple the regime through violence and establish an Islamic caliphate state. He was found guilty of conspiring to kill Hussein but found innocent of trying to change the Constitution due to lack of evidence.

Yasser Shahin: an Egyptian arrested in Evansville, Indiana and later released. He was initially held as a possible grand jury witness in the 9/11 case.

Abd Al Aziz Awad Abd Allah Al Shahrani: alias Abu Hajir Al Zubear Lazardi, a Saudi physical trainer from Riyadh who joined al Qaeda in Iraq on 19th Jumada al-thani 1428 (circa 2007), contributing a passport. His recruitment coordinator was Binder, whom he knew through Abu Salemeh. He arrived from Riyadh and Syria, where he gave 500 Saudi Rials and 10,000 Syrian lira to local contacts. He had experience as a boxing trainer. His brothers' phone numbers were 0569873893 and 0558718950.

Hossein Shahriarifar: alias of Hossein Dasgiri.

Ghalib Shahrur: a Hizballah member alleged by *Radio Free Lebanon* on September 19, 1986 to be one of the kidnappers of Frank Herbert Reed, director of the Lebanese International School in west Beirut on September 9, 1986.

Resul Bagher Nejad Shaian: variant of Rasoul Bagher Shaian.

Rasoul Bagher Shaian: variant Resul Bagher Nejad Shaian, variant Rasul-Baqer Sha'iyan, one of five Iranian diplomats arrested in Turkey on October 25, 1988 who were planning to kidnap Said Abu Hassan Mochhadezade, an anti-Khomeini engineer working in Erzincan who reportedly was a member of the Peoples Mujahideen. They were to be tried by a state security court in Istanbul State. The press reported that two of them were members of the Savama Iranian secret police; the other three were members of the embassy's bodyguard team. On October 28, 1988, he was expelled and flown out of Turkey.

Zahed Shaik: headed of the Muslim Brotherhood in Kuwait and brother of Khalid Sheikh Muhammad.

Abu Hazim al-Sha'ir: Saudi-based bin Laden operative.

Kamran Shaikh: alias of Kamram Akhtar.

'Abdallah Fadl 'Abd-al-'Aziz al-Sha'iri: alias Abu-'Ubayda, a Libyan university student of science from Darnah who was born in 1986 and joined al Qaeda in Iraq as a martyr on May 5, 2007, bringing his passport. His recruitment coordinator was Basit al-Sha'ri. He arrived from Libya via Egypt to Syria. His brother's phone number was 002189272642.

Rasul-Baqer Sha'iyan: variant of Rasoul Bagher Shaian.

Jamal Shaka: alias Abu Obieda Al Muhajer, a Moroccan from Casablanca who was born in 1985 and joined al Qaeda in Iraq on 16th Muharram (2007) as a martyr, contributing his ID and passport. His recruitment coordinator was Nabil, whom he knew through Abu Muhammad, who did a mission in Iraq. He flew from Morocco to Turkey to Syria, where he met Falah, Abu Essa, and Zyed. He brought 10,000 lira and 70 euros. His father's phone numbers were 0021266068281 and 0021274889968.

Fuad Shakar: one of ten Shi'ite Muslims identified in November 17, 1992 by the Lebanese newspaper *Nida' al-Watan* as suspected of instigating the kidnappings of U.S. hostages William Buckley, William Higgins, and Peter Kilburn.

Muhammad Khalaf Shakara: named on February 14, 2005 as one of Iraq's 29 most-wanted insurgents. A bounty of between $50,000 and $200,000 was offered.

Abdul Shakoor: alias of Ibrahim Rasul.

Fadi Shalabi: alias Abu-Haytham, variant Abu Hitham, a Syrian from Dar'a, variant Derah, who was born in 1982 and joined al Qaeda in Iraq on September 13, 2006. His phone numbers were 01580091 and 094303750. He contributed 1,300 lira. His recruitment coordinator was Abu-Basr, variant Abu Al Beser.

Abd Allah Shalali: alias Abu Talha, a Saudi from Riyadh who was born in 1984 and joined al Qaeda in Iraq as a fighter in 2007, contributing $50 and 50 euros, along with his passport. His recruitment coordinator in Lebanon was Shouieb, whom he knew via his father-in-law. In Syria, he met Abu Alla'a Abu Othman al Hajji. He brought $400. His phone number was 0021373481001.

'Adil Jum'ah Muhamad al-Sha'lali: alias Abu-'Umar, a Libyan from Darnah who joined al Qaeda in Iraq in 2007, bringing a "non-burned" passport. His recruitment coordinator was Umar. He flew from Egypt and Jordan to Damascus. His phone number was 00218924795394.

Saleh Dawoed al Shalami: alias Abu Youssef:a Libyan from Dernah who was born in 1986 and joined al Qaeda in Iraq as a martyr in 2006, bringing his passport. His recruitment coordinator, Al Mayet, came from his area. His brother Shoueb's phone number was 021892541531.

Khalied Abd al-Da'aiem al-Shalawi: alias Abu Haziefa, a Libyan from Darneh who was born in 1976 and joined al Qaeda in Iraq as a martyr circa 2006 or 2007, contributing $100, a watch, and his passport. His recruitment coordinator was Omar Shanani, whom he met via a friend. He flew to Syria via Egypt. While in Syria, he met Abu-Othman. His brother's phone number was 00218925540332.

Saud Abd Allah Al Shalawi: alias Abu al Barra'a al Ta'affi, a Saudi from Ta'aff who was born on 12/2/1405 Hijra who joined al Qaeda in Iraq on 1st Ramadan 1427 Hijra, bringing $920 and a watch. His brother Muhammad's phone number was 0566722337; his father's was 050579397; his brother Obieda's was 0556722337.

Noura Shalhoub: age 15, shot to death on February 25, 2002 after the Palestinian girl pulled out a knife and ran at an Israeli Army checkpoint near Tulkarm in the West Bank. Her suicide note said "I have decided to send a message to the occupation that there is no safety on our soil for Jews."

Khalid Jummah Masoud al Shalieah: alias Abu Musa'ab, a Libyan from Dernah who was born in 1984 and joined al Qaeda in Iraq on October 28, 2006, bringing $100, a watch, and a ring. His recruitment coordinator was Faraj. His phone numbers were 218927269608 and 21892748512.

Dr. Ramadan Abdullah Mohammad Shallah: alias Rashad, Mohamad el-Fatih, Mahmoud, Radwan, al-Shaer, Abu Abdullah, Ramadan Abdullah, founder and secretary general of Palestinian Islamic Jihad (PIJ), a terrorist front with headquarters in Damascus. The Western-educated native of Gaza was a professor of political science and economics. He was elected secretary general of the organization in 1995, two days after the assassination in Malta of Fathi Shaqaqi, the group's leader. He had been employed by the now-defunct World and Islam Studies Enterprise, based in Tampa, Florida. He is wanted for conspiracy to conduct the affairs of the PIJ through racketeering activities such as bombings, murder, extortion, and money laundering. He was listed as a "Specially Designated Terrorist" under U.S. law on November 27, 1995 and was indicted on 53 charges in the U.S. District Court, Middle District of Florida, in 2003. He was also named in the February 20, 2003 indictment of his friend, Sami Amin al-Arian, in Tampa, Florida, of conspiracy to commit murder via suicide attacks in Israel and the Palestinian territories, operating a criminal racketeering enterprise since 1984 that supports the PIJ terrorist organization, conspiracy to kill and maim people abroad, conspiracy to provide material support to the group,

extortion, visa fraud, perjury, money laundering, and other charges. The United States added
him to its most-wanted terrorists list on February 28, 2006. On February 12, 2007, the United
States offered $5 million for the arrest of Shal-
lah, then 49, in the Rewards for Justice program. The FBI said he planned and conducted
numerous bombings, murders, extortions, and
acts of racketeering. The Palestinian carries an
Egyptian passport. He was born on January 1,
1958. He is six feet one inch tall and weighs 225
pounds.

Abu-'Abdallah al-Shamali: variant of Abu Abd
Allah Al Shamalie.

Abu-'Umar al-Shamali: alias of Hasan Shilian
Muhammad al-Humdi, variant Hassan Shalian
Muhammad Al Hamdi.

Abu Abd Allah Al Shamalie: variant Abu-
'Abdallah al-Shamali, Saudi-based recruitment
coordinator for al Qaeda in Iraq foreign fighters
in 2007.

Ali Hussein Ali al-Shamari: age 35, one of three
suicide bombers who, on November 9, 2005,
attacked Western hotels in Amman, killing 59
and wounding more than 300. Abu Musab al-
Zarqawi's group Al Qaeda in Iraq claimed credit.
He was the husband of Sajida Mubarak Atrous al-
Rishawi, age 35, who, herself, was to be a suicide
bomber.

Badr Salim al-Shamari: alias of Badr Jiyad
Thamir Mutlaq al-Shammari.

Youssef Salem Al Shameri: alias Abu Yacoub,
a Saudi teacher from Riyadh who was born on
14/7/1404 Hijra and joined al Qaeda in Iraq
on November 17, 2006 as a martyr, bringing a
passport, 1,000 rials, and 3,000 lira. His recruitment coordinator was Abu Abdouh. His home
phone number was 0096612312979; his uncle's
was 0096612316369.

Ra'aed al Shamerie: a Saudi-based recruitment
coordinator for al Qaeda in Iraq foreign fighters
in 2007.

Nawaf Bin Shaiyem Saray Al Shamery: alias Abu
Sulaiman, a Saudi from Al Jawef who was born
in 1406 Hijra and joined al Qaeda in Iraq as a
martyr in 2007, contributing 3,100 of his 4,050
riyals, along with his passport and ID. His recruitment coordinator was Abu Abd Allah. He
met Abu Muhammad the smuggler in Syria. His
phone number was 00966553399449.

Abu Al Majahid Al Shami: alias of Anass Munier
Al Jumah.

Abu-al-Walid al-Shami: alias of Muhammad
Batal Muhammad Nizar, variant Muhammad Battel Muhammad Nizar.

Mahir Shami: named on February 14, 2005
as one of Iraq's 29 Most Wanted Insurgents. A
bounty of between $50,000 and $200,000 was
offered.

Tony Shamiyah: a member of the civil administration in Marj-Uyun charged on May
18, 1990 by the Israeli-backed Lebanese militia
with the assassination of William Bell Robinson, a U.S.-Lebanese social worker who ran
a center for mentally retarded children inside the Israeli-declared security zone in southern Lebanon by the Martyr Lula Ilyas 'Abbud
Group of the al-Rumaylah Martyrs Unit of the
Lebanese National Resistance Front on March
27, 1990. He and two other defendants were
among five individuals picked up in raids on
Rashayya al-Fukhkhar and Shab'a in southern
Lebanon.

Adnan Bin Ahmed Al Shamlan: alias Abu Al
Walied, a Syrian from Dye Al Zur Al Midan who
was born in 1985 and joined al Qaeda in Iraq in
2007, bringing 500 Syrian lira. He was deployed
to Al Anbr. His phone numbers were 01710793
and 051713085.

'Abd-al-Rahman Bin Muhammad Bin Farhan al-Shammari: alias Abu-Mus'ab, a Kuwaiti freelance smith from Al Hajra' who was born in 1984 and joined al Qaeda in Iraq on July 17, 2007 as a fighter, contributing $100, 100 Syrian lira, and 2,130 Saudi riyals, along with his passport and driver's license. His recruitment coordinator was Abu-'Abdallah, whom he knew via a friend. He arrived via Saudi Arabia and Jordan in Syria, where he met Abu-Hajir, who took 700 of his 3,600 Saudi Riyals and 4,000 Syrian lira. His phone numbers were 009656602295 and 009654576011.

Badr Jiyad Thamir Mutlaq al-Shammari: one of 11 Iraqis and three Kuwaitis arrested on April 13, 1993 by Kuwaiti authorities in a plot to assassinate former U.S. President George H. W. Bush with a bomb during his visit to Kuwait. He was a driver at the Ministry of Electricity and Water. He hosted several of the members of the network. On May 10, 1993, Kuwait ruled out extradition, saying it would try the group. On May 16, 1993, the Kuwaiti Attorney General denied press reports that the Kuwaiti had been released on bail. On June 4, 1994, the three-judge panel sentenced him to death. On March 20, 1995, a Kuwaiti high court overturned the bombing conspiracy conviction but sentenced him to five years in jail for smuggling alcohol.

Bandar 'Ajil Jabir al-Shammari: alias Hamdan Sa'ud Sa'd, 1 of 11 Iraqis and three Kuwaitis arrested on April 13, 1993 by Kuwaiti authorities in a plot to assassinate former U.S. President George H. W. Bush with a bomb during his visit to Kuwait. The Iraqi resident in Kuwait had a criminal record and was charged in several cases. He resided in the Zubayr area in Iraq and was believed to have sheltered three of the principal suspects. He had been deported from Kuwait after the Coalition invasion. On May 10, 1993, Kuwait ruled out extradition, saying it would try the group. On June 4, 1994, the three-judge panel sentenced him to death. On March 20, 1995, a Kuwaiti high court commuted the death sentence to life in prison.

Hadi 'Awdah Harjan al-Khalil al-Shammari: one of 11 Iraqis and three Kuwaitis arrested on April 13, 1993 by Kuwaiti authorities in a plot to assassinate former U.S. President George H. W. Bush with a bomb during his visit to Kuwait. The Iraqi resident of the al-Zubayr area was carrying drugs to sell inside the country and was to then share the proceeds with the rest of the network. On May 10, 1993, Kuwait ruled out extradition, saying it would try the group. On June 4, 1994, the three-judge panel sentenced him to six months.

Radi al-Shammari: one of two Jordanian terrorists arrested on January 21, 1991 in Bangkok, Thailand who were part of an international terrorist network financed and armed via Iraqi diplomatic pouches. He was deported on January 28, 1991, but ultimately flew to Nepal on January 31. He was not charged in Thailand but was arrested by Nepalese police upon arrival. Nepal deported him back to Bangkok on February 3, 1991. On February 7, he was deported to Athens.

Ra'id al-Shammari: a Saudi-based recruitment facilitator for al Qaeda in Iraq in 2006.

Salim Jiyad Thamir Mutlaq al-Shammri: variant of Salim Shiyad Thamir Mutlaq al-Shammari.

Salim Nasir Sabih Rumi al-Shammari: alias Khalid Farhan Salih, 1 of 11 Iraqis and three Kuwaitis arrested on April 13, 1993 by Kuwaiti authorities in a plot to assassinate former U.S. President George Bush with a bomb during his visit to Kuwait. The Iraqi was believed to be involved in reconnaissance against Coalition forces.

On May 10, 1993, Kuwait ruled out extradition, saying it would try the group. On May 16, 1993, the Kuwaiti Attorney General denied press reports that he had been released on bail. On June 4, 1994, the three-judge panel sentenced him to death. On March 20, 1995, a Kuwaiti high court commuted the death sentence to life in prison.

Yusuf Salim al-Shammari: alias Abu-Ya'qub, a Saudi teacher from Riyadh who was born on April

14, 1984 and joined al Qaeda in Iraq as a martyr on November 17, 2006, contributing 3,000 lira, 1,000 riyals, and his passport. His recruitment coordinator was Abu-'Abdah. His home phone number was 0096612312979; his uncle's was 0096612316369.

Hilal al-Shammut: preacher sentenced to hang on January 16, 1994 in connection with a plot foiled on June 26, 1993 to assassinate Jordanian King Hussein during the graduation ceremony at Muta University, a Jordanian military academy. He was also found guilty of belonging to the Islamic Liberation Party, which aimed to topple the regime through violence and establish an Islamic caliphate state. He was found guilty of conspiring to kill Hussein, but found innocent of trying to change the Constitution due to lack of evidence. The death sentence was commuted.

Hatim Ahmed Hamdan Al Shamrani: alias Abu Omar, a Saudi from Jeddah who was born in 1405 Hijra and joined al Qaeda in Iraq as a martyr in 2007, contributing his passport and ID. His recruitment coordinator was Abu Abd Allah, whom he knew through Abu Dajjanah. He flew to Syria, where he met Loua'aie, whom he disliked for taking his $100 and 1,000 rials of a friend and leaving them only $200. His phone number was 009666241428.

Musa'id Hasan 'Abdallah al-Shamrani: alias Abu-Jandal al-Tabuki, a Saudi electrician from Tabuk who was born in 1975 and joined al Qaeda in Iraq as a martyr on May 5, 2007, contributing 200 Saudi riyals and bringing $200, his passport and ID. His recruitment coordinator was Atif, whom he knew via a colleague at a mosque. He arrived from Riyadh via Amman to Damascus, where he met Abu-al-Abbas. Colleague Mish'al's home phone number was 0096644245934.

Muslih bin 'Ali bin 'A'id al-Shamrani: age 28, one of four Saudi terrorists who, on April 22, 1996, confessed to the November 13, 1995 bombing of a building used by U.S. military personnel in Saudi Arabia and said that they had planned other attacks but feared arrest. He claimed to have fought in the Afghan War. He was married and lived in Riyadh's al-'Arija' district. He had worked as a government employee before getting involved in business.

Nayef Shamri: a Saudi terrorist who died on September 6, 2005 following a three-day siege at a seaside villa in Damman's Almubarakia neighborhood in Saudi Arabia.

Saleh Salem Shaninah: alias Abu Salman Al Ghareeb, a Libyan born on February 28, 1982 who joined al Qaeda in Iraq in 2007.

Dr. Fathi al-Shaqaqi: secretary general of the Islamic Jihad Movement in Palestine in 1994. On January 23, 1995, U.S. President Bill Clinton ordered an immediate freeze on his U.S. assets, as his actions constituted a terrorist threat to the Middle East peace process. On October 26, 1995, he was assassinated in Sliema, Malta, by two gunmen on motorcycles. He was carrying a Libyan diplomatic passport for Ibrahim 'Ali al-Shawesh.

Sharad: alias of Bahij 'Abd-al-'Aziz al-Bahiji.

Khalaf Bin-Yusuf Bin-Khalaf al-Shar'an: alias Abu-Yusuf, a Saudi from al-Jawf who was born in 1983 and joined al Qaeda in Iraq on September 19, 2006, when he was assigned to al-Anbar. His recruitment coordinator was Abu-Sarab. He contributed 24,500 Liras and 4,700 Riyals. His father's phone number was 00966503344145, and his brother Muhammad's number was 00966503395125.

Ghassan Abdulah al-Sharbi: a Saudi held at Guantánamo Bay who was charged on May 30, 2008 by the Pentagon with having attended al Qaeda training camps and studying bomb making. He faced a life sentence.

Basit al-Sha'ri: Libya-based recruitment coordinator for al Qaeda in Iraq foreign fighters in 2007.

'Abid 'Abd-'Abid al-Shari: alias Abu-Mus'ab, a Saudi from al-Quriyat born in 1980 who joined al Qaeda in Iraq in 2007, bringing $500. His brother Abu'-Abd-al-Rahman's phone number was 059804282; his brother Abu-Hajir's was 0506399356; his brother 'Abdallah's was 0508720288.

Hamin Bani Shari: named on February 14, 2005 as one of Iraq's 29 most-wanted insurgents. A bounty of between $50,000 and $200,000 was offered.

Abd Al Aziz Bin Fayez Saleh Al Sharie: alias Abu Fayez, from Bilad Al Haramean, who was born in 1407 Hijra, joined al Qaeda in Iraq in 2007, bringing $520. His home phone number was 072812526; his mobile was 0506540727; Muhammad's mobile was 0504745627.

Ahmed Suleiman al Shariehi: alias Abu Annas, a Saudi who joined al Qaeda in Iraq as a martyr in 2007, bringing his passport, ID, 500 euros, and some U.S. cash. His recruitment coordinator was Sa'ad. His sister's phone number as 00966504257848; his father's was 00966504179053.

Muhamad Shariff: alias Abu Naji, an Algerian from Al Muse'ela who joined al Qaeda in Iraq as a martyr in 2007, contributing $50. He said he left his other valuables with a Syrian intelligence officer. His recruitment coordinator was Abu Abd Allah, whom he knew through Abd Al Malek; he as then connected to Samier and Jamal in Bash Garah. The phone numbers of his brothers were 0021372779627, 0021373637427, and 0021390839124.

Husayn 'Ali Bakr al-Sharnubi: arrested on October 15, 1994 by Egyptian police in connection with the October 14, 1994 stabbing of Naguib Mahfouz, the only Arab to receive the Nobel Prize for Literature, in a Cairo suburb.

Belal Abd Al Rahman Al Sharqaui: variant of Bilal 'Abd-al-Rahman al-Sharqawi.

Al-Haj Abdu Ali Sharqawi: a Yemeni arrested in Karachi in February 2002 on suspicion of involvement with al Qaeda. The *Washington Post* reported in December 2007 that he was held in Jordan for 19 months before being moved to Guantánamo.

Bilal 'Abd-al-Rahman al-Sharqawi: variant Belal Abd Al Rahman Al Sharqaui, alias Abu-'Abd-al-Rahman, a Jordanian from Amman who was born on December18, 1970 and joined al Qaeda in Iraq as a martyr on November 17, 2006, contributing his passport, ID, driver's license, $300, and 1,100 lira. His recruitment coordinator was 'Abd-al-Hamid. His brother's phone number was 4027488.

Mahmud Hasani Sharqi: named on February 14, 2005 as one of Iraq's 29 most-wanted insurgents. A bounty of between $50,000 and $200,000 was offered.

Hassan Ramadan Shaukani: an Egyptian Muslim militant hanged on July 17, 1993 by the Egyptian government for the April 20, 1993 attempted assassination of Information Minister Safwat al-Sharif in Heliopolis.

Salim Shiyad (variant Jiyad) Thamir Mutlaq al-Shammari: one of 11 Iraqis and three Kuwaitis arrested on April 13, 1993 by Kuwaiti authorities in a plot to assassinate former U.S. President George H. W. Bush with a bomb during his visit to Kuwait. The Kuwaiti was a lance corporal at the Petroleum Industry Protection Department in the Interior Ministry. He facilitated the movements of the two principals in the plot. On May 10, 1993, Kuwait ruled out extradition, saying it would try the group. On June 4, 1994, the three-judge panel sentenced him to five years.

'Abdal-Aziz Husayn 'Ali Muhamad Shams: member of a cell in Kuwait that set two bombs that exploded on July 10, 1989 in two streets leading to the Great Mosque in Mecca, killing a Pakistani and injuring 16 of the 1.5 million pilgrims from 100 countries attending the hajj. He allegedly went to the Iranian Embassy on June 22, 1989 to obtain the explosives. The Kuwaiti student of Saudi origin said he was recruited two years earlier to join the Followers of the Line of the Imam, a branch of Hizballah. He said he was involved in smuggling the explosives to Saudi Arabia. He claimed Iranian Sadiq 'Ali Reda was to give him money for the operation. He was also recruited to take part in the operation to serve the interests of Iran. He was present in the meetings in Medina and Mecca, and took part in the operation that took place near the Mosque.

Hoseini Shamsodin: an Iranian native of Tehran detained on July 6, 1994 by Philippine police for questioning in connection with the Abu Sayyaf group. He had an expired visa and passport.

Ismail Abu Shanab: senior Hamas figure who was called in by Israeli authorities for questioning after a Palestinian suicide bomber set off a bomb between two school buses on October 29, 1998.

Omar Shanani: a Libya-based recruitment coordinator for foreign fighters for al Qaeda in Iraq in 2006 and 2007.

Shankar: alias of Shaqir.

Rasmi al Shannaq: age 27, a Jordanian arrested by the FBI, Immigration and Naturalization Service, and State Department on June 25, 2002 in Baltimore for overstaying his visa. He lived with American Airlines flight 77, 9/11 Pentagon hijackers Nawaf Alhazmi and Hani Hanjour for two months in the summer of 2001 at a Northern Virginia apartment. On July 9, 2002, authorities detained 31 people, including Shannaq, who entered the United States using phony visas for which they paid $10,000 each from a Jordanian employee of the U.S. Embassy in Qatar in 2000 and 2001.

Abu-'Abd-al-Rahman al-Shanqiti: alias of Jadu Mamim Ahmad Lu'ubaydi.

Khaled Shanquiti: alias "The Mauritanian," he was involved in the bombing of the U.S. embassies in Kenya and Tanzania on August 7, 1998. He is a brother-in-law of Mohambedou Ould Slahi. President Bush ordered his U.S. assets frozen on September 24, 2001.

Fathi al-Shaqaqi: Palestinian Islamic Jihad leader who was killed by an unknown assassin in Malta on October 26, 1995.

Abu Shaqra: name on a forged Lebanese passport used by the four hijackers of a Kuwaiti Airbus A310 en route from Kuwait to Bangkok with intermediate stops in Dubai and Karachi on December 4, 1984.

Khalaf Bin Youssef Bin Khalaf Al Shara'an: alias Abu Youssef, Saudi from Jawaf who was born in 1403 Hijra and joined al Qaeda in Iraq on 26th Sha'aban 1427 Hijra (circa 2007), bringing 24,500 lira and 4,700 rials. His recruitment coordinator was Abu Sirab. His father's phone number was 00966503344145, his brother Muhammed's was 00966503395125.

Uzi Sharabaf: one of three masked gunmen who fired Kalashnikov submachine guns at students milling about a courtyard at the Hebron Islamic College in Israel on July 27, 1983. They also threw a grenade in the attack that killed three and wounded 30. He was arrested for the attack and sentenced to life in prison. On March 27, 1987, President Chaim Herzog commuted the sentences to 24 years each. On December 26, 1990, Israel freed him; a life sentence in Israel usually requires that the convict serve at least 20 years.

Muhammad Ibrahim Sharaf: founder and leader in the 1980s of the Yemeni Islamic Jihad. He had been a member of the Egyptian Islamic Jihad.

Samir Mohamed Hassan Sharara: a resident of Bint Jubayl village in southern Lebanon who hijacked a Gulf Air VC-10 after takeoff from Dubai on June 29, 1977. Armed with a pistol and two grenades, he forced the pilot to land at Doha International Airport in Qatar, where he demanded $125,000 and safe passage to an undisclosed nation. He said he wanted to publicize "south Lebanon, which is subjected every day to thousands of shells and savage, repeated aggressions." After he allowed the passengers to leave, Qatari troops boarded the plane and arrested him.

Bashir Ali Nasser Al-Sharari: born in Yemen in 1970, the Yemeni was believed by the FBI on February 11, 2002, to be planning a terrorist attack in the United States or on U.S. interests in Yemen.

Yusuf al-Sharidi: variant of Yasser Chraidi.

Bandar Bin-Zayn al-'Abidin Bin-Fawwaz al-Sharif: alias Abu-Jayb, a Saudi student from Mecca who was born on April 25, 1988 and joined al Qaeda in Iraq on May 21, 2007 as a combatant. His recruitment coordinator was Abu-'Abdallah, whom he knew through Abu-al-'Abbas. He traveled to Syria, where he met Abu-'Umar. His home phone number was 05564772; his mother's was 0501627527.

Bassam Abu Sharif: spokesman for the Popular Front for the Liberation of Palestine in 1972–1975. He was blinded in the right eye and lost several fingers when a book bomb exploded in his hands in the *al Hadaf* office in Lebanon on July 22, 1972. The book was titled *Days of Terror*.

Khalil Sharif: believed to be the shooter in the May 13, 1996 drive-by shooting by two Hamas gunmen who fired on Jewish settlers at a bus stop near Beit El, killing a U.S.-born seminarian and injuring three other people.

Mohamed Sharif: one of four gunmen posing as patients who, on October 22, 1995, shot to death Dr. Graziella Fumagalli, an Italian doctor working at a tuberculosis hospital in Marka, in her surgery, and wounding biologist Dr. Cristofo Andreoli. He remained at large.

Mohi Adin Sharif: variant of Muhi al-Din Sharif.

Muhi al-Din Sharif: variant Mohi Adin Sharif, a Hamas master bomber residing in Jerusalem whose body was found in Ramallah, West Bank, on March 29, 1998 after a car time bomb containing more than 100 pounds of explosives went off. Pathologists determined that he had been killed by gunfire three hours earlier. He provided the bomb that was used by Sufiyan Jabarin, 26-year-old Hamas suicide bomber who, on August 21, 1995, boarded Egged commuter bus Number 26 in Jerusalem and killed five people and injured 103.

Omar Khan Sharif: age 27, would-be British suicide bomber whose bomb failed to explode on April 29, 2003 at the Mike's Place restaurant in Tel Aviv, Israel. Sharif fled the scene after his bomb failed to detonate. He got rid of his coat and the explosives. He remained at large as of May 9. However, the State Department reported later that his body was found washed up on a Tel Aviv beach. He was born in Derby to an immigrant from Mirpur in the Pakistani-controlled section of Kashmir. His late father had opened Derby's first kebab stand and later owned launderettes and amusement arcades. The youngest of six children, Sharif boarded for two years at the $18,000/year prep school Foremarke Hall. He attended Kingston University in London, where he became a Muslim fundamentalist. He dropped out after a few months, married a woman who spoke little English and wore a burqa. They moved into a cheap row house in Derby near a radical mosque. They had two daughters, aged 3 and 7 as of 2003. He attended religious classes by Sheikh Omar Bakri Muhammed, Syrian-born leader of al-Muhajiroun (the Emigrants), a radical Islamic group.

He and fellow bomber Assif Muhammad Hanif were in Damascus in 2003, where Hanif attended an Arabic course at Damascus University. Sharif told friends he was going to study religion there.

The duo may have used plastic explosives they smuggled into Israel hidden in a Koran. They entered Israel at the Allenby Bridge border crossing with Jordan. Most of the injuries were blast injuries, rather than cuts from shrapnel.

As of May 9, three of Sharif's relatives were in custody his brother, Zahid Hussain Sharif, age 46; his sister, Paveen Akthor Sharif, age 35; and his wife, Tahari Shad Tabassum, age 27, all of Derby. They were held for failing to disclose information about acts of terrorism. Hussain was also charged with aiding and abetting acts of terrorism overseas.

Paveen Akthor Sharif: age 35, of Derby, UK, sister of Omar Khan Sharif. As of May 9, 2003, she was held in custody for failing to disclose information about acts of terrorism.

Sa'd al-Sharif: age 33 in 2001, alias Mustafa Muhammad Ahmed, Shayk Saiid, Mustafa Ahmad al-Hiawi, and Abu Mohammed, Laden's Saudi brother-in-law and financial chief. He was an explosives expert at the Jihad Wal Camp in Afghanistan, according to Jamal Ahmed al-Fadl, a witness in the African embassies bombing trial. His U.S. assets were ordered frozen on October 12, 2001.

Shaykh Said al-Sharif: al Qaeda financial aide listed by the *Washington Post* in late February 2008 as being at large.

Wisam 'Abdallah Jum'ah Al-Sharif: alias Abu-Muslim, a Libyan science student in the Geology Department in Benghazi who was born in 1985 and joined al Qaeda in Iraq as a martyr on July 28, 2007, contributing 3,000 liras, $100, 39,025 Libyan dinars, and 25 Egyptian piasters, along with his passport. His recruitment coordinator was al-Haj, whom he knew via Abu-Turab, who came with him. He went from Libya to Cairo to

Syria, where he met Abu-al-'Abbas. He still had 800 liras with him.

Zahid Hussain Sharif: age 46, of Derby, UK, brother of Omar Khan Sharif. As of May 9, 2003, he was held in custody for failing to disclose information about acts of terrorism and with aiding and abetting acts of terrorism overseas.

Nabil Sharitah: on February 7, 1994, he told the 29th Criminal Bench of the Berlin Regional Court that he did not transport the explosives used in the August 25, 1983 attack on the Maison de France French cultural center in Berlin, in which one person died and 22 were injured. However, he said that he gave explosives stored at the Syrian Embassy in East Berlin to Red Army Faction (RAF) member Johannes Weinrich only a few hours before the bombing. Sharitah was third secretary of the Syrian Embassy at the time and in charge of security. He had given himself up to German authorities.

Al Shariff: alias of Nadzmimie Sabtulah.

Muwafaq 'Abbas Shartah: one of five alleged Iraqi agents and members of the October 17 Movement for the Liberation of the Syrian People who were arrested by Syria in connection with the multiple bombings of public buses in Syria on April 16, 1986 that killed 27 people and wounded 100. The five were tried and convicted. They were executed on August 24, 1987.

Shashu: alias Abu-Bilah, who was born in 1986 and traveled from France to join al Qaeda in Iraq in 2007. His travel coordinator was Abu-Muhammad. He brought his passport and ID. His phone number was 490531918.

Habib Tanyus ash-Shartouni: variant of Habib Tanyus ash-Shartuni.

Habib Tanyus ash-Shartuni: variant Shartouni, allegedly confessed to the bombing on September 14, 1982 in east Beirut, Lebanon, that killed

President-elect Bashir Gemayel and eight others and wounded at least 50 people. The Phalange turned him over to the Lebanese government on April 26, 1983.

Abu Shattrey: alias of Ali Faraj Muhammad Suleiman.

Abu Shattri: alias of Ali Faraj Muhammad Soliman.

'Umar Jibril al-Shawahin: one of a group of Jordanian Afghans tried on December 21, 1994 by the Jordanian State Security Court for belonging to an illegal society, participating in a conspiracy to carry out terrorist acts, and possessing explosives for illegal purposes. The Muslim fundamentalists bombed cinemas, wounding nine people, including an attack on January 26, 1994 at an Amman cinema showing what they perceived to be pornographic films, and another bombing on February 1, 1994. The group had been seized in a crackdown on Muslim radicals in January 1994. Their trial began on August 27, 1994, when they were accused of planning to assassinate leading Jordanians, including 'Abd-al-Salam al-Majali, Jordan's former chief peace negotiator with Israel. One of those sentenced to death was Muhammad Jamal Khalifah, a Saudi fugitive son-in-law of Osama bin Laden. He was acquitted.

Ibrahim 'Ali al-Shawesh: name on Libyan diplomatic passport carried by Fathi Shaqaqi when he was shot to death in Malta on October 26, 1995.

Yasser Abu Shaweesh: on January 23, 2005, in a morning raid in Mainz, German police arrested Ibrahim Mohamed Khalil, age 29, a German citizen from Iraq who was suspected of planning suicide attacks in Germany, and, Shaweesh, 31, a Palestinian medical student living in Bonn. They were believed to have had contacts with Osama bin Laden, and were charged with belonging to a foreign terrorist organization. The Federal Prosecutor's Office said there was no indication that they had organized an al Qaeda cell in Germany. While in Afghanistan, where he trained before the 9/11 attacks, Khalil had contacts with bin Laden and Ramzi Binalshibh. Khalil fought U.S. forces for more than a year in Afghanistan and had high-ranking al Qaeda contacts who persuaded him to recruit suicide attackers in Europe. He moved to Germany in September 2002 to raise money and provide logistical support for al Qaeda. He had attempted unsuccessfully to obtain 48 grams of uranium from Luxembourg. Khalil recruited the Libyan-born Shaweesh for a suicide attack in Iraq. They had sought to raise money by taking out a $1 million life insurance policy on Yasser Abu S., who was to fake a fatal traffic accident. The duo had been under investigation since October 2004. Police searched four apartments in Mainz and Bonn.

The previous week, German police had detained nearly two dozen Islamic extremists.

German authorities had wiretapped the duo, and heard them make plans to move to the Netherlands, to obtain uranium for a dirty bomb that would kill Americans, and to recruit suicide bombers to go to Iraq. They talked about how to blend in to their surroundings. Khalil married a Syrian woman who had recently obtained German citizenship, which in turn permitted him to stay legally in Germany.

In late January, the judge ruled that there was enough evidence to hold them for trial.

Fa'iq Salih al-Shawish: one of a group of Jordanian Afghans sentenced on December 21, 1994 by the Jordanian State Security Court for belonging to an illegal society, participating in a conspiracy to carry out terrorist acts, and possessing explosives for illegal purposes. The Muslim fundamentalists bombed cinemas, wounding nine people, including an attack on January 26, 1994 at an Amman cinema showing what they perceived to be pornographic films, and another bombing on February 1, 1994. The group had been seized in a crackdown on Muslim radicals in January 1994. Their trial began on August 27, 1994, when they were accused of planning to assassinate leading Jordanians, including 'Abd-al-Salam al-Majali, Jordan's former chief peace negotiator with Israel. One of those sentenced to death was Muhammad Jamal Khalifah, a Saudi fugitive son-in-law of Osama bin Laden. Al-Shawish was sentenced to 7 and a half years.

Shawqi: alias Abu Haffis, an Algerian from Al Wadd who joined al Qaeda in Iraq as a fighter in 2007. He had experience with computers. His phone number was 021332217711.

'Ali Shawqi: alias of Muhammad Brazim Jayyusi, a Lebanese whose eight-day detention was ordered by Limassol's district court in connection with the Black June attack in which a grenade was thrown into the Shoham, Limassol, Cyprus offices of an Israeli shipping firm on September 23, 1981, injuring three female and two male Greek Cypriot employees.

Ka'b al-Shaybani: alias of Farid.

Sami al-Shayib: alias 'Isam, identified by Doha's *al-Sharq* on March 19, 1993 as a member of the Abu Nidal Group's Central Committee.

Al-Shaykh: alias of 'Abd al-Aziz Awda.

'Abdallah al-Shaykh: alias Abu-al-Zubayr al-Jaddawi, a Jeddah-based Saudi who was born on August 14, 1985 and joined al Qaeda in Iraq on September 13, 2006. His local recruiter was Abu-Hammam. He brought with him 1,351 riyals, $600, 5,950 lira, and a cell phone. He offered the phone numbers of Abu-'Umar: 0566551929 and 0503611521.

'Imad Ash-Shaykh: alias of Lieutenant 'Imad ad-Din Mustafa Shakir 'Ayyad, member of the Fatah Revolutionary Council who was killed on July 19, 1978 in an attack on the FRC offices in Tripoli, Libya by five members of Fatah.

Mujahid Shaykh: alias of Osama bin Laden.

Amir Hussein Shaykhan: on April 11, 2005, he confessed that he and a Syrian kidnapped French journalists Christian Chesnot of *RFI* and George Malbrunot of *Le Figaro* on August 19, 2004 in Iraq. The duo were freed in December 2004.

Abu-Shayma': a Lebanon-based recruitment coordinator for al Qaeda in Iraq in 2007.

Abu-Shayma': alias of Lakhlaf.

Ka'aen al Shebani: alias of Faried.

Basem Muhammad Shebli: alias Abu Omar, a Syrian from Dyr Al Zur who joined al Qaeda in Iraq as a martyr in 2007, bringing 15,500 lira. His recruitment coordinator was Al Hajji. His phone number was 310449.

Hanni Muhammad Al Shebli: alias Abu Al Zubear, a factory work from Al Quayem, Annizah who joined al Qaeda in Iraq as a fighter in 2007, bringing with him his passport, ID, bank book, and watch. He took a bus to Syria, where he was met by Abu Omar and Abu Ahamed. Loua'aie relieved him of 3,000 of his 10,000 rials. He said mujahedeen supporter Saleh could be contacted through his brother on his phone: 0096655880730. Al Shebli's home phone number was 009666346544.

Mohammed Shehada: age 25, a Jordanian convicted on July 11, 2007 by a Jordanian military court to three years of hard labor for plotting to attack Americans living in Jordan.

Salah Shehada: a leader of the Izzedine al-Qassam Brigades of Hamas who was killed on July 22, 2002 in an Israeli air strike.

Michael Shehadeh: on September 22, 2003, the Bush administration invoked the Patriot Act in the 16-year effort to deport him and Khader Hamide, two Palestinians who allegedly distributed magazines and raised funds in California for the Popular Front for the Liberation of

Palestine. Earlier court rulings had deemed the deportation unconstitutional because the duo was not involved in terrorist activity. In the earlier cases, they had been part of the LA Eight charged with violations of the McCarran-Walter Act against membership in communist organizations. On January 30, 2007, immigration Judge Bruce J. Einhorn dismissed a 20-year effort by the U.S. government to deport the two Palestinians after the FBI and Department of Homeland Security failed to turn over any potentially exculpatory information per orders in 1986, 1993, 1994, and 2005. They were represented by David Cole of the Center for Constitutional Rights, Marc Van Der Hout of the National Lawyers Guild, and Ahilan Arulanantham of the American Civil Liberties Union.

Abu Mustafa al-Sheibani: a leader of Shi'ite extremists based in Iran as of January 2008. His network included hundreds of members in several pro-Iranian insurgent groups in the south that specialize in roadside bombs against Americans and sabotage of UK forces in the area. His assets were subjected to financial sanctions by the U.S. Treasury on January 9, 2008 under Executive Order 13438.

Margalit Har-Sheif: age 22, convicted on June 14, 1998 by the Tel Aviv Magistrates Court of knowing Yigal Amir's intention to assassinate Israeli Prime Minister Yitzhak Rabin on November 4, 1995 and failing to inform the police. She said she did not believe him and thought he was trying to impress her. Her lawyer planned an appeal. On September 27, 1998, she was sentenced to nine months, with another 15 months suspended.

Khaled Awad Shehada: a 24-year-old Palestinian resident of the Jabaliya refugee camp in the Gaza Strip who, on December 5, 1993, opened fire with an Israeli-made automatic rifle as he boarded a public bus in Holon in central Israel, killing a 32-year-old reserve soldier. The bus driver shoved the killer out the door, then sped away. Other soldiers in the back of the bus fired on the terrorist, hitting him. Other soldiers at the bus stop also fired, killing the member of Islamic Jihad. His brother was active in the Islamic Jihad in Damascus, Syria. He had been allowed to exit Gaza on a student permit.

Moua'aied Khalef Shehaza: alias Abu Muhammad, a Syrian from Dye al Zur who had experience as a coordinator in Syria and who joined Al Qaeda in Iraq as a martyr in 2007, bringing 100 lira. His recruitment coordinator was Al Hajji. His phone number was 654736.

Marwan Al-Shehhi: age 23, of the United Arab Emirates (UAE), one of the al Qaeda hijackers who, on September 11, 2001, took over United Airlines flight 175, a B767 flying from Boston's Logan International Airport to Los Angeles International Airport with 65 people, including seven flight attendants and two pilots. The plane was diverted across New Jersey, pulled sharply right, and just missed crashing into two other airliners as it descended toward Manhattan. UA flight 175 crashed into New York City's 110-story World Trade Center South Tower at 9:05 A.M. He had resided in a Hamburg apartment with Muhammad Atta and had been enrolled in the local Technical University. German authorities said he was born in the UAE.

Fahad Shehri: arrested on March 18, 1997 by Canadian immigration officials. The Saudi had arrived in Canada in December 1996 and claimed refugee status. He said he was wanted for questioning in Saudi Arabia for the June 25, 1996 truck bombing of the U.S. military's compound at Khobar Towers near Dhahran that killed 19 U.S. airmen and wounded 547 others. He claimed he feared for his life. The U.S. and Riyadh said he was not a suspect. The Canadian government charged him with being a terrorist on March 26, 1997. Some reports indicated that he had bought weapons for Central Asian Muslim fighters. He was held in the Ottawa Detention Center.

Ahmed Darwish Al-Sheihhi: name used by one of three men carrying Omani passports who on September 9, 2001 left the Philippines in haste for Bangkok after being questioned by a policeman for videotaping the U.S. embassy on two separate days. Philippine police said they might have been making a bomb in their Manila Bayview Park Hotel room; traces of TNT were found in the room. Philippine authorities said their surnames were similar to three of the 9/11 hijackers' names. The trio flew from Bangkok separately on September 1 and 7.

Bader Darwis Homahhed Al-Sheihhi: name used by one of three men carrying Omani passports who, on September 9, 2001, left the Philippines in haste for Bangkok after being questioned by a policeman for videotaping the U.S. embassy on two separate days. Philippine police said they might have been making a bomb in their Manila Bayview Park Hotel room; traces of TNT were found in the room. Philippine authorities said their surnames were similar to three of the 9/11 hijackers' names. The trio flew from Bangkok separately on September 1 and 7.

Khaled Abdulla Mohammed Al-Sheihhi: name used by one of three men carrying Omani passports who on September 9, 2001 left the Philippines in haste for Bangkok after being questioned by a policeman for videotaping the US Embassy on two separate days. Philippine police said they might have been making a bomb in their Manila Bayview Park Hotel room; traces of TNT were found in the room. Philippine authorities said their surnames were similar to three of the 9/11 hijackers' names. The trio flew from Bangkok separately on September 1 and 7.

The Sheik: alias of 'Abd al-Aziz Awda.

Abd Allah Al Sheik: alias Abu Al Zubear al Jadawie, a Saudi from Jeddah who was born on 28/11/1405 Hijra and joined al Qaeda in Iraq on 20th Sha'aban 1427 Hijra (2007), bringing 1,351 rials, $660, a bag, and 5,950 lira. His recruitment coordinator was Abu Hmam. His phone numbers were 0566551929 and 0503611521.

Ahmad Omar Saeed Sheik: alias of Sheik Omar Saeed.

Mara'ai Hammed Omar al Sheik: alias Saraqah, a Libyan born in 1970 who joined al Qaeda in Iraq in 2007, bringing $100. He said Hassan's phone number was 0925152199; his uncle's was 0925128260; Rajab's was 0913798492; and Ramadan's was 0926243279.

Al Sheikh: alias of 'Abd al-Aziz Awda.

Abbas Hussain Sheikh: an Indian arrested as an accomplice to two men arrested on June 14, 2001 by Indian police for plotting to bomb the U.S. Embassy.

Jelani Abu Sheikh: sold the car to Saleh Ali Saleh Nabhan that he traded in to buy the green Mitsubishi SUV used in the November 28, 2002 suicide attack on the Israeli-owned Paradise Hotel in Kenya in which 16 died and 80 were injured.

Osman el-Sheikh: one of three Sudanese roommates of Fares Khalafalla, one of eight foreign Islamists arrested on June 24, 1993 by the FBI and charged with planning to bomb the UN headquarters building in Manhattan; 26 Federal Plaza, which includes the local FBI headquarters and other agencies; the Forty-Seventh Street diamond district, which is run principally by Orthodox Jews; and the Lincoln and Holland tunnels connecting Manhattan and New Jersey; and planning to assassinate Senator Alfonse M. D'Amato (R-NY), Assemblyman Dov Hiking, an Orthodox Jewish legislator from Brooklyn, UN Secretary General Boutros Boutros-Ghali, and Egyptian President Hosni Mubarak. He was arrested and held on a $75,000 bond because the Immigration and Naturalization Service said "the circumstances of their arrests indicate they may pose a threat to society." They had entered the United

States on tourist visas that had expired. They initially were not charged in the plot.

Sa'id Awlad al-Sheikh: alias Abu-Qutadah, a Moroccan from Jabal Rarsah, 'Uthman Bin-'Affan Street who was born in 1984 and joined al Qaeda in Iraq in 2007. He was assigned to al Anbar. His home phone number was 0021239711855; the house number was 195. His brother's home phone number was 0021261725481.

Hossein Sheikhattar: an arrest warrant was issued for the aide to the Iranian telecommunications minister in connection with the August 6, 1991 assassination of former Iranian Premier Shapur Bakhtiar in his Paris home.

David Shemtov: arrested on January 20, 1984 for supplying a hand grenade that was placed beneath a van owned by a leader of Israel's Peace Now movement that exploded during the group's demonstration on February 10, 1983 outside Prime Minister Menachem Begin's office. The grenade killed one person and injured nine.

Abdul Sherif: age 30, convicted on February 5, 2008 in a London court of 22 charges of failing to disclose information about terrorism and assisting an offender in connection with the failed copycat bombing of the London transit system in July 2005. He was sentenced to 10 years. The five defendants provided safe houses, passports, clothing, and food for the would-be bombers after the failed attacks. Sherif is the brother of Hussain Osman, a convicted bomber.

Abdul-Aziz el-Sherif: an emir of the Egyptian Islamic Jihad and associate of Ayman al-Zawahiri. His 1980s Basic Principles in Making Preparations for Jihad became the theological rationale for al Qaeda's terrorist campaign, as well as for that of other Islamists. He said that judges, lawyers, soldiers, police, and most of Egyptian society were apostates and thus legitimate targets for killing. He was arrested in Yemen in 2001 and extradited in 2004 to Egypt, where he was imprisoned. He was put in isolation in the Toura prison south of Cairo. In 2007, he reportedly had changed his rationale for armed struggle and was writing a jailhouse book to that effect.

Bassam Towfik Sherif: also known as Bassam Zayad, Popular Front for the Liberation of Palestine spokesman who took credit for the Japanese Red Army's attack on Lod Airport on May 30, 1972.

Sheroo: alias of Sher Mohammad Malikkheil.

Rida Shiban: a Lebanese national believed detained for questioning for his involvement with two terrorists who were trying to plant a 200-pound bomb at a building housing the U.S. Information Service Thomas Jefferson Library that exploded prematurely in Manila on January 19, 1991. He had been staying at the Travelers Inn a few hours before the bombing.

Abdesslam Issa Shibani: a Libyan intelligence officer believed to be linked to the September 19, 1989 bombing of the UTA DC-10 aircraft over Chad. Observers expected French Investigating Judge Jean-Louis Bruguiere to issue an arrest warrant following his July 5–18, 1996 visit to Libya. On June 12, 1998, France announced that it would try him, along with five other Libyans, in absentia. On March 10, 1999, a French antiterrorism court imposed life in prison on the six in absentia. If any of the six were to fall into French hands, they would automatically be given a retrial under French law. The prosecutor said the evidence showed that the Libyan officials had organized the attack. France had never formally requested extradition of the six. Qadhafi had earlier said he would turn the six over to France, but also had said he would consider making the six serve any sentence imposed by a French court in Libyan prison.

Milad Shibani: one of four accomplices of two Libyan intelligence officers arrested by the FBI on July 20, 1988 on charges of plotting to assassinate former National Security Council aide U.S.

Marine Colonel Oliver L. North. The Arlington, Virginia resident was the chair of the McLean, Virginia-based Peoples Committee for Libyan Students. U.S. Magistrate Leonie Brinkema set bond between $25,000 and $50,000. The group apparently was planning revenge against U.S. officials believed to have planned the April 1986 air raid against Libya in retaliation for Libyan involvement in several terrorist attacks. On July 22, he faced charges of violating his Arlington Carlyle House cooperatives' adults-only policy for living with his spouse and children and faced eviction. On July 28, 1988, a federal grand jury handed down a 40-count indictment, charging the group with conspiracy, money laundering, and violations of U.S. trade sanctions against Libya.

Mursad Shibbu: leader of the Lebanese Revolutionary Socialist Organization in the 1970s.

Abdel Hamid Shibli: one of two Black September members who were seriously injured when their explosives-laden car blew up on a Rome street on June 17, 1973. He was a Jordanian. It was believed they were driving their booby-trapped car toward their next mission, which may have been against the transit camp in Austria for Soviet Jewish émigrés. Some reports claim that Mossad arranged for the bombs' premature detonation.

Akram Sa'id Shihab: a Jordanian of Palestinian origin who resides in the Gaza Strip. He was wanted for questioning in the case of two masked gunmen who, on February 4, 1990, intercepted a Safaja Tours bus on the Ismailia–Cairo desert road, where they fired automatic weapons and threw 4 grenades, killing 10 and injuring 19. He spent four days at the Helio-Park Hotel in Heliopolis, a Cairo suburb, and made phone calls to Israel and Algeria during his stay.

Hassan Shihadah: name used by one of three terrorists reported by Paraguay's *Noticias* on August 31, 1994 to have entered the country on August 27, 1994 to conduct a bombing against the Jewish community in Buenos Aires. They were to travel from Barcelona, Spain via Hungary and Germany then to Rio de Janeiro or Sao Paulo, then to Foz do Iguacu or Asuncion, to Ciudad del Este, then onward with their explosives to Buenos Aires for a September 3 attack. He was born in 1969, was blond and bearded.

Shaykh Salah Shihadah: his release was demanded by the Hamas members who, on October 9, 1994, kidnapped Israeli Corporal Nachshon Mordekhay Wachsman from Jerusalem's 'Atarot junction.

Thirwat Shihata: an Egyptian Islamic Jihad operational planner who arrived in Iraq in mid-May 2002. Possibly the same person described subsequently. On September 24, 2001, President George W. Bush ordered his U.S. assets frozen.

Tharwat Salah Shihatah: fugitive sentenced to death on March 17, 1994 by the Higher Military Court in Cairo in connection with the November 25, 1993 bombing of the convoy of Egyptian Prime Minister Dr. 'Atif Sidqi that killed a 15-year-old girl and wounded 21 other people.

Riyadh Shikawi: possibly a Yemeni, believed by the FBI, on February 11, 2002, to be planning a terrorist attack in the United States or on U.S. interests in Yemen.

Khaled Shimmiri: age 20, a deranged (according to the Kuwaiti government) Kuwaiti junior traffic policeman who, on November 21, 2002, shot and seriously wounded two American soldiers who were driving between bases. Shimmiri fired on them at 10:30 A.M. after pulling them over on the highway between their headquarters at Camp Doha and Arifjan, a Kuwaiti base. The Americans, one injured in the face, the other in the shoulder, did not return fire. They were in a civilian vehicle and were not in uniform. The Kuwaiti was arrested in Saudi Arabia the next day and extradited to Kuwait on November 23. On March 5, 2003, he was convicted and sentenced to 15 years in prison. His attorney said he would appeal. Judge

Nayef Mutairat sentenced Shimmiri to ten years for attempted murder and five years for unlawful possession of a weapon, to be served consecutively. He also ordered Shimmiri to be dismissed from the Kuwaiti police force.

David Ben-Shimol: an Israeli soldier who was captured on November 2, 1984 following an attack on an Arab bus. He was also held for the September 22, 1984 grenade attack in a crowded Arab coffee shop in Jerusalem that injured four people. On April 18, 1985, he was convicted of both crimes.

Sayyid Fahmi al-Shinnawi: a famous Egyptian urologist who was 1 of 40 Shi'ite terrorists arrested in Egypt on August 19, 1989 for planning to carry out attacks against U.S., Israeli, Saudi, Iraqi, and Kuwaiti interests, including embassies and airlines. He had treated Ayatollah Khomeini in London.

Mohammad Ridha Ghulam Shirazi: an Iranian who was 1 of 13 members of the Iranian Lebanese Hizballah reported by Madrid *Diario 16* on October 20, 1987 as having entered Spain on October 13, 1987 to attack diplomats from Saudi Arabia, Kuwait, and Iraq.

Omar Shishani: age 47, arrested on July 17, 2002 by U.S. Customs agents when they discovered that the Jordanian-born man was carrying $12 million in false cashiers' checks as he arrived at Detroit Metropolitan Airport from Indonesia. He appeared on a watch list of people trained in Afghanistan by al Qaeda; his name had turned up in captured documents in Afghanistan. Shishani was carrying a U.S. passport and claimed to be a naturalized citizen. Investigators searching his bags found nine cashier's checks—two for $5 million each, two for $500,000 each, and five for $200,000 each. Six checks were posted for June; one for September 2002. The faked checks were supposedly issued by the Pomona, California branch of West America Bank (which does not have a Pomona branch). The checks had the

words "cashier's check" on them; the bank uses the term "official check." On July 23, a federal grand jury indicted Shishani on charges of possession of counterfeit security and smuggling merchandise into the United States. On July 24, U.S. District Court Magistrate Judge Donald A. Scheer ordered Shishani held without bond after prosecutors said he had acknowledged that Baharuddin Masse, who was listed on six of the checks, could be part of al Qaeda and that he had made "pro al Qaeda statements" and had named his daughter "al Qaeda." Shishani was carrying a photocopy of Masse's passport. Judge Scheer called Shishani a flight risk who faced 15 years in prison. The maximum penalty for the counterfeiting charge is 10 years and a $250,000 fine; on the other charge, 5 years and a $250,000 fine.

Shishani had previously lived in San Francisco and Napa, California. He claimed to be a salesman who had earned no commissions this year. He said his wife was a resident alien from Japan who works for Northwest Airlines. His family is from Chechnya. One source said he had served with the Jordanian army. He had claimed to come from a powerful Jordanian family with close relations to the king and the military. He claimed to have served in the Jordanian intelligence service from 1974 to 1976, and that his brother was commander of the Jordanian Special Forces. He had lived in the United States since 1979 and became a U.S. citizen in 1989, according to his lawyer. His attorney said he was merely a broker, carrying the checks for a client. Shishani had fired for Chapter 7 bankruptcy while living in San Francisco in 1991. He incorporated Shojoma Trading and Consulting Company, in Michigan in 1993, and dissolved it in 1996. He had no apparent source of income; his Northwest Airlines flight attendant wife was temporarily unemployed.

Members of the U.S. Joint Terrorism Task Force in Detroit searched Shishani's Dearborn, Michigan apartment the next day. Authorities found several financial documents, including a December 2000 net worth statement indicating $38.5 million in assets. His lawyer said he didn't even own his home, and authorities said the document could be a fake to be used in a scam.

A U.S. Secret Service agent was later suspended for writing an anti-Islam epithet ("Islam is Evil, Christ is King") on a Muslim prayer calendar in Shishani's home.

Jabir Shita: release from an Israeli jail was demanded on June 27, 1976 by the Popular Front for the Liberation of Palestine hijackers of Air France flight 139, an A300 flying from Tel Aviv to Paris and ultimately diverted to Entebbe.

Tawfiq wat al-Shiyar: one of six Muslims detained on May 26, 1989 at Larnaca, Cyprus for conspiring to murder General Michel 'Awn, leader of the Lebanese Phalangists, and for possession of arms, missiles, and munitions. The six were due to be tried by a Larnaca criminal court on October 9, 1989. On August 30, 1989, the Muslim 14 March group threatened to hijack a Cyprus Airlines plane if the government did not release them. The group seeks to avenge the 40 Lebanese Muslims who were killed by 'Awn's troops on March 14, 1989.

Nasser Shkirat: a 22-year-old who, on March 22, 1993, stabbed six Israeli Jews at Jerusalem's Kennedy High School with a kitchen knife. He held a Koran in the other hand.

Amer Shkokani: a Palestinian from El Bireh in the West Bank who, on May 24, 2002, tried to ram his car filled with explosives into a crowded Tel Aviv Studio 49 dance club. Eli Federman, a quick-thinking security guard, fired through the windshield. The driver fell from the car, which blew up before impact, injuring three passersby. Federman said "then I fired the rest of the bullets into his head," killing the terrorist. The al-Aqsa Martyrs Brigades claimed credit.

Mohamad Ibrahim Shnewer: age 22, born in Jordan, a U.S. citizen living in Cherry Hill, New Jersey and working as a taxi driver in Philadelphia, he was one of six men arrested by the FBI on May 27, 2007 in Cherry Hill, New Jersey planning on attacking Fort Dix and killing 100 soldiers with assault rifles and grenades. They were alleged to have conducted firearms training in the Pocono Mountains in Gouldsboro, Pennsylvania. The defendants used cell phones to conduct video surveillances. A Circuit City clerk spotted footage and jihad training videos they wanted transferred to DVD and alerted authorities in January 2006. An Egyptian military veteran worked with the FBI in befriending a suspect and taping conversations. The FBI described the cell as a leaderless homegrown group without apparent ties to al Qaeda, although other reports claimed Shnewer was the de facto leader. The group had considered Fort Monmouth in New Jersey; Dover Air Force Base in Delaware; the U.S. Coast Guard Building in Philadelphia; Fort Dix; and other locations. They picked Fort Dix because Serdar Tatar had delivered pizzas there from his family-owned Super Mario Pizza and had a map of the base. The group also planned to attack a U.S. naval base in Philadelphia just before the Army–Navy football game. He was the brother-in-law of the Duka brothers, who were also arrested. He was represented by attorney Rocco Cipparone. The six were ordered held without bail on May 11; only Shnewer had requested bail. He was charged with conspiring to kill military personnel, which carries a life sentence.

Shouieb: Lebanon-based recruitment coordinator of foreign fighters for al Qaeda in Iraq in 2007.

Yosef Shouli: a 23-year-old identified by the Israeli government on September 23, 1997 as one of four Palestinians living in the West Bank village of Asirah Shamaliya, north of Nablus, who were responsible for an attack on July 30, 1997 and the September 4, 1997 attack in which three Palestinians set off bombs in Ben Yehuda Street in Jerusalem, killing themselves, five others, and wounding 190 shoppers, including many foreign visitors, of whom some were American.

Hamid al-Shoumi: arrested on April 6, 2007 in Yemen after terrorists doused worshipers with fuel in a mosque, locked the doors, and torched the facility, wounding 33 people in Amran, south of Saada, where government troops are fighting Shi'ite Muslims who want to install a caliphate in the Sunni-dominated country.

Abdel Majid Shouraibi: a Moroccan expelled by the British Home Office to France on May 17, 1984 for "preparing acts of terrorism."

Bader Shourie: alias Abu Muhammad al Attawi, a Moroccan electrician from Casablanca who was born in 1982 and joined al Qaeda in Iraq as a martyr in 2007, contributing 100 euros and 45 lira and providing his passport and Spanish ID. His recruitment coordinator was Edriess. He arrived in Syria from Spain and Turkey. In Syria, he met Abu Muhammad, who took 50 of his 250 euros. His phone number was 00212621645.

Mohammed Shqeir: age 19, a Palestinian member of the Al-Aqsa Martyrs Brigades from Nablus, who, on October 27, 2002, set off a suicide bomb at a gas station in Ariel, a Jewish settlement in the West Bank, killing three soldiers and himself and wounding 20. He was grabbed by two bystanders and shot in the head by Israeli soldiers, who were unable to stop him from setting off his explosive belt as he fell. The Brigades said he was to "avenge the killing of Palestinian civilians by Israeli troops." Hamas separately claimed credit. The terrorist groups gave different names for the bomber. Hamas said he was Mohammad Bustami.

Muhammad 'Ali 'Ali al-Shraqawi: said by the Ethiopian Supreme State Security Prosecution on August 7, 1995 as being one of five terrorists who had confessed to training in the al-Kamp and Kangu camps in Khartoum with two of the nine Egyptian Islamic Group gunmen who, on June 25, 1995, fired on the armored limousine of Egyptian President Hosni Mubarak in Addis Ababa.

Taher Shriteh: a Gaza journalist who worked for *Reuters* and other foreign news organizations who was among the 1,200 Palestinians and other activists arrested by Israel after Hamas kidnapped Senior Master Sergeant Nissim Toledano on December 13, 1992.

Fadl Shrourou: chief spokesman for Ahmed Jibril, leader of the Popular Front for the Liberation of Palestine-General Command. He denied responsibility for the December 21, 1988 Lockerbie bombing of Pan Am 103 that killed 270 people.

Shuaib: alias of Ahmad Muhammad Hamid Ali.

Hamid Muhammad Shu'ayb: alias Abu-'Abd-al-Rahman, a Libyan born in 1984 who joined al Qaeda in Iraq in 2007. He said Tariq's phone number was 00218+926822096.

Jamal Shuayb: an Egyptian Islamic Jihad (EIJ) member who was deported by South Africa to Egypt in November 1998. He had been collecting funds from local Muslims and sending them to the EIJ in Egypt.

Fuad Shubaki: one of three men arrested on January 11, 2002 by the Palestinian Authority in connection with the *Karine*, a cargo ship that was boarded by Israeli navy commanders on January 3, 2002 in the Red Sea. They found 50 tons of weapons, including Katyusha rockets, antitank missiles, mortars, mines, and sniper rifles, believed to have originated in Iran and to be headed for the Palestinian Authority. The weapons were in quantities banned by the 1993 Oslo peace agreement. Israel said interrogation of the 13 crewmen determined that the arms smuggling was coordinated by Lebanese Hizballah. Shubaki was a major general in Yasser Arafat's security forces, whom Israel claimed is the Palestinians' main weapons buyer. On May 1, 2002, as part of a deal between Israel and the Palestinian Authority that led to Yasser Arafat's release from his besieged headquarters, the Palestinian Authority turned over to UK and

U.S. guards Fuad Shubaki, Arafat's chief accountant.

Muhamad Shubaki: one of four Arab terrorists who fired small arms and threw grenades at Jewish religious students in the West Bank on May 2, 1980, killing five settlers and injuring 17. The Palestine Liberation Organization's Unit of the Martyr Ibrahim Abu Safwat claimed credit. On September 16, 1980, Israeli security forces arrested the four terrorists plus six Fatah accomplices who had helped them hide in caves in the Hebron hills. Shubaki also admitted to the murder of Uriel and Hadassa Baraq, two Israeli tourists whose bodies were discovered on March 1, 1980 in the Bet Govrin region.

Layth Shubaylat: in a raid on a residence on October 3, 1992, Jordanian police uncovered weapons, documents, and photographs indicating that the Shabab al-Nafir al-Islami group planned to attack the U.S., UK, and French embassies. On October 5, the prosecutor told the State Security Court that the Lower House member had pleaded not guilty to charges of affiliation with a group plotting to overthrow the regime and possession of illegal weapons. The group had financial support from the Popular Front for the Liberation of Palestine-General Command.

Hani Muhammad al-Shubayli: alias Abu-al-Zubayr, a Saudi businessman from al-Qasim and 'Unayzah who joined al Qaeda in Iraq as a fighter in 2007, contributing his passport, ID, bank statements, and watch. He brought 10,000 riyals with him; his contacts in Syria, Abu-'Umar and Abu-Ahmad, requested 3,000 of them. He had arrived by caravan. His home phone number was 009666346544; Salah's number was 0096655880730.

Fu'ad Shudayfat: cadet sentenced to hang on January 16, 1994 in connection with a plot foiled on June 26, 1993 to assassinate Jordanian King Hussein during the graduation ceremony at Muta University, a Jordanian military academy. His sentence was commuted to 15 years at hard labor.

Abdel Labi Shudi: on June 11, 1980, he shot Libyan dissident Mohammed Saad Biget in a dispute as they lunched together in Rome. Shudi was arrested.

Shukran Shukran: release from an Israeli jail was demanded on June 27, 1976 by the Popular Front for the Liberation of Palestine hijackers of Air France flight 139, an A300 flying from Tel Aviv to Paris and ultimately diverted to Entebbe.

Ahmad Husayn Muhammad Shukri: on October 25, 1989, the Tel Aviv District Court imposed life plus 20 years on him for murdering Mikha'el Ashtamkar in Israel on September 7, 1989 and the next day trying to veer a bus traveling along the Jerusalem-Tel Aviv line into a ravine.

Adnan G. El Shukrijumah: variant Adnan G. el Shukri Jumah, Abu Arif, Ja'far al-Tayar, Jaffar al-Tayyar, Jafar Tayar, Jaafar al-Tayyar, a Saudi born on August 4, 1975 in Medina, Saudi Arabia and wanted in connection with possible terrorist threats against the United States. He carries a Guyanese passport, but is also believed to carry passports from Saudi Arabia, Canada, and Trinidad. He is about five feet four inches tall and weighs 132 pounds. The Rewards for Justice Program of the State Department offers $5 million for his capture. On March 25, 2003, the U.S. District Court for the Eastern District of Virginia issued a Material Witness Warrant for his arrest. He was believed possibly involved with al Qaeda terrorist activities.

A law enforcement spokesman said in March 2003 that he could be an organizer similar to Mohammad Atta, the 9/11 orchestrator. El Shukrijumah's name came up often in interrogations of Khalid Sheik Mohammed, the operations chief of al Qaeda. He was believed to have a connection to Jose Padilla, who was arrested in May 2002 on suspicion of planning to set off a radiological bomb in the U.S. The alias was also linked to the Oklahoma flight school where Zacarias Moussaoui studied aviation. He last entered the United States before 9/11 and left in 2001. Some authorities believed he was in Morocco or had reentered the United States illegally. The family had moved to Miramar, north of Miami, Florida, in 1995. His father is a prominent Muslim leader in that suburb and leads a prayer center, Masjid al Hijrah, next door to his home, which was searched by FBI agents. One of the suspect's addresses was a house in Pembroke Pines, Florida, where Padilla attended a mosque. The FBI said he had taken the battle name Ja'far al-Tayar (Ja'far the Pilot), used the alias Abu Arif, and had conferred with Ramzi Binalshibh, a 9/11 coordinator; field commander Abu Zubayda; and Khalid Sheik Mohammed, al Qaeda operations chief. He attended an al Qaeda explosives training camp in 2000, according to investigators. His name was also connected to Norman, Oklahoma, where Zacarias Moussaoui received flight training.

Adnan was the eldest of five children. He was born in 1975 in Saudi Arabia to a Guyanese father and Saudi mother. His father was the first Westerner to graduate from Medina's Islamic University. His father worked as a missionary in Trinidad and New York, leaving the family in Saudi Arabia.

The FBI rescinded a February alert issued against Mohammed Sher Mohammed Khan, an alias of El Shukrijumah.

On March 25, the FBI's Baltimore office said it wanted to question a Pakistani couple, Aafia Siddiqui, 31, and her husband, Mohammed Khan, age 33, about possible terrorist activities and their ties to El Shukrijumah. She resided in the Boston area, and had visited Gaithersburg, Maryland, in late December or January. She has a doctorate in neurological science and has studied at Massachusetts Institute of Technology (MIT) and Brandeis University, as well as in Houston, Texas. She listed her home as in Karachi. At MIT, she wrote a paper on how to set up a Muslim student organization. The duo are officers of the Institute

of Islamic Research and Teaching, Inc., of Roxbury, Massachusetts.

Within the week of the worldwide alert, the father lost his job as spiritual leader of the Masjid al Hijrah next door to his home. He had testified as a character witness for Clement Hampton-el, a member of his New York mosque who was sentenced to 35 years in prison for plotting an "urban terror war" along with the men accused of bombing the World Trade Center in 1993.

Adnan had also been a suspect in a plot by Imran Mandhai, currently serving 11 years after pleading guilty to conspiracy on charges of planning a "jihad cell" of 30 men that would target electrical substations, an armory, Jewish institutions, and Mount Rushmore. An FBI informant bugged Mandhai, who was heard naming Adnan as an accomplice. In spring 2001, Adnan refused to be an FBI informant. He left the country in May 2001.

On September 5, 2003, the FBI put out a worldwide alert for Shukrijumah, Abderraouf Jdey, Zubayr Al-Rimi, and Karim El Mejjati, who were believed to be engaged in planning for terrorist attacks, according to information provided by Khalid Sheik Mohammed, al Qaeda's operations chief. On May 25, 2004, the FBI put out another alert for him, saying that al Qaeda was believed to be planning a major attack for the summer.

Khalid Jum'ah Mas'ud al-Shu'liyyah: alias Abu-Musab, a Libyan from Darnah who was born in 1984 and joined al Qaeda in Iraq as a martyr on October 28, 2006, contributing cash, a watch, and a ring. His recruitment coordinator was Faraj. His phone numbers were 2189272690608 and 21927478512.

Sa'ud 'Abdallah al-Shulwi: alias Abu-al-Bara' al-Ta'ifi, a Saudi from Al-Ta'if-al-Jazirah who was born on November 6, 1984 and joined al Qaeda in Iraq on September 23, 2006, donating $920, his watch, and a cell phone. His recruitment coordinator was Abu-al-Fadil. His father's phone number was 0505790397, his brother Muhammad's was 0566722337, as was his brother 'Ubayd's.

Husayn Ahmad 'Ali Shumayt: a member of the Islamic Group in Egypt who was killed in July 1995 in Addis Ababa, Ethiopia. He had fled Egypt for Afghanistan a few years earlier. He moved to Peshawar, Pakistan before moving on. He was a prominent member of the Islamic Group's military wing in Qina. He was said by the Ethiopian Supreme State Security Prosecution on August 7, 1995 to have trained in the al-Kamp and Kangu camps in Khartoum with another of the nine Egyptian Islamic Group gunmen who, on June 25, 1995, fired on the armored limousine of Egyptian President Hosni Mubarak in Addis Ababa.

Karimah Shuqayr: an associate of Thurayya Kamal Sahyoun, who, on November 14, 1987, carried a ribboned Swiss chocolate box past security guards at the American University Hospital. A 1-kilogram TNT bomb attached to an Energa shell and nails inside exploded inside the box, killing her and six others and wounding 31. On November 20, 1987, Lebanese police announced that Shuqayr was the woman responsible for the box.

Ali Ahmad Shur: on June 2, 1985, Rome police discovered 1 pound of plastic explosives in a suitcase left by the Lebanese in his Hilton hotel room. The detonator had been accidentally destroyed and the suitcase had been abandoned.

Yasir Shuraydah: variant of Yasser Chraidi.

Ahmad Sulayman al-Shurayhi: variant of Ahmad Sulayman al-Shuray'i.

Ahmad Sulayman al-Shuray'i: variant al-Shurayhi, alias Abu-Anas, a Saudi from Riyadh who joined al Qaeda in Iraq as a suicide bomber in 2007, contributing 500 euros and $400. His recruitment coordinator was Sa'd. His sister's phone number was 00966504257848; his father's was 0096650441719053.

Badr Shuri: alias Abu-Muhammad al-'Atawi, a Moroccan electrician from Casablanca who was born in 1982 and joined al Qaeda in Iraq as a

suicide bomber in 2007, contributing 100 Euros, 45 liras, his passport, and a Spanish ID card. His recruitment coordinator was Idris. He flew via Spain and Turkey to Syria, where he met Abu-Muhammad, who took his 250 euros. His phone number was 00212621645.

Jaafar Shweikhat: a member of the Islamic Movement for Change in Syria who was executed in late 1996 for taking part in an attack on U.S. soldiers in Saudi Arabia in June 1996. The group claimed credit in his name for the bombing, on December 31, 1996, of a bus at the Intilak Center bus terminal in Damascus that killed 11 and injured 42.

Khatem Shweili: age 24, a Palestinian from the West Bank town of Hebron, who, on November 4, 2001, stepped from a Jerusalem sidewalk and fired a short-barreled M-16 assault rifle at Bus No. 25 carrying dozens of Israeli schoolgirls in Jerusalem. He emptied his magazine, killing two passengers and injuring dozens, five seriously. Nearly every window of the bus was blown out. An Israeli soldier, a policeman, and an armed civilian gunned down the terrorist. Islamic Jihad claimed credit.

Adel Siam: leader of the military wing of the Jihad who was shot to death by Egyptian police on April 4, 1994. He used a Yemeni passport, and was suspected of organizing several assassination attempts on government and media figures.

Nazih Al Sibaa: a Hamas leader in Jenin in the West Bank who helped plan suicide bombings. On February 16, 2002, he was killed by a car bomb. Palestinians said the car was booby trapped and set off by an overhead drone.

Haidi Zaynuhum al-Sifti: a pediatrician born in December 1958 who was identified by Egyptian police as being a suspect in the attempted assassination on August 13, 1987 by four gunmen who fired on Major General Muhammad al-Nabawi Isma'il, former deputy prime minister and interior minister, in front of his house in Cairo.

Abu Siham: alias of 'Atif Hammudah.

Abu Sijan: name given by an anonymous caller of one of the October 23, 1983 suicide bombers in Lebanon. A truck bomb at the Battalion Landing Team building at Beirut International Airport killed 241 U.S. Marines and injured more than 80 other soldiers, while a car bomb in Beirut's Ramel el-Baida district killed 58 French paratroopers and injured another 15.

Surinder Sikh: on January 24, 1990, Larnaca District Court issued an eight-day remand order for him from the Punjab after Larnaca police discovered a Walther pistol inside his suitcase. The pistol was wrapped in nylon and paper and concealed inside a tape recorder. It was found during an x-ray check on luggage about to be loaded on the Iraqi Airlines flight bound for Baghdad. Sikh was traveling to New Delhi via Baghdad. His passport indicated that his home address was Chakmander, Jaladhar.

Mohammed Siksik: age 20, a Palestinian suicide bomber who, on January 29, 2007, set off 9 to 17 pounds of explosives at the Lehamim Bakery in Eilat, killing three Israelis. Two of the dead were the bakery's owners; the third was a foreign worker from South America. Siksik, who was unemployed and had just witnessed the death of his newborn daughter, was from the northern Gaza town of Beit Lahiya. He was avenging his best friend's killing in the struggle against Israel. Islamic Jihad and the al-Aqsa Martyrs Brigades-Army of the Believers separately claimed credit.

Husayn Muhammad Simtayn: alias Husayn 'Ismat Sulayman, a member of the Islamic Jihad Organization (IJO), arrested by Turkish officials on April 10, 1987 with three others who had planned to kidnap Americans and Israelis living in Turkey and to attack U.S. consulates. The group had smuggled 91 kilograms of explosives into the country, intending to obtain the release of 200 colleagues imprisoned in Israel. He was

carrying a false passport and coded messages including the IJO Beirut headquarters' phone number and the phone number of Abu Muhammad, the IJO's Middle East operations chief in Beirut.

Murad al-Siouri: a former Yemeni Interior Ministry employee sentenced to five years on September 29, 2004 by a Yemeni court for helping USS *Cole* bomber Jamal al-Badawi in handling funds and forging identity papers.

Abu Sirab: Saudi-based recruitment coordinator for foreign fighters for al Qaeda in Iraq in 2007.

Husayn Shumayt Siraj: alias of Husayn Ahmad Shahid Ali.

Ibrahim Muhammad 'Abd-al-Rahman Sirbil: a Palestinian Muslim fundamentalist leader arrested by police in Jordan on August 25, 1992 after they uncovered a cache of weapons, explosives, documents, brochures, and videos linking him with an Islamic Jihad faction. On October 12, 1992, his trial began in the State Security Court. He was charged with affiliation with and collecting funds for an illegal group, and unlicensed possession of explosives and weapons. He was a native of Hebron and the occupied West Bank. The charge sheet said that he established the Islamic Jihad—Al-Aqsa Battalions in 1990 after splitting with Islamic Jihad. The first count carried a maximum penalty of six months. The charge of illegal possession of unlicensed explosives carried a minimum of 15 years in jail. The third charge of illegal possession of arms and ammunition carried three years. The fourth count of collecting $85,000 had an undetermined sentence.

Shaykh Ibrahim Sirbil: military chief of the Islamic Jihad in Jordan on January 1991.

Rustum Najib Sirhan: one of six Arabs for whom the Nicosia District Court issued an eight-day arrest warrant on May 30, 1989 in connection with the discovery two days earlier by fishermen of two Soviet-made SAM-7 missiles in the McKenzie seashore area near Larnaca International Airport. A group of six young Arabs were plotting to shoot down the helicopter of Lebanon's Christian leader, Major General Michel 'Awn, who was scheduled to arrive in Cyprus en route to Casablanca. All six were charged, inter alia, with illegal entry into Cyprus and with possession of weapons and explosives. On June 2, 1989, Lebanon requested extradition. On June 22, 1989, the Larnaca District Court set June 30 as the date for the opening of the preliminary hearing. On August 30, 1989, the Muslim 14 March group threatened to hijack a Cyprus Airlines plane if the government did not release them. The group seeks to avenge the 40 Lebanese Muslims who were killed by 'Awn's troops on March 14, 1989. The trial began on October 9, 1989. All pleaded guilty to illegally possessing and transporting weapons and explosives. Five pleaded guilty to illegal entry. The trial was moved from Larnaca to Nicosia for security reasons. On October 13, 1989, the court sentenced the six on eight charges. Five received jail sentences ranging from one to eight years; the sixth received one to five years. All of the penalties were to be concurrent, effective the date of arrest. The court president said he took the psychological state of the sixth accused into consideration in determining the verdict. On April 15, 1991, Cypriot authorities deported the six Lebanese to Beirut after they had served only 17 months of their sentences.

Salah Muhammad al-Siri: alias Abu-Hudhafah, a Yemeni weapons merchant from Ta'z who was born in 1979 and joined al Qaeda in Iraq as a martyr circa 2007, contributing $400, 50 Yemeni riyals, has passport, ID, medical report, and Army papers. His recruitment coordinator was 'Abd-al-Hay, whom he knew via Abu-Hamzah in his neighborhood. He flew from Sana'a to Wyria, where he met Abu'Umar al-Salmani, Abu-al'Abbas al-Jazi'ri, and Abu-Muhammad, whom he gave $300 of his $700. His phone number was 009674225036; his brother Walid Ahmad al-Siri's number is the same.

Yasser al-Siri: variant Yasir 'Ali al-Sirri, an Egyptian who ran the Islamic Observation Center in London, who was arrested in October 2001 on charges of providing the two bombers who killed Afghan Northern Alliance leader Ahmed Shah Massoud with a letter of recommendation that helped them get to Massoud. Information from al-Siri led to arrests in France and Belgium on November 26, 2001 of 14 Osama bin Laden contacts. Al-Siri had been living in the United Kingdom after requesting political asylum. He had been tried in absentia and sentenced to death in Egypt for the 1994 assassination attempt against then-Prime Minister Atef Sedki. On May 17, 2002, a London court began extradition proceedings. The naturalized U.S. citizen was wanted in the United States for sending money to Afghanistan to fund terrorism and for helping blind Sheik Omar Abd-al-Rahman. On July 29, 2002, a London court freed him after the Home Secretary declared that the U.S. Department of Justice had not provided sufficient evidence to warrant extradition. U.S. attorneys planned to file a new extradition request, based on conspiracy charges.

Murad al-Sirouri: among a group of conspirators who, in 2004, received prison terms of five to ten years in a Yemeni court in connection with the October 12, 2000 bombing of the USS *Cole*. As of May 2008, all were free.

Abu Sirrab: variant Serrab, a Saudi-based recruitment coordinator for al Qaeda in Iraq foreign fighters in 2006.

Yasir 'Ali al-Sirri: variant of Yasser al-Siri, fugitive sentenced to death on March 17, 1994 by the Higher Military Court in Cairo in connection with the November 25, 1993 bombing of the convoy of Egyptian Prime Minister Dr. 'Atif Sidqi that killed a 15-year-old girl and wounded 21 other people.

Yasser Sirri: held in the United Kingdom for links to the assassins of Afghan leader Ahmed Shah

Massoud on September 9, 2001. He was indicted with three others, including Lynne Stewart, on April 9, 2002 by Attorney General John Ashcroft for helping to pass unlawful messages between an Egyptian terrorist organization and Sheik Omar Abd-al-Rahman, who was serving a life sentence for plotting to blow up the World Trade Center and UN buildings in 1993. The four were also charged with providing "material support and resources" to the Egyptian Islamic Group. Sirri was in frequent contact with fellow defendant paralegal Ahmed Abd-al Sattar and provided financial support for the terrorists, according to the indictment.

Yasser Tawfik Sirri: at-large Egyptian Jihad terrorist who was one of 62 defendants tried in absentia in a military tribunal in Haekstep, Egypt beginning on February 1, 1999. Charges against 107 defendants included forgery, criminal conspiracy, subversion, membership in an outlawed group, plotting to carry out attacks on officials and police, attempting to prevent security forces from carrying out their jobs, and conspiracy to overthrow the government. He was a leader of the Islamic Observation Center in London.

'Abd-al-Rahman Sa'd Haris al-Sirwani: alias Abu-Sa'd, a Saudi from Mecca who was born on September 6, 1984 and joined al Qaeda in Iraq on October 10, 2006, contributing 100 and a cell phone. His recruitment coordinator was Abu-al-Zubayr. His brother's phone number was 00966502015503.

Subhi Abu Sita: alias of Mohammed Atef.

Subhi Abu Sitta: alias of Mohammed Atef.

Hussein Ibrahim Mahmoud Siyad: surviving member of a Fatah group that conducted Operation Martyr Kamal Adwan on March 11, 1978, seizing an Israeli tour bus and leaving 46 dead and 85 wounded before being stopped. He joined Fatah in 1977, trained in al-'Izziyah in southern Lebanon, then received training in handling explosives and weapons in Ad-Damur and al-Qasimiyah.

'Adil Siyam: wanted by Egyptian police in connection with the November 25, 1993 bombing of the convoy of Egyptian Prime Minister Dr. 'Atif Sidqi that killed a 15-year-old girl and wounded 21 other people. The *Middle East News Agency* (*MENA*) said they had also participated in the car bomb explosion in the al-Qulali area a few months earlier and the abortive attempt to assassinate UN Secretary General Dr. Boutros Boutros-Ghali during the Organization of African Unity summit in Cairo.

'Ummar Siyam: a resident of Gaza's Sabra neighborhood who walked to the Dizengoff Center, an enclosed Tel Aviv mall, where he set off a bomb near a bus on March 4, 1996, at 4:01 P.M., killing 20, including two Americans, and wounding 150. The Pupils of Ayash, a Hamas faction, claimed credit, as did Islamic Jihad.

Ohad Skornick: a religion student at Bar Ilan University who was arraigned by the Israeli government in connection with the November 4, 1995 assassination of Israeli Prime Minister Yitzak Rabin. He was charged with not acting to prevent a crime and was ordered held for five days.

Mohamedou Ould Slahi: Mauritanian citizen arrested January 26, 2000 after leaving Senegal by the Bureau of Mauritanian Security in conjunction with the Algerian terrorist bomb plot against the United States. He reportedly is a brother-in-law of a lieutenant of Osama bin Laden, Khaled Shanquiti, alias "The Mauritanian," who was involved in the bombing of the U.S. embassies in Kenya and Tanzania. Slahi had been living in Canada, which he left after the Canadian investigation of him started. He was often seen at the Assunna Mosque in Montreal. Slahi had been detained for a few hours at the Dakar, Senegal airport after arriving from Paris. After being questioned, he was permitted to travel to Nouakchott,

Mauritania. Senegal appeared unwilling to hold him without specific charges. His name was on an Interpol international watch list. Slahi had constant communications with a construction company in Khartoum, Sudan, that was owned by bin Laden and which was used as a front for al Qaeda. Slahi recently lived in Germany but arrived in Canada the previous fall. He worked closely with Mokhtar Haouari, an Algerian charged with being involved in the logistics of the plot. The United States was preparing an extradition request. Authorities were not sure whether he was the mastermind or a messenger in the plot. Mauritania freed Slahi on February 20, 2000. FBI agents had been permitted to submit questions during his incarceration and interrogation. He did not admit a role in the bomb plot.

On September 29, Mauritanian police arrested the former student of electrical engineering at Gerhard-Mercator University in Duisburg, Germany. He lived in Germany from the mid-1990s to September 1999, during which time he visited bin Laden camps in Afghanistan twice. In 1999, Ould Slahi moved to Canada, where he visited a Montreal mosque frequented by Islamic radicals plotting the millennium attacks in the United States. They included Ahmed Ressam. Ould Slahi might have activated the Canadian cell.

He is related through marriage to bin Laden associate Mahfouz Ould Walid, aka Abu Hafs, whose assets were ordered frozen by President Bush. Investigators believed Ould Slahi could have been directly involved in the 9/11 suicide hijacking plot.

He was rearrested in Nouakchott, Mauritania on November 2001 on suspicion of involvement with al Qaeda. The *Washington Post* said that he was held for eight months in Jordan. The *Post* claimed that as of December 2007, he was free in Mauritania.

Amor Sliti: on September 30, 2003, the 44-year-old was sentenced to five years for being an accomplice of Nizar Trabelsi, who planned to attack Kleine Brogel Air Base in Belgium by driving a car bomb into the canteen.

Dr. Richard Smith: alias of Ramzi Ahmed Yusuf.

Tasir Abu Snayna: one of four Arab terrorists who fired small arms and threw grenades at Jewish religious students in the West Bank on May 2, 1980, killing five settlers and injuring 17. Abu Snayna was from Hebron. The Palestine Liberation Organization's Unit of the Martyr Ibrahim Abu Safwat claimed credit. On September 16, 1980, Israeli security forces arrested the four terrorists plus six Fatah accomplices who had helped them hide in caves in the Hebron hills.

Abu Solaiman: variant of Abu Suleiman.

Abdel Halim Mohammad Atim Soliman: one of two Egyptians identified by the FBI as having ties to Hamas and the Islamic group who helped plan the February 26, 1993 World Trade Center (WTC) bombing. His fingerprints were found on manuals and magazines confiscated from WTC convict Ajaj when he was arrested at JFK Airport on September 2, 1992. They had been arrested in Denmark in April 1994 on suspicion of complicity in various arsons, attempted bombings, and plotting to disrupt a UN conference in Copenhagen, but were released without charge.

Ali Faraj Muhammad Soliman: alias Abu Shattri, a Libyan from Benghazi who was born in 1980 and joined al Qaeda in Iraq as a martyr in 2007, contributing his passport, 150 lira, and $160. He flew from Egypt to Jordan and on to Damascus, where he met Abu Omar and A'annas, whom he gave 2,000 lira. His brother's phone number is 002186230916.

Mohammed Ali Aboul-Ezz al-Mahdi Ibrahim Soliman: alias Sulieman, an Egyptian arrested by Brazilian Federal Police in April 2002 in the Tri-border city of Foz do Iguazu on the basis of an Egyptian government extradition request for his involvement in the 1997 al-Gama'at al-Islamiyya attack on tourists in Luxor, Egypt. The Brazilian Supreme Court released him on September 11,

2002 due to insufficient evidence to extradite him.

Nabil Ahmed Soliman: an Egyptian accused of participation in the assassination of Egyptian President Anwar Sadat in 1981. On November 1, 1997, a U.S. immigration judge declared that he must return to Egypt to face his punishment. His lawyer said he would appeal because he would face a firing squad.

Adel Ben Soltane: one of three Tunisians whose trial began on February 18, 2002 in Milan. The trio was convicted on May 17. (The State Department said four members of the Tunisian Combatant Group were sentenced in February to up to five years for providing false documentation and planning to acquire and transport arms and other illegal goods.) Judge Ambrogio Moccia said they would be expelled from Italy after serving their sentences. They had been cleared of several charges of supplying false documents and smuggling arms. He received four years and six months.

Mohammed Soltani: name on a Bahraini passport used by Hasan Ilyas Badr, who took part in several fedayeen attacks against Israeli interests in European capitals. He died when a bomb exploded prematurely in his room in London's Mount Royal Hotel on January 17, 1980. The May 15 Arab Organization claimed credit.

Alex Soriano: alias of Saifullah Mokhlis Yunos.

Salem Sa'ad Muhammad al Soua'aiere: alias Abu Al Abbas, a Saudi from Sharrouah who was born in 1982 and joined al Qaeda in Iraq as a martyr on 4 Rajab 1428. His recruitment coordinator was Sa'aied.

Saied Bin Abd al Qader Saleh Al Soua'aily: alias Abu Jabir, a Saudi from Kharaj who was born on 2/5/1396 and joined al Qaeda in Iraq as a martyr on November 2, 2006, bringing 30,000 lira, 1,000 rials, and a watch. His recruitment coordinator was Abu Ahmed. His home phone

number was 015455532; his brother Salem's was 05551044945.

Mustafa Soudeidan: one of two Eagles of the Palestinian Revolution, or possibly Saiqa terrorists who took five hostages on board diesel passenger train number 2590, which left Bratislava, Czechoslovakia and entered Marchegg, Austria on September 28, 1973. Two of the hostages escaped. The gunmen later took off for Vienna's Schwechat Airport, where they demanded that Austria close down the Schonau Castle facility for Soviet Jewish émigrés and not allow further émigré transit through Austria. The hostages were newly arrived Soviet Jews on their way to Israel. The Austrians agreed to safe passage. After refueling stops in Yugoslavia and Italy, the plane was denied landing by Tunisia and Algeria, and eventually landed in Libya. In December 1973, Libya announced that the duo had been released to fight against Israel. Some reports claimed that the duo had trained in a Popular Front for the Liberation of Palestine camp in Lebanon. One of them participated in the December 1975 Organization of Petroleum Exporting Countries raid.

Ziyad Bu Souhilah: alias Abu Mustafa, a Tunisian student from Tunis who was born in 1977 and joined al Qaeda in Iraq as a martyr in 2007, bringing his passport and driver's license. His recruitment coordinator, Ayemn, was a Tunisian who resided in Lebanon. He knew him through Radwan the Tunisian. His brother's phone number was 0021623216556.

Saleh Abdel Rahim Souwi: alias Salah Nazzal, a Hamas suicide bomber who, on October 19, 1994, set off his bomb on a Number 5 bus on Dizengoff Street in Tel Aviv's shopping district, killing 22 and wounding 48. He left a confessor videotape, claiming to live in Qalwiliah. He had participated in the 1987 intifadah, throwing rocks and bottles of flaming gasoline. On September 13, 1988, he was arrested and held until September 30, when he was released without charge. In 1989, while throwing a bottle in a confrontation with the

Army, Souwi's brother, Hussein, was shot in the head by an Israeli soldier. Souwi was detained for nearly a year starting in the summer of 1990. The next four years, he was in and out of detention.

Ishmail Hassan Sowan: variant Ismael, a Jordanian serving as a Palestine Liberation Organization (PLO) research assistant who was arrested on August 17, 1987 by Scotland Yard in a raid on a Westbourne Avenue flat in Hull, Humberside, under the Prevention of Terrorism Act. They seized 30 kilograms of Czech-made Semtex high explosives, four assault rifles, seven hand grenades, detonators and clocks for making bombs, eight magazines loaded with ammunition, and a large quantity of .38 mm and 9 mm ammunition in the dawn raid in connection with the killing of Ali Naji Awad al-Adhami, a Palestinian political cartoonist, on July 22, 1987. Sowan had been in the United Kingdom since 1984, studying for a degree at Bath University. He lived in the flat with his wife. He was charged with several arms offenses. Police suggested that the cache was to be used for an Arab terrorist blitz in Europe. On June 17, 1988, Sowan was sentenced to 11 years on weapons charges. The United Kingdom said he was a double agent recruited by Mossad to penetrate Fatah's Force 17, an elite PLO unit believed responsible for an assassination in the United Kingdom.

Ismael Sowan: variant of Ishmail Hassan Sowan.

Adel Nasser al Sowda: alias Abu Osama, one of six individuals killed on November 3, 2002 when a U.S. Predator unmanned aerial vehicle fired a Hellfire missile at their car in Yemen. Also killed was Abu Ali al-Harithi, a key suspect in the USS *Cole* bombing of October 12, 2000, and Kamal Derwish, a U.S. citizen who headed an al Qaeda cell in Lackawanna, New York that was wrapped up on September 14, 2002.

Mustafa Abu Srieh: one of two Palestinian terrorists who, on November 27, 2001, fired assault rifles on shoppers and pedestrians at the main bus station in Afula's main shopping district, killing a young man and woman and badly injuring nine other Israelis. One woman attacked a gunman, but they shot her at point-blank range. Two dozen others suffered minor injuries or shock. Police trapped the duo in a parking lot and shot them to death. They were from two Palestinian militant groups, the Islamic Jihad and the al-Aqsa Brigade. The duo had made a videotape in advance, saying that the attack was to avenge the deaths of Palestinian militants killed by Israel. Mustafa Abu Srieh of Islamic Jihad said "we hope our people will continue in the path of holy war." The other terrorist was Abdel Karim Abu Nafa, age 20, a Palestinian policeman and Fatah activist. The terrorists had stolen a white Subaru sedan with yellow Israeli license plates and drove directly to the bus station.

Abdelhafid Sriti: correspondent for Hizballah's *al-Manar* television and 1 of 32 people arrested on February 20, 2008 by Moroccan authorities who said they were a terrorist network linked to al Qaeda that planned to assassinate Cabinet members, army officers, and members of the local Jewish community. Some of the group belonged to al Badil al Hadari, an Islamist party the banning of which was announced the same day. The group had conducted holdups and sold stolen goods. One member worked with European criminals to steal $25.65 million from an armored truck in Luxembourg in 2000. The group also stole gold jewelry in Belgium, melting it down and selling it via a goldsmith who belonged to the group.

Ali Khaled Steitiye: age 39, a Lebanese who became a U.S. citizen–possibly fraudulently—in 2000. He was arrested in late October 2001 by Portland, Oregon police. He had used several Social Security numbers, according to police. He had a handgun tucked into his waistband. Police found a machete, 1,000 rounds of ammunition, fake credit cards, phony citizenship documents, and $20,000 in his apartment and car. September 11 was circled on his calendar. He had ties to Hamas and admitted to receiving firearms training in Lebanese camps several years earlier. He claimed to have lived mostly in the United States for the previous two decades. He was held without bail and a court in early December rejected his request for release. On December 12, he was charged with felony weapons violations for lying about his several felony convictions when he tried to purchase an assault rifle in August.

He became the key to the indictments on October 4, 2002 of six people from Portland, Oregon, including a former U.S. Army reservist, for conspiracy to join al Qaeda and the Taliban to wage war against the United States in Afghanistan after the 9/11 attacks. None had arrived in Afghanistan, although two were still at large and believed to be overseas. The five men and one woman were charged with conspiracy to levy war against the United States, conspiracy to provide material support to a terrorist group, and conspiracy to contribute services to al Qaeda and the Taliban. The indictment said that, in late 2001, five of them tried to go through China, Bangladesh, or Indonesia to Afghanistan to fight American soldiers, but failed to enter Pakistan because of visa and financial problems. The case began a fortnight after 9/11, when Mark Mercer, a deputy sheriff in Skamania County, Washington, saw five men in Middle Eastern clothes take target practice with a shotgun, a Chinese assault rifle, and a semiautomatic pistol in a private quarry in Washougal, Washington. A few weeks later, he noticed one of them on television being arrested on weapons charges. He called the FBI about Steitiye, a Hamas supporter who had received paramilitary training with pro-Palestinian militants in Lebanon. In October, FBI agents worked to find the four other shooters, but determined that they had left days earlier for Afghanistan.

Steitiye was named an unindicted coconspirator who lied in August 2001 to an Oregon gun dealer about a number of previous arrests and a felony conviction while purchasing an assault rifle. In September 2002, he was sentenced to 2 and a half years in prison on gun and fraud charges. Sheikh Mohamed Kariye, the imam of his mosque, the Islamic Center of Portland, had been indicted on charges of committing Social Security fraud during 1983 to 1995. Kariye had cofounded the Global Relief Foundation, which is under investigation for al Qaeda ties.

Ibrahim Suadan: one of two Palestinians believed to have kidnapped Shaykh Salman al-Sabah, a Kuwaiti prince and nephew of the king, and his 12-year-old daughter in Manila in July 1989.

Muhammad Bin Mishal Bin Ghodayb Al Sub'baie: alias Abu Muhaned Al Muhajer, a Saudi nongovernmental organization (NGO) employee from Riyadh who joined al Qaeda in Iraq in 2007 as a fighter. His recruitment coordinator was Abu A'annas, whom he knew via Saied Al Hadrey. He flew from Bahrain to Al Sharqiyah to Damascus, where he met Abu Omar, Abu Abd Allah, and Abu Sa'ad. He brought $100 and his passport. He gave his Syrian contacts 17,000 lira. He has experience with computers. His home phone number was 0096612480496; Abd Allah's was 00966504449106.

'Abd al-Jalid Khalid Ahmad al-Subbar: alias of 'Umar Mabruk.

Abu Sayf al-Sudani: alias of Fazul Abdallah Muhammad.

Abu Seif al Sudani: variant Abu Sayf al-Sudani, alias of Fazul Abdallah Muhammad.

Abu Taha al-Sudani: explosives expert believed killed on January 8, 2007, when the U.S. conducted an airstrike in Badmadow island off southern Somalia against al Qaeda terrorists.

Adel Ali Bayoumi Sudani: age 41, the head of the Egyptian Jihad's military wing, who was sentenced to death by an Egyptian military court on October 15, 1997.

Abu Sufian: age 25, an Iraqi with close ties to Abu Musab al Zarqawi, was 1 of 15 people arrested by Spanish authorities on December 19, 2005 on charges of setting up a recruiting network for al Qaeda that sent Islamic militants to Iraq. Police said at least two men were preparing to travel to Iraq as fighters. There was no evidence that they were preparing attacks in Spain, but they had materials to make explosives.

Isam al-Sufriti: wanted by Nicosia, Cyprus police in connection with the shooting of Hisham al-Sa'udi, a Yemeni Palestinian director of an offshore company, on January 31, 1985.

Muhammad Abdallah Slih Sughayr: one of three Saudis suspected of financing Abu Sayyaf, whose U.S. assets were blocked on October 10, 2007 by the U.S. Department of the Treasury.

Abu Suhayb: alias of Adam Yahiye Gadahn.

Abu-Suhayb: alias of 'Abd-al-'Aziz Bin-'Atiq Salih al-'Atiq.

Abu-Suhayb: alias of Ahmad 'Umar Bin-Sha'b al-Nahdi.

Abu-Suhayb: Saudi-based recruitment coordinator for foreign fighters for al Qaeda in Iraq in 2006.

Suhayl: Libyan-based recruitment coordinator for foreign fighters for al Qaeda in Iraq in 2006.

Abu Suhieb: alias of Abd Al Aziz Bin Attiq Saleh al Attiq.

Suhil: Libyan-based recruitment coordinator for foreign fighters for al Qaeda in Iraq in 2006.

'Adnan Sujud: on February 27, 1992, French Judge Jean-Louis Bruguiere issued an international arrest warrant for him in connection with the July 11, 1988 Abu Nidal attack on the Greek ship *City of Poros* that killed nine people and injured 80. The warrants charged him with murder and attempted murder. He was the only one of the four defendants thought to have been on the ship at the time of the attack. Greek authorities believed that Sujud threw grenades and sprayed passengers with gunfire.

Anwar Muhammad 'Atiyah Sukhour: variant of Anwar Muhammad 'Atiyah Sukkar.

Anwar Muhammad 'Atiyah Sukkar: variant Sukhour, 25-year-old Palestinian Islamic Jihad suicide bomber from Gaza City who, on January 22, 1995, set off his bomb outside a bus stop snack bar at the Beit Lid Junction of Israel, killing 18 soldiers and one civilian and wounding another 65 people. The carpenter had been detained twice for several days by Palestinian police, of which his father was a member.

Abu Sulaiman: alias of Nawaf Bin Shaiyem Saray Al Shamery.

Abu Gaith Sulaiman: variant of Sulaiman Abu Ghaith.

Abu Abed Sulaimani: a Saudi-based recruitment coordinator for al Qaeda in Iraq foreign fighters in 2007.

Abd Allah Abed Al Sulaimani: alias Abu Neimer al Ta'affi, a Saudi from Ta'aff who was born on 2/12/1411 Hijra and joined al Qaeda in Iraq on 1st Ramadan 1427 Hijra (2007), bringing $620, 4 riyals, and a watch. His recruitment coordinator was Abu Al Fadiel. His home phone number was 7311330; his father's phone numbers were 0503717554 and 0053410932.

Hussam Bin Muhsen Al Sulati: alias Abu Abd Allah, a Tunisian mechanical engineer from Matter who was born in 1981 and joined al Qaeda in Iraq as a fighter in 2007, contributing $100 and 10 Syrian lira, along with his passport, ID, and driver's license. He arrived from Turkey via Syria, where he met Abu Othman, who took his 3,000 Syrian lira and 430 Euros, but returned 100 Syrian lira. He was also in contact with Abu Mau'az from Sweden. His brother, Ameen Fankousha, is in Lebanon.

Sulayman: alias of 'Izzat Jaradat.

Sulayman: alias Bin-'Abbas, a Saudi fighter for al Qaeda in Iraq in 2w007. He owned a passport. His home phone number was 0096663390306; his cell was 0966505170309.

Abu-Sulayman: alias of Khalid 'Ad-al-Rahman al-Khlaywi.

Abu-Sulayman: alias of Ahmad Bin Mukhallad Bin Hamad al-Mutayri.

Abu-Sulayman: alias of Faraj 'Umran Muhammad.

Abu-Sulayman: alias of Hakim Muftah 'Ali al-Wahishi.

Abu-Sulayman: Saudi-based recruitment coordinator for foreign fighters for al Qaeda in Iraq in 2007.

Ahmad al-Rifa'i Sulayman: alias Abu-Muhammad al-Adhra'i, a Syrian from Dar'a who was born in 1983 and joined al Qaeda in Iraq on October 4, 2006. His recruitment coordinator was Ayman. His phone number was 0096315316315.

Husayn 'Ismat Sulayman: alias of Husayn Muhammad Simtayn.

Jihad Sulayman: an officer of the Lebanese Forces Party wanted for questioning in the January 26, 1994 bombing of the Sayyidat al-Najat Church in Beirut.

Mahmud Sulayman: one of two farmers in Imbabah who were arrested on January 5, 1993 by Egyptian investigators in Al-Minya for importing arms for terrorists in Asyut, in an ambush on the desert road in Al-Minya. The duo were carrying

four machine guns, two pistols, and 35 spare parts for weapons. They had previously been accused in seven cases of arms trading.

Al-Sayyid Salah al-Sayyid Sulayman: sentenced to death on March 17, 1994 by the Higher Military Court in Cairo in connection with the November 25, 1993 bombing of the convoy of Egyptian Prime Minister Dr. 'Atif Sidqi that killed a 15-year-old girl and wounded 21 other people. He was executed on May 3, 1994.

Sulayman Ibrahim Sulayman: variant Suleiman Ibrahim Suleiman, alias Abu-Khalid, from al-Qasim Buraydah, who was born on June 2, 1976 and joined al Qaeda in Iraq on October 4, 2006, contributing $100. His phone numbers were 0504955800, 0504955323, and 0504954500. His recruitment coordinator was Abu-Khalaf.

Abdallah Abid al-Sulaymani: alias Abu-Nimr al-Ta'ifi, a 15-year-old from al-Ta'if, Saudi Arabia who crossed into Iraq after arriving in Syria on September 23, 2006. He was born on June 14, 1991, according to what he told an al Qaeda in Iraq clerk when he joined the organization, making him the youngest individual listed in records that were captured at Sinjar in 2007 by coalition forces. He contributed $620, 4 riyals, his cell phone, and a watch. His recruitment coordinator was Abu-al-Fadl. His father's phone numbers were 0503717554 and 0553410932; his home number was 7311330.

Abu-'Abid Sulaymani: Saudi-based recruitment coordinator for al Qaeda in Iraq foreign fighters in 2006.

Sa'id Husayn Sulaymani: an Israeli Arab from Manshiya-Zabda arrested on March 4, 1996 and remanded into custody until March 20 for picking up a bomber in his grocery truck, hiding him in a crate, and driving him from Gaza to Tel Aviv for $1,100. The bomber then walked to the Dizengoff Center, an enclosed mall in Tel Aviv, where he set off a bomb near a bus on March 4, 1996, at 4:01 P.M., killing 20, including two Americans, and wounding 150. The Pupils of Ayash, a Hamas faction, claimed credit.

Suleiman: alias of Mohammed Ali Aboul-Ezz al-Mahdi Ibrahim Soliman.

Abu Suleiman: alias of Khalid Muhammad Abd Al Qader Mahmud Badqar.

Abu Suleiman: alias of Khalid Abd Al Rahman Al Khelaywai.

Abu Suleiman: alias of Mussa Ahmed Hussein Emarah Bib Hussein.

Abu Suleiman: alias of Hanni Abd Allah Al Quraishy.

Abu Suleiman: alias of Iyad Muhammad Tarkhan.

Abu Suleiman: a Palestinian believed to have provided money and mobile phones to the terrorists involved in the triple bombing on April 24, 2006 of a seaside promenade at the resort of Dahab, Egypt, killing 18 civilians, including six foreigners (among them a 10-year-old German boy who died in a taxi on the way to a hospital, a Swiss, a Russian, and a Lebanese woman, and two unidentified foreign women), and injuring 85, including three Italians and four Americans.

Ahmed al Rifa'aie Suleiman: alias Abu Muhammad Al Azruie, a Syrian from Dera'a who was born in 1983 and joined also Qaeda in Iraq on October 4, 2006. His recruitment coordinator was Aymen. His phone number was 0096315316315.

Ali Faraj Muhammad Suleiman: alias Abu Shattrey, a Libyan from Benghazi who was born in 1980 and joined al Qaeda in Iraq as a martyr in 2007, contributing 150 lira, $160, and his passport. He flew from Egypt and Jordan to Syria, where he met Abu Omar and Annas, who took

2,000 lira from him. His brother's phone number is 002186230916.

Hahmed Suleiman: a 21-year-old Egyptian student who was one of three Abdel Nasser Movement (the Palestine Revolution Movement also took credit) hijackers of an Egyptian B737 flying from Cairo to Luxor on August 23, 1976. They demanded the release of five would-be assassins from Egyptian jails. Commandos boarded the plane and overpowered and wounded all three hijackers. The trio said they received their directions in Libya, which promised $250,000 to divert the plane to Libya. On September 18, 1976, they were fined and sentenced to hard labor for life but were acquitted of charges of collusion with Libya.

Ibrahim Ahmad Suleiman: convicted in January 1997 of two counts of perjury for lying to the grand jury investigating the February 26, 1993 bombing of the World Trade Center. On November 24, 1998, U.S. District Court Judge Whitman Knapp passed a lighter sentence, amounting to time served of ten months. Suleiman faced immigration fraud charges in Texas. Suleiman denied traveling with Ahmad Ajaj despite extensive evidence to the contrary. He also denied handling a bombing manual even though his fingerprints were on it.

Mahab H. Suleiman: one of two members of the Popular Front for the Liberation of Palestine (PFLP) who threw grenades and fired a machine gun in Athens Airport at an El Al plane waiting to take off for New York on its way from Tel Aviv on December 26, 1968. Israeli passenger Leon Shirdan was killed and a stewardess suffered a fractured leg and spinal injuries when she jumped out of the plane. The PFLP duo were immediately arrested by Greek police; they were convicted and sentenced on March 26, 1970. Suleiman received 14 years and 3 months for interference with air traffic, arson, and illegal use and possession of explosives. Suleiman, age 19, was from Tripoli. The duo were freed on July 22, 1970 when six Palestinians hijacked an Olympic Airways plane to Beirut.

Sayed Ali Suleiman: arrested in Egypt on September 19, 1987 in connection with the killing of an Israeli diplomat at the Cairo trade fair in early 1986 and the attack on a U.S. Embassy station wagon on May 26, 1987 in Cairo by the Revolution Group.

Tulub Murdi Suleiman: on September 29, 2005, Egyptian police in the Sinai Peninsula shot to death Khaled Musaid and Suleiman in a gun battle in the Mount Halal area, near where fellow Sharm el-Sheik bombing suspect Moussa Badran had been shot earlier that day. The duo were suspected of having organized the multiple bombings on July 23, 2005 in the Sharm el-Sheik resort that killed 88 and wounded 119.

Yasser Suleiman: one of four terrorists who, on October 22, 1997, were hanged by the Egyptian government. The four were found guilty in January of killing policemen and attacking a tourist bus in 1993 and 1994. They were among 19 members of the outlawed Islamic Group who were tried for several offenses, including the murder of a police colonel. The four were convicted of plotting to kill senior state officials and tourists.

Sultan: Egypt-based recruitment coordinator for al Qaeda in Iraq foreign fighters in 2007.

Abu-Sulyman: alias of Iyad Muhammad Tarkhan.

Abu Sumahia: Saudi-based recruitment coordinator for al Qaeda in Iraq foreign fighters in 2007.

Aris Sumarsono: true name of Zulkarnaen.

Faysal Summaq: Syria's Ambassador to East Berlin in 1981 to 1989, he was arrested in Vienna, Austria on October 25, 1994 on charges of helping to provide 15 pounds of explosives to Popular Front for the Liberation of Palestine terrorist Ilich Ramirez Sanchez that were used in the 1983 attack on the French Cultural Center in Berlin. Germany requested extradition.

Mustafa Ibrahim Sunduqah: alias Husayn Bin-'Ali, identified by Doha's *al-Sharq* on March 19, 1993 as a member of the Abu Nidal Group's Central Committee and considered the real head of the revolutionary justice committee and one of the most prominent executioners.

Sunny: alias of Ataur Rahman.

Satam M. A. Al Suqami: age 25, one of the al Qaeda hijackers who, on September 11, 2001, took over American Airlines Flight 11, a B767 carrying 92 people, including nine flight attendants and two pilots, from Boston's Logan International Airport to Los Angeles International Airport. The plane was diverted over New York and crashed into New York City's 110-story World Trade Center North Tower at 8:45 A.M., killing all on board.

Hasan al-Sarai: variant of Hasan al-Surayhi.

Hasan al-Surayhi: variant al-Sarai, alias Abu-'Abd-al-Rahman al-Madani, a Saudi extradited to Saudi Arabia from Pakistan on February 3, 1996 in connection with the November 13, 1995 bombing of a building used by U.S. military personnel. He came from Medina and belonged to the al-Surayhi tribe, which lives in the al-Hijaz desert. He served in the Afghan war. He was married to a French woman, who visited him at his home in Renala Khurd in Pakistan, where he had resided since 1990.

Abu Hamzah al-Suri: alias of Faysal 'Uwayid.

Abu Musab al-Suri: alias of Mustafa Setmariam Nasar.

Abu Rida al-Suri: alias of Muhammed Bayazid, a Syrian physicist who attended the University of Arizona in the 1980s, befriended jihadists including Wadi al-Hage, and joined Usama bin laden in Afghanistan in the early 1990s. He developed business connections to Sudanese weapons of mass destruction-related entities. His name surfaced in al Qaeda's efforts to purchase Sudanese uranium.

Marwan Hadid al-Suri: age 38, alias Abu Marwan, an Al Qaeda paymaster who, on April 20, 2006, was shot to death in a gunfight outside Khaar, a Pakistani tribal area near the Afghan border. The Syrian-born operative was carrying documents indicating that he was an explosives expert and money carrier who distributed cash to al Qaeda members, including Abu Musab al-Zarqawi. His notebook included details and diagrams of bomb circuits and chemicals, including TNT and C-4. He paid families $2,500/family/quarter. Each family also received $500/child/quarter. Al-Suri had married a woman in Afghanistan, moved to Pakistan, and organized operations against the UN in Afghanistan. Police also found four hand grenades and a pistol on his body. Soldiers stopped a bus at a checkpoint, whereupon al-Suri shot one of the soldiers and was shot to death when he attempted a getaway.

Abdulslam al-Surir: alias of Ahmad Muhammad Hamid Ali.

Abu-Su'ud: Saudi-based recruitment coordinator for foreign fighters for al Qaeda in Iraq in 2007. His contacts included Thamir at 00966564490133 and Sulayman at 0096656919404.

Ahmed Suwailmi: a Saudi terrorist who died on September 6, 2005 following a three-day siege at a seaside villa in Damman's Almubarakia neighborhood in Saudi Arabia. He was the brother of Mohammed Abdel-Rahman Mohammed Suwailmi, who was initially reported to have died.

Mohammed Abdel-Rahman Mohammed Suwailmi: age 23, number 7 on the Saudi government's most-wanted terrorists list, was killed on December 27, 2005 following a shootout in the desert. He and a fellow terrorist shot to death two policemen outside Buraydah, northwest of Riyadh. They drove 12 miles southwest and fired on a security checkpoint near Al-Midhnab, killing another three officers. Police captured Suwailmi, who later died. Suwailmi was involved in recruiting and propaganda for Islamic militant groups and earlier shootings against police. In September, police had claimed he was among five militants killed in a gun battle in Dammam, but Suwailmi released an audiotape on the Internet to say he was alive. Police clarified on December 28 that Suwailmi's brother, Ahmed, had been killed in Dammam.

Ismail Abu-Suwayd: variant Ismail Abu Sweede, a Yemeni-based recruitment coordinator for al Qaeda in Iraq foreign fighters in 2006.

Sakr Abu Suwayd: alias of Abu Mus'ab al-Zarqawi.

Shaykh Ahmad Salim Suwaydan: variant Sheikh Ahmed Salim Swedan, alias Sheikh Ahmad Salem Suweidan, Sheikh Ahmed Salem Swedan, Sheikh Swedan, Sheikh Bahamadi, Ahmed Ally, Bahamad, Sheikh Bahamad, Ahmed the Tall, Admadal-Tawil, a Kenyan indicted on December 16, 1998 in the Southern District of New York for his involvement in the August 7, 1998 bombings of the U.S. embassies in Kenya and Tanzania; for conspiring to kill U.S. nationals; murder of U.S. nationals outside the United States; conspiracy to murder U.S. nationals outside of the United States; and attack on a federal facility resulting in death. He was believed to have brought the vehicles, including the 1987 Nissan Atlas truck that carried the bomb, as well as oxygen and acetylene tanks used in the Dar es Salaam attack. The Rewards for Justice Program offers $5 million for his apprehension. He is between five feet eight inches and six feet tall, and weighs 175 pounds. He has claimed to have been born in Mombasa, Kenya on April 9, 1960 and April 9, 1969.

Salem Saad bin Suweid: a Libyan member of al Qaeda arrested at an Amman home in connection with the October 28, 2002 assassination of U.S. Agency for International Development employee Laurence Foley. He told police that he had surveilled Foley for several days, then hid with a silenced 7 mm pistol behind Foley's car. Suweid had worn a bulletproof vest and had covered his face. He said he shot Foley at least six times and then ran to a rented getaway car driven by Yasser Fatih Ibrahim, a Jordanian who was also arrested and admitted his role. The duo said they were carrying out instructions by Ahmad Fadeel al-Khalaylah, alias Abu Musab al-Zarqawi, a Jordanian al Qaeda lieutenant they had met in Afghanistan when the trio were training in camps. On March 11, 2006, Suweid and Yasser Freihat, a Jordanian, were hanged before dawn for the murder of Foley.

Sheikh Ahmad Salem Suweidan: variant of Shaykh Ahmad Salim Suwaydan.

Ismail Abu Swaid: Yemeni-based recruitment coordinator for al Qaeda in Iraq foreign fighters in 2006.

Omran Ashur Swed: on October 30, 1984, he was deported to Tripoli, Libya in connection with several bombs that went off in London during mid-March 1984. Evidence was insufficient to press charges.

Sheikh Ahmed Salim Swedan: variant of Shaykh Ahmad Salim Suwaydan.

Ismail Abu Sweede: variant of Ismail Abu-Suwayd.

Sword of the Faith: alias of Nizar bin Mohammed Nawar.

Swift Sword: alias of Yusuf al-Ayeri.

Abu Syekh: alias of Umar Patek.

T

Muhammad Taa: one of three Lebanese arrested on July 28, 1994 by Costa Rican police in David when they tried to cross the Panamanian border with Costa Rica with false passports. They were suspected of involvement in the suicide bombing of ALAS flight HP-1202, a twin-engine Brazilian-made Embraer on July 19, 1994 that killed two crew and 19 passengers, including a dozen Israeli businessmen, shortly after the plane had left Colon Airport in Panama. The Partisans of God, believed to be an Hizballah cover name, claimed credit.

Abu al Barra'a al Ta'affi: alias of Saud Abd Allah Al Shalawi.

Abu Hamzza al Ta'affi: alias of Ahamed Ibrahim Hassan Ketto.

Abu Neimer al Ta'affi: alias of Abd Allah Abed Al Sulaimani.

Abu Zer al Ta'aiffi: alias of Shaker Salem Albieshi.

Mohammed Tabab: a Jordanian who was one of two terrorists arrested on March 15, 1973 in France, while attempting to smuggle explosives across the Italian–French border for use in attacks against the Israeli and Jordanian embassies as part of a Black September campaign. The two drove from a Lebanese Fatah base in a Mercedes carrying 35 pounds of plastique. The two Fatah members were imprisoned for six months and then expelled from France.

Omar Tabash: Palestinian suicide bomber who, on January 18, 2005, killed a member of Israel's Shin Bet domestic security force and wounded five soldiers, one seriously, and three other Shin Bet agents at an army checkpoint at the Gush Katif junction at the northern entrance to the Gush Katif settlement block along the Mediterranean coast of Gaza. The Islamic Resistance Movement (Hamas) claimed credit.

Yusuf at-Tabbal: leader of a group that was foiled in an assassination attempt against French President Mitterrand on June 3, 1982.

Tahari Shad Tabassum: age 27, wife of Omar Khan Sharif. As of May 9, 2003, she was held in custody for failing to disclose information about acts of terrorism.

Geri Mehed Tabet: a Libyan described by the *Washington Post* in April 1986 as having been in contact in October 1981 with 15 Sardinians who were arrested by Italian authorities in December 1982 as part of a Libyan plot to separate Sardinia from Italy.

Muhammad al Tabhini: variant of Muhammad al-Tubayhi.

Muhammad al-Tabihani: variant of Muhammad al-Tubayhi.

Mehdi Nejad Tabrizi: one of the five Guards of Islam gunmen who failed in an assassination attempt against Shahpour Bakhtiar, the Shah's last

Prime Minister, in Neuilly-sur-Seine, France on July 17, 1980. On March 10, 1982, a Nanterre jury sentenced four of them, including Tabrizi, to life in prison. His release was demanded on July 31, 1984 by the three Guardsmen of Islam hijackers of an Air France B737 flying from Frankfurt to Paris. On July 27, 1990, France pardoned the five. They were deported to Tehran that day.

Abu Zer al Tabouki: variant of Abu-Dhar al-Tabuki.

Abu-Dhar al-Tabuki: variant Abu Zer al Tabouki, alias of Nabil Salamah Salim al-Huwayti.

Abu-Dujanah al-Tabuki: alias of 'Adil Muhammad 'Abdallah Ruwayhil.

Abu-Jandal al-Tabuki: alias of Musa'id Hasan 'Abdallah al-Shamrani.

Mahfoud Tadjine: alias Abou Khalil Mahfoud, named on October 4, 1994 by the Algerian Armed Islamic Group (GIA) as its new amir (leader). He lives in the fundamentalist Algiers suburb of The Eucalyptuses, and was a GIA member since its founding in 1992.

Jalamat Tadrus: a woman from Egypt's al-Fayyum governorate, whose husband was a prominent member of the Iraqi Ba'ath Party before his death. She was a member of an Iraqi Ba'ath Party cell in Egypt arrested on April 13, 1991 on charges of plotting to carry out acts of sabotage and terrorism.

Hatim Tafish: one of four gunmen who, on March 6, 2004, disguised jeeps to look like Israeli army vehicles and tried to attack an Israeli military checkpoint at the Erez border crossing in the Gaza Strip. Palestinian Authority guards stopped them and shot to death at least four Palestinians before a large explosion took place, killing two Palestinian officers and wounding another 15 people. A car bomb had exploded nearby, apparently a diversion. Islamic Jihad, Hamas, and the al-Aqsa Martyrs Brigades jointly claimed credit, and said the dead were Omar Abu Said and Hatim Tafish of al-Aqsa, Mikdad Mbaied of Islamic Jihad and Mohammed Abu Daiah of Hamas.

Khaled Tagiuri: arrested by Bonn police in his hotel after arriving from Tripoli. He was believed part of an antidissident Libyan hit team.

Abi Tagrid: alias of Rafed Latif Sabah.

Abdul Rahman S. Taha: alias of 'Abd al-Rahman Yasin.

Ahmed Refai Taha: Egyptian al-Gamaat leader who was named as an unindicted co-conspirator on October 7, 1998 by a federal grand jury in New York for his role in the August 7, 1998 bombings of the U.S. embassies in Dar es Salaam, Tanzania, and Nairobi, Kenya.

Ali Shafik Ahmed Taha: alias Captain Rafat, one of three Popular Front for the Liberation of Palestine hijackers of an El Al B707 going from Rome to Tel Aviv's Lod Airport on July 22, 1968. The plane was diverted to Algiers, where the hijackers demanded the release of 1,200 Palestinian prisoners from Israeli jails. The Algerians held the trio at a military camp for the balance of the negotiations.

He joined Black September for a hijacking on May 8, 1972.

Commander Taha: alias of Taha Tagapaitedi.

Motan Mohamad Taha: name on the passport of one of three Lebanese arrested on July 28, 1994 by Costa Rican police in David when they tried to cross the Panamanian border with Costa Rica with false passports. They were suspected of involvement in the suicide bombing of ALAS flight HP-1202, a twin-engine Brazilian-made Embraer on July 19, 1994 that killed two crew and 19 passengers, including a dozen Israeli businessmen, shortly after the plane had left Colon Airport in Panama. The Partisans of God, believed to be a

Hizballah cover name, claimed credit. They reportedly were freed in August 1994.

Muhammad Taha: one of ten Shi'ite Muslims identified in November 17, 1992 by the Lebanese newspaper *Nida' al-Watan* as suspected of instigating the kidnappings of U.S. hostages William Buckley, William Higgins, and Peter Kilburn.

Mutawkil Taha: header of the Arab Writers Association whose release from prison was demanded by the two Palestinians who kidnapped U.S. citizen Chris George, director of the Save the Children Fund in Gaza, on June 22, 1989.

Sheik Abu Yasser Rifa'i Taha: in late July 1998, the exiled leader of Egypt's al-Gamaat al-Ismamiya said that the group was not a member of the Islamic Front for Holy War Against the Jews and Cruaders. He was military chief of the Egyptian Gama'at in June 2000.

Yahya Taha: a member of the Popular Front for the Liberation of Palestine's Central Committee who, on September 8, 1990, called for the Arab nation to rise against the U.S./Coalition activities against Iraq.

Midhat al-Tahawi: an Egyptian reserve Second Lieutenant and member of Gama'at who was sentenced to death by the Sidi Barrani military court on February 16, 1994 for having planned an assassination attempt against Egyptian President Hosni Mubarak, who was to visit the Sidi Barrani military base near the Libyan border.

Abdul Rahman S. Taher: alias of 'Abd al-Rahman Yasin.

Hasein Taher: variant Yasein Taher, Hasein Ther, age 24, residing in Lackawanna, a suburb of Buffalo, New York, who were identified as an al Qaeda-trained terrorist cell on American soil. The five had attended an al Qaeda training camp in Afghanistan, learning how to use assault rifles, handguns, and other weapons, in June 2001, and left the camp before the 9/11 attacks. They were charged with providing, attempting to provide, and conspiring to provide material support and resources to a foreign terrorist group (al Qaeda), which entail a maximum 15-year prison sentence. The recruits at the al-Farooq camp, which is located near Kandahar, were addressed by bin Laden. The camp was also attended by American Taliban John Walker Lindh.

The defendants were identified as Faysal Galab, age 26; Sahim Alwan, age 29; Yahya Goba, age 25; Safal Mosed, age 24; and Hasein Taher (variant Ther), age 24; who lived within a few blocks of one another. Two associates were believed to be in Yemen; another was out of the country. The associates, identified only as A, B, and C, included two U.S. citizens from Lackawanna, Pennsylvania. Prosecutors later identified the ringleader as unindicted co-conspirator Kamal Derwish, age 29, believed to be living in Yemen. The defendants were later joined by Mukhtar al-Bakri, age 22, who, with Alwan, admitted attending the camp.

At the September 19 bail hearing, Taher was represented by Rodney Persnius (variant Personius), who said that there was no proof his client was at the camp, but anyway, he didn't stay long.

The defendants were well-known in the local community. One was voted the high school's friendliest senior. Four are married; three have children.

The FBI had begun an investigation when the men came to Lackawanna in June 2001. The Bureau said there was no evidence that they were planning a specific attack in the United States.

Federal prosecutors noted on September 27 that some of the accused had tapes and documents in their homes that called for suicide operations against Islam's "enemies." On September 25, authorities searching Yasein Taher's Hamburg, New York apartment found a document that said "Martyrdom or self-sacrifice operations are those performed by one or more people against enemies far outstripping them in numbers and equipment. The form this usually takes nowadays is to wire up one's body, or a vehicle or suitcase with explosives, and then to enter into a conglomeration of the enemy, or in their vital facilities, and to detonate in an appropriate place there in order to cause the maximum losses in enemy ranks."

On October 8, Judge Schroeder released on $600,000 bond Sahim Alwan, but ordered the other five held without bail.

On October 21, a federal grand jury indicted the six on charges of providing and attempting to provide support to al Qaeda, and with conspiring to provide material support to the terrorists. They pleaded not guilty the next day to charges that they trained at an al Qaeda camp. They faced 15 years in prison.

On May 12, Taher pleaded guilty to supporting terrorism, admitting to learning to fire guns and grenade launchers at the camp. He acted against his attorney's advice. He was expected to receive an eight-year prison term when sentenced in September. Prosecutors said he was a member of a sleeper cell. The other men had been offered sentences of seven to ten years, contingent upon their cooperation in terrorism investigations. A conviction could entail a 15-year sentence.

On December 4, Taher, now age 25, was sentenced to eight years. He said "I'd just like to apologize to the court, my family, the community and most important my country. I know I've let a lot of people down."

Muhanad Taher: alias "the Engineer-4", age 26, who was believed to be one of the top bomb makers for Hamas. He was killed on June 30, 2002 by Israeli military forces. He was implicated in the June 18, 2002 suidice bombing of a bus in Jerusalem that killed 19 passengers and injured 55, the bombing in the summer of 2001 at a Tel Aviv disco that killed 21 people and wounded 120 others, and the Passover Seder attack on March 27, that killed 29 people and injured 140. The university graduate had become a regional leader of the Izzedine al Qassam Brigade. A second Hamas operative was killed and a third was critically wounded when Israeli troops fired on them in a Nablus house. Israeli authorities said Taher prepared numerous suicide bombers for their attacks.

Yasein Taher: variant of Hasein Taher.

Babak Taheri: one of three Iranians arrested on June 3, 1994 by police in Hat Yai, Thailand, in connection with the discovery on March 5, 1994 of a truck loaded with a ton of explosives in Thailand. Police believed that they planned assassination attempts against senior members of the U.S., Israeli, Pakistani, and other embassies, and that the truck bomb was to be used against the Israeli Embassy. On August 16, 1994, he was released for lack of evidence connecting him to the truck bomb.

Mohammed Reza Taheri-azar: age 22, a December 2005 University of North Carolina graduate from Iran, who on March 3, 2006, drove an SUV through The Pit, a popular campus watering hole, injuring nine people. He told police he did it "to avenge the deaths of Muslims around the world." In a 911 call, he said he aimed to "punish the government of the United States for their actions around the world." He appeared in Orange County District Court, charged with nine counts of attempted murder and nine counts of assault. Bail was set at $5.5 million. He was assigned a public defender. He said at the hearing he was "thankful for the opportunity to spread the will of Allah." The psychology and philosophy major had spent most of his life in the United States.

Midhat al-Tahhawi: one of three individuals sentenced to death on February 17, 1994 by a Cairo military court for plotting the assassination of President Mubarak by bombing Sidi Barrani Airport and the Presidential guest house in Marsa Matruh. Two of the defendants were executed by firing squad on February 28, 1994.

Abd Al Hakiem Omar Tahher: alias Abu Abd Allah, a Moroccan from Casablanca who was born on June 1, 1974 and joined al Qaeda in Iraq as a martyr on November 10, 2006, bringing a watch and passport. His recruitment coordinator was Saied. He said Hammed could be phoned on 002123593176; he also left the number 00212790.

'Abd-al-Hakim 'Umar Tahir: alias Abu-'Abdullah, a Moroccan from Casablanca who was born on June 1, 1974 and joined al Qaeda in Iraq as a martyr on November 10, 2006, contributing a watch, cell phone, and passport. His recruitment coordinator was Sa'id. He offered the phone number of Hamad: 0021213593176; he could also be reached on 0021279053712.

Adel Tahir: age 23, one of the five individuals without police records who, on May 16, 2003, conducted suicide bombings in Casablanca that killed 45 and wounded more than 100.

Fu'ad Abu-al-Tahir: alias of Muhammad al-Tahir.

Muhammad Tahir: a Palestinian arrested in connection with the April 26, 1985 bombing of the Geneva office of Libyan Arab Airlines, the bombing on the same date of the car of Ahmad Saqr, the Syrian Charge d'Affaires to the UN, and the placement of a bomb in the car of 'Abd al'Wahab Barakat, a Syrian diplomat and a nephew of President Hafiz al-Asad. On March 19, 1985, he was convicted of carrying out the bombings and sentenced to five years in prison. He admitted membership in the Marytyrs of Tal Za'Tar Organization.

Muhammad al-Tahir: alias Fu'ad Abu-al-Tahir, identified by Doha's *al-Sharq* on March 19, 1993 as a member of the Abu Nidal Group's Central Committee.

Shaykh Muhammad Abu Tahir: release from an Israeli jail was demanded on June 27, 1976 by the Popular Front for the Liberation of Palestine hijackers of Air France flight 139, an A300 flying from Tel Aviv to Paris and ultimately diverted to Entebbe.

Abderrahmane Tahiri: alias Mohamed Achraf, founder of the Martyrs for Morocco.

Hassan Tahrani: one of three Iranian youths who hijacked an Iran National Airlines B727 flying between Tehran, Abadan, and Kuwait on October 9, 1970 and diverted to Baghdad, Iraq. The trio threatened to blow up the plane with all passengers if Iran did not release 21 political prisoners. They injured a flight attendant. They were held by Iraqi authorities for questioning.

Samir Tahtah: age 28, a Moroccan arrested near Barcelona on June 15, 2005 as part of a cell of the Ansar al-Islam Army and al Qaeda in Iraq.

Abu-al-Bara' al-Ta'ifi: alias of Sa'ud 'Abdallah al-Shulwi.

Abu-Dhar al-Ta'ifi: alias of Shakir Salim al-Bishi.

Abu-Hamzah al-Ta'ifi: alias of Ahmad Ibrahim Hasan Katu.

Abu-Nimr al-Ta'ifi: alias of 'Abdallah 'Abid al-Sulaymani.

Abu-'Umar al-Ta'ifi: alias of 'Abd-al-Rahman Sa'id al-Ghamidi.

Sami Hussin Taiman: one of two hijackers of a British Airways flight from Bombay to London on March 3, 1974. The duo diverted the plane after its Beirut stopover and demanded to fly to Athens, where they intended to demand the release of Black September terrorists in the Athens airport attack on August 5, 1974. Greece denied landing permission, so the plane flew to Amsterdam's Schipol Airport. The terrorists allowed everyone to leave before torching the plane. The two were captured by police. The had claimed membership in the Palestine Liberation Army, but later the Organization of Arab Nationalist Youth for the Liberation of Palestine claimed credit. On June 6, 1974, a Dutch court convicted them on charges of air piracy and arms violations and sentenced them to five years. They were released on November 24, 1974, and flown to Tunis as part of an agreement reached with four hijackers of a British Airways plane in Dubai on November 22, 1974. On December 7, 1974, the two terrorists went to

Libya with the four hijackers who had demanded their release and five other terrorists released from Egypt. The two hijackers of the VC-10 apparently were given their freedom in Libya. Taiman's release was demanded on October 26, 1974 when two Arab terrorists and two Dutch criminals took 22 hostages at the prison chapel at Scheveningen, the Netherlands.

Khalid Ta'in: alias Abu-Isid, variant Abu-Usayd, an unemployed Algerian who was born on May 25, 1981 and joined al Qaeda in Iraq as a fighter on January 26, 2007. He contributed 1,150 lira, 75 dinars, and his passport. His recruitment coordinator was Sayid 'Ali, whom he met at a mosque. He flew to Damascus, where he met Abu-'Umar. He brought 150 euros. His phone number was 0021392261588824042.

Arif Tajjak: one of two accomplices of Ramzi Ahmad Yusuf who were arrested in March 1995 by Karachi, Pakistan police. He was implicated by Yusuf associate Ibrahim Rasul in terrorist activities in Karachi.

Andaleeb Takafka: age 20, a female Palestinian suicide bomber who, on April 12, 2002, set off an explosive belt at Jerusalem's Mahane Yehuda market's bus stop at 4 P.M., killing 6, including 2 Chinese citizens, wounding 90, 6 of them seriously, and destroying the bus while U.S. Secretary of State Colin Powell was meeting with Israeli Prime Minister Ariel Sharon. The blast left body parts and torn metal strewn across Jaffa Road. The al-Aqsa Martyrs Brigades claimed credit.

Takafka, whose name means "nightingale" in Arabic, lived in Beit Fajar, an isolated town south of Bethlehem, sewing in a clothes factory. She never talked of politics. Her parents remembered that she woke up before 6 A.M., made them tea, and left the house without saying a word. At her wake, her father, Khalil, said, "I am happy. All the girls should do it."

Mohamad Talao: named on March 21, 1994 as one of four suspects in the discovery on March 5, 1994 of a truck loaded with a ton of explosives

in Thailand. Police believed that they planned assassination attempts against senior members of the U.S., Israeli, Pakistani, and other embassies, and that the truck bomb was to be used against the Israeli Embassy.

Muhammad Abu Talb: variant of Muhammad Abu Talib.

Al-Kabir Talcan: variant Balkan, a Morrocan arrested in connection with the July 18, 1994 bombing of the Argentine-Israeli Mutual Aid Association (AIMA) in Buenos Aires that killed 96 and wounded 231. Hizballah was suspected. He entered Argentina on July 11, 1994.

Abu Taleb: Palestine Liberation Organization mediator who was believed to have been involved in the preparation and planning of the Red Eagles of the Palestinian Revolution takeover of the Egyptian Embassy in Ankara on July 13, 1979.

Ali Ghazi Taleb: a member of the Syrian Nationalist Social party of Lebanon who, on July 31, 1985, drove a suicide car bomb in Arnoun, Lebanon that killed a Lebanese civilian and injured two Israeli soldiers in the security zone of southern Lebanon.

Mustapha Taleb: one of six North African men arrested on January 5, 2003 by UK antiterrorist police after discovering traces of ricin, a toxin, in a north London apartment in the Wood Green district. The men were in their late teens, twenties, and thirties and were arrested in locations in north and east London. A woman detained with them was later released. They were held without charge under the UK's antiterrorist laws. Police said they were following a tip from French intelligence. A seventh man was grabbed on January 7. Some press reports said they were Algerians.

On January 11, police charged Mouloud Feddag; Sidali Feddag, Samir Feddag, age 26; and Mustapha Taleb, age 33, with possession of articles of value to a terrorist and being concerned in the development or production of chemical weapons. Nasreddine Fekhadji was charged with forgery and counterfeiting. A sixth man was arrested for possession of drugs and immigration offenses. The six were to appear in court on January 13. A seventh man, age 33, was turned over to immigration officials. Four of the North African men appeared in court for the first time on January 13. They were identified as Mouloud and Samir Feddag and Mustapha Taleb, along with a 17-year-old, whose name was withheld because of his age. They were charged with possession of articles for the "commission, preparation, or instigation of an act of terrorism" and with "being concerned in the development or production of chemical weapons."

Ricin traces were found in a house in Afghanistan in 2002 used by al Qaeda. There is no antidote. Police believed the suspects would kill a small number of people with the ricin to cause widespread panic. Some observers suggested that the terrorists intended to spike with ricin food that was to be delivered to a British military base. One of the detainees worked for a firm that served food on the base. The FBI issued a warning to local police about ricin on January 10.

On February 26, British authorities charged three men with conspiring to make chemical weapons. By April 2004, nine individuals associated with the ricin threat were charged with conspiracy to murder and other related charges. Their trials were slated for May and September 2004.

Abu Talha: alias of Muhammad Attia Al Amami.

Abu Talha: alias of Abu Baker Zaied Bin Houeraf.

Abu-Talhah: alias of Muhammad Salih Jarallah al-Khatib.

Abu Talha: alias of Muhammad Naeem Noor Khan.

Abu Talha: alias of Abd Allah Shalali.

Abu Talha: Mosul representative of Abu Musab al-Zarqawi in March 2005.

Abu-Talha: alias of Hafid.

Abdul Rahim al-Talhi: one of three Saudis suspected of financing Abu Sayyaf, whose U.S. assets were blocked on October 10, 2007 by the U.S. Department of the Treasury.

Jamal Muhsin al-Tali: alias of Jamal Mohammad Ahmad Ali al-Badawi.

Muhammad Abu Talib: variant Talb, linked to the December 21, 1988 Lockerbie bombing of Pan Am flight 103 in which 270 people died. He was one of 15 members of the Popular Front for the Liberation of Palestine-General Command (PFLP-GC) arrested on May 18, 1989 in Sweden on suspicion of involvement in explosions in Copenhagen and other crimes. On December 21, 1989, he was convicted of murder and gross destruction dangerous to the public and sentenced by the Uppsala town court to life in prison for setting off two bombs in Copenhagen in July 1985 against the synagogue and against the Northwest Orient Airlines office in which one person was killed and several others injured. He was found innocent of the bombing of Northwest Orient Airlines' office in Stockholm in April 1986. He was to be expelled from the country forever after the sentenced had been served (presumably, parole was a possibility). On November 2, 1989, the PFLP-GC denied that he was connected with the group. Some observers believed he was part of the Palestine Popular Struggle Front, headquartered in Damascus and financed by Libya. *ABC* quoted Swedish police as saying that he bought the clothing found in the suitcase in which the bomb on the flight Pan Am exploded. He visited Malta on October 19–26, 1988. He traveled to Cyprus on October 3–18, 1988, where some of the planning for the attack was believed to have taken place. He was one of 14 Arabs arrested on October 26, 1988 in Neuss, West Germany, where police found a weapons cache, including altitude-sensitive detonators that matched components used in the Lockerbie bomb.

He received SAM-3 missile training in the Soviet Union. He joined an Egyptian-sponsored Palestinian military unit in 1967 at age 15. While with the Popular Struggle Front, he returned to the USSR for training in political organizing. His wife, Jamilah al-Moghrabi, is a sister of one of his fellow defendants.

Taliban: alias of Muhammad Kabous.

Abu-Tamam: a Saudi-based recruiter of foreign fighters for al Qaeda in Iraq in 2006.

Mohammad Tamhidi: one of three suspected members of an Iranian hit squad who were released on April 6, 1984 by the Philippine Commission on Immigration and Deportation in spite of internal protests that the trio represented a threat to security. There were charges of a payoff. Some suspected them of involvement in the disappearance of nine pro-Shah Iranian students on August 16, 1983.

Sami Houssin Tamimah: variant Sami Hussin Taiman, participant in the March 3, 1974 hijacking of a British Airways flight from Bombay to London. His release was demanded on October 26, 1974 when two Arab terrorists and two Dutch criminals took 22 hostages at the prison chapel at Scheveningen, Netherlands. Authorities promised him a reduced sentence if he would not go along with the terrorists' demands. He subsequently aided in the negotiations, talking with his former compatriot, Adnan Ahmed Nuri, four times. Tamimah was released as a result of demands made by Arab nationalist Youth Organization for the Liberation of Palestine hijackers who seized a British Airways VC-10 in Dubai on November 21, 1974.

Ibrahim al-Tamimi: alias Tariq Muhammad, identified by Doha's *al-Sharq* on March 19, 1993 as a member of the Abu Nidal Group's Central Committee and its revolutionary justice committee.

Dr. Colonel Nadir al-Tamimi: assistant mufti of the Palestine National Liberation Army who, on August 9, 1990, issued a fatwa calling for attacks on Americans and Westerners in response to the U.S. blockade of Iraq.

Shaykh As'ad Bayyud al-Tamimi: a fundamentalist leader who resides in Amman and told *Reuters* that he had established the Islamic Jihad Movement-Bayt al-Maqdis in 1980. The group claimed credit for several anti-Israeli attacks, including that on a bus on the Tel Aviv–Jerusalem road in July 1989 in which 14 people were killed and 27 others wounded. The group threatened on April 24, 1990 to target U.S. citizens if the U.S. Senate did not retract within 10 days its resolution that Jerusalem is Israel's capital.

Jihad Ahmad Khalid al-Tanjirah: one of a group of Jordanian Afghans sentenced on December 21, 1994 by the Jordanian State Security Court for belonging to an illegal society, participating in a conspiracy to carry out terrorist acts, and possessing explosives for illegal purposes. The Muslim fundamentalists bombed cinemas, wounding nine people, including an attack on January 26, 1994 at an Amman cinema showing what they perceived to be pornographic films, and another bombing on February 1, 1994. The group had been seized in a crackdown on Muslim radicals in January 1994. Their trial began on August 27, 1994, when they were accused of planning to assassinate leading Jordanians, including 'Abd-al-Salam al-Majali, Jordan's former chief peace negotiator with Israel. One of those sentenced to death was Muhammad Jamal Khalifah, a Saudi fugitive son-in-law of Osama bin Laden. He was sentenced to life with hard labor.

Rima Tannous: one of four Black September hijackers, on May 8, 1972, of Sabena Airlines 517, a B707 flying the Vienna–Athens–Tel Aviv route over Zagreb. The group landed at Lod Airport in Israel and demanded the release of 317 fedayeen prisoners, most of them held at Ramleh prison. They threatened to blow up the plane and all aboard. She was captured when Israeli forces stormed the plane. The two male hijackers died in the rescue.

Tannous was an orphan who was reared by nuns. She entered nursing in Amman. She claimed that she was raped by a young man and then became a mistress to a Fatah doctor who gave her drugs. She said that she was forced to sleep with Fatah members and was beaten or refused morphine if she refused. She claimed that she was totally dependent upon Fatah for food and money. "I had to comply with their orders. I had as much free will as a robot." She was selected for a special course in sabotage and subjected to an intense loyalty test.

The two female hijackers were tried in a military court in the theater of the old British Army camp at Sarafand. They were charged for terrorist crimes in violation of point 58d of the 1945 British Mandatory Government's Defence (Emergency) Regulations and for being members of the unlawful El Fatah association, contrary to point 85.1.a. The women, claiming constraint according to section 17 of the Criminal Code Ordinance of 1936, said that they were forced to carry the arms and were not willing members of Fatah. The tribunal rejected that defense, noting tht the law allowed that defense only if there was an immediate threat of death or grievous harm, which did not appear to be the case. One of the judges demanded the death sentence for the women after they were found guilty of the three charges. His colleagues disagreed, and on August 14, 1972, the two were sentenced to life in prison.

Tannous' release was demanded by the four Black September terrorists who took over the Israeli Embassy in Bankok on December 28, 1972.

Ernesto Tanuz: a 64-year-old Syrian arrested on October 8, 1994 by Argentine police. He was an owner of the house where, the previous day, police had arrested 'Ali al-Hasan in connection with the July 18, 1994 bombing of the Argentine-Israeli Mutual Aid Association (AIMA) in Buenos Aires that killed 96 and wounded 231. His son, Julio, 24, was also detained.

Julio Tanuz: a 24-year-old Syrian arrested on October 8, 1994 by Argentine police. He was an owner of the house where, the previous day, police had arrested 'Ali al-Hasan in connection

with the July 18, 1994 bombing of the Argentine-Israeli Mutual Aid Association (AIMA) in Buenos Aires that killed 96 and wounded 231. His father, Ernesto, age 64, was also detained.

Hamid Taoube: a Lebanese-born Muslim with Australian citizenship who was arrested on January 25, 1991 in Australia after telling an undercover police officer of his plan to manufacture a bomb that he would carry onto a U.S.-bound plane, which he would then hijack to Iraq. He declined to enter a plea when he appeared in court on January 29, 1991. He was remanded into custody to appear again on February 18. He was charged with threatening to endanger the safety of an aircraft. He had phoned the Iraqi Embassy in Canberra and offered to hijack a plane. He was an unemployed welder who was separated from his wife and four children and who lived with his sister in Sydney. He had lived in the country for 15 years and had been on sickness benefits for nearly 6 years due to a back injury. He was refused bail.

Hesham al-Tarabili: arrested on September 14, 2002 by Brazilian authorities at Egypt's request in connection with the 1997 al-Gama'at al-Islamiyya attack on tourists in Luxor, Egypt.

Sulman Taraqi: variant of Salman Tariki.

Abu Tarek: alias of Habis Abdallah al-Sa'ub.

Charaabi Tarek: one of four Tunisians convicted by a Milan court on February 22, 2002 on terrorist charges, including criminal association with intent to transport arms, explosives, and chemicals, and falsifying 235 work permits, 130 driver's licenses, several foreign passports, and various blank documents. They were acquitted of charges of possession of arms and chemicals. The guilty verdicts were the first in Europe against al Qaeda operatives since the 9/11 attacks. The four belonged to the Salafist Group for Preaching and Combat, an Algerian wing of al Qaeda. He received four years. On April 19, 2002 the United States froze his assets.

Abu Tareq: in February 2005, a member of Islamic Jihad's Damascus, Syria-based political bureau.

Fatahi Tarhoni: a Libyan who, on April 6, 1985, shot to death Gebril Denali, a Libyan opponent of Muammar Qadhafi, in Bonn's Cathedral Square. Police arrested Tarhoni with the gun still in his hands.

Rajab Mukhtar Tarhuni: variant of Recep Muhtar Rohama Tarhuni.

Recep Muhtar Rohama Tarhuni: variant Rajab Mukhtar Tarhuni, one of two Libyans who, when stopped by police on April 18, 1986 in front of the U.S. officer's club in Ankara, Turkey, threw away a bag containing six grenades and ran. They were apprehended. The attack was to occur during a wedding party attended by 100 people. The terrorists were aided by a Libyan diplomat at the local embassy. On April 28, 1986, the duo were charged with conspiracy to kill a group of people and with smuggling arms. The duo had entered Turkey on April 16, 1986 and had contacted Umran Mansur, manager of the Libyan Arab Airlines office in Istanbul. He allegedly selected the target. The grenades were supplied by Mohammad Shaban Hassan, a Libyan Embassy employee in charge of administrative affairs who met with the duo on April 17 and 18. The trial began on May 13, 1986 in the State Security Court. On June 7, 1986, he was convicted of possession of explosives and was sentenced to five years in prison. The duo were acquitted of the more serious conspiracy charges. The Court of Appeals revoked the decision on the grounds that they were not punished for establishing an organization for the aim of committing a crime. During a retrial, the court insisted on its previous decision, causing a second revocation by the Court of Appeals Criminal Assembly. On April 14, 1988, he was sentenced to eight years and four months in prison for establishing an armed organization with the purpose of killing more than one person. He was also fined 62,500 Turkish lira.

Sulayman Bin 'Abd-al-'Aziz Sulayman al-Mulhim al-Tari: alias Abu-al-Bara', a Saudi from Riyadh who was born in 1985 and joined al Qaeda in Iraq in 2007 as a martyr, contributing $600 and 500 riyals, plus his passport. His recruitment coordinator was Abu-Su'ud. He arrived from Jodran and Syria, where he met Abu-'Uthman. His home phone number was 009662271799; his brother's was 00966556224662.

Mahdi Tarik: named used on an Iraqi passport by Abu Daoud to enter Poland in 1981.

Salman Tariki: variant Sulman Taraqi, a Libyan who was arrested on September 10, 1986 in Pakistan in connection with the hijacking by the Libyan Revolutionary Cells and the Organization of the Soldiers of God–Martyr Zulfikar Ali Bhutto Group, who took over Pan Am flight 73 at Karachi airport on September 5, 1986. The hijackers threw grenades and fired machine guns at the passengers, killing 22 and injuring 100 others. Police believed he was the mastermind of the attack, meeting with the Palestinians, arranging for weapons after casing the airport. He led authorities to a cache of East European weapons on the coast near Karachi.

Iyad Muhammad Tarkhan: alias Abu-Sulyman, variant Abu Suleiman, a Jordanian from Amman who was born on June 20, 1980 and joined al Qaeda in Iraq on November 18, 2006, intending to become a martyr. He contributed $180, 1,000 lira, a passport, a Jordanian military service ID, and his driver's license. His recruitment coordinator was 'Abd-al-Hamid. His home phone number was 0795937990; his brother's was 0795390377.

Abu Tariq: alias of Habis Abdallah al-Sa'ub.

Abu Tariq: a leader of al Qaeda in Iraq in the al-Layin and al-Mashadah sector near Balad as of November 3, 2007, when a U.S. military raid found his diary and will. His forces had shrunk from 600 to fewer than 20. He fled to Mosul.

Dr. Taufeeq: alias of Abu Faraj Farj.

Admadal-Tawil: alias of Shaykh Ahmad Salim Suwaydan.

Dia Tawil: a 19-year-old second-year engineering student at Bir Zeit University who made a farewell video for Hamas before he strapped on a nail bomb and walked in front of a bus station at a gas station at the Peace Rendezevous near the central Israeli border of the West Bank on March 27, 2001, killing two Israeli teenagers. His father, Hussein, was a nonviolent Communist Party militant. An uncle on his mother's side, Adnan Daghai, remains a Communist activist with the renamed People's Party. Paternal uncle Jamal is a leader of the Hamas political wing in Ramallah. Tawil had been slightly wounded in 2000 by a bullet at a Ramallah demonstration.

Khodr Tawil: Lebanese Brigadier General detained for the February 14, 2005 car bombing that killed former Lebanese Prime Minister Rafiq Hariri, age 60, as the billionaire was driving through central Beirut's waterfront just before lunchtime. Another 22 people died and more than 100 people were injured, including the Minister of Economy.

Al-'Adiliyah 'Abdallah Nasir Muhammad al-Tawq: on June 26, 1996, the Bahrain State Security Court sentenced him to life in prison for the February 11, 1996 bombing of the Diplomat Hotel in Manama, the January 17, 1996 bombing of the Le Royal Meridien Hotel, and the bombing of two branches of the Bahrain Corporation for International Shipping and Trade located in the Diplomatic Quarter.

Mustafa Sulayman al-Tawwab: a Lebanese who was one of 18 Arab terrorists reported by Madrid *Diario 16* on October 20, 1987 as having entered Spain in August to attack Middle Eastern diplomatic missions and assassinate Saudi Ambassador Muhammad Nuri Ibrahim. They had received weapons and casing reports on the ambassador

from a Lebanese student resident in Spain whose initials were HMI.

Ja'far al-Tayar: variant Jaffar al-Tayyar, Jafar Tayar, Jaafar al-Tayyar, aliases of Adnan G. El Shukrijumah.

'Abd-al-Hadi al-Saghir 'Abd-al-'Zaim Tayi': one of seven terrorists hanged on July 8, 1993 in the appeals prison in Cairo for attacks on tourist buses and installations in the al-Wajh al-Qiblio, Luxor, and Aswan areas, in accordance with the sentence handed down by the Supreme Military Court on April 22, 1993 in Case Number 6.

'Abd-al-Nabi Tayih: wanted in connection with the Muslim Group's October 21, 1992 attack on a tour bus near Dayrut, Egypt that killed a British tourist and injured two others. He was one of seven Islamic militants shot dead by police in a raid in Cairo on February 3, 1994.

Sidi al-Madani al-Tayyib: Osama bin Laden's chief financial officer in Sudan, he was captured by Saudi authorities in the spring of 1997. He is married to bin Laden's niece. He was pardoned "in return for exposing some of bin Laden's financial operations."

Zuher Hilal Mohamed al Tbaiti: one of three Saudi members of al Qaeda who were planning to attack U.S. and British warships in the Strait of Gibraltar. They were arrested by Moroccan police in May 2002. Two of the Saudis were married to Moroccans. They arrived in Morocco in late January via Lahore, Pakistan and either Qatar or Abu Dhabi. He was seen in Melilla, a Spanish enclave in northern Morocco. He married a Moroccan. He was under surveillance for a month, visiting Melilla and Ceuta, another Spanish enclave opposite Gibraltar. He was inquiring about buying Zodiac speedboats. In April, he was directed via a phone call to return to Saudi Arabia. He was arrested at Casablanca airport with fellow Saudi Hilal Jaber Alassiri and two Moroccan women. The detainees had $10,000 in case. They led authorities to Abdallah M'Sefer Ali al Ghamdi in another Moroccan city. The trio told authorities that after they had obtained the boats, a logistics team would bring in explosives and weapons, and a third, suicide team would conduct the operations. While in Afghanistan, Tbaiti and Alassiri had committed themselves to conduct eventual suicide operations. Moroccan authorities said the terrorists also planned, but later aborted, a local attack as well. They were arraigned in a Moroccan court on June 17, 2002, during which prosecutors said that the trio tried to recruit locals to al Qaeda and considered blowing up a café in central Marrakech and plotted a suicide attack against the local bus company. Alassiri argued against killing fellow Muslims, but Tbaiti said it was "justified by the nobleness of the operation." On February 21, 2003, a Moroccan court sentenced the three Saudi men to ten-year sentences for criminal conspiracy, use of false documents, and illegal stay in Morocco. They were acquitted of attempted sabotage and attempted homicide, according to defense attorney Khalil Idrissi.

The Teacher: alias of Ayman al-Zawahiri.

Adel Tebourski: on May 17, 2005, a Paris court sentenced him to two to seven years for association with a terrorist enterprise and providing logistical support to the killers of Ahmed Shah Massoud, who, on September 9, 2001, was assassinated in Afghanistan by al Qaeda terrorists posing as journalists.

George Teredjian: a Lebanese–Armenian employee of the Iraqi Embassy in Beirut who was believed to have driven the gunmen to the apartment Talib al-Suhayl al-Tamimi, a leading member of the London-based Free Iraqi Council opposition group in Beirut during the night of April 12, 1994. He was detained and charged with complicity.

William Edward Tesscher: name on a U.S. passport held by one of two suspected pro-Iraqi terrorists detained on February 17, 1991 by Philippines immigration police as the duo was about to board a Philippine Airlines flight to Tokyo's Narita Airport. He had a Pakistani passport in his luggage stamped by Baghdad immigration authorities. Pictures found in his luggage showed him posing with weapons at an undisclosed place. They were put under "custodial investigation" in Cebu on suspicion of planning to link up with the Japanese Red Army.

Youcef Ben Tetraoui: third-ranking leader of the Algerian Armed Islamic Group, who was killed on December 2, 1995 by Algerian security forces. He was an Afghan Arab who died at his hideout at Tebessa, east of Algiers. Repentant terrorists fingered his hideout, ending a search that began in 1992.

Abu Thabit: alias of Abd Allah Abu Baker Bawzeer.

Muhammad Bin Saud Bin Sa'ad Al Thabtie: alias Abu Sahour, a Saudi student from Mecca who was born on 7/2/1404 Hijra and joined al Qaeda in Iraq on 5th Jumada al-awal 1428 (2007) as a fighter, bringing 2,500 Saudi Riyals. His recruitment coordinator was Abu Abd Allah, whom he knew through Abu Al Abbnas. He arrived from Saudi Arabia to Iraq, where he met Abu Omar al Iraqi, whom he gave 8,000 Saudi Riyals. His mother's phone number was 055514772; his sister's was 0555228169.

Salah Thakore: name on a false Moroccan passport used by one of the three Egyptian Revolution hijackers of Egyptair flight 648 that had left Athens bound for Cairo on November 23, 1985.

Thamer: Saudi-based recruitment coordinator for al Qaeda in Iraq foreign fighters in 2006.

Abu Thamer: alias of Naif Abd Al Rahman Muhammad Al Saied.

Thamir: Saudi-based recruitment coordinator for foreign fighters for al Qaeda in Iraq in 2006.

Hasein Ther: variant of Hasein Taher.

Ahmad Thiab: an Iraqi who holds a Ph.D. in political science for whom Roanoke police were searching after they arrested nine men on March 5, 1997 suspected of laundering hundreds of thousands of dollars directed to Middle Eastern terrorist front organizations during the previous seven years. The suspects were held on federal murder, racketeering, narcotics, and extortion charges and were believed to have built a fortune via narcotics distribution, insurance scams involving arson, burglary, robbery, and fraud. The group owned or had a financial interest in 33 restaurants, convenience stores, and other shops. One of the front organizations was SAAR (expansion unknown), an investment-management agency that reportedly supports Hamas and that has ties to Usama Bin Ladin. The U.S. Attorney's Office for the Western District of Virginia identified the group as the Abed Family, named after the two brothers who controlled it, Joseph Abed and Abed Jamil Abdeljalil, both born in El Bireh, Palestinian Authority. They and four sons born in northern Virginia, along with a Jordanian, a Saudi, an Iraqi, and an American employee of the Postal Service, faced charges that could lead to life in prison.

Zuhair al-Thubaiti: the 9/11 Commission said that he was initially scheduled to be a 9/11 hijacker, but was pulled from the operation by al Qaeda leaders.

Fahad al Thumairy: Upon arriving in Los Angeles from Frankfurt on May 6, 2003, the 31-year-old Saudi consular official was informed that his visa had been revoked in March. He was barred from returning to the United States for five years, and put on an international flight two days later. He was suspected of having links to a terrorist group. He had been at the Saudi Consulate in Los Angeles since 1996, working in the Islamic and cultural affairs section.

Mani' Rashid al-Tikriti: identified on October 9, 1990 by the London-based Kuwaiti newspaper *al-Qabas al-Duwali* as being a leader of a worldwide Iraqi terrorist network. The paper claimed he was an aide to Barzan Ibrahim, and had served as a diplomat in Rome in 1983, where he was accused of collaborating with the Red Brigades and thus was expelled. He was later seen in the United Arab Emirates, where he allegedly hired Muhammad 'Abd-al-Hamid Hasan, a Jordanian, to assassinate a Gulf state's ambassasdor to Kuwait.

Sabbawi Ibrahim Hasan al-Tikriti: half brother of former Iraqi President Saddam Hussein and leader of a group of 25 Arab terrorists armed with missiles who were going to attack embassies of the Gulf War's allies on March 14, 1991, according to the Kuwaiti Embassy in Spain. The terrorists were using Sudanese passports and had departed from Soba, Sudan after being armed in Yemen.

Omar al-Timimi: age 37, an asylum seeker who was convicted on July 5, 2007 in a Manchester, United Kingdom court for possessing terrorism training manuals, including one showing how to use gas cylinders in car bombs. He was the head of a sleeper cell and had awaited orders since arriving in the United Kingdom from the Netherlands in 2002. He was arrested in 2006 on suspicion of money laundering. Police found on his computer bomb-making instructions, videos of executions of hostages, and information on detonators and explosives. He had links with terrorists in the Netherlands and with Junade Feroze, who was convicted in June 2007 for plotting to bomb targets in the United States and United Kingdom.

Salamulla Tippu: alias of Mohammed Alam Gir.

Abu-Tirab: alias of Al-Bara' Muhammad Sadiq.

Zineddine Tirouda: age 37, an Algerian born in the United States. An arrest warrant was issued on November 2, 2001. He was freed on bond, but charged with conspiring to illegally obtain U.S. passports and residency. The California Department of Transportation engineer once lived in the same apartment complex as Al-Bayoumi, who had contacts with some of the 9/11 hijackers, but claimed to have never met him.

Jihad Titi: age 18, a Palestinian suicide bomber who, on May 27, 2002, walked into a crowd of after-work shoppers at the sidewalk Village Café in a suburban Petah Tikva (seven miles east of Tel Aviv) strip mall and set off an explosion that killed an elderly Israeli woman, Ruth Peled, and her 18-month-old granddaughter, Sinai Kanaan, and injured more than 50 others. He wore blue jeans and a gray shirt. His bomb was packed with nails and shrapnel that sprayed the Em Hamoshavot strip mall and supermarket. The al-Aqsa Martyrs Brigades said it was retaliating for Israel's killing three Palestinian militants in a refugee camp near Nablus the previous week. The killer was a cousin of Mahmoud Titi, a militant in Nablus killed by an Israeli tank shell the previous week. Jihad's brother, Munir, was paralyzed from shrapnel wounds during an April invasion of the Balata refugee camp. Munir's 14-year-old son lost two fingers in that attack. Jihad recorded a video in which he said he would get revenge against the "pig government." Haleema, his mother, praised his act, saying that when he said goodbye to her, "I realized he was going to carry out a suicide attack. I said, 'Oh, son, I hope your operation will succeed.'"

Mahmoud Titi: a commander of the al-Aqsa Martyrs Brigades, who was killed by Israeli tank gunners on May 22, 2002 in Nablus.

Abdel Hakim Tizegha: age 29, arrested on December 24, 1999 by Bellevue, Washington police who charged him with illegally entering the country and eluding federal officers at the Canadian border. He was scheduled to appear before a federal magistrate on January 5, 2000. Press reports linked him to Ahmed Ressam and Abdel Ghani. Some observers believed that he was involved in a splinter group of the Algerian Armed Islamic Group (GIA) that broke with the GIA over a dispute regarding the targeting of fellow Muslims. On March 16, 2000, he pleaded guilty to illegal

re-entry and faced up to two years in prison and a $250,000 fine. On June 2, 2000, he reportedly was to be handed over to immigration authorities for probable deportation. He was sentenced by U.S. District Judge Barbara Rothstein to the time he had served since his arrest.

Jean-Marie Tjibao: leader of the Kanak Socialist National Liberation Front in New Caledonia in 1984.

Adel Tobbichi: Algerian arrested on June 21, 2002 in Montreal following a Dutch extradition request on charges of altering passports and other documents and providing them to terrorists planning to bomb the U.S. Embassy in Paris. He was extradited in July 2002. Dutch authorities had earlier arrested two French citizens in the plot. Rotterdam prosecutors said that wiretaps linked Jerome Courtailler and Mohammed Berkous, both 27, to Nizar Trabelsi, the would-be suicide bomber, who was under arrest in Belgium. He was acquitted on December 18, 2002, by a Rotterdam court, on charges of planning attacks on the U.S. embassy in Paris but turned over to immigration authorities.

Sheik Sobhi Tofailli: Hizballah commander reported by Jack Anderson and Dale Van Atta of planning the hijacking of a Kuwaiti A310 en route from Kuwait to Bangkok with intermediate stops in Dubai and Karachi on December 4, 1984.

Mohammad S. Tofighi: one of eight Iranian students arrested in the United States on November 15, 1979 for attempting to smuggle 3 disassembled Winchester 30.06 rifles, matching scopes, 15 boxes of ammunition, and a street map of Washington, DC with certain embassies marked, as one of the men was about to board TWA 900 from Baltimore-Washington International Airport to New York's JFK International Airport. The Iranians spoke of taking the rifles to Iran. They claimed to be attending Baltimore-area colleges, and were jailed on bonds ranging from

$25,000 to $250,000. The group was charged with dealing in firearms without a license, placing firearms on an interstate commercial airliner without notifying the carrier, and conspiracy. On November 26, 1979, charges were dismissed against him. Charges were also dropped against his wife, Shahla Amenli.

Avraham Toledano: a 58-year-old Israeli rabbi linked to the Kach ultra-nationalist movement who was arrested on November 26, 1993 by Israeli customs officials who discovered him trying to smuggle bomb-making materials and manuals from the United States into Tel Aviv's Ben Gurion Airport.

Usamah Tookan: signature used by one of the Palestinian gunmen who, on September 26, 1986, signed a statement asking their comrades not to seize hostages to obtain their release. He had been sentenced to life in Cyprus in February 1986 in connection with the takeover of an Israeli-owned yacht, the *First*, taking two Israeli hostages after killing a woman in the initial assault in Cyprus on September 25, 1985. After nine hours of negotiations, the terrorists killed the hostages and surrendered. Fatah Force 17 claimed credit.

Mohammad Toolabi: variant of Mohammod Reza Bahadoritoolabi and Mohammad Reza Bahadori Toolabi, one of eight Iranian students arrested in the United States on November 15, 1979 for attempting to smuggle 3 disassembled Winchester 30.06 rifles, matching scopes, 15 boxes of ammunition, and a street map of Washington, DC with certain embassies marked, as one of the men was about to board TWA 900 from Baltimore-Washington International Airport to New York's JFK International Airport.

Mohammad Reza Bahadori Toolabi: variant of Mohammad Toolabi

Henri Toronchik: one of two Israelis who took over a section of the West German Embassy in Tel Aviv on April 14, 1977 and surrendered five hours later. They were angered over the slow progress of and world apathy toward trials of Nazi war criminals.

Martinez Torres: alias of Ilich Ramirez Sanchez.

Toto: alias of Ismael Acmad.

Ali Ben Sassi Toumi: variant Ali Ben Sassi Touri. On January 26, 2005, the Italian Justice Ministry sent inspectors to Milan after Judge Clementina Forleo dropped terrorism charges against three Tunisians and two Moroccans on January 24, saying they were "guerrillas," not "terrorists." She said their actions in recruiting for and financing training camps in northern Iraq during the U.S.-led invasion did not "exceed the activity of a guerilla group." She claimed the 1999 UN Global Convention on Terrorism said that paramilitary activities in war zones could not be prosecuted according to international law unless they were designed to create terror among civilians and broke international humanitarian laws. Prosecutors said they would appeal. Maher Bouyahia and Ali Ben Sassi Toumi (variant Touri) were nonetheless given a three-year sentence for dealing with false documents and assisting illegal immigration; they had seven months left to serve.

Mohammed Ahmed al-Toumi: drunken Libyan who hijacked a Middle East Airways B707 flying from Benghazi to Beirut on August 16, 1973. He used two pistols to threaten the crew and passengers and divert the plane to Israel's Lod Airport. Israeli antiterrorist forces boarded the plane and overpowered him. He claimed that he wished to "show Israelis not all Arabs are enemies of Israel." He was committed to a mental institution on December 11, 1973.

Ali Ben Sassi Touri: variant of Ali Ben Sassi Toumi.

Karim Touzani: name on a stolen Belgian passport used by one of two al Qaeda suicide bombers who, on September 9, 2001, killed Afghan Northern Alliance leader Ahmed Shah Massoud.

Muhamed Tovanti: one of three Algerian hijackers of an Air Algerie Convair 640 flying from Annaba to Algiers on August 31, 1970. The trio wanted to fly to Albania to obtain political asylum, but the Albanian government refused to let the plane land. The group flew to Dubrovnik, Yugoslavia, where they surrendered to police.

Nizar Trabelsi: variant of Nizar Trabelzi.

Nizar Trabelzi: on September 13, 2001, Belgian police arrested the Tunisian former professional soccer player believed to have links to al Qaeda. Police seized from his apartment a submachine gun, ammunition, and chemical formulas for making explosives. Spain said he was in contact with six Algerian members of the Salafist Group for Call and Combat who had been arrested during the week. He had a longer criminal record and was linked to an individual arrested on the same day in the Netherlands. The group, also known as the Salafist Group for Preaching and Combat, was a dissident faction of Algeria's Armed Islamic Group. Trabelzi was in Spain at the same time as 9/11 hijacker Muhammad Atta, although there was no public evidence about whom Atta had contacted. Trabelsi was accused of planning to walk into the U.S. embassy in Paris with a bomb taped to his chest. Spanish police said they had seized equipment for faking documents. The group may have furnished passports, plane tickets, and credit cards to Islamic radicals. Spain also seized three pair of night-vision binoculars, a diary in which the writer said he wanted to be a suicide bomber, and videos showing Taliban attacks in Afghanistan. Similar charges were made on November 18 following another raid by Spanish police in which they found videos of attacks in Chechnya.

On Setpember 30, 2003, he was convicted of planning to bomb the NATO base at Kleine Brogel and sentenced to a decade in prison. He had admitted to planning to drive a car bomb into the cafeteria at Kleine Brogel, the Belgian air base believed to house U.S. nuclear weapons guarded by 100 U.S. troops. He said he intended to kill U.S. soldiers, not detonate the warheads. He said he had met Osama bin Laden in Afghanistan.

On December 21, 2007, Belgian police arrested 14 people allegedly seeking to forcibly free him.

Vicken Tscharkhutian: an Iraqi arrested on June 6, 1982 at Orly Airport in Paris for complicity in a Swiss bank bombing and the May 30, 1982 placement of a bomb at the Air Canada freight terminal at Los Angeles International Airport. On August 18, 1982, the Paris Appeals Court recommended against extradition of the Armenian Secret Army for the Liberation of Armenia member.

Younis Tsouli: Internet screen alias Irhabi007, a Moroccan living in London who served as a cyberterrorist for al Qaeda. In 2004, he posted a video of Abu Musab al-Zarqawi beheading American contractor Nicholas Berg in Iraq. He later broke into the servers of the Arkansas Highway Department and distributed al-Zarqawi's videos. He was also in contact with Syed Haris Ahmed, a Pakistani American, and Ehsanul Islam Sadequee, a Bangladeshi American, both of Atlanta, who, in March 2005, met with Canadian extremists in Toronto to explore attacking military bases and oil refineries. They gave him a video of potential U.S. targets, including fuel storage tanks on Interstate 95 near Lorton, Virginia, World Bank headquarters, the Pentagon, and the George Washington Masonic Memorial in Alexandria, Virginia. He was the administrator of the jihadi forum Muntada al-Ansar al-Islami, which had served as the propaganda outlet of Abu Musab al-Zarqawi. British authorities raided his apartment in West London in October 2005. He was logged on to youbombit.r8.org using his identity IRH007. On October 21, 2005, British police seized his hard drive that included photos of Washington locations and a CBRN (chemical biological radiological nuclear) vehicle. He was charged with possessing other computer slides showing how to make a car bomb, conspiring with fellow detainee Wassem Mughal, age 22, to cause explosions in the United Kingdom, and with Tariq al-Daour, age 19, to commit credit card fraud. Tsouli and Mughal were charged with conspiracy to murder and to cause an explosion. Prosecutors said they ran Web sites that linked terrorists in Denmark, Bosnia, Iraq, the United States, and United Kingdom. The sites included beheading videos. One of their laptops included a Power-Point presentation titled *The Illustrated Booby Trapping Course* that included how to create a suicide vest loaded with ball bearings. Tsouli had been asked by al Qaeda to translate into English its e-book, *The Tip of the Camel's Hump*. The trio also stole data for hundreds of credit cards, which they used to purchase supplies for operatives, and laundered money through 350 transactions at 43 Internet gambling sites, including www.absolutepoker.com, www.betfair.com, www.betonbet.com, www.canbet.com, www.eurobet.com, www.noblepoker.com, and www.paradisepoker.com, using 130 credit card accounts. He and his colleagues had made more than $3.5 million in fraudulent charges for global positioning system devices, night-vision goggles, sleeping bags, telephones, survival knives, hundreds of prepaid cell phones, tents, and more than 250 airline tickets using 110 different credit cards at 46 airline and travel agencies. They used 72 credit card accounts to register more than 180 domains at 95 Web-hosting firms in the United States and Europe. Al-Daour's computer contained 37,000 stolen credit card numbers. On July 5, 2007, a London court sentenced him to 10 years after he pleaded guilty to inciting murder on the Internet. He is the son of a Moroccan diplomat.

Yosef Tsuria: on June 14, 1984, he was convicted of plotting to blow up the El Aqsa Mosque. In a plea bargain, he was found guilty of illegal possession of explosives and impersonating an officer in a bid to purchase Uzi submachine gun silencers.

Shadi Abu Tubasi: age 22, of Jenin, Israeli citizen son of a Palestinian father and an Israeli Arab mother, and Palestinian Hamas suicide bomber who, on March 31, 2002, wearing a black jacket, set off several pounds of explosives wrapped around his torso at 2:30 P.M. at Haifa's Matza restaurant, killing 15 people, both Jews and Israeli Arabs, and injuring at least 36 others.

Muhammad al-Tubayhi: variant al-Tabihani, variant Muhammad al Tabhini, alias Abu-'Ayna' al-Muhajir, variant Abu al A'ainaa al Muhajer, a Saudi from Riyadh who joined al Qaeda in Iraq as a fighter in 2007, contributing his watch and bringing his passport. He met his recruitment coordinator, Abu-Sulayman, variant Abu Salman, variant Abu Salaman, via Sa'du Fahd al-'Anjan, variant Fahd al-Ghajman, variant Fahid al Ghagman, who introduced him to Sa'd Faldah, variant Sa'ad Feldah. His phone number was 0501222282. His spoke English.

Muhammed Tufail: on December 20, 2001, the Bush Administration placed him on the list of banned terrorists and froze his international funds.

Lt. Tufan: an Iranian policeman who was one of the hijackers of an Iran Air B727 en route from Bandar 'Abbas to Tehran on September 8, 1984 and diverted it to Iraq. The hijackers surrendered and requested political asylum, saying they staged the hijacking to oppose Khomeini's rule and that they supported former Prime Minister Shahpour Bahktiar.

Shaykh Subhi al-Tufayli: leader of the Followers of God, who lives in Lebanon. On July 24, 1994, the Argentine government instructed the Attorney General to request that Judge Galeano request his extradition in connection with the July 18, 1994 bombing of the Argentine-Israeli Mutual Aid Association (AIMA) in Buenos Aires that killed 96 and wounded 231. Hizballah was suspected. On July 29, Lebanon rejected the rquest, saying that there was no Ansarallah group and that no Lebanese were involved. Al-Tufayli also denied involvement.

Hasan Muhammad Tulays: variant Muhammad Hasan Tulays.

Muhammad Hasan Tulays: variant Hasan Muhammad Tulays, arrested while trying to park a booby-trapped car in al-Hazimiyah, Lebanon on February 6, 1987. The *Voice of Lebanon* reported on February 28, 1987 that he had confessed to firing six bullets on September 18, 1986 at Colonel Christian Goutierre, the French military attaché in Beirut, killing him. The Anti-Imperialist International Brigades, the Revolutionary Brigades, and the Front for Justice and Revenge separately claimed credit. On April 13, 1994, he was sentenced to life at hard labor for Goutierre's killing. At the time of the shooting, he was a corporal in the Lebanese army and a member of Islamic Resistance, Hizballah's military wing.

Ahmad Husni Tulbah: arrested on October 15, 1994 by Egyptian police in connection with the October 14, 1994 stabbing of Naguib Mahfouz, the only Arab to receive the Nobel Prize for Literature, in a Cairo suburb.

Abu-Tulhah: alias of 'Abd-al-Nasir Haws Bilqasim al-Saghir.

Abdallah Awlad al-Tumi: alias Abu-Muhammad, a Tunisian, age 36, a would-be martyr for al Qaeda in Iraq, according to the captured Sinjar documents. He flew from Turkey to Syria before entering Iraq in 2007. He provided the personnel offier with his marriage certificate, a knife, and $5,000 cash. He said he was a "massage specialist." He met his recruiter, Abu-'Ala, at a Dublin mosque. He was born on June 30, 1970. While in Syria, he met Abu-'Umar al Salmani. He brought with him $5,000, with which he was going to rent an apartment for four months.

Tung Kuei-sen: one of two bicyclists who, on October 15, 1984, assassinated Henry Liu, a prominent Chinese-American journalist who had authored several recent articles critical of the ruling Nationalist party in Taiwan, in his Daly City, California garage. On September 26, 1985, at the request of the United States, Brazilian authorities arrested him. He had earlier been in the Philippines and Japan. He was extradited to the United States. He was convicted on April 1988 after confessing. On May 11, 1988, a Redwood City, California court sentenced the Taiwanese gangster, a member of the United Bamboo Gang, to 27 years to life for the murder. He claimed the assassination was ordered by senior Taiwanese military officials. He said he was duped by Taiwan into believing it was a patriotic act.

'Isam Muhammad 'Abd-al-Rahman Tuni: executed by the Egyptian government on May 3, 1994 in connection with the November 25, 1993 bombing of the convoy of Egyptian Prime Minister Dr. 'Atif Sidqi that killed a 15-year-old girl and wounded 21 other people.

Zakariya Mahmud al-Tuni: a U.S. national of Egyptian origin who was arrested on June 25, 1993 by police in Al-Fayyum, south of Cairo, while in possession of 15 firearms, including automatic rifles, pistols, and a large quantity of ammunition. He was charged with inciting debauchery and obscenity for pornographic videotapes that were found in his possession. He entered Egypt in 1989. Security authorities believed he was associated with blind Sheik Omar Abd-al-Rahman, who lives in the United States and had been accused of several terrorist plots.

Abu Nasr al-Tunisi: believed by the FBI on February 11, 2002, to be planning a terrorist attack in the United States or on U.S. interests in Yemen.

Abu Usama al-Tunisi: a senior al Qaeda in Iraq leader who brought in foreign fighters and was believed to have seized and executed U.S. Pfc. Kristian Menchaca and Pfc. Thomas L. Tucker south of Baghdad on June 16, 2006. Their mutilated and booby-trapped bodies were found three days later, along with that of Spec. David J. Babineau, who died at a checkpoint. U.S. military officials said al-Tunisi had operated in Youssifiyah, southwest of Baghdad, since November 2004. On September 25, 2007, he was killed by a U.S. F-16 airstrike east of Karbala.

Abu Yusif al-Tunisi: alias Faker Ben Abdelaziz Boussora. The U.S. Rewards for Justice program issued a reward of $5 million for his arrest. As of early December 2006, he was still at large.

Faruq al-Tunisi: alias of Abderraouf Ben Habib Jdey.

Malik Tunisi: named on February 14, 2005 as one of Iraq's 29 most-wanted insurgents. A bounty of between $50,000 and $200,000 was offered.

The Tunisian: alias of Nizar bin Mohammed Nawar.

The Tunisian: alias of Sarhane Ben Abdelmajid Fakhet.

Abu-al-'Abbas al-Tunusi: alias of Samir.

Abu Turab: alias of Al Bara'a Muhammd Sadeq.

Abu-Turab: Saudi-based recruitment coordinator for foreign fighters for al Qaeda in Iraq in 2006.

Abu-Turab: alias of Muhammad Adam Muhammad al-Masmarani.

Abu-Turab: alias of 'Ali Mustafa Bal'idal-Qamati.

'Abd-al-Hamid Fahim 'Abdallah al-Turablisi: alias Abu-al-Walid, a Libyan from Darnah who was born in 1987 and signed up to be a martyr for al Qaeda in Iraq on May 9, 2007. His phone number was 218926230387. He contributed 200 Syrian Lira and $10. His coordinator was Saraj, whom he knew through a new acquaintance. He traveled via Libya, Egypt, and Syria to arrive in Iraq. While in Syria, he met Abu-'Abbas.

He brought $450 with him. He had been a student.

Owsan Ahmed al-Turaihi: alias Abu al-Jarrah, one of six individuals killed on November 3, 2002 when a U.S. Predator unmanned aerial vehicle fired a Hellfire missile at their car in Yemen. Also killed was Abu Ali al-Harithi, a key suspect in the USS *Cole* bombing of October 12, 2000 and Kamal Derwish, a U.S. citizen who headed an al Qaeda cell in Lackawanna, New York, that was wrapped up on September 14, 2002.

Waddud al Turk: an arrest warrant was issued after detectives of the Italian UCIGOC anti-terrorist squad, on July 31, 1990, identified the Abu Nidal member as an organizer of the October 25, 1984 terrorist attack in which the secretary of the United Arab Emirates Embassy in Italy was wounded and a woman companion slain. He was in custody in Pakistan after an attempted aerial hijacking.

Turki: alias of Abdul Hamid.

Al-Turki: alias of Mustafa 'Abd-al-Aziz Muhammad, identified by the Ethiopian government as one of the nine Egyptian Islamic Group gunmen who, on June 25, 1995, fired on the armored limousine of Egyptian President Hosni Mubarak in Addis Ababa.

Hassan Turki: listed by the U.S. Department of State in 2004 as having links to al Qaeda and running military training camps in Somalia. On March 3, 2008, a U.S. Navy Tomahawk missile was fired at a location in Dhobley, Somalia he was believed to be visiting.

Louai al-Turki: alias of Louai Sakka.

Abdullah Abdul-Aziz al-Tweijri: one of two al Qaeda car bombers who, on February 24, 2006, failed to disrupt Saudi oil supplies to the United States in an attack on the world's biggest oil processing plant. Both were on Saudi Arabia's 15 most-wanted list. One bomber drove his car into the gate, set off the bomb, and ripped a hole in the fence. The second bomber drove through the hole, but died when he set off his bomb after a fusillade from the police. The Saudi branch of al Qaeda claimed credit on a Web site for setting off two car bombs at the gates of the Abqaiq oil facility after guards fired on them. Oil prices jumped $2/barrel after the market heard reports that authorities fired on three cars a mile from the main entrance.

U

Abu-'Ubadah: alias of Salim Muhammad Salim al-'Isawi.

Shaykh 'Abd-al-Karim 'Ubady: his release was demanded by the Hamas members who, on October 9, 1994, kidnapped Israeli Corporal Nachshon Mordekhay Wachsman from Jerusalem's 'Atarot junction.

Abu Ubaida: al Qaeda senior trainer listed by the U.S. military in January 2002 as having died.

Abu Ubaidah: alias of Munir Ahmed Abdullah.

Muhammad 'Ubayd: one of the five Guards of Islam gunmen who failed in an assassination attempt against Shahpour Bakhtiar, the Shah's last Prime Minister, in Neuilly-sur-Seine, France on July 17, 1980.

Shayk 'Abd-al-Karim 'Ubayd: variant Obeid, whose release from an Israeli prison was demanded on September 18, 1991 by the Muslim kidnappers of British hostage Jack Mann.

Abu-'Ubayda: alias of 'Abdallah Fadl 'Abd-al-'Aziz al-Sha'iri.

Abu Ubaydah: a lieutenant of Osama bin Laden who, in 1992 to 1996, led attacks against government forces in Eritrea, Uganda, and the Ogaden region of Ethiopia.

Abu-'Ubaydah: alias of Ahmad Abd-al-Sayyid Hamad.

Abu-'Ubaydah: alias of Nizar Malak al-Hasan.

Abu-'Ubaydah: alias of Tariq Najib Hasan.

Abu-'Ubaydah: alias of Khalid al-Jarrah.

Abu-'Ubaydah: alias of Nabil.

Abu-'Ubaydah: alias of Tawfiq Muhammad al-Akhdar al-Rayhami.

Ahmad Hasan Kaka Ubaydi: named on February 14, 2005 as one of Iraq's 29 most-wanted insurgents. A bounty of between $50,000 and $200,000 was offered.

Abu Ubidah: alias of Muhammad Abd Allah Ramadan Umran.

Abu Ubidah: alias of Ahamed Abd al Sayed Hammed.

Abu Ubidah: alias of Ashour Edress Karami.

Abu Ubidah: alias of Abd al Hamied Omar Ali Al Sadai.

Yusuf 'Ubwani: indicted on March 24, 1994 in connection with the January 29, 1994 murder by the Al-Awja Palestinian organization in Beirut of Jordanian First Secretary Naeb Umran Maaitah. He was in jail on other charges.

'Ali al-'Udah: alias Abu-Mujahid, a Saudi from Bani 'Umar, Bishi, who was born on August 26, 1976 and entered Iraq on September 13,

2006, when he joined al Qaeda in Iraq. His phone numbers were 00966500803831 and 00966559321369. He contributed $1,200, 4,350 lira, 210 riyals, and his cell phone.

Muhammad Abd Allah al Ugayle: alias Abu Ya-coub, a Saudi from Jeddah who was born in 1986 and joined al Qaeda in Iraq as a fighter in 2007, providing his passport. His recruitment coordinator was Abu Usama, whom he knew via his friend Abu Shaker. He arrived by bus from Saudi Arabia to Jordan and Syria, where he met Abu Umar, Abu Umar the Tunisia, Abu Al Abbas, and Abu Muhammad Al Shayeb. He brought $1,400, 4,000 lira, and 70 riyals; they took all but $200. His home phone number was 0096626721489; Rahime's was 0096656938187.

Jussef Uhida: a Libyan who was arrested after three gunmen killed Abdel Belil Aref, a wealthy Libyan businessman, as he was dining at the Café du Paris on the Via Veneto in Rome on April 18, 1980. On October 6, 1986, the Italian government announced that, for "humanitarian motives," it had freed three convicted Libyan gunmen, including Uhida, in exchange for four Italians being held in Libya for the previous six years. A Red Cross plane flew the Libyans to Tripoli and returned with the Italians. Uhida had been serving a 26-year sentence for Aref's murder.

Najim Abdullah Zahwan Khalifah Ujayli: named on February 14, 2005 as one of Iraq's 29 most-wanted insurgents. A bounty of between $50,000 and $200,000 was offered.

'Adnan al-'Uklah: on February 18, 1982, the Moslem Brotherhood's Combatant Avant-Garde, outlawed in Syria in 1980, said it was headed by the former Syrian Army officer.

Saber Abu Ulla: variant of Saber Mohammed Farahat Abu Ele.

Shipon Ullah: age 23, one of three men arrested on March 22, 2007, by British police "on suspicion of the commission, preparation, or instigation of acts of terrorism" in the July 7, 2005 bombings of the London subway system. On July 5, 2007, British authorities charged the trio with conspiring with the bombers between November 1, 2004 and June 29, 2005, saying they handled reconnaissance and planning.

Umar: alias Abu Zir, an Algerian from Al Wadd who joined al Qaeda in Iraq as a fighter in 2007. His phone number was 0021390656709; Hafiez's was 0021375539485; brother Abd Al Razak Saqnie's was 021378359312.

'Umar: alias of Ahmad 'Abd-al-Azim Ahmad 'Abd-al-Rahman Fawwaz.

'Umar: alias Abu-'Asim, a Yemeni figher for al Qaeda in Iraq in 2007. He owned a watch, $100, and 1,300 lira. His phone number was 009677125795.

'Umar: alias Abu-al-Basir, a Saudi from Mecca who was sent on a suicide mission by al Qaeda in Iraq in 2007. He owned a passport and $412. His travel coordinator was Bassam. His home phone number was 5462930; his father's was 0503519490.

'Umar: alias Abu-'Abdallah al-Madani, a Saudi from al-Medina, variant Al-Madina al-Munaw-warah, who joined al Qaeda in Iraq in 2007 as a martyr, contributing $100 and 1,000 lira, along with his passport. His recruitment coordinator was Abu-Dujanh. His home phone numbers were 0552164505 and 0507331395.

'Umar: alias Abu-Dhar, an Algerian from al Wad who joined al Qaeda in Iraq as a fighter in 2007, bringing his ID card. He said Hafiz's phone number was 0021375539485 and 'Abd-al-Razzaq's was 0021390656709. He knew Shari' legal committee brother 'Abd-al-Razzaq Saqani, who could be found on 0021378359312.

Abu Umar: an Egyptian who was one of three al Qaeda suspects arrested by Pakistani authorities on January 9, 2003 after a gun battle in Karachi in which one of the terrorists threw a grenade. Police seized rifles; grenades; street maps of Karachi, Hyderabad, and Lahore; a satellite telephone; a laptop computer; suspicious documents; literature calling for a holy war; and more than $30,000 in cash (most of it American) from the terrorists' house. Two of the detainees claimed to be Abu Hamza of Yemen and Abu Umar of Egypt. Abu Umar's wife and three children were also detained. Seven other suspects were later released. They were all family members of Sabiha Shahid, a leader of the Jamaat-e-Islami party, who lived on the first floor. Police said they appeared to have entered Pakistan from Afghanistan in 2002.

Abu Umar: listed in the al Qaeda in Iraq Sinjar records as a Palestinian who crossed into Iraq to train al Qaeda fighters. He said he transited Dayr al-Zawr on his way to al-Qa'im, Iraq.

Abu-'Umar: a Syrian-based al Qaeda in Iraq travel facilitator in 2007.

Abu-'Umar: a Libyan-based recruiter for al Qaeda in Iraq in 2006

Abu-'Umar: alias of 'Abd-al-'Aziz 'Abd-al-Rabb Salih al-Yafi'.

Abu-'Umar: alias of Ahmad.

Abu-'Umar: alias of Haytham.

Abu-'Umar: alias of Majid 'Azzam Yahya al-Masura.

Abu-'Umar: alias of Sa'ud.

Abu-'Umar: alias of 'Adil Jum'ah Muhamad al-Sha'lali.

Midhat Mursi al-Sayid 'Umar: alias of Abu Khabab al-Masri.

Ziyad al-'Umar: on November 13, 1985, Italian authorities issued an arrest warrant for the Palestine Liberation Front member in connection with the hijacking of the Italian cruise ship *Achille Lauro* on October 7, 1985. The hijackers killed Leon Klinghoffer, age 69, an American confined to a wheelchair, and dumped the body overboard. The hijacking ended in Egypt. He had purchased the cruise tickets for the terrorists. On June 18, 1986, his Genoa trial began for murder and kidnapping. On July 10, 1986, he was sentenced in absentia to life in prison. On May 24, 1987, a Genoa appeals court upheld the conviction. On May 11, 1988, Italy's Supreme Court of Cassation confirmed an appeals court's life sentence for him.

Fakhri al-Umari: alias Abu Mohammed Omari, alias Mohammed Fakr Omari, Abu Daoud claimed that he had met with him in Sofia in August 1972 to plan the Black September Olympics attack of September 5, 1972. He was assassinated by a Palestine Liberation Organization bodyguard armed with an AK-47 on January 15, 1991.

Husayn Umari: alias Abu Ibrahim, an Iraqi for whom an international arrest warrant was issued in connection with the bombing in Orchard Street in London on December 25, 1983 near Marks and Spencer and Selfridges. He was believed to be living in South Yemen. His trial opened on December 13, 1989.

Islam al-'Umari: a fugitive in Sudan said by the Ethiopian Supreme State Security Prosecution on August 7, 1995 to have helped five terrorists who had confessed to training in the al-Kamp and Kangu camps in Khartoum with two of the nine Egyptian Islamic Group gunmen who, on June 25, 1995, fired on the armored limousine of Egyptian President Hosni Mubarak in Addis Ababa.

Muhamad al-'Umari: alias Abu Ibrahim, an eingineer who founded the 15 May terrorist group in 1979. He developed a moldable explosive that was believed to have been used in the Pan Am 103 bombing in December 21, 1988 that killed 270 and the UTA 772 bombing of September 19, 1989 that killed 171.

Abu-'Umayr: alias of 'Ali 'Uthman Hamd al-'Arfi.

Rashid al-'Umayshi: head of the Islamic Jihad Movement in Yemen believed to have been killed on February 2, 1993 in a clash with the army in Lahij, Yemen.

Umier: Libya-based recruitment coordinator for foreign fighters for al Qaeda in Iraq in 2007.

Muhammad Abd Allah Ramadan Umran: alias Abu Ubidah, a Libyan economics student from Dernah who was born in 1985 and joined al Qaeda in Iraq on 14/7/1428 Hijra (2007) as a martyr, contributing $103 and his passport. His recruitment coordinator was Umier, whom he knew via a friend. He traveled to Cairo and on to Syria, where he spent five days before entering Iraq. He met Abu Al Abbas in Syria. His phone number was 002187506606; his father's was 002185796589.

Muhammad Musa 'Umran: alias Abu-al-Walid, a Libyan born in 1985 who joined al Qaeda in Iraq on October 4, 2006, contributing $100 and a watch. His recruitment coordinator was Abu 'Umar. His phone number was 0926188074.

Yunis 'Umran: alias of Muhammad Dawud.

Kasim Unal: imam of the Sochaux mosque who was expelled from France in August 1994. He was a member of the Anatolian Federal Islamic State, a radical fundamentalist movement.

Al-'Unud: Saudi-based recruitment coordinator for al Qaeda in Iraq foreign fighters in 2007.

Ahmed Hassan al-Uqaily: age 33, arrested on October 7, 2004 by police in Nashville, Tennessee on illegal weapons charges during a sting operation set up after he threatened to "go jihad." The Iraqi-born man was putting into his car two disassembled machineguns, four disassembled hand grenades, and hundreds of rounds of ammunition he had purchased for $1,000 from an undercover agent. He had said he was angry about what was going on in Iraq, and intended to "go jihad" and blow up something.

Muhammad Khalifah 'Uqlah: one of 11 Iraqis and three Kuwaitis arrested on April 13, 1993 by Kuwaiti authorities in a plot to assassinate former U.S. President George H. W. Bush with a bomb during his visit to Kuwait. The 55-year-old Kuwaiti sheltered several of the suspects. On May 10, 1993, Kuwait ruled out extradition, saying it would try the group. On May 16, 1993, the Kuwaiti Attorney General denied press reports that Khalifah had been released on bail.

Mihrac Ural: Syrian leader in 1980 of the outlawed Turkish People's Liberation Party Acilciler organization. He married the secretary of Rif'at al-Asad, brother of the Syrian president.

Amin Faysal Ahmad al-'Urayfi: alias Abu-Wabir, a Yemeni factory worker from Sana'a who was born in 1986 and joined al Qaeda in Iraq as a fighter circa 2006 or 2007, bringing a passport and $100. He met his recruitment coordinator, Nabil, by way of Akram at a club. He flew to Syria, where he met 'Isa. His phone number was 009671306845. His paternal aunt's daughter's number was 00967777215095.

Rubi'i al-Urduni: alias of Abderraouf Ben Habib Jdey.

Abu Usama: alias of Ala'a Abd Allah Khan.

Abu Usama: alias of Fahid Muhammad Ali Alrawq.

Abu Usama: alias of Shaqueb Abd Al Latif.

Sa'ad Abu Abd al Rahman Abu Usama: Moroccan-based recruitment coordinator for Al Qaeda in Iraq foreign fighters in 2006.

Abu-Usamah: variant Abu Usama, alias of Badr Bin-'Id Bin-'Ali al-Qurni, variant Bader Bin Eied Bin Ali Al Qarni.

Abu-Usamah: alias of Usamah Adam Bilqasim al-'Abdi.

Abu-Usamah: Jordan-based recruitment coordinator for foreign fighters for al Qaeda in Iraq in 2006.

Abu-Usamah: alias of Shakub 'Abd-al-Latif.

Abu-'Usamah: alias of Fawaz.

'Umayr Usamah: Libya-based recruitment coordinator for al Qaeda in Iraq foreign fighters in 2007.

Abu-Usayd: alias of Khalid Ta'in.

Abu-Usayd: alias of Sami Ahsan Ahsan al-Jawfi.

Abu-Usayd: alias of Yasin.

Ali Hahmed Usman: a 35-year-old Palestinian who was one of three Abdel Nasser Movement (the Palestine Revolution Movement also took credit) hijackers of an Egyptian B737 flying from Cairo to Luxor on August 23, 1976. They demanded the release of five would-be assassins from Egyptian jails. Commandos boarded the plane and overpowered and wounded all three hijackers. The trio said they received their directions in Libya, which promised $250,000 to divert the plane to Libya. On September 18, 1976, they were fined and sentenced to hard labor for life but were acquitted of charges of collusion with Libya.

Ustaz: alias of Ayman al-Zawahiri.

Abu-'Ubaydah al-'Utaybi: alias of Muhammad Su'ud Muhammad al-Juday'i.

Adil Isma'il 'Isa al-'Utaybi: variant Ismail Eisa Otaibi, 1 of 11 Iraqis and three Kuwaitis arrested on April 13, 1993 by Kuwaiti authorities in a plot to assassinate former U.S. President H. W. George Bush with a bomb during his visit to Kuwait. The Iraqi participated in the operation and drove a van to be used in the attack. He hid explosives in the al-Barr area and informed police of their whereabouts upon his arrest. He sheltered three other suspects. He was a former convict. On May 10, 1993, Kuwait ruled out extradition, saying it would try the group. On May 16, 1993, the Kuwaiti Attorney General denied press reports that he had been released on bail. On June 4, 1994, the three-judge panel sentenced him to death. On March 20, 1995, a Kuwaiti high court commuted the death sentence to 15 years in prison.

'Awad Fayhan 'Awad al-'Utaybi: alias Abu-Walid, a Saudi from al-Qasim who was born in 1981 and joined al Qaeda in Iraq as a martyr circa 2007, contributing 200 riyals and a driver's license. He flew to Syria, then came over the border via Dir al-Zur. He met Ibrahim, his recruitment coordinator, through his maternal uncle. While in Syria, he met Najam and Lu'ay. He brought 800 riyals with him. He spoke English. His phone number was 00966552465215.

Faysal Sa'd al-'Utaybi: alias Abu-Sa'd, a Saudi from Riyadh who was born on February 28, 1979 and joined al Qaeda in Iraq on October 28, 2006 to become a martyr. His recruitment coordinator was Abu-Hudhayfah. He contributed 2,350 Syrian Lira and $600. His phone numbers were 0501010607 and 0554600656.

Hamid al-'Utaybi: alias Abu-Muhjin, a Saudi from Mecca who joined al Qaeda in Iraq on September 13, 2006, donating $900. He was born on August 18, 1981. His phone number was 0556555712. His recruitment coordinator was Abu-Tamam.

Sulayman Muhammad al-'Utaybi: alias Abu-Muhammad, a Saudi born in 1983 who joined al Qaeda in Iraq in 2007, bringing $100.

Sultan Radi al-'Utaybi: alias Abu-Dhar al-Makki, a Saudi from Mecca who was born on January 19, 1985 and joined al Qaeda in Iraq on October 14, 2006, contributing a watch and

845 riyals. His recruitment coordinator was Faysal. His brother's phone number was 0553272394; Munif's was 0566416525.

Fahd Bin-Khalaf Bin-Salih al-'Utayyi: alias 'Akramah. According to the captured Sinjar personnel records of al Qaeda in Iraq, he had lived in Riyadh, Saudi Arabia. He offered his brother's phone number of 0504228720. He was born in 1983. He arrived in Iraq on July 21, 2007, carrying a passport and ID card. He contributed 3,450 Syrian lira. His coordinator was Walid. He offered to be a fighter.

'Uthman: alias of Nawwaf al-Rawsan.

Abu-'Uthman: a Syrian-based travel facilitator for al Qaeda in Iraq in 2007.

Ahmad Isma'il 'Uthman: sentenced to death on March 17, 1994 by the Higher Military Court in Cairo in connection with the November 25, 1993 bombing of the convoy of Egyptian Prime Minister Dr. 'Atif Sidqi that killed a 15-year-old girl and wounded 21 other people.

Bilal Ali Uthman: age 26, one of two members of the Isbat Al Ansar, a Sunni Muslim radical group with bin Laden links arrested in early October 2001 by Lebanese authorities in Tripoli. The two were handed to the military prosecutor's office for involvement in terrorist activities, arms trafficking, and planning to conduct other acts targeting U.S. interests in the region.

Ibrahim Abu Uthman: driver on December 11, 2007 of a truck bomb with 1,800 pounds of explosives that targeted the UN High Commission for Refugees and the UN Development Program offices in the Hydra district of Algeria, killing 17 UN staffers, including six Algerians, a Senegalese, a Dane, and a Philippine citizen. Five of the dead were foreigners, including two Chinese. Another three foreign UN employees—two Chinese and one Lebanese—were hospitalized. The body count rose to 17 at the UN facility and totaled

at least 37 for the two bombings by December 14, when rescue workers found more corpses in the rubble. The Algerian newspaper *El Watan* claimed that 72 people died and 200 were wounded; *El Khabar*, a daily paper, said health officials had tallied 67 dead. Seven survivors were pulled from chunks of concrete. One was a woman, age 40, whose legs were amputated at a local hospital. Al Qaeda in the Islamic Maghreb, the remnants of the Salafist Group for Preaching and Combat, claimed credit in an Internet posting on the al-Hisbah Islamic Network. The group said the UN facility was "the headquarters of the international infidels' den." An Algerian security officer said the perpetrators were two convicted terrorists who had been freed in an amnesty. One of the bombers, 64, was in an advanced stage of cancer. The other was a 32-year-old from a poor suburb.

Jihad Muhammad 'Uthman: on October 25, 1984, he fired at Muhammad al-Sudiyah, United Arab Emirates Vice Consul in Rome, killing Nushin Montaseri, an Iranian student and injuring al-Sudiyah. The Jordanian was later arrested and confessed. The Arab Revolutionary Brigades took credit.

Omar Mahmoud Uthman: alias Abu Qatada al-Filistini, possibly in London, a senior agent for Osama bin Laden in Europe, his U.S. assets were ordered frozen on October 12, 2001.

Faysal 'Uwayid: alias Abu-Hamzah al-Suri, a Syrian from Dayr Az Zur who was born in 1990 and joined al Qaeda in Iraq in 2007, contributing 350 lira. His recruitment coordinator was Barakat. He also met Abu-Muhammad in Syria. His home phone number was 655426.

Zahi Salah al-'Uwayqah: alias Abu-Bakr, a Saudi student from Jawf al-Sakakah who was born in 1985 and joined al Qaeda in Iraq on June 1, 2007 as a martyr, contributing 16,300 Saudi Riyals. His recruiter coordinator was Abu-'Abfdallah, whom he knew through a person who works with him. In Syria, he met Abu-'Uthman, age 25, who took his 900 Syrian liras, leaving him with 1,650 Saudi riyals. He met muhajidin support Slaih Shakir Shiekh Abu-Sayaff. His phone numbers were 009666257652 and 00966503396649.

Abu-Uways: alias of Awas 'Ali 'Abd-al-Karim.

Captain 'Abbas Mul-Uyuz: an intelligence officer in the Iraqi Republican Guards whom Egyptian Interior Minister Muhammad 'Abd-al-Halim Musa said, on April 3, 1991, was involved in an Iraqi-sponsored terrorist operation.

Mohammed Uzair: killed in early April 1995 by unidentified gunmen. He was a suspect in the March 8, 1995 lethal shooting of two U.S. consulate officials and wounding of a third in a morning ambush on a white Toyota Hiace minivan taking the diplomats to the Consulate in Karachi, Pakistan.

V

Gholamreza Vahidju: charged by Iran with hijacking an Iranian plane from Tehran to Bushehr in 1984 and diverting to Cairo. He allegedly collaborated with a dismissed military person. He was arrested in Iran. He had lived in Iraq and Paris. On November 12, 1995, Tehran television reported the Vahidju, son of Hasan, had confessed to the hijacking.

Ali Rad Vakili: an Iranian briefly detained by French police who later believed that he was a member of the hit squad that, on August 6, 1991, stabbed to death former Iranian Premier Shapur Bakhtiar in his Paris home. He and an associate had tried to enter Switzerland on August 7 with forged visas in Turkish passports in the names of Musa Kocer and Ali Kaya. They were turned over to French authorities, who released them because they had valid French visas. On August 14, the People's Mujahedeen exile group said he was a member of the Al Qoods (Jerusalem) Force, a terrorist unit in the Iranian Revolutionary Guard. Paris *Agence France Presse* reported on August 16 that he had escaped detection at a Geneva hotel because the local police computer had broken down, preventing an identity check of the man who had checked into the Hotel Windsor as Musa Kocer. Police missed the arrest by three hours. However, Geneva police arrested him on August 21 as he was walking on a beach before dawn. He was extradited to France on August 27 and charged in Paris with murder and criminal association in connection with terrorism. On December 6, 1994, a Paris terrorism court convicted him and sentenced him to life in prison.

Bertan Valentino: an Italian believed to be an Iraqi detained on May 2, 1992 by Ecuadoran police in Quito on suspicion of involvement in the March 17, 1992 car bombing at the Israeli Embassy in Buenos Aires that killed 29 and injured 252. He and six Iranian Hizballah members had intended to go to Canada via the United States. On May 9, the Crime Investigation Division in Quito said that the group was not involved in the bombing, but would be deported to Iran through Bogota and Caracas. They were released on May 12, 1992 and given 72 hours to leave the country.

Dr. Paul Vijay: alias of Ramzi Ahmed Yusuf.

W

Tariq Mursi Wabbah: an Egyptian Islamic Jihad member who was deported by South Africa to Egypt in November 1998. He had been collecting funds from local Muslims and sending them to the Egyptian Islamic Jihad in Egypt.

Abu-Wabir: alias of Amin Faysal Ahmad al-'Urayfi.

Khalid Abdul Wadood: alias of 'Abdallah Ahmad 'Abdallah.

Abu Musab Abdel Wadoud: alias of Abdelmalek Droukdel.

Alyan Muhammad Ali al-Wa'eli: born in Yemen in 1970, the Yemeni was believed by the FBI, on February 11, 2002, to be planning a terrorist attack in the United States or on U.S. interests in Yemen.

Ammar Abadah Nasser al-Wa'eli: born in Yemen in 1977, the Yemeni was believed by the FBI, on February 11, 2002, to be planning a terrorist attack in the United States or on U.S. interests in Yemen.

'Abd-al-Wahab: alias Abu-Hammam, a Yemeni fighter for al Qaeda in Iraq in 2007. He owned $100 and a passport. His phone number was 00967304736.

Osameh al-Wahaidy: age 41, of Fayetteville, a Jordanian employed as a spiritual leader at the Auburn Correctional Facility and as a math instructor at the State University of New York at Oswego, who was one of five men connected to the Islamic Assembly of North America (IANA), a Saudi charity that operates out of Ann Arbor, Michigan, who were indicted by federal authorities on February 26, 2003, in connection with two money-raising and distribution efforts. He was one of four Arab men living near Syracuse accused of conspiracy to evade U.S. sanctions against Iraq by raising $2.7 million for individuals in Baghdad through the Help the Needy charity (an IANA affiliate). The funds were placed in New York banks, then laundered through an account at the Jordan Islamic Bank in Amman before they were distributed to people in Baghdad. The four were charged with conspiracy and violation of the International Emergency Economic Powers Act, which makes it illegal to send money to Iraq. Two of the men could face 265 years in prison and fines of more than $14 million. The other two faced five years in prison and a $250,000 fine.

Abdal-Rahman Wahbah: an Egyptian member of the Damascus-based Arabism's Egypt (Misr al-'Urubah) who was captured in the Jabal al-Rayhani area of Lebanon on August 22, 1987 after the group attacked a South Lebanese Army patrol.

Husan 'Uways Wahbah: acquitted on July 16, 1994 by a Cairo military court of involvement with the Vanguard of the Conquest gunmen who, on August 18, 1993, fired on the motorcade of Egyptian Interior Minister Hassan Alfi.

Mohammed Waheed: thought to be responsible for planting a bomb on December 2, 1982 in the former Iraqi Consulate in Thailand that killed

Thailand's top bomb disposal expert and injured 17 other people. The Mujabbar Bakr Commando Group claimed credit.

Naser Said Abdel Wahib: on July 27, 1980, he threw two hand grenades into a crowd of 40 Jews, most of them teens waiting to take a bus to summer camp from the Antwerp, Belgium, Agoudath Israeli cultural center to the Ardennes. One person died and 20 others were injured. He carried a Moroccan identity document but was believed to be a Lebanese. After a chase by witnesses, police arrested him. He was carrying a pistol and several magazines of ammunition. On August 1, 1980, an Antwerp court remanded him to custody. The Popular Front for the Liberation of Palestine and Abu Nidal's Fatah-Revolutionary Council claimed credit. On January 12, 1991, he was freed after serving more than ten years of a life term. In turn, Abu Nidal Organization kidnappers released four Belgian hostages they had taken prisoners on November 8, 1987 after attacking the *Silco* yacht in the Mediterranean Sea off Lebanon.

Yusef Majid Wahib: an Iraqi sentenced to ten years in prison by the Kuwaiti State Security Court in 1984 in connection with the December 12, 1983 truck bombing of the administrative building of the U.S. Embassy in Kuwait, killing four people and injuring 59. As of April 1987, none of the death sentences had been carried out. The release of 17 of the 25 prisoners in the case was demanded on numerous occasions by the Islamic Jihad in return for Americans held captive in Lebanon beginning in 1986.

Usamah Bin-'Abd-al-Rahman al-Wahibi: alias Abu-'Abd-al-Rahman, a Saudi from Riyadh who was born on July 12, 1983 and joined al Qaeda in Iraq on October 28, 2006 to provide legal services. He contributed two mobile phones and a flash memory card. His recruitment coordinator was Abu-Sarab. His phone number was 0503239223.

Wahid: alias of Matarawy Mohammed Said Saleh, identified on July 7, 1993 by federal prosecutors as a tenth suspect in the plot broken up by the

FBI on June 24, 1993 involving individuals who were charged with planning to bomb the UN headquarters building in Manhattan; 26 Federal Plaza, which includes the local FBI headquarters and other agencies; the 47th Street diamond district, which is run principally by Orthodox Jews; and the Lincoln and Holland tunnels connecting Manhattan and New Jersey; and planning to assassinate Senator Alfonse M. D'Amato (R-NY), Assemblyman Dov Hiking, an Orthodox Jewish legislator from Brooklyn, UN Secretary General Boutros Boutros-Ghali, and Egyptian President Hosni Mubarak.

Abu-Wahid: alias of Murad.

Hakim Muftah 'Ali al-Wahishi: alias Abu-Sulayman, a Libyan from Benghazi who was born in 1986 and joined al Qaeda in Iraq in 2007, bringing 24 Libyan dinars. He said 'Ali Muftah's phone number was 925111744; Tariq's was 092511-7051.

Walid: alias Abu-'Abd-al-Rahman, a Libyan member of al Qaeda in Iraq in 2007 who was to conduct a suicide mission in Tall 'Afar in Mosul Governorate. His friend 'Uthman al-Manzini's phone number was 00218927111255.

Abu Walid: alias of Ibrahim Bin Muhammad Al Shabi.

Abu-al-Walid: alias of Khalid.

Abu-al-Walid: Saudi-based recruitment coordinator for al Qaeda in Iraq foreign fighters in 2007.

Abu-al-Walid: alias of Muhammad.

Abu-al-Walid: alias of Muhammad Nasir al-Dusari.

Khalfallah 'Abd-al-Mu'min Walid: alias Abu-Mus'ab, an Algerian who joined al Qaeda in Iraq in 2007, bringing $855. His personnel coordinators were Abu-Jalal and Abu-Haydfar. His phone number was 0021332248457.

Wahidi: one of 44 Bahrainis arrested on June 4, 1996 and charged with plotting to overthrow the government. He claimed to report directly to Iranian leader Ayatollah Ali Khameni, and had asked the group to gather information on U.S. forces in Bahrain, where the U.S. Fifth Fleet is based. One suspect said that the group had been trained by Hizballah in Lebanon. The group claimed to be the military wing of Hizballah Bahrain.

Muhammad Ahmad al-Shaykh al-Wahmawi: one of a group of Jordanian Afghans tried on December 21, 1994 by the Jordanian State Security Court for belonging to an illegal society, participating in a conspiracy to carry out terrorist acts, and possessing explosives for illegal purposes. The Muslim fundamentalists bombed cinemas that wounded nine people, including an attack on January 26, 1994 at an Amman cinema showing what they perceived to be pornographic films, and another bombing on February 1, 1994. The group had been seized in a crackdown on Muslim radicals in January 1994. Their trial began on August 27, 1994, when they were accused of planning to assassinate leading Jordanians, including 'Abd-al-Salam al-Majali, Jordan's former chief peace negotiator with Israel. One of those sentenced to death was Muhammad Jamal Khalifah, a Saudi fugitive son-in-law of Usama bin Laden. He was acquitted.

Isma'il al-Wahwah: sentenced to hang on January 16, 1994 in connection with a plot foiled on June 26, 1993 to assassinate Jordanian King Hussein during the graduation ceremony at Muta University, a Jordanian military academy. He was also found guilty of belonging to the Islamic Liberation Party, which aimed to topple the regime through violence and establish an Islamic caliphate state. He was found guilty of conspiring to kill Hussein, but found innocent of trying to change the Constitution due to lack of evidence.

Abu Wa'il: a former member of the Abu Nidal group who was shot in the head in front of his house in the Shatila camp in Lebanon on December 8, 1987.

Abu Al Wailed: alias of Turkey Bin Abd Al Aziz Bin Ibrahim.

Abd Al Rahman Suleiman Al Wakeel: alias Abu Omar, a teacher who was born in 1401 Hijra and joined al Qaeda in Iraq as a fighter in 2007, contributing 10,200 euros, his passport, and a watch. He took a bus from Jordan to Syria, where he met Abu Othman, who took his 3,000 rials. His phone number was 0096664431108.

Adman Waki: age 28, a Syrian arrested on December 28, 2004 by Spanish police in Irun near the French border in connection with the March 11, 2004 al Qaeda bombings of commuter trains that killed 200 and injured 2,000.

'Abd al-Wakim: an Iraqi whose eight-day detention was ordered by Limassol's district court in connection with the Black June attack in which a grenade was thrown into the Shoham, Limassol, Cyprus offices of an Israeli shipping firm on September 23, 1981, injuring three female and two male Greek Cypriot employees.

Saad ad-Din Wali: name on a forged Iraqi passport used by Black September leader Abu Daoud when he traveled to Sofia in 1972 to buy arms for Fatah. He was credited with planning the September 1972 Munich Olympics massacre. He was arrested in February 1973 in Amman, Jordan. He would figure prominently in a 1977 extradition squabble among Israel, West Germany, and France.

Walid: alias Abu al-Lahd, a Popular Front for the Liberation of Palestine member whom *Ha'aretz* claimed on November 13, 1986 was 1 of the masked suicide terrorists who fired on and threw grenades at worshippers in the Neve Shalom, Istanbul, Turkey synagogue on September 6, 1986, doused the 21 corpses with gasoline, and set them alight. Two terrorists who had barred the door died in the attack when their grenades exploded in their hands. A third escaped. The attack was claimed by the Islamic Jihad, Abu Nidal, the Northern Arab League, the Islamic Resistance, the

Palestinian Resistance Organization, the Fighting International Front—'Amrush Martyr Group, and the Organization of the Unity of the Arab North.

Walid: alias of Mahir al-Rawsan.

Walid: on July 6, 1988, Pakistani district court judge Zafar Ahmed Babar ended an eight-month trial in a special court in Rawalpindi's Adiyala maximum security prison and sentenced the Lebanese to death by hanging for the September 5, 1986 hijacking of a Pan Am B747 and for killing 11 passengers at Karachi airport. There was insufficient evidence to convict five terrorists of the deaths of 11 other passengers. The hijacker mastermind, Sulayman al-Turki, said that the group would appeal the sentences and if they were freed, "we would hijack a U.S. airliner once again." The court also passed a total jail sentence of 257 years for each of the accused on several other charges of murder, conspiracy to hijack, possession of illegal arms, and confinement of the passengers. The terrorists had 30 days to appeal against the verdict and the sentence in Lahore's High Court. On July 28, 1988, the press reported that the terrorists reversed their decision not to appeal.

Walid: suspected of al Qaeda membership, he escaped from a Yemeni prison on July 3, 2002. He had been arrested earlier in the year in the desert near the Oman–Yemen border and handed over to Yemeni authorities on charges of trying to enter the country illegally. He was in his thirties, and had fled Afghanistan after fighting U.S. forces in the Tora Bora region in December. He had been transferred in June from a prison in Sana'a to Aden, where several other al Qaeda suspects were held.

Walid: Syrian-based travel facilitator for al Qaeda in Iraq foreign fighters in 2007.

Abu Walid: spokesman for the al-Aqsa Martyrs Brigades in February 2008.

Abu-Walid: alias of 'Awad Fayhan 'Awad al-'Utaybi.

Abu al-Walid: alias of Turky Bin-'Abd-al'Aziz Bi-Ibrahim.

Abu-al-Walid: alias of 'Abd-al-Hamid Fahim 'Abdallah al-Turablisi.

Abu-al-Walid: alias of Muhammad Musa 'Umran.

Abu-al-Walid: alias of Ahmad Farhat Ahmad.

Abu al-Walid: according to the captured Sinjar personnel records of al Qaeda in Iraq, a student who arrived in Iraq on May 9, 2007, having traveled from Darnah, Libya. He hoped to become a martyr. He signed up through coordinator Bashar and contributed several thousand Syrian lira. His Syrian coordinator was Abu 'Abbas.

Abu-al-Walid: alias of Turky Bin-'Abd-al'Aziz Bin-Ibrahim.

Abu-al-Walid: alias of Jum'ah Hamad al-Muhaiydi Sakran.

Khaled Abul Walid: one of six Palestine Popular Struggle Front (some reports say it was the Popular Front for the Liberation of Palestine) hijackers of an Olympics Airways B727 flying from Beirut to Athens on July 22, 1970. In Athens, the hijackers negotiated for the release of seven Arab terrorists who were being held for the December 21, 1969 attack on an El Al airliner, the December 21, 1969 attempted hijacking of a TWA plane, and the November 27, 1968 attack on the El Al office in Athens. The Greek government agreed to continue the trial of the November terrorists on July 24, sentencing the duo to 11 and 18 years, respectively, then let them go free. The seven freed terrorists flew to Cairo.

Mahfouz Ould al-Walid: alias of Abu Hafs al-Mauritania.

Walied: Saudi-based recruitment coordinator for foreign fighters for al Qaeda in Iraq in 2007.

Abu Al Walied: alias of Khalid Muhammad Rakan Al Murshed.

Abu Al Walied: alias of Abd Al Aziz Khalid Al Hazeel.

Abu Al Walied: alias of Muhammad Mussa Oumran.

Abu Al Walied: alias of Jum'ah Hamad al-Muhaiydi Sakran.

Abu Al Walied: alias of Adnan Bin Ahmed Al Shamlan.

Abu Al Walied: alias of Ahmed Farahat Ahmed.

Aliyah Wani: age 22, one of the Islamic militants who conducted several coordinated attacks against 11 police posts in 3 Thai provinces, leaving 112 people dead on April 28, 2004; 107 of the dead were militants. He was the only one of six attackers to get out alive from their raid in Yupo. He was shot in the leg. He said a stranger had persuaded his group to attack the police station to obtain weapons.

Majdi Abu-Wardah: credited by Hamas with being one of the bombers who, on February 24, 1996, set off a bomb on the No. 18 Egged bus in Jerusalem that killed 23 people and injured 49 and another bomb at an Ashqelon soldiers' hitchhiking post that killed two and injured 31. He was reportedly a resident of the al-Fawwar refugee camp near Nablus.

Mohammed Abu Warden: a 21-year-old student at an Islamic teachers college who was arrested on March 1996 by Palestinian security forces on suspicion of being the mastermind of three of the last four bombings in the area. He was convicted of recruiting three suicide bombers.

Yasir Arafat approved a sentenced of life at hard labor.

William James Wardel: alias of Nahed al Warfelly.

Nahed al Warfelly: alias William James Wardel, an Iraqi who carries a British passport and was one of five men detained by the Immigration Police in January 1991 as part of a terrorist plot against U.S., UK, Israeli, and Australian installations and airlines.

Misbah Saied Al Warghami: variant of Musbah Sa'id al-Warghami.

Musbah Sa'id al-Warghami: variant Misbah Saied Al Warghami, alias Abu-Miqdad, variant Abu Muqtad, a Tunisian clerk from Bin Zert who was born on July 22, 1981 and joined al Qaeda in Iraq on November 18, 2006 to become a martyr. He contributed an ID card. His recruitment coordinator was Abu-'Umar. His cousin's phone number was 0021696472072.

Jamal Warrayat: a Palestinian from Jordan and a naturalized U.S. citizen who, on April 16, 1991, was convicted in U.S. District Court in Newark, New Jersey of making a threat against U.S. President George H. W. Bush. He phoned the Iraqi Embassy and offered to kill President Bush. The Embassy was unresponsive.

Rada Hassen al-Mossa al-Wassny: one of 16 Middle Eastern terrorists the Saudi Embassy told Thai officials, on March 20, 1990, were planning to attack Saudi diplomats and officials overseas. He carried a Lebanese passport.

'Adil al-Watari: variant of 'Adil al-Watri.

Adel al Watery: variant of 'Adil al-Watri.

'Adil al-Watri: variant Adel al Watery, variant al-Watari, a Yemen-based recruitment coordinator for al Qaeda in Iraq foreign fighters in 2007.

'Adil al-Watari: variant of 'Adil al-Watri, variant Adel al Watery.

Salim 'Umar Sa'id Ba-Wazir: alias Abu-Muthanna, a Yemeni student from Hadramaut who was born in 1984 and joined al Qaeda in Iraq as a fighter in 2007, providing his passport and watch. His recruitment coordinator was Ahmad. He arrived in Damascus from Yemen by plane via Malaysia. In Syria he met Abu-'Uthman and al-Hajji, to whom he gave $1,500. He had experience with weapons. His home phone number was 352390, but he asked that the personnel officer "not inform the women."

Mussbah Mahmud Werfalli: a Libyan diplomat identified by Rageb Hammouda Daghdugh, a Libyan arrested in Rome on February 5, 1985 carrying a Walther P-38 pistol and $25,000 in checks issued by the Libyan People's Bureau. He claimed Werfalli and another Libyan had given him the money and gun to assassinate U.S. Ambassador Maxwell Rabb and the envoys from Egypt and Saudi Arabia. Werfalli was protected by diplomatic immunity, but was ordered to leave Italy. In April 1986, the Italian courts issued an arrest warrant for Werfalli, who was believed to be in Malta.

Wisam: alias Abu-al-'Abbas, a Jordanian member of al Qaeda in Iraq who was to conduct a suicide mission in Mosul in 2007. He owned 2,050 Syrian lira and a wristwatch. His colleague Abu-Wa'il's phone number was 0096264893098.

Nasir al-Wuhayshi: leader of al Qaeda in Yemen as of summer 2007. He was a former secretary of Osama bin Laden and had escaped from a Yemeni prison along with one of the USS *Cole* attack masterminds, Jamal al-Badawi, in 2006.

'Abd al-Hamid Wusaym: a Jordanian arrested on September 24, 1981 in connection with the Black June attack in which a grenade was thrown into the Shoham, Limassol, Cyprus offices of an Israeli shipping firm on September 23, 1981, injuring three female and two male Greek Cypriot employees.

Y

Yequti'el Ben-Ya-aqov: identified on March 13, 1994 by Israeli authorities as a leader of the extremist group Kahana Lives, which the Cabinet unanimously banned for being a terrorist group.

Atamnia Yacine: age 33, an Algerian, arrested by Bangkok police on August 24, 2005 on charges of possessing 180 fake French and Spanish passports and overstaying his visa. Thai police believe he supplied the fake IDs used in the July 7, 2005 bombings of the London subway system.

Abu Yacoub: alias of Muhammad Abd Allah al Ugayle.

Abu Yacoub: alias of Muhammad Abu Abd Allah Al Oujaylly.

Abu Yacoub: alias of Abd Al Munaem Essa Muhammad Ouqaiel.

Abu Yacoub: alias of Youssef Salem Al Shameri.

Charles Yacoub: a Montreal resident of Lebanese descent who, on April 7, 1989, hijacked a new York-bound Greyhound bus carrying 11 passengers from Montreal and forced it to drive onto the grounds of the Canadian Parliament in Ottawa, 100 miles west. He wanted to draw attention to his demands that Syrian troops leave Lebanon and release Lebanese prisoners. He surrendered to the Mounties.

Ibrahim Salih Mohammed al-Yacoub: variant of Ibraham Salih Muhammad al-Yaqub.

Abd Al Aziz Abd Al Rab Saleh Al Yafea'a: variant of 'Abd-al-'Aziz 'Abd-al-Rabb Salih al-Yafi'.

Al-Yafei: name on a forged Lebanese passport used by the four hijackers of a Kuwaiti A310 en route from Kuwait to Bangkok with intermediate stops in Dubai and Karachi on December 4, 1984.

'Abd-al-'Aziz 'Abd-al-Rabb Salih al-Yafi': variant Abd Al Aziz Abd Al Rab Saleh Al Yafea'a, alias Abu-'Umar, variant Abu Omar, a Saudi from Riyadh who was born on April 6, 1979 and joined al Qaeda in Iraq on November 17, 2006 to become a martyr. He contributed a passport and watch. His brothers' phone numbers were 00967733758083 and 00966506192733.

Abdul Rahman al-Yafi: a Yemeni arrested in Cairo in October 2000 on suspicion of involvement with al Qaeda. The *Washington Post* reported that he was held in Jordan for four months, but was free in Yemen as of December 2007.

Ali al-Yafi: alleged leader of the four hijackers of a Kuwaiti A310 en route from Kuwait to Bangkok with intermediate stops in Dubai and Karachi on December 4, 1984.

A. J. Yaghi: one of two male Lebanese hijackers of a South African Airways B727 flying from Salisbury, Rhodesia to Johannesburg, South Africa on May 24, 1972. The duo threatened to blow up the plane. At a refueling stop in Salisbury, they let some of the passengers deplane. In Blantyre, Malawi, they demanded money from the

Anglo-American Mining Company. The next day, all passengers and crew escaped. Troops fired on the jet, and the hijackers were captured. On September 18, 1972, they were sentenced to 11 years. They were released in Malawi in 1974. Some reports claim that they then went to Cairo, while others said they were deported to Zambia on May 21, 1974.

Abdellah Yahia: a member of the Algerian Islamic Group (GIA) and leader of the Eucalypti district in Algiers who was believed to be the leader of the four Algerian Islamic extremists who, on December 24, 1994, hijacked an Air France A300 on the ground at Algiers's Houari Boumedienne Airport and killed a Vietnamese trade councilor and an Algerian policeman. The hijackers were killed in a rescue attempt at Marseilles airport. His mother participated in airport negotiations.

Abu Yahiya: alias of Ahamed Tewfik al A'azri.

Muhammad Anwar Rafiia'a Yahiya: alias Abu Abd al Kabeer, who, according to the captured Sinjar records of al Qaeda in Iraq (Islamic State of Iraq), was born on March 10, 1990. He lived in Dernah, Libya and came to Iraq via Egypt and Syria, assisted by Abu Abbas and coordinator Bashar. He brought with him 700 Libyan dinars, and contributed 2000 Syria lira and $12. The student offered to be a martyr.

'Abdallah Hamid Yahya: a Sudanese who was one of 18 Arab terrorists reported by Madrid *Diario 16* on October 20, 1987 as having entered Spain in August to attack Middle Eastern diplomatic missions and assassinate Saudi Ambassador Muhammad Nuri Ibrahim. They had received weapons and casing reports on the ambassador from a Lebanese student resident in Spain whose initials were HMI.

Abu-Yahya: alias of Ahmad Tawfiq al-Adhari.

Abu-Yahya: alias of 'Abd-al-Hadi Muhamad 'Abdallah al-Dulaymi.

Abu-Yahya: alias of 'Ali Muhammad 'Abd-Rab Hamid Khudayr.

Adel Yahya: age 23, a north Londoner from the Tottenham area, who was arrested by British police on December 20, 2005 at 5 A.M. as he arrived at Gatwick Airport on a flight from Addis Ababa, Ethiopia, in connection with the abortive plot to set off bombs in the London subway system on July 21, 2005. He had been out of the country since June. He was held on suspicion of the commission, preparation, or instigation of acts of terrorism. His trial began on January 15, 2007. Defendants Yassin Hassan Omar, Yahya, and Muktar Said Ibrahim attended the Finsbury Park mosque to hear jihadist sermons by Abu Hamza Masri, who was convicted in 2006 for soliciting murder and inciting racial hatred.

On July 10, 2007, the jury was unable to reach a verdict on defendants Asiedu and Yahya and was dismissed. The judge gave prosecutors until the next morning to seek a retrial. Retrials were scheduled. On November 20, 2007, a British court sentenced Asiedu to 33 years in prison. He had admitted to a charge of conspiracy to cause explosions.

Muhammad Anwar Rafi' Yahya: alias Abu-'Abd al-Kabir, a Libyan student from Darnah who was born on October 16, 1990 and joined al Qaeda in Iraq as a martyr on May 9, 2007, contributing 2,000 Syrian lira and $12. His recruitment coordinator was Bashar. He arrived via Libya and Egypt to Damascus, where he met Abu-'Abbas. He brought 700 Libyan dinars.

Mourad Yala: was arrested in Geleen, the Netherlands, in April 2003 on suspicion of falsifying passports. He was released in 2004 and deported to Spain. The *Telegraaf* reported in October 2004 that Yala was suspected by Spanish investigators of developing technology for converting laptop computers into time bombs. He was among 18 suspected terrorists being held by Spanish authorities on November 8, 2004.

Ali Yamal: variant Lyal Jamal, a Lebanese who was believed to have set off a suicide bomb on ALAS flight HP-1202, a twin-engine Brazilian-made Embraer on July 19, 1994 killing two crew and 19 passengers, including a dozen Israeli businessmen, shortly after the plane had left Colon Airport in Panama. The Partisans of God, believed to be an Hizballah cover name, claimed credit.

Abu-al-Fida' al-Yamani: alias of Al-Mutakkil Ala-Allah Mahdi al-Dabarah.

Abu-Haydarah al-Yamani: alias of 'Ali Ahmad 'Ali Hammud.

Abu Hazifah Al Yamani: alias of Abd Al Rahman Muhammad Ouqael.

Abu Al Jarah Al Yamani: alias of Yaser Hassan Ahmed Ammer.

Rabhi Yamar: alleged member of the Islamic Salvation Front who was arrested for involvement in the August 26, 1992 bombing of the Air France ticket counter at Houari Boumedienne Airport in Algeria that killed 12 people and wounded 128. Public sessions of his trial began on May 4, 1993. On May 26, 1993, a special Algiers judicial council sentenced him to ten years.

Abu-al-Yaqin: alias of Sa'id.

Muhammad Yaqout: a member of the Egyptian Jihad group arrested by Yemeni authorities on April 20, 2008. The group was suspected of being connected with terrorists who attack U.S. targets in Sana'a. Authorities said he was behind two mortar attacks against the U.S. Embassy on March 18 and a residential compound housing U.S. and other Western citizens on April 6. He had been arrested in August 2007 after a suicide car bombing killed eight Spanish tourists in Marib on July 2, 2007. He was released after two months.

Ya'qub: Saudi-based recruitment coordinator for foreign fighters for al Qaeda in Iraq in 2006.

Abu-Ya'qub: alias of Yusuf Salim al-Shammari.

Ibraham Salih Muhammad al-Yaqub: variant Ibrahim Salih Mohammed al-Yacoub, indicted in the Eastern District of Virginia for the June 25, 1996 bombing of the Khobar Towers military housing complex in Dhahran, Saudi Arabia. He is wanted on multiple conspiracy charges against U.S. nationals and property, including conspiracy to kill U.S. nationals; conspiracy to murder U.S. employees; conspiracy and use of weapons of mass destruction against U.S. nationals; conspiracy to destroy U.S. property; conspiracy to attack national defense utilities; bombing resulting in death; murder while using a destructive device during a crime of violence; and murder and attempted murder of federal employees. The Rewards for Justice Program offers $5 million for his apprehension. He claims to have been born on October 16, 1966 in Tarut, Saudi Arabia. He is five feet four inches tall and weighs 150 pounds.

Imad Eddin Barakat Yarkas: variant Emaz Edim Baraktyarkas, alias Abu Dahdah. On November 13, 2001, Madrid and Granada police arrested nine members of the Mujahedeen Movement, which has ties to al Qaeda, and accused them of recruiting members to carry out terrorist attacks. The arrests followed two years of investigations. The leader was initially identified Yarkas, a Syrian with Spanish nationality. The other eight were from Tunisia and Algeria. Spain did not offer details on the terrorists' targets. The next day, police identified three more Islamic suspects. Police seized videos of Islamic guerrilla activities, hunting rifles, swords, fake IDs, and a large amount of cash. Spain—and other European nations—expressed concern about extraditing suspects to the United States for trial by military tribunals announced by President Bush.

On November 17, 11 suspected members of an al Qaeda cell were arraigned. On November 19, Spanish officials said that eight al Qaeda cell members arrested in Madrid and Granada had a role in preparing the September 11 attacks. Judge Baltasar Garzon ordered eight of them held without bail, because they "were directly related with the preparation and development of the attacks perpetrated by the suicide pilots on September 11." Judge Garzon charged them with membership in an armed group and possession of forged documents. They were also accused of recruiting young Muslim men for training at terrorist camps in Indonesia. They also reportedly sheltered Chechnya rebels and obtained medical treatment for al Qaeda members. They conducted robberies and credit card fraud and provided false documents to al Qaeda visitors. They also forwarded money to Hamburg. The group had connections to Mohamed Bensakhria, head of the Frankfurt-based cell that planned a terrorist attack in Strasbourg, France. He was arrested in the summer of 2001 and extradited to France. The group also had connections to six Algerians detained in Spain on September 26 who were charged with belonging to the Salafist Group for Preaching and Combat, a bin Laden-funded Algerian group. The charges were based on documents and intercepted phone conversations of detainee Yarkas, al Qaeda's leader in Spain. His name and phone number were in a document found in a search of a Hamburg apartment of a bin Laden associate. Police believe hijacker leader Atta could have met with some of them when he visited Spain in January and July. The group had links to Mamoun Darkazanli. Judge Garzon released three others who were arrested on November 13, but ordered them to report regularly to the authorities.

Yarkas, a father of four, was picked up at his central Madrid apartment. He met with bin Laden twice and was in close contact with Muhammad Atef. Yarkas earned $2,000/month, but traveled often to Yemen, Saudi Arabia, the United Arab Emirates, Senegal, and Indonesia and throughout Europe, visiting the UK ten times. He met bin Laden associates in the United Kingdom.

On March 13, 2004, the imprisoned Yarkas was questioned by the investigating judge in connection with the March 11, 2004 multiple bombings of trains in Madrid that killed 200 and wounded 2,000.

On April 21, 2005, the trial began of al Qaeda suspects in Spain linked to the 9/11 attacks. Among them was Yarkas, age 42, who faced 40 years each for nearly 3,000 counts of accessory to murder, recruiting Islamic fighters to go to Bosnia and Afghanistan, and membership in a terrorist organization. On July 5, 2005, Yarkas told a court he was innocent, and the prosecution's claim that they were a Spanish al Qaeda cell was a "myth." On September 26, 2005, a Spanish court convicted Yarkas and sentenced him to 27 years in prison for conspiring with al Qaeda and the 9/11 hijackers. On April 6, 2006, a Spanish prosecutor told the Spanish Supreme Court that the conviction of Yarkas should be overturned for lack of evidence. On June 1, 2006, Spain's Supreme Court threw out his conviction, citing lack of proof. He had been sentenced to 27 years. He would still serve 12 years for leading a terrorist group.

On April 16, 2008, Judge Ismael Moreno of the National Court indicted Syrian-born Imad Eddin Barakat Yarkas, age 44; Syria-born Muhamed Galeb Kalaje Zouaydi, age 47; and Bassam Dalati Satut, age 48, on suspicion of financing terrorist cells. The indictment said that the duo removed $76,500 in December 2006 from Zouaydi's company and gave the money to Yarkas. Yarkas was charged with membership in a terrorist organization. The trio were arraigned on April 24, denying the charges.

Hijad Yarmur: East Jerusalem resident arrested as one of the Hamas terrorists who, on October 9, 1994, kidnapped Israeli Corporal Nachshon Mordekhay Wachsman from Jerusalem's 'Atarot junction. He took the videotape from the kidnappers to the Gaza Strip to mislead investigators. He also led the Israeli security forces to the house in which the hostage was held.

Abu Yaser: alias of Muhammad Bin Sabber Bin Muhammad al A'anzi.

Yasin: alias of 'Abd-al-Karim al-Naji 'Abd-al-Radi Ahmad, an Egyptian Islamic Group terrorist who was arrested after the failed June 26, 1995 assassination attempt against Egyptian President Hosni Mubarak in Addis Ababa, Ethiopia.

Yasin: alias Abu-Usayd, variant Abu Asid, a Saudi from Mecca who joined al Qaeda in Iraq as a fighter in 2007, bringing his passport. His recruitment coordinator was Abu-'Uthman. His home phone number was 5346636.

Yasin: alias Abu-M'awiah, a Yemeni fighter for al Qaeda in Iraq in 2007 who owned $100 and his passport. His phone number was 00967245732.

'Abd al-Latif Yasin: arrested on August 12, 1985 by the Egyptian prosecutor's office on charges of communicating with Libya to the detriment of Egypt's political status and receiving a bribe from Libya to commit murder in the foiled plot to assassinate Ghayth Said al-Mabruk, a political refugee living in Alexandria, Egypt, on August 6, 1985. When arrested, he and two others had a machine gun and pistol. They were later found guilty and sentenced to death.

'Abd al-Rahman Said Yasin: variant Abdul Rahman Yasin, alias Aboud Yasin, Abdul Rahman S. Taha, Abdul Rahman S. Taher, wanted for participating in the terrorist bombing of the World Trade Center (WTC) in New York City on February 26, 1993, which resulted in six deaths, the wounding of 1,000 others, and significant destruction of property and commerce. He is wanted for damage by means of fire or explosives; damage by means of fire or an explosive to U.S. property; transport in interstate commerce of an explosive; destruction of motor vehicles or motor vehicle facilities; conspiracy to commit offense or defraud the United States; aiding and abetting; assault of a federal officer in the line of duty; commission of a crime of violence through the use of a deadly weapon or device. The Rewards for Justice program offers $5 million for his apprehension. He claims to have been born in Saudi Arabia on April 10, 1960. He also claimed to have been born in Bloomington, Indiana. He is five feet ten inches tall and

weighs 180 pounds. The Jersey City resident was indicted in August 4, 1993, charged with mixing the chemicals, including the nitroglycerin, for the WTC bomb. Seven days after the bombing, he boarded a flight to Amman, Jordan. He was also suspected of involvement in Ramzi Ahmad Yusuf's Boyinka plot to bomb 11 U.S. airliners flying from the Philippines to the United States.

The Iraqi American was a grad student in engineering. The FBI interviewed him within six days of the 1993 WTC bombing. He was the roommate of Mohammed Salameh, the Jordanian who parked the bomb-laden van in the underground parking garage. Yasin helped mix the explosives in a storage locker in Jersey City. He left for Jordan and ended up in Iraq, where he worked for the Saddam Hussein government. He refused to return to New York for trial as a coconspirator.

He might have a chemical burn on his right thigh. He takes medication for epilepsy.

Abou Yasin: alias of 'Abd al-Rahman Said Yasin.

Izat Yasin: identified by the Ethiopian government as the foreign deputy coordinator of the nine Egyptian Islamic Group gunmen who, on June 25, 1995, fired on the armored limousine of Egyptian President Hosni Mubarak in Addis Ababa.

Mohammed Yasin: alias Ustad Osama, in his thirties, an explosives expert who manufactures "suicide jackets" for Harkat-e-Jihad. He met with London 7-7-05 train bomber Sidique Khan in Pakistan in the fall of 2004.

Shaykh Ahmad Yasin: variant Sheikh Ahmed Yassein, Sheik Ahmed Yassin, founder of the Islamic Resistance Movement (Hamas) on December 14, 1987. His release from prison was demanded by the two Palestinians who kidnapped U.S. citizen Chris George, director of the Save the Children Fund in Gaza, on June 22, 1989; and by the Hamas members who, on October 9, 1994, kidnapped Israeli Corporal Nachshon Mordekhay Wachsman from Jerusalem's 'Atarot junction. He was freed in September 1997 by the Israelis when Jordan agreed to release two Mossad agents into Israeli custody. Hamas's founder and spiritual leader was 61, a quadriplegic who is nearly blind. He had served eight years of a life sentence for ordering the killings of Palestinians who collaborated with Israel. He issued a call for moderation, saying he was ready to coexist with Israelis as long as Palestinian rights are respected. On August 22, 2003, President Bush froze his assets and called on allies to join him by cutting off European sources of donations to Hamas. He died on March 22, 2004 when Israeli AH-64 Apache helicopter gunships fired three missiles at him as he was being pushed in a wheelchair from 5:30 A.M. prayers at Gaza City's Islamic Group Mosque, a few yards from his modest residence. The blasts killed him, three of his bodyguards, and four other followers, and wounded at least 15 others, including two of his sons. Israeli Prime Minister Ariel Sharon said he personally authorized the assassination.

Tall al'Yasin: release from an Israeli jail was demanded on June 27, 1976 by the Popular Front for the Liberation of Palestine hijackers of Air France 139, an Aerospatiale Airbus A300 flying from Tel Aviv to Paris and ultimately diverted to Entebbe.

Abu-Yasir: alias of Muhammad Bin-Subbar Bin-Muhammad al-'Anazi.

Abu-Yasir: alias of Farid.

Abu-Yasir: alias of 'Abd-al-Rahman Ahmad Nasir Khatir.

Abu-Yasir: alias of 'Abd-al-Rahim Bin-Hamdun.

Salah Yasir: Fatah dissident who, in a July 1977 interview with Madrid's *Cambio* in Algiers, vowed to kill several Arab personalities, including Yasir Arafat.

Yassir Yasiri: a second-tier al Qaeda operative arrested on March 15, 2003 in Lahore, Pakistan.

Sheikh Ahmed Yassein: variant of Shaykh Ahmad Yasin.

Abu Yasser: alias of Abd Al Rahman Ahamed Nasser Khatter.

Ehab Yousri Yassin: while being chased by Cairo police on April 30, 2005, he jumped from a bridge and set off a nail bomb, killing himself and injuring six people. He was wanted in connection with the bomb that exploded on a motorcycle on April 7, 2005 near a tour group in Cairo's historic Khan al-Khalili bazaar, killing three people, along with the terrorist, and wounded 18, including four Americans. The previously unknown Islamic Pride Brigades took credit on the Internet.

Two hours later and 2½ miles away, his sister and his fiancé fired three times from their car at a tour bus going to a Cairo historic Islamic site. Two people–not the tourists–were injured and the veiled gunwomen, both in their twenties, were killed. Some witnesses said the police fired on the terrorists; others said the girls turned their guns on themselves.

Fawaz Yassin: Chief of the Palestine Liberation Organization (PLO) office in Khartoum; believed to have organized the March 1, 1973 Black September takeover of the Saudi Embassy in Khartoum in which two U.S. diplomats and one Belgian diplomat were murdered. Libyan leader Muammar Qadhafi refused an extradition request and helped him to a sanctuary in the People's Democratic Republic of Yemen. A Sudanese court indicted him on five counts, including murder. The six defendants were convicted of murder on June 24, 1974 and sentenced to life, but Sudanese President Gaafar el-Nimeiry immediately commuted each sentence to seven years. He announced that the group would be handed over to the PLO. They were flown to Cairo the next day. It appears that Egypt placed the group at the disposal of the PLO in November 1974.

Sheik Ahmed Yassin: variant of Shaykh Ahmad Yasin.

Touwafik Yassin: a 25-year-old identified by the Israeli government on September 23, 1997 as one of four Palestinians living in the West Bank village of Asirah Shamaliya, north of Nablus, who were responsible for an attack on July 30, 1997 and the September 4, 1997 attack in which three Palestinians set off bombs in Ben Yehuda Street in Jerusalem, killing themselves, five others, and wounding 190 shoppers, including many foreign visitors, among whom were Americans.

Salah Abdul Karim Yassine: a Palestinian arrested in November 2000 in Paraguay after threatening to bomb the U.S. and Israeli embassies in Asuncion. He was charged with possession of false documents and entering the country illegally. He was alleged to be obtaining $100,000 in financing while living in Ciudad del Este. He said he was making the threats as a joke. He remained in prison at the end of December 2000.

Yayah: alias of Adam Yahiye Gadahn.

Dara Yazdani-Amiri: one of four people arrested by London police on December 14, 1988 during a demonstration in front of the offices of Iran Air. They had attacked three computers of the firm, and were to face charges of criminal damage and violent disorder on January 5, 1989.

Amir Muhammad Yazdi: a lieutenant in Savama, the Iranian intelligence organization, who was believed to have been one of the gunmen who shot and critically wounded Arab League deputy director Midhat al-Hiyali, an Iraqi, in Palaio Psikhiko, Athens, Greece, on December 21, 1987. Yazdi had arrived in Greece the previous day through Volos and was traveling on a Jordanian passport.

Mustafa Abu al-Yazeed: variant of Mustafa Abu al-Yazid.

Yazid: alias Abu-Muhammad, a Jordanian member of al Qaeda in Iraq in 2007 who owned a passport and whose phone number was 0777480805.

Boutiche Yazid: one of four Islamic extremists who were hunted down and shot to death by police after the terrorists, on March 28, 1994. assassinated Konstatin Kukushkin, a driver at the Russian Embassy, and senior Algerian diplomat Belkacem Touati in front of his wife and children in Bordj el Kiffan.

Mustafa Abu al-Yazid: variant Yazeed, as of July 2007, he was 51 years old and al Qaeda's liaison with the Taliban and the group's leader in Afghanistan. The Egyptian is a trained accountant who had served as bin Laden's financial manager in the Sudan in the 1990s. He was one of the original members of al Qaeda's Shura Council (the group's ruling group). He served time in the early 1980s in prison with al Qaeda deputy Ayman al-Zawahiri after both were convicted on charges of participation in the assassination of Egyptian President Anwar Sadat. He ran the group's finance committee from 1995 to 2007.

Abdul Kareem Yazijy: age 35, who might have been one of the nine suicide bombers who killed 25 people on May 12, 2003 in Riyadh.

On May 6, 2003, Saudi television showed the faces of 19 men, including 17 Saudis, a Yemeni, and an Iraqi (who held Kuwaiti and Canadian citizenship) being sought following the discovery of a large arms cache in Riyadh. Authorities said the terrorists planned attacks in the kingdom. After a gunfight with police in which the getaway car was damaged, the suspects stole vehicles and fled into a densely populated section of the city. Yazijy was one of the 19. The government later said the terrorists planned attacks on the royal family—including the defense minister, Prince Sultan, and his brother, the interior minister, Prince Nayef—and received their orders directly from Osama bin Laden. The government offered a reward of $80,000 for information leading to the cell and $10,000 for information about the terrorists.

His younger brother, Abdullah, called on him to turn himself in, and noted that he had disappeared 18 months earlier. He had a long history of "emotional instability," according to Abdullah. His brother went to Afghanistan for a few months in 1990 and later worked for two years in Sarajevo for the Saudi charity Supreme Committee for the Collection of Donations for Bosnia-Herzegovnia, which was raided in 2002 for al Qaeda ties.

Abdul-Rahman Mohammed Mohammed Yazji: suspected in the 2003 bombing of the Riyadh housing complex for foreigners that killed 17 people. He died in a gun battle with Saudi authorities on April 3–6, 2005 in a walled compound in Ar Rass.

Alireza Yeganeh: a seaman arrested after eight Iranian students were arrested in the United States on November 15, 1979 for attempting to smuggle 3 disassembled Winchester 30.06 rifles, matching scopes, 15 boxes of ammunition, and a street map of Washington, DC with certain embassies marked, as one of the men was about to board TWA 900 from Baltimore-Washington International Airport to New York's JFK International Airport. Yeganeh was held for conspiracy and dealing in firearms without a license.

Abu-al-Jarrah al-Yemeni: alias of Yasir Hasan Ahmad 'Amir.

Abu-Bashir al-Yemeni: al Qaeda training camp commander listed by U.S. Central Command on January 8, 2002 as being at large.

Abu Huthaifah al-Yemeni: alias of Fahd Mohammed Ahmed al-Quso.

Abu Saleh al-Yemeni: al Qaeda operational facilitator listed by the U.S. Central Command on January 8, 2002 as having died.

Haitham al-Yemeni: a senior al Qaeda leader who was killed by a Predator-fired missile near the Afghanistan-Pakistan border on May 13, 2005.

Husam Yemeni: an Ansara-Islam member captured by U.S. troops in mid-January 2004.

Souhib al Abi al-Yemeni: variant of Suhayb al-Abiyy al-Yemeni.

Suhayb al-Abiyy al-Yemeni: Souhib al Abi al-Yemeni, variant alias of Yazid Humud 'Abdallah.

Ahmad Fathi Yihia: age 22, an Islamic Jihad (IJ) member from Kufeirat, near Jenin, who, on July 7, 2003, set off a bomb during the night that killed Mazal Afari, age 65, in the living room of her Kfar Yavetz home. Yihia died when the roof collapsed. Three of Afari's grandchildren were slightly injured. An IJ spokesman said the bombing was not sanctioned by the leadership, which had agreed to a three-month truce.

Noam Yinon: on May 26, 1984, he pleaded guilty to involvement in the attempted bombing on April 27, 1984of five buses of the Kalandia Bus Company, an Arab-owned company serving the Arab portion of East Jerusalem and the West Bank. He was one of 27 individuals believed to belong to Terror Against Terror. His case was separated from the others in a plea bargain. The army reserve paratrooper was convicted of hauling 50 army-issue antipersonnel mines for the Jewish terrorist group. In early June 1984, he was sentenced to 18 months in jail and 18 months probation.

Tahir Yoldashev: leader of the Islamic Movement of Uzbekistan, which has links to Osama bin Laden.

Marco Antonio Yon Sosa: leader of the Guatemalan Revolutionary Movement of November 13. The Mexican government announced that he and two of his followers had been shot to death near the Guatemalan border on May 16, 1970. He was a lieutenant in the Guatemalan Army until 1960, when he joined a rebellion against President Miguel Ydigoras Fuentes.

Abou Youcef: alias of Mourad Khelil.

Boulesbaa Youcef: alleged member of the Islamic Salvation Front who was arrested for involvement in the August 26, 1992 bombing of the Air France ticket counter at Houari Boumedienne Airport in Algeria that killed 12 people and wounded 128. Public sessions of his trial began on May 4, 1993. On May 26, 1993, a special Algiers judicial council passed death sentenced on 38 defendants, including him. The council found him guilty of actual direct participation in the crime as well as taking part in an aggression with the aim of destroying the governing regime.

Georges Fouad Nicolas Younan: one of three individuals arrested in Richford, Vermont on October 23, 1987 after they illegally crossed into the United States from Canada with a terrorist bomb made from two metal canisters filled with smokeless gunpowder. A black hood found with the bomb and bomb-making equipment resembled hoods used in terrorist attacks in the Middle East. On October 28, 1987, U.S. Magistrate Jerome J. Niedermeier ordered them held without bail. They said they were Canadian citizens living in Montreal, but were believed to be Lebanese. On May 17, 1988, the U.S. government reported that the trio were members of the Syrian Social National Party, a Syrian terrorist organization that assassinated Lebanese President-Elect Bashir Gemayel in 1982. Younan was found guilty by a jury of several explosives violations and an immigration violation. He could face 35 years in prison.

Bahij Mohammed Younis: Jordanian arrested on October 28, 1981 by Austrian police while in possession of submachine guns, other small firearms, several hand grenades, and several passports. He was believed to be a mastermind behind several Palestinian terrorist attacks. On October 22, 1982, he was sentenced to life in prison in connection to the May 1, 1981, murder in Austria of Heinz Nittel, president of the Austrian-Israeli Friendship League, a leading Socialist Party official, and head of the Vienna Traffic Department. Abu Nidal's Al Asifah organization claimed credit for the assassination.

Fawaz Younis: variant Yunis, variant Rida Yunus, alias Nazeeh, leader of the six Brigades of the Marches of Lebanese Resistance hijackers who took over Royal Jordanian Airlines flight 402, a B727 boarding passengers at Beirut International Airport on June 11, 1985. The plane hopscotched through Europe and the Middle East. The hijackers escaped after setting off a bomb on the plane in Beirut. On September 13, 1987, the FBI arrested the Lebanese Shi'ite, who was believed to have been the spokesman identified as Nazih. At the time of his arrest, Younis was lured onto the *Skunk Kilo* yacht off the Cyprus coast by a friend, in hopes of buying drugs. He was taken to a U.S. Navy vessel that headed west for a rendezvous off Corsica with the U.S. aircraft carrier Saratoga. He was then flown to Andrews Air Force Base and held at Quantico Marine Base. He pleaded not guilty on September 17, 1987 in a ten-minute hearing before U.S. magistrate Jean F. Dwyer in Washington, DC, to a five-count indictment of conspiracy, destruction of an aircraft, and hostage taking, the latter count of which carries a life term. On October 7, 1987, he was arraigned in a federal court on charges of air piracy, placing a destructive device aboard an aircraft, committing violence aboard an aircraft, and aiding and abetting a hijacking. On February 12, 1988, U.S. District Judge Barrington D. Parker ruled that he could be charged with leading the hijacking of the Jordanian airliner but not with assaulting passengers and blowing up the Royal Jordanian Airline jet at Beirut International Airport. Parker refused to dismiss six conspiracy and hijacking counts under the 1984 Hostage Taking Act, and upheld the use of Navy vessels that transported him. However, on February 23, 1988, Judge Parker threw out Younis's written confession and all other statements he made to the FBI shortly after his arrest. On October 14, 1988, the U.S. Court of Appeals for the District of Columbia Circuit overturned Parker's decision. On March 14, 1989, the U.S. District Court in Washington, DC convicted him of air piracy and taking of hostages. He was found not guilty on three counts of blowing up the aircraft and threatening or harming the passengers.

On October 4, 1989, he was sentenced to 30 years in prison. On January 29, 1991, the U.S. Court of Appeals for the District of Columbia upheld the conviction. On March 29, 1993, the Jabal Lubnan Public Prosecution Office indicted him for hijacking the Jordanian plane and blowing it up. His attorney requested extradition.

On March 28, 2005, the United States deported him to Lebanon. He served almost 16 years in prison. He was released from federal prison in Petersburg, Virginia, in February 2005 and deported to Lebanon for being an illegal immigrant.

Qari Mohammed Yousaf: a Taliban spokesman who claimed credit for a January 15, 2006 suicide car-bomb attack against a Canadian military convoy in southern Afghanistan that killed two civilians and Glyn Berry, age 59, Canada's senior diplomat in the south and political director of a 250-member provincial reconstruction team.

Saeed son of Yousaf: one of five Libyans arrested on March 27, 1993 by police in Peshawar, Pakistan at a checkpoint near the Gulbahar crossing. Police found in their vehicle two .30 pistols and 30 cartridges, fake passport stamps, U.S. dollars, and Pakistani currency.

Mohammed Yousef: one of three terrorists who, on July 11, 1988, fired machine guns and threw hand grenades at the City of Poros, a Greek island ferryboat that was carrying tourists in the Aegean Sea, killing 11 and injuring 98.

Rafik Mohamad Yousef: age 31, arrested on December 3, 2004 at a safe house of three radical Islamic members of the Iraqi group Ansar al-Islam, hours before they planned to attack Iraqi Prime Minister Ayad Allawi during a state visit. On November 16, 2005, Germany charged Ata Abdoulaziz Rashid; Mazen Ali Hussein, age 23; and Yousef with plotting to assassinate Allawi. Their trial began on June 19, 2006.

Ramzi Ahmed Yousef: variant Yusuf, sentenced on January 8, 1998 to life plus 240 years for the World Trade Center bombing of February 26, 1993. He had also plotted with Wali Khan to bomb a dozen U.S. airliners over the Pacific in the Bojinka plot and to assassinate Pope John Paul II and U.S. President Bill Clinton in Manila.

Siraj Yousif: a Sudanese UN diplomat who left the United States in July 1995. He was suspected of involvement in the World Trade Center bombing on February 26, 1993 as well as the group that was arrested on June 24, 1993 for plotting to bomb several New York City landmarks, including the UN building, and for planning to assassinate Egyptian President Husni Mubarak during a visit to the United States.

Sufuwan Mahmoud Yousri: convicted on September 21, 2003, by an Israeli military court of being the getaway driver on March 26, 2002 during a roadside ambush in which gunmen shot to death a Swiss woman and a Turkish man from the Temporary International Presence in Hebron. An injured survivor–a Turkish Army officer–said the killer was a Palestinian in military garb. Yousri received two consecutive life sentences.

Youssef: alias of Ali Shafik Ahmed Taha, frequent hijacker for various Palestinian terrorist organizations.

Youssef: Abu Hurierah, a Syrian from Al-Ladhiqiha who joined al Qaeda in Iraq in 2007. His phone number was 04147844.

Abu Youssef: alias of Khalaf Bin Youssef Bin Khalaf Al Shara'an.

Abu Youssef: alias of Mussa Ibrahim Muhammad Al Murshid.

Abu Youssef: alias of Saleh Dawoed al Shalami.

Abu Youssef: alias of Mohammed Youssef el Najjar. In 1973, Black September detainee Abu Daoud said that he had been a key planner of the November 28, 1971 assassination of Jordanian

Prime Minister Wasfi Tell in Cairo. At the time, Abu Youssef was a member of the Palestine Liberation Organization's political department and chairman of the Higher Committee for Palestinian Affairs in Lebanon. He apparently died on April 10, 1973 in an Israeli raid on Black September facilities in Beirut.

Ahmed Farouk Hassan Youssef: alias Abu Abd Allah, an Egyptian doctor from Al Sharqiah who was born in 1976 and joined al Qaeda in Iraq as a fighter in 2007, contributing his passport and certificates. His recruitment coordinator was Sultan, whom he knew through Fahid at work. He came from Jeddah to Syria, where he met Abu Omar. While there, Loua'aie took $1,000 of his $1,200. He complained about Loua'aie's bad treatment of him. His phone number was 0020552180324.

Ashraf Saeed Youssef: arrested on April 30, 2005 by Cairo police in connection with the bomb that exploded on a motorcycle on April 7, 2005 near a tour group in Cairo's historic Khan al-Khalili bazaar, killing three people, along with the terrorist, and wounded 18, including four Americans. The previously unknown Islamic Pride Brigades took credit on the Internet.

Mohamed Hesham Youssef: who was serving a sentence in Egypt on terrorism charges, was indicted in Florida on September 16, 2004, with Adham Amin Hassoun for providing financial support and recruitment for al Qaeda and other terrorist groups fighting in Afghanistan, Chechnya, Kosovo, and Somalia, and for helping Jose Padilla (arrested on May 8, 2002 in the "dirty bomb" case) to attend Afghan terrorist training camps. The U.S. District Court in Miami charged them each with two counts of providing material support to terrorists. The indictment said that between 1994 and 2001, Hassoun wrote more than two dozen checks totalling $53,000 to support terrorists. Many were written to the Holy Land Foundation and Global Relief Foundation charities, which funneled money to terrorists.

Yaaqoub Youssef: variant of Bassam Ya'qub Yusuf.

Yasser Sheik Youssef: alias Abu Obieda, a Syrian from Ladhiqiha who was born in 1977 and joined al Qaeda in Iraq on 22nd Ramadan 1427 Hijra, bringing 850 euros, a watch, and a bracelet.

Abu Yuhud: Fatah dissident who, in a July 1977 interview with Madrid's *Cambio* in Algiers, vowed to killed several Arab personalities, including Yasir Arafat.

Ragis Yunes: alias Abu Daghana, a Moroccan from Casablanca who was born in 1982 and joined al Qaeda in Iraq as a martyr in 2007, contributing 60 Turkish lira, 3,105 lira, his passport, and ID. His recruitment coordinator was Ibrahim, whom he knew through his brother Rashied. He traveled from Turkey by bus to Syria, where he met Rabi and Loua'ai, who took his luggage. He was carrying 120 euros. His phone number was 0021267213556.

Buhayj Yunis: identified by Doha's *al-Sharq* on March 19, 1993 as a former member of the Abu Nidal Group. He was sentenced to prison in Austria after a terrorist operation, announced his resignation from the group, and saw his sentence suspended.

Fawaz Yunis: variant of Fawaz Younis.

Mohammad Yunis: age 18, on April 15, 2003, fired a rifle at and threw hand grenades inside a commercial trucking terminal at the Karni (variant Qarni) border crossing between Israel and the Gaza Strip. In the shootout, the Hamas gunman and two Israelis died, one perhaps from friendly fire.

Mohammed Yunis: arrested in Jordan on October 1986 and believed to be the second in command in the plot that led to the July 24, 1985 assassination of Ziyad al-Sati, the first secretary of the Jordanian embassy in Ankara. The Islamic Jihad Organization and Black September separately claimed credit. Turkey requested extradition.

Bahi Yuniz: variant of Bahij Mohammed Younis.

Mokhlis Yunos: variant alias of Saifullah Yunos.

Abu-Yunus: alias of Sami Bin Rashid Bin Sulayman al-Sayyifi.

Rida Yunus: variant of Fawaz Younis.

Ahmed Mohammed Yusef: a Palestinian born in Syria who told Israeli television viewers on June 6, 1990 that he and other Libyan-supported Palestine Liberation Front occupants of two Palestinian speedboats heading toward Tel Aviv and nearby Mediterranean beaches on May 30, 19990 had intended to murder civilians.

Abu Yusif: alias of Muhammad.

Adnan Muhammad Yusif: an Iraqi infantry soldier carrying a Brazilian passport issued in 1973, was detained at the border town of Paso de Los Libres, Corrientes Province, Argentina, while trying to leave the country on July 18, 1994. He was questioned in connection with the July 18, 1994 bombing of the Argentine-Israeli Mutual Aid Association (AIMA) in Buenos Aires that killed 96 and wounded 231. Hizballah was suspected. He was released on July 22 for lack of evidence.

Abu Yussrr: alias of Mustafa Mohamed Fadhil.

Amad Yussuf: one of two Palestinians believed to have kidnapped Shaykh Salman al-Sabah, a Kuwaiti prince and nephew of the king, and his 12-year-old daughter in Manila in July 1989.

Yusuf: alias Abu Hurayrah, a Syrian from al-Ladhiqiyyah with a production degree who joined al Qaeda in Iraq in 2007. His phone number was 04147844.

'Abd-al-Baqi Yusuf: one of two terrorists killed in a shootout with police a day after terrorists, on February 4, 1994, attacked worshippers in the Ansar al-Sunnah mosque in Khartoum, killing 19 worshippers and injuring several others.

Abu-Yusuf: alias of Khalaf Bin-Yusuf Bin-Khalaf al-Shar'an.

Abu-Yusuf: alias of Musa Ibrahim Muhammad al-Murshid.

Abu-Yusuf: alias of Muhammad.

'Adli Yusuf: a member of the Palestine Liberation Organization diplomatic mission in Nicosia who, on February 1, 1990, was arrested following a police chase after he and another individual were involved in a nighttime shooting involving machine guns in the Ayios Dhometios, Nicosia area while trying to sell heroin and hashish.

Ali Yusuf: alias of Hasan Marwan (or Marwan Hasan), an Egyptian (or Jordanian) who was arrested on August 29, 1981 by Austrian police after he fired a Polish PN-63 machine pistol and threw grenades into a Vienna, Austria synagogue, killing two and injuring 20. He was believed to be connected to the May 1, 1981, murder in Austria of Heinz Nittel, president of the Austrian-Israeli Friendship League, a leading Socialist Party official, and head of the Vienna Traffic Department. Abu Nidal's Al Asifah organization claimed credit for the assassination. Yusuf was wounded in the synagogue attack. Police later received a phone call from a man with an Arab accent who threatened to bomb three movie theaters if the synagogue terrorists were not released. On January 21, 1982, a Vienna court sentenced Yusuf to life imprisonment for the Nittel murder. Yusuf testified in the case against Bahij Mohammed Younis, who was sentenced to life for masterminding the Nittel murder and the grenade attack.

Bassam Yaaqoub Yusuf: variant Ya'qub Yussef, a 28-year-old Iraqi arrested by Lebanese security forces on February 17, 1997. He was hiding in a convent. He was suspected of involvement in political assassinations of Iraqi opposition figures in London, Morocco, Kuwait, and Albania for the Iraqi intelligence services. Judge Khalid Hammud, the government assistant commissioner at the military court, said the Iraqi intelligence agent was born in 1969. His last entry into Lebanon was on October 15, 1996. He resided at a monastery in Mount Lebanon. He was found in possession of documents showing that he was involved in operations in four countries and reported to Abu Ahmad in Jordan in 1996, where he received instructions on his next operations. Yusuf and Ahmad allegedly traveled to Morocco, where Yusuf killed an Iraqi opposition figure on September 15, 1996. Yusuf allegedly also worked as a veterinarian for Iraqi intelligence and had an affair with a Lebanese girl.

Darrar Yusuf: alias of Mahmud Ayat Ahmad al-Katib, a Fatah member who fired three shots at Husayn Muhammad 'Ali, an Iraqi Embassy employee, who died in Libya on August 17, 1978. Yusuf was carrying a Jordanian passport, which he had used in traveling from Damascus on August 12. It was charged that he was told to assassinate the ambassador by Khalid Abdullah, who provided his revolver.

Hamdi Abu Yusuf: alias of Isma'il 'Abd-al-Latif Yusuf.

Ibrahim Tawfik Yusuf: variant Youssef, alias Abu Hija, a 34-year-old Catholic Palestinian who trained the Japanese Red Army group who attacked Israel's Lod Airport on May 30, 1972. He and three other Popular Front for the Liberation of Palestine (PFLP) terrorists driving in a car fired 200 bullets from their machineguns and threw three incendiary grenades at El Al flight 432, a B720B scheduled to fly from Zurich to Tel Aviv, as it was taxiing down the runway on February 18, 1969. The pilot was killed. They were sentenced to 12 years hard labor for murder by a Winterthur court on December 22, 1969, but released after the September 6, 1970 hijacking of a Swissair plane by the PFLP. The group said they were "trained in Jordan and some of them left Syria to carry out their attack in Zurich."

Isma'il 'Abd-al-Latif Yusuf: alias Hamdi Abu Yusuf, identified by Doha's *al-Sharq* on March 19, 1993 as a member of the Abu Nidal Group's Central Committee.

Jamal Fayiz al-Yusuf: a member of Hizballah-Palestine's Muhammad al-Khawajah group who on July 18, 1995 shot to death two Israeli youths, one of them a soldier, who were hiking in a nature reserve in Wadi al-Qilt on the West Bank.

Na'im 'Uthman Yusuf: one of five Palestinians arrested on July 9, 1987 when Egyptian authorities discovered an Iranian-backed terrorist group that had chosen a governorate in Lower Egypt for their operations. Police seized explosives from a group collaborating with the al-Jihad Organization.

Qari Mohammed Yusuf: an Afghan who claims to be a videographer for as-Sahab, the al Qaeda media production unit. The Pashto-speaker said he lives in Kunduz, and has links with the Taliban.

Ramzi Ahmed Yusuf: variant Yousef, alias Abdul Basit, Naji Oweida Haddad, Abdul Basit Mahmood, Abdul Karim, Dr. Richard Smith, Dr. Paul Vijay, Adam Ali Qasim, Amaldo Forlani (he had 21 aliases), Kuwaiti-born planner of the February 26, 1993 bombing of the World Trade Center (WTC). He also plotted to set off bombs in a dozen U.S.-destined planes. He also planned to crash a hijacked plane into the McLean, Virginia headquarters of the Central Intelligence Agency. On March 31, 1993, federal prosecutors in Manhattan indicted him. He was believed to have escaped to Egypt. He had resided at the same Jersey City address once occupied by Mohammed A. Salameh, who had rented the truck used in the WTC bombing. In August 1993, the United States offered a $2 million reward for his arrest. He was indicted for the WTC blast. Yusuf was arrested in the Sokawa rest house in Islamabad, Pakistan on February 7, 1995 and extradited to the United States in February 1995. He had been identified by Ishtiaque (variant Istiayaak) Parker, a South African Muslim who lived across from his rooming house. He pleaded not guilty to 11 felony charges in the WTC bombing.

The Islamabad-based *Pakistan* paper claimed that he had planned to set off bombs at the Israeli consulate in Bombay and the Israeli Embassy in New Delhi. It said he was involved in the bombings of the Israeli embassies in London and Buenos Aires and had contacts with the Afghan mujahidin and Kashmiri nationalists. A Pakistani, Abdul Shakoor, implicated him in a bombing in Mashad, Iran on June 20, 1994 in which 25 died and 70 were injured. Pakistani police said he intended to kill Prime Minister Bhutto on December 24, 1993 when she was in the Nursery Area in Karachi. Bhutto had earlier claimed that Yusuf had tried to kill her in September 1993 when he drove a car with explosives towards the Bilawal House in Karachi. He accidentally detonated the bomb he intended to place under a manhole cover near her home in Karachi. He was treated for injuries to his hands and released.

Yusuf escaped from his Manila apartment on January 6, 1995 when fire broke out when he and associate Said Ahmed were mixing explosive chemicals in the kitchen sink as part of a plot to assassinate the Pope.

He was brought back to the United States on February 8, 1995 after his arrest in Islamabad, Pakistan on February 7, 1995.

On April 1, 1995, Philippine authorities indicted him on charges of plotting to assassinate the Pope and bombing the Philippine Airlines B747 in December. On April 13, 1995, U.S. prosecutors indicted him with the bombing of an airliner on December 11, 1994 that killed Japanese passenger Haruki Ikegami and injured ten people, and of planning to bomb other U.S. airliners in the Bojinka plot. The bombing charge carried the death penalty. He was believed to have boarded the plane in Manila, placed a bomb under a seat in a life-vest holder, then gotten off the plane at Cebu before it left for Tokyo.

His Filipina girlfriend was Carol Santiago.

On April 2, 1995, Pakistani authorities charged him with illegal possession of explosives. The next day, Abdul Shakur claimed that Yusuf was involved in a plot against Prime Minister Bhutto, but that a bomb exploded in Yusuf's hands. He was taken to the Civil Hospital under the name Khalid Ali, then moved to Aga Khan Hospital under the name Adam Baluch.

In an interview with London's *al Hayat* on April 11, 1995, he said his real name was Abdul Basit Balouchi, born and raised in Kuwait. He had used the name Abdel Basit Abdel Karim when he obtained a Pakistani passport in New York in 1992. He had used 20 other aliases. When he arrived at JFK International Airport on September 1, 1992, his airline ticket was for Azam Mohammed, and his picture ID card was for Kharram Kahn. He said his father was from Pakistan and his mother was Palestinian. His grandmother lived in Haifa, Israel. He claimed he graduated from the Swansea Institute in the United Kingdom in 1989 with a degree in electrical engineering.

On April 13, 1995, federal officials in New York charged him with conspiring with others to plant bombs on numerous commercial U.S. aircraft.

In a prison interview with London's *al-Majallah*, he claimed that he had used the aliases Ahmad Rashid, Ibrahim Kamal, 'Abd-al-Basit 'Abd-al-Karim, and Abd-al-Basit-al-Balushi. He had been reported as being Kuwaiti, Pakistani, Iraqi, and Palestinian. He claimed to speak Arabic, English, Urdu, and Baluchi.

On October 5, 1995, the United States, in New York City, charged that he possessed a letter threatening to kill Philippine President Fidel Ramos and poison the Philippine water supply. The letter demanded the release from a Philippine jail of his colleague, Abdal Hakim Murad, who was arrested in January in a raid in Manila.

His release was demanded on November 13, 1995 by the group that set off a car bomb in a parking lot of a building belonging to the Saudi

National Guard in Riyadh, killing five American military trainers and wounding 60 others.

On February 23, 1996, he was indicted for the December 1, 1994 bombing of the Green-belt Theater in Manila, Philippines, that injured several moviegoers.

On September 5, 1996, he was found guilty on all seven counts in the conspiracy to set off the airplane bombs. Defense attorneys said they would appeal.

He was sentenced to life in prison in 1997.

His release was demanded on March 20, 2000 by the Abu Sayyaf rebels, who took more than 70 hostages, many of them children from 2 Philippine schools.

On April 4, 2003, the U.S. Court of Appeals of the Second Circuit upheld his convictions in the February 26, 1993 World Trade Center bombing and the Boyinka plot.

Sa'id Ibrahim Yusuf: one of three men arrested for the November 24, 1985 Abu Nidal Group assassination of Husayn 'Ali Ibrahim al-Bitar and his son, Mohammad, in the Al-Rashid suburb of Amman, Jordan. The trio entered Jordan on November 14 from Kuwait carrying Jordanian passports.

Shawqi Muhammad Yusuf: alias Munir Ahmad, identified by Doha's *al-Sharq* on March 19, 1993 as a member of the Abu Nidal group's Political Bureau.

Yasir Shaykh Yusuf: alias Abu-'Ubaydah Iyad, a Syrian from Latakia who was born in 1977 and joined al Qaeda in Iraq on October 14, 2006, contributing a cell phone, 850 euros, a bracelet, and a watch.

Z

Abu-Yasir al-Maki Z.: alias of Muhammad.

Rashid Z.: alias Abu-al-'Abbas, a Tunisian fighter for al Qaeda in Iraq in 2007, who owned a passport, $200 and 300 lira. His phone number was 002167130190.

Bilal Muhammad al Za'ari: alias Abu Ammer, a Moroccan from Tanjah who was born on August 10, 1988 and joined al Qaeda in Iraq on 22nd Ramadan 1427 Hijra (2006), bringing an MP3 player and $100. His recruitment coordinator was Sa'ad. His phone number was 0021270977574.

Ahmad Sami Zaarour: a Lebanese arrested on March 1, 1991 in a Bad Segeberg apartment by Schleswig-Holstein CID officers on suspicion of being the person who set off a hand grenade on February 26, 1991 on the fourth floor of central Berlin's Hotel Boulevard on the main Kurfuerstendamm shopping avenue. The short gunman fired a submachine gun at three U.S. government employees before escaping. Police said the attacker was an albino with short blond hair and blue eyes.

Salam Ibrahim El-Zaatari: a Lebanese arrested on October 28, 2001 by Pittsburgh police as he was attempting to board a Northwest Airlines flight bound for Beirut by way of Detroit and Amsterdam. He was carrying a retractable knife. He said he was unaware that the 9/11 hijackers had carried similar box cutters, even though his luggage had several news clippings about the attacks.

Zacharia: variant Zechariah, alias of Lieutenant Abdel Aziz al Atrash, one of the May 8, 1972 Black September hijackers of Sabena Airlines flight 517, a B707 flying the Vienna-Athens-Tel Aviv route over Zagreb. He died when Israeli forces stormed the plane.

Hasan Hasan Zad: a Lebanese and one of eight Hizballah terrorists who were arrested in Spain on November 24, 1989 when police discovered that they had cached several kilograms of Exogen C-4 explosives in jam jars in the port of Valencia and Madrid. He used a Brazilian passport and acted as the postman for the network between Lebanon and Spain. He had also brought explosives into Valencia.

Eden Natan Zada: age 19, AWOL Israeli Army Jewish settler who, on August 4, 2005, in Army uniform and wearing a skullcap and thick beard, boarded Egged Bus No. 165 from Haifa traveling to Shfaram, an Arab town, and opened fire with his M-16, killing four Palestinians and wounding 10. Passengers killed him before he could escape. Zada was a member of the Kach terrorist group. He had left his post on June 14, and moved to the West Bank settlement of Tapuah, a stronghold of Jewish radicals. Prime Minister Ariel Sharon called it an "act of Jewish terrorism." Zada was jailed for life. He committed suicide on December 22, 2006.

Muhammad Nayif al-Zadah: on July 25, 1985, a Lebanese military prosecutor called for the death penalty for the Palestinian's involvement in suicide bomb attacks against the U.S. embassy in Beirut on April 18, 1983, in which an Islamic Jihad truck bomb killed 64 people and injured 123; and for the December 15, 1981 car bombing of the Iraqi embassy that killed 61 and injured more than 100.

Qari Mohammed Zafar: an Al Qaeda operative hiding in the tribal area of Pakistan and the local leader of Lashkar-e-Jhangvi, an outlawed militant group with ties to al Qaeda. His religious title of Qari means that he had memorized the Koran. He was linked to a group of three men arrested in Karachi in late February 2007 carrying a suicide vest. He was believed to have recruited the consulate bombing team that killed several people in a suicide bombing against the U.S. consulate on March 2, 2006.

Maher Zagha: age 34, a Jordanian who attended college in New York, was one of five men connected to the Islamic Assembly of North America (IANA), a Saudi charity that operates out of Ann Arbor, Michigan, who were indicted by federal authorities on February 26, 2003, in connection with two money-raising and distribution efforts. He was one of four Arab men living near Syracuse accused of conspiracy to evade U.S. sanctions against Iraq by raising $2.7 million for individuals in Baghdad through the Help the Needy charity (an IANA affiliate). The funds were placed in New York banks, then laundered through an account at the Jordan Islamic Bank in Amman before they were distributed to people in Baghdad. The four were charged with conspiracy and violation of the International Emergency Economic Powers Act, which makes it illegal to send money to Iraq. Two of the men could face 265 years in prison and fines of more than $14 million. The other two faced five years in prison and a $250,000 fine.

Mahmoud Zahar: variant of Mahmoud Zahhar, a Hamas spokesman in Gaza City in 2002.

Abu Zahayr: name given as the leader of the six Brigade of the Marches of Lebanese Resistance hijackers who took over Royal Jordanian Airlines flight 402, a B727 boarding passengers at Beirut International Airport on June 11, 1985. The plane hopscotched through Europe and the Middle East. The hijackers escaped after setting off a bomb on the plane in Beirut.

Ahmad Zahedi: one of 57 people of Middle Eastern and North African origin arrested by French police on June 3, 1987 in connection with the discovery of an arms, explosives, and drugs cache in Fontainebleau forest, south of Paris, the previous week. Threats had been made by the Committee for Solidarity with Arab and Middle East Political Prisoners. He was ordered out of the country.

Ehsan Zahedi: a Mujahidin-e Khalq Organization member arrested by Iranian authorities after the November 9, 1993 bombing of the French Embassy and Air France office in Tehran.

Mohammad Zahedi: an Iranian tried with two Arabs who were arrested in April 1979 trying to smuggle 50 kilograms of explosives through Austria into West Germany. He denied membership in any Palestinian organization. He said he had been hired by Mohammad Hamadi to bring a car from Europe to Beirut. On July 20, 1979, the Passau regional court sentenced him to four months for forging documents and unlawful entry into West Germany.

Hisham Abdel-Zaher: arrested by Egyptian police in connection with the February 26, 1993 bombing of the Wadi el-Nil coffee shop in Tahrir Square in Cairo in which four people were killed and 16 wounded. He was tried with 48 other fundamentalist suspects on March 9, 1993 at the military court complex in the Hakstep area east of Cairo. They were charged with damaging national unity and social peace by calling for a change of the system of government and damaging the national economy by attacking tourism. Some were also charged with attempted murder in eight attacks on tour buses and Nile cruise ships. They faced possible death sentences. They were also accused of belonging to an underground organization, attempting to overthrow the government, and illegal possession of arms and explosives. During the trial, Abdel-Zaher shouted that the Islamic

Group was led by Sheik Omar Abdul Rahman, an exiled cleric in the United States whose followers were responsible for the bombing of the World Trade Center, also on February 26, 1993.

Mahmoud Zahhar: variant Zahar, Hamas spokesman in the Gaza Strip who was among the 1,200 Palestinians and other activists arrested by Israel after Hamas kidnapped Senior Master Sergeant Nissim Toledano on December 13, 1992. On June 25, 1995, Palestinian police arrested him after Hamas claimed credit for bombing a Jewish settlement. He was called in by Israeli authorities for questioning after a Palestinian suicide bomber set off a bomb between two school buses on October 29, 1998. By May 2002, he remained a Hamas spokesman.

Abdul Zahir: an Afghan man suspected of al Qaeda membership who was charged on January 20, 2006, by federal authorities in the United States in the March 2002 grenade attack that wounded three journalists in Gardez. He was also charged with paying other al Qaeda members to conduct terrorist attacks against coalition forces, conspiracy, aiding the enemy, and attacking civilians. He had been held at the U.S. prison in Guantánamo Bay, Cuba, since being detained in July 2002. He had been in Afghanistan from 1997 until his capture. He had worked as a courier and translator, and moved more than $50,000 to terrorists. He also produced anti-U.S. leaflets to recruit Afghans living near the U.S. embassy and U.S. military bases. He was charged with working with two other terrorists in the grenade attack that seriously injured a Canadian reporter for the *Toronto Star*.

Abu Zahra: alias of Mustafa Ibrahim Ahmad, an Iraqi sentenced, in absentia, to death by the Kuwaiti State Security Court in 1984 in connection with the December 12, 1983 truck bombing of the administrative building of the U.S. embassy in Kuwait, killing four people and injuring 59. As of April 1987, none of the death sentences had been carried out. The release of 17 of the 25 prisoners in the case was demanded on numerous occasions by the Islamic Jihad in return for Americans held captive in Lebanon beginning in 1986.

Yasin Hasan Muhammad Zahrah: one of a group of Jordanian Afghans sentenced to death on December 21, 1994 by the Jordanian State Security Court for belonging to an illegal society, participating in a conspiracy to carry out terrorist acts, and possessing explosives for illegal purposes. The Muslim fundamentalists bombed cinemas, wounding nine people, including an attack on January 26, 1994 at an Amman cinema showing what they perceived to be pornographic films, and another bombing on February 1, 1994. The group had been seized in a crackdown on Muslim radicals in January 1994. Their trial began on August 27, 1994, when they were accused of planning to assassinate leading Jordanians, including 'Abd-al-Salam al-Majali, Jordan's former chief peace negotiator with Israel. One of those sentenced to death was Muhammad Jamal Khalifah, a Saudi fugitive son-in-law of Usama bin Laden.

Abu-Rashash al-Zahrani: alias of Sa'id.

Faris al-Zahrani: on Saudi Arabia's list of 26 most-wanted terrorists, he was arrested on August 5, 2004 in the mountainous region in the south. His messages were displayed on the Web site of al Qaeda on the Arabian Peninsula. He was one of three clerics on the list, and thought to have taken a leadership position after Saudi forces killed its leader, Abdulaziz al-Muqrin in June.

Khalid Saeed Shmad al-Zahrani: the 9/11 Commission said that he was initially scheduled to be a 9/11 hijacker, but could not acquire a U.S. visa.

Sami Rajab Ahmad al-Zahrani: alias Abu-al-Zubayr, a Saudi student from Jeddah who was born in 1986 and joined al Qaeda in Iraq as a martyr in 2007. His recruitment coordinator was Abu-'Abdallah. He flew to Syria, where he met Abu-'Umar and Abu-al-Harith. His father's phone number was 0556363877; his brother's was 0556600366.

Yahya Bin-Rajab Bin-'Isa al-Zahrani: alias Abu-Yahya al-Kinani, a Saudi from Mecca who was born in 1980 and joined al Qaeda in Iraq in 2007. His recruitment coordinator was Abu-'Abdallah.

Yassin al-Zaiban: one of three off-duty security guards who hijacked a Royal Jordanian Airlines Caravelle 50 flying between Amman and Aqaba on November 5, 1974 and diverted to Benghazi, Libya, where they were granted political asylum. The hijackers were members of the Jordanian Free Officers Movement.

Abdul Zaid: alias of Abdul-Sattar Hisham.

Ahmed Zaid: one of two Popular Front for the Liberation of Palestine-General Command-Black September-Nationalist Youth Group for the Liberation of Palestine terrorists who told two vacationing British women that they were Persians and gave them an electronic music device to bring with them on an El Al B707 flying from Rome to Tel Aviv on August 16, 1972. The device had a bomb inside, which exploded shortly after takeoff. The plane landed safely in Rome. Rome police arrested the men, who were identified as an Iraqi and a Jordanian. In February 1973, they disappeared from Italy after being given provisional liberty on the grounds that the bomb "was not adequate to destroy the airliner."

Mohammad Abbas Zaida: alias Abu Khalid, who allegedly sent four Palestine Liberation Front (PLF) terrorists to hijack the Italian cruise ship *Achille Lauro* on October 7, 1985. They killed Leon Klinghoffer, age 69, an American confined to a wheelchair, and dumped the body overboard. The hijacking ended in Egypt. The plan was to conduct a suicide mission in Ashdod, Egypt, but the terrorists were discovered and forced to act earlier, thus seizing the boat. On November 13,

1985, Italian authorities issued an arrest warrant for the PLF member.

Tewfik Hussein Zaiden: one of two would-be Fatah hijackers of an Alia Caravelle flying from Beirut to Amman on October 4, 1971. One of the Palestinian hijackers was killed during the flight when overpowered by security guards. The woman had attempted to pull the pin from a grenade she had carried on board inside a wig. They wanted to divert the plane to Iraq.

Rady Zaiter: Lebanese leader of a Quito-based cocaine ring suspected of funneling cash to Hizballah. He was arrested in Colombia on June 22, 2005.

Zaini Zakaria: the 9/11 Commission said that he was initially scheduled to be a 9/11 hijacker. In February 2006, Malaysian and Southeast Asian security officials told the media that Zakaria, 38, a Malaysian engineer who was to participate as a pilot in a second wave of al Qaeda 9/11-style hijackings on the U.S. West Coast, had been in Malaysian custody since December 2002. He got cold feet after seeing the carnage of 9/11, and did not want to become an Islamic martyr. Two other men in the plot were Zacarias Moussaoui and Tunisian-born naturalized Canadian citizen Aberraouf Jdey, who remained at large, according to the *Associated Press*. Zakaria had been in al Qaeda camps in Afghanistan in 1999; while there, he met Riduan Isamuddin, alias Hambali. Upon his return to Malaysia in 1999, Zakaria enrolled in flight school and earned a license to fly a small plane. He looked into Australian jet pilot licenses. On 9/11, it dawned on him what al Qaeda had in mind for him, and he backed out. Zakaria had been represented by attorney Saiful Izham Ramli; his new attorney was Edmund Bon.

Abu-Zakariyah: alias of Salih.

Raid Zakarna: a 19-year-old Palestinian who, on April 6, 1994, drove an Opel car bomb next to an

Egged bus number 340 at a bus stop in 'Afula, Israel, killing eight, including himself, and wounding more than 50 people. The car was packed with natural gas canisters, nails, and explosives. He was from the northern West Bank village of Kabatiya. He had served time in prison during the intifada. Hamas and Islamic Jihad claimed credit.

Yasir Zaki: wanted in connection with the Muslim Group's October 21, 1992 attack on a tour bus near Dayrut, Egypt that killed a British tourist and injured two others. He was one of seven Islamic militants shot dead by police in a raid in Cairo on February 3, 1994.

Abu Zakker: alias of Ali Bin Riad.

Marwan Zalloum: an al-Aqsa Brigades leader who was killed on April 22, 2002 by an Israeli helicopter attack on his car.

Mohammed Haydar Zammar: age 41, a naturalized German citizen of Syrian origin who was captured in Casablanca, Morocco in December 2001. The former locksmith was reported missing by his family after he left Hamburg, Germany, for Morocco on October 27, 2001. He was taken to Syria, and as of mid-December 2006, remained in prison. He was linked with those involved with the Hamburg cell that was behind the 9/11 attacks. He was suspected of recruiting Mohammed Atta and other Hamburg hijackers circa 1997 at his local mosque and linking them to the al Qaeda Afghan-based leaders. Although he was questioned by German police after the 9/11 attacks, they did not have enough evidence to hold him. In July 2001, he was detained while in transit in Jordan for several days before being deported to Germany. On October 25, the 300-pound Zammar was issued a temporary one-year passport. He left the country ostensibly to obtain a divorce from a Moroccan woman. Moroccan authorities said he left the country for Spain; Spanish officials said he did not arrive. His partner said he had trained at an al Qaeda Afghan camp and had fought in Bosnia. Syria held him on a long-standing charge of involvement in a bomb plot.

On February 11, 2007, a Syrian security court sentenced him to 12 years in prison. He initially was sentenced to death for membership in the Muslim Brotherhood, but the sentence was commuted. He had moved to Germany with his father in 1972 and received German citizenship a decade later. He was represented by attorney Mohanad al-Husni.

Ayman bin Mohammed Amin Saeed Abu Zanad: age 30, a Palestinian carrying an Egyptian travel document, who, on October 6, 2001, set off a remote-controlled (some reports said he was a suicide bomber) bomb in front of a shop that was closed for prayers in Khobar, Saudi Arabia, killing one American and one non-Saudi, and injuring an American, a Briton, and two Filipinos. It was not clear whether the attack was related to the September 11 attacks. Palestinian Ambassador Mustafa Hashem Sheikh said the attack was likely aimed at harming Saudi-Palestinian ties, rather than tied to the September 11 attacks. On November 14, the Saudi Interior Ministry said he was the first Palestinian suicide bomber in the country. His father found in his room "two valid Indian passports with his name and photograph."

Ja'far Abu-Zanjah: alias Abu-'Abbas. According to the captured Sinjar personnel records of al Qaeda in Iraq, his address was Algiers, Algeria; phone number 0021321263630; home, 0021371614213. He was born in 1981. He arrived in Damascus by plane, with the assistance of a friend. In Syria, he met 'Abd-al-Hadi, who had "weak vision." He brought with him 150 euros. He worked as a security guard at home, and wanted to be a "fighter." He arrived in Iraq on February 15, 2007. His coordinator was Samir.

Ahmed Zaoui: leader of the Algerian Armed Islamic Group who reportedly had been staying in Belgium in mid-1994. French authorities wanted to question him in connection with lethal attacks on French soil. On September 4, 1995, his trial in Belgium, along with that of a dozen other Islamic militants, began following his arrest in March 1995.

Nordine Zaouli: Algiers-born hijacker on December 10, 1993 of an Air France flight from Paris's Roissy airport to Nice, who demanded to go to Libya. He surrendered in Nice's Cote-d'Azur airport. He had a police record for armed robbery and other crimes and was on a list of people not permitted in France.

Yusef Zaqout: one of three 15-year-old Palestinian boys who, on April 23, 2002, were shot to death near the Netzarim settlement by Israeli soldiers firing a .50 caliber machine gun. The trio had planned to set off a crude pipe bomb, and were also armed with knives. The trio had competed for top honors at Salahuddin School in Gaza City. They left confessor letters to their families, saying they were seeking to be heroes. Hamas condemned the boys' gesture and forbade adolescent attacks.

Muhammad Abu Zarat: one of four Palestinian terrorists who were found guilty on February 17, 1983 in Turkey and again sentenced to death for their part in the July 13, 1979 raid on the Egyptian Embassy in Ankara that resulted in the death of two security guards. They had been tried twice before at the Ankara Martial law Command's First Military Court and the Ankara First High Criminal Court, but both times their sentences were annulled.

Bilal Muhammad al-Za'ri: alias Abu-'Amir, a Moroccan from Tangier who was born on August 10, 1988 and joined al Qaeda in Iraq on October 14, 2006, contributing $100 and an MP3 player. His recruitment coordinator was Sa'd. His phone number was 0021270977574.

Muhammad Zari: arrested by Stockholm police on December 18, 2001, the Egyptian asylum-seeker faced years in prison in Egypt for membership in an Islamic terrorist group. He was put on a plane to Egypt.

Ne'matollah Zarifi: one of 57 people of Middle Eastern and North African origin arrested by French police on June 3, 1987 in connection with the discovery of an arms, explosives, and drugs cache in Fontainebleau forest, south of Paris, the previous week. Threats had been made by the Committee for Solidarity with Arab and Middle East Political Prisoners. He was ordered out of the country.

Imed Ben Zarkaoui: leader of a Milan-based network that was wrapped up on November 6, 2007 in coordinated raids in Italy, France, Portugal, and the United Kingdom that netted 17 Algerians and Tunisians suspected of terrorist ties in Salafist jihadi militant cells that were recruiting would-be suicide bombers for Iraq and Afghanistan. Milan prosecutors ordered the raids in Milan, Bergamo, Verese, and Reggio Emilia. Police found poisons, remote detonators, and manuals. The leaders were identified as Dridi Sabri, Mehidi Ben Nasr, and Imed Ben Zarkaoui, all operating in Italy. Three suspects remained at large. Police said the investigation began in 2003. The detainees were charged with illegal immigration, falsifying ID documents, and helping to hide people sought for terrorist activity.

Abd al Kafi Muhammad Othman Zarmouh: variant of Abd-al-Kafi Muhammad 'Uthman Zarmuh.

Abd-al-Kafi Muhammad 'Uthman Zarmuh: variant Abd al Kafi Muhammad Othman Zarmouh, alias Abu-al-Bara', a Libyan from Masratah who was born on December 19, 1987 and joined al Qaeda in Iraq on October 1, 2006, contributing $200 and a watch. His home phone number was 0021851625524; his brother's was 00218913806006. His recruitment coordinator was Abu-al-Layth, variant Liyth.

Abu Islam Al Zarqaui: variant of Abu-Islam al-Zarqawi.

Abu Ra'aied al Zarqaui: alias of Muhammad Hammed Ali Al Banawi.

Abu-Islam al-Zarqawi: variant Abu Islam Al Zarqaui, alias of Muhammad Islam 'Umar Musa Hajjaj.

Abu-Isma'il al-Zarqawi: alias of 'Amir Qasim Muflih al-Jardat.

Abu Mus'ab al-Zarqawi: most common alias of Ahmad Fadil Nazzai al-Khalaylah, variant Ahmad Fadil al-Khalailah, alias Abu Ahmad, alias Abu Muhammad, alias Sakr Abu Suwayd, Jordanian-born leader of al Qaeda in Iraq.

Zarqawi was wanted for his role in a plot to bomb hotels in Amman and Europe in December 1999.

Two gunmen in the October 28, 2002 assassination of Laurence Foley, a U.S. Agency for International Development employee in Amman, said they were acting on the orders of the Jordanian al Qaeda lieutenant they had met in Afghanistan when the trio were training in camps. al Zarqawi provided $10,000 for the attack, along with another $32,000 for additional attacks. On April 6, 2004, a Jordanian court sentenced him to death for the Foley murder.

Moroccan authorities said on June 2, 2003 that he was behind the five May 16, 2003 suicide bombings in Casablanca that killed 45 and wounded more than 100. He obtained $50,000 to $70,000 from al Qaeda for the attacks.

He was responsible for planning and participating in scores of bombings, assassinations, beheadings, and other terrorist attacks during the coalition occupation of Iraq in 2005 and 2006. The radical Sunni was believed to be al Qaeda's chemical weapons chief. On October 17, 2004, Jordan's military prosecutor indicted al-Zarqawi and 12 other Muslim militants in the plot broken up in March 2004 that Jordanian authorities said involved a chemical weapon attack that could have killed 80,000.

On February 14, 2005, the Iraqi government named him as one of its 29 most-wanted insurgents. He called for an "all out war" against Shi'a Muslims in September 2005. On March 20, 2005, a Jordanian military court sentenced him 15 years in prison for planning an attack on the Jordanian Embassy in Baghdad and other sites.

On February 15, 2006, a Jordanian court sentenced to death al-Zarqawi and eight other men for plotting chemical attacks against sites in Jordan in 2004. Zarqawi and three others remained at large.

He was killed by coalition forces in an airstrike on June 7, 2006. The State Department's Rewards for Justice Program had offered $25 million for his apprehension.

Abu-Ra'id al-Zarqawi: alias of Muhammad Hamid 'Ali al-Banawi.

Amin Aminah Sulayman Za'rul: variant Za'rur, a Lebanese arrested on August 14, 1986 by Larnaca, Cyprus while carrying a loaded pistol and 18 hand grenades in his suitcase. He was scheduled to appear in court on September 22, 1986 on charges of possessing and carrying arms and explosives. His release was demanded on September 5, 1986 by the four hijackers of the Libyan Revolutionary Cells and the Organization of the Soldiers of God—Martyr Zulfikar Ali Bhutto Group who took over Pan Am flight 73 at Karachi airport. He was given a seven-year sentence. On January 10, 1987, a bomb consisting of dynamite in a drain pipe exploded at a Larnaca apartment building on Sofronios Khristodhoulou Street; he had lived on the ground floor of the building. A note at the site of the bombing demanded his release. Hizballah was suspected.

Amin Aminah Sulayman Za'rur: variant of Amin Aminah Sulayman Za'rul.

Mustaq Ahmad Zarzar: alias of Mushtaq Zargat.

Mohammed Zaul: age 23, married father of a young son, from the village of Hussan, west of Bethlehem, on February 22, 2004 killed eight and wounded more than 50 when he set off a bomb on an Egged Number 14 bus at the intersection of of Emek Rafaim and King David Streets near

Liberty Bell Park in an upscale Jerusalem neighborhood at 8:27 A.M., during the Sunday morning rush hour. The al-Aqsa Martyrs Brigades claimed credit.

Dr. Ayman Muhammad Rabi al-Zawahiri: alias Abu Muhammad, Abu Fatima, Muhammad Ibrahim, Abu Abdallah, Abu al-Mu'iz, The Doctor, The Teacher, Nur, Ustaz, Abu Mohammed, Abu Mohammed Nur al-Deen, Abdel Muaz, deputy to Osama bin Laden of al Qaeda. A physician and religious/ideological leader of al Qaeda, who founded the Egyptian Gamaat, his military trial in absentia in Haekstep, Egypt began on February 1, 1999. The military court sentenced him to death on April 18, 1999. He earlier had spent time in Egyptian jails for radical fundamentalist activities. He issued frequent audio and video tapes to the Internet and *al Jazeera* following his and Osama bin Laden's fleeing Afghanistan after the September 11, 2001 attacks in the United States. He was born in Egypt on June 19, 1951. He was named as an unindicted co-conspirator on October 7, 1998 by a federal grand jury in New York for his role in the August 7, 1998 bombings of the U.S. embassies in Dar es Salaam, Tanzania and Nairobi, Kenya. He has also been charged with the murder of Americans outside the United States, conspiracy to murder U.S. nationals outside the United States, and an attack on a federal facility resulting in death. The State Department's Rewards for Justice Program offers $25 million for his apprehension.

Khalid al-Zawahiri: reportedly Ayman's son, he was arrested on February 24, 2004 in Pakistan.

Mohammad Zawahiri: younger brother of Ayman Zawahiri, he was announced by Egypt on March 4, 2004 as being held in detention. Observers believed he had been held for at least three years. He was sentenced to death in absentia in 1999 for his role in attacks by the Egyptian Islamic Jihad.

'Abd al-Rahman Zawan: one of three Libyans invited to leave Spain on December 20, 1985 when secret service agents uncovered the Libyans' plot to assassinate exile Libyan opposite leader Dr. al-Muqayrif. The trio had worked for the Libyan Embassy in Madrid, but did not have diplomatic status. They left within three weeks.

Suhayl Qasim Ahmad al-Zawawi: Saudi arrested on September 1, 1994 by Cairo airport authorities after finding that his bag contained 12 magazines for a machine gun, a rifle, a pistol, 3 iron sticks, an electric detonator, 2 tear gas canisters, and a machine gun cooling jacket. He was planning on boarding a Saudi flight for Riyadh.

Bassam Zayad: also known as Bassam Towfik Sherif, Popular Front for the Liberation of Palestine spokesman who took credit for the Japanese Red Army's attack on Lod Airport on May 30, 1972.

Muhmad Mansur Zayada: one of two Israeli Arabs from Lod who were members of the Popular Front for the Liberation of Palestine who, on May 8, 1988, were sentenced to life in prison for throwing a grenade at a bus at the Meteorological Junction in June 1987.

'Abd-al-Hamid Muhammad Abu-Zayd: arrested on October 15, 1994 by Egyptian police in connection with the October 14, 1994 stabbing of Naguib Mahfouz, the only Arab to receive the Nobel Prize for Literature, in a Cairo suburb.

Abu-Zayd: alias of 'Abd-al-Razzaq Kunima.

Abu-Zayd: alias of Jamal Ahshush.

Hamza Abu Zayd: variant Abu Zeid, variant Hamzah Abu Sa'id. On January 15, 1991, he assassinated Salah Khalaf, Fatah's deputy chief; Fakhri al-Umari, aide to Salah Khalaf; and Hayel Abdel-Hamid, the Palestine Liberation Organization's (PLO) security chief whom he had served as bodyguard, in Tunis. He then grabbed Abdel-Hamid's wife and daughter and held them hostage for six hours, demanding to go to the airport and fly to freedom. He surrendered to Tunisian police and the PLO. He had contacts with the Abu Nidal Organization. He was turned over to the PLO after a month's incarceration and flown to Yemen. On April 7, 1991, a Palestinian military tribunal meeting in Yemen sentenced him to death. He was executed.

He apparently left Abdel-Hamid's employ in 1985 and visited Hungary, Poland, Yugoslavia, Cyprus, and the Philippines. He was recruited by the Abu Nidal group in Eastern Europe in December 1987.

Hassan Abu Zayd: age 20, an Islamic Jihad suicide bomber who, on October 26, 2005, set off explosives he was carrying in a bag outside the Falafel Barzalai restaurant, among a row of market stalls in Hadera, Israel, a coastal city, killing at least five Israelis and wounding more than two dozen others. Islamic Jihad (IJ) had threatened to retaliate for the killing of Luay Saadi, an IJ West Bank military leader by Israeli forces in Tulkarm on October 24. Abu Zayd came from Qabatiya on the northern West Bank. Israeli jets retaliated the next day. An airstrike on the Jabalya refugee camp in the northern Gaza Strip killed eight Palestinians, including Shadi Mahanna, IJ's commander in northern Gaza, and his deputy, Mohammed Qandeel. Police also arrested the bomber's father.

Zaydan: alias of Thabit 'Abd-al-Karim Mahmad.

'ali Zaydan: alias Haytham, identified by Doha's *al-Sharq* on March 19, 1993 as a member of the Abu Nidal Group's Central Committee and an officer in the intelligence administration.

Abu Zayeb: alias of Ahamed Bin Muhammad Bin Dakhiel Allah Al Balwii.

Abu Zayed: alias of Abd Al Razak Konima.

Abu Zayed: alias of Jamal Ahshoush.

Mohammed Mohsen Yahya Zayed: one of two Yemenis arrested in Germany and extradited to the United States, where they were prosecuted in 2005 for conspiracy to send money from Brooklyn to Hamas and al Qaeda. His colleague, Sheik Mohammed Ali Hassan al-Moayad, claimed to have sent millions to the groups. Evidence included documents obtained in Afghanistan, Yemen, and Croatia, sources in the United Kingdom and Israel, and electronic surveillance of their hotel room in Germany where they stayed in 2003. On March 10, 2005, Zayed was convicted of conspiring to funnel money to al Qaeda and Hamas. Zayed was convicted of attempting to provide material support to Hamas but acquitted of attempting to aid al Qaeda. Defense attorneys said they would appeal. Zayed was represented by Jonathan Marks. On September 1, 2005, Zayed was sentenced to 45 years. As of 2007, he was held in the Florence supermax prison in Colorado.

Shaykh Mubarak Salih Mashan al-Zayidi: chief of the Yemeni Jahm tribe that, on November 25, 1993, kidnapped Haynes R. Mahoney, director of the U.S. Information Service in Yemen, from his jeep as he drove to a Sanaa hotel. Al-Zayidi was an ex-army officer and former leader of a pro-Iraqi political group.

Halit Adil Zayit: arrested on August 7, 1979 by Turkish authorities for assisting the four Red Eagles of the Palestinian Revolution in their takeover of the Egyptian Embassy in Ankara on July 13, 1979. Police found at the hideout a Kalashnikov rifle, 20 knives, 150 rounds of ammunition, a bulletproof vest, and two hand radio receivers.

'Atif az-Zayn: lone hijacker on July 21, 1984 of a Middle East Airlines B727 flying from Abu Dhabi to Beirut. He threatened to explode a bottle of liquid unless the plane went back to Abu Dhabi, where he wanted to visit with his children. He also demanded the liberation of south Lebanon and a promise by the Lebanese government to give more attention to the south. He also demanded a news conference in Beirut. He surrendered.

Khalil Mahmud al-Zayn: a Lebanese who was 1 of 18 Arab terrorists reported by Madrid

Diario 16 on October 20, 1987 as having entered Spain in August to attack Middle Eastern diplomatic missions and assassinate Saudi Ambassador Muhammad Nuri Ibrahim. They had received weapons and casing reports on the ambassador from a Lebanese student resident in Spain whose initials were HMI.

Abu-Zaynab: alias of Jamal.

Abd Al Rahman Al Vaitouri Hammed Al Zaytoni: variant of 'Abd-al-Rahman al-Fayturi Hamad al-Zaytuni.

'Abd-al-Rahman al-Fayturi Hamad al-Zaytuni: variant Abd Al Rahman Al Vaitouri Hammed Al Zaytoni, alias Abu-Mus'ab, variant Abu Musa'ab, a Libyan student from Sarat who was born on May 18, 1987 and joined al Qaeda in Iraq to become a martyr on November 17, 2006, bringing his passport. His recruitment coordinator was 'Abdallah. His brother's phone number was 00218925857021.

Ben Zouz Zebda: alleged member of the Islamic Salvation Front who was arrested for involvement in the August 26, 1992 bombing of the Air France ticket counter at Houari Boumedienne Airport in Algeria that killed 12 people and wounded 128. Public sessions of his trial began on May 4, 1993. On May 26, 1993, a special Algiers judicial council acquitted him.

Khaled Zeer: a 24-year-old Jerusalem area leader of the Hamas military wing who was shot and killed by police in Arab East Jerusalem on November 26, 1993 when he fired on them while trying to escape custody.

Nasrollah Shanbe Zehi: convicted on February 18, 2007 in the February 14, 2007 bombing in Iran that killed 11 members of the Revolutionary Guard. The Sunni Muslim group Jundallah (God's Brigade) claimed credit. He was hanged on February 19 at the site of the attack.

Ibrahim Sado Ibrahim al Zehika: a Jordanian who was tried in absentia and, on January 7, 1987, sentenced to life in prison for setting off two time bombs at popular cafes in Kuwait on July 11, 1985 that killed 10 and injured 87.

Zeid: a Syrian-based Moroccan who was the principal accomplice of Saad al-Houssaini, alias The Chemist.

Hamza Abu Zeid: variant of Hamza Abu Zayd.

Mustafa Awad Abu Zeid: Palestine Liberation Organization secretary in Tripoli, Libya, who was blinded by a parcel bomb on October 25, 1972.

Abdallah el-Zein: On March 8, 1998, the Israeli *Yediot Aharonot* claimed that the Lebanese-born individual was tied to the 1992 bombing of the Israeli Embassy in Buenos Aires and the July 18, 1994 bombing of the Buenos Aires Argentine-Israeli Mutual Aid Association in which 86 people were killed and 300 injured. On February 19, 1998, Switzerland caught five Mossad agents trying to bug a Bern apartment where he once lived.

Nadia Zekra: detained on January 17, 1995 in London under the Prevention of Terrorism Act on suspicion of the July 26, 1994 car bombing of the Israeli Embassy in London that injured 14 people. The 48-year-old remained in custody as of March 22, 1995. On June 22, 1995, British antiterrorist police said that a group of wealthy, well-educated, leftist secular Palestinians led by Zekra, a Knightsbridge housewife, were responsible for the attacks on the embassy and a north London building that housed Jewish and Israeli charities. They all lived in an upscale London neighborhood near the Israeli Embassy. All six people arrested were Palestinians who had been residents of the United Kingdom for years. Zekra was accused of conspiring to detonate bombs. The group might have been members of a breakaway faction of the Syrian-supported Popular Front for the Liberation of Palestine. Zekra was accused of driving and parking the car bomb. The mother of two teen sons, she graduated from a Jordanian university's sociology department. She lived for years in Kuwait before moving to London in the 1980s. Her husband was a wealthy Palestinian businessman. She posted an $800,000 cash bail and property pledges in April 1994. On July 24, 1996, the 'Akko Magistrates Court in Israel announced it would extend the remand of Zekra, now age 30, by 10 days. On November 4, 1996, a London judge freed her for lack of evidence. She was to be freed formally the next day when the judge was to instruct the jury to find her not guilty. The prosecution had claimed that she had driven the car carrying the bomb. The judge said that the guard who testified against her had claimed she was fairly tall and stocky, which did not match Zekra.

Omar Zemiri: one of three gang members who escaped during a March 29, 1996 raid by police in Roubaix, France on a hideout of Algerians and Moroccan terrorists who had committed a series of bank, armored car, service station, and convenience store robberies during which bystanders were shot down. More than 1,000 shots were fired in the gun battle, which ended with four Algerians burning alive. The gang members were associated with a mosque in Lille known for preaching radical theology to disaffected North African immigrants. He said the group was attempting to finance a jihad.

Redouane Zenimi: a member of a Spanish al Qaeda cell broken up by arrests on May 14, 2004. The group, which reported to Abderrazak Mahjdoub and Abu Musab al-Zarqawi, provided financing to the rest of the European network. Zarqawi ordered Abderrazak Mahdjoub and Abdelahi Djaouat to travel to Damascus in March 2003 with the intention of going to Iraq. The duo were arrested in Syria.

Saleh Hussein Ali al-Zenu: alias Abu Hammam, one of six individuals killed on November 3, 2002 when a U.S. Predator unmanned aerial vehicle fired a Hellfire missile at their car in Yemen. Also killed was Abu Ali al-Harithi, a key suspect in

the USS *Cole* bombing on October 12, 2000 and Kamal Derwish, a U.S. citizen who headed an al Qaeda cell in Lackawanna, New York that was wrapped up on September 14, 2002.

Abu Zer: alias of Ibrahim Bin Masoud Sa'ad.

Muhammad Abu Zera: one of four Red Eagles of the Palestinian Revolution terrorists who took over the Egyptian Embassy in Ankara on July 13, 1979. He was born in Darha, Syria in 1960. The four were indicted on July 28, 1979 by the Ankara martial law command military tribunal for carrying out hostile acts aimed at damaging relations between Turkey and Egypt; premeditated murder; smuggling, possessing, and using bombs; threatening the liberty of more than one person; and other armed acts. On October 25, 1979, a military court sentenced the four Palestinians to two death sentences each for killing two Turkish guards in the attack. On May 23, 1980, Turkey's supreme military court threw out the death sentences and ordered a retrial in a civilian court. On December 23, 1980, an Ankara criminal court sentenced the four Palestinian terrorists to death.

Parviz Zerafatkhah: a Mujahidin-e Khalq Organization member killed by Iranian authorities after the November 9, 1993 bombing of the French Embassy and Air France office in Tehran. Iran claimed he was killed while trying to flee Iran from the Ilam western border point.

Muhammad el-Zery: suspected Islamic radical arrested in Sweden and later expelled by Swedish officials on December 18, 2001. After 9/11, he had been deemed a security risk, despite earlier being granted political asylum. In October 2003, he was released without having faced trial or charges. He was placed under surveillance, which continued as of mid-December 2006.

Djemal Zetouni: variant of Djamal Zitouni.

Zeyad: Libya-based recruitment coordinator for al Qaeda in Iraq foreign fighters in 2007.

Isnu Zhbgeen: one of three Arab Nationalist Youth for the Liberation of Palestine hijackers of a KLM B747 flying from Beirut to New Delhi and Tokyo on November 25, 1973. The hijackers forced the pilot to fly to Damascus, where the plane was denied refueling privileges. It flew on to Nicosia, Cyprus, where the group demanded the release of seven of their colleagues who were jailed in April 1973 for attacks in Cyprus against Israeli interests. The demands were rejected, but the seven were quietly amnestied by President Makarios and flown to Cairo on December 6. The plane next flew to Tripoli, Libya, where they were rebuffed, and then landed at Valletta, Malta, where the gunmen freed all of the 247 passengers and eight flight attendants. They flew on to Dubai on November 28. KLM agreed to halt transporting arms to Israel. The Dutch government pledged on November 25 not to "allow the opening of offices or camps for Soviet Jews going to Israel" and banning "transportation of weapons or volunteers for Israel." The hijackers went on to Aden, South Yemen, but were denied landing permission. They returned to Dubai, where they surrendered after promises of safe passage to an undisclosed country. On December 8, 1973, the hijackers were taken to Abu Dhabi, where they presumably were turned over to the Palestine Liberation Organization.

Mouaki Bannani Ziad: alleged member of the Islamic Salvation Front who was arrested for involvement in the August 26, 1992 bombing of the Air France ticket counter at Houari Boumedienne Airport in Algeria that killed 12 people and wounded 128. Public sessions of his trial began on May 4, 1993. On May 26, 1993, a special Algiers judicial council sentenced him to a year in jail.

Mustafa Zibri: alias Abu Ali Mustafa, the head of the Popular Front for the Liberation of Palestine, who was killed on August 27, 2001 in an Israeli missile attack.

Hasan Marzuq Raghib al-Zidani: alias Abu-Jandal, a Saudi who joined al Qaeda in Iraq in 2007, bringing $756 and 37 Syria lira. His personnel coordinators were Abu-al-Harith and Abu-'Abd-al-Hadi. His uncle's phone numbers were 00569948244342 and 0096638126769.

Sheik Abd-al-Majid al-Zindani: head of al-Iman University, an Islamist university in Sana'a, Yemen, he had fought with Osama bin Laden against the Soviets in Afghanistan. In 2004, the United States and UN declared him a terrorist who recruited for al Qaeda camps and raised money for weapons for terrorist groups. Among his students was John Walker Lindh, an American who later joined the Taliban.

Mohamed Zineddine: alias Sa'id, alias Mourad, alia Mehdi, a Moroccan born in 1960 in Chgrane, Khouribga Province, Morocco, sentenced in absentia to life in prison in 1985 for smuggling arms and munitions from Algeria to Morocco. He had been living in Algeria from the 1970s into 1994.

Abu Zir: alias of Umar.

Abu Zir: alias of Fahied.

Abu-Zir: alias of Ahmad Muhammad Muhsin Salah, variant Ahmed Muhammad Mohsen Saleh.

Haytham al-Zir: a Palestinian Islamic Jihad member whose trial for setting off a bomb that killed seven people in Patras, Greece on April 19, 1991 began on May 8, 1992 in a courtroom within the Kordhallos prison in Piraeus. He was sentenced by an Athens appeals court on July 6, 1992 to three years for handling arms and explosives.

Jihad al-Zir: a Palestinian Islamic Jihad member whose trial for setting off a bomb that killed seven people in Patras, Greece on April 19, 1991 began on May 8, 1992 in a courtroom within the Kordhallos prison in Piraeus. He was acquitted by an Athens appeals court on July 6, 1992.

Djamal Zitouni: variant Jamal Zitouni, variant Djemal Zetouni, a former militant of the Algerian Islamic Salvation Front accused by French security services of being a leader of an armed gang active in the Bir Khadem area that was responsible for an August 3, 1994 attack on a French school, Max Marchand, in Ain Allah, Algiers that killed five French nationals. He was also suspected of killing two other French nationals in Bir Khadem and two Yugoslavs in the Teklea garden in Ben Aknoun. On November 18, 1994, London's *al-Sharq al-Awsat* reported that he had replaced Abou Khalil Mahfoud as the Armed Islamic Group's leader in Algeria. He reportedly died in late 1996 under mysterious circumstances, and was succeeded by Antar Zouabri, who died on July 22, 1997 in a gun battle with authorities.

Jamal Zitouni: variant of Djamal Zitouni.

Abdellah Ziyad: variant Abdelylah Ziyad, alias Rachid, alias Abdelmalek Bachir, born in Casablana, Morocco in 1958, he was believed to be a leading member of the Moroccan Islamic Youth Movement in France's Chartres region. He was believed to be running weapons between France and Morocco in mid-1994. He was sentenced in absentia to life in prison in 1985 for smuggling arms and munitions to Morocco from Algeria.

Abdelylah Ziyad: variant of Abdellah Ziyad.

Khalil Ziyad: arrested in Jordan on December 29, 1999, the FBI said he was a Florida-based procurement agent for Osama bin Laden, specializing in computers, satellite telephones, and covert surveillance equipment. Jordan did not publicly reveal the arrest and later released him. However, *Time* magazine reported that he was cooperating with the FBI and providing information about bin Laden's U.S. operations.

Muhammad Salih Musa Ziyadah: one of a group of Jordanian Afghans tried on December 21, 1994

by the Jordanian State Security Court for belonging to an illegal society, participating in a conspiracy to carry out terrorist acts, and possessing explosives for illegal purposes. The Muslim fundamentalists bombed cinemas, wounding nine people, including an attack on January 26, 1994 at an Amman cinema showing what they perceived to be pornographic films, and another bombing on February 1, 1994. The group had been seized in a crackdown on Muslim radicals in January 1994. Their trial began on August 27, 1994, when they were accused of planning to assassinate leading Jordanians, including 'Abd-al-Salam al-Majali, Jordan's former chief peace negotiator with Israel. One of those sentenced to death was Muhammad Jamal Khalifah, a Saudi fugitive son-in-law of Osama bin Laden. He was acquitted.

Hasan 'Umar Zizo: alias of Ali Sayyid Muhamed Mustafa al-Bakri.

Karam Zohdi: one of the leaders of the al-Gamaat al-Islamiya who helped plot the October 1981 assassination of President Anwar Sadat. He was sentenced to life in prison for ordering the murder. He was released from prison on September 28, 2003, expressing regret for the murder.

Osama Abdel Zomar: variant of Abd al-Usamah al-Zumar.

Aboud el-Zomoor: serving a 40-year sentence for taking part in the October 6, 1981 assassination of Egyptian President Anwar Sadat. On June 25, 1998, Egyptian police uncovered a plot by 17 suspected Islamic militants to kidnap Americans in Egypt and swap them with jailed terrorists, including Aboud el-Zomoor. The militants were trying to revive Islamic Jihad.

Lt. Col. Abu Abdel Latif Zomor: Egyptian Army intelligence officer linked to the Egyptian Muslim Brotherhood assassination of Egyptian President Anwar Sadat on October 6, 1981. Zomor was captured in a gun battle between police and Muslim extremists at the Giza Pyramids on October 17, 1981. His brother was also arrested. He was sentenced to life on March 6, 1982.

Tariq Zomor: brother of Abu Abdel Latif Zomor. Both were sentenced to life on March 6, 1982 in connection with the October 6, 1981 assassination of Egyptian President Anwar Sadat.

Antar Zouabri: leader of the Armed Islamic Group (GIA) who died at age 27 in a gun battle with Algerian army troops on July 22, 1997. He and 100 of his followers died in the ancient tunnels where the group was hiding near Tipasa, Algeria. The son of a shoemaker had succeeded Jamal Zitouni, who died in late 1996 under mysterious circumstances.

Sources differ on his fate. Other sources reported that GIA's leader since 1996 died in a 2 and a half hour gun battle on February 8, 2002.

Bashar Zoualha: a 24-year-old identified by the Israeli government on September 23, 1997 as one of four Palestinians living in the West Bank village of Asirah Shamaliya, north of Nablus, who were responsible for an attack on July 30, 1997 and the September 4, 1997 attack in which three Palestinians set off bombs in Ben Yehuda Street in Jerusalem, killing themselves, five others, and wounding 190 shoppers, including many foreign visitors, among whom were Americans.

Muhammed Galeb Kalaje Zouaydi: a Syrian-born builder and real estate developer in Madrid accused of helping finance bin Laden's operations. He was arrested on April 23, 2002 by Spanish police. He was arraigned, charged with "multiple crimes of terrorism," and ordered held indefinitely without bail by antiterrorism judge Baltasar Garzon. He was represented by attorney Maria Angeles Ruiz Martinez. The judge said there was evidence that he had sent money to suspects in Germany linked with 9/11 hijack leader Mohamed Atta. On October 18, 2002, the Department of the Treasury designated the Illinois-based Global Relief Foundation, one of the country's largest Muslim charities, as a terrorist organization, because it had received more than $200,000 from Zouaydi. On April 21, 2005, the trial began of al Qaeda suspects in Spain linked to the 9/11 attacks. Among them was Zouaydi, age 44, who allegedly funneled $800,000 to radical Islamists, including al Qaeda. He was represented by attorney Manuel Tuero. He was eventually sentenced for membership in a terrorist group and sentenced to nine years in prison.

On April 16, 2008, Judge Ismael Moreno of the National Court indicted Syrian-born Imad Eddin Barakat Yarkas, 44; Syria-born Muhamed Galeb Kalaje Zouaydi, 47; and Bassam Dalati Satut, 48, on suspicion of financing terrorist cells. The indictment said that two of them removed $76,500 in December 2006 from Zouaydi's company and gave the money to Yarkas. He was charged with membership in a terrorist organization. The trio were arraigned on April 24, denying the charges.

Jamal Zougam: age 30, listed in a 9/11 indictment as an al Qaeda operative, although he was not indicted. On March 13, 2004, Spain arrested him for questioning. He was linked to the cell phone and cell phone card found in a gym bag linked to the March 11, 2004 multiple bombings of trains in Madrid that killed 200 and wounded 2,000. He had a criminal record in Spain. He had been under surveillance since the May 2003 bombings in Casablanca, Morocco. He owned a cell phone shop in Madrid. The Moroccan merchant was charged on April 11, 2006, by Judge Juan del Olmo of providing the cell phones used as detonators in the backpack bombs. Four witnesses said he had placed dark blue bags under seats in trains that blew up. He is the half brother of Mohamed Chaoui, with whom, on March 19, 2004, he was charged with belonging to a terrorist organization, four counts of terrorism, 190 counts of murder, 1,400 counts of attempted murder, and auto theft. On October 31, 2007, a Spanish court convicted him of membership in a jihadist terrorist cell and of terrorist murder.

Mohammed Zozad: name on a Lebanese passport used by a man who checked into the Kreoli Hotel in Glifada, Greece in June 1988. He was believed to be part of a group that was going to car bomb a U.S. military base in Greece, but the bomb exploded prematurely, killing the two terrorists.

Abdel Wael Zuaiter: Fatah representative in Italy who was born in Nablus, Jordan. The Jordanian had resided in Rome for 16 years and was employed as a translator for the Libyan Embassy. He was assassinated by two gunmen on October 16, 1972. The Jordanian Embassy said that he was a nephew of Akram Zuaiter, Jordan's Ambassador in Beirut, but declined to confirm reports that he was a second cousin of Yasir Arafat. He had been questioned in connection with the attempt by two Jordanians to blow up an Israeli airliner on August 17, 1972. The Israelis claimed that he worked for Black September (BSO) and Razd. He was also questioned after the BSO bombing of a Trieste pipeline in August 1972. His brother was expelled from West Germany after the Olympics attack. The Israelis believed that he was BSO's chief in Italy, and held him responsible for the hijacking of a Rome-Tel Aviv flight to Algeria on July 22, 1968 and the explosion of a bomb on an El Al B707 in August 1972. He had been a public apologist for the Munich attack, claiming that the Israelis plotted to have the hostages killed so that they could gain world sympathy.

Zayn Abidin Muhammed Hussein Abu Zubaida: more commonly known as Abu Zubaydah.

Mohammed Abu Zubayda: variant of Abu Zubaydah.

Abu Zubaydah: variant Mohammed Abu Zubayda, alias Zayn al-Abidin Muhammad Husayn, variant Mohammed Hussein Zein-al-Abideen, variant Zayn Abidin Muhammed Hussein Abu Zubaida, head of al Qaeda logistics and smuggling operations. He was linked to a host of al Qaeda terrorists, including Khalil Deek, with whom he had a $3,000 joint bank account. Jordanian officials told the press on February 29, 2000 that they believed he was a key member of a plot to attack Israelis, Americans, and other Christian tourists. He was among 14 plotters who remained at large.

He was born in 1973 and went to Afghanistan as a teen, where he met bin Laden. The Gaza Strip resident was believed to be a member of bin Laden's inner circle. He fled to Afghanistan after directing the plot from Pakistan. He was believed to be in contact with the Algerians charged in a separate attempt to bomb targets in the United States. Some believed he was communications chief and coordinator of al Qaeda operations outside Afghanistan. He also served as a gatekeeper for bin Laden's training camps in Afghanistan.

On September 24, 2001, President George W. Bush ordered his U.S. assets frozen.

He was arrested in Pakistan on March 27, 2002.

On September 6, 2006, President George W. Bush announced that the last 14 detainees would be transferred from secret foreign prisons to the military detention facility at Guantánamo Bay. The group was identified as Abu Zubaydah, Khalid Sheikh Mohammed, Ramzi Binalshibh, Mustafa Ahmad al-Hawsawi, Hambali, Majid Khan, Lillie, Ali Abd al-Aziz Ali, Ahmed Khalfan Ghailani, Abd al-Rahim al-Nashiri, Abu Faraj al-Libi, Zubair, Walid bin Attash, and Gouled Hassan Dourad.

On March 27, 2007, during his hearing before the military combatant status review tribunal at Guantánamo Bay, he denied membership in al Qaeda and said he differed with its approach to jihad. The Pentagon charged that he was the administrative director of the Khaldan training camp in Afghanistan, and that he had forged documents and was the travel facilitator for al Qaeda. He had helped Abu Musab al-Zarqawi sneak into Iraq from Afghanistan in November 2001.

On August 9, 2007, the Pentagon declared him an enemy combatant, a legal status that permitted the military authorities to hold him indefinitely at the detention center and put him on trial for war crimes.

Abu-al-Zubayr: Saudi-based recruiter of foreign fighters for al Qaeda in Iraq in 2006 and 2007 who attended a Saudi university where he found several volunteer suicide bombers.

Abu-al-Zubayr: alias of Walid Bin-'Abdallah 'Ali al-Khudayri.

Abu-al-Zubayr: alias of Bilal Ahmad Bin-'Abbud.

Abu-al-Zubayr: alias of al-Raway'i Salim Sa'id al-Sa'iri.

Abu-al-Zubayr: alias of Hani Muhammad al-Shubayli.

Abu-al-Zubayr: alias of Sami Rajab Ahmad al-Zahrani.

Abu-al-Zubayr: alias of Talal Muhammad al-Najashi.

Abu-al-Zubayr: alias of Fawwaz Shabbab al-Ruqi.

Al-Zubayr: Saudi-based recruitment coordinator for foreign fighters for al Qaeda in Iraq in 2006.

Abu Zubear: alias of Walied Abd Allah Al Hamzi.

Abu Al Zubear: alias of Hisham.

Abu Al Zubear: alias of Abd al Aziz Bin Ibrahim Bin Abd Al Aziz Al Majed.

Abu Al Zubear: alias of Ali Abd Allah Muhamad Al Assmarie.

Abu Al Zubear: alias of Abd Al Qader Abd Al Aziz Al Sha'aerie.

Abu Al Zubear: alias of Hamdi Ali Ramadan Al Aeyraj.

Abu Al Zubear: alias of Hanni Muhammad Al Shebli.

Abu Al Zubear: alias of Walied Bin Abd Allah Ali Al Khoudairi.

Abu Al Zubear: alias of Belal Ahmad Bin Aboud.

Salem Omar Zubeidy: a Libyan from either Denver or Ann Arbor, charged as an accomplice of two Libyan intelligence officers arrested by the FBI on July 20, 1988 of plotting to assassinate former National Security Council aide Marine Colonel Oliver L. North. He was a former chair of the McLean, Virginia-based Peoples Committee for Libyan Students. U.S. Magistrate Leonie Brinkema set bond between $25,000 and $50,000. The group apparently was planning revenge against U.S. officials believed to have planned the April 1986 air raid against Libya in retaliation for Libyan involvement in several terrorist attacks. On July 28, 1988, a federal grand jury handed down a 40-count indictment, charging the group with conspiracy, money laundering, and violations of U.S. trade sanctions against Libya.

Mahdi Mohammad Zubeyde: claimed to be innocent and merely fighting for the liberation of Palestine when his trial began at the Fourth High Criminal Court in Istanbul on November 4, 1977 for the attack in Istanbul Airport in August 1976 that led to the deaths of four and injuries to 20 others. He and Mohammad Rashid Husayn had been sentenced to life in prison for murder and causing injuries, but the supreme court of appeals reversed the sentences. The prosecutor asked for 5 to 10 years for infiltrating arms into Turkey.

Ahmad Bin-Shubat Bin-'Abd-al-Rahman al-Zufayri: alias Abu-Wiham al-Hadrawi, a Saudi licensed electrician and student from Safr al-Batim who joined al Qaeda in Iraq on August 21, 2007 as a suicide bomber, contributing 1,305 Saudi riyals and his passport. His recruitment coordinator was Abu-'Abdallah. He arrived in Syria by bus, meeting Abu-'Umar. His phone number was 037223785.

Yusef Ali Mohammed Zughayar: one of two terrorists who set off a car bomb in Jerusalem's Mahane Yehuda central street market, killing themselves and wounding 21 Israelis. The bomb apparently went off prematurely. Islamic Jihad took credit, and threatened more attacks to derail the Wye accords. At least six activists were detained. Palestinian Authority officials said that the terrorists came from Anata and Silat Harithiya. The duo met in an Israeli jail and were identified as Yusef Ali Mohammed Zughayar, age 22, and Seleiman Musa Dahayneh, age 24, who had been married for three months to Zughayar's sister, Basma.

Akram az-Zughbi: alias Ibrahim ad-Dayah, a Syrian who was arrested on March 16, 1979 at Cairo airport for being a member of Saiqa who was sent by Syrian intelligence to blow up the Foreign Ministry building opposite the Arab League building and conduct two other operations of his choosing. His release was demanded by terrorists who took over the Egyptian Embassy in Ankara, Turkey on July 13, 1979. He was from the Hawran district of Syrian. He was recruited by Wadi Ali Hawriyah, alias Abu Ahmad, of Saiqa, Bilal Hasan, alias Abu Mazin, commander of Saiqa's militia, and Abu Ali, commander of the Saiqa security forces and his deputy Abu Salim. Ad-Dayah was trained at Ad-Damur camp in Beirut.

Basil al-Zughul: cadet sentenced to hang on January 16, 1994 in connection with a plot foiled on June 26, 1993 to assassinate Jordanian King Hussein during the graduation ceremony at Muta University, a Jordanian military academy. His sentence was commuted to 15 years at hard labor.

Karam Zuhdi: the Egyptian Gama'at intended to obtain his release in the November 17, 1997 attack in Luxor at the Hatshepsut Temple that killed 58 foreign tourists and four Egyptians and wounded 26 other tourists.

Abbud al-Zumar: a former leader of the Egyptian Islamic Jihad (EIJ) who remained behind bars in 2007. He was believed to have supported former EIJ leader Abdul-Aziz el-Sherif's renunciation of terrorism.

Abd al-Usamah al-Zumar: variant Osama Abdel Zomar, a Palestinian student living in Varese, Italy, who was arrested on November 22, 1982 by border police in Kipi, Greece, when customs officials found 60 kilograms of dynamite, detonators, and other material hidden in a Mercedes with a Bari license plate. He was sentenced to 20 months on the border charge and, in 1987, to an additional 20 months for weapons concealment. He finished his sentence on November 29, 1988, but was held in prison pending an extradition decision. On March 23, 1985, the Italian media reported that Greece had decided to extradite him to Italy for the October 9, 1982 attack on Rome's main synagogue with hand grenades and submachine guns in which a two-year-old boy died and 37 persons were injured. On December 6, 1988, Greece rejected Italy's extradition request and deported the Abu Nidal member to Libya. On May 24, 1989, a Rome criminal court judge sentenced him in absentia to life in prison following his conviction for organizing the attack. Zumar had served in Rome as president of a group of Palestinian students in Italy.

Amin Saad Muhammad al-Zumari: born in Saudi Arabia or Yemen in 1968, a Yemeni believed by the FBI on February 11, 2002 to be planning a terrorist attack in the United States or on U.S. interests in Yemen.

Abbud al-Zummar: The Egyptian Gama'at intended to obtain his release in the November 17, 1997 attack in Luxor at the Hatshepsut Temple that killed 58 foreign tourists and four Egyptians and wounded 26 other tourists.

Zurwaq: Libya-based recruitment coordinator for al Qaeda in Iraq foreign fighters in 2007.

Sulayman al-Zuyud: cadet sentenced to hang on January 16, 1994 in connection with a plot foiled on June 26, 1993 to assassinate Jordanian King Hussein during the graduation ceremony at Muta University, a Jordanian military academy. His sentence was commuted to 15 years at hard labor.

INDEX

About the Author

EDWARD F. MICKOLUS is President of Vinyard Software and is the author of more than a dozen books on international terrorism and scores of articles on political science, history, and psychology. He holds an MA, M.Phil., and Ph.D. in political science from Yale University. He is the author of *Terrorism, 2005–2007: A Chronology* (PSI, 2008) and *Terrorism, 2002–2004: A Chronology* [3 Volumes] (PSI, 2006). He is a Professor at Harrison-Middleton University Henley-Putnam University, and a member of the Speakers Bureau of the International Spy Museum. Mickolus recently retired from the Central Intelligence Agency, where he had served for more than 33 years, receiving the Career Intelligence Medal and National Clandestine Service Medal.